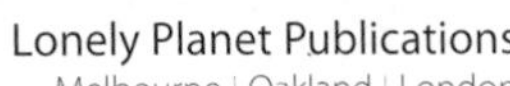

Tom Downs

New Orleans

Introducing New Orleans

New Orleans has always been a see-it-while-it's-still-there sort of destination. The city has always been surrounded by water, and mad-as-hell hurricanes have always threatened to whirl in off the Gulf of Mexico. From the beginning, Mother Nature has had her own plans for the sinking, bowl-like floodplains, reclaimed swamps and natural levees on which the city stands. New Orleanians don't just live with that fact. They've made high art out of it. Their city has always been a rare, tragic beauty. And, Katrina be damned, New Orleans is still here, folks, with its swelling love of life and a new, fresh eye on the future.

Let's not mince words. The future of New Orleans is shaky and uncertain. Memories and thoughts of the hurricane and the difficult road ahead linger over every conversation. No matter what direction the city goes in, though, New Orleans can't help but continue to be unique, beautiful and eternally intriguing. The city will always have its sultry weather, its exotic architecture, its beguiling history. More importantly, it will always embrace and nurture its culture, its festivals, its joie de vivre.

That's the way it should be. It's what we love about this city. It's a city with grace, pluck and an indomitable human spirit. Whatever happens next here carries with it rich and varied traditions.

Tourism is considered the strongest stick arching over New Orleans' quicksand. The historic neighborhoods along the high ground are all intact and primed to go. The historic Creole restaurants, the po'boy joints, the bars, nightclubs, hotels, museums and art galleries are open for business, and in many cases are already jumping with the same verve they had before Katrina. Jazz Fest, Mardi Gras and a dozen other fine festivals are all going strong. The population is slowly coming back, though it's obvious that not everyone will return, and old neighborhoods and communities have begun to resemble their former selves.

All of this is remarkable considering what happened here in the late summer of 2005, and the vivid and expansive evidence of the catastrophe that still surrounds the higher ground. A significant event took place here, one with heavy environmental, social and political ramifications. The visitor to New Orleans ought to get around town a bit, bear witness to what has happened and consider the serious implications. But New Orleans is not a depressing place. See what happened, take that understanding home with you – but not without first ducking back into the safe haven of the living city and having the time of your life.

previous pages *Wrought iron gate of Gallier House (p139), Banjo player in Jackson Sq (p136)*

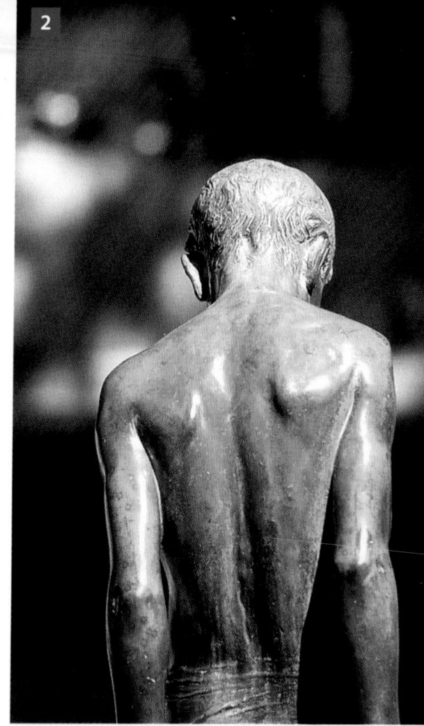

1 *Fog shrouded banks of the Mississippi River (p144)* **2** *Statue in City Park (p161)* **3** *Classic car and brightly painted houses in the French Quarter (p135)*

1 *Alligator in the Audubon Zoological Gardens (p158)*
2 *Wares on display at the Historic Voodoo Museum (p140)*
3 *Paintings outside the Cabildo (p138), Jackson Sq*

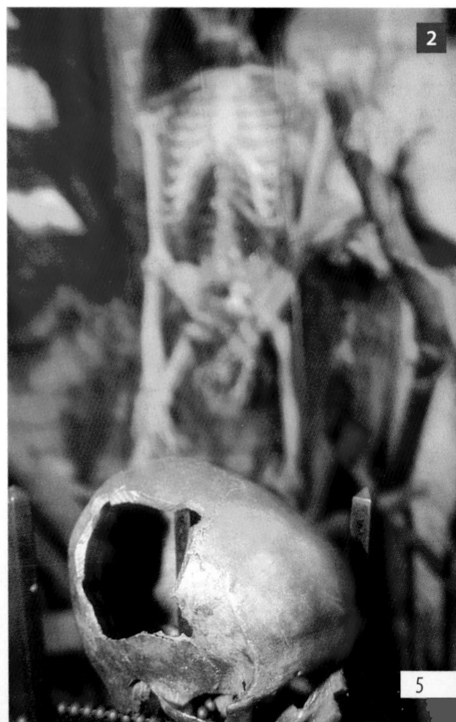

1 *Cajun sauces in the French Market (p221)* **2** *Classic New Orleans breaded catfish*
3 *Chef preparing meals at Emeril Lagasse's Nola (p184), French Quarter*

1 *Street jazz (p77)* **2** *Bourbon St (p200), French Quarter*
3 *Couple drinking in bar on Bourbon St (p200)*

following page *Streamboat Natchez (p145) on the Mississippi River*

STEAMER
NATCHEZ
PORT OF NEW ORLEANS

Published by Lonely Planet Publications Pty Ltd
ABN 36 005 607 983

Australia Head Office, Locked Bag 1, Footscray, Victoria 3011, ☎ 03 8379 8000, fax 03 8379 8111, talk2us@lonelyplanet.com.au

USA 150 Linden St, Oakland, CA 94607, ☎ 510 893 8555, toll free 800 275 8555, fax 510 893 8572, info@lonelyplanet.com

UK 72–82 Rosebery Ave, Clerkenwell, London, EC1R 4RW, ☎ 020 7841 9000, fax 020 7841 9001, go@lonelyplanet.co.uk

Printed by SNP Security Printing Pte Ltd, Singapore

Contents

Introducing New Orleans 3
City Life 11
Mardi Gras & Jazz Fest 31
Arts 55
Architecture 67
Music 75
Food 85
History 105
The Wrath of Katrina 119
Sights 131
Walking Tours 165
Eating 175
Entertainment & Nightlife 197
Shopping 219
Sleeping 235
Excursions 251
Directory 271
Glossary 285
Index 296
Maps 305
Rebuilding New Orleans 320

The Author

Tom Downs

Tom has been writing about New Orleans for Lonely Planet since 1999. His first experience with the city came during a summer break while he was in college. He was drawn to New Orleans after seeing the film *Down by Law,* in which the city appeared extremely exotic and dangerous to him. He was fascinated that such a place could be found in America. He hitched a ride in a Volkswagen from San Francisco to New Orleans, asked to be dropped off in front of the Hummingbird Hotel (now long gone), checked in and tried to get a job washing dishes in the greasy-spoon café downstairs. Failing that (no local references!), he managed to get work moving old office furniture. It wasn't much fun, especially in the torpid month of July, and he doesn't recommend this activity for visitors. But the place dug its hooks into him, and from that point on he has made semi-annual visits, with numerous forays into Cajun Country, the Mississippi Delta and Memphis. He loves this part of the country, but nevertheless continues to call Oakland, California, home. He lives with his wife, Fawn, and their kids in a house near a lake filled with geese.

Tom's Top New Orleans Day

I'll wake up with my groovy gal Fawn in our suite at the Soniat House (p241). We'll take our morning coffee on the balcony, then mosey up Chartres St towards Jackson Square (p136), then turn up Pirate's Alley for a look at books in Faulkner House (p140). On Royal St we'll drop by for a visit at the Historic New Orleans Collection (p139) because we always dig the huge portraits and paintings there, and the volunteers are so well behaved. Then we'll catch a cab to the Garden District (p156), have a quick walk past the glorious old houses, and end up on Magazine St to see some galleries (p213) and clothing stores (p222). Fawn will pick out a cute little 'baby doll' get-up at House of Lounge (p232) and I'll have my face shaved at Aidan Gill (p231) and we'll be feeling pretty much ready for action. After a stop at Parasol's (p189) in the Irish Channel for roast beef po'boys, we'll head down to the Ogden Museum of Southern Art (p155) in the Warehouse District. By the time we're done there, we'll both remark that we haven't had a real drink all day, so we'll head back to the French Quarter for a late afternoon whiskey at Napoleon House (p201). We'll discuss our dinner plans, decide not to rush it, and take an unhurried walk in the lower Quarter. We'll have a look at the fun shops (p220) filled to the rafters with old knickknacks along Lower Decatur St. This is just around the block from our hotel, so we'll head back for a shower before cabbing back Uptown for a late dinner at Dick & Jenny's (p192), where the atmosphere is both fun and romantic and the food's great. We'll feel uplifted and ready to go all night. Live music (p206) will just be starting up in the clubs. We'll go either to the Maple Leaf Bar (p209) in the Riverbend, or back downtown for some club hopping in the Faubourg Marigny. If I have my druthers we'll end up at the R Bar (p203). It's a short walk from there back to our hotel, and I love walking in this part of town late at night. I'll be feeling plenty satisfied at the end of a day like this, but I'll still have scores of ideas for the next day.

LONELY PLANET AUTHORS

Why is our travel information the best in the world? It's simple: our authors are independent, dedicated travelers. They don't research using just the Internet or phone, and they don't take freebies in exchange for positive coverage. They travel widely, to all the popular spots and off the beaten track. They personally visit thousands of hotels, restaurants, cafés, bars, galleries, palaces, museums and more – and they take pride in getting all the details right, and telling it how it is. For more, see the authors section on **www.lonelyplanet.com**.

City Life

New Orleans Today 12

City Calendar 14

Culture 19

Identity 19

Lifestyle 20

Religion 21

Fashion 22

Sports 23

Media 23

Language 24

Economy & Costs 25

Government & Politics 26

Environment 26

Climate 27

The Land 27

Green New Orleans 28

Urban Planning & Development 29

City Life

NEW ORLEANS TODAY

Right now, the city is progressing slowly out of the fog of crisis and toward a hazy horizon. New Orleanians will for many years be coming to terms with the fact that their city has been irrevocably changed. Few are able to go an hour without thinking or talking about the hurricane, and some worry that, as time passes, the city is getting used to the wreckage. For the first time in decades the city must look ahead, seeking its own future.

LOWDOWN

Population 250,000 (anticipated by the end of 2007)
Time zone Central (GMT minus six hours)
3-star room $150-250
Coffee $1.50
Po'boy $7
Essential drink Abita Amber $4
No-no Putting off your next trip to New Orleans

New Orleans is currently two cities: the city that is there, the island and the Dead Zone, populated by the people who have come back home and can muster up a healthy optimism; and the city that isn't there, the people scattered across the USA, unsure if they'll ever come back. Gradually, more and more of the latter are likely to move on with their lives elsewhere.

The pre–Civil War footprint of the city, on the higher ground that follows the natural levee inside the curve of the Mississippi River, was least affected by Hurricane Katrina and appears poised to thrive again. The French Quarter, the Marigny, the Central Business District (CBD), the Garden District, Uptown, Carrollton and Esplanade Ridge are pretty much intact and open for business. By early 2006 the shops and galleries on Magazine St, from the Lower Garden District all the way up to Audubon Park, were already hopping again. One could walk those streets on a Saturday afternoon and momentarily forget about the vast, incomprehensible devastation still scattered across the great bowl of the inner city. Six months after Hurricane Katrina, most of the city, from upper-class Lakeview to the impoverished Lower Ninth Ward, remained a ghost town, completely in disarray. To say the least, there is a strange disconnect between different parts of town.

Restaurant in French Quarter

In the surviving neighborhoods, one quickly senses strong communities bound together more tightly than ever before. Small local restaurants such as Liuzza's by the Track and Coop's Place in the Quarter are jam-packed with local customers, determined to spend their money in ways that help preserve some of the unique character of their city.

At the same time, many businesses in the French Quarter have suffered through some frustratingly slow months. Joe DiSalvo, owner of Faulkner House Bookshop on Pirates Alley, says he's had days when just one book has sold. On some evenings you can walk into Arnaud's restaurant at 9pm to find the place empty.

Regardless how quickly the tourism industry rebounds, as no doubt it will, the people of New Orleans faced difficult decisions and major developments in Katrina's wake. At the time of writing, it was estimated that up to 70% of the city's population remained outside the city. Some were housed within commuting distance of New Orleans, while the vast majority were living in other cities nationwide. Many were in Houston, TX, six hours' drive west of New Orleans. Some were as far away as Seattle, WA. It was unclear how many of these people would eventually return to New Orleans. The prevailing estimate, based on early polls among New Orleanians displaced by Katrina, indicated the city's population would eventually rebound to about half its pre-Katrina size. That would make New Orleans a smallish city of 250,000 souls.

New laborers, many of them from Latin America, have already moved into the city on a semipermanent basis. As long as construction work is available, as it should be for many years, these new arrivals can be expected to stay and possibly settle in the city. Their numbers are likely to grow if service industry jobs are left unclaimed by uprooted New Orleanians.

HOT CONVERSATION TOPICS

Whether you are sitting on a barstool or taking a guided tour, the best way to get to know the locals is by asking pertinent questions. Here are some suggestions that are sure to get them to open up with a harsh laugh, a thoughtful comment or a groan.

- Were you in town during Katrina?
- What's new about the 'new' New Orleans?
- What would happen if the city were to flood all over again in the next couple of years?
- FEMA trailers – chick magnets, or what? (Trying to lighten things up a bit.)
- True or False: this town needs more festivals.
- Where are all the librarian conventioneers? Bourbon St ain't the same without 'em.
- Whattya think of them fancy new parking meters?
- Where can I get some good gumbo around here?
- Can you guess where I got my shoes?
- Y'all speak French here, don't you?

The current population in New Orleans, numbering anywhere from 80,000 to 130,000, consists of people who lived on higher ground and who lost relatively little during the hurricane and flooding. A small number of die-hard New Orleanians have returned to water-sopped homes and begun the process of stripping down, rewiring and resurfacing. The result, at first anyway, was that New Orleans was inhabited by an unusually high proportion of middle-class and wealthy residents. (See Demographic Shift, p19, for more details.)

The atmosphere is interesting, to say the least. Grassroots political efforts are gaining momentum in a city that, historically, has a jaundiced view of its politics. Weekly town-hall meetings occur regularly as citizens and small-business people form neighborhood groups intent on reversing a history of corrupt politics. Locals have weighty issues on their minds, and most seem ready to talk about their city even with concerned strangers.

The talk isn't all gloomy. Most of the people you'll meet in New Orleans feel they are reclaiming their city, and they generally share a tough, chin-up character. The threat of flooding has always loomed large over New Orleans, and after a flood passes through, those still standing know they've dodged a bullet.

Race remains a crackly undercurrent to most of what goes on in New Orleans. Whites, who quickly returned to the city in great numbers, bristled at Mayor Nagin's promise to make New Orleans a 'chocolate city' once again. Nagin, in making a direct appeal to the thousands of blacks who had yet to come back, seemed to be overlooking the majority of people who had already begun to rebuild their neighborhoods, and many took offense. Nagin, himself black, has long had an image problem with black voters, and he was clearly trying to make amends. Alienating the current population wasn't the most savvy move with an election looming. Nagin miraculously overcame this PR snafu in time for the May 2006 election, which he won over Mitch Landrieu. Locals never warmed to Landrieu, a liberal democrat whose father 'Moon' Landrieu had been mayor in the 1970s and whose sister Mary Landrieu currently serves in the US Senate. Nagin is still seen as a political outsider, while well established political families like the Landrieu clan represent a New Orleans of the past.

The 'new' New Orleans, whatever that turns out to mean, is not likely to avoid controversy. It doesn't appear likely that the entire city will be rebuilt. As people awaited finalization of plans for the city's future, a palpable anger rose in some sectors, particularly among some blacks, who suspected their well-established communities were about to get shafted. The 'Bring New Orleans Back Commission,' appointed by Nagin, has proposed shrinking

TOP TEN NEW ORLEANS BOOKS

Don't just get bombed on Bourbon St. Get to know America's most interesting city by reading about it. Here's a short syllabus for your pretrip studies.

1 Dead in Attic – A collection of Chris Rose's compelling post-Katrina columns, which initially appeared in the *Times-Picayune*.

Why New Orleans Matters – By Tom Piazza, this is an evocative, almost elegiac overview of New Orleans culture set in context of the natural threats hovering in the city's future.

Mon Amour: Twenty Years of Writing about New Orleans – Andrei Codrescu's book reads like a love letter tinged with sadness, but filled with humor, irony and appreciation for a rare city.

Up from the Cradle of Jazz – A highly readable inroad to the city's musical heritage, from jazz to R&B and funk, by Jason Berry, Jonathan Foose and Tad Jones.

French Quarter Manual – An attractive, illustrated overview of architectural styles and features commonly found in the French Quarter, by Malcolm Heard.

New Orleans Cemeteries: Life in the Cities of the Dead – By self-proclaimed cemetery hound Rob Florence, *New Orleans Cemeteries* delves into some of the more intriguing stories about New Orleans' fascinating boneyards.

Managing Ignatius: The Lunacy of Lucky Dogs and Life in the Quarter – The real-life account of Jerry E Strahan, who for 20 years managed the Lucky Dog company. Needless to say, he had no shortage of humorous and astonishing material.

Mardi Gras Indians – A full-color collection of photos and text by Michael P Smith that is both fascinating and beautiful.

Bayou Farewell – Mike Tidwell visits the disappearing Cajun Wetlands and uncovers a unique Cajun culture threatened by environmental changes.

Historical Atlas of Louisiana – by Charles Robert Goins and John Michael Caldwell, this is an engrossing, cartographic history of the state, with routes of Native American migration and colonial exploration, along with pages of maps and text specific to New Orleans.

the footprint of the city in order to consolidate the city's devastated infrastructure. Without singling out particular neighborhoods, the commission recommended converting some parts of town into parklands.

The Lower Ninth Ward leaps to mind when such scenarios are discussed, and a few residents in that part of town are standing their ground. Spray-painted signs appear on houses, saying, 'Coming Back Home' and 'No Bull Dozers.' A nonprofit organization called 'Common Grounds' has established a toolshed in the neighborhood and recruits volunteers to help locals rebuild their homes. Some people were living in white FEMA trailers hooked up to generators in front of their wrecked houses, a clear sign they intend to fix up their homes. Unfortunately, for the foreseeable future anyone who rebuilds in these parts of town will have to do without city services and infrastructure like hospital and ambulance services, police patrols, road maintenance and all utilities.

CITY CALENDAR

Any excuse for a drink, a dance or a parade, New Orleanians are like kids when it comes to holidays. The city has many holidays and festivals of its own, as well as all of the federal holidays, and often does 'em better'n anywhere else. Still, Christmas in New Orleans is really just a warm-up for Mardi Gras. If you're prone to postholiday blues, that doesn't happen here. There's always another big event on the horizon.

JANUARY

To help offset the chilly weather, January is an event-filled month. And, while it's cool and sometimes clammy, the weather here is balmy compared to the Midwest.

SUGAR BOWL

☎ 525-8573

This NCAA football game between two of the nation's top-ranking college teams takes place on New Year's Day. It originated in 1935 and fills the Superdome to capacity every year. In 2006, the Superdome wasn't ready for the game, but expect its return in 2007.

BATTLE OF NEW ORLEANS CELEBRATION

☎ 281-0510

On the weekend closest to January 8, volunteers stage a re-creation of the decisive victory over the British in the War of 1812 at the original battleground in Chalmette National Historical Park. The highlight is the Saturday night tour, illuminated by lanterns, through battleground encampments. A noontime commemoration on Sunday in Jackson Sq features a military color guard in period dress. Chalmette Battlefield was badly damaged by Hurricane Katrina, and there is no word when this event will resume. But it will.

MARTIN LUTHER KING JR DAY

St Claude Ave

On the third Monday in January, a charming midday parade, replete with brass bands, makes its way from the Bywater to the Tremé District, down St Claude Ave.

MARDI GRAS PARADES

Early Carnival parades in January or February tend to be the most outlandish, such as the annual Krewe du Vieux parade that passes right through the French Quarter. Early in the Carnival season each year, the *Times-Picayune* runs a 'Carnival Central' section with maps of all the parades. See p37 for more information.

FEBRUARY

Mardi Gras kicks into gear in February, making it the most festive time of year in New Orleans. The weather sometimes has plans of its own, but figuratively speaking it rarely rains on the parade.

MARDI GRAS PARADES

St Charles Ave & Canal St

The greatest free show on earth really heats up during the three weeks before Mardi Gras, culminating with multiple parades each day. Routes vary, but the largest krewes stage massive parades, with elaborate floats and marching bands, that run along sections of St Charles Ave and Canal St. None enter the French Quarter. See the Mardi Gras & Jazz Fest chapter for more information.

MARDI GRAS DAY

In February or early March, the outrageous activity reaches a crescendo as the French Quarter nearly bursts with costumed celebrants. It all ends at midnight with the beginning of Lent.

MARCH

You might think things would slow down after Mardi Gras, but no. March is fun-filled and the weather is often sweet in the early spring. To cap it off, the Easter Bunny hops through town on a Sunday morning in March or April.

ST PATRICK'S DAY

Just when you thought the city would calm down, the festivities pick up again on March 17. At 6pm the annual Jim Monaghan parade, honoring the late owner of **Molly's at the Market** (p201) bar, brings musicians and green-painted people together in the French Quarter. The parade ends up at Molly's. There's a simultaneous pub crawl disguised as a parade starting in the Bywater, at the corner of Burgundy and Piety Sts, and ending on Bourbon St in the Quarter. Even if these rowdy parades don't actually collide, you can easily jump the banks of one stream and find your way

UNIQUE EVENTS

New Orleans has all kinds of holidays that aren't celebrated anywhere else. Here are the best of 'em.

French Quarter Festival – Take Jazz Fest, cancel the 'headliners' (usually Sting or someone like that), move it to the French Quarter and reduce it to a single three-day weekend and you've got the FQF.

Jazz Fest – We didn't mean to suggest Jazz Fest isn't still the king of music festivals.

Carnival – They do this in other parts of the world, but not quite like they do it in New Orleans.

Voodoo Music Experience – Big-time rock and punk acts give the Decatur St crowd a chance to let off steam.

Tennessee Williams Literary Festival – The playwright was a character, and New Orleans is good theater. It all makes perfect sense.

into the other. On the previous Sunday, the big Uptown/Irish Channel parade makes its way down Magazine St. Along the way, riders on the parade floats pelt bystanders with cabbages and potatoes. Follow them to **Parasol's** (p189), where a huge block party is a heel-kickin' good time.

INDIAN SUNDAY

www.mardigrasindians.com

St Joseph's Night, March 19, is a big masking event for black Indian gangs. After sunset, the Indians come out in their finery, and often their suits of feathers and beads are even more elaborate than they were on Mardi Gras. The confrontations between rival gangs can be intense, though rarely violent. If wandering the backstreets at night isn't your cup of tea, on the following Sunday, the Indians emerge for the last time for the Indian Sunday parade. It's a much more relaxed and showy affair, which works to the audience's benefit. Bring a camera and get some amazing shots. The parade has no fixed route, but traditionally has gone through the heart of Mid-City. With the neighborhood slow to recover from Hurricane Katrina, the event may undergo some changes. Check the website above, or call the **Backstreet Cultural Museum** (p146) for information.

TENNESSEE WILLIAMS LITERARY FESTIVAL

☎ 581-1144; www.tennesseewilliams.net

The end of March features a four-day fête in the playwright's honor. Tennessee Williams lived in the French Quarter early in his career, and thereafter called New Orleans his 'spiritual home.' Attendees of the event attempt to keep his spirit alive with a 'Stell-a-a-a!' shouting contest, along with colorful walking tours, theater events, film screenings, literary celebrity interviews and the usual quantities of food and alcohol. The festival runs through the last weekend of the month, with events held at theaters, restaurants and hotels in the French Quarter.

APRIL

Jazz Fest is obviously the big tamale at the end of the month, but New Orleans cranks up to that level with some superb smaller festivals. Climate-wise, it does not get any better than April.

FRENCH QUARTER FESTIVAL

☎ 800-673-5725; www.fqfi.org, www.nola.com/fqfest

One of New Orleans' finest music festivals, the French Quarter Fest no longer feels like a warm-up for Jazz Fest. It follows a similar formula of celebrating superb music and scrumptious food, but this one has the advantage of a smaller size, intimate Vieux Carré setting, and free admission. But when we say 'smaller,' we don't mean puny. The fest's 15 stages spaced throughout the Quarter showcase jazz, funk, Latin rhythms, Cajun, brass bands, R&B and more over a period of three days. Dozens of the city's most popular restaurants operate food stalls in Jackson Sq and elsewhere in the Quarter. The French Quarter Festival is held during the second or third weekend of April.

LOUISIANA CRAWFISH FESTIVAL

☎ 271-3836; 8200 W Judge Perez Dr, Chalmette, Louisiana

A huge crawfish feed qualifies as the epitome of southern Louisiana culture, and that's just what this is. It's fun for the entire family, with rides, games, live Cajun music and an array of dishes featuring crawfish. It's in nearby Chalmette (drive down Claiborne Ave and you'll find yourself in Chalmette), in early April.

JAZZ FEST

The **Fair Grounds Race Track** – and, at night, the whole town – reverberates with good sounds, plus food and crafts, over two weekends in the latter part of April and early May. See p49 for more details.

MAY

The mercury starts rising and the festival season slows down a bit in May. Still, it's not an unpleasant time to visit. Jazz Fest carries over into the first weekend of the month (see above).

WINE & FOOD EXPERIENCE

☎ 529-9463; www.nowfe.com

Well, this is just an excuse to act all high-brow with strangers, but it's fun if you like wine and food. And who in New Orleans doesn't? You sign on (and pay a pretty penny) for various plans. 'Experiences' may include a vintner dinner, with wine-and-food pairings being the primary focus; an evening street fair on Royal St, made jolly by wine and song; and a whole host of tastings, seminars and brunches.

JUNE

With summer comes humidity and frequent showers. Locals start vacationing, and musicians often go on tour.

FRENCH MARKET CREOLE TOMATO FESTIVAL

☎ 522-2621; www.frenchquarter.com/events

Whether you say 'to-may-toe' or 'to-mah-toe,' you're sure to dig this celebration of the delta-bred red natives. If you're quickly tomatoed out, there's plenty of food and entertainment, and a gospel choir marches the Quarter singing the praises of the big tomato. It takes place in the **French Market** during the second weekend of the month.

JULY

Some fun events are held in the muggy month of July.

INDEPENDENCE DAY

Since the Civil War, some folks in these parts have regarded July 4 as a 'Yank' holiday. But whenever there's a war on, as there always seems to be these days, you can count on a rise in patriotism in New Orleans. Besides, New Orleanians are not known to pass up a good time. Food stalls and entertainment stages are set up on the riverfront, and fireworks light up the sky over the 'Old Man' – that's the Mississippi River, not Uncle Sam.

ESSENCE MUSIC FESTIVAL

www.essence.com/essence/emf

Contemporary African American vibes are what this festival offers. *Essence* magazine sponsors a star-studded lineup of R&B, hip-hop, jazz and blues performances at the **Superdome**. Started in 1995, the event regularly has big name black recording artists, along with an array of stalls selling arts and crafts and delectable foods. In 2006, with the Superdome out of commission, Essence moved its act to Houston, TX, and it wasn't certain whether it would ever return to New Orleans. The event is held on Independence Day weekend.

TALES OF THE COCKTAIL

☎ 343-4285; www.talesofthecocktail.com

Sure, Bourbon St seems to be holding a 24/7 festival of booze 365 days a year, but this three-day event, begun in 2003, sets its sights a little higher. Appreciating the art of 'mixology' is the main point, and getting lit up is only an incidental part of the fun. If it sounds a little highbrow, well, it is. But that's no excuse for shying away from the free cocktail hour, which kicks off the event in the Hotel Monteleone. This is also a literary event – perhaps in the same spirit in which *Playboy* is a literary magazine. For at some of the events you get to hear knowledgeable writers talk about booze and bartending, while you try interesting sorts of new drinks. You'll very likely learn some cool history to share with your barfly friends back home.

AUGUST

The weather's about as bad as it gets, but by now New Orleanians are acclimated to the saunalike atmosphere. It's hot and sultry, and when Southern Decadence starts, things get pretty wild. Unfortunately, hurricane season kicks into high gear at around this time – and lasts the rest of the year.

SATCHMO SUMMERFEST

www.fqfi.org, www.nola.com/satchmofest

Louis Armstrong's birthday, August 4, is celebrated with four days of music and food in the French Quarter. Three stages present local talents in 'trad' jazz, contemporary jazz and brass bands. The entertainment is free, and the food stalls offer festival staples such as po'boys, red beans and jambalaya at reasonable prices. At night the clubs hop, and seminars are conducted by notable jazz writers throughout the fest for serious music fans. It's tight like that.

SOUTHERN DECADENCE

www.southerndecadence.com

Billing itself as the 'Gay Mardi Gras,' this five-day festival celebrates gay culture in the lower Quarter. Expect music, food, dancing in the streets and a general boost in the city's gay population as thousands of visitors show up for the party. The Sunday parade is everything you'd expect from a city with a vital gay community, as well as rich traditions in masking and cross-dressing. One of the city's most entertaining events.

Musicians busking outside street café

OCTOBER

Fall brings cooler weather and spooks and more fun.

VOODOO MUSIC EXPERIENCE

www.voodoomusicfest.com

In New Orleans rock and roll tends to get overlooked, but not during Halloween weekend when Voodoo rocks City Park. Kudos to Voodoo for putting a tremendous lineup on stage in 2005, just two months after Hurricane Katrina nearly washed the city away. That year's event featured the Nine Inch Nails, the Foo Fighters, the Flaming Lips, Queens of the Stone Age, Billy Idol, Social Distortion, the New York Dolls, Ryan Adams, Cake and Joss Stone. Needless to say, Voodoo kicked Katrina's fat ass outta town.

HALLOWEEN

Celebrated on October 31, Halloween is a holiday not taken lightly in New Orleans. Most of the fun is to be found in the giant costume party throughout the French Quarter. It's a big holiday for gay locals and tourists, with a lot of action centering around the Bourbon Pub & Parade Disco (p204).

NOVEMBER

Having a more holiday-starved calendar, the rest of the country goes into what is generally called 'The Holidays' in November. New Orleans can do that too. Thanksgiving kicks things off on the third Thursday of the month.

ALL SAINTS DAY

This being New Orleans, with its beautiful cities of the dead, you can expect to encounter memorable activities on November 1. The cemeteries fill with people, some of them fairly eccentric, who come to pay their respects to ancestors and recently departed family and friends. It is by no means morbid or sad, as many people have picnics and parties. It wouldn't be out of line for a family to serve gumbo from a pot beside the family crypt. Interesting traditions are carried out, as many people spruce up the monuments and decorate them with creative memorials, some of which qualify as folk art. St Louis Cemetery No 1 (p147) and, around the corner, St Louis Cemetery No 2 are the easiest to drop in at, but pretty much any cemetery in town will have something going on.

CELEBRATION IN THE OAKS

If overenthusiastic displays of holiday lights and decorations turn you on, you might want to check out the colorful constellations at City Park. It's a unique New Orleans take on the spirit of Christmas in America – a little bit Vegas, a little bit Disneyland, with 2 miles of the park's magnificent oak trees providing the superstructure. You can view it in its entirety from your car (turn off those headlamps) or in a horse-drawn carriage. A separate walking tour visits the botanical gardens and carousel area. The huge power cord is plugged into the socket every night after dark, from the last week of November through to the first week in January. Admission is $10 per motor vehicle and $5 per person for the walking tour.

DECEMBER

White Christmases are extremely rare in New Orleans, but on some days you can see your breath. Count on over-the-top displays of holiday spirit on front lawns all over town. Plus oak trees lit up like…well, like Christmas trees.

CHRISTMAS NEW ORLEANS STYLE

☎ **522-5730; www.fqfi.org**

During the month of December, St Charles Ave is a festival of light, as many of New Orleans' poshest homes are lavishly decorated and illuminated for the holidays. This is also a great time to tour historic homes. The lobby of the **Fairmont Hotel** in the CBD is transformed into a gaudy but charming Christmas grotto, its walls and ceiling concealed by shredded cotton. And of course, the Celebration in the Oaks continues all through the month. On Christmas Eve, **St Louis Cathedral** attracts a tremendous crowd for its midnight choral mass. Many restaurants offer réveillon dinners on Christmas Eve. **French Quarter Festivals** can provide a complete schedule of events, open homes and réveillon menus.

FEUX DE JOIE

☎ **524-0814**

'Fires of joy' light the way along the Mississippi River levees above Orleans Parish and below Baton Rouge in December and on Christmas Eve (December 24). To reach the giant bonfires you must either endure incredible traffic along the narrow River Rd, or drop a pretty penny to see the fires from a riverboat. Another option is to take I-10 to La Place (27 miles) or even Burnside (50 miles) to see the spectacle.

NEW YEAR'S EVE

Revelers – mostly drunk tourists – pack the French Quarter, especially around **Jackson Brewery**, where the Baby New Year is dropped from the roof at midnight. Adding to the frenzy are thousands of college football fans, in town for the annual Sugar Bowl, which takes place on New Year's Day.

CULTURE

IDENTITY

More than anywhere else in America, the people of New Orleans identify very deeply with their city. This strong affiliation, which crosses racial and sociological lines, is rooted in a common appreciation for the city's rich multicultural traditions. All New Orleanians grow up eating gumbo (an African-French hybrid) and, regardless of their religious beliefs, they all celebrate Mardi Gras, a Catholic holiday with pagan roots. Above all else, everyone who lives here understands and appreciates the uniqueness of their city. It has always been a place apart, and it always will be.

DEMOGRAPHIC SHIFT

Before Katrina, Orleans Parish was home to approximately 500,000 people. African Americans held a considerable majority, with 67% of the population, making New Orleans one of the 'blackest' cities in the US. Whites comprised just over 30% and the remainder was mostly Hispanic and Vietnamese. These figures are predicted to change dramatically as the population resettles. Some projections have suggested the future New Orleans will be a city of about 250,000 people, though it is easy to imagine this figure rising considerably once the city is actually rebuilt. New Orleans will likely continue to be very diverse, perhaps more than before. The number of blacks is expected to reduce significantly, the Hispanic population is increasing and possibly the city will have a white majority.

ONLY IN NEW ORLEANS

An expression often heard in New Orleans is 'Only in New Orleans.' Even native-born denizens of the city are moved from time to time to utter these words while shaking their heads in wonder. Every day the city will confound you, make you laugh, move you to tears and get beneath your skin like no other. The following 'only in New Orleans' experiences are all available to the tourist.

- Dance to zydeco music and bowl a few frames at **Mid-City Lanes Rock & Bowl** (p209).
- Chomp on oyster po'boys at **Parasol's** (p189).
- Join the second-line at a jazz funeral or second-line parade.
- Party with a lifelike Ernie K-Doe statue at **Ernie K-Doe Mother-in-Law Lounge** (p203).
- Be in that number when the **Saints** (p215) go 'falling down' at the Superdome.
- Buy Faulkner novels in a house once lived in by the author at **Faulkner House Bookstore** (p224).
- See Mardi Gras Indians in action on **Indian Sunday** (p16).
- Chomp on muffuletta sandwiches at the **Central Grocery** (p180).
- Sleep in a stylish Creole town house at **Soniat House** (p241).

In the parts of the city hardest hit by Hurricane Katrina, the primary hope for the future lies in the love people have for their city. After even a few years in other parts of the country, should the opportunity present itself, native New Orleanians are likely to feel compelled to return home to family and communities.

While New Orleanians may share a common love for the city, cultural divisions are also strong. Economic and geographic lines roughly parallel race lines, and white and black societies generally coexist separately. Before Katrina struck, you needed only to walk from the Garden District to an Uptown housing project to see the extremes in wealth and the racial breakdown. (The future of those projects is a topic of much discussion in the city's plans for renewal.) However, there has always been a broad cultural crossover zone rarely seen in other US cities. In bars, clubs and public events around the Quarter and Faubourg Marigny, you'll often encounter a healthy mix of whites and blacks.

New Orleans has always had a sizable community of non-natives, drawn to the city's lifestyle. Many of these people indulge in the local culture with more gusto than the natives. New Orleans' creative orb continues to attract young adventurous and artistic people. Hit a few lower Decatur St bars or Magazine St galleries and you'll tap into scenes that are vital to the city without necessarily being from the city. Some of these people were the first to hurry back and pick up the pieces after Hurricane Katrina. Almost every art gallery in town reopened within months of the disaster, and the grungy bars on Decatur St bounced back long before the tourists returned to Bourbon St.

Gays in great numbers have been attracted to New Orleans' permissive Mardi Gras atmosphere, and contribute to the city's artistic culture. They have also helped restore many historic homes in the French Quarter (primarily the lower half and to the lake side of Bourbon St) and in the Faubourg Marigny.

The Marigny, in the past five to 10 years, has become a major draw for young professionals, many of them multimedia types whose incomes are not dependent on the local economy. They've introduced cosmopolitan fashion tastes and distributed their disposable income along Frenchmen St. Some of the French Quarter's early retirees and time-share types introduce a minimal 'Conch Republic' vibe with their straw hats and leisure clothing, but there is an even greater number of holdouts from the 1970s, who arrived young and now are not so young.

LIFESTYLE

Life in New Orleans is celebratory, and partylike public events frequently bring the city together. Mardi Gras is the ultimate holiday, claimed in one way or other by all sectors of society, and much of what goes on, goes on in the streets. The people of New Orleans are up for a good time, and they're generous about sharing what they have with each other and even with out-of-town visitors. These qualities are unlikely to succumb to the post-Katrina blues, as the main motivation for many of the people who returned to New Orleans was to keep alive the special spirit of the place.

Music and food are of course key ingredients in New Orleans life, which is why so many places that feature live music also serve food, whether it involves table service or barbecue dished out on the sidewalk. Musicians and chefs are generally part of the party, rather than entertainers or celebrities. So, while Kermit Ruffins' photo may appear in every magazine in town, if you're at his gig at Vaughan's (p208), he'll mingle with the crowd between sets and even dish up some barbecue from the back of his own truck.

On a more private level, rich traditions keep family ties relatively strong among the poor and the wealthy. More than in any other US city, old families in New Orleans, many going back 100 or 200 years, live in the same neighborhoods, worship in the same churches, bury their dead in the same crypts, eat in the same restaurants, belong to the same Social Aid and Pleasure Clubs, play the same musical instruments, even take on the same trades and professions generation after generation. For some, New Orleans is confining, offering little opportunity for 'finding yourself.' However, many of the people who have lived their entire lives in the city seem content, as if they cannot imagine life having turned out differently. This may seem foreign for visitors from places where it seems like everyone wants to get away.

RELIGION

Roman Catholics predominate in New Orleans and the Cajun Country of southern Louisiana, creating an anachronism amid the Protestant 'Bible Belt' that shapes much of the South. French and Spanish heritage, along with a later influx of Irish, among others, accounts for the Catholic preeminence. Slaveholders were required by Bienville's 1724 Code Noir to baptize and instruct their slaves in the Catholic faith – an edict not rigidly followed. Nevertheless, Catholicism is not uncommon among blacks today, although the influx of blacks from throughout the South during the mid-20th century brought many Baptists to the city. In the months after Katrina, there was no early indication whether Creole Catholic families were more likely to return than the more recent Baptists, though religious affiliation may indeed influence such decisions for many families.

New Orleans' signature celebration – Mardi Gras – is rooted in Catholic beliefs. Carnival begins on 'Twelfth Night,' (January 6; the twelfth night following Christmas), and continues to Mardi Gras, or 'Fat Tuesday,' which is the day before Ash Wednesday.

Religious paraphernalia

MUCH ADO ABOUT VOODOO

Voodoo has in no small way contributed to New Orleans' reputation as the 'least American city in America.' It is perceived as both a colorful spectacle and a frightening glimpse of the supernatural, and this has proved to be an irresistible combination. Scores of shops selling voodoo dolls, gris-gris (amulets) and other exotic items attest to the fact that visitors to New Orleans can't help but buy into the mystique of voodoo.

All the hype aside, voodoo has remained a vital form of spiritual expression for thousands of practitioners. It came to the New World via the French colony of St Domingue (now Haiti), where slaves from West Africa were able to continue their religious traditions. A hybrid voodoo developed on the island, as people from many different tribal communities contributed various spiritual practices – including animism, snake worship, ancestor worship and making sacrifices to deities, called *loas*.

In St Domingue, voodoo played an integral role in the slave rebellions that led to Haitian independence at the end of the 18th century. (Haiti is, in fact, the second-oldest nation in the Americas, having gained its independence just 28 years after the USA.) Haitian *vodoun* cults became military units as *vodoun* priests urged their followers to fight for freedom, and the bravery of the rebels was probably abetted by vodoun charms carried for protection. Haitian landowners fled the island, many settling with their slaves in New Orleans.

In New Orleans, voodoo fused with Catholic beliefs as saints and deities became interchangeable for followers of both religions. And it grew extremely popular as more people turned to voodoo conjurers for advice, fortune telling, herbal medicine, love charms and revenge against their enemies. These conjurers became increasingly influential in the community, and some of the more successful were wealthy and often controversial.

Little is known about the famous 19th-century diviners with spectacular names like Doctor John, Doctor Yah Yah and Sanité Dédé. Even the facts about the life of Marie Laveau, the most famous voodoo queen, continue to baffle historians. Half a century or more after their deaths, their biographies were written by historians who relied solely on hearsay and scant newspaper clippings. But no matter how true or false, their stories are fascinating.

The sights chapter has information about existing voodoo temples (p143) and a voodoo museum (p140). Also see Voodoo Queen on p143.

Catholics traditionally feast (hence 'Carnival,' with the Latin root 'carne' or meat) before Ash Wednesday, the beginning of Lent and a period of penitence that continues until Easter; see p33.

Slaves and immigrants from Haiti also perpetuated their own belief systems brought from West Africa. Voodoo rooted itself in New Orleans as in other parts of the New World – particularly in places like Brazil and the Caribbean. Central African women of the Fon and Yoruba tribes were especially influential on the plantation estates and at gatherings at Congo Sq (now Louis Armstrong Park). Much conjecture about voodoo focuses on its mystery and on ceremonies where worshipers enter a trance. Small temples like the Voodoo Spiritual Temple at 828 N Rampart St continue to serve worshipers.

Protestant Americans settled in the Uptown area and built the great churches that line St Charles Ave. After WWII the influx of African Americans from the rural South increased the Protestant presence in town.

FASHION

Among Uptown and workaday people neatness is considered a reflection of self pride. Downtown, including in the French Quarter, a certain amount of sloppiness isn't ordinarily frowned upon. (The impeccable older women who volunteer as docents at the Historic New Orleans Collection, for instance, will be perfectly cordial to a younger man who is clean shaven but doesn't appear to have combed his hair.) Individuality, not sloppiness, is considered the object in the creative-leaning downtown faubourgs.

Short pants are worn by men and women in summer, but Uptown men are less likely to wear shorts than downtown men. Uptowners are more likely to tuck in shirts (even into shorts) and keep hair neatly combed even on the balmiest of days.

Casual attire is not acceptable at traditional Creole restaurants, such as Antoine's or Brennan's. For men, jackets, but not necessarily ties, are required at most of these old-line establishments.

Hats, while no longer in fashion, are also not really a novelty in New Orleans. Men and women are both likely to wear them. A local hat store, Meyer the Hatter, changes its inventory from season to season – heavier felt hats in the fall and winter, floppier straw ones in spring and summer. You can ask to see felt hats in summer, but your choices will be limited and the salesperson may think of you as not really a hat person.

There is a fairly high concentration of Goths, in black duds and with black hair, along lower Decatur St.

Now for the subject of disrobing in public. If there are any rules on this, they would have to be, 'If you must do it, do it on Bourbon St, and afterwards be sure to tell everyone how drunk you were when you did it.'

However, few rules apply during Mardi Gras weekend. Outrageousness is the whole idea of Mardi Gras. Grease paint, gaudy-colored clothing (the more gold-and-silver lamé the better), sexual suggestiveness and cross-dressing (even among straights) are all acceptable. On Mardi Gras, lewdness, while not rampant, is more common than usual and not considered offensive as long as personal space is respected.

SPORTS

College and professional football is big all over the South, and New Orleans is no exception. The biggest show in town has always been the Saints, who have been martyred on many a Sunday over the years. The **Saints** play in the NFC South Division, and returned to play eight home games at the Superdome in the 2006 season. The NFL promised to keep the team in New Orleans as long as ticket sales and TV revenue remained high enough.

The **Tulane Green Wave** plays NCAA Division I football at the Superdome. The best and most exciting Tulane game is a battle with long-standing rival Louisiana State University (LSU) from Baton Rouge.

The local NBA team, the **Hornets**, seemed less committed to returning to New Orleans after Hurricane Katrina. The team played in Oklahoma City for the 2005 season, which began after the hurricane, and then decided to stay away for another season (the team was slated to play six games in New Orleans Arena, keeping ties to the city alive). The team's future remained sketchy beyond that. It was assumed, in order to sell tickets, that most of the city's pre-Katrina population would need to return.

The University of New Orleans Privateers basketball team is quite good; games are played at the **UNO Kiefer Lakefront Arena** (☎ 280-6100). At Tulane, women's and men's games are played at the small but very lively **Avron B Fogelman Arena** (☎ 865-5000) on campus.

New Orleans does not have a Major League Baseball team, but minor league baseball is always fun. Fans sit close to the field and watch as young prospects strive to prove they're ready to play in the big league. The **AAA Zephyrs** toss the old bean around the horn at Zephyr Field. They play 72 home games from April to September.

Tulane and UNO baseball games are worth spending a lazy afternoon watching. Tulane plays on campus, while UNO games take place at the larger Privateer Park on the lakefront. In late February, baseball teams from Louisiana face off against Mississippi teams in the **Winn-Dixie Showdown**, a three-day series of triple-headers in the Superdome.

If heading down to the track to put a few bucks on a pony's nose seems more in keeping with the character of old New Orleans, see the Fair Grounds Race Track (p160) for more information.

Outside the city, you'll find out why Louisiana touts itself as 'the Sportsman's Paradise.' Fishing has always been a way of life in the bayous and swamps across the southern part of the state. The region is rich in largemouth bass, speckled trout and striped bass. For every pickup truck you spot on Louisiana's highways and byways, rest assured there's a small fishing boat stored behind a house or tied to a dock somewhere.

MEDIA

New Orleans' only daily newspaper is the *Times-Picayune*. The *Times-Pic* has not traditionally drawn praise for its journalism, but staff certainly stepped up to the plate during Hurricane Katrina (even though the paper's own offices were shut down) and coverage of the city's

> **WORTHWHILE WEBSITES**
>
> While you're planning your trip, get up to speed on local New Orleans news, culture and events by checking out the following websites.
>
> **Gambit** www.bestofneworleans.com
>
> **Louisiana Weekly** www.louisianaweekly.com
>
> **Offbeat** www.offbeat.com
>
> **Times-Picayune** www.nola.com

redevelopment has been very good. In April 2006 the newspaper was honored with two Pulitzers for its coverage of Katrina. Chris Rose's column is essential reading for anyone who cares about the city. The paper offers visitors a daily entertainment calendar, and a glimpse of local society.

For alternative news and entertainment listings, pick up a copy of the free weekly newspaper *Gambit*. Its sporadic distribution makes it somewhat difficult to find; it's surprisingly scarce in coffee shops. The monthly *Offbeat* magazine provides a complete music and entertainment calendar with good reviews of local performances and recordings. It's available free at record stores and coffee shops.

The *Louisiana Weekly*, which has been published in New Orleans since 1925, offers an African American perspective on local and regional politics and events. The paper has covered the hurricane and recovery from a decidedly different perspective, ranging from the middle ground to the far left; interesting to get a fuller picture of how New Orleanians see things.

Where New Orleans is a monthly publication that offers maps of attractions; it's strictly for visitors.

A few magazines about the South deserve a mention. The *Oxford American*, published in William Faulkner's hometown of Oxford, Mississippi, is sort of the *New Yorker* magazine for the South. It deals with modern Southern culture generally, with a literary and somewhat intellectual sensibility.

WWOZ FM90.7 is the city's best station for music, playing nonstop music from New Orleans and Louisiana. For more on the station and its programs, see WWOZ, the Sound of New Orleans on p82.

WSMB AM1350 is worth listening to in the afternoon, from 4pm to 7pm, when Tom Fitzmorris' 'The Food Show' airs. Locals get passionate about food, discussing everything from recipes for gumbo to where to get the best oysters.

Station WWNO FM89.9 broadcasts a predominantly classical format but plays jazz from 10:30pm to 1am. It's the city's only National Public Radio affiliate, offering morning and evening news programs.

News and literary programming is broadcast by WRBH FM88.3.

LANGUAGE

Visitors expecting to hear French will be greatly disappointed. You are likely to hear the familiar Southern drawl, with 'y'all' being a common way to address one person or an entire crowd. At all levels of society it is common to drop the final 'g' in gerunds: 'I'm goin' to the shoppin' mall to get a swimmin' suit.'

> **TALK LIKE A NEW ORLEANIAN**
>
> As you would expect in a city that calls a 'hero sandwich' a 'po'boy,' New Orleanians tend to put their own dressing on the English language. All the time people stare right at you and say 'where y'at.' They aren't really asking where you're at though, they just want to know how you're doing. And they don't want a downer reply. People also say they're 'makin groceries' when they're heading down to the supermarket.
>
> The French Quarter is commonly referred to as the Vieux Carré (Voo Carray), meaning 'old quarter.' Sidewalks are called banquets. The expression 'Laissez les bon temps roulez' (Let the good times roll) is heard all the time.
>
> New Orleans streets with French names featuring corrupted pronunciations include Decatur (De-*cay*-ter), Burgundy (Bur-*gun*-dee), Esplanade (Es-plan-*aid*), Chartres (*Char*-ters) and Carondelet (Car-ahn-dah-*lette*).
>
> The calliope organ heard on Mississippi steamboats is pronounced 'cah-lie-o-pee,' but the old Calliope housing project is typically called 'Cally-ope.'

Traces of New Orleans' old 'Yat' dialect are still heard around town. Apart from city-specific expressions, Yat sounds an awful lot like the traditional Brooklyn accent, and it reflects the same Irish, Italian and German roots. French terms survive from the Creole days, but pronunciation is not always faithful. See Talk Like a New Orleanian, opposite, for a short primer on local talk.

ECONOMY & COSTS

Hurricane Katrina caused a fiscal crisis unprecedented in the US. All of New Orleans' industries were affected. The city was completely shut down for weeks, and months later economic recovery progressed slowly.

The Port of New Orleans, one of the nation's largest, remained shut for two weeks after the storm, leading to price jumps across the US in coffee and other goods that enter the country at New Orleans. Before Katrina, the port saw some 6000 ocean vessels each year, and by the end of 2005 traffic had improved to 65% of its pre-Katrina levels. For New Orleans, the dip meant losses in docking fees, storage rents, distribution income and banking fees. However, the port is expected to fully recover.

The oil industry in Louisiana seemed to sail through the crisis as the dip in local production was partially offset by a temporary hike in oil prices. At full capacity, Louisiana produces 19% of the country's natural gas reserves and 11% of the country's petroleum. Also affected by Katrina was the local fishing industry, which provides more than one-fourth of the US's seafood annually. This trade too is expected to recover, although overfishing and a general decline of sea life worldwide is likely to have a great impact in Louisiana. The storm surge, by pushing destructive amounts of salt water into the state's fresh waterways, decimated inland crawfish populations, which were expected to decline to 20% of the normal level for the 2006 season. The wholesale price doubled.

Tourism, which in the year prior to Katrina netted $5.5 billion for the city (with 10.1 million visitors coming to New Orleans in 2004), saw a huge dip in revenue long after the hurricane. Vacationers, who typically stay away from the parts of town hardest hit by the floods, seemed deterred by the imagined devastation of the French Quarter. Business in restaurants, bars and retail shops in the French Quarter, which all rely heavily on the tourist trade, was far below normal months after the storm. Elsewhere in town, such as Magazine St in the Garden District, recovered fairly quickly on the strength of overwhelming local support.

A large part of the tourism industry in New Orleans is conventions, which in an ordinary year occupy the Ernest Morial Convention Center every week. In the wake of Katrina, dozens of conventions scheduled for 2006 pulled out of New Orleans. Cleanup and restoration efforts got the Convention Center back in operational condition in early 2006, but tradeshow and convention business weren't expected to fully recover for another year or so.

A fully recovered tourism industry is seen as key to New Orleans' future. The slow return of visitors to the French Quarter, the CBD and the Garden District, long after they had recovered from the storms, hurt a city that desperately needed a boost. The city government suffered as its tax base shrank, further hamstringing city-funded efforts in the recovery. On an individual level, a large percentage of the 75,000 citizens employed in tourism-related industries were out of work.

The huge drop in the local population hurt the economy as local businesses struggled to fill staff positions. The city suffered a severe housing shortage, and resulting skyrocketing rents deterred service workers from coming back. Local fast-food chains were offering signing bonuses and wages up to $10 per hour for jobs that normally pay at or just above the minimum wage of $5.15 per hour. As parts of the city are rebuilt, increased housing ought to help bring down rents and increase labor in the city, but it is likely to take several years before a balance is finally reached.

For tourists, costs are not greatly changed in post-Katrina New Orleans. While the drop in tourism would ordinarily mean lower hotel rates, a shortage of hotel rooms resulted from the crisis, as many rooms were occupied by FEMA employees and homeless New Orleanians. Available hotel rooms were consequently going at peak season rates, making it difficult to find a double room for less than $150 per night. As more rooms became available in 2006, and as big tourist draws like Jazz Fest took place, prices were expected to fluctuate more. Expensive Creole restaurants and cheap mom-and-pop dives opened soon after Katrina, making it possible to spend anywhere from $5 to $100 for an excellent New Orleans meal. Car-rental rates held at about $40 per day for a compact Chevy or similar vehicle.

The temporary loss of the St Charles Streetcar line made travelers moving between the French Quarter and the Garden District more reliant on taxis. And while fewer taxis were available during early 2006, the rates were legally fixed. A ride from Canal St to Jackson St costs about $6. The fare from the airport is fixed at $28 for up to two passengers.

GOVERNMENT & POLITICS

New Orleans is governed by an elected mayor and a legislative city council. Council members represent five political districts of the city, which will need to be redrawn after the redevelopment of New Orleans.

New Orleans and Louisiana politics have always been rife with cronyism and corruption. In the early 20th century 'political machines' ran City Hall and the rest of the state. The Regular Democratic Organization, known as the 'Old Regulars,' ran things for decades. So did 'the boss,' Mayor Martin Behrman, who sat in the mayor's chair from 1904 to 1920, and again in 1924. More recently the Morial family held the mayorship for the best part of four decades, with father Ernest 'Dutch' Morial heading the city from 1978 to 1986 and son Marc Morial taking over from 1994 to 2002. At the time of the younger Morial's departure many positions in the city government were occupied by family and friends of the Morials. In the 2002 election Richard Pennington's defeat was in part brought about by his presumed affiliation with the Morials. Political outsider Ray Nagin scored an overwhelming upset victory. Nagin's win was seen as a boost for reformers, but his anticorruption campaign didn't go much further than crackdowns in the Taxicab Bureau and the Utilities Department.

In the late 1920s Huey P Long (who chose for himself the nickname the 'Kingfish') formed a statewide political machine that outlived Long himself. Long, a populist candidate who single-handedly unseated the Old Regulars, served a single term as the governor, from 1928 to 1932. He continued to rule the state from Washington, DC, where he served as US senator before he was assassinated in 1935. His less-influential brother, Earl Long, was governor three times, beginning in 1939, when he replaced Governor Richard Leche, the Kingfish's appointed heir, who resigned during a corruption scandal. Earl Long, fondly remembered for his well-publicized affair with stripper Blaze Starr, was re-elected to alternating single terms in 1948 and 1956. His wife had him committed to a mental institution for a short period during his final term in office, and the governor got himself released only after firing the hospital administrator and replacing him with a more sympathetic administrator.

The real power in the city has been behind the scenes, at times, in the hands of bankers, newspapermen and other businessmen in New Orleans' tightly knit elite clubs. The presidents of the Hiberia, Whitney and Canal banks, and members of the highly exclusive Boston Club, the Pickwick Club and the Louisiana Club, have traditionally wielded an inordinate amount of political power in the city.

State and local politics have all too often served the needs of big business while overlooking such critical issues as public schools, long among the worst in the country, and crime. The New Orleans Police Department (NOPD) was notoriously corrupt for decades, until a mid-1990s shakedown helped restore some semblance of dignity.

ENVIRONMENT

The damage wrought by the aftermath of Hurricane Katrina, though devastating for so much of the city, was not the cataclysmic event long foreseen by ecologists. Nature seems to have her own plans for southern Louisiana and, despite consistent human efforts to stave off the inevitable, New Orleans remains an enjoy-it-while-you-can sort of place.

CLIMATE

The Gulf of Mexico provides New Orleans with plenty of moisture – the city receives about 60in of rainfall annually. No season is immune from rain.

In March, April and May the weather is quite variable, with plenty of rain; but when spring arrives, it brings long stretches of sunny, mild days that are perfect for the festivals.

Summer from June to August is hot and steamy; your clothes stick to your skin and you never feel properly dry. Brief afternoon showers, with thunder thrown in for dramatic effect, occur almost daily. On long summer days you can expect about eight or more hours of sunshine, out of a possible 14 hours. The months of September and October are the most likely to offer clear, temperate weather.

Winter temperatures average a comfortable 54°F, yet occasional drops in temperature, combined with the damp atmosphere, can chill you to the bone. Snow is rare in New Orleans. During December's short days, fog and rain conspire to allow only 4½ hours of sunshine a day.

Localized river fog often forms from December to May.

HURRICANE SEASON

Hurricanes – tropical cyclones in the Western Atlantic Ocean and the Gulf of Mexico – strike anytime from June 1 to November 30, with the greatest frequency in late summer and early autumn. In especially busy years, hurricanes can occur well into December, even January.

A developing hurricane passes through several stages. A tropical depression is the formative stage, and a tropical storm is a strengthened tropical depression, with wind speeds between 39mph and 73mph. A Category One hurricane brings winds between 74mph and 95mph. This can produce a storm surge, or large waves, which can flood coastal roads. The most intense is a Category Five hurricane, with sustained winds of 156mph or greater.

Hurricanes are sighted well in advance, though their exact course can never be predicted. There are two distinct stages of alert: a Hurricane Watch, issued when a hurricane *may* strike in the area within the next 36 to 48 hours, and a Hurricane Warning, issued when a hurricane is likely to strike the area.

THE LAND

The first important factor to consider is that New Orleans is surrounded by water. The city stands between the Mississippi River, which curls like a devilish snake around much of the city, and Lake Pontchartrain, a large saltwater body connected to the Gulf of Mexico. Swamps and marshes cover much of the remaining area around the city.

The land the city stands on has been wrested from the Mississippi's natural floodplain. The oldest parts of town adhere to the high ground, which are in fact natural levees created by the Mississippi depositing soil there during floods. The moniker 'Crescent City' comes from this old footprint on the natural levees, which got its shape by forming along the curve of the river. The high ground in New Orleans is just a few feet above sea level. Much of the rest of the city is below sea level, forming a bowl that obviously remains vulnerable to flooding, despite man-made levees. The city's elevation averages 2ft below sea level. And it is sinking.

Most of Louisiana and Mississippi was formed over millennia by the Mississippi, which spilled huge amounts of soil toward the gulf, forming sandbars and land. The river constantly shifted its course as it deposited more land into the Gulf, forever fanning east then west and back, pushing the coast further south. The river continually changed its course in search of shorter paths to the Gulf. The land it created was of a fine and loose soil, excellent for planting. It also gradually sinks under its own weight, in a process known as subsidence. Before the levees were put in place, flooding regularly replenished the soil and offset this subsidence. The 'bowl' that flooded after Hurricane Katrina is partly land that has subsided, and partly former swamp.

New Orleans is surrounded by 130 miles of levees. The US Army Corps of Engineers built and maintains these levees, which have kept the Mississippi River on a fixed course for more than a century (see p144). You'll see the levee from Jackson Sq, in the French Quarter, as it

Swamps of Louisiana

rises like an evenly graded hill and hides the river from view. You can also walk along the levee for an up-close look at it and one of the world's most powerful rivers.

The other important factor for New Orleans is its proximity to the Gulf of Mexico, and its vulnerability to the storm systems generated there. The Atlantic hurricane season lasts approximately half a year, from early summer to late fall. The 2005 hurricane season was particularly brutal, with a record 27 tropical storms spawning 15 hurricanes. Of the five to make landfall, two, Katrina and Rita, slammed southern Louisiana within a three-week period. Katrina was by far the most destructive, but Rita was actually stronger.

Neither Katrina nor Rita was a direct, cataclysmic hit on New Orleans. Had the eye of either storm passed over the city, damage from wind and flying debris may well have exceeded damage done by flooding. In such an event, neighborhoods on the higher ground would not have been spared. New Orleanians must continue to brace themselves for a disaster of that magnitude. With Hurricane Ivan having struck near the city in 2004, it seems Louisiana is experiencing major hurricanes with increased frequency.

Hurricanes cause floods by pushing in surging volumes of water from the Gulf. New Orleans is exposed to Gulf storm surges via Lake Pontchartrain, which is connected to the Gulf, and via the Industrial Canal, which links up with the Gulf, Lake Pontchartrain and the Mississippi River. Surging Gulf waters can be far more difficult to predict than rising river tides. Storm surges rise up like tsunamis, lunging upward as they squeeze through narrow canals. River floods, by contrast, can be observed far upstream, often weeks in advance.

GREEN NEW ORLEANS

Hurricane Katrina caused extensive environmental damage by washing waters contaminated with sewage, petroleum, lead and other toxins over 80% of New Orleans. And the 12 million tons of debris caused by destroyed buildings and trees was estimated to have created three decades' worth of landfill. In the rush to clean up the devastated areas, some environmentalists feared not enough precautions were taken to ensure the toxic agents were safely disposed of. Consequently, further cleanup is necessary as these parts of town are redeveloped.

Katrina also pointed out the urgency of addressing the state's long-ignored coastal erosion. South of New Orleans, some 25 miles of coast – an area roughly equivalent to the size of Manhattan – is lost each year due in part to subsidence of the natural floodplains. Erosion is further enhanced by the extensive canal network dredged for oil production, and the wakes of shipping traffic wears away at the delicate edges of these canals. Quickly disappearing are miles of bird refuges, home to more than half of North America's bird species, as well as freshwater homes to Louisiana's treasured crawfish bounty. The Cajun fishermen who have maintained their unique lifestyle for so many generations are facing the reality that their lifestyle and their home are endangered. For New Orleans, the loss of these wetlands makes the city more vulnerable to hurricanes, as the diminishing land buffer enables hurricanes to maintain full strength nearer to the city. For similar reasons, New Orleans will only become more vulnerable to storm surges like the one that followed Hurricane Katrina.

A plan to offset coastal erosion, calling for some controlled flooding of the lower Mississippi and restoration of offshore islands, was drawn up in the early 1990s, but hasn't yet been implemented. Mike Tidwell's book *Bayou Farewell* is a compelling look at what is lost in environmental and cultural terms.

By sending storm surges up the Mississippi River Gulf Outlet, a canal dug to provide more direct access from the Gulf to the Port of New Orleans, Katrina made a decisive case for closing down the environmentally destructive outlet. MRGO, as the outlet is called, is a huge intrusion in an extremely delicate ecosystem. At 76 miles long, it is longer than the Panama Canal, and it passes from a saltwater body deep into low-lying freshwater marshlands. Erosion has expanded the canal to three times its original width, and more than 11,000 acres of cypress swamp and 19,000 acres of marsh have been lost to saltwater intrusion. Vegetation and wildlife have also disappeared. Ironically, the anticipated shipping traffic never really materialized, and it has cost tens of millions annually to maintain the canal. During Hurricanes Katrina and Rita, levees all along MRGO were breached, causing flooding to St Bernard Parish and leading to the Industrial Canal breach that decimated the Lower Ninth Ward. In September 2005 Louisiana's senators urged Congress to stop funding MRGO's maintenance, hoping the canal would naturally refill if dredging stopped.

URBAN PLANNING & DEVELOPMENT

After Hurricane Katrina damaged or destroyed 80% of New Orleans' mostly residential areas, the city faced some daunting redevelopment decisions, and few of the solutions were likely to escape controversy. However, there was real hope that out of the tragedy some positive changes could be brought about.

FUTURE FLOOD PROTECTION

After Hurricanes Katrina and Rita it became disturbingly clear that most, if not all, of the flooding had resulted from engineering problems on the inland floodwalls that failed during the storms. Breaches at the 17th St and London Canals, which led to flooding throughout the lakeside of town, were clearly due to design failure, as the soil beneath the canals shifted and undermined the floodwalls well before the water level had reached their tops. The floodwall along the Industrial Canal, through the Lower Ninth Ward, appeared to have also performed below design specifications, as there was no sign the walls had been overtopped by the storm surge. The Army Corps of Engineers, which built the floodwalls and maintains them, argued the Industrial Canal breach was not caused by human error, instead, claiming the 14ft walls were designed to contain only 12.5ft of water. That excuse didn't appear to hold water, however, as local officials and engineers offered ample evidence to counter the Corps' slippery logic.

Meanwhile, the Army Corps of Engineers began rebuilding the failed floodwalls to pre-Katrina specs, which promised protection in the event of a Category Three storm. Katrina was measured at Category Three when it made landfall on the Gulf Coast, so New Orleanians were less than reassured by this development. The State of Louisiana urged for taller and stronger floodwalls built to withstand Category Five storm surges. The state also demanded improved drainage in the city, wetlands restoration to help buffer New Orleans against hurricanes, and for sea walls at spillways and canals entering from the Gulf. The Feds balked at the project, which some estimated would cost $32 billion and take decades to complete.

The Army Corps of Engineers did agree to strengthen the 17th St Canal by adding new floodgates, improved pumps and new levees along the canal. And as the breached Industrial Canal wall was rebuilt, some argued that the opposite side, which did not breach during Katrina, would be the vulnerable side in future storm surges. Ultimately, it seems, there's no winning when the opponent is water.

In early 2006 the mayor's appointed 'Bring New Orleans Back Commission' released its initial plan for the future, which at that stage remained exploratory but put forth some major changes.

Top on the list of controversial issues was the proposal to shrink the city footprint to accommodate what is likely to be a far smaller population in the future New Orleans. Part of the thinking behind the reduced footprint plan was to make it easier and more economical to rebuild infrastructure, including city streets and drainage, in the redeveloped areas. Some of the decimated areas were likely to be sparsely populated, and the commission put the onus on residents to declare their intention to return before any commitment was made toward rebuilding. A smaller footprint was also thought of as a way to reduce the flood prone area of the city.

The commission also proposed plans for new housing tracts in the areas that will be redeveloped, with mix-income properties rather than the housing projects that for decades have been mired in poverty and crime. Such tracts, possibly slated for devastated parts of Mid-City, may be modeled on the River Garden development near the Lower Garden District. New regulations may also require that homes in flood zones be elevated. The plan recommended developing a light-rail system and adding new parks and bike paths throughout the city.

Mardi Gras & Jazz Fest

Mardi Gras 32
History 33
Experiencing Carnival 37
New Orleans Jazz & Heritage Festival 49
History 50
Experiencing Jazz Fest 51

Mardi Gras & Jazz Fest

In February or March each year New Orleans expands on the Fat Tuesday concept with a 10-day festival during which the fun steadily intensifies until the entire city is certifiably insane. That's Carnival, or Mardi Gras, for you. Then the city does it again for Jazz Fest, which also falls over a 10-day period. Both festivals flout the old showbiz adage of leaving 'em wanting more. These festivals deliver course after course until no one is left standing. You simply can't take any more. But many people will come back again next year, and year after year after that.

Samba dancer sashaying through the French Quarter

Mardi Gras is a deeply rooted tradition in New Orleans that goes all the way back to the city's origins as a French colony. In 1699 on Lundi Gras (Mardi Gras Eve), Pierre Le Moyne, Sieur d'Iberville, took possession of the Louisiana territory and named his first encampment Pointe de Mardi Gras. Since then, New Orleans' Mardi Gras has evolved into one of the greatest spectacles in the world.

Jazz Fest, while dating back only to 1970, is not to be outdone by Mardi Gras. By showcasing music, food and the arts, Jazz Fest celebrates the culture that is so integral to life in New Orleans. As a tourist attraction, Jazz Fest is on a par with Mardi Gras. In the 2006 comeback year, visitors pouring into New Orleans for Jazz Fest outnumbered those who came for Mardi Gras. It was the great show of faith the city so badly needed from out-of-town fanatics.

Both festivals are tremendous and unique events. If we had our pick, we'd say do both.

MARDI GRAS

Carnival is New Orleans' leviathan holiday – a beautiful, undulating, snakelike festival that first rears its head on January 6 (the Feast of the Epiphany) and weeks later unfolds in all its startling, fire-breathing glory to terrify and delight the millions who come to the city to worship it.

In New Orleans, Mardi Gras operates on the subconscious. It's the flame that burns in the city's soul, the elaborate overture that tells us what the city is all about. It's a baroque fantasy, a vibrant flower, a circus, a nightmare, a temptation from the devil. It permeates all levels of New Orleans society. Families of all classes and colors come out before each parade. All over the city imaginative people create theatrical costumes for seasonal masquerade parties.

Above all, Mardi Gras is a hell of a party, and New Orleans, in its characteristic generosity, welcomes travelers from around the world to join in the revelry.

HISTORY

To understand and appreciate Mardi Gras it is helpful to first become familiar with its history, for many of the traditions that shape the holiday today actually acquired their significance decades, even centuries ago.

Pagan Rites

Carnival's pagan origins are not lost on anyone in New Orleans. Carnival can be traced all the way back to the ancient Greeks, who held prespring festivals that could be downright decadent. The Romans took up the torch, and added oil to the flames, with their Lupercalia, which was celebrated in an atmosphere of characteristic debauchery. During Lupercalia, all social order broke down as citizens and slaves, men and women cavorted in masks and costumes and behaved in a totally lawless and licentious manner. Sadism, masochism and prostitution were the order of the day, followed by a period of recovery and introspection. An ox was sacrificed, and its blood was believed to wash away the sins of the people. Similar pagan rites were practiced by Druid priests in France, culminating in the sacrifice of a bull.

The early Catholic Church failed to appreciate these traditions, but after trying unsuccessfully to suppress them, the church eventually co-opted the spring rite and fit it into the Christian calendar. In Rome, it came to be known as *carnevale* (farewell to the flesh), referring to the fasting that began on Ash Wednesday. For many centuries the celebration, lasting several days, continued to be characterized by chaos and public lewdness, with a pervading sense of violence in the air.

MEET THE BOYS ON THE BATTLEFRONT

The most significant African American tradition of Carnival began in 1885 when a Mardi Gras Indian gang, calling itself the Creole Wild West, paraded the city's backstreets on Mardi Gras. Their elaborately beaded and feathered suits and headdresses made a huge impression, and many more black Indian gangs soon followed – the Wild Tchoupitoulas, Yellow Pocahontas and Golden Eagles, among many others. The new tradition, some say, signified respect for Native Americans who constantly fought US expansion in the New World. A canon of black Indian songs was passed down from generation to generation, with lyrics often fusing English, Creole French, Choctaw and African words until their meaning was obscure.

From the beginning, 'masking Indian' was a serious proposition. Tribes became organized fighting units headed by a Big Chief, with Spy Boys, Flag Boys and Wild Men carrying out carefully defined roles. Tremendous pride was evident in the costly and expertly sewn suits, and when two gangs crossed paths, an intense confrontation would ensue as members of each tribe sized each other up. Often violence would break out. As is the case with many of Mardi Gras' strongest traditions, this was no mere amusement.

Big Chiefs became pillars of communities, and some became legends – among them Big Chief Jolly of the Wild Tchoupitoulas and Tootie Montana of the Yellow Pocahontas. Chief Jolly, an uncle of the Neville Brothers, made his mark by recording black Indian classics backed by The Meters. Bo Dollis and the Wild Magnolias are one of the most dynamic Indian performers, and they appear at clubs in New Orleans and at Jazz Fest.

Over the years, black Indian suits gained recognition as extravagant works of folk art, and they are exhibited as such at the **Backstreet Cultural Museum** (p146), at the **Presbytère** (p137) and at **Jazz Fest** (p49). Layers of meaningful mosaics are designed and created in patterns of neatly stitched sequins. Multilayered feathered headdresses – particularly those of the big chiefs – are more elaborate and flamboyant than the headgear worn by Las Vegas show performers. The making of a new suit can take the better part of a year.

After Hurricane Katrina, the fate of the Mardi Gras Indians was in doubt. Most of the gangs hailed from the city's worst-hit neighborhoods, and the Indians had scattered across the country. Many were unable to sew new suits for Mardi Gras 2006, but an encouraging number came back and made their presence known on the streets. As Big Chief Victor Harris of the Spirit of Fi Yi Yi gang told *OffBeat* magazine, 'Even though it's sort of a ghost town, we have to bring the spirit out of the ghost.'

Visitors not in town for Mardi Gras are likely to have other opportunities to see them at **Jazz Fest**, or occasionally performing in clubs like **Tipitina's** (p209). The Indians also parade annually on **St Joseph's Night** (roughly midway through the Lenten season) and on **Super Sunday** (p16).

In Venice by the 17th century, a sophisticated theatrical sensibility turned Carnival into a baroque masquerade in which citizens transformed themselves into characters of the commedia dell'arte and ran rampant on the city's streets. The festival continued to thumb its nose at social conventions, and a preponderance of satyr costumes indicates the holiday's pagan origins had not been forgotten. This theatrical form of Carnival became the custom in France, and variations of it spread to French outposts in the New World.

Creole Carnival

Early generations of Creoles loved to dance, and they celebrated the Carnival season with balls and a full calendar of music and theater. The Creoles also had a penchant for masking, and on Mardi Gras the people of the city would emerge from their homes wearing grotesque, sometimes diabolical, disguises.

From the beginning the spirit of Carnival appears to have crossed race lines and permeated every level of society. Early on, Creoles of color held Carnival balls to which slaves were sometimes invited. The popularity of masking among blacks was made evident by an ordinance, passed during Spanish rule, which prohibited blacks from masking. The fear was that blacks, effectively disguising their color, might easily invade elite white balls. Several times, masking was altogether outlawed by authorities who distrusted the way in which masks undermined the established social order. This didn't stop people from masking, though, and on Mardi Gras, the citizenry tended to blend into an unruly, desegregated mob.

Carnival remained primarily a Creole celebration for several decades after the Louisiana Purchase made New Orleans a US city, and Creoles continued to elaborate on the festivities. By the 1830s parades replete with ornamented carriages, musicians and masked equestrians had become an important part of the Mardi Gras celebration. But the public splendor was short-lived, and by the mid-19th century Creole Carnival revelers had begun withdrawing into their ballrooms. Many Creoles lamented that New Orleans had become too American, too practical-minded, to sustain such a fanciful holiday as Mardi Gras.

Carnival's 'Golden Age'

Mardi Gras was saved not by Creoles, but by a secretive group of wealthy Anglos who resided in the Garden District. Calling themselves the **Mistick Krewe of Comus**, these men made their first public appearance after dark, their spectacular horse-drawn floats illuminated by flambeaux (torches) on Mardi Gras in 1857. On that night, the stage was set for Carnival as we know it today.

New clubs modeled themselves on the Comus, calling themselves 'krewes' (a deliberately quirky spelling of 'crews'). **Rex** first appeared in 1872, **Momus** a year later and **Proteus** in 1882. Pompous parades, presided over by a king, coursed through the streets at night, delighting audiences with elaborately decorated, torch-lit floats fashioned from horse-drawn carriages. Mythological and sometimes satirical themes defined the parades, making these processions coherent theatrical works on wheels. The parades would end at a theater or the opera house, where exclusive balls would close out the evening.

These old-line krewes were (and for the most part remain) highly secretive societies comprising the cities wealthiest, most powerful men. They are to New Orleans as the nobility is to Europe, and their parades are often cynically regarded as condescending gestures from the privileged class to the masses. Rex naturally anointed his annual king the 'King of Carnival,' and his krewe also contributed several lasting traditions. He contributed the official colors of Carnival – purple, green and gold, which New Orleanians continue to work into their Mardi Gras attire – and the anthem of Carnival, a corny tune called 'If I Ever Cease to Love.' Additionally, the Rex parade featured floats that depicted biting political satire, which would become a recurring motif shared by other krewes.

But Comus' king remained the true king of Carnival. Whereas the identity of Rex's king was generally known to the public, the Comus' true identity was a carefully guarded secret. On Mardi Gras, Rex paid his respects to Comus by visiting him at his ball. These odd traditions are steadfastly observed to this day.

DOING FAT TUESDAY

There is a lot going on throughout the day on Mardi Gras, and it ain't all pretty. Your day can turn into a dog's breakfast if you don't have a plan. Take stock of what you want to check out, and figure out the where and when of it. We have our own rotund agenda for a Fat Tuesday that takes in Mardi Gras Indians, the big Zulu and Rex parades, some key walking parades and enough time for partying in the French Quarter and Faubourg Marigny.

Firstly, know that Mardi Gras is an all-day affair, and it's going to feel like you're going full throttle the entire way. Fortunately, fun and excitement on this scale will spur you to superhuman feats. For some, this means drinking booze from dawn till dissolution. Scarf some food wherever you can. Pace yourself, and you'll avoid the crash and vomit phase. But don't be a wet blanket. Approach the day as a migratory bird approaches flight over a large body of water.

Some things happen early. Mardi Gras Indians don't operate on a schedule, but often congregate at the **Backstreet Cultural Museum** (p146) in the early morning. Drop by around 10am, when the museum starts its 'open house.' If you don't spot any Indians in this vicinity, you might try Congo Sq in **Louis Armstrong Park** (p146).

On Rampart St you can catch **Zulu** as it reaches the end of its route. Then make your way back into the French Quarter to see the **Society of St Anne** walking parade, which reaches the Quarter around 11am or so. If you're in costume, you can just file in, joining the revelry as it makes its way to Canal St. Here, you'll meet up with the **Rex** parade.

The afternoon is a good time to hang out in the Quarter, which by now is a big masquerade party. Back at the Backstreet Cultural Museum, a cool party might be in full swing (you'll know about it if you stopped by earlier). Keep an eye out for the **Krewe of Cosmic Debris**, a fun krewe that usually hits a bunch of bars in the Quarter before ending up on Frenchmen St for a big musical street party that lasts on into the evening. At the **R Bar**, also in the Marigny, another raging party spills out onto Royal St.

Carnival rose to new heights during the years that followed the Civil War, and as New Orleans coped with the hardship and insult of 'carpetbag' rule, the importance of Mardi Gras as the cultural focal point of the year was cemented. At times, the seriousness with which Carnival was regarded in New Orleans was exhibited in rather extreme ways. In 1890 two parades, those of Comus and Proteus, reached the edge of the French Quarter at the same time. In a heated dispute over which krewe would enter the Quarter first, several krewe members appeared ready to draw swords, but the confrontation was resolved without violence.

Many enduring black traditions emerged around the turn of the 20th century. The spectacular **Mardi Gras Indians** began to appear in 1885 (see Meet the Boys on the Battlefront, p33). The **skull-and-bones gang** (influenced, some think, by Mexican Day of the Dead artwork), wearing comical skeleton suits, chased frightened little kids around neighborhoods on Mardi Gras morning. Their purported 'purpose' was to put a little fear in the youngsters in order to make the kids behave. A band of prostitutes calling themselves the **Baby Dolls** also began masking on Mardi Gras. Dressed in bloomers and bonnets, they danced from bar to bar, turning tricks along the way. You still might run into Baby Dolls today, but they probably won't be turning tricks.

The black krewe of **Zulu** first appeared in 1909, with members initially calling themselves the Tramps and parading on foot. By 1916, when the Zulu Social Aid & Pleasure Club was incorporated, the krewe had floats, and its antics deliberately spoofed the pomposity of elite white krewes. Zulu members paraded in black face, and their dress was a wickedly absurd interpretation of African tribal culture, as if to say, 'Is this really how you see us?' Krewe hierarchy included a witch doctor, a mayor, the absurdly uppity Mr Big Shot and a phalanx of tribal warriors bearing shields and wearing grass skirts. In time, Zulu's members would include some of the city's more prominent black citizens. Jazz star Louis Armstrong reigned as King Zulu in 1949, and although his float broke into pieces during the parade (fortunately, in front of a bar), he had no complaints. As he summed up the experience, 'I always been a Zulu, but King, man, this is the stuff.'

Modern Carnival

The 20th century has seen the coming and going of dozens of different krewes, each adding to the diversity and interest of Carnival. **Iris**, a women's krewe, was formed in 1917 and began parading in 1959. Gay krewes began forming in the late '50s, with **Petronius**, the oldest gay krewe still in existence, staging its first ball in 1962. (Petronius is not a parading krewe.)

Today's 'superkrewes' began forming in the 1960s. **Endymion** debuted as a modest neighborhood parade in 1967; now its parades and floats are the largest, with nearly 2000 riders and one of its immense floats measuring 240ft in length. Endymion is so big, its ball is held in the Louisiana Superdome. While Endymion was still fledgling, **Bacchus**, which began in 1969, shaped the trend for bigger things to come. From its start, Bacchus deliberately set out to break Carnival tradition, wowing its audiences by anointing celebrity monarchs (including Bob Hope, Jackie Gleason, Kirk Douglas and William Shatner) and opening its ball to the paid public. **Orpheus**, a superkrewe founded by musician Harry Connick Jr, first appeared in the mid-1990s.

Tradition was dealt a blow when the old-line krewes Comus, Proteus and Momus stopped parading in the early 1990s. City council member Dorothy Mae Taylor challenged these all-white krewes to integrate, and their response was to retreat from the streets, continuing their elite Carnival traditions in private.

Despite many changes, and although rambunctious tourists generally outnumber rowdy locals during Mardi Gras, the holiday continues to mark the zenith of New Orleans' festive annual calendar. And despite the grayish ooze of trash, spilled beer, piss and vomit that's ground into the city's gutters by thoughtless mobs, a hearty spirit manages to shine through, somehow linking today's Carnival to those of 18th-century France and even to the Lupercalia of ancient Rome. The masking tradition, carried out primarily in the French Quarter and Faubourg Marigny, upholds an ancient and enchanting Mardi Gras aesthetic. Night parades continue to haunt St Charles Ave and Canal St with surreal and terrifying floats, Mephistophelian masked riders and infernal flambeaux. The skull-and-bones gangs and black Indians continue to carry out their spontaneous rituals. When it comes right down to it, the good, the bad and the ugly are all parts of Mardi Gras tradition.

A Gras Like No Other

The parades were shorter, some of the floats looked a little ragged, crowds were smaller and people less rowdy than usual. But Mardi Gras 2006, taking place just six months after Hurricane Katrina, was loaded with significance. Despite scattered protests that celebrating Carnival would be inappropriate, the city urged itself on with a strident determination and its people came together to show what they're made of. With a warm, homespun quality, it turned a pretty sweet party.

For many, Mardi Gras was a homecoming. With very little yet accomplished in sorting out the devastated city's future, New Orleanians converged on their city from hotels and apartments across the country. Their presence was an affirmation of spirit and, hopefully, a harbinger for the city's future. The desire to return to New Orleans, and to keep the city's traditions alive, was palpable in every event. The message was clear: the party would go on, but not without them.

The Krewe of Dreux, a Gentilly group, paraded through the heart of its flood-ravaged district. It was a strange, Fellini-esque sight, so many people in goofy attire amid such desolation. But it was their own desolation, and veiled in their frivolity was a very serious sense of optimism, hope and defiance. Mardi Gras Indians, many of them scattered across the US, reconvened in New Orleans, where some marched in the Lower Ninth Ward. Zulu, the city's largest African American krewe, paraded down St Charles Ave, accompanied for the first time by 20 Zulu dancers from South Africa. Once the participants reached the parade's customary terminus at Armstrong Park, however, most members continued on foot through severely damaged Mid-City neighborhoods, where many of the krewe members lived.

The sardonic humor that is always a significant part of Mardi Gras was especially acute in 2006. Carnival floats were mockingly draped with the blue tarpaulins that covered so many damaged roofs after Katrina. Krewe d'Etat had floats celebrating 'Olympic' sports, such as 'Breach Volleyball' and 'Looter Shooting.' And WWOZ radio announced that the new Krewe of FEMA (Federal Emergency Management Agency) would make its inaugural appearance on Ash Wednesday – hilariously, a day too late.

To be sure, there was a touch of sadness about this Mardi Gras. As Andrei Codrescu wrote, 'Mardi Gras feels more like Dia de los Muertos.' Maybe so. Or perhaps it can be likened to the point in a jazz funeral when a somber procession turns into a more joyous second-line parade. The city needed to let go of its grief so that it could move forward. For that, Mardi Gras came just in time.

EXPERIENCING CARNIVAL

Carnival begins slowly, with related events, parties and parades becoming more frequent as Mardi Gras nears. (Mardi Gras, translating as 'Fat Tuesday,' is used here specifically to refer to the actual day, rather than to the entire season; Carnival refers to the season from January 6 to Fat Tuesday.) During the final, culminating weekend, particularly on Lundi Gras and Mardi Gras, many things are scheduled to occur simultaneously, and you will have to make some decisions. Preplanning and prioritizing are definitely in order, as getting around town grows more difficult with each passing day (a bicycle will grant you the greatest mobility). Be prepared to improvise a little.

Parades

PARADING KREWES

The parade season is a 12-day period beginning two Fridays before Fat Tuesday. Most of the early parades are charming, almost neighborly processions that whet your appetite for the later parades, which increase in size and grandeur by the day, until the awesome spectacles of the superkrewes emerge during the final weekend.

A popular preseason night procession, usually held three Saturdays before Fat Tuesday, is that of the **Krewe du Vieux** (see Taking the Piss Out of Carnival, p38). By parading before the official parade season and forgoing motorized floats (nearly all krewe members are on foot), Krewe du Vieux is permitted to pass through the French Quarter. It's a throwback to the old days, before floats and crowds grew too large, when parading krewes typically traversed the Quarter while onlookers packed the sidewalks and balconies. The themes of this notoriously bawdy and satirical krewe clearly aim to offend puritanical types.

NOBLESSE OBLIGE

Parading Carnival krewes don't just aim to entertain the masses – they come bearing gifts. Krewe members aboard floats toss trinkets, called 'throws,' to eager mobs clamoring for free booty.

It is important to impress upon Carnival virgins that getting your share is not passive work. Regardless of how cheap or garish the throws are, people want 'em. You have to plea for the sympathy of krewe members, and once a throw is airborne you often have to fend off aggressive rivals. It's all in good fun, of course, but it helps to have a little competitive drive.

The traditional plea 'Throw me something, mister!' is a holdover from the days when all krewe members were men. You'll still hear people say it, but if you're addressing a woman, a simple 'Throw me something!' will suffice.

The standard item tossed from Carnival floats is a string of plastic beads. By the end of Mardi Gras, aggressive throw-catchers can proudly drape several pounds of beads around their necks.

Quantity isn't the only issue. Creative throws, such as Zulu's famous hand-painted coconuts, are among Carnival's highest prizes. 'Medallion beads' (or 'krewe beads') bearing an emblem representing the krewe are also highly sought after. Doubloons (minted aluminum coins bearing krewe insignia and themes) are popular collectors' items. Other things you may acquire along a parade route range from plastic cups to bags of potato chips.

The smaller, common plastic beads coveted by spectators a generation ago have come to be called 'tree beads,' for their ignominious fate is to be tossed into the branches of the live oaks along St Charles Ave, where some actually hang on long enough to see the following year's Carnival. They can also be strung together to make elegant Christmas tree ornaments.

A word of caution: when a throw lands on the street, claim it by stepping on it, then pick it up. If you try to pick it up without first stepping on it, someone else will surely step on your fingers – and then insist that the object is by rights theirs!

Krewes that traditionally parade during the first weekend are **Pontchartrain**, with a Mid-City promenade known for its stellar marching-band contests; the **Knights of Sparta**, with an Uptown night parade that features traditional touches like flambeaux carriers and a mule-drawn float; and **Carrollton**, an 80-year-old krewe that rolls down St Charles Ave on Sunday afternoon.

In some years, parades are held every night of the subsequent week, getting larger as the final weekend gets near. Toward the end of the week, the highly secretive **Knights of Babylon** presents its attractive traditional parade, replete with flambeaux and riding lieutenants (eerily reminiscent of hooded Klansmen); it follows the Uptown route, but continues toward the lake on Canal St and down Basin St for a few blocks. On the Friday night before Mardi Gras, Uptown is the domain of **Hermes**, with its beautiful nighttime spectacle maintaining the aloof mystery of 19th-century Carnival processions. Hermes is followed directly by **Le Krewe d'Etat**, whose name is a clever, satirical pun: d'Etat is ruled by a dictator, rather than a king. However menacing this modern krewe may be, d'Etat's floats and costumes reflect fairly traditional standards of beauty.

Mardi Gras weekend is lit up by the entrance of the superkrewes, with their monstrous floats and endless processions of celebrities, marching bands, Shriner buggies, military units and police officers. The superkrewes always take the 'bigger is better' approach to the fullest allowable extent, and are as flashy as a Vegas revue. The crowds of spectators also grow larger by the day, and that comfortable corner you'd staked out for yourself earlier in the week is now likely to be overrun by tourists. All of these considerations aside, if you've been in town all week, you'll be ready for something bigger by this time. (A few nonsuperkrewes parade on the weekend as well.)

The all-women's krewe, **Iris**, parades down St Charles Ave with more than 30 floats and 750 krewe members. Iris is usually followed by **Tucks** (see Taking the Piss Out of Carnival, below), an irreverent krewe with the inspired alliterative motto of 'Booze, Beer, Bourbon, Broads'.

On Saturday night the megakrewe **Endymion** stages its spectacular parade and Extravaganza, as it calls its ball in the Superdome. With about 1900 riders on nearly 30 enormous, luminescent floats rolling down Canal St from Mid-City, the Endymion parade is one of

TAKING THE PISS OUT OF CARNIVAL

New Orleans' old-line Carnival krewes enjoy a bit of satire, but mostly just create an aura of pompous mystery with their secret kings and queens and their exclusive balls. No doubt they enjoy themselves and their own exquisiteness. But for we common folk, the most fun to be had during Mardi Gras is with the smart-asses. For many, the whole point of Carnival is to crack wise about pretty much anything. And while they're taking the piss out of authority figures and the most vaunted traditions of Carnival itself, they manage to have as much fun as anyone anywhere.

The **Krewe of Mystic Orphans and Misfits** (aka MOMs) does a commendable job of mocking the elites. MOMs' titular heads are King Quasimodo the Megamillion and Queen Inertia the Inumerable. MOMs has some serious fun at its raging masquerade ball, held annually at Blaine Kern's Mardi Gras World, amid the grand floats of bigger krewes. The ball is not exclusive, but it is by invitation only. Make friends in town and you might find your way in.

More accessible are the marching krewes, such as the bawdy **Krewe du Vieux** (www.kreweduvieux.org), whose rocking walking parade through the French Quarter two weeks before Mardi Gras weekend is reason enough to do Mardi Gras earlier than the rest of the tourists. The krewe's annual themes tend to challenge accepted notions of good taste, and awful puns are *de rigueur*. The 2006 theme was 'C'est Levee.' Get it? In spite of itself, Krewe du Vieux has become a cherished tradition, with the only float parade going through the French Quarter. After the parade, its ball, the raucous Krewe du Vieux Doo, is open to the public (admission $20). See the krewe's website for information.

For mockery that's even less gracefully articulated, don't miss the parade of the **Krewe of Tucks** (www.kreweoftucks.com), which got its name from an old bar and celebrates the frat-boy virtues of beer, broads and beads. Its parade is the only one that spectators are allowed to throw things at, although you're really only supposed to toss unwanted beads into the giant toilet on one of its floats. Anyone can join this most undiscriminating of krewes, ride in its parade and party at its ball. See the krewe's website for information.

Not anyone can join the **Krewe of Barkus**, however, as it's strictly for dogs. Founded in 1993 (by humans on behalf of their dogs), this canine krewe has a king and queen. On Sunday before Mardi Gras, some 1500 costumed pooches sniff the streets and piss on fire hydrants in a parade with floats and marching bands.

the season's most electrifying events. Endymion always has celebrity marshals, and the krewe's massive 240ft steamboat float is the biggest in New Orleans.

On Sunday night the **Bacchus** superkrewe wows an enraptured crowd along St Charles Ave with its celebrity monarch (it was Michael Keaton in 2006) and a gorgeous fleet of crowd-pleasing floats.

Monday night is parade night for **Proteus**, one of the oldest krewes to have a parade. Proteus' parade is an old-school affair, replete with riding lieutenants, flambeaux and lovely hand-painted floats. The main event of the evening is staged by **Orpheus**, a spirited and stylish superkrewe founded by singer-pianist Harry Connick Jr (who hails from New Orleans). Connick rides annually, and he always enlists a handful of movie stars and musicians to join his 1200-member krewe. Orpheus is such a huge parade, you may have to wait several hours before seeing the famous 140ft Leviathan float. It's a spectacular float, and most people are glad they waited.

Participant in costume for Mardi Gras parade

On Mardi Gras morning **Zulu** rolls its loosely themed and slightly run-down floats along Jackson Ave, where the atmosphere is very different from the standard parade routes. Folks set up their barbecues on the sidewalk and krewe members distribute their prized hand-painted coconuts to a lucky few in the crowd. When Zulu reaches St Charles Ave, it follows the Uptown route toward Gallier Hall (p151) for a spell before ending up on Orleans St and the Tremé District.

Zulu typically runs blithely behind schedule while the 'King of Carnival,' **Rex**, waits further Uptown for clearance on St Charles Ave. Rex's parade is, naturally, a much more restrained and haughty affair, with the monarch himself looking like he's been plucked from a deck of cards, as he smiles benignly upon his subjects. Rex's floats are beautifully constructed and hand-painted, but in terms of throws, some loot-hungry spectators frequently note Rex's shocking stinginess.

On Mardi Gras afternoon you can continue to watch parades. The populist spirit of the **truck parades** (haphazardly decorated semis loaded up with people line-dancing and throwing beads) is sociologically interesting but minimally entertaining. If you've been in town all weekend you'll be paraded-out by this time and there's plenty going on elsewhere around town.

PARADE ROUTES

There are two primary Carnival parade routes in Orleans Parish. The **Uptown parade route** typically follows St Charles Ave from Napoleon St to Canal St (where these parades actually begin and end can vary, but this stretch is fairly constant). The Zulu parade departs from this course by rolling down Jackson Ave until it reaches St Charles Ave, at which point it follows the standard route toward Canal St. The **Mid-City parade route** begins near City Park and follows Orleans Ave to Carrollton Ave and then onto Canal St, down toward the French Quarter, hooking into the Central Business District (CBD) in order to pass the grandstands at Gallier Hall.

These lengthy routes, which can take several hours for some of the larger krewes to traverse, obviously afford many vantage points from which to see the parades. But your choice is fairly straightforward: either head away from the crowded Quarter to get a more

THE LAW OF MARDI GRAS

New Orleans has fostered a reputation as a permissive city, and Mardi Gras is obviously a time of unbridled debauchery. But don't come expecting utter lawlessness. Overall, the New Orleans Police Department does a commendable job maintaining order, despite immense, spirited crowds consuming unbelievable quantities of liquor. Along parade routes and in the French Quarter, cops are everywhere. If their ranks appear to have swelled, it's because the entire force is working long shifts, with little time for rest in between. Rule No 1 is don't push your luck with tired cops!

Surprisingly, the presence of so many overworked cops does not interfere with the general merriment of Carnival. The attitude of the police during Carnival is to let people have their fun, but officers draw the line at potentially dangerous behavior. If a cop tells you to watch what you're doing, don't try to argue. If you start with the 'Aw, but ossiffer…' routine, you're likely to end up in the slammer until Ash Wednesday.

Many special laws go into effect during Carnival. Here are a few that visitors ought to bear in mind:

- Do not park your car along a parade route within two hours of the start of a parade – it's guaranteed that your car will be towed.
- Do not cross police barriers unless permitted to do so by an officer.
- During parades, do not cross the street if it means stepping between members of marching bands or in front of moving floats.
- It is against the law to throw anything at the floats (except for Tucks' toilet float).
- Police tend to look the other way (figuratively, anyway) while women expose their breasts in the French Quarter. But don't expect the same tolerance elsewhere.
- It isn't true that it's okay to have sex in public.

'neighborhood' feel, or stick close to the corner of Canal St and St Charles Ave, where the crowds are thickest and a raucous, sometimes bawdy party atmosphere prevails. Grandstands (with paid admission) are set up along St Charles Ave in the area between Lee Circle and Gallier Hall, and parading krewe members tend to go into a bead-tossing frenzy through this corridor.

If catching throws is of highest priority, here's a tip: near the end of parade routes, krewe members often discover they've been too conservative early on, and they tend to let loose. However, by this time the excitement level of the parade may already have passed its crescendo.

WALKING PARADES

On Mardi Gras there are many 'unofficial' walking parades that are worth seeking out and, in some cases, even joining.

The **Jefferson City Buzzards**, a walking club that has been moseying from bar to bar on Mardi Gras morn since 1890, starts out at 6:45am at Laurel St near Audubon Park. If you're into drinking early, you are likely to run into them at drinking establishments between there and the French Quarter. Since 1961, jazzman Pete Fountain's **Half-Fast Walking Club** has been making similar bar-hopping rounds, starting out from Commander's Palace at around 8am.

Downtown has its own morning activities, the biggest event being the parade of the **Society of St Anne**. This is a gloriously creative costume pageant – krewe members, clad in elaborate hats, capes, makeup and masks or, in some cases, in very little at all, march through the Bywater, Faubourg Marigny and the Quarter to the jazzy rhythms of the Storyville Stompers. The parade starts around 10am in the Bywater, and the colorful procession, which strives to re-create scenes from 19th-century oil paintings of French Mardi Gras, flows down Royal St all the way to Canal St, where it sometimes arrives in time to run into the Rex parade.

Another costume-oriented downtown walking parade is that of the **Krewe of Cosmic Debris**, which convenes at around noon in Marigny. The krewe's wandering musical voyage through the Quarter is largely determined by which bars it elects to patronize along the way.

(Continued on page 49)

Mardi Gras &
Jazz Fest

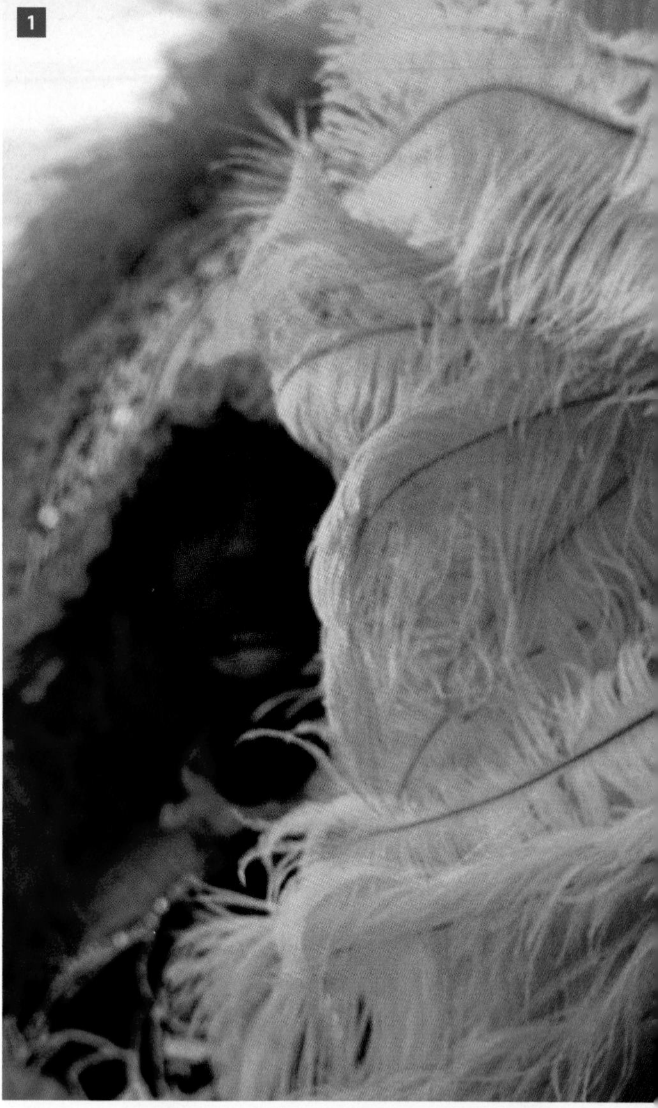

previous page *Colorfully costumed reveler, Mardi Gras (p32)*

1 *Flamboyant costumes (p49)*
2 *Decorated dolls*

1 *Colorful detail of a Mardi Gras float (p37)*
2 *Mardi Gras mask (p49)*
3 *Reveler in costume*

opposite page *Float in Rex parade (p39)*

1 *Parade performer in costume* **2** *Trumpet players in walking parade (p40)* **3** *Children in costume parade*

1 *Musician in wild costume, Jazz Fest (p49)* **2** *Fans dancing* **3** *Acoustic blues artist*

1 *Capturing the moment*
2 *Musician takes the stage (p52)*

following page
Performer on stage

(Continued from page 40)

Costume Contests

Mardi Gras is a citywide costume party, and many New Orleanians take a dim view of visitors who crash their party without a costume. Needless to say, they take costumes seriously. On Fat Tuesday, exquisitely attired maskers, human beasts and exhibitionists mingle, and a spirit unique to Mardi Gras animates the streets; this is all-ages material, folks.

This unbound creativity is distilled into two costume contests – a high-proof one for adults and a watered-down one for the entire family. The notorious **Bourbon St Awards**, attracting a large number of gay contestants, is staged not on Bourbon St (as it once was) but in front of the Rawhide Bar at Burgundy and St Ann Sts; it begins at noon. The cleaner **Mardi Gras Maskathon** is held in front of the Meridien Hotel on Canal St, after the Rex parade concludes.

MARDI GRAS MASK MARKET

The main point of Mardi Gras is to wear a mask. If you're unprepared for this, never fear, for an astounding selection of high quality handmade masks is available at the outdoor Mask Market. Artisans from around the country show their wares in stalls set up in Dutch Alley, behind the French Market, Sunday through Monday leading up to Mardi Gras. A live music stage is set up there too.

Balls

You can't expect to roll into town on Friday night and on Fat Tuesday gain admittance to one of the invitation-only society functions that typify the Carnival ball season. You can, however, buy your way into a party put on by one of the more modern krewes, including **Orpheus** (☎ 822-7211), **Tucks** (☎ 288-2481), **Bacchus** (www.kreweofbacchus.org) and **Endymion** (☎ 736-0160; www.endymion.org). Gay krewes include **Petronius** (☎ 525-4498) and the **Lords of Leather** (☎ 347-0659).

Information

The glossy magazine *Arthur Hardy's Mardi Gras Guide* (www.mardigrasneworleans.com; Mardi Gras Guide, 602 Metairie Rd, Metairie, LA 70005; $7) is an indispensable source of information and a worthwhile souvenir. Published by an obsessive Carnival aficionado, the annual publication appears in bookstores each year before Twelfth Night (January 6). It includes parade schedules, route maps and loads of history and commentaries that give an in-depth understanding of the entire culture of Carnival. Similar information is offered by the *Gambit Weekly*, which publishes a Carnival edition during February or March, depending on the date of Mardi Gras. *OffBeat*, a music magazine, offers invaluable information on Mardi Gras–related events.

FUTURE MARDI GRAS DATES

Mardi Gras can occur on any Tuesday between February 3 and March 9, depending on the date of Easter. Dates for the next several years:

- 2007 February 20
- 2008 February 5
- 2009 February 24
- 2010 February 16
- 2011 March 8

NEW ORLEANS JAZZ & HERITAGE FESTIVAL

Jazz Fest sums up everything that would be lost if the world were to lose New Orleans. Much more than Mardi Gras, with its secret balls and sparkly trinkets, Jazz Fest reflects the tremendous generosity of New Orleans. It's a big-hearted, open-armed party that welcomes the world to share in the city's bounty. Jazz Fest celebrates the exotic and the fun, and the crowds, while huge, are civilized and appreciative.

Of course the Fest is first and foremost about music, but it isn't just about jazz. The multitude of stages and tents feature everything that pours in and out of jazz – blues, Gospel,

Afro-Caribbean, folk, country, zydeco, Cajun, funky brass, and on and on. The music shares the marquee with the unique and varied food of southern Louisiana, served up in great portions during the festival. Second-line parades, a uniquely New Orleanian phenomenon, part crowds and pull people along with them. The astonishing spectacle of the Mardi Gras Indians always has a show-stopping effect. But the show doesn't stop – not until the sun starts to go down on the second Sunday.

Indeed, Jazz Fest is more than just a festival. Ordinarily New Orleans entertains itself like no other city in the US, but during Jazz Fest some of the city's most loyal fans from around the world pour into the little city, and New Orleans kicks everything up a notch. For 10 or 11 days the city rocks round the clock. Clubs and restaurants are packed to the gills, and jazzy beats and bluesy grooves keep the rafters shaking till dawn most nights. The town's full of musicians and artists and characters. Don't just sit there. Join 'em.

HISTORY

Jazz Fest began in 1970, and of course the idea of staging a big music festival in New Orleans couldn't have been more natural. George Wein had already organized the well-established Newport Jazz Festival, so he was brought to New Orleans to launch a similar tradition. Wein hired Quint Davis to help in the promotion of the project. Both men are still in charge of organizing the event each year.

The first festival, held in Louis Armstrong Park (p146), featured a remarkable lineup of legendary artists, including Duke Ellington, Mahalia Jackson, Clifton Chenier, Fats Domino and The Meters. Mardi Gras Indians performed, and every now and then a second-line parade swept through the audience. The ingredients were already in place for a major cultural event with a genuine regional significance. Outside talent, such as Ellington, complimented the local talent as well as beefed up the event's exposure.

Only 350 people attended that first Jazz Fest. It's startling to think there was so little interest. Most likely, the low numbers were due to poor promotion outside of New Orleans. Out-of-towners arrived in much greater numbers for the '71 fest, and with them came a far stronger local response. To accommodate another anticipated jump in attendance, the fest was moved to the far larger Fair Grounds Race Track a year later, and Jazz Fest really hasn't looked back since. By the late 1970s the festival had grown from one weekend to two, with already many legendary moments solidifying the event's cultural importance. Mesmerizing performances by the likes of James Booker, the Neville Brothers and Professor Longhair have been recorded for all posterity. The musical lineup soon expanded to include big-time national acts, such as Lenny Kravitz, Sting and Bruce Springsteen, as well as international acts from South America, the Caribbean and Africa.

The festival may have peaked in 2001, when some 650,000 people attended and 12 stages featured nearly every kind of music with the possible exception of Goth. The years since have seen some much-needed slimming down of the numbers, but the festival remains immense, with all the high-profile talent and new discoveries you'd expect, and it continues to draw die-hard regulars who come to New Orleans year after year for the Jazz Fest.

The 2006 fest drew impressive crowds, though the number of stages was reduced to nine. With Jazz Fest providing the first real boost for local tourism since Hurricane Katrina, it was a case of a cultural event really coming through for its city.

BIG BONES FOR BIG SHOTS

Jazz Fest ticket prices cost $40 per day or $120 for a full weekend. It's a bargain, when you consider how much entertainment is packed into the eight-hour days. Tickets entitle you entry to the Fair Grounds, and then you're on your own to shuffle through the crowd from tent to stage. Occasionally, if you arrive late for a popular act, you might be refused entry to a full tent. Tickets can be purchased at the gate, or in advance through the Jazz Fest website (www.nojazzfest.com). **Ticketmaster** (www.ticketmaster.com) also sells Jazz Fest tickets.

For an added advantage, the **Big Chief VIP Experience** ($500 for a weekend) is a privilege pass that entitles you to be ushered to seating near the front of each stage. And you'll always get in. An extra $100 gets you a parking place. Purchase your Big Chief pass in advance through the Jazz Fest website or Ticketmaster.

EXPERIENCING JAZZ FEST

Some people choose to do Jazz Fest over and over again, year after year, so obviously there's something addictive about the experience. It doesn't hurt that there are umpteen ways to approach this gargantuan feast of music, food and culture. It hosts three three-ring circuses and a city of concessionaires crammed into a single horse track, so get oriented, sort out your priorities, confer with your pals, and head to the Fair Grounds.

Young fans getting into the spirit at Jazz Fest

Setting the Stage

The first thing to decide is whether or not to go to New Orleans during Jazz Fest instead of at a different time of year. It's not a difficult decision to make. If you don't mind spending your days at a race track without being able to bet on horses, and you are an unabashed lover of music and New Orleans culture, this is absolutely your party. All you need to ask yourself is: one weekend or two? And if one's enough, then which one?

Noone will laugh if you choose one weekend. The drawback is you may have to pick your dates before the Fest schedule is announced. Some early planners book their hotel room a year in advance – for some, this year's room was secured with a deposit when they checked out after last year's fest. The schedule isn't announced until early February at the earliest. However, there's a statistical logic to making blindfolded decisions in this way, as both weekends are always packed equally with big-name show-stoppers and unheard of talents from the nearby swamps and faubourgs. Sometimes you'll miss out on a personal favorite if you're not attending every day of the fest, but in the end something along the way will make up for the loss.

For those who make their Jazz Fest plans late – that's to say, after February – there's the advantage of knowing the schedule and the disadvantage of not having your pick of hotel rooms. Free-spenders are still likely to find a pricey suite of rooms in the French Quarter at this point, but thrifty types with particular tastes might be a little frustrated if they've waited this long to make up their minds to go to the fest. Our advice for novices is make your plans and reserve your rooms in November or December.

Of course, planning ahead to do both weekends removes the doubts and uncertainties and doubles your pleasure. If you decide to do both weekends, you'll have four days for bopping around town, or maybe driving out to Cajun Country. No matter what, be prepared for an overcrowded city full of people who share your passion for music, food and nightclubbing. It's a competitive but jovial crowd.

Once your dates and rooms are secured and the schedule is released, you can begin to plot out your days at the Fair Grounds.

You can also begin to assemble your get-up. Your threads, babe. For the most spirited attendees, Jazz Fest is another excuse to don a costume in New Orleans. The snazzier/sillier/louder, the better. Having your duds in order is the surest way to make friends and influence people at Jazz Fest. It's another aspect of the show.

Once in New Orleans, get your hands on the latest *OffBeat* magazine. Grab two – one as a keeper, the other to tear out essentials like the Fair Grounds map and the Fest schedule. Study these, fold 'em up, keep 'em in your pocket at all times. You'll want to know the who/what/where.

At the Fair Grounds

It takes a well-bred racehorse about two minutes to circumnavigate the Fair Grounds track, but the average human will require up to 10 minutes to get from one stage to the next. The only way to get from stage to stage is to walk or half-jog through dense crowds and all kinds of tempting food stalls and vendors.

On entering through the Sauvage St gate, for some, Life's Reward is already found. The **Gospel Tent**, while no longer a well-kept festival secret, remains a cherished chapel of earth-shaking musical performances. Chances are, for all but the most devout gospel music enthusiasts, nearly all of the talent here will be new to you – and maybe later you won't remember the names of half the southern church choirs and quartets you've stomped your feet with. But you'll never forget the exhilarating experience of live gospel music. This is one of the reasons why Jazz Fest has so many repeat visitors.

Also on the pavement near the Sauvage St gate is the **Jazz Tent**. The lineup here leans more toward the contemporary side of things. You might see Irvin Mayfield, Terence Blanchard, Astral Project, Donald Harrison Jr, Ellis Marsalis or Nicolas Payton on this stage.

To take in the infield stages, follow the track in a counterclockwise direction, as the ponies do. The **Jazz & Heritage Stage** is a smaller stage where brass bands and the Mardi Gras Indians perform. Suitably enough, the **Backstreet Cultural Museum** (p146) has an exhibit in the next little tent over.

The **Economy Hall Tent** is where all those buck-jumpin', parasol-twirlin' Fest-goers end up. You'll stomp your feet to 'trad' jazz with the likes of the Preservation Hall Jazz Band, Walter Payton, the Dukes of Disneyland, the Young Tuxedo Brass Band, Tremé Brass Band and Pete Fountain. These elder statesmen are strong as oxen, so expect to see 'em in years to come. Dozens of **food stalls** (see Food & Drink, opposite) line up behind Economy Hall.

Turn into a corridor midway along the grandstand to reach the Winners' Circle, which during Jazz Fest is transformed into the **Lagniappe Stage**. Here the entertainment is varied. The stage's isolation from the rest of the fairgrounds makes it ideal for intimate performances by singers and small ensembles – the type of acts that do well in clubs but don't always translate to outdoor festivals. Lounge singers might follow acoustic blues performers on this stage. This is also where interviews are done. Local writers chat with music legends.

Up in the grandstand, in the glassed-in areas where big shots wait for their ponies to run, take a look at the photo and art exhibits.

From the grandstand, get back on track. The **Kid's Tent** (opposite) is next, with playful troubadours and nonstop puppet shows who make a special plea to the young at heart. Heading around the track's curve gets you to the **Blues Tent**. Traditionally, this stage was next to the Gospel Tent, but it was moved here in 2006. Maybe it'll get moved back. Either way, this is where you are likely to catch blues, R&B and funk acts like Snooks Eaglin, Etta James and The Meters. The Blues Tent also integrates rock acts like the Radiators and Cowboy Mouth. Sometimes popular funky brass bands such as Rebirth end up here.

Cajun and zydeco music is the emphasis at the **Fais Do-Do Stage**. If CJ Chenier, DL Menard, Geno Delafose, Rosie Ledet and

FEST SURVIVAL KIT

Eight hours in the sun in New Orleans, even on a day so exhilarating as a day at Jazz Fest, is always to some degree an endurance test. Throw in booze and the chance of rain and, well it ain't exactly Verdun, but you'll want to be properly equipped. Here's a quick checklist.

Essentials

- sunscreen
- hat
- shades
- bottled water
- *OffBeat* magazine
- camera
- rain poncho (if you don't like the look of that sky)
- Cajun shrimp boots (again, if rain and muddy grounds are likely)

Nonessentials (but some people like 'em)

- folding chair (the kind of portable seats GCI and Crazy Creek make for hike-in campers)
- blanket to sit on
- goofy get-up

SURPRISE ATTACKS

The Jazz Fest schedule inevitably lists a healthy mix of musicians everyone has heard of and some that nobody outside of New Orleans knows about. Keep your ears to the ground, and some of the unknowns will soon become familiar names to you. Each year Jazz Fest delivers surprise discoveries that everyone talks about.

At the 2005 Fest, a nearly unheard-of Mississippi singer named **Bobby Lounge** attracted national attention for his soulful, earth-shaking performance. He was attached to an iron lung and accompanied by a lovely contortionist in a nurse suit, and he simply belted out some unforgettable original lyrics to songs with titles like 'I Remember the Night Your Trailer Burned Down.' Lounge then disappeared completely from the limelight. He was back at the Fair Grounds in 2006, this time eagerly anticipated by thousands.

Each year also promises emotionally charged appearances by local talents such as **Mahogany Brass Band**, fronted by trumpeter Brice Miller. It's a traditional brass outfit whose performances go way beyond nostalgia – Miller simply pulls his audience in and rules the moment. The same can be said of **Big Chief Bo Dollis and the Wild Magnolias**. Dollis is a compelling singer who guts it out on every number. This guy means business, and with his gang of fully suited Indians backing him up, he simply blows his audience away.

You're bound to discover dozens of comparable Jazz Fest moments. This thing isn't scripted. Each year promises its own set of surprises.

Beasoleil are at Jazz Fest this year – and they almost always are – then you'll find 'em here. Sometimes local roots rockers like the Iguanas also take the Fais Do-Do Stage.

Following the direction of the ponies once again gets you to Congo Sq, a legendary Jazz Fest stage. It's a big stage with an expansive patch of grass to accommodate huge crowds. The stage has become the venue for world acts from Africa and Latin America. The lineup tends to be completely different each year, and there's often a buzz about performers who are making rare appearances in the US. Past performers have included Los Van Van from Cuba and King Sunny Adé from Nigeria. Congo Sq is not so easily defined, however, as rapper Juvenile has also worked the stage here, as have countless brass bands and some of the bigger Mardi Gras Indian gangs. The Ohio Players headlined Congo Sq in 2006.

By far the biggest stage in the infield is the **Acura Stage**, where the biggest names appear. The audience here stretches clear across the infield, with a giant, high-resolution video screen beaming the performances to those so far from the stage they can only hear the performances. A lot of people plant picnic blankets in front of the stage first thing in the morning and stay there all day. If you're buzzing around the infield like a hummingbird, chances are you won't reach the front row here (unless you have a Big Chief VIP pass). The headliners vary from year to year, and many of them have little or no connection to New Orleans or the culture that this festival professes to celebrate. But who's to complain about a live performance by Bruce Springsteen? Earlier in the day the stage is often taken over by the locals, such as Irma Thomas or Big Chief Bo Dollis and the Wild Magnolias.

Jazz Fest for Kids

There is plenty of fun for the young 'uns at Jazz Fest, most of it concentrated in the **Children's Cultural Village**, **Storytellers Pavilion** and **Kids' Tent**. Dancing, sing-alongs, captivating stories, puppet shows and hands-on arts and crafts are happening all day long. The talent is usually worth catching even if you're not a kid. Local living legends David and Roselyn often appear. They have that authentic traveling troubadour style and a deep well of timeless tunes to draw on. Off campus, **Big Top Gallery and Three Ring Circus** (see Live Music for the Whole Family, p210) stages 'Kids Fest' between the weekends, with family-oriented entertainment.

Food & Drink

Among the crowds at the Fair Grounds there are always scores of people holding plates of food and looking very satisfied. At some point you're sure to be one of these people. Fest food vendors cook up some fine vittles, much of it reflecting regional tastes. Many stalls seem to have a cult following and return to the Fest year after year. Lines can be long, but this is Louisiana. People are patient and friendly, which makes the wait bearable.

There are usually two concentrated food areas, plus scattered stalls around the Fair Grounds. Most of the vendors' signs are basically menus – what the sign says is what they sell. So it's not difficult to find what you're hankering for. The food is not dirt cheap, but considering they have a captive, hungry audience the vendors could probably gouge prices. To their credit, they don't.

Some of the more popular Fest foods are fried soft-shell crab, Crawfish Monica (cream crawfish sauce over fusilli pasta), crawfish bread, cochon de lait (roast suckling pig), po'boys, spinach and artichoke casserole, Cuban sandwiches and Palmer's Jamaican chicken. Of course, you'll also find great jambalaya, red beans and fried catfish. Second-liners always recommend the 'ya ka mein,' an Asian noodle soup that's commonly sold along parade routes. The beer selection's limited to MGD and Fosters, but what the hell – finely crafted microbrews don't really go with the climate or this kind of food. You can also refresh yourself with rose-mint iced tea, mango freezes (like a smoothie), or a syrupy sno-ball. Café du Monde's café au lait will pick you up if your mojo's beginning to flag.

Shopping at the Fest

Shopping and having to carry a lot of stuff around a music festival might not sound like something a sane person would do, but some of the vendors at the Fair Grounds have desirable stuff for sale: posters, photographs, paintings, jewelry, African drums, CDs and DVDs. Even if you're deaf to the vendors' siren song, check out such shops as the one operated by accordion-maker **Clarence 'Junior' Martin**. Admire lovely hand-crafted button accordions of the sort played by zydeco sweetheart Rosie Ledet (the best advertisement the squeeze box ever had). **Hamacher Woodworks & Engraving** has a nice stall packed with finely crafted bowls made from pecan and other regional hardwoods. Very nice stuff. **Jazz Fest Live** sells recordings of performances you saw maybe two hours ago, so you can relive the experience at home.

Off-Campus Highlights

When the last band has finished its set on the Fair Grounds, take a victory lap around the track and catch a cab to your favorite restaurant. You might want to have a copy of *OffBeat* in hand. While waiting for your cab and then your table, you can consider your evening plans. Hopefully you still have a little gas in the tank, because there's a lot going on in the clubs around town. All the clubs will have stacked the deck for every night during the festival – including all the off-nights between the two weekends.

Aside from standout gigs and jam sessions raising the rafters in the clubs, several annual events accompany Jazz Fest. **Piano Night** is a tradition in which the hottest piano players take turns at the ivories and basically try to out-play each other. Don't expect routine performances from anyone who takes the House of Blues (p206) stage during this event. It's usually on the Monday after the first weekend.

All day every day during the Fest – that's on the two weekends and the weekdays in between – the **Louisiana Music Factory** (p226) has free shows. There's something in the air during Jazz Fest, so the performances are charged with an energy you wouldn't expect to find at a free show in an overcrowded record shop.

In 2006, percussionist Washboard Chaz inaugurated **Chaz Fest**, which hopefully will continue for years to come. It's a one-day music festival held on the Thursday between the two weekends from noon to 10pm. The first year's lineup featured hard-working artists (like Chaz) who play the city's clubs nearly every night year round. It was held at the **Truck Farm** (3020 St Claude Ave) in the Bywater. See the Chaz Fest website (www.chazfestival.com) for info.

It's also worth poking around the web to see what sorts of smaller one-off events are going on. Some musicians host parties, barbecues and crawfish boils in their backyards or favorite bars and invite the public to join them. That's the kind of people New Orleanians are.

Arts

Painting 56
Historic Paintings 57
Outsider Art 58
Modern & Contemporary Painting 58
Photography 59
Pottery 61
Literature 61
Theater & Performing Arts 63
Theater 63
Classical Music & Opera 64
Ballet 64
Cinema & Television 64

Arts

The arts of New Orleans go far beyond the proliferation of dabbers you'll meet around Jackson Sq, who can always eke out a living by hawking quaint scenes of the French Quarter. Over the centuries standouts in the Louisiana arts scene have produced truly brilliant work by turning sharp eyes on city and regional themes, or by departing entirely from the Vieux Carré aesthetic. The history of New Orleans is recorded in brilliant paintings left behind by the French and Spanish, and in haunting Storyville photographs. Great writers have always come from this part of the country, and many more have had productive sojourns in New Orleans. The city has had fertile homegrown movements in pottery and theater and, of late, Hollywood film production is becoming increasingly common in the 'Big Easy's' atmospheric quarters.

Museum of Art (p163), City Park

Feeding much of this creativity is the intense appreciation of art held by the locals. Many of the city's Creole cottages and antebellum mansions are full of art. In the aftermath of Hurricane Katrina the New Orleans Conservation Guild took in thousands of storm-damaged paintings, demonstrating that even while recovering from major disasters, New Orleanians place art high on their lists of priorities. Tastes run the gamut, from traditional to envelope-pushing. Galleries were quick to reopen after Katrina, and within a few months many reported business being fairly good, considering the lack of tourists.

New Orleans is a city of good museums that are generally strong in local and regional art. Reputable galleries turn up in great numbers all over town. The city supports several distinct arts hubs. Royal St is the main stem of the mostly mainstream French Quarter arts scene, where savvy self-marketers have opened shop among the expensive antique shops. More down to earth (and lower in price) are the up-and-coming galleries along lower Decatur St. On the strength of the monthly Bywater Art Market and the New Orleans Center for Creative Arts (NOCCA), an educational facility for young artists, the low-rent Bywater is a fertile artistic zone. More highbrow are the quality galleries of Julia Row in the Warehouse District. Upbeat Magazine St has several dispersed blocks of excellent galleries (see p210 for listings).

The city's arts grow more vital all the time, and through regular tours of the galleries a dedicated art lover could easily assemble an impressive private collection here.

PAINTING

Painters have always found inspiration in New Orleans' timeworn architecture and oak-shaded avenues, as well as in the surrounding watery landscapes of marshland, cypress, oak and Spanish moss. The creative current seems to be growing stronger, even after Hurricane Katrina, and now is a very good time to get familiar with the local scene.

HISTORIC PAINTINGS

Edgar Degas had family connections with New Orleans, and a visit in the early 1870s brought about *The Cotton Exchange in New Orleans* (1873), perhaps the most recognizable and valuable work of art produced in the city. However, seeing the actual painting requires a visit to the Musée Municipal in Pau, France.

Art in New Orleans goes back much further than that, though. Our most vivid images of early New Orleans are from paintings, many of them on view in local museums. The Historic New Orleans Collection is particularly strong in works portraying the old city.

Among the earliest paintings of New Orleans is François Gérard Jollain's *Le Commerce que les Indiens du Mexique Font avec les Francois au Port du Missisipi* [sic] (c 1720). The painting is a superb historical artifact, though it is historically (and hysterically) inaccurate. It was a work of propaganda, commissioned by John Law's Company of the Indies, and it depicts French traders, Catholic missionaries and Native Americans in harmonious coexistence amid tropical palms and snow-capped peaks.

Much later, John William Hill and Benjamin Franklin Smith, two fine lithographers from New York, drew and printed a razor-sharp, bird's-eye view of the Central Business District (CBD), with the French Quarter and the Mississippi in the background, in *New Orleans from St Patrick's Church* (1852).

We also have many rural scenes that give an idea of what much of Greater New Orleans was like before the city expanded beyond the raised ground. Country roads lead into town through swamps and grasslands, with the edge of cypress forests in the background. The artists were likely aware that this scenery was disappearing. The results are often bittersweet, and sometimes a tad romantic. Frederick Arthur Callender's *New Orleans from Algiers Point* (1893), Lulu King Saxon's *Uptown Street* (1890) and Andres Molinary's *Old Gentilly Road* (1890) are fine works that depict slow-paced country scenes. Rutted roads scarcely hint at the bustle of the city, though in Callender's painting smokestacks loom in the distance.

John Antrobus, an English painter, was in Louisiana long enough to cast a cold eye on the condition of slaves. His *Plantation Burial* (1860) is a moving scene set in a darkly forested graveyard for slaves that completely lacks the condescension so typical of other paintings of African Americans from the time. Carolina-based William Aiken Walker was perhaps the most famous painter of slave scenes, and his travels through the South in the 19th century often brought him to Louisiana. The Historic New Orleans Collection has a gallery dedicated to Walker's work, and also has the superior Antrobus painting.

Clarence Millet (1897–1959), a native of Hahnville, LA, studied painting in New York before settling in New Orleans. Some of his work is in the Ogden Museum of Art. His *Old New Orleans* (1943) is a nostalgic, stylistically modern scene of cobblestones and horse-drawn carriages. *Spring Comes to the Mississippi* (1955) is an evocative rendition of the *batture* dwellers who lived in raised shanties between the river and levee. Far better is Millett's more realistic work of the 1950s. *Violet Locks* (1950) is an exceptional depiction of a lock keeper facing the Mississippi River at flood stage. *Batture Shanty at Riverbend* (1956) captures the river's awesome beauty and the awkwardness of human attempts to settle along it.

JOHN JAMES AUDUBON

Among the most famous painters to work in southern Louisiana was John James Audubon (1785–1851), who briefly resided at 706 Barracks St in the French Quarter and on the Oakley Plantation in West Feliciana Parish in the early 1820s. Audubon made regular follow-up visits to the region while undertaking to paint all of the birds of North America.

Audubon, a Frenchman born in St Domingue (now Haiti), was self-taught as a painter. He sketched in pencil and used pastels and watercolors for color and shading. Some of his backgrounds were actually painted by assistants. His illustrations are life-sized, the birds skillfully rendered in impeccable detail, and look very lifelike.

But his models were all dead. Audubon sought them out and shot them with very fine birdshot. He wired them up in agreeable poses before sketching. His writings indicate he often shot more than 100 birds in a day, and he was never unaware if a bird was nearing extinction.

Audubon completed 435 bird pictures, 80 of them in Louisiana. He had 200 sets of the entire collection beautifully engraved and printed for a ready market in Europe and North America.

OUTSIDER ART

The South has long been known for its rich folk-art traditions, now fashionably referred to as 'outsider' art, and New Orleans is a good place to seek out reasonably priced works for your collection back home. The very best paintings demonstrate highly individualistic techniques developed in complete isolation from the art world. Many great outsider works are in museums, but true gems can also be found in galleries and shops on Magazine St.

Clementine Hunter (1886–1988), an African American woman whose life spanned most of the 20th century, developed her wonderful painting style while living a quiet life in Louisiana's Cane River Parish. Self-taught, illiterate, and often too poor to buy art supplies, she nevertheless produced sophisticated work. She had a keen eye for color, blending and combining hues with subtlety, and out of pure resourcefulness she occasionally substituted canvas with window shades and paper bags. Her simply composed scenes tell stories culled from her own experience. Many of her works hang in the Ogden Museum.

Roy Ferdinand (1959–2004) was another self-taught African American artist who specialized in what he termed 'urban realism.' His paintings capture life in the ghetto, with hip-hoppers and 'black urban warriors' amid the shotgun houses and fences of New Orleans' backstreets. Voodoo and Santaria images are frequent motifs in Ferdinand's finely detailed work. The Ogden Museum (p155) and the Barrister's Gallery (p213) both exhibit pieces by him.

Nilo Lanzas, a native Nicaraguan who moved to New Orleans in 1956, began painting late in life. He was self-taught, frequently applying his oils to wood. In his unique, accessible style, he has depicted such scenes as OJ Simpson, Saddam Hussein and Al Capone together in hell. The New Orleans Museum of Art owns some of his best work, but you can also visit Berta's and Mina's Antiquities (p213), a gallery operated by Lanzas' daughter, and buy something if it strikes you.

The local artist who calls himself 'Frenchy' has attracted attention with his exuberant style. The main attraction with his work, especially his series of live musical performances, is that it is created in the moment. It's spontaneous art that draws on the energy of dynamic human events.

Alabama artist Anton Haardt also owns a gallery on Magazine St (p213), which generally features a handful of excellent outsider art from around the South.

MODERN & CONTEMPORARY PAINTING

New Orleans isn't widely known for its modern sensibilities, possibly reflecting how difficult it can be to keep up with the times in such an old-fashioned town. But with a respected arts department at Tulane University (p158) and an adventurous spirit in the local arts market, excellent work is constantly showing in the city's galleries.

Two influential painters ushering in the 20th century were the brothers Woodward, transplants from New England. William Woodward (1859–1939), who founded the architecture school at Tulane, made finely rendered drawings and prints of the French Quarter. Younger brother Ellsworth Woodward (1861–1939) was the more accomplished artist, having trained at the Rhode Island School of Design and in Europe. He wielded artistic influence as dean of Newcomb Art School, and produced a few masterpieces of his own. *Backyard in Covington* (c 1939), a study in oils, is on view at the Historic New Orleans Collection. Other works by Ellsworth, including many fine watercolor landscapes and French Quarter scenes, hang in the Ogden Museum.

Knute Heldner (1886–1952), Swedish born, spent much of his professional life in New Orleans. In the '30s, Heldner painted landscapes, street scenes and portraits in New Orleans and around Louisiana for the Works Projects Administration (WPA; previously Works Progress Administration) Federal Art Project. The Ogden Museum holds many of his works, including some haunting bayou landscapes.

John McCrady painted in New Orleans for three decades, producing provocative works such as *The Parade – Orleans and Dauphine Streets* (1950). This one's excellent. A gaudy Mardi Gras Parade, illuminated by flambeaux, rolls through the French Quarter, while a cartoony cutaway reveals life going on inside one of the buildings. Some amusing, idealized body movement going on in there (though it's PG-13).

Wonderful modern portraits include Angela Gregory's *Time Goes By* (1925), a painterly and contemplative rendition of the elderly Ellsworth Woodward; and Emily Alberta Collier's *Seated Mulatto Woman* (1938), a lovely study in warm hues.

To get oriented in the contemporary scene, the Contemporary Arts Center is a good start. So to is the Ogden Museum's Michael Brown and Linda Green Collection, which has been assembled through selective culling of local galleries over the past 30 odd years.

The Ogden's collection includes some fine pieces by Justin Forbes. His *Neo-American Gothic* (1996), depicts a young slacker couple, the woman obviously with child, standing in front of a motel with a shovel and a potted snake plant. It's comical in the way only the truth keenly observed can be. The late Ida Kohlmeyer's abstract-expressionist works are also on display at the Ogden, having been rescued by her family from Hurricane Katrina and deposited there for safekeeping. Kohlmeyer, a Newcomb alumnus, created intensely personal and sharply colorful works, some of which reflect the influence of Joan Miró'.

ART MUSEUMS

The city's museums are excellent places to see what's been going on all these years in New Orleans' art scene, from the 18th century to the present. In this book, museums are covered in greater depth in the Sights chapter.

Ogden Museum of Southern Art (p155) – The art of the beautiful South is what this place is all about. The collection has grown from one man's obsession into a first-rate repository of the region's painting and sculpture.

Historic New Orleans Collection (p139) – Take the Merieult History tour here to view historic paintings and artifacts from Louisiana's earliest days to the 20th century. It's an astounding collection.

New Orleans Museum of Art (p163) – New Orleans' premier arts institution displays the works of European masters and also has quality collections of Asian and Native American arts. First-rate traveling exhibits set up camp here as well.

Contemporary Arts Center (p153) – Lacks a permanent collection, making it like a gallery/performance space compound for living arts.

The tiresome Blue Dog series has become his cashcow, but Cajun artist George Rodrigue has produced quality work over the years. Having trained in Los Angeles in the '60s, his creative roots are in pop art, not folk art. But one of his finer pieces is *Aioli Dinner* (1971), a pastoral scene depicting an outdoor Cajun supper, with men seated around a long table amid women, children and live oaks draped in Spanish moss. It is in the New Orleans Museum of Art. Rodrigue's sad-eyed Blue Dog, by the way, originated in the French myth of the *loup-garou* (werewolf), popular in Cajun culture. Rodrigue more recently has done topical hurricane paintings. Rodrigue has a gallery on Royal St (see p211).

Jazz Fest posters in recent years have been prints of paintings by James Michalopoulos, who is noted mostly for highly expressive architectural studies. Demand for rare prints of Michalopoulos' 2001 portrait of Louis Armstrong has driven the price up to $2500. His gallery is on Bienville St (see p211).

PHOTOGRAPHY

New Orleans, being a city that loves parades, has been subjected to a continuous parade of photographers since the medium's early days. Local museums have photography exhibits, but the best place to go is A Gallery for Fine Photography (p210) in the French Quarter.

The grandfather of today's New Orleans photographers would have to be EJ Bellocq, a native New Orleanian whose portraits of Storyville prostitutes captured the lost, haunted and decadent beauty of old New Orleans. (See Storyville Trollops, p60.)

William Henry Jackson (1843–1942) spent some time taking pictures around New Orleans in 1897. The master photographer is best known for his panoramic landscapes of the American West, when that part of the country was still considered the frontier. His *Cotton on the Levee at New Orleans* is a significant record of the city at the turn of the 20th century. Jackson's streetscapes of Canal St and the French Quarter reveal a graceful city at a time of great change.

STORYVILLE TROLLOPS

During his lifetime Ernest J Bellocq (1873–1949) was known in New Orleans as a journeyman photographer, and later in life as a somewhat eccentric character in the French Quarter. It wasn't known until after his death that he had compiled the portraits of Storyville prostitutes that would be celebrated for their graceful beauty and historic value.

Bellocq took his Storyville photographs around 1912 with an 8in x 10in view camera. All of his subjects posed willingly in their own private rooms in the posh pleasure palaces and lowly cribs of the district. Uneven lighting often comes from open windows, and in some instances the plates are scratched – faces were deliberately scraped from some – but these imperfections fail to diminish the intrigue and beauty of the images.

After his death, 89 of Bellocq's glass plates were discovered in an antique shop. No original prints survive. The emergence of Bellocq's art was accompanied by shadowy rumors of the photographer's comportment and physical stature. Suddenly Bellocq was remembered as an insane hydrocephalic hunchback. The image is undeniably appealing – a twitching, large-headed hunchback skulking the red-light district with an expensive large-format camera – but sadly none of it is true. Bellocq may have grown senile in old age, but a rare photo of him as a younger man shows him to be normal looking.

Lee Friedlander, himself a master of the photographic medium, purchased the entire collection of plates in 1967 and began making prints, some of which showed in an exhibit at the Museum of Modern Art in 1970. Friedlander's prints are made on period gold-tone printing paper, and are not tampered with in the darkroom.

A beautiful large-format book of Bellocq's work is out of print and now fetches collectors' prices. A Gallery of Fine Photography (p210) usually exhibits some of the gorgeous prints made by Friedlander.

The 1920s saw an emergence of local talents who formed the New Orleans Camera Club. This group included Eugene Delacroix (1892–1967), whose soft and tinted shots reflect the Steiglitz influence, and Joseph 'Pops' Whitesell (1876–1958), whose group portraits have a more documentary quality.

Among the dozens of professional shutter masters who passed through southern Louisiana during the WPA years, Fonville Winans stayed on and recorded images of Cajun Country for over 50 years. Winans bought a boat to get deep into the bayous, where he mingled with trappers, fishers and shrimpers. His *The Oysterman* (1934) and *Dixie Belles* (1938) are outstanding images of a world gone by.

Walker Evans was among those passing through in the '30s, and he took many photographs of old houses in New Orleans and in Louisiana's Plantation Country. An untitled frame of a woman in a feathered hat standing in front of a French Quarter barber shop, taken in 1935, is Evans' most memorable image of the Crescent City.

Swiss-born Robert Frank also visited New Orleans while taking the photos that comprised his landmark exhibit and book *The Americans* (1959). From that collection, *Trolly – New Orleans* captures the tension of segregation simply by framing the side of a streetcar, with well-to-do whites staring out the front windows and a sad-eyed black man staring out a back window.

East Coaster Lee Friedlander has made frequent photographic journeys to New Orleans, and devoted an entire book to the city, his lovely *The Jazz People of New Orleans* (published in 1992). The best of the collection are photos of musical legends such as Johnny St Cyr, Papa Jack Laine, Isidore Barbarin and Roosevelt Sykes appearing very much at ease in their own homes. Friedlander's greatest contribution to the arts in New Orleans, however, has been his careful management of EJ Bellocq's original glass plates, which Friedlander owns and exclusively prints.

Michael P Smith, a local photographer, made his mark taking color images of Mardi Gras Indians in action, mostly during the 1980s when the Indians were not so well documented as they are now. Many of Smith's shots of musicians during the 1970s and '80s are excellent, and his Professor Longhair poster is highly collectible. Christopher Porché West's formal portraits of Mardi Gras Indians are exquisite, capturing perfectly exposed images of the intricate artistry of the Indians' suits in controlled studio settings. Porché West's Gallery is in the Bywater (p231).

Photographers continue to produce beautiful black-and-white images of the city and its people. Louis Sahuc owns Photo Works on Chartres St (p227), and Johnny Donnels has a gallery on St Peter St (p226).

POTTERY

The Newcomb Art School's pottery department established a name for itself in the early 20th century. Ellsworth Woodward, dean of the school, encouraged a regional emphasis that spawned a local movement. Today, original Newcomb pottery is highly sought after, and the tradition is kept very much alive by contemporary artists. In the art-nouveau tradition, Newcomb pottery is noted for its natural motifs inspired by regional flora and fauna. Clay from the north shore of Lake Pontchartrain is typically used.

The work of Sadie Irvine (1887–1970) with live oak motifs stands out as some of the most recognizable Newcomb pieces.

LITERATURE

Ever since Samuel Clemens acquired his Mark Twain pseudonym while piloting a steamboat on the Mississippi River, New Orleans has made an impression on American writers. You can pay homage to past greats at the March literary festival celebrating Tennessee Williams (see p16).

George Washington Cable (1844–1925), described by Twain as 'the South's finest literary genius,' abhorred slavery and racism. He touched many Creole nerves with his fictional books *Old Creole Days* and, especially, *The Grandissimes,* both of which were set in New Orleans. His essays in *The Negro Question* (1885) are an indictment of the Code Noir and make compelling arguments for civil rights.

Author Kate Chopin (1851–1904) spent 14 years in New Orleans and southern Louisiana after marrying a cotton broker. She wrote her evocative accounts of the Creoles and Cajuns after returning to St Louis as a widow in 1882. Her second novel, *The Awakening,* was originally condemned for its portrayal of a young woman's adultery, but it was rediscovered in the 1970s as a masterpiece that evokes the region while chronicling a woman's discontent. Also look for her nonfiction books *Bayou Folk* (1894) and *A Night in Acadie* (1897).

Sherwood Anderson (1876–1941) was already considered among America's best short-story writers when he moved to New Orleans in 1920. His signature work, *Winesburg, Ohio,* had already put him at the forefront of American letters. He stayed about five years, but made a lasting impact during that time. His short story *A Meeting South,* set in the French Quarter, is by turns hauntingly beautiful and, here and there, a little too quaint. Anderson was a regular contributor to a local literary rag, the *Double Dealer,* which helped put New Orleans on the literary map, and his presence in the city attracted many other writers who would add to the city's growing literary cachet. F Scott Fitzgerald (1896–1940) and John Dos Passos (1896–1970) both took up residence in the city for short periods while writing early works. But the most significant arrival was William Faulkner (1897–1962), who then considered himself a poet.

Faulkner House (p140), at 624 Pirate's Alley, is where Faulkner briefly stayed, at the onset of his career. Faulkner penned his first novel, *Soldier's Pay,* during his

FIVE CHOICE NOLA READS

Many books capture the humor, the culture, the crime or the spooky allure of New Orleans. Prime yourself for your visit by indulging in all of the following Crescent City classics.

A Confederacy of Dunces – John Kennedy Toole's crazy novel is now looked upon as *the* New Orleans classic, and even after Katrina the spirit of our so-called hero, one misshapen Ignatius Reilly, still seems to lurk in the Crescent City.

A Streetcar Named Desire – Plays don't always make good reading, but Tennessee Williams' New Orleans masterpiece does.

Jolie Blon's Bounce – A most terrifying villain lights up this James Lee Burke thriller, but hero Dave Robicheaux comes out on top – barely.

A Walk on the Wild Side – Scintillating prose, lurid absurdity and screwball characters make it obvious that New Orleans and author Nelson Algren were made for each other.

Interview with the Vampire – You simply can't say you've familiarized yourself with the literature of New Orleans until you've gotten to know Anne Rice's charismatic Lestat.

GO WITH ROBICHEAUX

It's no mystery why the crime genre has found a home in the tainted realm of southern Louisiana. The region is known for corrupt politicians, notorious law enforcement officers, pervasive violence, race tensions, a highly visible sex trade, colorful characters and dark swamps, where anything can happen without anyone needing to know about it. There are countless authors setting mysteries in the Big Easy and in bayous and mansions in the vicinity of the city.

But, hands down, James Lee Burke (1936–) is top of the class in his field. His popular Dave Robicheaux (ro-bih-*cho*) novels, 14 strong and not about to stop, are densely plotted and tautly written, and shrewdly exploit the twisted culture, politics and atmosphere of New Iberia and New Orleans. James Lee Burke's books get better with each installment, but to get you started check out *Jolie Blon's Bounce* (2002) or *The Neon Rain* (1995).

six-month stint in New Orleans, and his second novel, *The Mosquitoes* (1926), is set in New Orleans. It is for his later works such as *Light in August* (1932), *The Sound and the Fury* (1929) and *As I Lay Dying* (1932), all written at his home in northern Mississippi, that Faulkner was canonized as one of America's greatest writers.

Truman Capote was by mere chance born in New Orleans while his parents sojourned there. In the mid-1940s Capote returned to New Orleans long enough to write *Other Voices, Other Rooms.*

Robert Penn Warren's novel *All the King's Men* (1946) won a Pulitzer for portraying Louisiana politics in the era of Governor Huey Long. Warren then went on to win more Pulitzer prizes for *Promises* in 1958 and *Now and Then* in 1979.

Francis Parkinson Keyes' *Dinner at Antoine's* (1948) was a bestseller. She lived at 1113 Chartres St.

Nelson Algren is rightfully claimed by Chicagoans, but one of his most influential novels, *A Walk on the Wild Side* (1956), is set largely in New Orleans' decaying Storyville district. The hilarious saga of a Depression-era scamp named Dove Linkhorn, it established a high-water mark for bizarre character studies and beautiful prose that would be the aim of later Crescent City novels.

Shirley Ann Grau writes fiction about the American South with a sympathetic eye toward African American women. Among her works set in New Orleans are *The Hard Blue Sky* (1958) and *The House on Coliseum Street* (1961).

Walker Percy's first novel, *The Moviegoer* (1961), is an existentialist portrayal of a young New Orleans stockbroker, Binx Bolling, whose despair and relationship with his cousin Kate are revealed against a muted Mardi Gras background.

John Kennedy Toole rose to posthumous notoriety when his unforgettable portrayal of hot-dog vendor Ignatius Reilly in *A Confederacy of Dunces* (1980) was published after the author's suicide. No other book so readily prepares the first-time visitor for the hapless and semidysfunctional personalities that abound through all spectrums of New Orleans society.

Romanian-born novelist and poet Andrei Codrescu is best known for his travelogue commentary on the vagaries of US culture, *Road Scholar* (1993), which was turned into a film. His offerings also include a collection of essays, *The Muse is Always Half-Dressed in New Orleans* (1993). Codrescu lives in New Orleans and writes a weekly commentary called 'Penny Post' for the *Gambit.*

Cult author and Georgia-native Harry Crewes chose New Orleans as the backdrop for his brilliantly crafted novel, *The Knockout Artist* (1987), about a washed-up boxer who entertains at Uptown parties by knocking himself out. Tim Gautreaux, a student under Walker Percy at Tulane, has established himself as a fine regional storyteller. His collection of short stories *Welding with Children* (1999) takes a consistently hard look at the moral fiber of his home state.

Elmore Leonard, who has done well with Detroit and Florida for his literary palate, was actually born in New Orleans. His novel *Bandits* (1987) is set in New Orleans. In a shift from his regional nonfiction work, Tony Dunbar wrote the New Orleans detective novels *Crooked Man* (1994) and *City of Beads* (1995), featuring the Dubonnet Tubby character. For yet another story about the mob in New Orleans, check out John Grisham's *The Client* (1993).

THEATER & PERFORMING ARTS

New Orleans has many of the high cultural institutions one expects from a major city. But if the city shrinks significantly, opera, ballet, symphony and many theaters may find it financially difficult to keep afloat. In the immediate aftermath of Katrina, most of the performing arts were making a valiant stand.

THEATER

In terms of its contribution to the American dramatic arts, New Orleans theater can pretty much be summed up with two words: Tennessee Williams. While living at 632 St Peter St, Williams (1911–83) wrote *A Streetcar Named Desire* (1947), which portrayed Blanche Dubois' descent from an elite plantation existence to life in the Quarter with her sister and lowbrow brother-in-law Stanley Kowalski. As Williams descended along a path of alcohol and drug abuse, his pathos became increasingly evident in works such as *Suddenly Last Summer* (1956), which was set against a decadent New Orleans background.

Small companies define the local scene. Hurricane Katrina slowed things down a bit locally, but by spring 2006 most of the small companies were back in action. The larger Broadway shows were slow to return, however, as the Saenger Theater, where big shows play, was badly damaged in the floods. Companies worth checking out include Le Petit Théâtre du Vieux Carré (p214), founded in 1916, and Southern Repertory Theater (p214), which stages its productions at the Shops at Canal Place.

THE GOTH QUEEN OF NEW ORLEANS

Anne Rice (1941) was born in New Orleans with a boy's name: Howard Allen O'Brien. She didn't like the name, and at a very young age chose to be called Anne. Much later, she married a man named Stan and took his last name.

She established her credentials as a gripping and erotic storyteller in the occult genre. Her bestselling vampire and witchcraft novels include *Interview with the Vampire* (1976), followed by *The Vampire Lestat* (1985), *The Queen of the Damned* (1988) and *Lasher* (1993), among others. *The Feast of All Saints* (1979), a semifictional account of free persons of color in antebellum New Orleans, is noteworthy for capturing an intriguing period and culture in New Orleans' history. If you yearn for more of her erotica, without the gore, look for books penned by AN Roquelaure, a Rice pseudonym.

Rice has been known to pull creative publicity stunts. The author, who at times vaguely resembles actress Kathleen Turner, staged her own funeral at Lafayette Cemetery No 1 in July 1995. She pulled out all the stops, hiring a jazz band and a horse-drawn hearse, and fans and photographers formed a lively funeral procession. Rice looked very pleased with herself as she lay in a cushy, silk-lined coffin. She stopped short of being shoved into a crypt, opting instead to be taken to a bookstore across the street.

Rice no longer lives in New Orleans, having moved to sunny La Jolla, CA, after the death of her husband. She moved a few months before Hurricane Katrina struck the city. In 2005 Rice alienated some of her audience by announcing that she had returned to the Catholic Church and would devote several years to writing a trilogy chronicling the life of Jesus.

Check out Rice's website (www.annerice.com) for regular dispatches in flowery prose from the author. It is fascinating to see how aware Rice is of everything written about her in print and on the web – she responds to criticisms made on Amazon.com and even in obscure blogs.

Horse and carriage before Anne Rice's former home, as described in the Mayfair Chronicles

TENNESSEE WILLIAMS

One of the US's greatest playwrights, Thomas Lanier 'Tennessee' Williams (1911–83) grew up in Clarksdale, MS, and St Louis, MO, and he took his nickname from his father's home state of Tennessee. But New Orleans was a frequent home for him during his peripatetic professional life, and he wrote his most famous plays in and about New Orleans. In turn, his New Orleans works rate among the best literary achievements from the Crescent City.

Williams penned *A Streetcar Named Desire* while residing at 632 St Peter St in the French Quarter. In Blanche Dubois and Stanley Kowalski, the play introduced two of the most memorable characters of the American theater, and its tense and sultry mood remains for many a prevailing image of the French Quarter. Williams won a Pulitzer after the play appeared on Broadway, with Marlon Brando setting the bar out of reach for all future Stanleys. Brando reprised his role in the film version – essential viewing if you're brushing up on New Orleans culture. The streetcar line from which the play gets its suggestive name ran down to Desire St in the Bywater, but the tracks were pulled up long ago. Noisy drunks in the French Quarter still holler 'Stella-a-a-a!' while walking back to their hotel rooms at night, however.

The ultramelodramatic *Suddenly Last Summer* is set in a Garden District mansion, and deals somewhat coyly with the subject of homosexuality. Williams, who was gay, was known to prowl gay bars, which by the 1940s were plentiful in the French Quarter.

New Orleans' annual Tennessee Williams Literary Festival (p16) takes place in March, a great time to explore the French Quarter's literary and dramatic sides.

CLASSICAL MUSIC & OPERA

When New Orleans was a Creole city its tastes were culturally sophisticated by North American standards. The city staged the first opera in the Americas, in 1796, and by the end of the 19th century the grand New Orleans Opera House stood on Bourbon St. The Opera House burned down in 1919, and the city was operaless for more than two decades. The city's opera rarely causes much of a stir, but remains an important part of the local culture. In March 2006 the opera, joined by Placido Domingo and other international stars, performed a benefit gala for victims of Hurricane Katrina.

The Louisiana Philharmonic Orchestra (LPO) temporarily lost its home, the Orpheum Theatre, which was badly damaged by Hurricane Katrina. But during the spring 2006 season the Philharmonic made appearances at other venues around town, such as Loyola University's Roussell Hall, Tulane University's Dixon Hall and at City Park. The LPO is unusual for being owned by the musicians, who formed the company in the 1990s after a labor disagreement with the New Orleans Symphony was not resolved. For more information about the city's music scene, see the New Orleans Music chapter (p75).

BALLET

The financially strapped New Orleans Ballet Association (NOBA), founded in 1969, usually runs a few productions annually. The season is very short, and is fleshed out with presentations by visiting dance companies from around the world. Performances are at the Theater of the Performing Arts in Armstrong Park.

CINEMA & TELEVISION

Before Hurricane Katrina, New Orleans had been establishing itself as a popular site for location shoots of blockbuster Hollywood films. With a growing community of quality support crew and extras, the city was touting itself as 'Hollywood South.' That trend may well continue, as most of the neighborhoods that location scouts drool over survived the hurricane and look as cinematic as ever.

Recent activity in the city includes the 2006 remake of *All the King's Men,* starring Sean Penn as a Louisiana politician modeled on Huey Long. As an interesting side note, Penn, having shot his scenes in New Orleans before Katrina happened, returned to the flooded city during the weeklong struggle to help get people out.

Director Wayne Wang and actress Queen Latifah were recently in New Orleans to shoot *Last Holiday* (2006). Latifah plays a woman who learns she is dying. She travels from New Orleans to Europe to enjoy her last days, then…well, we won't spoil the ending.

In 2004 *A Love Song for Bobby Long* (2004), starring John Travolta and Scarlett Johansson, was filmed in New Orleans. He plays Bobby, an alcoholic former literature professor languishing in an Uptown shotgun house. She's a moody, recently orphaned teen. Needless to say, they meet and discover an unexpected connection.

The highest-grossing film shot locally is director Oliver Stone's controversial *JFK* (1991), which includes numerous French Quarter scenes. Another hit, *Dead Man Walking* (1996), stars Susan Sarandon and Sean Penn in a true story about Sister Helen Prejean, a New Orleans resident who devotes time to death-row inmates and inspires discussion about the state's death penalty.

Andrei Codrescu's witty *Road Scholar* (1994) begins with his driving lessons in New Orleans before he hurtles across the US in a '59 Cadillac convertible.

Dennis Hopper and Peter Fonda play bikers in *Easy Rider,* the 1969 film classic. The scene of the two smoking pot in St Louis Cemetery No 1 upset the locals, since it introduced legions of youth to the New Orleans party scene.

Blaze Star, former governor Earl Long's main squeeze, told her story in an autobiography made into the 1989 movie *Blaze,* starring Paul Newman. Former governor Huey Long (Earl's brother) known as the 'Kingfish,' has been fictionalized in the Oscar-winning *All the King's Men* (1949), based on Robert Penn Warren's bestseller, and in *A Lion is in the Streets* (1953).

The musical genre, for which New Orleans once served as a staple location, has faded since 1958, when Elvis Presley starred in *King Creole.* Archives, however, are rich with footage of tap dancer Bill 'Bojangles' Robinson in *Dixiana* (1930) and jazz singer Billie Holiday's only screen appearance in *New Orleans* (1947). Louis Armstrong performed in *Hello Dolly!* (1969).

Hollywood has adapted many of Tennessee Williams' plays for film. His persistent portrayal of sexual repression and obsession often features New Orleans as a suitably decadent setting. In *Suddenly Last Summer* (1959), Katherine Hepburn as Violet Venable plots the forced lobotomy of her niece, played by Elizabeth Taylor, to preserve the reputation of her sexually irrepressible homosexual son. Vivian Leigh won an Oscar for best actress opposite a brutish Marlon Brando in *A Streetcar Named Desire* (1951), which also featured Oscar-winning supporting roles from Kim Hunter and Karl Malden. Filmed in and near the French Quarter, it deals with madness and rape. For more information, see Tennessee Williams, opposite.

Writer-director Jim Jarmusch's black-and-white film *Down by Law* (1986) stars avant-garde jazzman John Lurie, grizzled crooner Tom Waits and the crown prince of Italian slapstick, Oscar winner Roberto Benigni, as three down-and-outs at Orleans Parish Prison. The repartee between the three is the stuff of comic legend.

Louis Malle's *Pretty Baby* (1978), starring Brooke Shields as a pubescent streetwalker, was shot on location at the Columns Hotel. Julia Roberts plays a Tulane law student in *The Pelican Brief* (1993), a film adaptation of John Grisham's bestseller. *Interview with the Vampire* (1994) features Tom Cruise and Brad Pitt in the big-screen version of Anne Rice's novel.

New Orleans police officers would never use French terms such as *cher,* as did the fictional cops in *The Big Easy* (1987). Its star, Dennis Quaid, was also in *Undercover Blues* (1993). Even devout fans of James Lee Burke's detective novels may flinch at the gratuitous violence in the screen adaptation of *Heaven's Prisoners* (1996), starring Alec Baldwin.

THE HANDS BEHIND MR BILL

Fans of classic *Saturday Night Live* (SNL) will remember Mr Bill, the little Play-Doh man with the high-pitched voice who helplessly cried 'Oh no-o-o-o!' as he was abused by his little clay friends. The hands that moved the action and also guest-starred belonged to Walter Williams of New Orleans.

Mr Bill was a regular fixture on SNL from 1978 to 1980. Williams revived the character for the Fox Family Channel in 1998. You can still enjoy the primitive little action figure by renting or purchasing the DVD collection, 'Mr Bill's Disasterpiece Theater Definitive Collection.'

FIVE CHOICE NOLA FILMS

Whether made on the streets of New Orleans or on a soundstage, some excellent flicks have drawn from the city's sultry, decadent and loony environment. These films capture the 'Big Easy' in its multifarious guises.

A Streetcar Named Desire (1951; Elia Kazan) – New Orleans' seamy side, with some definitive casting: Brando as Stanley Kowalski and Vivienne Leigh as Blanche Dubois.

Down by Law (1986; Jim Jarmusch) – The opening shots, taken from a moving car panning past shotgun houses and housing projects, captures a side of New Orleans that we'll never know again.

King Creole (1958; Michael Curtiz) – One of Elvis' better films, with Michael Curtiz of *Casablanca* renown behind the camera. The King dominates, but New Orleans plays a key supporting role. Stagey, but has some great scenes of the French Quarter and seedy nightclubs.

New Orleans Exposed (2005) – Filmed just before Katrina wiped out much of the back of town area, this shoestring documentary delves into the housing projects where some of the city's biggest rap stars and most notorious criminals lived. It's a harrowing look at the flip side of the Big Easy.

Abbott & Costello Go to Mars (1953) – We gotta be kidding, right? Well, see for yourself. The old-school comic duo thinks it is going to Mars, but ends up in New Orleans during Mardi Gras. Needless to say, the old chums never catch on to the fact they haven't left the planet Earth.

Just to show there's no accounting for taste, we highly recommend *Abbott & Costello Go to Mars* (1953), in which Costello is scared witless by Mardi Gras floats and masked New Orleanians. Anyone who's ever had a surreal Mardi Gras experience will relate to it.

Michael Beaudreaux (*boo*-dro) stars in *The Louisiana Story* (1945), a semidocumentary about a young Cajun boy who scouted the swamps for oil drillers. The film's point of view – that Cajun culture and livelihoods can coexist with modern technology – is thrown into question because the Standard Oil Company helped fund the production.

Another essential documentary that explores an uncelebrated side of the city's culture is *New Orleans Exposed* (2005). It captures life in the city's back of town before Katrina depopulated the area. It's a low-budget but completely engrossing look at the city's murderous side, as well as the hip-hop artists who articulated the life there.

Other Hollywood films set in New Orleans, such as *Candyman II* and *Zombie vs Mardi Gras,* had short runs at the box office. Nevertheless, *Zombie* has become something of a cult classic.

Architecture

French Colonial House 69
Spanish Colonial House 69
Creole Town House 70
Creole Cottage 70
Shotgun House 71
American Town House 71
Federal 71
Greek Revival 71
Five-Bay Center Hall House 71
Two-Level Gallery House 72
Italianate 72
Gothic Revival 72
Beaux Arts 72
Second Empire 73
21st-Century Changes 73

Architecture

New Orleans' architectural strength is in its great quantity of 19th-century homes, and in the uncommon cohesion of so many of its historic neighborhoods. The city has no fewer than 17 historic districts on the National Register. Several, including Mid-City, Gentilly Terrace and Parkview, were devastated by floods after Hurricane Katrina. The French Quarter and the Garden District, which were spared flooding, have long been considered the two standouts. But, really, if you could relocate an entire neighborhood such as the Tremé, the Marigny or the Irish Channel to another city, these districts would stand out as architectural treasure troves. Such is the depth of New Orleans' historic housing stock.

The French Quarter and Garden District nicely illustrate the pronounced difference between the Creole and the American influences that defined Old New Orleans. The Quarter and the Creole 'faubourgs' downriver from Canal St are densely packed with stuccoed brick structures built in various architectural styles and housing types rarely found in other US cities. The wide lots and luxuriant wooden houses of the Garden District, upriver from the French Quarter, more closely resemble upscale homes found throughout the South. Here we see a spectacular quantity and variety of architectural gems. Uptown, further upriver, the display intensifies to the point of near-gaudiness. New Orleans was an exceedingly wealthy city when this part of town was developed, in the decades preceding the Civil War, and these neighborhoods remain decidedly upmarket today.

Because New Orleans has always been vulnerable to flooding, the city was first built on the highest ground. At the time of the Civil War, the city's footprint still adhered more or less to the natural levees created by the shifting Mississippi River. Consequently, the floods that followed Hurricane Katrina spared the oldest parts of the city. In these historic neighborhoods, damage caused by wind was for the most part repaired within the following months. As the city's population has reduced back to mid-19th century numbers, some urban planners have proposed shrinking its extents back to the high ground.

In the following pages we'll identify some of the most common types of houses (Creole cottages, town houses, shotgun houses etc) found in New Orleans' historic districts. While we're at it, we'll also point out some of the more prevalent architectural styles (Greek revival,

Colorful houses on St Ann St, French Quarter

TEN NOT TO MISS

When roaming New Orleans' historic neighborhoods, keep your eyes peeled for these architectural gems.

St Louis Cathedral (p137) – New Orleans' most recognized building anchors Jackson Sq in the French Quarter.

LaBranche Buildings (p167) – Stop and admire the great variety of cast-iron balcony rails that wrap around this block of buildings. You might also spot some wrought iron in the mix.

Napoleon House (p201) – Have a decadent cocktail in the rustic courtyard of this grand old Creole town house.

Jean Lafitte's Blacksmith Shop (p201) – The pirate's humble cottage, listing slightly to one side, looks like a relic from the French outpost. It actually was built in the Spanish period.

Gallier Hall (p151) – The epitome of Greek revival pomp and circumstance, the hall overlooks Lafayette Sq.

Louise McGehee School (p168) – This extravagant Second Empire mansion stands out in the opulent Garden District.

Pitot House (p161) – Built in the Spanish period, this plantation house reflects an older, French-colonial style.

Madame John's Legacy (below) – A wide French-colonial plantation home stands out in the compressed Quarter.

Ursuline Convent (p142) – In the French Quarter, this is the lone survivor from the French period.

Charles Briggs' House (p168) – A rare and striking Gothic revival mansion in the Garden District.

Italianate etc) found in the city. If you're planning to really explore New Orleans' historic neighborhoods, be sure to stop by the **Preservation Resource Center** (p155) in the Warehouse District for maps and free literature about landmark buildings in all areas of the city.

FRENCH COLONIAL HOUSE

Surviving structures from the French period are extremely rare. New Orleans was a French colony only from its founding in 1718 until the Spanish took over in 1762, and it was really a small outpost at that time. Twice during the Spanish period fires destroyed much of the town. Only one French Quarter building, the **Ursuline Convent** (p142), remains from the French period. The convent was built in a style suitable to the climate of French Canada, but the French quickly recognized that the Caribbean styles were more appropriate in steamy New Orleans. A few houses built during the Spanish period and later have French-colonial trappings.

Madame John's Legacy, at 628 Dumaine St, dates to 1788 but in many ways reflects the French style. It is often described as a French plantation house. It's marked by a steep, hipped roof, casement windows and batten shutters. In common with French plantation houses in the Caribbean, it has galleries – covered porches – that help keep the house cool in summer. Galleries shaded rooms from direct light and from rainfall. Residents could ventilate the house by leaving windows and doors open during the day. This house has narrow open spaces around all four sides, indicating the streets of the town were not so tightly packed during the French period as they became during the Spanish period. Out on Bayou St John the **Pitot House** (p161) also has signature French-colonial components.

Briquette entre poteaux, in which brick fills the spaces between vertical and diagonal posts, was common to French-colonial houses, and this style endured during the Spanish period. This structure is visible where stucco is cleared to expose the exterior walls of **Lafitte's Blacksmith Shop**, 941 Bourbon St (p201), and on the side of the **Hotel St Pierre**, at 911 Burgundy St. Neither of these buildings would otherwise be considered French colonial.

SPANISH COLONIAL HOUSE

During the town's Spanish period, adjacent buildings were designed to rub shoulders, with no space between, which created the continuous (though subtly varying) façade we now see along so many streets in the French Quarter. The signature type of home of this period is the two-story town house, with commercial space on the ground floor and residential quarters upstairs. The space between houses – the courtyard – represented a significant piece of well-shaded and private outdoor space. The courtyard was used like a family room.

LOCAL ARCHITECTURAL IDIOMS

The architectural terminology used in Louisiana and especially in New Orleans is a patois of French and English. Here are a few terms you may encounter on architectural tours or in books on the subject. We've thrown in a few geographic terms, as you're likely to hear those as well.

abat vent – An overhang, like an extended eve, that shades the front of Creole cottages. The same thing on a shotgun house is called an overhang.

banquette (bankee) –A term for sidewalk, passed down from the Creoles.

briquette entre poteaux – Similar to English half-timber construction, except that bricks are used to fill the intervening wall space between posts

entresol – A low-ceilinged mezzanine. Found in some Creole town houses.

gallery – A covered porch with the roof supported by arches or columns.

garde de frise – An iron grate separating two adjacent balconies, sometimes fan-shaped, often with small devil's pitchforks on top. They deterred thieves and could keep a daughter separated from the boy next door.

loggia – A gallery that is attached to the back of a house and opens up on the courtyard.

neutral ground – The median in the middle of the street.

A covered space along the back of the house, the loggia, served as a sort of courtyard gallery, and within it a curved stairway led to the upstairs living spaces. A carriageway linked the courtyard to the street. Arches, tiled roofs and balconies with ornate wrought-iron railings became common. Often, servants quarters occupied part of the courtyard area.

The house at **729-733 Royal St** was built in the Spanish era and retains much of its original character.

CREOLE TOWN HOUSE

Very few buildings survive from the Spanish-colonial period, and not all the survivors reflect the Spanish style. But the Creoles of New Orleans appreciated Spanish architecture and regularly applied its key elements (especially the courtyard, carriageway and loggia) to the town houses that are so common in the French Quarter still.

Most surviving examples date from the American period. An especially elaborate, three-story example of the Creole town house, with key Spanish elements, is **Napoleon House**, 500 Chartres St (p201).

CREOLE COTTAGE

Free-standing cottages pop up all over the French Quarter and the Faubourg Marigny. The most common type of cottage is the Creole cottage, which while simple is not necessarily small. High-pitched gabled roofs are a signature quality, and dormers on some of the roofs indicate upstairs living spaces. The front of the house usually has two casement doors, sometimes four. Where there are two doors, the other two openings are windows. These openings are often shuttered to shield the interior space from sidewalk traffic, passing just inches away. An extension of the roof overhangs part of the sidewalk.

The airy floor plan is as simple as can be, with four interconnected chambers, each with an opening (a door or window) to the side of the house. Ceilings are high. There is usually space on the sides of the house for exposed access to a back courtyard. At the back of the house there is a gallery, often with arched openings to the courtyard.

Simple Creole cottages probably started to appear during the Spanish period. Over time they became more stylish, reflecting Victorian tastes with intricate fanlights, ornately carved eve brackets and elaborately designed dormers. In some instances the form is expanded to include two full floors, plus dormers. But structurally, and in terms of floor plan, Creole cottages tended to vary little, for this style of house was well suited to the French Quarter's urban density and Louisiana's steamy climate. The house at **936 St Peter St** is a Creole cottage, although the Corinthian pilasters that frame the façade are not at all typical. In the Marigny, the double cottage at **1809-11 Dauphine St** is an even better example. Similar houses can be seen throughout the neighborhood.

SHOTGUN HOUSE

During the latter half of the 19th century, as New Orleans grew, the shotgun house became a more popular type of single-family dwelling than the Creole cottage. Shotgun houses were inexpensive homes that could be built on narrow property lots, and they were built in great numbers all over New Orleans. The name shotgun supposedly suggests that a bullet could be fired from front to back through the open doorways of all of the rooms, but in truth only the most basic shotgun has its doors lined up so perfectly. Walk along Orleans or St Anne Sts toward Rampart St and you'll see rows of shotguns with four-step stoops and finely trimmed eves.

The most basic 'single-shotgun' house is a row of rooms with doors leading from one to the next. As there is no hall, you have to pass through each room to get from the front to the back of the house. These houses are freestanding, with narrow spaces along either side of the house. Windows on both sides encourage cross-ventilation and keep the rooms cool. High ceilings also help with ventilation. The interiors are often comfortable and adorned with Victorian flourishes.

'Double-shotguns' are duplexes, with mirror-image halves traditionally forming two homes. Many double-shotguns have been converted into large single homes. Some shotguns, called 'camel-back shotguns', have a 2nd floor above the back of the house.

AMERICAN TOWN HOUSE

The town house (see Spanish Colonial House, p69) was popular among Anglo-Americans, but the Americans had their own style. They replaced the open carriageway with a closed hall leading from the front to the back of the house. They also had no commercial space on the ground floor. Americans tended not to conduct their business at home.

You'll see American town houses throughout the Quarter, but some stand out. **Gallier House** (p139) is a landmark designed by James Gallier Jr that is open for tours. The house has both a carriageway and hallway, and for Gallier it was a conscious fusion of the two styles.

FEDERAL

Federal-style architecture, with its restrained grace and Classic Roman references, may not be representative of the New Orleans aesthetic. However, architect Benjamin Henry Latrobe's **Louisiana State Bank** (401 Royal St) is a local landmark that reflects the straightforward geometry, plain surfaces and fine detail of the Federal style. Note the elegant, slightly pitched beams over the second-story windows and the narrow arched dormers. Slender wrought-iron balconies extend just far enough to allow the parting of casement shutters to peek out to wave hello. The influence of this style can be observed in many town houses in the French Quarter. Simply patterned cornices commonly found on cottages often represent a Federal influence.

GREEK REVIVAL

Perhaps no other style symbolizes the wealth and showiness of mid-19th century America than Greek revival architecture. The style, which is readily recognizable for its tall columns, was inspired by such classics as the Parthenon. Greek revival houses can be found in droves along St Charles Ave Uptown and in the Garden District. A nice example is the raised villa at **2127 Prytania St**. In the French Quarter you'll see grand Greek revival entryways at **840 Conti St** and **1303 Bourbon St**.

New Orleans' best example of monumental Greek revival architecture, with its columned porticos and stolid structure, is **Gallier Hall** (p151). The **US Mint Building** (p142) is another public building with strong Greek revival features.

FIVE-BAY CENTER HALL HOUSE

The 1½-story, center hall house became common with the arrival of more Anglo-Americans to New Orleans after the Louisiana Purchase in 1803. The raised center hall house, found in the Garden District and Uptown, became the most common type. It stands on a pier foundation 2ft to 8ft above ground, and its columned front gallery spans the entire width of the house. The front door leads directly into the center hall and is flanked by two windows to each side. The roof is gabled and usually has a dormer to illuminate an upstairs room. This type of house is clad in wood.

TWO-LEVEL GALLERY HOUSE

This type of home is most common in the Lower Garden and Garden Districts, although a few can be seen along lower Chartres St in the French Quarter and along Esplanade Ave, heading toward the lake. It's a two-story house, set back from the sidewalk, with front galleries on both levels. Each level has three or four openings, with doors usually to one side. Stately box columns are common.

ITALIANATE

The Italianate style gained popularity after the Civil War. Although the style originally drew its influence from the stately villas of Tuscany, you won't necessarily recognize the connection in New Orleans. You're more likely to identify certain details that mark the Italianate style, including wide roof overhangs with closely spaced brackets or double-brackets. Segmental arches, frequently used over doors and windows, and the ever-popular decorative boxlike parapets over galleries are also commonly identified as Italianate features. You'll find such details on many different types of buildings in New Orleans. On the outskirts of the French Quarter, the town house at **547 Esplanade Ave** has a graceful Italianate entrance and signature double eve brackets.

GOTHIC REVIVAL

The Gothic revival style, typically identified by its steeply pitched gable roofs, pointed arched windows, occasional gingerbread trim and twisting, polygonal chimneys, is not common in New Orleans, but the city has some stellar examples. Chief among them is the **Charles Briggs House** (p168) in the Garden District. **Greenville Hall** (p159), an extension of Loyola University, is in the steamboat Gothic style.

BEAUX ARTS

The hefty beaux-arts style, with its grand scale and cold stone siding, is atypical of the more earthy architecture New Orleans is known for. In the heart of the French Quarter, the beaux-arts **State Supreme Court Building** (p168) dwarfs its neighbors, but nevertheless has an

House laced with cast iron ornamentation in the Garden District

CAGED BEAUTIES

Several components contribute to the unique appeal of the architecture of New Orleans, but perhaps none makes so instant an impression as the ironwork that adorns the city's many balconies and galleries.

Some beautiful wrought-ironwork remains from the Spanish period. Wrought by hand, these railings have segmented geometric patterns, fine bars and forged arrows. Some have monograms. Have a look at the high-quality wrought-iron balcony rails on the **Cabildo** (p138) and the **Presbytère** (p137).

The innovation of casting iron made mass-production possible. During the 1850s, after Madame Pontalba added the cast-iron railings to her prominent **Pontalba Buildings** (p136), the entire town went mad for ironwork. Cast iron made it possible to integrate complex patterns and shapely filigrees into designs. Decorative motifs such as flowers and ears of corn became not only possible, but popular.

You'll also find wrought- and cast-iron fences and gates around some of the crypts in **St Louis Cemetery No 1** (p147).

impressive beauty that defies its context. Opposite, the building at **410-414 Chartres St**, which houses the research center of the Historic New Orleans Collection (p139), boasts staunch beaux arts features on a relatively modest scale. The terracotta-clad **Hotel Monteleone** (p241) displays some of the finer, more decorative features of the style.

SECOND EMPIRE

The Second Empire style made its way to New Orleans from France via the East Coast during the Reconstruction period. It is marked by mansard roofs, prominent dormers and rounded moldings over the windows and doors. In New Orleans, where classical styles remained influential, the Second Empire style was more restrained than elsewhere. Good examples are the **Louise McGehee School** (p168) in the Garden District and the house at **1437 Eighth St**, also in the Garden District.

21ST-CENTURY CHANGES

In the years ahead, and perhaps for decades to come, New Orleans will be rebuilding and reforming. In some of the flooded areas, homes need to be stripped, rewired, reinsulated, replastered, recarpeted and refurnished. In the most devastated parts of town, where some 200,000 homes are beyond repair, new streets, sewers and power lines will need to be installed before rebuilding can begin. It is not clear if areas such as the Lower Ninth Ward or New Orleans East will be rebuilt or turned into parklands. The residents of such neighborhoods who decide to stay in New Orleans will need housing. So too will the residents of Mid-City housing projects, which remained empty six months after Katrina. It is unlikely these structures will be repaired, as the city was already closing down housing projects around town before Katrina came.

A possible model for future developments can be seen in the Lower Garden District, where construction on the River Garden development began in 2003 and had already been largely completed when Hurricane Katrina struck. The development, which replaces a demolished housing project and some warehouses, is a mix of federally subsidized housing, market-rate rental properties and condominiums. Building styles approximate New Orleans

THE ARTISANS

New Orleans' great wealth of well-preserved, historic buildings is a credit to the plasterers, lathers, blacksmiths, masons and carpenters who have maintained these traditional skills in an age when bland box housing has become the norm everywhere else in the US.

Artisans in New Orleans are often members of families with proud traditions in the trades, and many are black Creoles who lost their homes when Hurricane Katrina blew through town. After Katrina, a good percentage of the city's artisans scattered across the country. It remains to be seen how many of these families will choose to reclaim their city and rebuild their homes and communities.

traditions, with a combination of row houses and bungalows replete with shuttered openings and wrought-iron railings. But its wide street plan is more in line with car-friendly suburban America, and its commercial centerpiece is a large Wal-Mart. It's a pseudo-historic vision for the future that some decry as soulless. We drove up and down the streets of the River Garden after Hurricane Katrina, but as the city was still fairly subdued at the time it was impossible to assess whether a vital community had begun to coalesce there. In its favor, the development hadn't been subjected to flooding.

Another, less Utopian possibility is to simply let residents rebuild their old neighborhoods, flooding hazards be damned. This approach is likely to require enforcing strict building codes in historic areas, which would likely slow down the city's recovery. At this point, the city isn't even promising it will provide services to some of the more remote parts of the city, but just the same some citizens are vowing to claim what's theirs and rebuild.

Music

Jazz 77
Jazz Pioneers 77
Jazz Resurgence 78
Rebirth of Brass 79
Blues 80
R&B & Funk 80
Cajun & Zydeco 82
Rock, Roots & Indie 83
Hip-Hop 84

Music

Saxaphone player, French Quarter

After Hurricane Katrina, it was infrequently said but generally understood that the true litmus test for the health of the 'new' New Orleans would lie in its music. If, in the new New Orleans, the city's music scene could survive and thrive, then New Orleans would be alright. It is still too early to say for certain what the outcome will be, but the early vital signs are encouraging. When the doctor last checked the city's pulse, what she heard was a tight little Bucktown shuffle.

Although some local bands remain splintered, with band members scattered to places like Houston and New York, most musicians were quick to re-establish themselves in New Orleans. However, the truth of it is that local musicians have always felt the pull of brighter lights and bigger cities to see whether they can make it outside the city's comfortable scene. Many do make it, but many more realise there's really no place like home when that home is New Orleans.

By early 2006 the city's most popular weekly gigs were again packing big crowds, and Jazz Fest that year was a homecoming for even more musicians – for many of whom just being on stage again in their hometown was a tearful and emotional experience. The pull to return, to establish new roots in the city's fertile soil is very, very strong.

Like never before, music is very important to New Orleans. This is a celebratory city. Parades happen nearly every day, and 'parade' in New Orleans means 'second-line' – just look for the marching brass band and file in after it. There's your parade. Funerals, parties, brunches, festivals, fireworks, steamboat rides down the Mississippi – all are accompanied by music.

The city's history can be traced in its music. The French and their descendants, the Creoles, were mad about ballroom dancing and opera. New Orleans boasted two opera companies before any other US city had even one. Meanwhile, slaves and free persons of color preserved African music and dance at public markets such as Congo Sq. These European and African influences inevitably came together when French-speaking black Creoles, who prided themselves on their musicianship and training, began livening up traditional European dance tunes by adding African rhythms. From there, jazz was an inevitability.

The postwar influx of non-Creole blacks from elsewhere around the South was accompanied by a flourishing of blues, R&B, soul and funk music. And, as things will do, it all came full circle. All of these influences poured into the 1980s brass band renewal that's going strong to this day.

JAZZ

A proliferation of brass instruments after the Civil War led to a brass-band craze that spread throughout the South and the Midwest, and many musicians of the postwar generation learned how to play without learning how to read sheet music. These untrained musicians 'faked' their way through a song, playing by ear and by memory, often deviating from the written melody. Thus, improvisation became another way to breathe extra life into musical arrangements. The stage was set for jazz. New Orleans, as nearly everyone knows, was at the center of the birth of this American musical form.

JAZZ PIONEERS

One of the most problematic figures in jazz history is **Charles 'Buddy' Bolden**, New Orleans' first 'King of Jazz.' Very little is known about the cornetist's life or music, and no recordings survive. The details of this legend paint an attractive, larger-than-life man, indicating that he made a huge impression on those who saw him play. Some said Bolden 'broke his heart' when he performed, while others mused that he would 'blow his brains out' by playing so loud. One eyewitness account asserted that his cornet once exploded as he played it.

But the exaggeration veiling the actual truth about Bolden cannot cheapen his stature. For roughly a decade, between 1895 and 1906, he dominated a town already crowded with stellar musicians. People were drawn in by Bolden's expressive and energetic playing, and audiences deserted the halls where rival dance bands were performing when word spread that Bolden was playing somewhere else in town. Naturally, all the young musicians of New Orleans wanted to be just like him, and his influence was widely felt.

Sadly, Bolden went insane while still at the top of the New Orleans music scene. He was institutionalized for 25 years, oblivious to the fact that, after his abrupt departure from the scene, jazz had spread worldwide and had developed into many new styles. When Bolden died, he was already long forgotten. Bolden is buried in an unmarked grave in Holt Cemetery.

After Bolden, New Orleans enjoyed a series of cornet-playing kings, including **Freddie Keppard**, **Bunk Johnson** and **Joe 'King' Oliver**. While Keppard's star passed over like a comet and

POST-KATRINA IPOD MIX

Culling New Orleans' vast reservoir of songs, we've compiled a musical soundtrack to reflect the emotional roller coaster of recent events in the city. Surely music will be the salvation of New Orleans. So load up your iPod, or whatever you're using these days, with some old and new tunes from the Crescent City. Paring down to just 25 songs (limited to one per artist in our list) is not really necessary, so add or subtract to the list as you see fit.

Irma Thomas – It's Raining

Clarence 'Frogman' Henry – Ain't Got No Home

Jelly Roll Morton – Don't You Leave Me Here

Henry Red Allen – Feelin' Drowsy

Sidney Bechet – Old Stack O'Lee Blues

Johnny Adams – I Won't Cry

Aaron Neville – Tell It Like It Is

Fats Domino – Walkin' to New Orleans

Professor Longhair – Tipitina

Dr John – Right Place Wrong Time

Tremé Brass Band – Gimme My Money Back

Huey 'Piano' Smith – Rockin' Pneumonia and the Boogie Woogie Flu

King Oliver – Stop Crying

Eddie Bo – Check Mr Popeye

Shirley and Lee – Let the Good Times Roll

Al Johnson – Carnival Time

James Andrews – Got Me a New Love Thing

Cory Harris and Henry Butler – Shake What Your Mama Gave You

The Meters – Cissy Strut

Nicholas Payton – Cannabis Leaf Rag 1

Los Hombres Calientes – New Second Line

Sugarboy Crawford – Jock-a-Mo

Dixie Cups – Iko Iko

Ernie K-Doe – Te Ta Te Ta Ta

Louis Armstrong – When the Saints Go Marching In

Bunk languished in obscurity until he was rediscovered by 'trad' jazz enthusiasts in the 1940s, Oliver made a break for Chicago, where his Creole Jazz Band reached a much larger audience. Those who followed Oliver's career say his sudden fame was deserved but that he was past his prime when he reached Chicago. He was soon overshadowed by his protégé, **Louis Armstrong**, whom Oliver summoned from New Orleans in 1922. Together with Baby Dodds, Johnny Dodds and Lil Hardin (Armstrong's wife), Oliver and Armstrong made many seminal jazz recordings, including 'Dippermouth Blues.' By the late '20s, Oliver had lost his chops – and his teeth – and his career quickly went south. He hocked his horn and ended up supporting himself as a fruit vendor in Savannah, GA, where he died in 1938.

Pianist **Jelly Roll Morton** was a controversial character – he falsely claimed to have 'invented' jazz while performing in a Storyville bordello in 1902 – but he had uncommon talents in composition and arrangement. **Kid Ory**, who hailed from nearby La Place, LA, was also important in the development of jazz. His expressive 'tailgate' style on the trombone accompanied many of the first jazz stars, including Louis Armstrong, and when Ory moved his band to Los Angeles in 1919, he introduced jazz to the West Coast.

Sidney Bechet was the first jazz musician to make his mark on the soprano saxophone, an instrument he played with vibrato and deep, often moody feeling. For 14 years clarinetist **Barney Bigard** was a key member of the Duke Ellington Orchestra. **Henry 'Red' Allen** was born across the river in Algiers, where he began playing in his father's marching band at age eight.

The Barbarin family is legendary in New Orleans for producing some of the city's best-loved musicians, including drummer **Paul Barbarin** and his nephew, banjo and guitar player **Danny Barker**. Barker also wrote many popular tunes for his wife, singer **Blue Lu Barker**. Members of the Barbarin family are still playing in New Orleans today.

Louis Prima also hailed from New Orleans, and although the Italian trumpet maestro (composer of 'Sing Sing Sing' and 'Just a Gigolo') became linked to the Las Vegas entertainment scene, when his time was up he came home and was laid to rest in Metairie Cemetery.

JAZZ RESURGENCE

When **Wynton Marsalis** released his first album in 1982, he was only 19 years old – and yet music critics proclaimed him a genius. Not since Louis Armstrong had a New Orleans jazz musician been so well received on the national scene. It was the start of good things to come. Soon, Wynton's older brother **Branford Marsalis** was also making waves, and other young musicians who were studying with Winton and Branford's father, **Ellis Marsalis**, at the New Orleans Center for the Creative Arts, formed the nucleus of a New Orleans jazz revival. These included pianist-crooner **Harry Connick Jr** and trumpeters **Terence Blanchard** and **Roy Hargrove**. This wasn't another resuscitation of 'trad' jazz, though. The young turks of the '80s were

SATCH

Although he is sometimes referred to as 'King Louis,' in the world of jazz Louis Armstrong (1901–71) is really beyond royal sobriquets. The self-deprecating Armstrong is more widely remembered as 'Satchmo' – or 'Satch' for short.

Armstrong made his greatest contributions to music during the 1920s, when he began to modify the New Orleans sound. New Orleans jazz had always emphasized ensemble playing, but, to showcase his unique gifts, Armstrong shaped his arrangements specifically to support his own driving, improvised solos. With his cornet riding above the ensemble, songs such as 'Muskrat Ramble' and 'Yes! I'm in the Barrel' had an intensity not heard before. If the music sounds all too familiar today, it's because Armstrong's influence was so far-reaching.

As his popularity grew, Armstrong became the consummate showman, singing, jiving and mugging for his audience. His tours of Europe helped spread the popularity of jazz worldwide.

All of this, incredibly, was accomplished by the son of a prostitute. Armstrong grew up on the outskirts of New Orleans' notorious Storyville district, where he and fellow street urchins would sing on the streets for pennies. While residing in the Waifs' Home for troubled youth, he began to learn the trumpet, and, obviously, he was a natural talent. Armstrong's big break came in 1922, when King Oliver hired him to play in his band in Chicago. Satch never looked back. He only returned to New Orleans to play the occasional gig and, in 1949, to assume the role of Zulu on Mardi Gras. He lived for several decades in a nondescript house in Queens, New York.

clearly products of the post–Miles Davis and John Coltrane world. Since their beginnings in New Orleans, many have relocated to other parts of the country, where media exposure and more money tend to be available. Blanchard's achievements include soundtracks to many of filmmaker Spike Lee's joints.

The flow of talent from New Orleans hasn't ceased. **Henry Butler**, a blind pianist with extraordinarily quick hands, moved to Colorado after Hurricane Katrina destroyed his home in the Lower Ninth Ward. Hopefully the move proves to be a temporary one. Butler has pursued several musical paths, from straight jazz to blues, funk and Latin. Don't miss an opportunity to see him perform live if/when he returns to the Crescent City.

Trumpeter **Nicholas Payton** began his career recording classic New Orleans standards with a modern musical approach. He joined forces with the ancient legend Buck Clayton in a Grammy-winning performance of 'Stardust.' More recently, Payton has experimented with blending jazz-psychedelic-funk fusion styles with hip-hop and digital effects. You can hear his groovy new sound on the album *Sonic Trance*.

Trumpeter **Kermit Ruffins** is one of the most entertaining musicians in town. His shows at Vaughan's (p208) every Thursday night always pack the house and often attract other musicians, who come for the chance to play with Kermit's band, the Barbecue Swingers. Another trumpet player to watch is **Irvin Mayfield**, who with legendary percussionist **Bill Sumners** has formed the popular outfit **Los Hombres Calientes**. They've got a good thing going with their intense concoction of wildly expressive and percussive Latin jazz, and they put on a great live show.

Trumpet player **James Andrews** is a fixture on the local club scene. His album *Satchmo of the Ghetto* was produced by Allen Toussaint and features Dr John tinkling the ivories on some tracks. Andrews hails from an illustrious family of young musicians. **Trombone Shorty**, a local celebrity since he was about eight years old, is his younger brother. **Donald Harrison Jr** (namesake son of the late Mardi Gras Indian chief), an inspired contemporary jazz innovator on alto sax, made a name for himself in New York City before returning to his native New Orleans. He's followed his father's footsteps as a community leader and Mardi Gras Indian.

REBIRTH OF BRASS

It could reasonably be argued that modern New Orleans music began with marching brass bands. Mobile brass outfits parading through the city's backstreets for funerals and benevolent society 'second-line' parades during the late 19th century pretty much set the tone for things to come – Buddy Bolden, Freddie Keppard and even Louis Armstrong grew up idolizing the horn players, who frequently played along the streets where these future jazz innovators lived. While early-20th-century ensembles such as the Excelsior, Onward and Olympia brass bands never became nationally recognized, their tradition did not die. Many brass bands today, including the current generation of the Onward, Olympia and Tremé brass bands, still play very traditional New Orleans music, although surely they're jazzier than pre-20th-century bands were.

The brass band scene received a welcome infusion of new blood in the late 1970s with the emergence of the **Dirty Dozen Brass Band**. The Dirty Dozen was anything but traditional, fusing diverse styles of music from 'trad' jazz to funk, R&B and modern jazz. No longer a marching band, the Dirty Dozen continues to perform in clubs around town, and tours frequently. It paved the way for the much funkier and streetwise **Rebirth Brass Band**, formed in 1983. Original members of Rebirth, including trumpeter Kermit Ruffins, have moved on, but a younger crew of musicians has kept the band alive, and it remains one of the most popular groups in New Orleans, where Rebirth performs regular club gigs. **Tremé Brass Band**, headed by Uncle Lionel Batiste on the bass drum, is a nice mix of elder statesmen and young guns, mixing in traditional New Orleans jazz with original numbers with a little funk hitch to the beat.

Brass music has evolved in interesting ways, sometimes fusing with reggae and even hip-hop. Rappin' trombone player **Coolbone** is at the forefront of what he terms the 'brasshop' movement. The **Soul Rebels** also borrow freely from hip-hop for their innovative brass arrangements. **Bonerama** infuses the genre with the funk of The Meters and the loaded energy of Jimi Hendrix.

RIP TUBA

At the **Backstreet Cultural Museum** (p146), Anita Francis flicked on the lights in the Jazz Funeral Room, where 4in x 5in photos and newspaper obituaries have been taped to one wall. There were some familiar faces. One display honored **Tootie Montana**, Big Chief of the Yellow Pocahontas, whose death in early 2005 made the national papers. It was a big funeral, all the Indians and a big crowd came out to say goodbye to a great man, she said.

Nearby, photos of **Anthony 'Tuba Fats' Lacen** caught my eye. Anyone who's been to New Orleans would have recognized the big, quiet man whose tuba looked unusually small on his shoulder. Tuba Fats had been a recognizable fixture on Jackson Sq and in second-line parades for years. Photographers looking for a definitive image of New Orleans music naturally gravitated toward Tuba. Millions of music lovers had shuffled and buck-jumped to his solid bass lines. Anita smiled fondly, 'Yeah, Tuba passed. January '05. He had the biggest funeral.'

'Bigger than Tootie's, even?'

'Oh yeah, everybody loved Tuba. He played all the parades. He was an Indian long time ago. He went to South Africa, not long before he died. His friends the Zulus, from Africa, they come here for the funeral. The Indians come. And the musicians come. It lasted three days. Three days for the funeral. Biggest funeral I remember.'

BLUES

Despite its proximity to the Mississippi Delta, where the blues began, New Orleans never became a blues capital the way Chicago did. The blues have always been the domain of guitarists and harp players, and New Orleans has always been primarily a brass and ivory city. But it has never lacked great blues artists. Asked to name the king of New Orleans blues, a local musician is likely to name trumpeter Louis Armstrong, whose blues-based solos of the 1920s and 1930s were equal in expression and originality to those of any Delta guitarist of his day.

New Orleans has also been home to a few great blues guitarists, beginning with Mississippi native Eddie Jones, who preferred to be known as **Guitar Slim**. By the '50s Guitar Slim was based in New Orleans, where he packed patrons into nightclubs like the Dew Drop Inn. He wooed audiences with his anguished vocal style and agitated guitar licks. His biggest hit – a gift from the devil, he said – was 'The Things I Used to Do,' which sold a million copies. Other New Orleans blues guitarists include living legends **Earl King**, whose 'Trick Bag' and 'Come on Baby' are essential items on any New Orleans jukebox, and blind guitarist **Snooks Eaglin**.

If you're venturing into the Mississippi Delta you'll find a lot more blues. See p268 before hitting Hwy 61. Better yet, grab a copy of Lonely Planet's *Road Trip: Blues & BBQ*.

R&B & FUNK

Although New Orleans is still widely regarded as a jazz city, it is just as much an R&B and funk city. Since the 1950s and 1960s the city has been churning out popular singers, drummers and piano players in truly mind-boggling numbers.

New Orleans owes its solid reputation as a breeding ground for piano players to a man named Henry Roeland Byrd – otherwise known as **Professor Longhair**. His rhythmic rumba and boogie-woogie style of playing propelled him to local success with tunes such as 'Tipitina' (for which the legendary nightclub is named) and 'Go to the Mardi Gras.' He did not tour, though, and his name soon faded away. His style of playing, however, lived on in younger pianists like **Huey 'Piano' Smith**, who recorded 'Rockin' Pneumonia and the Boogie Woogie Flu,' and the eye-patched genius **James Booker**. Virtually every piano player to come from New Orleans in the past 50 years has had to acknowledge Fess' influence. In 1970, Professor Longhair was barely making a living sweeping floors when promoter Quint Davis tracked him down and booked him for that spring's Jazz Fest. His performance launched a decade of long-overdue recognition for one of New Orleans' great performers. He died in 1980.

While Professor Longhair was still mired in obscurity, some very unforgettable tunes came out of the Crescent City to rock the nation. 'Lawdy Miss Clawdy' was cut by **Lloyd Price**, with a backup band that included **Dave Bartholomew** and **Fats Domino**, the duo credited with shaping the 'New Orleans sound.' Bartholomew's trademark arrangements, built on soulful horns and a solid backbeat laid down by drummer Earl Palmer, can be heard on many of the big hits of the '50s, including some of Little Richard's early recordings. In collaboration with Bartholomew, Domino would go on to become one of the city's most successful musicians, recording a string of hit singles including 'Blueberry Hill,' 'My Blue Heaven' and 'Ain't that a Shame.' Domino continues to perform (he often appears at Jazz Fest), but his home in the Lower Ninth Ward was flooded and at the time of writing he was residing outside New Orleans.

The familiar expression 'see you later, alligator' naturally resulted in a catchy New Orleans pop song, recorded by **Bobby Charles** in 1955. The often-covered 'Ooh Poo Pah Doo' is also a local creation, and was first sung by **Jessie Hill**. Other stars to emerge from the Crescent City during this period were the late, great **Johnny Adams**, who wooed the city with smooth, gut-wrenching ballads, and the dynamic pop duo **Shirley and Lee**, whose 'Let the Good Times Roll' became standard fare on radio playlists nationwide.

In the 1960s R&B in New Orleans and elsewhere fell under the spell of **Allen Toussaint**, a talented producer, songwriter and musician whose legion of hits is legendary. As the producer and talent developer at Minit Records, he exhibited a remarkable adaptability in molding songs to suit the talents of many of New Orleans' diverse young artists. The formula worked for **Ernie K-Doe**, who hit pay dirt with the disgruntled but catchy 'Mother In Law,' a chart-topper in 1961, and the coy 'A Certain Girl.' Toussaint also wrote and produced the **Lee Dorsey** hit 'Working in the Coal Mine,' which couldn't have been more different from the K-Doe songs.

Irma Thomas, the 'Soul Queen of New Orleans,' also frequently collaborated with Toussaint. The former waitress was discovered in a talent show and was soon recording hits such as the sassy anthem 'Time Is on My Side' (later covered by the Rolling Stones) and the touching, autobiographical 'Wish Someone Would Care.' A number of Toussaint-penned ballads, including 'It's Raining' and 'Ruler of My Heart,' lent definition to her body of work.

Toussaint's most enduring and successful partnership was with the Neville Brothers, who have reigned as the 'first family' of New Orleans music for four decades. **Aaron Neville**, whose soulful falsetto hallmarks one of the most instantly recognizable voices in pop music, began working with Toussaint in 1960, when his first hit single, the menacing but pretty 'Over You,' was recorded. The association later yielded the gorgeous 'Let's Live.' But 'Tell It Like It Is' (1967), recorded without Toussaint, is the biggest national hit of Aaron's career.

EXPERIENCING NOLA MUSIC

You don't have to try very hard to catch music in New Orleans, because music is everywhere in the city. Much of what you'll hear as you walk through the French Quarter is either canned zydeco music (designed to lure free-spenders into shops) or cover bands rumbling out danceable grooves in Bourbon St bars. Rest assured, this is far from the bottom of the well. To really familiarize yourself with New Orleans music, follow the following simple steps.

- Before your trip, tune into **WWOZ** (p82) Internet stream, which broadcasts local music round the clock. And if driving in the New Orleans area, keep your radio dialed to FM90.7.
- Your first shopping stop should be the **Louisiana Music Factory** (p226). This excellent record store specializes in the music of Louisiana and has listening stations to sample recent releases and re-releases.
- In the afternoon, stroll through Jackson Sq, where you're likely to see the local **buskers** (p136) working for tips.
- Catch **weekly gigs** (p206), such as Bob French at Donna's Bar, Rebirth at the Maple Leaf or Kermit at Vaughan's.
- Do the bar-hopper's **Nightlife Crawl** (p172) walking tour outlined in this book to take in clubs along lower Decatur and Frenchmen Sts.
- Don't miss legendary **Tipitina's** (p209) club, and while there pay your respects to Professor Longhair's statue.
- Visit the R&B hit maker **Ernie K-Doe's Mother-in-Law Lounge** (p203) bar, opened before his death and lovingly maintained as an entertaining tribute.
- Drop by the **Jazz National Historic Park** (p142) headquarters at noon to catch live music and discussions about New Orleans music.
- Stages are set up around the Quarter and musicians perform all weekend during the **French Quarter Festival** (p16).
- The **New Orleans Jazz & Heritage Festival** (p49) is a music-lover's smorgasbord packed into two weekends.

Art Neville, a piano player from the Professor Longhair school, began performing with a group called the Hawkettes in the mid-'50s. In the late '60s he formed the group Art Neville and the New Orleans Sound with guitarist Leo Nocentelli, bassist George Porter Jr and drummer Zigaboo Modeliste, a group that would soon change its name to **The Meters** and define New Orleans funk music. The Meters later joined forces with George Landry, who as Big Chief Jolly was head of the Wild Tchoupitoulas Mardi Gras Indian gang (see Meet the Boys on the Battlefront, p33). Landry also happened to be an uncle of the Nevilles. When **Wild Tchoupitoulas** began performing funk- and reggae-based Indian anthems (such as 'Meet de Boys on de Battlefront') in the mid-'70s, it was the first time the four Neville brothers performed together – Charles and Cyrille rounded out the quartet. More recently, Aaron's son Ivan has joined the group.

The Meters and Allen Toussaint also contributed to the success of **Dr John**, who recorded his bestselling album *Right Place Wrong Time* with their support in 1973. Dr John began life as Mac Rebennack. He played guitar as a sideman for many New Orleans artists during the late '50s, but switched to the piano after his left index finger was shot off and sewn back on. He moved to Los Angeles and toured with Sonny and Cher in the mid-'60s before carving out his own unique blend of psychoactive soul and voodoo rock that have made him an enduring cult figure.

Current musicians to check out include **Davell Crawford** (grandson of Sugarboy Crawford, of 'Jock-A-Mo' fame), a funk-driven tour de force on piano and Hammond B-3. The man can sing. The funk quintet **Galactic** has been laying down intricate rhythms since the early 1990s. The group has forged ahead as an instrumental band since 2004, when lead singer Theryl DeClouet left the band. **Papa Grows Funk**, with its Hammond-organ grooves, has established a reputation that goes beyond New Orleans.

CAJUN & ZYDECO

The traditional music of rural southern Louisiana began with dances – waltzes, quadrilles and two-steps. The 20th century brought innovations that led to two separate types of music. Cajun music is the music of the white Cajun people and zydeco is the music of French-speaking blacks who share the region.

The traditional Cajun ensemble comprised a fiddle, diatonic button accordion, guitar and triangle (the metal percussion instrument common to symphony orchestras and kindergarten music class). **Joe Falcon** was the first Cajun recording star, and probably the

WWOZ, THE SOUND OF NEW ORLEANS

For complete immersion in New Orleans music, tune in to community radio WWOZ (90.7FM) or pick up the station's Internet stream (www.wwoz.org). Known locally as OZ (oh-*zee*), the station broadcasts the music of southern Louisiana, with a healthy mix of 'trad' and modern jazz, blues, R&B, Cajun and zydeco. Some shows concentrate on world music, but most stick close to home. There's no shortage of material.

WWOZ went on the air in December 1980, and for several years broadcast from a bare-bones studio upstairs from Tipitina's nightclub. Legendary shows at Tip's were broadcast live simply by dropping a microphone through a hole in the floor. The studio has since moved to Louis Armstrong Park, and the station is now managed and subsidized by The New Orleans Jazz & Heritage Foundation, which also organizes Jazz Fest.

The station's massive collection of LPs, CDs and recordings of live shows survived Hurricane Katrina with few casualties. After the hurricanes, OZ streamed online from a remote host in New Jersey while its studio remained out of commission. It's back in Armstrong Park, with most of the same DJs as before.

Some highlights on WWOZ's weekly calendar (all times US Central):

Trad Jazz with Bob French (9-11am Tue & Fri)

Blues & R&B with Jivin' Gene (7-10pm Tue)

Jazz Roots with Tom Morgan (9-11am Wed)

R&B & Blues with David Torkanowsky (2-4pm Thu)

Old Time Country & Bluegrass with Hazel the Delta Rambler (10am-noon Sun)

Cajun & Zydeco with Charles Laborde & Jim Hobbs (noon-2pm Sun)

Kitchen Sink (10pm-midnight Sun-Thu)

first Cajun musician who was successful enough to quit his day job as a farmer. In the 1930s the **Hackberry Ramblers** were the first Cajun outfit to appeal to an audience beyond Acadiana. No doubt, the infusion of Western Swing influences helped boost the Ramblers' popularity.

Around the same time, blacks such as **Amadé Ardoin** and **Adam Fontenot** maintained similar musical traditions. Ardoin's plaintive music, originally called 'la la,' included a simple number called 'Les Haricot Sont Pas Salés' (the snap beans aren't salted). *Les haricot,* as pronounced in Louisiana, easily morphed into zydeco. As this new music formed, it drew from Caribbean music and the blues. Today, it is a decidedly louder music than Cajun, with a more exuberant, syncopated beat. Zydeco accordionists prefer the piano-accordion, and the rhythm section usually includes a *frottoir,* a metal washboardlike instrument that's worn like armor and played with spoons.

Live music on Bourbon St

Zydeco didn't really take off until the 1950s, when **Clarence Garlow** released one of Louisiana's enduring standards, 'Bon Ton Roula,' which made the national R&B charts. That smash hit was followed by **Boozoo Chavis**' infectious 'Paper in My Shoe,' and, soon afterwards, by the emergence of zydeco's biggest star, **Clifton Chenier**. While he played accordion and sang in French much of the time, Chenier gave the music a decidedly R&B feel, and his recordings for the California-based Arhoolie label helped popularize the music well beyond the Louisiana state line.

A Cajun revival began in the 1960s with the **Balfa Brothers** and **Marc Savoy**, who stripped the music back down to its roots, revealing its traditional beauty to a wide national audience. Savoy still performs regularly, along with his wife Ann Savoy, at his accordion shop in Mamou (p254).

Hard-traveling **Beausoleil** is probably the most widely known Cajun band playing today. You're more likely to catch them touring through your home town than you are in Louisiana, unless there's a festival on. **DL Menard**, looking very much the aged farmer, still performs at festivals and the occasional gig.

Popular zydeco artists such as **Queen Ida**, **CJ Chenier** (Clifton's son) and **Buckwheat Zydeco** are often on the road but play frequent gigs in Louisiana. **Chris Ardoin**, **Rockin' Dopsie**, **Rosie Ledet** and **Geno Delafose** are easier to catch closer to home. Artists' websites are a good place to check out performance schedules.

ROCK, ROOTS & INDIE

New Orleans rock boils down to a few longtime standouts, most of whom sound like updated versions of the Doobie Brothers (who are not a local product). The **Radiators**, going strong for over 25 years, clearly lead the pack. They're a jam band that draws on the rich veins of swamp rock and R&B, and they have an extremely loyal following in town and from abroad.

Cowboy Mouth, headed by legendary drummer Fred LeBlanc, has been rocking the city since the early '90s. Their song 'Take Me Back to New Orleans' gained new significance in the weeks after Katrina forced a complete evacuation of the city. **Better than Ezra** also hails from New Orleans. Their song 'King of New Orleans' is a local anthem of sorts, and 'WWOZ' is a catchy tribute to the radio station.

The **Iguanas** are a roots band who create some cool grooves by melding R&B–based rock with liberal doses of Mexican conjunto and Chicano rock sounds.

The **Subdudes** combine a similar rock-funk sensibility. Their 2006 release *Behind the Levee* reaches the higher ground with a track called 'Looking at You,' featuring zydeco singer Rosie Ledet.

TRENT REZNOR'S NEW ORLEANS

Nine Inch Nails front man Trent Reznor lived in New Orleans' Garden District from 1995 to 2005. The brooding songwriter lived in the 1850s mansion at 2425 Coliseum St, and he converted an Uptown mortuary into his personal studio. He was fairly reclusive in the 'Big Easy,' never really delving into the local music clubs. He said he was drawn not to the local jazz and R&B scenes, but to the city's atmosphere and 'weird spirituality.' While living in New Orleans Reznor recorded two NIN albums and produced Marilyn Manson's album *Antichrist Superstar* for his Nothing record label.

Reznor sold his house in March 2005 for $1.8 million and moved to Los Angeles. In October, Nine Inch Nails headlined the Voodoo Experience in New Orleans, less than two months after the city was devastated by Hurricane Katrina.

HIP-HOP

It perhaps follows that a predominantly African American city widely known as the 'murder capital of America' should have had a thriving gangsta rap scene. The city's dangerous back of town neighborhoods and housing projects served as a petrie dish for hustlers looking for alternative sources of income to drug dealing. That part of town was completely shut down by Katrina, and if you ask anyone who has genuine influence over the city's renewal, none will espouse bringing back the 'down-South hustla' aspect of the city's culture. But such things don't come about by official design, so who knows, maybe New Orleans will be back on the hip-hop map by the end of the decade.

The biggest rap star to come out of the 'Big Easy' is **Juvenile**, whose 'bounce' rap style relies on danceable mixes designed to make the girls' azzes wiggle. His album *400 Degreez* went platinum many times over. **Soulja Slim** was an up-and-comer with a huge local following who didn't fare so well as Juvie. Soulja, a product of an Uptown housing project, was gunned down in November 2003.

The New Orleans hip-hop scene has revolved around successful independent labels such as Cash Money, which put rapper **Lil Wayne** in the limelight. Underground rap impresario **Master P** runs his No Limit label in Baton Rouge.

Food

The Culture of Louisiana Cuisine 86
Creole, Cajun & Soul 86
History 87
How New Orleanians Eat 88

Staples & Specialties 89
Seafood 89
Meats 91
Gumbo 92
Breads & Sandwiches 92
Rice & Beans 93
Grits & Cornbread 94
Herbs, Spices & Seasonings 94
Sauces 94
Vegetables 95
Fruits 95
Sweet Treats 96

Drinks of New Orleans 97
Alcoholic Drinks 97
Nonalcoholic Drinks 98

Celebrating With Food 99
Home Cooking 99
Special Events 99

Where to Eat & Drink 101
Old-line Creole 101
Contemporary Cuisine 101
Neighborhood Joints 102
Oyster Bars 102
Diners 102
Po'boy Shops & Other Fast Food 102
Foreign Fare 102

Vegetarians & Vegans 103

Eating With Kids 103

A Louisiana Gumbo Party 104
Louisiana Chicken & Okra Gumbo 104

Food

Food is a big deal in New Orleans. From its earliest days to the present, the people of New Orleans have honed a fine taste for subtle, rich, heartwarming dishes. Local tastes are for flavors that linger pleasantly, like good gravy, in your taste bud memory bank. Food has always been an integral part of the local culture and economy, probably never more so than it is now. During the months following Hurricane Katrina, reports of restaurant openings were a daily boost to morale in a city that desperately needed every encouragement.

Soft-shell crab with new potatoes and almonds

In terms of ingredients and culinary creations, southern Louisiana's fertile soil and wetlands provide an abundance of seafood, herbs, peppers and produce for the pantry. The local cuisine has much in common with the food you'll find in the South, as well as elsewhere in the US, but in important ways it stands out. Creole and Cajun cuisine both originated in southern Louisiana, giving New Orleans a culinary cachet that no other city in North America can match.

The local dining scene is anchored by some long-established Creole restaurants that maintain deep traditions going back to the French-colonial period. But each generation of chefs seems to introduce new innovations, and the city is always a hotbed of contemporary cuisine. But make no mistake, from tumbledown po'boy shops to streamlined American diners and caféteria-style Soul Food joints, the city's low-cost, workaday eateries are every bit as vital and rewarding as the white-tablecloth establishments.

So if you're visiting New Orleans for the first time or the 100th, jump in mouth-first. Get to know the tremendously hospitable people who make this treasured city great by breaking bread with them. You'll quickly discover that the heart, color and exuberance of the people of New Orleans is the true source of the city's vibrant cuisine.

THE CULTURE OF LOUISIANA CUISINE

What makes New Orleans unique is its strong cultural connections to Louisiana's Cajun Country, the southern USA, France and the Caribbean. The cuisine of New Orleans bears the influence of an extraordinarily diverse range of people. Native Americans, French colonials, Creoles, African slaves, free persons of color, Acadians (Cajuns), and immigrants from Europe, the Caribbean and Latin America have all contributed ingredients, tastes and kitchen techniques. Today the local cuisine is enhanced by a spirit of innovation that helps keep standards up to date.

CREOLE, CAJUN & SOUL

When we speak of contemporary New Orleans food, we're actually speaking of the unique mixing of three dominant cooking styles – Creole, Cajun and Soul Food – commonly associated with both the city and the state of Louisiana. The first two are native to predominantly French southern Louisiana, while Soul Food is popular throughout the American South.

Buttery-rich, refined and sophisticated, Creole cuisine is the food of the city and the delicious legacy of the city's French heritage. Dishes such as the delicate *poisson en papillote* (fish cooked in parchment paper) and shrimp rémoulade (p95) are prime examples of how the chefs of New Orleans reflect the city's French roots, while using local ingredients and incorporating contributions of the other cultures that have passed through the port city. On the whole, Creole cuisine is smooth and rich, with a tip of the hat to the sauces and formal presentations of the French motherland.

Rustic, flavorful and bold, Cajun food is the food of the country – in this case, the southern Louisiana marshes, bayous (tributaries) and prairies west of New Orleans proper. Often mistakenly attributed to New Orleans, Cajun food has its physical and cultural roots with the rural settlers from British Maritime Canada. When the French Acadians arrived in Louisiana (see p113) they brought their unique frontier cuisine and adapted it to the remote areas of what is now alternately called Acadiana, Acadian Louisiana or Cajun Country. The long-simmering single pot dishes (such as crawfish étouffée, shrimp jambalaya and roux-based gumbo) reflected the survival-oriented frontier traditions of the Acadians – simple foods based on the varied bounty of the land.

Broadly speaking, Soul Food – as well as its closely related cousin, southern country-style food – is derived from British cuisine and adapted with indigenous ingredients and the cooking techniques of African slaves and African American hired cooks. The often-blurred distinction between the southern cooking of blacks and whites is the quality of the raw ingredients. As a general rule, southern country-style cooking starts with the pick of the crop or carcass, and Soul Food stews up the rest. Crispy fried chicken, okra smothered with tomatoes, collard greens cooked with salt pork, hearty yellow cornbread and fluffy raised biscuits are common to both styles of cooking. Soul Food includes such delicacies as turkey neck stew, pigs' feet and chitterlings (tripe).

UNDERSTANDING THE MENU

If you're not from the United States, the typical American restaurant meal is divided into three sections: the appetizer (starting course), entrée (main course) and dessert. Most restaurants will present a printed menu and have the daily specials recited by the waitstaff. At country restaurants that serve plate lunches the menu might be completely verbal, so pay attention if you don't see a blackboard or printed menus.

You may also encounter specialized restaurants that only serve one item cooked in a particular way, for example fried catfish or boiled crawfish. In this case, all you have to do is say how much you want as the food will be sold by the plate, pound or piece.

HISTORY

When the French arrived in Louisiana, they found a climate and natural environment very different from that of France. From the indigenous Attakapas, Chitamacha and Houma, the Europeans learned how to source oysters, crawfish, crabs, shrimp, turtle, speckled trout and

SOUL FOOD *Charmaine O'Brien*

In early days, African slaves may have been preparing meals for wealthy white families, but they certainly weren't eating the same food. The white families ate the hams of the pig and the slaves made do with the ribs, offal, feet and skin. The white folks ate vegetables such as turnips and the slaves got the green tops. Slaves were given molasses (used as a flavoring), cornmeal and whatever else was left over or considered second-rate.

Slaves were usually permitted to keep their own small patch of herbs and vegetables as well as a few chickens, and out of this they created their own family meals. Food was often deep-fried in pig fat, which was readily available. They stewed poor-quality meat for hours to tenderize it and develop its flavor. While the slaves had little choice in the foods they ate, they came to develop a rich, hearty, delicious cuisine – including greens, chitterlings (tripe), cornbread and ham hocks – we now know as Soul Food.

Soul Food is not indigenous to southern Louisiana like Creole and Cajun food, and while you will find Soul Food all over the southern US, the version you eat in Louisiana will have more pepper, spice and garlic.

catfish. They also found wild game such as pigeon, rabbit, dove, squirrel, duck and deer. The indigenous people pointed out plant life such as wild greens, onions, berries, beans, pumpkins, squash, watermelon, peaches and corn (maize). Also, not insignificantly, the French picked up the native technique of pounding leaves from the sassafras tree into a flavorful powder that they called *filé* (*fee*-lay).

The rich sauces and pureed soups common to the homeland were adapted with the fresh ingredients of the New World. A hybrid cuisine developed, named for the descendants of French settlers, the Creoles. Creole families in New Orleans often owned slaves of African descent. Slave cooks interpreted French dishes loosely, frequently adding their own touches – this led to a predominant local style. Among the African contributions to New Orleans' cuisine was the use of okra, which is most famously featured in Creole gumbo (see p92).

The arrival of the Cajuns in the 18th century led to another new regional cuisine, although not in New Orleans directly. Cajun cuisine, now popular worldwide, originated as country fare. Although New Orleans has a few old-line Cajun restaurants, it really wasn't until chef Paul Prudhomme rose to fame that the city became known as a mecca for Cajun cuisine. (See Paul Prudhomme, p184, for more details.)

Napoleon's quick sale of the Mississippi River basin in 1803 to the fledgling United States brought Anglo-American settlers (and their trademark foods) to northern Louisiana. Other groups flocked to New Orleans, which was by then a crucial river port and point of entry into the US. Free black settlers from Afro-Caribbean Haiti and Santo Domingo came to the city, as did slaves from Senegambian West Africa. Italians (mostly from Sicily) settled here in record numbers, bringing their distinctive dishes and adding red gravy (spiced tomato sauce) to the developing Creole culinary style. Freed slaves from other American states made their way here following the American Civil War. Germans arrived and set up wheat farms outside the city. Irish fleeing the Great Potato Famine populated the neighborhoods near the French Quarter. Toward the end of the 20th century, waves of Vietnamese and Central American immigrants came to New Orleans and made their contribution to the city's diverse living cuisine.

HOW NEW ORLEANIANS EAT

For the average resident of New Orleans, food is much more than simple sustenance. It's a hobby, a constant topic of conversation and a borderline obsession. Food (with its corollary activities of procuring, cooking and eating) is the collective passion at the core of New Orleans' distinctive local culture.

Unlike other American cities, where the exceptional restaurants occupy the upper end of the cost spectrum, New Orleans has a well developed mid-priced and even low-end restaurant scene, which are enjoyed by people from all walks of life. Many of the city's trademark dishes – overstuffed seafood po'boys and garlicky muffulettas – were invented and popularized by the poorer segments of the city's population.

The classic morning meal of beignets (warm, sugar-dusted French doughnuts) and café au lait (coffee with milk) is a leisurely indulgence, but gallons of hot coffee is more the norm. Breakfast is a relatively small deal compared with the midday meal. Lunch is a time

SUNDAY BRUNCH

In New Orleans, Sunday brunch is an important family tradition. The concept of brunch was originally shaped by the demands of the Catholic Church, which required the faithful to fast from midnight Saturday until after mass on Sunday.

By the time you left church, not only were you spiritually refreshed but also mighty peckish. But it was too late for breakfast and too early for lunch, so brunch was devised as an in-between sort of meal and popularized by such old-line Creole restaurants as Brennan's (p185) and Commander's Palace (p190). Grillades and grits (grilled beef or veal slices braised in tomato sauce and served with cooked mush of coarse-grained hominy) is a classic New Orleans brunch dish. Jazz bands were added to the mix, and the tradition of the 'Jazz Brunch' is now a common Sunday morning repast. New Orleans may not be the devout Catholic city it once was, but brunch remains a very popular meal among tourists who can afford the pricey egg dishes and morning cocktails referred to as 'eye-openers' (p97).

for social gatherings and business dealings, and a chance to sample the city's restaurant fare at cut-rate prices. The city's economic and social strata mingle at lunch counters and tiny diners across town, comparing notes on the day's special – a rich bowl of crawfish bisque or a roast beef po'boy dripping with rich brown gravy. Taking the evening meal (referred to as either dinner or supper) at a restaurant is generally reserved for special occasions, even if it's to commemorate the fact that it's just Wednesday night. Impulsive between-meal snacks are relatively common, since you have to have something to go along with your morning coffee. And your afternoon coffee. And all the cups of coffee in between.

Many family traditions are observed with large meals in the home, preferably with a multigenerational group in attendance. Often special dishes are prepared for family gatherings, such as baked ham for Sunday dinner, jambalaya for a sister's birthday, or duck and sausage gumbo to celebrate a successful hunting trip.

There are no real surprises with etiquette, as eating here is generally a relaxed affair. If you know how to eat politely in a restaurant or at home with your in-laws, you'll be fine. If you are eating at someone's home, a small gift and words of praise for the meal will see you invited back. In home situations, serving food from a communal dish (also called serving 'family style') is common. The food will be placed in the middle of the table for you to help yourself. Make sure you use serving utensils, and not your personal cutlery to take food from a communal dish. If you are dining with a family, they may say grace before the meal. If this is unfamiliar to you, just bow your head and follow the family's lead.

Eating here can be a robust activity that often requires getting down and dirty with your food. For example, it's impossible to eat an overstuffed po'boy without wrestling the huge sandwich into submission – a very difficult task for dainty eaters. Likewise, if you are eating boiled crawfish, dive in hands-first and watch your companions for the correct protocol.

STAPLES & SPECIALTIES

Some of the staples available in southern Louisiana can be found almost anywhere there is immediate access to abundant seawater and freshwater life, wild game, and common grains and vegetables. But by and large what the cooks of New Orleans do with these foodstuffs is unparalleled elsewhere.

SEAFOOD

Many staple dishes of Louisiana cuisine feature creatures yanked from the state's intricate wetlands – saltwater, freshwater and brackish marshes. Most of these dishes end up on tables throughout the Crescent City.

Fish

Local fish such as snapper, speckled trout, pompano and flounder are all used in straightforward Creole preparations, usually with copious amounts of butter. Trout meunière features delicate fillets of the Gulf fish lightly dusted in flour, pan-fried in butter and topped with lemon butter sauce. A simple grilled pompano is transformed into pompano Pontchartrain with the topping of sautéed lump crabmeat (p90). Cajun cooks turn redfish or snapper into flavorful dishes like court-bouillon (a robust, spicy tomato-based dish rich with peppers and spices). Dredged in cornmeal and deep-fried, the catfish is a stalwart of the Soul Food pantheon.

CATFISH

Until recent years, the catfish had a bit of an image problem. With its natural freshwater habitat in muddy rivers and ponds, the bottom-feeding catfish *(Ictalurus furcatus)* vacuums the watery floors for tasty morsels. Unfortunately, this means it also ingests a fair amount of sludge, pesticide and post-industrial goop. Consequently, the catfish has traditionally been the food for poor folks.

Thanks to modern farming techniques, the whiskered wonder has risen to new levels of acceptance. The taste of the fish was transformed when it was farmed in clean ponds and fed compressed grain pellets. For aqua farmers, catfish are an attractive proposition since they are easy to breed and grow quickly. The catfish is now akin to an aquatic chicken; it's widely available, cheap, easy to cook and has a fairly neutral flavor.

Crabs

The tasty blue crab is indigenous to southern Louisiana and is a prized local specialty. During the lengthy crab season (April to October) these delicious-tasting shellfish are available fresh-boiled at informal restaurants and boiling points across the state. The rest of the year, sweet chunks of peeled meat (usually described as 'lump' crabmeat) make flavorful fillings for stuffed eggplant and is the basis for crunchy crab cakes (fried patties of crab, breadcrumbs and seasonings). You'll also find it in seafood gumbos (p92).

SOFT-SHELL CRAB

Travelers fortunate enough to visit during the earlier part of crab season can indulge in a prized delicacy. As part of its molting process, the blue crab sheds its shell three or four times a year for the first few years of its life. If caught more or less in its birthday suit, they can be eaten whole, shell and all. Soft-shelled crabs are usually pan-fried with browned butter sauce or stuffed with various seafood mixtures.

Patrons of the New Orleans Jazz and Heritage Festival (Jazz Fest; p49) can enjoy soft-shelled crab in its popular po'boy incarnation. Once fried, the crabs are cut in half and inserted into a crusty sandwich roll in the legs-up position for easy snacking on the crispy appendages. Jokingly referred to as the 'bug po'boy' or 'spider sandwich,' it's a great way to taste the season's best in between stages.

Shrimp

Culled from the nearby Gulf of Mexico (and, increasingly, from farms), these little critters feature on just about every menu in southern Louisiana. Shrimp is the star attraction in Cajun shrimp étouffée (shrimp smothered in gravy), fried in an overflowing shrimp loaf (po'boy) and chilled in a shrimp rémoulade.

The barbecued shrimp featured on many local menus is misleadingly named. The shrimp are not grilled, but are pan-fried in their shells (heads on) with butter, olive oil, garlic, Worcestershire sauce, black pepper and other spices. Even in upmarket establishments, patrons who order this dish are given a paper bib to minimize splatter-related dry-cleaning bills.

Oysters

These salty bivalves can be found in coastal waters throughout the Northern Hemisphere, but in New Orleans, oysters, even in the simplest form, are considered high art. In oyster bars all over town, patrons watch with reverence as the oysters are ritualistically shucked – by the dozen or half-dozen – and served raw on the half-shell. Just add a dash of horseradish and a squirt of lemon, and slurp it down whole.

Farmed 'ersters,' as they're called in the local 'Yat' dialect, are available year round, but are best in the colder months (the months that have an 'r' in their names) when they're plump and salty.

Oysters also make their way into many Creole and Cajun specialties, including oyster soup, oyster casserole, gumbos and rice dressing (p93). They are also commonly coated in seasoned cornmeal and deep-fried for a classic po'boy filling. Old-line Creole establishments typically feature elaborate dishes like Oysters Rockefeller (named after John D because they're so rich), which are baked in the shell with a mixture of chopped spinach, breadcrumbs and aromatic vegetables.

ERSTER WARNING

You're likely to see elaborately worded disclaimers on signs and menus of oyster bars. They commonly read as follows: 'There may be a risk associated with consuming raw shellfish as is the case with other raw protein products. If you suffer from chronic illness of the liver, stomach, or blood, or have other immune disorders, you should eat these products fully cooked.'

The lawyers have spoken. Now belly up for a 'dozen raw and a beer' and slurp away.

Crawfish

If caricatures of this crustacean on souvenir T-shirts, billboards and brochures are any indication, the crawfish is king of Louisiana. During springtime it features on just about every menu in the state. If you leave Louisiana without once tasting crawfish, you had better book a ticket back.

Resembling tiny lobsters, crawfish can either be served fresh-boiled or in the form of prepeeled tail meat. When crawfish are in season – from early December to mid-July, but best from mid-February – the most popular way to enjoy them is boiled. You can try boiled crawfish at a no-nonsense seafood restaurant called a 'boiling point,' where crawfish are served on aluminum beer trays. Being only a few inches in length, you need to eat a lot of crawfish to make a meal, and about 4lb to 5lb (2kg to 2½kg) of the little creatures per person is usual.

Crawfish also form the foundation for well-known Cajun dishes such as crawfish étouffée (crawfish smothered in gravy), crawfish boulettes (fried stuffing balls), crawfish jambalaya (p93) and the labor-intensive crawfish bisque. In this classic Cajun delicacy, boiled crawfish heads are filled with a sausagelike stuffing made of crawfish tails. They are then simmered in a rich roux-based crawfish soup, and served over white rice.

THE CRAWFISH LEGEND

When the Acadians were forced to leave Nova Scotia, the local lobsters (very loyal shellfish, indeed) decided to follow their adopted humans to Louisiana. During the arduous marathon swim, the crustaceans lost a lot of weight and most of their size. By the time the lobsters reached the bayous and swamps of southern Louisiana to reunite with their beloved proto-Cajuns, they had transformed into the Acadian's smaller, and now-totemic, crawfish.

MEATS

Pork, Sausage & Ham

Pork is popular throughout the South, where every part of the animal can be prepared in countless ways. While ham and pork chops are as popular here as anywhere else, Louisiana naturally has a few porcine specialties of its own. Most popular is andouille (ahn-*doo*-wee), a spicy smoked sausage that turns up in gumbo and jambalaya.

Boudin is a tasty Cajun sausage made with pork, pork liver, cooked rice and spices. *Boudin blanc* (white *boudin*) is a popular quick bite, sold by the link in ready-to-eat form in groceries, meat markets and gas stations all over Acadiana. To eat one, cut a link in half, insert an open end into your mouth, and slowly squeeze the filling out. (Eating the elastic casing is considered questionable.) The hard-to-find *boudin rouge* (red *boudin*) contains the blood of the freshly slaughtered pig. *Boudin rouge* can't be sold commercially due to health regulations governing the use of blood in products, but it is still made by families and some butchers on the side.

Gratons (called 'cracklings' elsewhere in the South) are made by cooking down pork skin until most of the fat is rendered and the skin itself is golden and crisp. It's a very popular snack throughout the region.

Tasso is another highly prized butcher-shop specialty. It's basically a lean chunk of ham, cured with *filé* (crushed sassafras leaves) and other seasonings, and then smoked until it reaches the tough consistency of beef jerky. Small portions add flavor to soups, sauces and beans.

The bits that are usually discarded elsewhere are used in inventive ways in the Deep South, and you can choose from pickled pigs' feet, chitterlings (tripe; also known as 'chitlins') or smoked ham hocks.

Poultry

You can eat chicken stuffed, roasted, barbecued, stewed, fricasséed and swimming with gooey dumplings. Chunks of chicken can turn up in your jambalaya or sauce *piquante* (spicy tomato-based stew). Southern country-style fried chicken is also popular in New Orleans.

Turkey has made a jump from the Thanksgiving table to become a more workaday dish. For a really fowl feast, look out for the turducken (a turkey stuffed with a duck stuffed with a chicken). Some enterprising Cajun cooks put their crawfish boiling rigs to use in wintertime for deep-frying whole turkeys.

Beef & Wild Game

Though not as popular as seafood or pork, beef does find its way into countless dishes in its ground form – as in rice dressings, stuffed bell peppers and Creole-Italian meat sauces. Younger milky veal is used in many more-refined Creole dishes, such as tender veal scallops topped with mushrooms bordelaise.

The fertile wetlands and dense northern forests of Louisiana provide habitats for a wide variety of furred and feathered creatures, such as deer, duck, geese and quail. Being an adaptive bunch, the inhabitants of the state have cultivated a taste for all of them. Even alligator and turtle meat turn up in a variety of Cajun soups and dishes.

Barbecue

Barbecue isn't the spiritual issue that it is in nearby Texas or Memphis, but there are small joints in the city and countryside. When you can get hold of good barbecue it can be anything from pork ribs to chicken, mutton and hot links, accompanied by soft white bread, coleslaw, potato salad, pinto beans and plenty of beer or sweet soda. Dig in mano a mano, as true barbecue is a no-utensils affair.

GUMBO

The most representative dish of New Orleans is gumbo, a spicy, full-bodied soup/stew, and no cook in the city is without a personal recipe for it. The ingredients – which can include products from the sea, land and air – vary from cook to cook, and pot to pot. It is traditionally served over starchy steamed rice.

For any Louisiana cook, gumbo is the personal interpretation of a classic process and their own highly individualized culinary thumbprint. Close to the coast, you can find gumbos teeming with all manner of seafood (oysters, jumbo shrimp, half-shelled crabs), while prairie-bred Cajuns turn to their barnyard and smokehouse traditions for inspiration. Creole cooks in New Orleans often add tomato to their gumbos.

The distinctively thick texture that separates gumbo from the broth-based soup family comes from the use of various thickening agents: dark roux, okra or the late addition of *filé*.

BREADS & SANDWICHES

As you might expect from a Franco-centric culture, New Orleans enjoys its daily bread, whether it be a hot loaf wrapped in restaurant linen or the omnipresent po'boy. The trademark bread of the Crescent City is an oblong French loaf, with a crispy crust and feather-light interior. It's wider than the classic thin baguettes of Europe, and well suited for sopping up sauces and soups.

Po'Boys

Travelers may know this versatile specialty by one of its other names: submarine, grinder, or hoagie to name but a few. But make no mistake, New Orleans' po'boy looms large in the city's food culture. They are the fast food of Louisiana, served everywhere from neighborhood groceries to interstate gas stations. You'll find some great little po'boy shops Uptown.

The name was once apt. The mythology maintains that originally po'boys were hollowed-out loaves layered with cheap ingredients – such as potatoes and brown gravy – and served to striking workers, vagabonds, or other 'poor boys.' When modern eaters consider the po'boy's gargantuan size, it is obvious it's built to sustain hard-working people. You can order half a po'boy and be satisfied.

You can stuff the bread with anything that's edible, but New Orleans classics include fried shrimp, oysters or catfish, roast beef dripping in gravy, roast pork, crawfish, soft-shell crab or even French fries soaked in gravy.

When you order a po'boy, your server will ask if you want it 'dressed,' meaning with mayonnaise, shredded iceberg lettuce and tomato slices. Just say yes.

Muffulettas

It's only a slight exaggeration to say that New Orleans muffulettas are the size of manhole covers. Named for a round sesame-crusted loaf, muffulettas are layered with various selections from the local Sicilian deli tradition, including Genoa salami, shaved ham, mortadella and sliced provolone cheese. The signature spread – a salty olive salad with pickled vegetables, herbs, garlic and olive oil – is what defines the sandwich, though. It's a flavorful, greasy mess.

Muffulettas are a great option for frustrated vegetarians traveling in New Orleans, as they can easily be made without meat.

The muffuletta, in all its glory

RICE & BEANS

When a poor man's meal in French Louisiana doesn't come wrapped in a crunchy po'boy roll, odds are that it's served on a bed of white rice. Louisiana rice consumption is considerably higher than that of the rest of the nation, and even rivals that of some Asian countries. Rice is the staple grain of both Creole and Cajun cuisines.

Rice fields dominate the marshy lands of the Cajun Prairie. The texture is somewhere between glutinous Japanese sushi rice and the fluffier American long-grain varieties. The starchy texture helps the rice keep its integrity whether it's covered in a pool of shrimp étouffée or acting as sausage filler in links of hot Cajun *boudin*. The drier, more discreet grains of long-grain rice are more common in dishes from the Anglo-influenced Soul Food traditions of northern Louisiana, such as hoppin' John (rice and black-eyed peas).

As an inexpensive and easily prepared source of protein, beans have played an integral role in the culinary history of New Orleans, as well as in the rest of Louisiana.

Jambalaya

Hearty, rice-based jambalaya (johm-buh-*lie*-uh) is a Louisiana classic. It is loosely based on Spain's paella, although in practical terms it's probably closer to *arroz con pollo* (chicken and rice). Jambalaya can include just about any combination of fowl, shellfish or meat, but usually includes ham, hence the dish's name (derived from the French *jambon* or the Spanish *jamón*). The meaty ingredients are sautéed with onions, pepper and celery, and cooked with raw rice and water into a flavorful mix of textures. You'll find jambalaya at restaurants and food stalls during music, food or cultural festivals. It is flavorful, easy to eat and festive.

Rice Dressing

It's a regional call whether you refer to this chicken, pork and rice mélange as rice dressing (the traditional Cajun name) or dirty rice (a Deep South slang variant). Either way, it's a tasty way to use the giblets from a roast chicken or holiday turkey, and any leftover rice.

Red Beans & Rice

A poor man's meal rich in smoky flavor, the combination of red beans and rice is a lunch tradition synonymous with Mondays throughout the state, especially in New Orleans. Monday was traditionally wash day, and in the days before large household appliances it took all day to hand-wash the family laundry. So a pot of red beans would go on the stove along with the ham bone left over from Sunday dinner, and the longer it cooked, the better it tasted. By the time the washing was finished, supper was ready.

In the absence of red beans, larger maroon kidney beans are often used. The flavoring meat can also be spicy andouille sausage or chunks of pork *tasso,* a long-smoked Cajun specialty. Black-eyed peas, a hearty Soul Food staple, are creamy beige with a single dark spot (the eye) near the center. Black-eyed peas are traditionally cooked with a flavoring meat (ham hocks and salt pork are common).

No matter what type of beans are on the table, locals typically reach for a trusted pepper sauce (below) before digging in.

GRITS & CORNBREAD

Corn, introduced to European settlers by the Native Americans, is a keystone staple of American cuisine. Around wet New Orleans, where wheat doesn't grow well, corn is used in a variety of breads and other dishes. Dried corn, when ground into a coarse meal, is suitable for coating oysters and catfish before deep-frying.

Dried hominy grits are prepared as a porridge (similar in texture to polenta) and are served as a breakfast side option at any Southern diner. On their own grits can be a tad bland, but add a chunk of butter, a shake of black pepper and a few squirts of hot sauce and they become an addictive morning ritual.

Cornbread is the simple, everyday bread most often seen on southern country-style and Soul Food menus. It comes in many variations, including muffins, corn sticks (cornbread baked in corn-shaped moulds), crackling bread (cornbread with cracklings added) and hush puppies (balls of deep-fried cornbread batter).

HERBS, SPICES & SEASONINGS

The trademark herbs and spices of Louisiana cooking illustrate how the state's culinary traditions melded the bold flavors from European traditions with indigenous ingredients (*filé*, bay leaves) to form a culinary synthesis. The emphasis in the Creole cooking of New Orleans is on balanced flavors, rather than on spices that overwhelm the palate. Cajun dishes are generally hotter. Cajun cooks usually use a blend of salt, peppers, spices and dried herbs. Similar mixes can be purchased commercially, but, buyer beware, as some companies go heavy with cayenne at the expense of a balanced flavor.

A small bottle of Louisiana pepper sauce can be found, along with the ubiquitous salt and pepper shakers, on every table in New Orleans. Usually a fermented mix of pepper pods, salt and vinegar, pepper sauces have departed from the standard red-pepper variety in recent years. Avery Island's McIlhenny dynasty, the manufacturers of the omnipresent Tabasco sauce, has recently expanded its line to include other peppery bases such as green jalapeno, mild garlic and the painful habanero chili.

Brownish Creole mustard, more rustic and flavorful than its yellow American counterpart, is similar to a European whole-grain mustard except that the mustard seeds are marinated in vinegar during preparation. It's a vital ingredient in shrimp rémoulade.

Parsley and green onions are important finishing herbs in Cajun cuisine. Usually minced and added at the last stage of cooking, they provide a distinctly 'green' flavor to gumbos, jambalayas and other classic dishes. Whole bay leaves are commonly used to flavor many savory dishes, particularly long-cooked beans.

Seafood boil, also known as crab and shrimp boil, can contain a blend of bay leaves, mustard seeds, cayenne pepper, peppercorns, cloves and allspice.

SAUCES

Another French hand-me-down, highly refined sauces add flavor and warmth to many Creole dishes. Many Cajun and Creole recipes begin with a roux, which hails from French cuisine. This classic concoction is the primary thickener and flavoring agent in gumbos, étouffée and other Louisiana standbys. It imbues a dish with a rich and deep, nutty flavor.

Being able 'to roux' is a fundamental skill in the Louisiana cooking repertoire. When picking a shade of roux, many cooks follow this rule: the darker the meat, the lighter the roux. This means chicken gumbo calls for a dark roux, while heartier game meats (such as venison) call for a lighter roux.

The New Orleans take on rémoulade is a spicy sauce that greatly differs from the French mayonnaise-based classic. New Orleans recipes for this sauce sometimes call for a base of tomato ketchup spiked with horseradish, red pepper and Creole mustard. You're likely to find it on chilled shrimp as shrimp rémoulade.

Mayonnaise in Louisiana is considered a relative of the French original, rather than a bland white sandwich spread. In many homes and restaurants, you'll find a pale yellow version of this continental classic in dishes, or on salads such as potato salad and coleslaw. Hollandaise sauce, rich with eggs and butter, is an important ingredient in more upscale brunch offerings, such as eggs benedict, eggs sardou and trout margeury. Béarnaise sauce is a common variant on hollandaise that includes a mixture of herbs, shallots and vinegar.

Cocktail sauce makes regular appearances at oyster bars and crawfish boils. It's a simple concoction with ketchup, prepared horseradish, pepper sauce and lemon.

VEGETABLES

With its long growing season and rich soil, the land around New Orleans yields a wide range of farm fresh vegetables. Whether they're brought in for sale at the French Market (p138) or purchased from roadside vendors, the products of Louisiana gardens are an essential part of the local culinary tradition.

Okra came with the African slaves and has made a distinct culinary impression on the Deep South as a whole. Okra has a significant amount of mucilage (also known as 'goo'), and is used as the primary thickener in traditional Creole gumbo. It can also be served as crispy pickled pods, or breaded and deep-fried until crunchy.

Significant native vegetables include a vast variety of squash that choke the markets during the summer season. A native variety of sweet potato is known as 'Louisiana yam.' If you see yams on a menu, you can safely assume it is actually sweet potato. Actual yams, brought by slaves from Africa, are also widely available. Candied yams are a popular side dish served with roasted meats.

Turnips, mustard and collard greens – individually or in combination – are Soul Food regulars. The greens are usually cooked with a chunk of flavoring meat (usually some sort of pork), sprinkled with a bit of pepper sauce, and served with cornbread.

Italian cooks in the city like to transform the eggplant into eggplant parmagiana, which is cooked with red gravy (spiced tomato sauce). Similar preparations await the mirliton, a vegetable squash eaten throughout Latin America, where it is known as 'chayote.'

The home gardens of Louisiana produce their fair share of green beans. The French *les haricots* is said to have morphed into the term 'zydeco,' appellation for the music of the rural blacks in Cajun Country.

FRUITS

While most fruit is shipped in from someplace else, some tasty specialties are grown locally. Ponchatoula, northwest of New Orleans, produces strawberries that are tangy and sweet. Along roadsides and fencerows throughout the state sweet and tart dewberries grow in sticky brambles When the summer berries turn deep purple, intrepid pickers hit the bushes, braving sharp thorns and snakebite for a bucket load. Another roadside sign to look for in southern Louisiana is one advertising Ruston peaches, a popular summer fruit eaten fresh, or baked into dessert pies.

THE HOLY TRINITY

The combination of three vegetables – white onion, sweet green bell pepper and celery – is popular enough in Cajun and Creole cooking to warrant the nickname, 'The Holy Trinity.' Local dishes such as gumbo, red beans, court bouillon and sauce *piquante* (spicy tomato-based stew) all require this flavorful trio be sautéed in the initial stages of the cooking process. Their collective importance is similar to the *mirepoix* (base of onion, celery and carrot) in continental French cuisine. In many dishes, garlic is also added, but that messes up the Biblical metaphor. The sweet bell pepper sometimes goes it alone as a dinner course, filled with meat and bread stuffing.

The homegrown Creole tomato can be integrated into a wide variety of dishes. Creole cooks are likely to add the flavorful fruit to their gumbo and jambalaya recipes. Cajuns are likely to smother okra or summer squash with a tomato or two. But at peak tomato season, you only need to slice them up, sprinkle a little salt and serve.

Watermelons grow well in the semitropical conditions and are commonly purchased from roadside truck stands during summer. Oranges grow around Port Sulphur, south of New Orleans, and the Washington orange is its specialty.

SWEET TREATS

Collectively, New Orleanians have a famously sweet tooth. The desserts of the region give ample incentive to save a little room, which is not easy to do, considering the predominance of tasty and filling starters and main courses.

Pecans & Pralines

Though the peanut rules many other southern states, the pecan is Louisiana's nut of choice. Pecans are indigenous to the region and were often used in cooking by the Native Americans. While driving the backroads in the north of the region you will see deep shady groves of huge pecan trees. Pecans are used mostly in sweet dishes and are a common ingredient in stuffing for poultry and vegetables. Pecan pralines (*praw*-leens in Louisiana) are an extremely popular sweet treat.

Beignets

Not so much a dessert as a round-the-clock breakfast specialty akin to the common doughnut. Flat squares of dough are flash-fried to a golden, puffy glory, dusted liberally with powdered (confectioner's, or icing) sugar, and served scorching hot. Good any time of day (even after a big meal) with a cup of rich café au lait (p98). Ground zero for this treat is Café du Monde (p178) in the French Quarter.

Bread Pudding

A specialty in New Orleans and Acadiana, this custardy creation is a good use for leftover bread. Variations in New Orleans generally involve copious amounts of butter, eggs and cream and will usually come topped with a bourbon-spiked sugar sauce. In recent years cooks have taken to adding white chocolate and other ingredients to spice up this simple fare.

Pies

The Deep South's traditional dessert is usually available in a variety of flavors and served with a cup of steaming hot coffee. The baking process is relatively simple and the fillings are infinitely variable – a crust can be filled with fresh berries, gooey pecans, coconut cream, apples, rhubarb, custard or lemon curd topped with mile-high meringue.

Fried pies, similar to the Central American empanada, are a popular convenience dessert. A flaky crust is wrapped around fruit or custard fillings and deep-fried in fat or lard.

Making pralines

Bananas Foster

This now infamous dish of sliced bananas, brown sugar, spices, butter and various liqueurs was made famous at Brennan's Restaurant (p185) in the French Quarter, and is now a New Orleans dessert standard. The bananas are sautéed (usually tableside) in a flood of butter and sugar, reduced to a thick sauce, and then flamed with strong rum and a well-placed match. This preparation is served over rich vanilla ice cream.

DRINKS OF NEW ORLEANS

New Orleans has certainly earned its international reputation for debauchery. From the intimacy of neighborly beer joints to the over-the-top extravaganza of the carnival season, the city has a gloriously excessive drinking culture. The party is fueled by beverages, ranging from watery beer to sophisticated cocktails. It's not all alcoholic, however. When in New Orleans, be sure to sober up with a pot of chicory coffee and soften things up at lunchtime with a frosty root beer.

ALCOHOLIC DRINKS

In the same way that gourmands attempt to eat their way across the city, hard-drinking pilgrims often try to sample the countless (and often near-flammable) specialty drinks of New Orleans. In a town where barrooms never seem to close, and even breakfast has a cocktail course, you can expect bottle-based indulgences to be plentiful and varied. Whether you prefer your poison on the rocks, on draft, in a snifter, or in a go cup, there will always be a range of 'adult beverages' within easy reach.

Eye-Openers

Cocktails in the morning hours are a bit decadent, even in New Orleans. But decadence is more acceptable here than elsewhere. If you require a 'hair of the dog that bit you,' the traditional hangover cure, New Orleans can accommodate the need.

Brunch wouldn't be popular without beverages with a little kick. The Absinthe Suissesse, a tame holdover from New Orleans' absinthe binge (prior to it being outlawed in the early 20th century), is a rich, licorice-flavored concoction that's more cream than booze. The subtle mix of Herbsaint, heavy cream and orgeat (primarily almond) syrup makes for a smooth start to any New Orleans morning after.

The Ramos Gin Fizz, named for 19th-century New Orleans bartender Henry Ramos, is a rich, frothy blend of gin, cream, egg whites, extra-fine sugar, fizzy water and a splash of orange-flower water.

The Mint Julep is more popular in other parts of the South, particularly in Louisville, KY, where it is traditionally drunk in great quantities on Derby Day. But most self-respecting barkeeps in New Orleans know how to properly mix bourbon, sugar and muddled mint. It makes an ideal afternoon refreshment on hot days.

Classic New Orleans Cocktails

Local classics such as the Sazerac, Pimm's Cup and Cafe Brulot represent the best of old-school New Orleans cocktail culture. Though each of these drinks have internationally known counterparts, drinking one here requires a slightly adventurous palate and a sense of local history. All of them are at their best when prepared by a bartender who is at least 70 years old.

Sazerac is a potent whiskey drink that uses either rye or bourbon as its primary ingredient, with aromatic bitters (including the locally produced Peychaud's), a bit of sugar and a swish of Herbsaint.

Pimm's Cup is a summer refresher traditionally associated with the infamous French Quarter bar, Napoleon House (p201). It's a simple mix of the British gin-based liqueur (Pimm's No 1) topped with soda or ginger ale.

Cafe Brulot is more of an after-dinner experience than a cocktail. On your table, spices, sugar and brandy are heated to the flaming point and ignited for dramatic effect; strong brewed coffee is then added.

Tourist Drinks

The bars on Bourbon St feature many beverages that have a local New Orleans cachet, like the Hurricane. These drinks are standards for those hell-bent on a French Quarter party experience. Much-imitated, and often more festive than substantial, these libations have contributed to many tales of blurry Mardi Gras mayhem.

The Hurricane was made famous by the French Quarter bar Pat O'Brien's (p202). It's a towering rum drink that gets its bright pink hue from the healthy portion of passion fruit juice. Frozen daiquiris, by New Orleans' definition, are a class of alcoholic Slurpees that come in all the brightest colors of the spectrum.

Beer

New Orleans' most famous surviving brewery is Dixie, founded in 1907. The flavor of the flagship lager isn't noticeably different from the national brands, but it's worth reaching for an ice-cold Dixie 'long neck' for a local change. Dixie also produces a couple of other mystique-heavy beers – Blackened Voodoo Lager and Jazz Amber Lite – which are longer on image than taste.

The most widespread microbrews hail from the Abita Brewery (p264). From its standard amber ale to more ambitious Mardi Gras bock and seasonal Jockimo stout, Abita beers provide a welcome local alternative to the usual corporate lagers. Other good bets include local brewpubs such as the Crescent City Brewhouse (p181) in the French Quarter.

Wine

Generally, the wines savored in New Orleans' fine restaurants have been shipped in from far afield, because the humid conditions of the region are unsuitable for the growing of wine grapes.

NONALCOHOLIC DRINKS

Coffee & Chicory

Kick-start your first day in New Orleans with a visit to the French Quarter's illustrious Café du Monde (p178). Here you'll find perhaps the best coffee in town – deep, dark, smoky French-roasted chicory coffee, cut with equal parts of hot milk – and the gold standard of beignets.

COCKTAIL COCKAMAMIE

It should come as no surprise that New Orleans claims to have invented the whole concept of having a drink for the hell of it – that is, having a cocktail. As always, the Crescent City backs up the claim with a good story that may well explain the origin of the word 'cocktail.'

The story begins with a man named Peychaud, who settled in New Orleans after fleeing the 18th-century slave uprisings in St Domingue (now Haiti). He opened an apothecary on Royal St, where, we are told, he developed a penchant for drinking brandy from an eggcup. The concept appealed to the people of New Orleans, and Peychaud began serving drinks in this fashion at his shop. (One might wonder why people were so willing to drink from an eggcup, but read on…)

The eggcup, of course, was not called an eggcup in French-speaking New Orleans. It was called a *coquetier;* well it was called that until Peychaud's inebriated patrons began mispronouncing it. The term evolved – much as the word Acadian turned into Cajun – from 'coquetier' to 'cock-tay' to 'cocktail.' In time, the eggcup was disposed of in favor of a regular glass, and other liquor came to be more popular than brandy, but the name stuck.

Chicory, a roasted herb root, is often mixed with ground coffee, resulting in Creole coffee or New Orleans blend. Originally used to 'extend' scarce coffee beans during hard times, chicory continues to be added for a fuller-bodied flavor.

ROOT BEER OF CHOICE

The Native Americans made tea from the roots of the sassafras tree, and it is from this original usage that root beer owes its creation. These days, Louisianans drink twice as much root beer as the American average. This is largely a credit to the local Barq's root beer, created by Ed Barq in 1898 at his home in nearby Biloxi, Mississippi. This carbonated New Orleans institution goes well with the hot weather and full-flavored food. Barq's, widely available in cans and bottles, is the only local brand, although it was recently acquired by The Coca-Cola Company.

Iced Tea

In hot and humid Louisiana, iced tea is more than just a drink – it's a form of air-conditioning in a tall, sweaty glass. Preparation of the common beverage couldn't be simpler – it's simply chilled regular tea poured over ice and garnished with a lemon wedge or mint leaves. No milk, please.

When you order iced tea at a restaurant, it is usually a bottomless cup and will be regularly refilled. If you want a proper English cup of tea, specify 'hot tea' or you'll get a tall, ice-filled glass instead of a steaming mug.

CELEBRATING WITH FOOD

New Orleans loves its food, and it pulls out all the stops for big holidays and events. Naturally, this means good eating and lots of drinking. After all, the city's biggest holiday is 'Fat Tuesday.'

HOME COOKING

It is always a great honor to be invited to someone's home for dinner while traveling, and as New Orleanians are a hospitable people, they consider having a guest an occasion; however, don't expect a seven-course Creole meal. New Orleanians generally dine out when the occasion calls for so extravagant a spread. Your host is likely to have a more modest repertoire. Many home cooks have a personal gumbo recipe and can capably prepare local seafood and meat dishes. Generally, expect American and southern standards with a dash of Creole and Cajun flavor.

Some New Orleanians with backyards have adopted the Cajun tradition of holding crawfish boils during the late spring. If you are invited to a crawfish boil, expect a large cross-generational crowd of extended family and friends. It's a boisterous, informal affair, with lots of lager beer and piles of crawfish. If you're squeamish about biting into crustaceans then you aren't going to make many friends, so come hungry and ready to put away a few pounds of the little critters.

SPECIAL EVENTS

The local calendar seems to have more holidays than regular work days (see the City Calendar, p14). On some of these special days it's all about the food.

Carnival

Carnival season in New Orleans means a flurry of private celebrations and gatherings that precede parades, balls or other seasonal parties. Food can range from chill-chasing chicken sauce *piquante* to fancy hors d'oeuvre, or delicate finger sandwiches filled with ham salad and cheesy artichoke dip. For devout Catholics, Mardi Gras is the last day of feasting before somber Lent begins on the morrow. Although the number of people partaking in Lenten vows may have dropped, the tradition of meat-feasting on 'Fat Tuesday' continues, and tables – both private and commercial – overflow with New Orleans favorites like steak, ribs, roasts and baked hams. For more information about Mardi Gras, see p32.

KING CAKES

Of all Mardi Gras' traditions, none is more kitschy than the king cake. Every year, on Twelfth Night (January 6), the first king cakes emerge from bakeries all over New Orleans and soon appear in offices – including the mayor's – and at Twelfth Night parties throughout the city.

The king cake is an oval, spongy Danish pastry with gooey icing and purple, green and gold sugar on top. More importantly, it always contains an inedible peanut-size plastic baby somewhere inside. The baby is the key – it's what perpetuates the king cake tradition. The rule is, whoever is served the piece of cake with the baby inside (careful – don't swallow that baby!) has to buy the next cake. Some office workers eat king cake five days a week between Twelfth Night and Mardi Gras.

The king cake originated in 1870, when the Twelfth Night Revelers used it to select a queen for the 'Lord of Misrule,' and a Carnival tradition was born. Early king cakes contained an uncooked golden bean instead of a baby, and the recipient of the bean was crowned king or queen of a Carnival krewe. That ritual is still maintained by some krewes, but such important matters are no longer left to chance. The bean, or baby, is always planted in the piece of cake served to a preselected king or queen. It seems the king cake has lost some of its clout.

Nevertheless, these cakes are big business in this city. One local bakery chain claims they sell 30,000 king cakes a day. According to local statisticians, 750,000 king cakes are consumed every year in the New Orleans metropolitan area.

Jazz & Heritage Festival

People show up hungry for this one. Over two weekends from the end of April, Jazz Fest is a nonstop flurry of amazing live music and an opportunity to sample the diverse cuisines of the region. Some of the Jazz Fest food booths enjoy a unique level of celebrity, equal to the musical acts that grace the major stages. Die-hard fans and repeat customers invariably have food factored into their festival routine. As an added bonus, the festival coincides with the peak seasons for crawfish and soft-shell crab. Each night for the duration the festival, expect long lines outside nearly every restaurant in town. See p53 for further details on Jazz Fest.

Thanksgiving

Louisiana's contributions to the American Thanksgiving tradition are the deep-fried turkey and the turducken. The deep-frying technique requires a standard oversized crawfish pot and a high-output propane burner. The bird is rubbed down with Cajun spices and, with a comically large syringe, injected with pepper sauce before it is submerged into the hot oil. Once cooked, the meat is moist and flavorful (with an added zing from the injected marinade) without the slightest trace of oil. The skin is crispy and spicy with a little caramelized sweetness.

The turducken, meanwhile, is an extravagant combination of turkey, duck and chicken. Chicken, being the smallest of the three, is stuffed inside a duck, which in turn fills the cavity of a turkey. It may sound like a bird-brained idea, but, for some, the holidays wouldn't be the same without it.

Christmas Season

The natives of Louisiana take the rich, edible traditions of Christmas very seriously. Sugar-dusted cookies, sticky homemade candies, moist cakes, and special group cocktails (such as eggnog) make their yearly appearance. A gumbo made from the Thanksgiving turkey may be the centerpiece of a pre-Christmas meal. Baked hams and roast beef make perpetual snacking the norm. During the cold months of December and January, Gulf oysters are at their plumpest, so the versatile shellfish shows up on party tables as stew, soup and gumbo.

On Christmas morning a huge breakfast is served and tables are piled high with fluffy biscuits, *pain perdu* ('lost bread,' a baguette-based version of eggy French toast), salty bacon or the New Orleans classic grits and grillades (grilled beef braised in tomato sauce).

St Patrick's Day

In a city looking for any excuse to revel, an event celebrating Ireland's patron saint is not to be missed. Crowds follow a festive parade from the French Quarter into the Irish Channel. Along the way the participants make regular stops at various bars to enjoy that most American (and disgusting) of St Paddy specialties, beer dyed green with food coloring. Not the most flavorful of traditions, but in the end, a party's a party. Of course, corned beef and cabbage appear on tables and in bars all over the city.

The Feast of St Joseph

Every March 19, two days after the Irish celebrate their favorite saint, the Sicilian community honors their patron, St Joseph, with feasts and elaborate rituals. At church services the altars heave with food arranged to represent crosses, crowns of thorns, sacred hearts, palm leaves, chalices and St Joseph's staff. After mass, all are welcome to dig in. Check the newspaper for churches holding services that day.

Cajun Fais Do-Do

Originally referring to any organized Cajun dance (be it at home or in the community), the term *fais do-do* now refers mainly to outdoor street dances that take place during local festivals. Unchanging, however, is that young and old alike dance to the irresistible rhythms of fiddles and accordions et al. The basic Cajun step is a flowing partner dance with waltz, two-step and more complex jitterbug variations. Some clubs in New Orleans may hold the occasional *fais do-do,* but the best place to experience one is out in the country.

The dancing traditionally begins after dinner and replenishment is usually required by midnight. During the interlude, you might dig into a chicken gumbo, rich beef stew cooked with plenty of onions and thyme, or links of *boudin,* then down another beer to cool your sweat.

The name *fais do-do* comes from the French sweet nothings that mothers whisper to their babies to send them off to sleep. In the old days, mothers would coo their children to sleep (do do, *bebe,* do do) in a quiet room attached to the dancehall.

WHERE TO EAT & DRINK

From simple lunch counters to white linen Creole institutions, New Orleans' high-spirited restaurant scene forms the cornerstone of social life for locals. The city has a glorious abundance of top-notch restaurants, suitable for every budget and taste.

OLD-LINE CREOLE

The fancy food that made New Orleans famous generally comes with a formal, historical atmosphere. On your plate, expect butter-rich sauces, continental French influences and local seafood. Service and decorum at these local institutions are definitively old school – it's not uncommon for the waitstaff to be 30-year veterans. Diners will be expected to adhere to a semiformal dress code – jackets for gentlemen. If you can afford the relatively steep price tag (main courses between $20 to $35), a meal at one of the old-line Creole institutions is a wonderful 'old New Orleans' experience. The budget conscious can dress up for a lunchtime excursion, which is significantly less expensive than dinner seatings. Reservations are usually required. See Creole Classics (p178) for a list of New Orleans' old-line establishments.

CONTEMPORARY CUISINE

The global flavors of fusion cuisine and the essentialist simplicity of new American cuisine have led to exciting interpretations of classic dishes that aren't bound by the rules of tradition. New Orleans' chefs, always eager to experiment with unfamiliar flavors, have come up

RADIO TO MAKE YOU HUNGRY

Turn your radio dial to Tom Fitzmorris' 'The Food Show' to get total immersion in New Orleans' food culture. The program, which airs weekdays from 4pm to 7pm on WSMB AM1350, is a call-in show, hosted by one of the city's leading restaurant critics. Fitzmorris also has a great radio voice and a long-standing passion for the local cuisine. Conversations range across the board, including debates over recipes and restaurants, and are both informative and colorful.

with cuisines that they call Contemporary Creole, Nouveau Cajun, Louisiana Fusion or new New Orleans Food. Dishes from these kitchens can include crunchy fried rabbit with *tasso* cream sauce or panéed Gulf trout with vermouth crème fraîche and poached oysters. Expect upscale prices, service and wine selections at these fine-dining establishments; the atmosphere will also tend toward the more stylish, as will the crowds. To get into the hottest new restaurants, book ahead as far in advance as possible.

NEIGHBORHOOD JOINTS

For unfussy and reasonably priced regional dishes, go where the locals go, the no-frills neighborhood restaurant. The pick of this bracket all share similar characteristics: they've been around for generations; they've been staffed by the same waiters and cooks for decades; and the clientele will vary from construction workers in overalls to white-collar types. The décor at a neighborhood joint may lack the polish of a high-end restaurant, but these places are less concerned with appearances than with high-quality food and unpretentious service. Reservations are rarely accepted (exceptions are sometimes made for large groups), and some function on a 'cash or local check only' basis. See Five Choice Neighborhood Joints, p186.

OYSTER BARS

Even if you're a bit squeamish about eating seafood, no trip to New Orleans is complete without a 'dozen raw and a beer' at a local oyster bar. Hard-working shuckers work like banter-friendly sushi chefs as they rip through piles of rocky shells, with gloved hands and blunt, thick-bladed oyster knives. Hardcore oyster bars can be a little intimidating for the newcomer, like you've just stepped into the ceremonies of an arcane culinary cult. Regular patrons each have their own oyster ritual, which takes on meditative qualities. It's fun to watch the different routines – slurp, pause and stare into space is the most common. The salty gulps are usually punctuated with sips of cold beer.

DINERS

Specializing in short-order cooking and long-simmering plate lunches, diners provide an inexpensive opportunity to sample traditional fare with quick service. Some diners stay open around the clock to accommodate insomniacs and postnightclub hunger pangs. Food ranges from burgers, sandwiches, pies and waffles to more regional dishes such as gumbo, jambalaya, étouffée, red beans and rice, fried seafood and the ever-present po'boy.

PO'BOY SHOPS & OTHER FAST FOOD

New Orleans has quick, inexpensive midday fare at its countless po'boy shops, neighborhood groceries and even gas stations. In the realm of plastic franchise restaurants, a local chain called 'Popeye's' specializes in spicy fried chicken and serves fast-food versions of regional dishes such as shrimp étouffée and jambalaya.

FOREIGN FARE

In a city that loves to eat, new discoveries and influences are always welcome, and you'll notice that foreign influences are even creeping into many upscale restaurants. You'll also find a wide variety of ethnic restaurants in the confines of the Crescent City.

Italian is the most popular ethnic cuisine in town, especially the locally adapted Creolized version. The riverfront side of the French Quarter was the original home of the Sicilian community, and there are still some Sicilian-run family restaurants peppered throughout the city's other neighborhoods.

New Orleans has a high concentration of Vietnamese immigrants, and their spicy national cuisine fits in well with local tastes. The same goes for the well-established Cuban and Cuban-American communities. The city also has a few good sushi restaurants.

VEGETARIANS & VEGANS

The same cooking techniques that make Louisiana food so flavorful can also make mealtime rather challenging for the vegetarian traveler. The common use of 'flavoring meats' and meat-based stocks means that many apparently flesh-free vegetable dishes may well include a bit of ham, sausage or seafood. It's not that the cooks of Louisiana are out to persecute the herbivorous diner – it's just that they come from a thoroughly omnivorous heritage.

However, as the average American becomes more aware of the flesh-free aesthetic, more options are appearing on the local restaurant scene. There are restaurants catering exclusively to vegetarians, and most upscale places will be able to assemble something, even if they don't have vegetarian dishes on the menu. Italian restaurants, with their pastas and tomato-based red gravy dishes, are good bets.

With some planning, you will be able to enjoy the regional cuisine without compromise or despair. Firstly, if you can make an exception for seafood, you will have no problems. Seafood is one of the region's culinary strengths, although you should double-check with staff because sausage and ham can also be added, particularly in seafood gumbo.

Gumbo z'herbes, a green gumbo made with a hearty variety of turnip, collard, spinach and other greens, is a meatless Lenten staple that many Creole restaurants offer year round. Just ask whether the roux was made with butter or oil, and if there are any pork products used in the cooking process. Neighborhood joints shouldn't provide any difficulty as they will invariably have bean-and-vegetable side dishes, which you can combine to make up a substantial meal. While vegetables and beans used to be cooked in pigs' fat, these days most places use vegetable oil, although you should check first. A muffuletta without the Italian meats (cheeses and olive salad only) is a good way to sample a reasonable meatless facsimile of the local sandwich specialty. It will be easier to find vegetarian infrastructure in New Orleans, but if you're out in Cajun Country don't overlook local diners, which will have a wide selection of vegetable dishes for the choosing. Vegans should steer clear of cornbread, since it's usually prepared with a batter that includes eggs and milk.

There are no vegetarian restaurants in New Orleans, but a few make above-average overtures to nonmeat-eaters. Hookah Cafe (p186), Slim Goodie's Diner (p189) and Angeli on Decatur (p179) all have vegetarian standards on their menus. Contemporary restaurants such as Gabrielle (p193) and Bayona (p183) almost always have vegetarian specials.

EATING WITH KIDS

New Orleans has always been child friendly. In the wake of Hurricane Katrina many families remained outside the city while public schools were closed. It was feared that among the inevitable changes wrought by the hurricane, possibly the new city would be one with far fewer children. However, in such abnormal times kids are often fawned over, so visitors with the brood in tow will feel welcome in most of the city's eateries.

Dining out has always been a family affair in New Orleans. Even old-line Creole establishments with their haughty waiters and multicourse meals are accustomed to serving kids of all ages. The question, really, is whether or not your tots are amenable to dressing up and sitting still. Also consider whether the distinctive food served in these traditional restaurants is likely to go over well.

High-end contemporary restaurants are often less stuffy than the Creole places, but they can also be less child friendly. The chefs in these places are often regarded as culinary Picassos unwilling to alter a finely crafted dish to suit a child's taste buds.

A youngster's best bet is the neighborhood joint, the diner, the po'boy shop, where menu offerings are less foreign and adventurous. Many of these places offer children's menus. The touristy places in the French Quarter are always accommodating, though they don't often serve the best food. The Crescent City Brewhouse serves decent, all-American fare and offers mom and dad an opportunity to sample some local brews without going to a bar.

If your child is set on a dish that may contain cayenne pepper or other seasonings, ask about the spice level before ordering. Often your server can either ask the cooks to ratchet down the spice level or suggest an appropriately tame alternative.

A LOUISIANA GUMBO PARTY

If after your trip you want to invite your friends over for a home-cooked New Orleans feast, you can't do much better than to prepare a heartwarming pot of gumbo. No other food is as representative of the cuisine New Orleans has to offer. What follows is a gumbo you can make almost anywhere.

LOUISIANA CHICKEN & OKRA GUMBO

Ingredients

2/3 cup	neutral-flavored oil (for the roux)
2/3 cup	flour (for the roux)
10oz (300g)	tomatoes, diced
6 cups	chicken stock
2 tblsp	Tabasco sauce
2 tblsp	tomato paste
5 tblsp	Worcestershire sauce
2 tsp	dried thyme leaves
2 tsp	dried oregano leaves
1 tsp	ground cayenne pepper
1 tsp	ground white pepper
2 cups	fresh okra, sliced
3	garlic cloves, crushed
2	chickens, quartered
1	small onion, peeled
1	large red bell pepper, diced
1	large green bell pepper, diced
2	onions, diced
2	stalks celery, diced
1	bay leaf
	sea salt to taste
	freshly ground pepper to taste
	filé powder
	pepper sauce to taste

Simmer the chicken in eight cups (2L) of water with the garlic cloves and the small onion for about an hour. Remove the chicken from the pot and discard the garlic and onion. Skim all the fat from the chicken stock. If you have the time, the easiest way to do this is to put it in the refrigerator overnight and lift off the solidified fat in the morning. When the chicken has cooled, removed the meat from the bones and discard the bones and skin.

In a heavy soup pot that will hold at least eight quarts (8L), make a dark brown roux with the oil and flour.

When the roux is the desired color, turn off the heat and add the peppers, onion and celery, sautéing until the vegetables are soft (about five minutes). Add the tomatoes, Worcestershire, Tabasco, tomato paste, bay leaf, thyme, oregano, cayenne and white pepper. Stir thoroughly. Slowly whisk in the skimmed chicken stock a little at a time, making sure there are no lumps. Cook over a medium heat for 20 minutes. Add the okra and chicken meat and continue cooking for another 30 minutes. Season with salt and pepper as required. Remember, the gumbo should be fairly thick.

To serve, mound half a cup of steamed rice in a bowl. Ladle gumbo around the rice. Serve with pepper sauce and *filé* powder.

Makes 12 servings.

History

The Recent Past 106

From The Beginning 108

- Native Inhabitants 108
- European Exploration 109
- French & Spanish New Orleans 109
- Antebellum Prosperity 111
- Slaves & Free People of Color 112
- A Demographic Gumbo 113
- Union Occupation 114
- A City Divided 115
- Into the 20th Century 116
- 20th Century Shifts 117
- Preservation & Tourism 118

History

THE RECENT PAST

In the early summer of 2005, Hurricane Katrina was nothing but a sparkle in the ocean's eye. While people in New Orleans were concerned with many of the big issues common to all American cities, some of the news that summer was of the 'only in New Orleans' variety. The overall mood in the city was cautiously optimistic.

The summer began on a sad note, with the death of Big Chief Allison 'Tootie' Montana. Montana, head of the Yellow Pocahontas Mardi Gras Indians gang, suffered a heart attack while addressing the City Council. He was making a plea against perceived police abuses of Indian gangs, and his final words were, 'I want this to stop!' Then he collapsed. Montana, 82, was taken to hospital and pronounced dead on arrival. His jazz funeral was marked by a grandiosity fit for a departed head of state. Montana had been widely regarded as a hero in New Orleans, having been honored by usually fractious Indian gangs as the 'chief of chiefs.'

Meanwhile the city's controversial mayor, C Ray Nagin, was three years into his first term in office and remained somewhat enigmatic. A black businessman who had never before run for public office, Nagin stood apart from the career politicians and political dynasties that had ruled New Orleans for so many years. He also frequently stood apart from his own political party. A Democrat, he had contributed to the campaign of George W Bush in the 2000 presidential election. In Louisiana's gubernatorial election of 2003, he endorsed a conservative Republican candidate over the eventual winner, Democrat Kathleen Blanco. And in the 2004 presidential election he voiced support for Democrat John Kerry with evident reluctance.

In the 2002 mayoral race Nagin was a long-shot whose often colorfully expressed frustrations with Louisiana politics resonated with voters. His self-financed campaign held the promise of political independence rarely seen in the smoke-filled rooms of Louisiana's political arena. He convincingly won a run-off against Police Chief Richard Pennington, taking 59% of the vote. He was slightly more popular with white voters than with black voters.

Nagin quickly made an impression. He initiated an anticorruption campaign and followed through by cracking down on the Taxicab Bureau, the Utilities Department and the city vehicle inspection workers. With some fanfare TV news teams recorded

Steamboat on the Mississippi River

TIMELINE

1718 — Bienville founds Nouvelle Orléans, which is populated by nuns, convicts, slaves and immigrants

1750s — Cajuns begin to arrive in southern Louisiana

footage of government employees being arrested; Nagin's own nephew was put behind bars.

Pennington had been hugely popular as police chief. He had cleaned up an infamously corrupt department, and was credited with New Orleans' declining crime rate in the late 1990s. However, those numbers reversed in the early 2000s, and by 2004 New Orleans' murder rate climbed to 10 times the national average. More than 260 people were killed in the city that year.

Crime and poverty tend to go hand-in-hand, so let's review the numbers. New Orleans in the first half of the decade had a high, 28% poverty rate. Roughly one-fourth of the city's families subsisted on $15,000 a year, or less. (By comparison, a college grad accepting entry-level work in New York City struggles to make ends meet on about twice that amount.) However, compared with most American cities, the cost of living in New Orleans is relatively low, and supportive family and community traditions are strong. The proportion of welfare recipients in New Orleans was below 4% following welfare reform, putting it in league with other major cities in the US. And in some of the city's poorest neighborhoods, such as the Lower Ninth Ward, the percentage of homeowners was as high as in the far wealthier Garden District. Unemployment in the city was officially about 5%.

FIVE CHOICE HISTORY BOOKS

Aspects of New Orleans' fascinating history have been committed to paper by some mighty fine writers. Here is a selection of readable inroads into the Crescent City's past.

Rising Tide: The Great Mississippi Flood of 1927 and How It Changed America – An important and engrossing study of the politics of flood control in the lower Mississippi Valley by John M Barry. Especially pertinent in post-Katrina New Orleans.

Storyville – Al Rose takes a serious look at the city's notorious red-light district, but doesn't miss the intrigue and allure of the old hood.

The Free People of Color of New Orleans – Mary Gehman's engrossing overview of an integral ingredient of New Orleans' cultural gumbo.

Frenchmen, Desire, Good Children & Other Streets of New Orleans – Cartoonist John Churchill Chase sticks with the most colorful aspects of New Orleans' history – and manages 260 pages of highly enjoyable reading.

New Orleans –An easy-to-digest, general history of the city by John R Kemp.

The local economy hadn't been strong, or very diverse, in decades. The New Orleans Metropolitan Convention and Visitors Bureau boasted some $4.9 billion had been pumped into the regional economy by out-of-town visitors in 2004, making tourism the number one industry. The number of visitors in the city frequently was equal to the number of residents. In some parts of town, tourism had very little impact, but throughout the first half of 2005, residents in the French Quarter were sounding alarms about the wear and tear on their old neighborhood. Large tour buses, officially banned from the Quarter, regularly swiped signs and dented cast-iron balcony posts. In July 2005 the City Council surprisingly approved a new large hotel development on Iberville St. Mayor Nagin vetoed the project, which, had it passed, would have effectively ended a 36-year moratorium on hotel development in the Quarter. French Quarter residents also made considerable noise when the city installed 6ft-tall, solar-powered parking meters and new trash bins emblazoned with advertisements.

Possibly driving the activism in the Old Quarter was the steady rise in property values. Citywide, real estate saw an 11% jump in the first half of 2005. The average price of single-family homes sold in the French Quarter increased by 17% from 2004 prices, to nearly $900,000. Andrei Codrescu commented in his July 5 column in the *Gambit*, 'The real estate boom is driven by an incredible number of bad gamblers who are hoping to cash in before the inevitable happens.'

A hopeful sign for the economy was the growing presence of the film industry. New Orleans had begun touting itself as 'Hollywood South,' as more feature films and TV shows were shot on location in the city. Films such as *Ray* (with Oscar-winner Jamie Foxx) and *All*

1762
France hands the Louisiana Territory over to Spain

1791
The arrival of French-speaking migrants from St Domingue doubles New Orleans' population

the King's Men (with Sean Penn in the 'Kingfish'-inspired role) were filmed in part in New Orleans. While the industry was not locally based, frequent production in the city meant regular work for hundreds of set and costume designers, camera assistants, sound assistants, carpenters, hairdressers, grips and extras. In the fall of 2005 shooting was scheduled to begin in New Orleans of a Jerry Bruckheimer film called *Deja Vu,* starring Denzel Washington. But those plans were put on hold when Hurricane Katrina appeared on the horizon.

Hurricane Katrina had started up near the Bahamas and whirled across southern Florida into the Gulf of Mexico. It was a Category One hurricane when it entered the Gulf, but as it approached the coast of Louisiana and Mississippi it gained strength and became Category Five – the highest level. New Orleans braced for the possibility of a direct, catastrophic blow. On August 27 Mayor Nagin called for a mandatory evacuation of the city. It was the first time in the city's history that all its residents were required to leave.

See the Wrath of Katrina chapter (p120) for a detailed account of the disaster.

FROM THE BEGINNING

Many aspects of New Orleans' culture today – street names, food, Mardi Gras – suggest a profound influence left behind by the French and Spanish, who took turns governing the waterlogged outpost before the Americans absorbed it. It is equally significant that African culture, often with Caribbean influences, has always held a stronger sway here than elsewhere in the US. Of course, being a major capital of the South has determined many events in the city's history and contributes to its character today.

By North American standards, New Orleans is an old city, and the depth of its history has always been cherished by locals. An important part of post-Katrina rebuilding involves preserving the unique multicultural character that is very consciously rooted in the city's extraordinary history.

NATIVE INHABITANTS

The French weren't the first to claim ownership of southern Louisiana. Settlements can be traced back 10,000 years. The Tchefuncte arrived after 700 BC building small, scattered settlements with circular shelters made from poles and covered with mud-caked thatch.

After 1700, Europeans documented numerous direct contacts with local tribes. Seven small tribes known collectively as the Muskogeans lived north of Lake Pontchartrain and occasionally settled along the banks of the Mississippi River. They spoke Choctaw dialects but were not members of the larger Choctaw nation. One band, the Quinapisa, attacked the expedition led by French-explorer René Robert Cavelier La Salle, and later settled above New Orleans on the Mississippi River as the tribe fled an epidemic in 1718. Other tribes south of New Orleans inhabited the bayous in Barataria and the lower course of the Mississippi. Native foods included maize, beans, wild rice, squash and ground sassafras leaves.

Europeans adapted to the region's extreme environment by observing the eating and hunting habits of these indigenous peoples. But the interaction was not mutually beneficial. Most indigenous groups suffered from epidemics introduced by the Europeans, while many others were captured by slave traders. Those who survived either of these fates were most likely absorbed by the Houma and Choctaw tribes, who at that time were moving westward in flight from English and Chickasaw slave raids. The Houma thrived in isolated coastal bayous from Terrebonne to Lafourche up until the 1940s, when oil exploration began in southern Louisiana and disturbed their way of life.

Alliances between escaped African slaves and Native Americans were not uncommon. Early French settlers also sometimes married Native American women. Today, some 19,000 Louisianans identify themselves as American Indian, but a great number of these people are culturally and racially mixed.

1803	1815
Napoleon reclaims Louisiana, then sells the entire territory to the US for $15 million	General Andrew Jackson leads US troops in the battle of New Orleans

EUROPEAN EXPLORATION

Europeans probably first saw the mouth of the Mississippi River as early as 1519, when the Spanish explorer Alonso Alvarez de Pineda is believed to have come upon it. Word of such an entryway to the heart of North America reached Europe, and several explorers attempted to find it.

Many of those who did find the Mississippi met tragic ends. The Spanish conquistador Hernando de Soto's overland expedition from Florida to the Mississippi was a grueling three-year trek through some of the most inhospitable terrain in North America. In 1542, de Soto reached the Mississippi, where his reward was a watery grave in the river's gulf-bound muddy waters. After de Soto's experience, further exploration of the Mississippi was put off for well over a century.

In 1682, La Salle headed an expedition of 23 Frenchmen and 18 Native Americans that probed southward from French outposts on the Great Lakes. Upon reaching the Gulf of Mexico, he staged a ceremony to claim the Mississippi River and all its tributaries for France. This was no modest claim, for it included not only the entire river from Minnesota to the Gulf, but a considerable part of North America, extending from the Rockies to the Alleghenies. La Salle honored King Louis XIV in naming the area Louisiana. His maps inaccurately (and perhaps deliberately) showed the Mississippi River in the vicinity of Matagorda Bay (Texas), suspiciously close to New Spain's silver mines, which would have directly challenged Spain's claims there. In fact, upon his return to the region, La Salle bypassed the mouth of the Mississippi – again, perhaps intentionally – and he was murdered in Texas in 1687.

The Mississippi continued to elude ships on the Gulf until 1699, when Canadian-born Pierre Le Moyne, Sieur d'Iberville, and his younger brother Jean-Baptiste Le Moyne, Sieur de Bienville, located the muddy outflow. They encamped 40 miles downriver from present-day New Orleans on the eve of Mardi Gras and, knowing their countrymen would be celebrating the pre-Lenten holiday, christened the small spit of land Pointe de Mardi Gras – a name that would later have special cultural significance for New Orleans. With a Native American guide, Iberville and Bienville sailed upstream, pausing to note the narrow portage to Lake Pontchartrain along Bayou St John in what would later become New Orleans.

FRENCH & SPANISH NEW ORLEANS

Iberville died of yellow fever in 1706, but Bienville remained in Louisiana to found Nouvelle Orléans – so named in honor of the duc d'Orléans – in 1718. Bienville chose a small patch of relatively high ground beside the Bayou St John, which connected the Mississippi to Lake Pontchartrain and thereby offered more direct access to the Gulf of Mexico. Factoring in the site's strategic position, Bienville's party decided to overlook the hazards of perennial flooding and mosquito-borne diseases. Engineer Adrien de Pauger's severe grid plan, drawn in 1722, still delineates the French Quarter today.

From the start, the objective was to populate Louisiana and to make a productive commercial port out of New Orleans. Promotion of the endeavor fell into the hands of the shrewd Scotsman John Law, head of the Company of the West, an important branch of the Company of the Indies, which controlled trade between France and the rest of the world. While Bienville's original group of 30 ex-convicts, six carpenters and four Canadians struggled against floods and yellow-fever epidemics, Law busily portrayed Louisiana as heaven on earth to unsuspecting French, Germans and Swiss, who soon began arriving in New Orleans by the shipload. To augment these numbers, additional convicts and prostitutes were freed from French jails if they agreed to relocate to Louisiana. This inauspicious start to the colony would have an indelible impact on the city's character for generations to come.

The colony was not a tremendous economic success, and due to the harsh realities of life in New Orleans civilian immigration was slow – especially by women. The colonists

1830s
Marie Laveau becomes Voodoo Queen of New Orleans

1840
Antoine's opens for business

created an exchange economy based on smuggling and local trade. To increase the female population, the Ursuline nuns brought young, marriageable women with them in 1728. They were known as 'casket girls' because they packed their belongings in casket-shaped boxes. Such grim imagery was consistent with the prevailing outlook of the times. New Orleans was already establishing itself as, and gaining a reputation for being, a loosely civilized outpost. Looking about her, one recently arrived nun commented that 'the devil here has a very large empire.'

In a secret treaty, one year before the Seven Years' War (1756–63) ended, France handed the unprofitable Louisiana Territory to King Charles III of Spain. In return, France gained an ally in its war against England. For the Spanish, Louisiana represented a buffer between its possessions in New Spain and the English colonies along the Atlantic coast. Spanish-governor Antonio de Ulloa didn't arrive in New Orleans until 1766.

The locals bitterly resented becoming Spanish subjects. However, the 'Frenchness' of New Orleans was little affected for the duration of Spain's control. Spain sent a small garrison and few financial resources. Ulloa spoke no French, and after he attempted to forbid trade with French islands, a rebel force drove him from office in 1768. In response, Spain sent

A GENTLEMAN AND A PIRATE

Jean Lafitte, New Orleans' celebrated pirate, is a peculiar legend whose story frequently strays into the realm of mythology. Historical accounts seem overeager to stress his patriotism, while excusing some of his more suspect activities, which included raiding ships and slave running. His biographers typically emphasize his well-mannered, swaggering style. One thing's for sure, he's an alluring figure who fits right in with the New Orleans' mystique.

Lafitte's origins are hazy (he may have been from France, St Domingue or the Cajun Wetlands), but by the time of the Louisiana Purchase he was already a highly public figure in New Orleans. He supplied stolen and smuggled goods to the remote, oft-deprived city. From his compound on the island of Grande Terre in Barataria Bay, about 40 miles south of New Orleans, Lafitte led a band of some 1000 pirates who plundered Spanish ships sailing in the Gulf of Mexico. (Technically, Lafitte could insist he was a 'privateer,' working on behalf of the state of Cartegena, which was battling Spain for its independence.) His brother Pierre kept a blacksmith shop in the city, where in fact he oversaw the wholesale and retail of the pirates' loot. Through the labyrinthine waterways of southern Louisiana, Lafitte's men transported clothes, spices and furnishings past US customs officials. In the city he sold his coveted merchandise at below market prices. Obviously, he was a very popular outlaw in the city. He mixed with the best society (including Mayor Nicolas Girod), ate and drank in the finest restaurants and had his pick of women.

Lafitte also imported slaves from the Caribbean after the import and export of slaves had been outlawed in the US. Again, by skirting customs tariffs, he was able to sell this 'merchandise' at deep discounts. Louisiana officials tended to look the other way. Most local politicians were the pirate's friends and customers.

Governor WCC Claiborne, who took office in 1803, saw things differently. He put a price on Lafitte's head, to the sum of $500. Lafitte countered by putting a price of $1000 on Claiborne's head, and hid out in the swamps, where Claiborne's bounty-hunters couldn't track him down. Thus, the French-speaking pirate wittily outfoxed US authorities, earning his way into the hearts of the Creole city forever. When Claiborne finally tracked Lafitte down and arrested him, Lafitte was sprung on bail, disappeared again to the swamps and flouted all orders to appear in court. The battle between these two men seems to have entertained New Orleanians for the better part of a decade.

When the Royal Navy threatened to invade New Orleans during the War of 1812, Lafitte offered to help block British passage from the Gulf. In return he asked that Claiborne stop hounding the pirates. Claiborne refused, but General Andrew Jackson arrived in town and agreed to Lafitte's terms. Whether Lafitte's pirates in fact helped much in the Battle of New Orleans (1815) is sometimes questioned. But for many it's a matter of faith that Lafitte proved himself a true patriot on behalf of the stars and stripes.

In any case, it doesn't appear that the US held up its half of the bargain. In 1817 Lafitte was forced to leave Barataria. In Galveston, Texas, he set up another small kingdom of pirates and outlaws, but he was rousted off the island by the US Navy four years later. He and his flotilla of ships disappeared in the night, never to be heard of again. Some historians think he may have ended up in Illinois or St Louis. That's not a very romantic ending. Others simply surmise that Lafitte and his band of corsairs were wiped out in a hurricane.

1853

Yellow-fever epidemic claims the lives of almost 8000 citizens

1857

The Mistick Krewe of Comus launches modern Mardi Gras with a torch-lit night parade

2600 troops led by General Alejandro O'Reilly, an Irishman who had joined the Spanish military originally to fight England in the Seven Years' War. 'Bloody' O'Reilly, as he came to be known, squashed the rebellion and then eased trade regulations.

An enduring impact left by the Spanish was the architecture of the old city. After fires decimated the French Quarter in 1788 and 1794, much of the French Quarter was rebuilt by the Spanish. Consequently, the quaint Old Quarter with plastered façades we know today is not French, as its name would suggest, but predominantly Spanish in style.

The Spanish sensed they might eventually have to fight the expansion-minded Americans to retain control of the lower Mississippi. Hence, Spain jumped at Napoleon Bonaparte's offer to retake control of Louisiana in 1800.

ANTEBELLUM PROSPERITY

While Napoleon Bonaparte was waging war in Europe, the US was expanding westward into the Ohio River Valley. Napoleon needed cash to finance his wars, and US President Thomas Jefferson coveted control of the Mississippi River and the port of New Orleans. American merchants were already playing a rapidly increasing role in the commerce of New Orleans. Nevertheless, the US minister in Paris, Robert Livingston, was astonished by Bonaparte's offer to sell the entire Louisiana Territory – an act that would double the US's national domain – at a price of $15 million. On December 20, 1803, the American flag was raised.

Little cheer arose from the Creole community, which envisaged Americans arriving in droves with their puritanical work ethic. The Americans' Protestant beliefs and support for English common law jarred with the Catholic Creole way of life. In 1808 the territorial legislature sought to preserve Creole culture by adopting elements of Spanish and French law – especially the Napoleonic Code as it related to equity, succession and family. Elements of the code persist in Louisiana today.

New Orleans grew quickly as Americans moved to the increasingly busy port to make their fortunes. In the age of steamboats and flatboats, New Orleans was obviously well positioned to be the financial and commercial capital of the western USA. Almost all of the goods shipped in and out of the vast Mississippi River Valley and the Deep South, passed through New Orleans. The city teemed with customs officials, factors, agents, bankers, stevedores, warehouse laborers, lawyers and insurance companies. As commissions poured into the city by the boatload, antebellum New Orleans became the fourth-wealthiest city in the world. Of America's ports and financial centers, only New York was bigger.

The city's populace spilled beyond the borders of the French Quarter. In the 1830s Samuel Jarvis Peters (1801–55), a wholesale merchant from Quebec, bought plantation land upriver from the French Quarter to build a community. Peters helped create a distinctly American section, beginning with today's CBD, that's separated from the Creole Quarter by broad Canal St. He married into a Creole family and epitomized the American entrepreneur operating within the Creole host community.

Oak Alley Plantation (p286)

1862

New Orleans is taken by the Union and occupied for the duration of the Civil War

1880s

Mardi Gras Indians begin to appear on Mardi Gras

ANDREW JACKSON & THE WAR OF 1812

A month after Louisiana's admission to the Union as the 18th state in 1812, President James Madison declared war against the British. Madison's unpopular action barely registered with New Orleans' residents until a British force assembled in Jamaica.

General Andrew Jackson arrived in Louisiana in November 1814, but locals were suspicious of his intentions when he imposed martial law. Their distrust of Jackson lessened when the British landed on the Louisiana coast.

Jackson convinced Jean Lafitte to side with the American forces in exchange for amnesty, thereby gaining the help of the pirate's band of sharpshooters and his considerable arsenal of weapons. Jackson also enlisted free black battalions and Choctaws.

The Battle of New Orleans at Chalmette, just four miles from the French Quarter, was a one-sided victory for the Americans, with nearly 900 British losses versus only 13 US losses. Word soon reached New Orleans that the battle had actually begun after the US and Britain agreed to end the war. But the decisive American victory clearly put a lid on British designs on the Louisiana Territory.

Developers further transformed the 15 riverbank plantations into lush American suburbs. By 1835 the New Orleans & Carrollton Railroad began providing a horse-drawn streetcar service along St Charles Ave, linking the growing communities of Lafayette, Jefferson and Carrollton. Today, these one-time suburbs are all part of Uptown New Orleans. Creole families that benefited from the city's flourishing economy built their opulent homes along Esplanade Ave, from the Quarter all the way out to City Park.

Obviously, the wealthy chose the highest ground for their gorgeous enclaves. But the city also expanded into low-lying wetlands that had to be drained. Underprivileged immigrants and blacks settled the city's swampy periphery, including an area eventually called the Ninth Ward. These poor, flood-prone neighborhoods would be hardest hit in September 2005.

On a much lighter note, the late 1850s saw the revival of Carnival. The old Creole tradition, now propelled by Americans, hit the streets of New Orleans as a much grander affair than ever before. (See p33 for more Carnival history.) Americans also assumed control of the municipal government in 1852, further illustrating the erosion of Creole influence in New Orleans.

SLAVES & FREE PEOPLE OF COLOR

From the beginning, people of African descent were a very important part of the city's population; many households in New Orleans included a few slaves. Equally significant, though, was the city's considerable number of blacks who were free in the antebellum period.

The French brought some 1300 African slaves to New Orleans in the city's first decade. In 1724, French Louisianans adopted the Code Noir (Black Code), a document which carefully restricted the social position of blacks, but also addressed some of the needs of slaves and accorded certain privileges to free persons of color. Under the Code Noir, abused slaves could legally sue their masters. The number of slaves in the city grew to thousands by the time of the Civil War. In the city slaves usually served in the household, as cooks, maids, butlers and footmen.

Slaves in French and Spanish Louisiana were allowed to retain much more of their African culture than slaves in other parts of the USA. Drumming and dancing were permitted during nonworking hours, and since the 1740s free blacks and slaves were allowed to congregate at the huge produce market at Congo Sq (initially called Place des Negres), just beyond the city's ramparts. The Congo Sq market was a cultural brewing pot unlike anything else in the country, and immense crowds (including occasional tourists from the East Coast and Europe) showed up to witness complicated polyrhythmic drumming and dances that, by stuffy European standards, were considered highly exotic

1895–1905

Buddy Bolden reigns as the first 'King of Jazz'

1897

Storyville, New Orleans' infamous red-light district, is established and suggestive. Congo Sq today is a quiet corner of Louis Armstrong Park, on Rampart St. Radio station WWOZ is headquartered nearby, and the square usually livens up with events during Jazz Fest.

Additionally, thousands more slaves were sold at public auctions held throughout the Vieux Carré. By the mid-19th century New Orleans had become the largest slave-trading center in the country. With the import of slaves outlawed, smugglers such as the 'pirate' Jean Lafitte (see A Gentleman and a Pirate, p110) brought slaves into New Orleans by way of the state's bayous and swamps. As the price of slaves rose to $2000 or more, depending on their skill levels, slave numbers fell in the city. By the 1850s the influx of Irish laborers presented an inexpensive alternative with very little cash commitment required of the employer.

Long before the start of the Civil War, New Orleans had the South's largest population of free blacks. In Creole New Orleans they were known as *les gens de couleur libre*. Throughout the 18th and 19th centuries, it was not altogether uncommon for slaves to be granted their freedom after years of loyal service. Sometimes the mixed offspring of slaves and owners were granted their freedom. Skilled slaves were often allowed to hire themselves out, working jobs on the side until they were able to earn enough money to buy their freedom. The Code Noir permitted free blacks to own property and conduct business. Many made a decent living as skilled carpenters and blacksmiths.

The city's free blacks typically identified with Creole culture, speaking French and attending Mass on Sunday. Trained musicianship was prized among many families, and orchestras of free black musicians regularly performed at wealthy Creole balls. The free blacks of New Orleans were considered a highly cultured class who probably enjoyed a higher quality of life than blacks anywhere else in the US. They were often well educated, and some owned land and even had slaves of their own. But they didn't share all the rights and privileges of white Creoles and Americans. They were not entitled to vote or serve in juries, and while going about their business blacks were sometimes required to show identification in order to prove that they were not slaves.

Affairs between the races was socially accepted, but interracial marriages were not. The *plaçage* was a cultural institution whereby white Creole men 'kept' light-skinned black women, providing them with a handsome wardrobe and a cottage in the Vieux Carré, and supporting any resulting children. Subtle gradations of mixed color led to a complex class structure in which those with the least African blood tended to enjoy the greatest privileges. (Octoroons, for instance, who were in theory one-eighth black, rated higher than quadroons, who were one-quarter black.)

The multiple classes of blacks in New Orleans greatly enhanced the cultural gumbo that made New Orleans such a unique and fascinating place. The city's cuisine, music, religion and holiday traditions are all enriched by the influence of Creole-African culture.

A DEMOGRAPHIC GUMBO

The multicultural stew was by no means limited to people of African descent, and the European influence expanded well beyond the French. The Creoles could only loosely be defined as being of French descent. The progeny of unions between French Creoles and Native Americans and blacks of varying shades also considered themselves Creole. Early German immigrants to the city frequently Gallicized their names, began to speak French and blended in.

When the French Acadians began to arrive in Louisiana in 1755, however, they did not blend into New Orleans' French-speaking society. The Cajuns, as they are now called, had been deported by the British from Nova Scotia in 1755 after refusing to pledge allegiance to England. Aboard unseaworthy ships they headed south, but the largely illiterate, Catholic peasants were unwanted in the American colonies. Francophile New Orleans seemed a more natural home for the Cajuns, but even here the citified Creoles regarded them as

1901	1906
Louis Armstrong is born on August 4	The muffuletta sandwich is invented at the Central Grocery

YELLOW FEVER

New Orleans' reputation as an unhealthy place was widespread and well deserved during the 18th and 19th centuries, when its residents were ravaged not so much by wild living but by the horrors of yellow fever. Symptoms of the disease showed themselves suddenly, and death soon followed. An 1853 epidemic resulted in almost 8000 deaths; that was about 10% of the residents who remained in the city after some 30,000 had fled.

Yellow fever's primary victims were male immigrants, children and laborers, many of whom lived and worked in squalid conditions. Yet no one was immune, and entire families were often lost. Numerous orphanages arose to care for children who survived their parents.

Some of the supposed treatments only hastened death, including exorbitant bloodletting and large doses of calomel, a poisonous mercury compound, whose horrid effects mortified skin and bone, causing them to slough away. In 1836 one visiting physician commented, 'We have drawn enough blood to float a steamboat and given enough calomel to freight her'.

Morticians were overworked and underpaid during these epidemics. In the rush to entomb the dead, who were believed to be contagious, funeral services were often dispensed with. Cemeteries became putrid, fouled by the mass of bodies that could not be interred quickly enough.

In 1881, Dr Carlos J Finlay, a Cuban, revealed that the disease was spread by mosquitoes, and his findings were confirmed by Walter Reed in 1905. Health authorities in Louisiana urged people to screen their homes and eliminate mosquito-breeding grounds, but New Orleans suffered one last epidemic in 1905.

country trash. The Cajuns fanned out of the city into the upland prairies of western Louisiana, where they were able to resume their lifestyle of raising livestock. For three decades, wandering Acadians continued to arrive in Louisiana in the forced migration they called *le grand dérangement.*

Other former-French subjects soon arrived from St Domingue (now Haiti). The slave revolt there in 1791 established St Domingue as the second independent nation in the Americas. Following that, thousands of slaveholders fled with their slaves to Louisiana, where they helped bolster French-speaking Creole traditions. During the following two decades, thousands of former slaves also relocated from St Domingue to New Orleans as free people of color. This influx doubled the city's population and injected an indelible trace of Caribbean culture that remains in evidence to this day. Their most obvious contribution was the practice of voodoo, which became popular in New Orleans during the 19th century.

Antebellum New Orleans was the second-largest gateway, after New York, for a steady flow of immigrants entering the US. As the Civil War approached, nearly half of the city's population was foreign born. Most were from Ireland, Germany or France. The Irish, in particular, were largely unskilled and took grueling, often hazardous work building levees and digging canals. Their wages were low enough to justify hiring them rather than risk the lives of $2000 slaves. They settled the low-rent sector between the Garden District and the docks that is still known as the Irish Channel.

Despite the Napoleonic Code's mandate for Jewish expulsion, and an anti-Semitic, Southern Christian culture, trade practices led to tolerance of Jewish merchants. Alsatian Jews augmented the small Jewish community in New Orleans, and by 1828 they had established a synagogue. Judah Touro, whose estate was valued at $4 million upon his death in 1854, funded orphanages and hospitals that would serve Jews and Christians alike.

UNION OCCUPATION

At the dawn of the Civil War, New Orleans was by far the most prosperous city south of the Mason-Dixon Line, and had commercial ties to the North and to the rest of the world. However, Louisiana was a slave state, and New Orleans was a slave city, and it was over

1927	1936
During the Great Mississippi Flood, the levee is dynamited in St Bernard Parish, flooding residents there to protect New Orleans	Vieux Carré Commission founded to regulate moderations made to French Quarter exteriors

this very issue that the nation hurtled toward civil war. On January 26, 1861, Louisiana became the sixth state to secede from the Union, and on March 21 the state joined the Confederacy.

The war didn't reach New Orleans until a year later. The Union readily achieved its objective to control the lower Mississippi River, and captured New Orleans in April 1862. It was the first Confederate city to be captured, and it would be occupied until the war's end in 1865. For the duration of the war, New Orleans was embroiled in petty rivalries between the locals and their oppressors from the North.

New Orleanians, otherwise famous for their hospitality, didn't take too kindly to the occupation government or its leader, Major General Benjamin 'Beast' Butler. As his nickname suggests, Butler was not intent on winning the hearts of the city's populace, and his presence unified the city in its hatred of him and the North. Soon after the US flag went up in front of the US Mint, a local man named William Mumford cut it down. Butler established the severe tone of his administration by having the man hanged from the very same flagpole. Under Butler's rule, property was confiscated from citizens who refused to pledge loyalty to the Union.

On the other hand, Butler was also credited with giving the Quarter a much-needed clean-up, building orphanages, improving the school system and putting thousands of unemployed – both white and black – to work. But he didn't stay in New Orleans long enough to implement Lincoln's plans for 'reconstructing' the city. Those plans, blueprints for the Reconstruction of the South that followed the war, went into effect in December 1863, a year after Butler returned to the North.

A CITY DIVIDED

The 'Free State of Louisiana,' which included only occupied parts of the state, was readmitted to the Union. Slavery was abolished and the right to vote was soon extended to a few select blacks. But the road to equality would not be a smooth one, as quickly became clear. The move to extend suffrage to all black men, in 1863, sparked a bloody riot, and after an exceedingly violent police response the melee ended with 36 casualties. All but two were black. It was a grim beginning for the Reconstruction period, foreshadowing an endless series of race-related struggles that would leave the people of New Orleans hardened, embittered and battered.

At the war's end Louisiana's state constitution was redrawn. Causing no small amount of resentment among white Southerners, full suffrage was granted to blacks, but the same rights were denied to former Confederate soldiers and rebel sympathizers. This obviously paved the way for northern government officials – derisively called 'carpetbaggers' – who were voted into office throughout the South. Emboldened, blacks began challenging discrimination laws, such as those forbidding them from riding 'white' streetcars, and racial skirmishes regularly flared up around town.

White-supremacist groups such as the Ku Klux Klan began to appear throughout the South. In New Orleans, organizations called the Knights of the White Camellia and the Crescent City Democratic Club initiated a reign of terror that targeted blacks and claimed several hundred lives during a particularly bloody few weeks. In the 1870s the White League was formed, with the twin purposes of ousting what it considered to be an 'Africanized' government (elected in part by newly enfranchised black voters) and ridding the state government of Northerners and Reconstructionists.

By all appearances, the White League was arming itself for an all-out war. Police and the state militia attempted to block a shipment of guns in 1874, and after in an ensuing 'battle' the scalawag Governor William Pitt Kellogg was ousted from office for five days. Federal troops entered the city to restore order.

Although Reconstruction officially ended in 1877, New Orleans remained at war with itself for many decades after. Many of the civil liberties that blacks were supposed to have

1955

Fats Domino records hit record 'Ain't that a Shame'

1960

Federal marshalls escort black children into their classrooms as schools are desegregated gained after the Civil War would be reversed by what became known as Jim Crow law, which reinforced and in some ways increased segregation and inequality between blacks and whites.

With its educated class of black Creoles, New Orleans was a natural setting for the early Civil Rights movement. In 1896, a New Orleans man named Homer Plessy, whose one-eighth African lineage subjected him to Jim Crow restrictions, challenged Louisiana's segregation laws in the landmark *Plessy* v. *Ferguson* case. Although Plessy's case exposed the arbitrary nature of Jim Crow law, the US Supreme Court interpreted the Constitution as providing for political, not social, equality and ruled to uphold 'separate but equal' statutes. Separate buses, water fountains, bathrooms, eating places and courtroom Bibles became fixtures of the segregated landscape. Louisiana law made it illegal to serve alcohol to whites and blacks under the same roof, even if the bar had a partition for segregation.

'Separate but equal' remained the law of the land until the Plessy case was overturned by *Brown* v. *the Board of Education* in 1954. Congress passed the Civil Rights Act in 1964.

INTO THE 20TH CENTURY

As the 20th century dawned, manufacturing, shipping, trade and banking all resumed, but New Orleans would never again enjoy the prosperity of its antebellum period. The turn of the century was a formative period in which New Orleans became known as a very different sort of city.

Most important was the emergence of a new musical style brewing in the city. Called 'jass' and later jazz, the new music brought together black Creole musicianship and African American rhythms. It also benefited from a proliferation of brass and wind instruments that accompanied the emergence of marching bands during the war years. As jazz spread worldwide, the music became a signature of New Orleans much as impressionist painting had become synonymous with Paris. See p76 for more on the innovators who contributed to this vibrant explosion of creativity in the 'Big Easy.'

The early years of jazz coincided with the golden age of Storyville, New Orleans' notorious red-light district. Houses of ill repute, catering to the natural and unnatural needs of men, had always operated all over town. But by the 1890s prostitution was such a flourishing business that it began to invade even the city's finer neighborhoods. Politicians, having little hope of ending the trade, sought at least to contain and control it. The district, to the lakeside of the French Quarter, was intended as a well-demarcated zone where prostitution would be regulated by health officials.

Storyville quickly gained renown as a modern Gomorrah, a domain of whores, pimps, madams, card cheats, drug peddlers and a tragic number of wanton street urchins. The district's very existence rested on its ability to foster and nurture any form of depravity. Some Storyville houses were sordid cribs enlivened by barrelhouse piano players like Jelly Roll Morton, a jazz pioneer who was also a card cheat and pimp. But many houses were posh Taj Mahals of ill repute.

WWI spelled the end for Storyville. In 1917, Secretary of the Navy Joseph Daniels ordered the district officially closed, expressing the navy's fears that legalized prostitution would cause the spread of social diseases among servicemen based at a New Orleans training camp. However, prostitution continued illegally along the same streets until the district was razed in the 1940s.

A CLEAN STORY

It is ironic that Storyville bears the name of Sidney Story, the city official who proposed the notorious district of ill repute in 1897. Story is generally believed to have led a squeaky-clean life, which in New Orleans at that time qualified as a saintly achievement. He wanted to contain vice, not celebrate it, and he certainly never wished for his name to be used in association with it. Those who lived and plied their trades in Storyville, apparently feeling no gratitude for Mr Story, simply called their stomping grounds 'the District.'

1965
Hurricane Betsy, the billion-dollar hurricane, batters the 'Big Easy'

1970
Jazz Fest held for the first time

New Orleans continued to escape the natural calamities that were always thought to be the city's destiny, but there was seemingly nothing to be done to offset human folly. The great Mississippi Flood of 1927, which inundated dozens of counties from Illinois down to Louisiana, generated natural fear in New Orleans. To the north, the great river broke its levees in 145 places and washed over 27,000 sq miles (70,000 sq km). Among the hardest hit area was the Mississippi Delta, where thousands of destitute, black field hands, after struggling mightily to bolster the levees, were stranded for months afterward. The upriver levee breaks greatly reduced the threat to New Orleans, but as an unnecessary precaution the city's bankers and power brokers arranged for the destruction of levees in St Bernard Parish, downriver from the city, thus deliberately flooding out some 10,000 residents there. This blatant effort to protect the wealthier communities at the expense of poorer areas would not be forgotten. It fed conspiracy theories that ran rampant after Hurricane Katrina, as people observed the familiar pattern of devastation in poorer areas while wealthier zones such as the French Quarter and Garden District survived.

20TH CENTURY SHIFTS

In the 1930s, oil companies began dredging canals and laying a massive pipe infrastructure throughout the bayou region to the southwest of New Orleans. This new industry contributed to erosion of Louisiana's coastal wetlands, and today the wetlands are disappearing at an alarming rate. Some Cajun towns on Bayou Lafouche have already shrunk down to a smattering of buildings and trailers on wood pilings. Refineries crowd up along the Mississippi River between New Orleans and Baton Rouge. But gas and oil brought a new source of wealth to New Orleans' CBD, where national oil companies opened their offices. The State of Louisiana produces one-fifth of the nation's oil and one-fourth of the nation's natural gas today.

New Orleans was inundated with military troops and personnel during WWII. German U-boats sank many allied ships in the Gulf of Mexico, but New Orleans was never directly threatened. With war came manufacturing jobs. Airplane parts and Higgins boats, used for shuttling troops and supplies to the beach during the Normandy invasion, were built in New Orleans. For the duration of the war Mardi Gras was canceled.

The demographics of the city were changing. During the 'white flight' years, chiefly after WWII, black residents moved out of the rural South and into the cities of the North as well as Southern cities such as New Orleans. Most whites responded by relocating to the suburbs. Desegregation laws finally brought an end to Jim Crow legislation, but traditions shaped by racism were not so easily reversed. In 1960, as schools were desegregated, federal marshals had to escort black schoolchildren to their classrooms, to protect them from white protestors. The tragic irony is that as many whites moved their children into private schools, many formerly all-white public schools became nearly all-black. The underfunded public schools declined drastically.

New Orleans' quaint cityscape also changed during the postwar years. A new elevated freeway runs above Claiborne Ave. The neutral ground in the middle of the thoroughfare, once overgrown with trees, was paved for parking. Elevated freeways were also built along the uptown edge of the CBD, cutting immediately above Lee Circle. High-rise office buildings and hotels shot up around the CBD in the 1970s, towering over the low-lying Vieux Carré. In the mid-1970s the Louisiana Superdome opened. A huge hubcap of a building, the Superdome hosts NFL football games, the annual Sugar Bowl college game, and occasional Super Bowls and presidential conventions. It also served as a temporary refugee camp during the aftermath of Hurricane Katrina (see p125).

In 1978 New Orleans elected its first black mayor, Ernest 'Dutch' Morial, marking a major shift in the city's political history. Morial, a Democrat, appointed blacks and women to many city posts during his two terms in office. Morial's tenure ended in 1986, and in 1994 his son, Marc Morial, was elected mayor and then re-elected in 1998. In 2001 the

1978
New Orleans' first black mayor, Ernest 'Dutch' Morial, is elected

1987
The Saints post their first winning season since joining the NFL in 1967

younger Morial attempted to pass a referendum permitting him to run for a third term, but the city electorate turned him down. Another African American, businessman Ray Nagin, became mayor in 2002.

PRESERVATION & TOURISM

During the first few decades of the 20th century, the French Quarter was no longer a center for business, having been long overshadowed by the American sector and the CBD. It was an old and crumbling district, with almost all of its buildings dating from before the Civil War, and by this time it was heavily populated by large families of working-class immigrants and blacks. The lower Quarter was largely populated by Sicilian immigrants, many of whom worked the port and the farmers market and opened Italian restaurants. It was a bustling, if decrepit, neighborhood that was no doubt full of vitality.

The issue of preservation arose as prominent citizens began to recognize the architectural value of the French Quarter. The Vieux Carré Commission was founded in 1936 to regulate exterior modifications made to the historic buildings. Gentrification began to take its course as wealthy New Orleanians began to purchase property in the French Quarter, driving up the value of real estate and eventually nudging out the Quarter's poorer residents. A similar process took place in many other neighborhoods in the city, such as the Garden District and the Faubourg Marigny. New Orleans currently has 17 National Register historic districts. Cemetery-preservation societies have taken on similar responsibility for protecting dozens of landmark bone-yards throughout the city.

As New Orleans accentuated its antiquity, tourism increased. Bourbon St became largely oriented toward the tourist trade, with souvenir shops and touristy bars opening up along the street. To accommodate the tourist influx, large-scale hotels were built in the heart of the French Quarter in the traditional architectural styles. As the oil boom of the 1970s went bust in the 1980s, tourism became the rock of the local economy. Conventioneers and vacationers regularly outnumbered locals on the weekend, spending cash and spilling beer, primarily in the French Quarter.

Tourist dollars meant job opportunities for locals, and also helped prop up some of the city's specialty industries, namely in the field of food. New Orleans effectively promoted its unique cuisine as reason enough to visit the city, and some restaurants propped up their chefs to celebrity status. In addition, the city became a magnate for ambitious Cajun chefs, such as Paul Prudhomme, who gained international renown while working at Commander's Palace in the Garden District and then his own K-Paul's restaurant (p184) in the French Quarter. Chef Prudhomme's rise to fame was directly responsible for an international appreciation of Cajun food, which previously was little known outside southern Louisiana.

2002
Long-shot Ray Nagin wins election and becomes major of New Orleans

2005
Storm surge following Hurricane Katrina floods 80% of New Orleans

The Wrath of Katrina

A History of Hurricanes	120
The Gathering Storm	122
The Cyclone Blows Through	123
Levee Failure	124
An Appalling Scene	125
George to the Rescue	127
Militarized Zone	128
Baby Steps Back	129
What the Future Holds	130

The Wrath of Katrina

New Orleans is an elaborate sand-castle city, built in a precarious low-lying region near the Gulf of Mexico. Major hurricanes twirl through the region every summer and fall, tearing trees and buildings out of the ground and sending the surging sea inland. The city is fortified by levees and floodwalls that don't always bear up when the game is on the line. An event like Hurricane Katrina had long been feared. It was expected, actually. The question, really, was how much of the city would be left after the tide washed away. During the last week of August in 2005, as Hurricane Katrina whirled on its treacherous path through the Gulf of Mexico toward New Orleans, the world waited with dread to see what would become of a beloved and unique American city.

The great tragedy is that Katrina was foreseeable, and it was also preventable. The city's levee system could have been better maintained, and it could even have been improved to withstand greater storms. And, of course, the horrible aftermath could have been avoided with better planning, communication and crisis response at all levels of leadership.

As it turned out, Katrina was the most significant single event in New Orleans' history, at least since the Civil War and possibly going back to the Louisiana Purchase. Many important parts of the city – in fact, most parts of town that a tourist would be interested in seeing – are enjoying a swift comeback. But New Orleans will be in recovery mode for years, if not decades, to come. The city has survived large storms in the past, so bouncing back and fatalistically awaiting the next cataclysmic storm is nothing new for New Orleanians. The city will surely let the good times roll again.

THE SAFFIR-SIMPSON SCALE

The intensity of hurricanes is measured according to the Saffir-Simpson Scale. The determining factor is wind speed. Storm surges (see p122), which pose a particular threat for New Orleans, correlate to a storm's intensity. Katrina was a Category Five over the Gulf of Mexico and a Category Three by the time it reached New Orleans.

Tropical Storm Winds 39-73mph, storm surge less than 4ft

Category One Winds 74-95mph, storm surge 4-5ft

Category Two Winds 96-110mph, storm surge 6-8ft

Category Three Winds 111-130mph, storm surge 9-12ft

Category Four Winds 131-155mph, storm surge 13-18ft

Category Five Winds greater than 155mph, storm surge greater than 18ft

A HISTORY OF HURRICANES

For New Orleans, every hurricane season appears to be another turn at the Wheel of Misfortune. To its fatalistic citizens, ever aware that the city's levee system would easily be overwhelmed by a major hurricane, it has always seemed to be a matter of time before the city would be laid to waste by a cataclysmic hurricane. Major hurricanes, of Category Three strength or worse, hit the Gulf Coast within 100 miles of New Orleans every 10 years on average. So far the city has been spared a house-flattening direct hit. However, New Orleans has survived many near misses and has endured hurricane-induced flooding on many occasions.

In September 1965 Hurricane Betsy became known as 'Billion Dollar Betsy' after setting a new high watermark for destruction costs. (The damage topped $1.4 billion.) Betsy's winds of 105mph created a storm surge that breached levees and flooded large parts of Gentilly and the Lower Ninth Ward.

In 1969 Hurricane Camille, a near miss for New Orleans, slammed the coast just 55 miles east of the city. Incredibly, Camille's storm surge, backed by 190mph winds, forced the Mississippi River to flow backwards as far north as New Orleans. But the river did not overtop its levees.

In 1992, Hurricane Andrew, a Category Five hurricane on the Saffir-Simpson Scale (see opposite), destroyed $44 billion worth of south Florida real estate. From there Andrew spun through the Gulf and up toward Louisiana, but it had already weakened to a Category Three hurricane and swung to the west of New Orleans.

Hurricane Ivan, the strongest Atlantic cyclone of 2004, followed an extraordinary looping path and struck the Gulf Coast twice after inflicting most of its wrath on the island of Granada. Ivan was a major hurricane as it hit the Alabama coast, then it crossed the Atlantic seaboard and doubled back down to the Gulf before making landfall in Louisiana. It had downgraded considerably to tropical-storm levels by that time.

Hurricane Katrina in the Gulf of Mexico

In recent years there has been a disturbing increase of strong hurricanes on the Gulf. The 2005 season saw more storms, and stronger storms, than any year previously. Four hurricanes in 2004–5 made the top-10 list of strongest tropical cyclones in recorded history. Three of these – Wilma, Rita and Katrina – occurred in a three-month period. Katrina and Rita, occurring less than a month apart, both struck Louisiana. It is believed that rising temperatures of the ocean, brought about by global warming, has caused this intensification of Atlantic storms. If so, the trend can be expected to continue and possibly worsen.

THE GATHERING STORM

Hurricane Katrina developed from a tropical depression first spotted over the Bahamas on August 23, 2005. On the following day the system intensified into a tropical storm, at which point it was named Katrina. On Thursday, August 25 it increased to a Category One hurricane as it made landfall in Florida. Katrina cut across the Everglades, north of Miami, and entered the Gulf of Mexico just six hours later. Seven people died in Florida as a result of Katrina's violent foray through the state.

The storm momentarily weakened, but back on water it rapidly regained strength and, alarmingly, doubled in size. By Saturday, August 27, Katrina had become a Category Three hurricane, and overnight it upgraded to Category Five. For a short time it was the strongest hurricane ever recorded in the Gulf, and it had set course for the mouth of the Mississippi River.

Computer models had already put New Orleans and Lake Pontchartrain directly in Katrina's path – a scenario that, if realized, would likely spell total devastation for the city. Governor Kathleen Blanco declared a state of emergency in Louisiana and requested federal assistance. President Bush was vacationing at his ranch in Crawford, TX, but the White House announced that the Federal Emergency Management Agency (FEMA) had been authorized to 'alleviate the impacts' of Katrina.

Early Sunday morning a strong sense of urgency managed to come through in a dryly worded National Weather Service advisory that now described Katrina as a 'potentially catastrophic Category Five hurricane.' People living on the Gulf Coast were advised to 'protect life and property' as quickly as possible.

Two hours later, Mayor Ray Nagin ordered an unprecedented mandatory evacuation of the city, warning that Katrina's storm surge would likely 'topple' the city's levee system. For those unable to leave the city, Nagin said, the Louisiana Superdome would be set up as a refuge of 'last resort.'

SCOURGE OF THE STORM SURGE

Hurricanes represent a double threat for coastal communities. While intense winds wreak havoc on roofs, trees and power lines, a surging sea pounds the coast with devastating waves and flows up rivers and channels to flood inland areas. On rare occasions, storm surges caused by particularly intense hurricanes can reach heights of 20ft to 30ft.

Wind causes a storm surge by pushing down on the sea and creating currents that move ahead of the storm's eye. As these currents travel from deep water onto the continental shelf the water is forced up. On the coast, waves generally rise gradually, peaking within a few hours and subsiding to normal levels within six to 12 hours. These surging waves pound the coast incessantly and barrier islands can disappear altogether. The rising sea seeks any available path. Narrow rivers and channels can have a funnel effect, forcing water levels even higher.

New Orleans is not on the coast, but numerous waterways run from the city through the flat terrain of southern Louisiana to the Gulf of Mexico. Hurricanes can push water into Lake Pontchartrain, which is an estuary at the city's northern edge, and up man-made channels such as the Mississippi River Gulf Outlet. Even the river itself can surge during a hurricane. Since most of New Orleans is below sea level and surrounded by water, the city is especially vulnerable to floods. Canals run throughout the city to divert incoming water away. Floodwalls and levees protecting the city before Hurricane Katrina struck were designed to contain 14ft of surge – sufficient for your average Category Three hurricane. It had long been feared that a stronger hurricane would flood New Orleans.

Katrina's storm surge was measured at about 11ft in New Orleans, but the city's floodwalls failed to withstand the pressure. On the Mississippi Coast, where Katrina hit directly, waves of almost 30ft were reported.

RIDING IT OUT

About 80% of New Orleans' population left town before Hurricane Katrina hit, which is seen as a better-than-average evacuation. Katrina, which was a Category Five hurricane over the Gulf of Mexico, was taken seriously by a great majority of the city's residents. Normally, far more people choose to ignore hurricane alerts and usually don't regret riding out the storm. False alarms are far more common than direct hits. When a hurricane swings wide of the city you might expect intense winds, fallen trees and power outages. These are inconveniences many are willing to put up with.

Hurricane parties had become a tradition in New Orleans. People would hunker down in their homes with candles, wine and beer. When the winds came, adventurous types would even go outside and grab onto a tree or a pole to see what it felt like to have the air lift their feet off the ground. Some bars would stay open during storms. Usually, the storm would subside within a few hours and life would soon return to normal. This tradition, no doubt, will not be as popular in post-Katrina New Orleans.

Leaving, on the other hand, is always a huge hassle. You have to board up the house, pack the car, and then sit in bumper-to-bumper traffic for hours, all the while feeling like a sitting duck if the traffic doesn't move out of the hurricane's path in time. You stay in a crummy motel somewhere in northern Louisiana, or crowd into relatives' homes, and after the storm passes you return home in more haltingly slow traffic. Of course, the devastation wrought by Katrina supports the better-safe-than-sorry view.

Some people, out of concern for looting, opt to stay home to protect their property. They prefer to accept the risks of staying over the risks of leaving. Unfortunately, Katrina's aftermath only confirmed the worst fears of these vigilante holdouts.

Throughout the city, from the Lower Ninth Ward to the Riverbend, many residents left the city, while others hunkered down with little more than a flashlight and a cooler filled with beer. Many hotels in the French Quarter were fully booked, and took in more guests as staff and families sought refuge there. Across the metropolitan area, roughly 200,000 people, including the poor, the elderly and tourists with no wheels of their own, were either unable to heed the warnings or, for reasons all their own, decided to ride out the storm.

Later in the day, the National Weather Service issued a dire warning for New Orleanians staying in the city. If a storm surge topped the levees, at least half the city's homes would be severely damaged, power outages would last weeks and a shortage of drinking water would 'make human suffering incredible by modern standards,' the report stated.

THE CYCLONE BLOWS THROUGH

On Sunday night, many storm watchers permitted themselves a cautious sigh of relief as the storm weakened and spiraled east of New Orleans. Katrina made landfall near the Mississippi–Louisiana state line just before midnight on the 28th. By sunup Monday morning, the storm had passed.

Still, Katrina wreaked havoc on New Orleans. Throughout the city shingles had been sheared from roofs, windows had been shattered and massive oak trees were literally pulled out of the ground by their roots. Part of the roof was pealed off the Superdome, where up to 20,000 people had taken refuge. Power lines and telephone poles lay in tangled heaps and debris was scattered over the city's streets. Eight to 10in of rain fell unrelentingly, backing up the sewer system and flooding lawns and streets.

Still, it appeared the city had been spared the worst. Katrina had not been the dreaded 'nightmare scenario' of a direct hit. The brunt of the storm's force had slammed into the Mississippi coast, where entire towns were simply obliterated by winds far exceeding 100mph and by lurching 30ft waves that struck coastal communities with the impact of tsunamis.

The Louisiana National Guard announced it had received hundreds of reports of levees being topped in New Orleans, but the National Guard was unable to confirm these reports. In reality the water had risen close to 11ft high. The city's levee system had been designed to withstand up to 14ft of water. Water poured from the lake into the city's canals and wind-blown swells may have splashed over the tops, but not enough to cause serious flooding. The heavy rain may have caused some of the city's lowest areas to flood by a few inches.

However, surging waters applied unrelenting pressure in all directions, seeking out weak spots in the floodwalls. Early Monday morning they found what they were looking for.

LEVEE FAILURE

The news gradually came out that floodwalls along the 17th St Canal had failed and that water was pouring into the city at a steady rate. Residents in the Lakeview neighborhood, alongside which the 17th St Canal runs, saw water rising about 3in every 20 minutes. The water rose slowly, as pumps in the canal continued to siphon water away from the breach, but the breach widened and soon the pumps were overmatched.

In the Lower Ninth Ward, large concrete sections of floodwall lining the Industrial Canal gave way one by one. Crushing waves tumbled into the neighborhood, lifting houses off their foundations and battering them about like unmoored boats. The breach widened several hundred feet, exposing five or six city blocks to instant flooding. The water spread out from there and kept rising. Residents had little time to crawl upstairs into attics, and those who made it that far had to hammer their way through their roofs. Some people didn't have hammers; many homes were completely submerged.

The Mississippi River Gulf Outlet breached its levees in several places, flooding New Orleans East and St Bernard Parish. Later in the day, another breach occurred along the London Ave Canal in the Filmore, just east of City Park. However, in a triumph for the Army Corps of Engineers, the Mississippi River did not breach its levees.

The storm had moved north and the sky began to clear. Yet water continued to rise and spread throughout the city all that day. Water flowed in great currents throughout the city's lowlands, the entire 'bowl' of the city that is below sea level. It flooded City Park. The wealthy neighborhoods to either side of the park, from Lakeview to Gentilly Terrace, were in water up to the eves of one-story houses. Gentilly Terrace was under water. St Roch, the Seventh Ward and much of the Tremé were flooded several feet. Mid-City and Gert Town were inundated. The Lower Ninth Ward was an underwater ruin. In all, 80% of the city had reverted to a semitoxic swamp.

The only good news was that the oldest parts of the city – the neighborhoods on the high ground nearest the river – were spared. The water miraculously stopped rising at Rampart St, just outside the French Quarter. A few inches lapped St Claude Ave, along the edge of the Marigny and Bywater. Esplanade Ave, laid atop a narrow ridge leading from the Quarter to Metairie, had not been flooded. Most of the Central Business District looked fine. All

Inner Harbor Navigational Canal Levee breaks

of Uptown, the Garden District, the Lower Garden District and the Riverbend were high and dry.

The *Times-Picayune* had reporters on the ground and by afternoon was posting periodic updates on its website. By evening, the paper seemed to have a grasp on the magnitude of the catastrophe as its reporters communicated from the city's flood zones. In Baton Rouge, FEMA chief Michael Brown belatedly asked his boss, Homeland Security Secretary Michael Chertoff, to send medical and emergency response employees to New Orleans. Governor Blanco was requesting help from President Bush. Memos circulated the White House about the breached levees. Bush, meanwhile, spent the day appearing at photo ops around the country. The President met with Secretary Chertoff early in the day to discuss unrelated issues. Chertoff said he went to sleep Monday night still unaware that New Orleans was flooding.

As Chertoff tucked himself in bed, a *Times-Pic* reporter noted that, on the lakeside of town, the croaking of frogs was 'deafening.' By all indications, nature was reclaiming a major American city. More than a hundred thousand people were trapped in the city, and thousands were dying. And water kept flowing in.

WHY THE LEVEES BROKE

New Orleans' levee system was supposedly designed to withstand a storm of Katrina's magnitude, and yet the city was devastated by floods that covered some 80% of the city. In the worst-hit parts of town, single-story homes were completely submerged as Lake Pontchartrain poured through floodwalls that were supposed to have protected New Orleans.

The engineers who inspected the breach sites concluded that the levee system failed due to design flaws. Floodwalls along the 17th St, London Ave and Industrial canals were not overtopped by rising waters. They were undermined by weak underlying soil that shifted beneath the concrete walls. The surging waters passing through these canals had added scouring power, and the increased volume and weight added tremendous pressure on the floodwalls. As the earthen foundations gave way, the walls broke down.

AN APPALLING SCENE

The White House's nonresponse would mystify the nation all week, culminating with a Thursday-night radio appearance by Mayor Ray Nagin, who urged Bush and crew to 'get off your asses and do something…let's fix the biggest goddamn crisis in the history of this country.' By that time, the situation in New Orleans had devolved into chaos, death and lawlessness.

Engineers tried to stop the incoming waters by dropping 3000lb sandbags from helicopters onto the levee breaches, to no avail. A foul stench filled the city as water filled streets and houses, bringing with it silt, chemicals, gasoline and sewage. Poisonous snakes swam down residential streets. Bloated human bodies floated in the muck. People climbed trees to get above the deluge. Others congregated on the elevated I-10 and I-610 freeways. Under clear skies the temperature rose to the usual steaminess of late August.

Initially 500 police officers did not report for duty (two, it turned out, had committed suicide), leaving a depleted force to deal with increasingly angry citizens badly needing help. The Louisiana National Guard was also at less than full force, with most of its troops deployed to Iraq. Nevertheless, the search-and-rescue effort had begun. Fleets of boats, piloted by firefighters, police, Coast Guards and sport fishers dispersed throughout the flooded streets of the city looking for stranded survivors. People found in attics and balconies, and on rooftops were taken to the nearest high ground or to the Superdome, where they were simply dropped off with the vague hope that they would be transported from there to better facilities. Thousands of people were missing, including legendary R&B musician Fats Domino who for several days was feared dead. The living had clear priority over the dead, as Mayor Nagin indecorously noted: 'We're not even dealing with dead bodies. They're just pushing them on the side.'

Fires broke out around town, some caused by arson. With fire trucks unable to reach the fires, entire houses – in some cases several adjacent houses – simply burned to the ground.

CHOICE WORDS

As disaster turned into catastrophe in New Orleans, politicians far and wide groped for words. Some had poignant things to say, while most simply vented frustration or put their feet in their mouths. We're concerned primarily with the latter categories here.

- 'This is, to put it mildly, the big one, I think.' – FEMA Chief Michael Brown in a briefing to President Bush.
- 'We don't ask them to pack up in 24 hours unless it's a real emergency.' – Michael Chertoff, Secretary of the Department of Homeland Security, explaining the slow arrival of military personnel to New Orleans.
- 'There's a lot of boats and choppers headed that way. Boats and choppers headed that way. It just takes a while to float 'em!" President George Bush, on ABC's Good Morning America.
- 'Don't tell me 40,000 people are coming here. They're not here. It's too doggone late.' – Mayor Ray Nagin, on WWL-AM radio in New Orleans.
- 'This is a national emergency. This is a national disgrace.' Terry Ebbert, head of New Orleans' Emergency Operations.
- 'Get people to higher ground and have the feds and the state airlift supplies to them – that was the plan, man.' – Ray Nagin.

Looters ran rampant while law enforcement officials were preoccupied with getting people to dry land. Most homes and shops were unprotected. Pharmacies were raided for prescription drugs; electronics stores and clothing stores were ransacked. A huge Wal-Mart store was relieved of its entire stock of firearms. 'Gangs of armed men' roamed the city, one official reported. Another claimed the French Quarter was 'under attack.' Some of these crimes occurred in full view of police, who were preoccupied with getting hurricane victims to dry ground. People carted stolen goods in garbage cans and on inflatable mattresses. Dozens of carjackings, murders and rapes were witnessed, though not confirmed. Rumors, some horribly exaggerated, swirled about the level of violence in the city.

Some of the looting, however, was legitimate, considering the circumstances. Too many people were stuck in the city with too little food and water, while stores and restaurants were fully stocked and abandoned, with food likely to rot in refrigerators that no longer had power.

Louis Armstrong Airport was converted into a triage center, with rows of people on stretchers and wheelchairs filling the waiting rooms.

In the Superdome, where the number of refugees rose as high as 25,000, food and water ran out, electricity was cut off and the uneasy crowd waited in darkness with no air or working toilets. Babies had no diapers and the infirm were in need of medicine. Fights broke out and fires flared in trash receptacles. Hundreds of buses had been promised to take people out of the city, but were slow to come.

When emergency vehicles approached the Superdome, they encountered an unruly and hostile crowd. Military helicopters were shot at while trying to airlift sick people from the dome's parking lot.

Thousands of people drifted over to the Convention Center hoping to catch buses that never showed up. It had become an ad-hoc refugee center, with little to offer the people who waited there. Food and water drops inevitably caused hoards to fight it out over insufficient supplies. Doctors were frightened off by rushing crowds. Corpses sagged in wheelchairs and sprawled on the sidewalk, no longer drawing the attention of the crowds that milled around them. The police department reported sending 88 police officers who were 'beaten back by an angry mob.'

For three hideous days the unruly situation in New Orleans seemed only to intensify. TV cameras were able to get in and cover appalling scenes for the world to see.

Not until Thursday – the fourth day after the floods began – did buses begin to arrive at the Superdome and the Convention Center. FEMA chief Michael Brown said he hadn't been aware of the crowds at the Convention Center until Thursday, even though it had been in the news all week.

Delirious and aggressive crowds fought to get on each bus and were eventually carried out of the city, mostly to refugee centers such as the Astrodome in Houston, where cots and food awaited. On Thursday and Friday some 28,000 National Guard Troops arrived from around the country to restore order and to help evacuate the city. New Orleans was, for the time being, uninhabitable.

GEORGE TO THE RESCUE

On Friday morning, as he flew aboard Air Force One to make his first visit in New Orleans, President Bush watched a DVD of newscasts from the week. White House aides made the DVD for the President because they felt the horrific reality of the situation hadn't sunk in yet. However, the president had suffered an eight-point drop in his approval rating in less than a week.

In New Orleans, Bush toured the devastated area with an army of firefighters standing behind him. TV crews followed the commander in chief as he made an appearance at the sight of the 17th St Canal breach. Some said the workers and machinery repairing the floodwalls at the time were part of an orchestrated photo op to create the illusion that everything was under control in New Orleans. Senator Mary Landrieu of Louisiana said the crews disappeared after the president and the media left the scene.

Bush's appearance followed a week of far more compelling news stories. For days the media had broadcast images of unprecedented desperation in an American city. Repeatedly, New Orleanians who stopped to talk before TV cameras shook their heads and said they'd lost everything, didn't know if their families were safe, had no idea where they'd go or how they would pull their lives together. The nation had helplessly watched the ugly scenes as civilization broke down in New Orleans. The question on everyone's mind was, 'How could this be happening in this country?'

Perhaps most disturbing was that almost all of the people trapped in New Orleans were black. It seemed stark evidence of deep-seeded problems in the country that went far deeper than the political bungling and disorganized response that, on the surface, defined this crisis. The poverty and vulnerability of blacks in New Orleans was on full view for the world to see.

In truth, thousands of whites lost everything as well. The first neighborhoods to be washed out by the 17th St Canal breach were predominantly white. The floodwaters merely sought lower ground, not caring who lived on that ground. But, as Katrina highlighted for the world to see, in New Orleans the most flood-prone areas are generally inhabited by the poorest people, and the poorest people are predominantly black. Relatively few whites seemed to resort to taking refuge in the Superdome or at the Convention Center – even taking into account New Orleans' pre-Katrina population was about 30% white. TV audiences could observe this on the news and draw their own conclusions about the apparent indifference of the nation's leaders.

Comparisons to the 9/11 tragedy appeared to be on many people's lips, but seemed mostly intended to rouse a national response, as the attack on the World Trade Center had

CONSPIRACY THEORY

Wherever there's a levee breach, there's a conspiracy theory right behind it. The flooding of the Lower Ninth Ward was no different. Not long after the neighborhood was virtually smashed to bits by crushing waves, the rumors ran rampant. Conspiracy theorists, aided by online bloggers, suggested the walls lining the Lower Ninth Ward side of the Industrial Canal had been dynamited by city leaders intent on protecting wealthier neighborhoods. Take a look at a map and it's plain to see that had the other side of the canal breached, the French Quarter may well have suffered devastating floods. You can't underestimate the fat cats of any era.

The idea took root easily because it had many precedents. With levees, as soon as one side is breached, the pressure instantly subsides on the other side. Up and down the Mississippi River, farmers and townsfolk have always had to keep armed vigil on their levees, watching for dynamiters from the other side. And, of course, there were also the well-known events of 1927. That year, as much of the Mississippi River overtopped its levees, local bankers and politicians evacuated the poor residents of St Bernard Parish and blew the levee there in order to spare New Orleans. It was a case in which no conspiracy theories were needed – the power brokers simply did their dastardly deed in the open, sanctioned by the government.

But no incriminating evidence has turned up in the Ninth Ward. Some ear-witnesses claim to have heard an explosion just as their homes were overwhelmed by the floods. Could have been dynamite. Or, more likely, just the sound of a huge concrete wall cracking open with 12ft of water gushing through it, turning houses into driftwood in a single blow.

ACCOUNTABILITY TIME

The political finger-pointing that followed Hurricane Katrina only emphasized that Katrina was a natural disaster made worse by human error. Nothing can be done to prevent a hurricane, but the effects of Katrina were magnified by levee failures and poor emergency response. As New Orleans struggled to get back some semblance of normalcy, assessment of the disaster showed flaws at all levels of government.

- Concrete floodwalls, built atop earthen levees, failed not because the water overtopped them, but due to design flaws. The Army Corps of Engineers was responsible for designing, building and maintaining the levees and floodwalls.
- In 2003 New Orleans received a $7 million grant to establish effective emergency communications systems, but the money seemingly vanished. Communication in the city was almost completely shut down after Katrina, making it impossible for police, firefighters and medics to run a coordinated response.
- Mayor Ray Nagin didn't call for his mandatory evacuation until the morning of August 28, less than 18 hours before the storm reached New Orleans.
- No plan was in place to provide public transport out of the city for people who lacked cars.
- The Superdome was established as a 'refuge of last resort' for those unable to leave the city, but food, water and medical supplies were not sufficient for the number of people who stayed there or the length of time they stayed.
- Governor Kathleen Blanco tried to get help from the White House, but she didn't specify exactly what Louisiana needed from the federal government until the fourth day of flooding.
- FEMA Director Michael Brown was indecisive and ineffective in getting available support in place after the storm. FEMA promised buses to expedite the evacuation of the flooded city, but it took most of the week for buses to materialize.
- Brown reported directly to Michael Chertoff, Secretary of the Department of Homeland Security, but the two failed to communicate during the crisis. Chertoff seemed thoroughly out of touch as he publicly downplayed the extent of the disaster.
- President George Bush's leadership style has always been top-down. An effective federal response needed to come from him, particularly since Brown and Chertoff, his appointees, were ill-suited to their jobs. Troops and federal emergency support arrived on Bush's orders, but too late to prevent a week of agony and tragedy in New Orleans.

done for New York. Similar comparisons to the chaos in Baghdad were more apt in reflecting the breadth of suffering and the complete breakdown of law and order. The difference, for better or worse, was that Baghdad had US troops on the ground.

MILITARIZED ZONE

On Friday and Saturday, the ravaged city abruptly turned into a militarized zone. The city's desolation seemed complete as army trucks and tanks filed into town and the remaining civilians were evacuated. National Guard troops went from house to house, finding people, pets and bodies. Over the ensuing weeks the floodwaters receded back into the lake and canals with the help of pumps. For over two weeks the city was clinically dead. Military checkpoints prevented civilians from returning to their homes. Feral cats and dogs roamed neighborhoods as the SPCA attempted to reign them in.

The displaced people of New Orleans – some took offense to the term 'refugee' – were transported to Houston, TX, Baton Rouge and Atlanta, GA. Many were given bus tickets to anywhere in the country. Within days Hurricane Katrina victims were scattered far and wide, from Seattle, WA, to Atlanta, and for half a year FEMA would be paying hotel bills across the USA. Many of these people had little hope of returning to New Orleans. Perhaps out of anger, many said they had no desire to live in New Orleans again.

Nagin targeted September 19th for the reopening of the city's least damaged neighborhoods and some residents returned. It was important that the city start showing some signs of life, to get the recovery underway. But Hurricane Rita spun into the Gulf of Mexico on September 20.

Rita quickly intensified into a Category Five hurricane as it reached the middle of the Gulf. It was stronger than Katrina and, like Katrina, appeared intent on making landfall just below New Orleans. Again the city was evacuated, this time completely. The city's collapsed floodwalls still lay in ruins and Rita's storm surge would surely flood the city.

Rita weakened and changed course, striking at the Louisiana–Texas border on September 24. The hurricane's 15ft storm surge reached New Orleans a day ahead of the storm's eye and, sure enough, much of the city was again under several feet of water. The aftermath was fairly straightforward this time, as there was no one in need of rescue.

The Louisiana coastal wetlands took a huge environmental hit, though. Rita and Katrina combined to wash away some 118 sq miles of wetlands. Salt water flowed into fresh water ecosystems, killing trees and fish. Some 2.3 million gallons of oil were spilled off the coast.

BABY STEPS BACK

Nagin reopened parts of the city once again on September 30. Residents along the high ground, including the French Quarter and Garden Districts, returned to a city eerily quiet and small. Most of New Orleans remained a devastated wasteland that went completely dark at night. Some neighborhoods, such as the Marigny, reopened but residents had no gas supply. The city, having marinated for weeks in the salty sludge, still smelled swampy. Troops and armed guards of police forces from around the country seemed to outnumber civilians, and a curfew kept people off the streets at night. For several months, the city's murder rate was zero. But suicides were up.

Some blocks looked perfectly normal except for a few fallen trees or the blackened hull of a home that had burned down. There was a jarring contrast between the part of New Orleans coming back to life, which some called the 'Island,' and the devastated 'Dead Zone.' On the Island, debris was being cleared away and businesses were reopening. Heading toward the lake along Canal St, a bathtub ring left by the floodwaters, was prominently visible on the sides of vacant buildings. The line started ankle high at Rampart St, just outside the French Quarter, and from there steadily rose toward the eves – 'rising' being a relative concept in a city with a convex, below-sea-level topography. The line itself was as straight as a carpenter's level. Debris piled up 10ft high or more on sidewalks and neutral grounds. Everywhere, trees and plants that hadn't blown over during the storms appeared to be in shock, leafless and nearly lifeless.

Not all was bleak and depressing. Dozens of restaurants reopened every week, despite being understaffed and having limited access to commonly used ingredients. Some restaurants, like Paul Prudhomme's K-Paul's, provided free meals for patrons cut off from their incomes. 'If you're hungry, we want to feed you,' Prudhomme announced. Such gestures engendered a sense of goodwill and common cause among the people who had returned to the city. People ate out more often than usual, partly because not everyone had gas at home and partly because it was the most optimistic thing they could do.

The population slowly increased – an estimated 60,000 people were sleeping in the city by November, and approximately twice that number were in town during weekdays. Tourists trickled into town on Saturday and Sunday. For months, every day saw reunions as neighbors and familiar faces returned, and people commiserated, passed on news and shared horror stories. Like never before, the city's populace seemed politically motivated as groups met in informal town-hall meetings to bat around ideas for the future of their city. The mayor formed a Bring New Orleans Back Commission to plan for the city's future, and residents wanted to make certain their voices would be heard.

Each week saw symbolic reopenings of local institutions, such Café du Monde, which reopened its doors in mid-October. A week later, the Voodoo Experience rock festival, with Nine Inch Nails headlining, took place as scheduled. Nobody argued these developments made things right, but they were seen to be big steps in the right direction.

So was the quick return of many of the city's artists and gallery owners. Along Julia St in the Warehouse District and up and down Magazine St galleries opened their doors and held openings. Live music performances, like Kermit Ruffins' weekly gig at Vaughan's, were charged events in which locals reconnected and, in a way, reaffirmed their faith in their city. People had weighty issues on their minds, but it was reassuring to see a return of New Orleans culture. It seemed New Orleanians – at least those who were back – were making a stand. Government services such as mail delivery and garbage pickup were irregular at best, but the city's spirit would survive.

After some deliberation, the city decided to plan a smaller Mardi Gras in February and Jazz Fest in April. Not going ahead with important events like these would amount to surrender. On December 31 New Orleans rang in the New Year with its longstanding tradition of dropping a gumbo pot from the Jackson Brewery in Jackson Sq. The crowd was smaller than usual, with very few tourists, but in the air was a sense that the city was turning the page, moving ahead into its uncertain future with its pride and love of life intact.

For the thousands of displaced New Orleanians, still in motels around the country, the future was much less certain. The New Year signified a passage of time with no clarification on when, or if, their neighborhoods would be cleaned up or rebuilt. A January second-line parade urged blacks back from Mississippi and Texas, and many returned to parade the streets of the Tremé. It was a statement of intent, that the community was still alive. But the parade ended in a shooting, casting a pall not only over the day but over the future.

WHAT THE FUTURE HOLDS

With parts of New Orleans recovering quickly from Hurricane Katrina, and vast tracks languishing long after the storms, New Orleans seemed poised to bring about positive changes, but was also at risk of losing an integral aspect of its unique character. As the mayor's Bring New Orleans Back Commission drafted plans for the city's future, and as local and national politicians haggled over how much money Washington ought to pitch in for the city's recovery, it seemed clear that the soul of the city was at stake.

Rebuilding the city was seen as an opportunity to address ongoing problems such as the high crime rate and the woeful school district. Some in the city seemed content to simply not rebuild the city's poorest, most crime-ridden neighborhoods. In late 2005 it wasn't lost on many that the city's crime problem had been transferred over to Houston, TX, where a huge portion of New Orleans' displaced residents were now living. Others proposed alternatives to the prison-block style housing that had previously been provided for low-income families. Mixed-income developments modeled on the River Garden area (p73) were offered as a better solution that would help draw the city's poorest residents out of a seemingly perpetual hopeless cycle.

It remains unclear just how things will play out. A key question is how many displaced New Orleanians will return to the city. A smaller New Orleans almost surely will mean a wealthier and, as some say, a 'whiter' city. A January 2006 poll suggested as many as 80% of the city's black displaced residents might never return. If so, the new New Orleans may not be the creative, multicultural stew that has nurtured so much art and, especially, music. But surely, as rebuilding begins, many will change their minds and return to their one-of-a-kind hometown.

Big factors determining which way the city's future will go are improved levees and time. Levees engineered to withstand greater storm surges will make it safer to live in the city and more affordable to insure homes. With the war in Iraq siphoning some $9 billion a month from the national treasury, the Bush Administration seemed reluctant to commit funding (estimated at over $30 billion) for an ambitious levee project on US soil. The longer it takes for rebuilding to get underway, the harder it will be for people who have relocated to pull up stakes again and reclaim their homes in New Orleans.

Early drafts of the Bring New Orleans Back Commission plans assumed a smaller population. The commission called for reducing the city's footprint, converting the most flood-prone neighborhoods into parkland, and introducing more bike paths and light-rail transit lines to help make New Orleans more environmentally sound. Meanwhile, a group representing low-income musicians took steps in early 2006 to ensure that an important segment of the population was re-established. The resulting Musicians' Village in the Upper Ninth Ward will be finished before the rest of the city sees concerted rebuilding efforts. Possibly other independent community groups will follow suit.

Sights

Itineraries 133
Organized Tours 134

French Quarter 135
Jackson Square 136
French Market 138
Royal Street 138
Elsewhere in the French Quarter 139
Mississippi River 144

Tremé District 145

Faubourg Marigny & Bywater 148

CBD & Warehouse District 150
CBD 151
Warehouse District 151

Lower Garden District 155

Garden District 156
Irish Channel 157

Uptown & Riverbend 157

Esplanade Ridge & Bayou St John 160
Bayou St John 160

City Park & Around 161

Sights

New Orleans is a city of small and interesting neighborhoods that are worth exploring even if you don't have too definite an idea of what you're looking for. Just about everything most travelers are interested in seeing can be found on the high ground that did not flood after Hurricane Katrina. The French Quarter, the Marigny, the Warehouse District and the entire length of Magazine St, through the Lower Garden District to Uptown, were spared. In these parts of town, great little museums, landmark buildings and oak-shaded medians turn up amid quirky shops and art galleries, and intimate cafés and bars.

Wrought-iron balconies, French Quarter

The French Quarter, or Vieux Carré (voo car-*ray*), is the original city as planned by the French in the early 18th century. This is still where most of the fun happens in New Orleans, especially for tourists. The Quarter and the Creole suburbs (Marigny, Tremé and Bywater) formed the heart of Creole New Orleans, downriver from Canal St. The old American sector, now the Central Business District, is immediately upriver from Canal St.

Upriver from the town square, riverside plantations extended from the levee toward the lake in long, narrow, rectangular plots. Their typical depth of 40 arpents (one arpent is just under an acre) roughly coincides with Claiborne Ave, which paralleled the river, while St Charles Ave was intended to split the properties at the 20-arpent line. Anglo Americans subsequently subdivided and settled this area, generally referred to as Uptown.

A subtle ridge of high ground near Bayou St John, that once served as an early portage route between the river and the lake, attracted early plantation houses and other substantial homes, and became known as Esplanade Ridge. Other bayou ridges include Metairie (*met-ar-ee*) and Gentilly. These areas also mostly avoided flooding after Hurricane Katrina.

WHERE ARE YOU AT?

The Mississippi River serves as a false compass in New Orleans. While it's true that the river flows from north to south, it curves *under* New Orleans and thus is actually flowing from west to east where it passes the French Quarter. So, when locals give directions, they rarely indicate north/south/east/west.

Directions, upriver or downriver, are relative to the water flow, which bends to all points of the compass; for example: 'The Convention Center is upriver from (or above) the French Quarter,' even though a compass would show that the Convention Center is south-southwest.

In addition, the river and Lake Ponchartrain serve as landmarks in 'riverside' or 'lakeside' directions: 'You'll find Louis Armstrong Park on the lakeside of the French Quarter – head toward the lake and you'll find it,' and 'Preservation Hall is on St Peter St toward the river from Bourbon St.'

Canal St divides uptown from downtown. However, to add confusion, a large part of the city, from the Garden District to the Riverbend, is commonly referred to as Uptown. Because of the vagaries of the river, Uptown streets are labeled 'south' and downtown streets are 'north.'

ITINERARIES

One Day

Our sympathies if you have just one day in New Orleans. We'll assume this means a full 24 hours and that you're not going to waste any time on sleep. Start at the **Cafe du Monde** (p178) for café au lait and beignets. Stroll through beautiful **Jackson Square** (p136), down Pirates Alley and along **Royal Street** (p138) to take in the French Quarter's historic architecture. Spend an hour at the **Historic New Orleans Collection** (p139) to see interesting exhibits and art of the old city. Have a cup of gumbo, an oily muffaletta and an Abita ale at **Napoleon House** (p201). Hop in a cab to the **Garden District** (p168) for an afternoon stroll. Check out the historic houses and do some shopping and gallery hopping on Magazine St. Have a cocktail on the front porch of the **Columns Hotel** (p205), then treat yourself to superb regional cuisine at **Dick & Jenny's** (p192), **Brigsten's** (p193) or **Commander's Palace** (p190). Taxi back to the lower Quarter for some bar hopping. Hit any of the dives on Decatur St, be sure to drop in to see what's going on at **Oswald's Speakeasy** (p202) and mosey on down to Frenchmen St in the Faubourg Marigny for some bar and club hopping. If you have nowhere to lay your head, you can always double back to Cafe du Monde for more coffee.

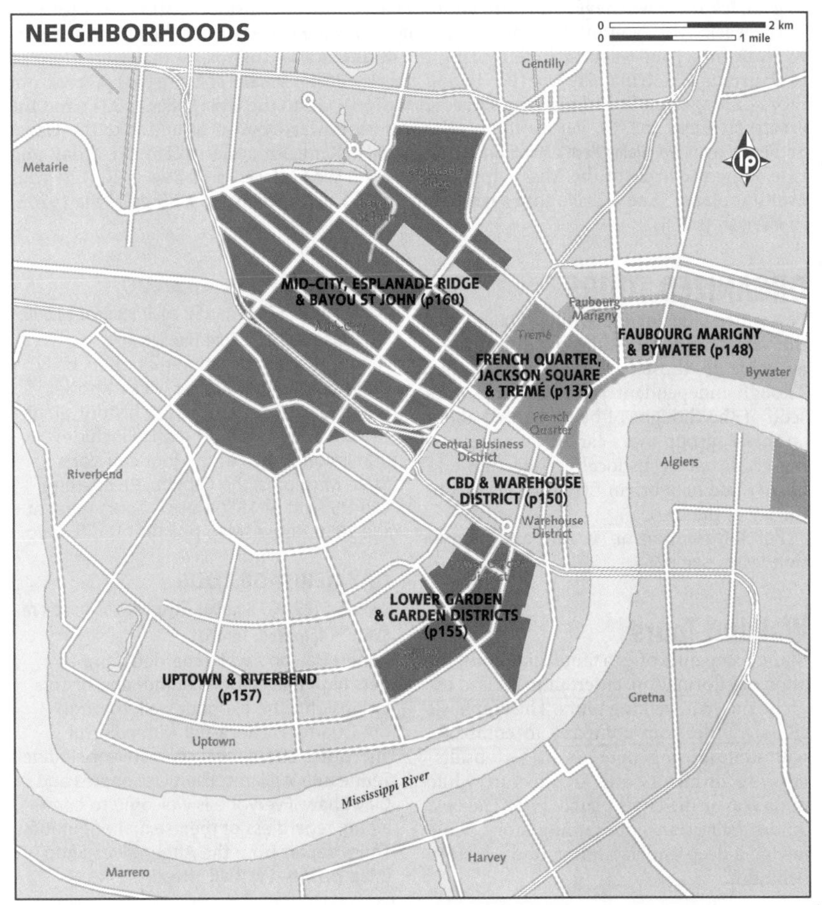

Three Days

Check into a hotel in the lower Quarter and make it your mission to really familiarize yourself with this historic district. Make a daily excursion to another part of town. Day one can be a little less intense than what's spelled out for the one-day itinerary. Day two might include a visit to the Warehouse District art galleries and museums, and lunch at **Mothers** (p187). Visit the **Ogden Museum of Southern Art** (p155) and the **Confederate Museum** (p152), or admire the WWII exhibits at the **National World War II Museum** (p154). Hop aboard the St Charles Ave Streetcar, if its running, for a quick ride back to the French Quarter. Have dinner at a laid-back dive, such as **Coop's** (p179) or **Fiorella's** (p180) then swing by **Donna's Bar & Grill** (p206) for live music. On day three check out **St Louis Cemetery No 1** (p147) in the morning. Have a leisurely lunch at **Galatoire's** (p182), then take a tour of **Gallier House Museum** (p139) to see what life was like in the Creole days or check out the **Historic Voodoo Museum** (p140). Have your last supper in a contemporary restaurant.

One Week

A week provides ample time to become a regular customer in a favored café or bar with enough room for a two- or three-day excursion out of town. You'll also have more time to do the things you want to do in the French Quarter, so you won't feel the constant pull to get back there whenever you're in another part of town. Consider renting a car for part of the week. Also, you might consider staying somewhere else besides the Quarter. Sights to work into your week include touring the **devastated areas** (opposite) that were flooded by Hurricane Katrina, **City Park** (p161) and the **New Orleans Museum of Art** (p163). Check out more of Magazine St and visit the **Audubon Zoo** (p158). Go to the **Green Market** (p231) and the **Bywater Art Market** (p230). Peruse the junk stores on Lower Decatur St and take the Canal St Ferry over to **Blaine Kern's Mardi Gras World** (p154). Rent a bicycle (p216) for a day and ride along the levee of the Mississippi. Include the **Mid-City Lanes Rock & Bowl** (p209) in your evening plans. Take a drive into **Cajun Country** (p257) or through the **Mississippi Delta** (p265) to **Memphis** (p268).

ORGANIZED TOURS

Few other cities in the United States offer the variety of worthwhile organized tours available to those visiting New Orleans. Though independent travelers sometimes scoff at the thought of being herded about en masse, group tours can be an entertaining crash course in local architecture and history and help orient first-time visitors to the lay of the land.

For information on swamp and plantation tours, see p253.

Walking Tours

Many companies offer a tantalizing combination of information, entertainment and exercise on their walking tours. The emphasis shifts a little from company to company, with some leaning more toward serious discussions of history and architecture while others favor the city's pliable lore. The best guides ballast an entertaining story while having a deep understanding of the history behind it.

FRIENDS OF THE CABILDO

☎ 523-3939; 523 St Ann St; adult/student $12/10; ⏲ tours 10am & 1:30pm Thu-Sun

A nonprofit organization that offers daily two-hour French Quarter walks. Knowledgeable guides emphasize history, architecture and folklore. The price includes admission to two of the four Louisiana State Museums: the Cabildo, Presbytère, Old US Mint or 1850 House. Tours meet at the 1850 House (Map pp310–11) gift shop.

GAY HERITAGE TOUR

☎ 945-6789; 909 Bourbon St; groups of 4 or more $20; ⏲ 4pm Wed, 1pm Sat

Robert Batson's well-regarded company gets high marks for its humor and historical insight. The 2½-hour walk through the Quarter is chock-full with colorful anecdotes about local characters including Tennessee Williams, Ellen DeGeneres and Clay Shaw. Everyone is welcome to come along, regardless of their sexual orientation. Tours depart from the Alternatives Shop (Map pp310–11). Call ahead.

JEAN LAFITTE NATIONAL HISTORIC PARK

☎ 589-2636; nolabienville@aol.com; 419 Decatur St; tours free; 9:30am

Free walks of the French Quarter led by park rangers. The tours are limited to 30 people and are very popular. To get tickets, you must arrive at the park office (Map pp310–11) at 9am, and each person must show up for their own ticket.

HISTORIC NEW ORLEANS TOURS

☎ 947-2120; www.tourneworleans.com; adult/child $15/7; 10am daily, 1pm Mon-Sat

Author Robert Florence's company runs a range of quality tours through the French Quarter, the Garden District and St Louis Cemetery No 1. The Cemetery-Voodoo tour is a classy and informative jaunt into some of New Orleans' more mysterious realms, and includes a visit to Priestess Miriam's Voodoo Spiritual Temple (p143) – it's an exhilarating side of New Orleans that few visitors dare to see.

Carriage Rides

A leisurely carriage ride through the French Quarter can make you wonder why cars ever replaced horses. Tour guides offering carriage rides through the French Quarter are certified by the city – which means that they at least have a modest understanding of the Quarter's history. However, be aware that Mark Twain's admonition, 'Get your facts first, then you can distort them all you please,' certainly applies to the carriage-guide business. Historical embellishment is commonplace.

ROYAL CARRIAGES

☎ 943-8820; www.neworleanscarriages.com; 30-min tour for up to 4 people $50; 8:30am-midnight

Carriages depart day and night from Jackson Sq. You will not be disappointed if you consider the tours to be fun orientation rides.

Bus Tours

Bus tours all too frequently represent the cheesiest way for tourists to experience a city, which is why we would not ordinarily recommend any for New Orleans. However, this time around we will make one exception…

GRAY LINE KATRINA TOUR

☎ 569-1401, 800-535-7786; www.graylineneworleans.com; adult/child $35/28; 9am & 1pm

The idea of a Gray Line bus tour of neighborhoods devastated by Hurricane Katrina might sound too similar to rubbernecking at a wreck on the highway. But if you feel it's important to witness the destruction, and you lack a friend to drive you around the vast area that was flooded, then you should hop aboard and do so guilt-free. Most of the people of New Orleans would prefer that visitors to the city see the devastated areas rather than pretend nothing happened here in the summer of 2005. While it's true that Gray Line hopes to profit from the tours, the company's approach has been tasteful and sensitive, rather than sensational. In fact, at the time of writing, if the tour had a weakness it would be that it does not include the most shocking wreckage of the Lower Ninth Ward. The bus passes through the vast lakeside neighborhoods, and some of the tour guides actually hail from the ruins. While it is guaranteed to take years for New Orleans to clean up the Katrina mess, the devastation is likely to be less visible as time goes by – ask locals if this tour is still worth taking before dropping $35.

FRENCH QUARTER

Eating p178, Shopping p223, Sleeping p238

Locals call it the Vieux Carré, or 'Old Quarter,' but the French Quarter is much more than a historic district. It is the cultural and geographic focal point of New Orleans. Though the Quarter is very touristy, the locals have not completely surrendered it to out-of-town visitors. Contrary to the neighborhood's ribald Bourbon St image, you are never more than two or three blocks from a quiet residential street with a solitary local bar, a burgeoning flower shop or a bookstore guarded by a docile dog.

There is no denying the Quarter's appeal. It's walkable, picturesque, always busy and filled with an extraordinary range of great restaurants, bars, nightclubs, courtyard cafés, art galleries, rummage shops and quirky museums. And, of course, the Quarter has row upon row of 19th-century Creole townhouses and charming cottages, and Victorian-era shotgun houses. The architectural splendor is seen in details such as ornate cast-iron balconies, wooden shutters, fan lights and courtyards. A visitor can walk these blocks time and time again and on each occasion notice something new that had never caught their eye before.

At its heart is Jackson Sq, a public garden defined by striking architectural symmetry and the daily cultural chaos that surrounds it. It's possible to spend the better part of a day here acquainting yourself with New Orleans' history at the four Louisiana State Museums, and catching the ever-changing street scene from a sidewalk bench.

The Quarter's grid street plan was laid out in 1722 by engineer Adrien de Pauger. For many decades it *was* New Orleans – a tiny settlement on the river, surrounded by swamps and plantations. A canal and portage linked it to the Bayou St John. After the Louisiana Purchase prompted an influx of Anglo Americans, the French Quarter remained the heart of the Creole city, while the Americans settled Uptown.

By the early 20th century, the Quarter had deteriorated into a run-down, densely populated, working-class neighborhood. In the 1930s wealthy residents such as the Williamses, whose home is now part of the Historic New Orleans Collection, began to restore some of the Quarter's old townhouses, spawning a preservation movement that ultimately saved the Quarter from demolition. At that time, the city purchased historic properties like the Pontalba Buildings overlooking Jackson Sq, and federal funding helped restore the French Market. The entire Vieux Carré was declared a historic district and most of its buildings acquired landmark status.

Since the 1930s, the population in the Quarter has plummeted from more than 12,000 to about 5000 today.

Orientation

The French Quarter is a compact grid of six blocks by 13. It's bounded by the Mississippi River levee, Canal St, Rampart St and Esplanade Ave. Jackson Sq, the heart of the old city, is perfectly centered on the riverside of the Quarter. The upper Quarter, nearest Canal St, is most touristy. Below Orleans Ave (which divides the quarter in half) things quiet down, and most of the buildings are private residences with the odd corner shop or guesthouse thrown in.

TRANSPORTATION

Bus Buses skirt the Quarter's periphery, but none go through the middle of the neighborhood. The 55 bus runs down Decatur St, through the Marigny and out to UNO on Lake Ponchartrain. The 5 bus runs on N Peters and through the Marigny and Bywater. The 11 bus runs from Canal St along the entire length of Magazine St, to Audubon Park. The 42 bus runs on Canal St through Mid-City all the way to City Park. The 88 bus runs on Rampart St and St Claude Ave to the Bywater.

Streetcar The 2 Riverfront streetcar edges the levee side of the French Quarter from Esplanade Ave (near the Faubourg Marigny) to the Convention Center (in the Warehouse District). When it's operating, the St Charles Ave streetcar runs from Canal St along St Charles Ave through the CBD, the Garden District and Uptown. The 45 streetcar runs on Canal St from the river through Mid-City (temporarily only as far as Crozat).

Ferry The Canal St Ferry crosses the Mississippi River to Algiers Point. It docks near the foot of Canal St.

Parking There is a large public parking lot at the Shops at Canal Place, where Canal St meets the levee. Metered parking is available on most streets, but pay close attention to restrictions (posted on signs). Street parking is easier in the lower Quarter.

JACKSON SQUARE

Jackson Sq is a traditional public square with a cathedral overlooking an impeccably landscaped open space. The square has a striking architectural symmetry that is rarely seen in the United States, where city planning is usually more free form. The identical, block-long Pontalba Buildings overlook the square, and the nearly identical Cabildo and Presbytère structures flank St Louis Cathedral, the square's centerpiece. Taken as a whole, with its surrounding architecture and concentration of artisans, fortune-tellers and entertainers who share the stone-paved walkway with pedestrian traffic, it's one of the country's finer public spaces.

The square was part of Adrien de Pauger's original city plans laid out in 1722, and it began its life as a military parade ground called Place d'Armes. Madame Micaëla Pontalba transformed the muddy grounds into beautiful groomed gardens and renamed the square to honor Andrew Jackson, who led the American forces in the Battle of New Orleans before serving two terms as the seventh president of the USA (1829–37).

In the middle of the park stands **Jackson monument** – Clark Mills' bronze equestrian statue of Jackson, which was unveiled in 1856. The inscription, 'The Union Must and Shall be Preserved,' was an added – and locally unwelcome – sentiment from General Benjamin Butler, the Yankee commander of occupying forces in 1862.

PRESBYTÈRE Map pp310-11

☎ 568-6968; 751 Chartres St; adult/senior & student $6/5, child under 12 free; 9am-5pm Tue-Sun

Although architect Gilberto Guillemard originally designed the Presbytère (1791) to be a rectory for the St Louis Cathedral, the building was never directly used by the church after it was completed in 1813. Instead, the cathedral administrators rented the building to the city for use as a courthouse before selling it to them in 1853. Ownership was transferred to the Louisiana State Museum in 1911.

The Presbytère has a permanent exhibit, called 'Mardi Gras: It's Carnival Time in New Orleans,' that is essential viewing for visitors wanting to learn a little bit more about Louisianan culture. The exhibit delves into all of the major topics with vibrant displays of masks and costumes, parade floats, Mardi Gras–Indian suits and historic photographs. Documentary videos and detailed signage help convey the meaning behind many of Mardi Gras' more complicated traditions.

ST LOUIS CATHEDRAL Map pp310-11

☎ 525-9585; donations accepted; 9am-5pm Mon-Sat, 1-5pm Sun

The architectural pearl of the French Quarter is the triple-spired Cathedral of St Louis, King of France. St Louis Cathedral was the focal point for the Catholic community of Creole New Orleans, and remains an important cultural landmark today. Intriguingly, voodoo queen Marie Laveau, who practiced a hybrid voodoo–Catholicism, worshiped here during the height of her influence in the mid-19th century. During the Christmas Eve midnight Mass the cathedral draws a large, standing-room-only crowd of worshipers.

In 1722 a hurricane destroyed the first of three churches built here by the St Louis Parish, established in 1720. Architect Don Gilberto Guillemard dedicated the present cathedral on Christmas Eve in 1794, only weeks after it was saved from a devastating fire by a combination of shifting winds and a firebreak provided by the empty lot where the original Cabildo had burned down six years earlier. Extensive remodeling from 1849 to 1851 was designed by French-trained architect JNB DePouilly. In 1850, the cathedral was designated as the metropolitan church of the Archdiocese of New Orleans. Pope Paul VI awarded it the rank of minor basilica in 1964.

Buried in the cathedral is its Spanish benefactor, Don Andrés Almonaster y Roxas, who also financed the Cabildo and the initial construction of the Presbytère – not bad for a minor official who arrived in New Orleans as a poor Spanish notary. He gained his wealth from rents after he acquired real estate facing the Place d'Armes. His daughter, Madame Pontalba, later built the Pontalba Buildings to complete Jackson Sq.

1850 HOUSE MUSEUM Map pp310-11

☎ 568-6968; 523 St Ann St; adult/senior & student $3/2, child under 12 free; 9am-5pm Tue-Sun

The 1850 House is one of the apartments in the lower Pontalba Building. Madame Micaëla Pontalba, daughter of Don Andrés Almonaster y Roxas, continued her father's improvements around Jackson Sq by building the long rows of red-brick apartments flanking the upper and lower portions of the square. She was also responsible for renaming the once-barren parade grounds, the Place d'Armes, after her friend Andrew Jackson. Initial plans for the apartments were drawn by the noted architect James Gallier Sr. In 1927, the lower Pontalba Building was bequeathed by William Ratcliffe Irby to the Louisiana State Museum, and three years later the city acquired the upper Pontalba Building, where Micaëla once lived.

Now, knowledgeable volunteers from the Friends of the Cabildo give tours of the apartment, which includes the central court and servants' quarters with period furnishings throughout. Innovations include the use of bricks imported from the East Coast, extended porches to create covered

HISTORIC HOUSE TOURS

New Orleans offers a nice array of fine old houses that are open for tours. The following list includes a few of the more significant homes. The two earliest homes on the list represent French-colonial city and plantation houses.

1850 House – lower Pontalba Buildings (p137)

Beauregard-Keyes House (opposite)

Gallier House (opposite)

Hermann-Grima House (p140)

Merieult House (opposite)

Pitot House (p161)

walkways, and the upstairs galleries, which have cast-iron railings in place of wrought iron. Repeated along the railings are the initials AP, signifying the union of the Almonaster and Pontalba wealth.

When guides are not available visitors can roam the house at their leisure.

CABILDO Map pp310-11

☎ 568-6968; 701 Chartres St; adult/senior & student $6/5, child under 12 free; 🕑 9am-5pm Tue-Sun

The first Cabildo was a single-story structure destroyed by the Good Friday fire of 1788. Reconstruction was delayed by the city's more pressing need for a prison, cathedral, and police and fire stations. It turned out to be fortuitous that architect Gilberto Guillemard, who was busy with the St Louis Cathedral, did not hurry the reconstruction. The December 1794 fire would have likely destroyed a new Cabildo and the almost completed cathedral as well. Tenants in the rebuilt Cabildo, dedicated in 1799, have included the Spanish Council (for which the building is named), the City Hall government from 1803 to 1853, the Louisiana Supreme Court from 1853 to 1910 and the Louisiana State Museum from 1911 to the present.

Three floors of exhibits emphasize the significance of New Orleans in a regional, national and even international context. It is a challenge to see it all in part of a day. You might try to survey the lower floor, paying attention to the pre-Columbian Native American artifacts and the colonial exhibits that most interest you. You can overlook Jackson Sq from the Sala Capitular (Spanish Council room) on the 2nd floor. This is where the Louisiana Purchase documents were signed, transferring the extensive territory from Napoleonic France to the US. Other displays depict the Battle of New Orleans, including the role of free blacks and members of the Choctaw tribe in Major General Andrew Jackson's force, which decisively defeated General Packenham's British troops in 1814. The 3rd-floor exhibits of racial and ethnic groups from the American period are among the most interesting, with artifacts and shocking depictions of African slaves next to Civil War military displays that show free people of color in support of the Confederacy.

FRENCH MARKET

For more than 200 years, New Orleanians have been trading goods on this spot (Map pp310–11) beside the river levee. Decatur St was originally called Rue du Quai, and then Rue de la Levée, before naval hero Stephen Decatur was honored by having the street named for him in 1870. The Spanish built the first meat-and-produce market here in 1791, but it was destroyed by hurricane and fire. In 1813, city-surveyor Jacques Tanesse designed a replacement market, the Halle des Boucheries (Meat Market), at 900 Decatur St. Adjacent to it, an open colonnade called the Vegetable Market (now anchored by Café du Monde) was designed in 1813.

During the 1930s the Works Progress Administration (WPA) extensively renovated – and in some respects, remodeled – the city-managed French Market from St Ann to Barracks Sts. The cupolas atop the old Meat Market were added at this point, and the sturdy colonnade that runs the length of the Market also dates from that period. Further remodeling and landscaping were done in the early 1970s.

In addition to Café du Monde (p178), the French Market is home to a produce market, a flea market and many permanent shops and vendors selling tourist curios and gifts; see p223 for more information.

ROYAL STREET

With block after block of high-end antique shops, galleries and potted ferns hanging from cast-iron balconies, Royal St is New Orleans' most elegant street. Royal changes in character as it stretches from Canal St to Esplanade Ave, becoming quieter and more residential at its lower end. Along the way, the street has courtyard cafés and gift shops that lure strollers in off the sidewalk.

GALLIER HOUSE MUSEUM Map pp310-11

☎ 525-5661; www.hgghh.org; 1118 Royal St; adult/senior $6/5, child under 8 free; tours hourly 10am-3pm Mon-Fri

New Orleans owes much of its architectural heritage to James Gallier Sr and James Gallier Jr, architects renowned for their Greek-revival designs. In 1857 Gallier Jr began work on this impressive French Quarter town house, incorporating numerous innovations, such as interior plumbing, skylights and ceiling vents, into the design. A cistern provided fresh water to the kitchen, which in turn provided hot water to the upstairs bath. It is carefully furnished with period pieces. There are also intact slave quarters out back – once you see these, you'll recognize them throughout the Quarter.

HISTORIC NEW ORLEANS COLLECTION Map pp310-11

☎ 523-4662; www.hnoc.org; 533 Royal St

The Historic New Orleans Collection offers tourists a fascinating history lesson. Housed in a complex of historic buildings, anchored by **Merieult House**, the museum has displayed private collections of art and historical documents that seem to have an equal pull on visitors, local researchers and foreign scholars.

The rotating exhibits of **Williams Gallery** (admission free; 10am-4:30pm Tue-Sat) provide visitors with an opportunity to gain an understanding of different aspects of local history. For example, one past exhibit featured historical photographs, videos and oral histories to document the enormous influence émigrés from St Domingue had in New Orleans at the beginning of the 19th century – the exhibit made the case that French Creole culture was given a much needed infusion at a time when the city was undergoing its initial transformation into an American city.

Upstairs, the **Merieult History Tour** offers a version of Louisiana's past that is meticulously researched. The handsome gallery displays are housed in the landmark Merieult House, built in 1792 (the building is a rare survivor of the 1794 fire). Showcased are the original transfer documents of the 1803 Louisiana Purchase. If the guide leaves something out, you can pick up a handy listing of each room's contents to find out more on your own. The tour is a bit fast paced, considering how much of the material here is worth closer inspection. See if your guide will pause now and then while you inspect the many early maps showing the city's evolution, or such disturbing items as an 1849 broadside advertising '24 Head of Slaves' (individual children for sale for $500 or entire families for $2400). Nevertheless, no better, short introduction to the history of the city is available.

In back, the 1889 **Williams Residence** is an almost overlooked part of the tour. The wealthy Williams family had eccentric taste, exemplified not only by their purchasing this townhouse in 1938, in what was then considered a dowdy neighborhood by the city's elite. The Williamses filled their home with art and furniture collected in their world travels, and from the look of things they entertained often. The tour is a peek back at an unusual time in the city's history. Tours are given Tuesday to Saturday at 10am, 11am, 2pm and 3pm. The cost is $4.

In 1996, the Historic New Orleans Collection moved its research facilities, the **Williams Research Center** (☎ 523-4662; 410 Chartres St; 10am-4:30pm Tue-Sat) to a beautifully refurbished police station. It really isn't of interest to the casual visitor, but if you have specific queries about almost any building in New Orleans the staff at this research center can help. The archives contain more than 300,000 images and a comprehensive block-by-block survey of the French Quarter. Ink pens are not permitted inside.

ELSEWHERE IN THE FRENCH QUARTER

BEAUREGARD-KEYES HOUSE

Map pp310-11

☎ 523-7257; 1113 Chartres St; tours adult/child $5/2

Greek-revival structures like Beauregard-Keyes House, built in 1826, are uncommon in the French Quarter. Confederate General Pierre Gustave Toutant Beauregard, a native of Louisiana, lived in this house for only 18 months. General Beauregard became an instant hero throughout the South when he commanded the first shots of the Civil War, at Fort Sumter in Charleston, South Carolina.

The house's other illustrious resident stayed far longer. Author Francis Parkinson Keyes lived here from 1942 until her death in 1970. Beginning in 1926, she became well known for her serialized travel correspondence in *Good Housekeeping*. She published 51 novels, including many that were set locally, such as *Crescent Carnival* (1942), the best-seller *Dinner at Antoine's* (1948) and *Steamboat Gothic* (1952). Her novel *Madame Castel's Lodger* (1962) is set in this house.

Period pieces decorate the house, while Keyes' doll and ceramic collections occupy the back cottage. Tours operate on the hour from 10am to 3pm Monday to Saturday. A gift shop offers most of Francis Parkinson Keyes' books.

FAULKNER HOUSE Map pp310-11

☎ 524-2940; 624 Pirate's Alley; 🕑 10am-6pm

Considered one of the greatest American novelists, William Faulkner (1897–1962) briefly rented an apartment in a town house on Pirate's Alley in 1925. (At the time, the narrow passageway was called Orleans Alley). While living in the city he described as a 'courtesan, not old and yet no longer young,' Faulkner worked for the *Times-Picayune* and consorted with local literati, including the well-established author Sherwood Anderson, who was then also living in New Orleans. Anderson helped Faulkner publish his first novel, *Soldier's Pay* (1926). Faulkner contributed to the *Double Dealer,* a literary magazine published in New Orleans. The house is now home to Joe DeSalvo, who runs a bookstore in the front rooms.

NEW ORLEANS PHARMACY MUSEUM

Map pp310-11

☎ 565-8027; www.pharmacymuseum.org; 514 Chartres St; adult/child $5/4; 🕑 10am-5pm Tue-Sun

The Pharmacy Museum is a beautifully preserved shop with ancient display cases filled with intriguing little bottles. The shop was established in 1816 by Louis J Dufilho at a time when pharmaceutical arts were newly established. The museum claims Dufilho was the nation's first licensed pharmacist, but his practices would be considered suspect today. He dispensed gold-coated

Hermann-Grima House

pills to the wealthy, and opium, alcohol and cannabis to those who needed to feel better for less money. As a bonus, the museum also displays items from the traveling collection of the Museum of the American Cocktail – 19th-century bar supplies and photos. The cocktail, after all, is rumored to have originated in another pharmacy around the block from here.

HERMANN-GRIMA HOUSE Map pp310-11

☎ 525-5661; www.hgghh.org; 820 St Louis St; tours adult/senior $6/5; 🕑 tours 10am, 11am, noon, 2pm & 3pm Mon-Fri

Samuel Hermann, a Jewish merchant who married a Catholic woman, introduced the American-style Federal design to the Quarter in 1831. Hermann sold the house in 1844 to Judge Grima, a slaveholder, after he reportedly lost $2 million during the national financial panic of 1837. Cooking demonstrations in the authentic open-hearth kitchen are a special treat on Thursdays from October to May.

HISTORIC VOODOO MUSEUM

Map pp310-11

☎ 523-7685; 724 Dumaine St; adult/child $7/3.50; 🕑 11am-5pm

This fascinating museum has an intricately arrayed collection of voodoo artifacts and is worth visiting. Tours of the museum are self-guided, and some of the items raise questions for which there is seemingly no answer. Carefully read the handout as you pass through the rooms; otherwise, there is little to explain the exhibited arcane.

HULA MAE'S LAUNDRY Map pp310-11

☎ 522-1336; 840 N Rampart St; ⏲ 10am-9pm

Cossimo Matassa's J&M Music shop, where New Orleans musicians recorded some of the biggest R&B hits in the 1950s, closed down years ago, but the site, now a busy laundromat, contains a few items of interest to music fanatics. The pebbly J&M sign is still inlaid on the front threshold. Inside, by the dryers and folding tables, one wall is dedicated to a photo-and-history exhibit that tells some of the story behind this historic spot. It was here that Fats Domino and Dave Bartholomew established the 'New Orleans Sound,' and countless oldies but goodies, including Lloyd Price's 'Lawdy Miss Clawdy,' were recorded right there where those people are folding their clothes.

MASPERO'S EXCHANGE Map pp310-11

☎ 524-8990; 440 Chartres St

Pierre Maspero operated La Bourse de Maspero, a coffeehouse and one of many slave-trading houses in New Orleans. Maspero was a tenant in the building that now houses the restaurant Maspero's Exchange – not to be confused with Café Maspero on Decatur St. Regular markets for the abhorrent trade in human chattel occurred on Exchange Alley (now Exchange Place), between Conti and Canal Sts. Following the Good Friday fire of 1788, Don Juan Paillet built this structure, that later became the scene of slave trading, with an entresol (a mezzanine floor with a low ceiling that was visible from the exterior through the arched windows). This cramped little room, at the time only reached through a ceiling door from the bottom floor, is where the African slaves are said to have been imprisoned while awaiting their sale. This room now serves as a dining room – a rather tasteless use of the space.

One other historical note about Maspero's is worth mentioning: with British troops approaching in 1814, this building served as the headquarters for the local Committee of Public Safety, charged with marshaling citizens to fight under General Andrew Jackson.

MUSÉE CONTI HISTORICAL WAX MUSEUM Map pp310-11

☎ 525-2605; 917 Conti St; adult/senior/child $6.75/6.25/5.75; ⏲ 10am-5:30pm

Every city in America with a tourism industry of any size must have a wax museum, right? New Orleans' version, the Musée Conti waxes nostalgic about local historical figures including Andrew Jackson, Huey Long, Louis Armstrong and Napoleon Bonaparte (caught in the bathtub for some reason); the lifelike exhibits then detour

A FULL DAY OF FUN FOR KIDS

New Orleans isn't just about booze, broads and beads. Kids can have fun here too. In fact, contrary to popular misconception, New Orleans rates among the most family-friendly travel destinations in the US. The city is full of sights you can go to with the young 'uns in tow.

The **Big Top Gallery and Three Ring Circus** (Map pp312–13; ☎ 569-2700; www.3rcp.com; 1638 Clio St) is an arts and education center that offers workshops for kids and adults. The center also shows films and has art exhibits and music shows that should appeal to the entire family.

The **House of Broel** (Map pp312–13; ☎ 522-2220; www.houseofbroel.com; 2220 St Charles Ave; adult/child $10/5; ⏲ 10am-5pm Mon-Sat) has a dollhouse museum that appeals primarily to girls with very frilly taste. The collection includes 15 large houses that are architecturally impressive (hey, don't look at Dad, he doesn't have time to make one of these). Some of the houses are miniature vignettes of antebellum life, populated by mini Rhetts and Scarletts.

Elsewhere in this chapter (and in other chapters) you'll find many listings of sites that will appeal to children.

- Audubon Zoo (p158)
- Aquarium of the Americas (p152)
- Blaine Kern's Mardi Gras World (p154)
- City Park (p161)
- Louisiana Children's Museum (p154)
- Musée Conti Wax Museum (above)
- River boat cruises (p145)
- Southern Fossil & Mineral Exchange (p232)
- Storyland (p162)
- St Charles Streetcar (p275)

suddenly toward more sensational personalities like Frankenstein's monster (chained down, for your protection) and the Swamp Thing (unchained!). Some of your favorite celebrities, past and present, are sure to be on hand.

NEW ORLEANS JAZZ NATIONAL HISTORIC PARK Map pp310-11

877-520-0677; 916 N Peters St; admission free; 9am-5pm

The headquarters of the Jazz National Historic Park doesn't have much to offer yet – there's no historic exhibit pulling all the stops. Such a thing is sorely missing in the 'Cradle of Jazz.' However, the center does have educational musical programs on most days of the week. Many of the park rangers are musicians and knowledgeable lecturers, and their presentations discuss musical developments, cultural changes, regional styles, myths, legends and musical techniques in relation to the broad subject of jazz. At some point, the center is supposed to relocate to a permanent headquarters in Louis Armstrong Park.

OLD US MINT Map pp310-11

568-6968; 400 Esplanade Ave

This large, unremarkable Greek-revival building looks out of place among the smaller Creole houses of the lower Quarter. It's roof was badly damaged during Hurricane Katrina so the **New Orleans Jazz Exhibit** and the **Houma Indian Arts Museum** are likely to remained closed for some time while the building is repaired.

From 1838 to 1861 and again from 1879 to 1910, the New Orleans Mint struck US coinage bearing the 'O' mint mark. The Confederate States of America briefly produced coins after seizing the mint in 1861. After serving as a US Mint, a federal prison and a US Coast Guard office, the building was transferred to the Louisiana State Museum, which opened its doors to the public in the 1980s.

When it reopens, the jazz exhibit is worth a visit to see dented horns, busted snare drums and homemade gut-stringed bass fiddles played by some of the Crescent City's most cherished artists. The Houma Arts exhibit is an impressive and often humorous collection of colorful wood carvings depicting men and animals – many of them life-sized.

URSULINE CONVENT Map pp310-11

529-3040; 1112 Chartres St; adult/senior/child $5/4/2, child under 8 free; tours 10am, 11am, 1pm, 2pm & 3pm Tue-Fri, 11:15am, 1pm & 2pm Sat & Sun

After a five-month voyage from Rouen in France, 12 Ursuline nuns arrived in New Orleans in 1727 to provide care at the French garrison's miserable little hospital and to educate the women of the colony. The French Colonial Army planned and built the existing convent and girls' school between 1745 and 1752, making it the oldest structure in the French Quarter and the Mississippi Valley. The convent is also one of the few surviving examples of French-colonial architecture in New Orleans, though it probably reflects a design style more common to French Canada than balmier New Orleans. The Ursuline nuns occupied the building until 1824, at which point they moved Uptown.

The Ursuline order had a missionary bent, but it achieved its goals through advancing the literacy rate of women of all races and social levels. In New Orleans their school admitted French, Native American and African American girls. Free persons and slaves alike were educated. By the mid-18th century, the literacy rate among women in the colony was an astounding 71% – higher than for men.

The Ursulines, having quickly observed that an unusually high proportion of the colony's women were working the world's oldest profession, brought marriageable teenage girls from France. The girls arrived with their clothes packed in coffin-like trunks and thus became known as the 'casket girls.' They were educated by the nuns and brought up to make proper wives for the French men of New Orleans. Over the centuries, the casket-girl legacy became more sensational as some in New Orleans surmised the wood boxes may have contained French vampires. The fun with nuns never stops.

Guided tours of the fully restored convent include a visit to the Chapel of Archbishops, built in 1845. The chapel's stained-glass windows pay tribute to the Battle of New Orleans (Andrew Jackson credited his victory to the Ursulines' prayers for divine intervention) and to the Sisters of the Holy Family, the black Creole nuns established in 1842 by Archbishop Antoine Blanc.

US CUSTOM HOUSE Map pp310-11

423 Canal St

The fortresslike US Custom House covers a square block. Construction on it began in 1849 and was supervised by Lieutenant PGT Beauregard, who later commanded Confederate forces. During the Reconstruction period after the Civil War, it served as the headquarters for African Americans in the Republican party. Blacks held a majority in the Louisiana legislature, and two African Americans filled the office of lieutenant governor: Oscar J Dunn and Pickney Benton Stewart Pinchback. Meetings took place in the enormous **Marble Hall** on the 2nd floor.

The construction of the building is also interesting. A cofferdam surrounded the excavation while the foundation was under construction; cotton bales used to seal the dam gave rise to stories that the building was founded on bales of cotton. Despite a mat of cypress timbers, the foundation has settled about 3ft under the weight of the brick and granite structure. All four sides of the building are identical.

VOODOO SPIRITUAL TEMPLE

Map pp310-11

☎ 522-9627; 828 N Rampart St; donations accepted; 🕑 10:30am-5pm Mon-Fri, sometimes Sat

A visit to Priestess Miriam Williams' Voodoo Spiritual Temple will convince you that the practice of voodoo is alive and well in New Orleans. Priestess Miriam founded the Voodoo Spiritual Temple in a converted storefront two doors down from Hula Mae's Laundry in 1990. The site she chose is just a few blocks from Congo Sq, where Marie Laveau is said to have performed theatrical public rituals in the mid-19th century. In Miriam's dimly lit temple, altars to many deities are endowed with such worldly offerings as cigarettes, liquor, money, candles, toys, photographs and statuettes, and the walls are covered with colorfully patterned cloths. In a back room, a snake relaxes in its vivarium and on the odd occasion, with a transfixed countenance, Priestess Miriam will take it out and lift it up, the snake appearing to move its body according to her will. In an adjacent shop Miriam

VOODOO QUEEN

Voodoo became wildly popular in New Orleans after it was introduced to the city by black émigrés from St Domingue at the beginning of the 19th century, but very little is known with certainty about the legendary 19th-century Voodoo Queen Marie Laveau, who gained fame and fortune by shrewdly exploiting the mystique of voodoo. Though details of her life are shrouded in myth and misconception, what has been passed down from generation to generation indeed makes a fascinating story.

She was born in 1794, a French-speaking Catholic of mixed black and white ancestry. Invariably described as beautiful and charismatic, at age 25 she married a man named Paris, who died a few years later. She became known as the widow Paris. She had 15 children with another man named Glapion. Glapion is believed to have migrated from St Domingue, and may have been Marie Laveau's first connection to voodoo.

In the 1830s she established herself as the city's pre-eminent voodoo queen, and her influence crossed racial lines. Mostly she reeled in stray husbands and helped people avenge wrongs done to them. According to legend, she earned her house on St Anne St as payment for ensuring a young man's acquittal in a rape or murder trial.

She apparently had some tricks up her sleeve. She is said to have worked as a hairdresser in the homes of upper-class white women, and it was not uncommon for these women to share society gossip while having their hair done. In this way, Laveau gained a thorough familiarity with the vagaries of the elite, and she astutely perceived the value of such information. At the peak of her reign as Voodoo Queen, she employed a network of spies, most of them household servants in upper-class homes.

Reports on Laveau's activities suggest that there was much more to her practice than nonpractitioners were permitted to witness – which probably makes these reports suspect. However, part of the Laveau legend involves rituals she presided over in the countryside around New Orleans. According to sensational accounts, related after her death, Laveau's followers danced naked around bonfires, drinking blood and slithering on the ground like snakes before engaging in all-out orgies.

A brothel out by Lake Pontchartrain, called Maison Blanche, was reputedly operated by Marie Laveau. But it is uncertain if this was the same Marie Laveau – for, confusingly, there were actually two people known as Marie Laveau, the second being the daughter of the original Marie Laveau. It is unclear where the influence of one gave over to the other. The elder Marie Laveau died in 1881 and is believed to be buried in St Louis Cemetery No 1. The daughter lived into the early 20th century.

does a modest trade in books, postcards, votive candles and other assorted voodoo artifacts.

To neophyte eyes (all are welcome to visit the Voodoo Spiritual Temple), the temple is exotic and thrilling. Miriam, herself, is an impressive presence with her face beaming proudly and her hair radiating upward. Miriam is unconcerned that her shop or the dramatic handling of the snake might conform to prevailing misconceptions about voodoo: 'It's OK that people should have a false opinion of voodoo, because all conceptions are initially false. Ideas progress toward the truth. Every thought is a misconception until something in it touches the thinker in some way. That's what voodoo is like. It is silent. It is an energy that vibrates into our minds.'

CHEZ VODUN Map pp310-11
☎ 558-0653; www.chezvodun.com; 822 N Rampart St
This large space, with an aroused Legba statue guarding its entry, offers a tourist-friendly introduction to the voodoo religion. Within it are the Temple of Pythons, an active place of worship; a gift shop that sells voodoo art and artifacts; a hookah parlor; and a bar that serves voodoo martinis. Presiding over the Saturday-night ceremonies is Dr Sharon Caulder, a scholar, author and voodoo chief who conducts healing rites for members of the audience. In the tradition of voodoo (and other religions too, of course), spirituality and theatrics go hand in hand. Visitors are welcome.

MISSISSIPPI RIVER

Every visitor to New Orleans ought to take at least a short stroll on the Mississippi River levee to see if Old Man River is still rollin' along. For though the mighty river constantly flows by the city, and is actually several feet higher than the city, from the streets it is hidden from view and you might easily forget it is there. But without it there would be no New Orleans. The river has shaped the geography of a huge part of the USA, and it has factored in much of the country's history as well.

The Mississippi is no lazy river. You will not see anyone in their right mind attempt to swim across it. Through New Orleans, the river's depth averages about 200ft. Its immense volume of water and sand roils with tremendous, turbulent force, whirling and eddying and scouring at the banks of snakelike curves.

It runs some 2400 miles from Minnesota to the Gulf of Mexico, and its drainage basin extends from the Rockies to the Alleghenies, covering 40% of the continental US. All of the rain that falls in this vast area ultimately ends up in the Gulf, and most of it is carried there by the Mississippi. The Platte, the Missouri, the Ohio, the Cumberland and the Arkansas – mighty rivers themselves – all feed into the Mississippi, which carries their waters past New Orleans. The Mississippi drains more water than the Nile. Only the Amazon and the Congo carry a greater volume of water to the sea.

Along with all that water, the Mississippi moves up to several million tons of sediment into the Gulf every day. Thus, the river has shifted more than 1000 cu miles of earth from north to south, depositing soil into the Gulf and spreading it to the east and west as the river changed its course. The land that is Louisiana and much of the states of Mississippi and Alabama was created by the river.

The river's name is a corruption of the old Ojibwe *Misi-ziibi* (great river). For early European settlers to the Mississippi Valley, the river initially proved too unruly to serve as a viable route into the heart of the country. The advent of the steamboat in 1807 changed that. During the early part of the 19th century New Orleans' population mushroomed, largely as a result of river traffic and trade. The river connects major cities such as Minneapolis, MN; St Louis, MO; Memphis, TN; and Baton Rouge and New Orleans.

It is natural for deltaic rivers to flood regularly and periodically change course, and preventing the Mississippi from flooding is no simple engineering feat. The river has proven more than mere levees can handle on several occasions, most notoriously in 1927, when the river breached levees in 145 places. That spring, some 27,000 sq miles of farmland, from Illinois to southern Louisiana, turned into a raging sea, up to 30ft deep in places, that flowed steadily down to the Gulf. Entire towns were washed away and a million people were driven from their homes. It took several months for the flooding to recede back

MISSISSIPPI RIVERBOATS

New Orleans' current fleet of steamboats are theme-park copies of the old glories that plied the Mississippi River in Mark Twain's day. Gone are the hoop-skirted ladies, wax-mustachioed gents, round-the-clock crap games and bawdy tinkling on off-tune upright pianos. In their place are pudgy tourists clad in white shorts, Bourbon St T-shirts and tennis shoes, who are content to rest their plump bottoms on plastic stadium seats. The evenings are given over to urbane jazz cruises. The calliope organ survives, but even this unique musical instrument loses some of its panache when applied to modern schmaltz like 'Tie a Yellow Ribbon on the Old Oak Tree.' Alas, romance is forever relegated to the past.

Still, few visitors to New Orleans can resist the opportunity to get out on the Mississippi and watch the old paddle wheel propel them upriver and back down for a spell. It's a relaxing pastime that the entire family can enjoy.

Some steamboat trips have actual destinations. The battlefields of Chalmette are just a little way downriver from New Orleans, and the Audubon Zoo is a short ride upriver from the Aquarium of the Americas.

John James Audubon Riverboat (Map pp310–11; ☎ 586-8777; www.auduboninstitute.org; round-trip adult/child $17/8.50) runs daily short trips between the Aquarium of the Americas and Audubon Park and Zoo. The boat moves slowly and the journey takes one hour. Combination tickets for the two attractions and the boat ride are available.

New Orleans Paddlewheels (☎ 524-0814, 800-445-4109; www.neworleanspaddlewheels.com; adult/child $16/11, jazz dinner cruise $56/29, without dinner $30/18) has two boats, the **Creole Queen** (Map pp308–9) and the **Cajun Queen** (Map pp310–11), that run one-hour cruises on the river. The two-hour dinner-and-jazz cruise, featuring a live Dixieland jazz combo, boards nightly at 7pm and departs at 8pm. When Chalmette Battlefield is reopened, expect the company to resume cruises to that historic site. For all cruises, passengers board at the Canal St Wharf.

Steamboat Natchez (Map pp310–11; ☎ 586-8777, 800-233-2628; www.steamboatnatchez.com; trips $16-22, jazz cruise adult/child $31.50/15.75, cruise & dinner adult/teen/child $54/27/$11.25) doesn't go to Chalmette or the zoo, but it's the closest thing to an authentic steamboat running out of New Orleans today. The *Natchez* is steam-powered and has a bonafide calliope on board (an organist performs your favorite pop classics on the 11:30am and 2:30pm cruises). The evening dinner-and-jazz cruise takes off at 7pm nightly. The *Natchez* boards behind the Jackson Brewery.

to within the river's banks. New Orleans, however, remained high and dry, as north of the city the floodwaters chose the Atchafalaya River's shorter path to the Gulf.

There are numerous benches along the levee in the French Quarter, which on mild sunny days call out for a picnic. The levee is good for a stretch of the legs. You can also get out on the water by hopping aboard the Canal St Ferry (see p152) or a steamboat river cruise (see above).

TREMÉ DISTRICT

Eating p185

Hard times have befallen this historic district. Long home to an impoverished African American community, the Tremé was slammed by Hurricane Katrina. Though flooding wasn't as huge a problem here as it was elsewhere, much of the district's already shaky architecture was severely battered by the hurricane's winds. Ancient, gnarly oak trees fell in every direction, and many of the neighborhood's residents, having scattered to all corners of the country, were slow to return. But Tremé will surely bounce back. The neighborhood has too much history and culture to be forsaken for long.

Ne'er do well Claude Tremé, an émigré from France, did a stint in jail for killing a slave, then married up and inherited his in-laws' vast and prized piece of property just beyond the limits of the French Quarter. He sold the land to the city in 1810, and the Faubourg Tremé was laid out as a suburb two years later. In time the Tremé was populated predominantly by mixed-race Creoles and, only relatively recently, by African Americans from elsewhere in the South.

Most people who wander into the Tremé District share an interest in African American culture. The neighborhood has some essential cultural sights and a historic church. Louis Armstrong Park and St Louis Cemetery No 1 are immediately above the Tremé's residential streets. Also, this is where you'd be most likely to encounter a jazz funeral. However, shops and businesses are few and far between, and at night walking the streets of the neighborhood can be risky.

Orientation

The Tremé is adjacent to the French Quarter, toward the lake. The actual residential neighborhood is bound by Rampart St,

TRANSPORTATION

Bus The 88 bus runs on Rampart St, between the Tremé and the French Quarter, and connects to the Bywater along St Claude Ave.
Parking Street parking is generally easy to come by.

Louis Armstrong Park, Claiborne Ave and Esplanade Ave. Louis Armstrong Park is also on Rampart St, and St Louis Cemetery, just beyond the park, is on the corner of Basin and St Louis Sts.

BACKSTREET CULTURAL MUSEUM

Map pp310-11

☎ 522-4806; www.backstreetmuseum.org; 1116 St Claude Ave; donations accepted; 10am-5pm Tue-Sat, call ahead

Make this fascinating and folksy repository your first stop in the Tremé. It's a none-too-slick museum that celebrates the city's many unique African American traditions, including Mardi Gras Indians, second-line parades and jazz funerals. (The term 'backstreet' refers to New Orleans' 'back o' town,' or the poor black neighborhoods from which so much of the city's culture brews.) While funding is clearly at a shoestring level, the exhibits are exceptional. The curator, Silvester Francis, is a collector and self-taught documentarian whose personal involvement in the community gives him access to a spectacular array of artifacts and archival footage.

The museum is, appropriately enough (considering the jazz funeral angle), in the former Blandin's Funeral Home, where the original neon sign is intact. The building is actually an old house, and the front parlors are where you'll see exhibits of Mardi Gras–Indian suits, social aid and pleasure club banners, and some extraordinary raw video footage of Indians on the march. Francis, a photographer and filmmaker who has documented parades and backstreet events since 1980, is just about as knowledgeable as anybody on these subjects. His guided tours can sometimes gloss over the more fascinating details and history – there is really too much to be said about any of these interesting subjects on a short tour – so be sure to ask him lots of questions as he (or his wife) guides you from room to room. Occasionally, special events are held in the Backstreet Cultural Museum that have stellar entertainment. The museum is bustling with activity during Mardi Gras.

LOUIS ARMSTRONG PARK Map pp310-11

The park, which commemorates legendary jazz cornetist Louis Armstrong, is usually very quiet and some consider it unsafe to wander into alone, especially at night. The park is surrounded by fences that project an unwelcoming atmosphere. That's too bad, because a public space with a jazzy name on this particular spot makes sense and, one would think, really ought to be a cultural focal point for New Orleans.

In the mid-19th century, the area was just outside the city's walls (Rampart St, as the name suggests, was the town limit), and slaves and free persons of color met in a market here called Congo Sq. African music and dances were permitted here, while in the rest of the US people of African descent were forced to repress their traditional culture. In the early 20th century, Storyville, a hotbed of early jazz music among other things (see p60), occupied the adjacent neighborhood, to the lakeside of Basin St. Ironically, most of this area's historic architecture was razed in the 1950s to clear space for the park and for housing projects.

Seeing the **Louis Armstrong statue** is the most popular reason to go inside the park, and

FEMA TRAILERS

While passing through some of New Orleans' hard-hit areas, you might notice white, 30ft trailers parked in front of badly damaged houses. These are the FEMA trailers you may have heard about. The Federal Emergency Management Agency (FEMA) lent these out to people displaced by Hurricane Katrina. The trailers serve as temporary housing for those waiting for their homes to be repaired. For many, the best place to park it is in front of their real home. After Hurricane Katrina, the sight of a few trailers parked on a devastated block was an encouraging sign, indicating the intention of at least some of the neighbors to revive the neighborhood. Such signs can be catchy, inspiring more to return.

The trailers sparked controversy when FEMA attempted to set up group sites in city parks. Many local property owners, envisioning long-term, crime-ridden trailer slums, took a 'not in my backyard' attitude toward these sites, which FEMA was then forced to put on hold.

while you're here, also check out the **bust of Sidney Bechet**, a tribute to the jazz clarinetist. Other structures here include the **Mahalia Jackson Theater** and the **Municipal Auditorium**, where music and other cultural events take place. The radio station WWOZ airs out of Armstrong park.

The park's lighted **arched entrance**, at the corner of Rampart and St Ann Sts, is picturesque in a dated sort of way and really creates a festive Carnival atmosphere when the bare bulbs that spell 'Louis Armstrong Park' are lit up. (Unfortunately, when the bulbs burn out, weeks and months sometimes go by before they are replaced.) **Congo Square**, located on roughly the same spot as the 19th-century market, is a quiet corner of the park where musicians sometimes play. During Jazz Fest, cultural events are held here.

In the future, the **New Orleans Jazz National Historic Park** (☎ 589-4806) will be based at **Perseverance Hall** in the park. Tune in to WWOZ (see p82) and other cultural media to learn about concerts and parades sponsored by the National Park Service.

ST AUGUSTINE'S CHURCH Map pp310-11

☎ 525-5934; 1210 Governor Nicholls St

St Aug's, the second-oldest African American Catholic church in the country, was a casualty of Hurricane Katrina. The Archdiocese of New Orleans decided to close the historic parish after Katrina tore metal sheathing from the steeple and caused some $400,000 in water damage. The building still stands and, as an auxiliary of the St Peter Claver Parish, events are still held here from time to time. (At this writing, after vehement protests from the African American Catholic community, the diocese was considering reopening the church for a trial period.)

Designed by JNB DePouilly, who later rebuilt St Louis Cathedral, St Augustine's opened in 1841. It was where Creoles, émigrés from St Domingue and free persons of color came to worship. Separate pews were also designated for slaves, which was unusual for the time. Many jazz pioneers and Civil Rights heroes worshipped at St Aug's, including jazz clarinetist Sidney Bechet, who was baptized here. In recent decades, the neighborhood has been increasingly populated by Baptists, and church attendance has dropped significantly.

Call the church to see if it's possible to arrange a visit. One of St Augustine's

St Louis Cemetery No 1

stained-glass panels depicts the Sisters of the Holy Family, the order of black Creole nuns founded in 1842 by Henriette Delille and Archbishop Antoine Blanc. There is also a Tomb of the Unknown Slave.

ST LOUIS CEMETERY NO 1 Map pp310-11

admission free; 🕒 8am-3pm

New Orleans' oldest cemetery (it dates from 1789), St Louis Cemetery No 1 has a rare beauty, enhanced by natural decay wrought by time. If you visit just one cemetery, make it this one near the French Quarter. Time and a willingness to explore the grounds are essential. Wandering at your own leisure, you can appreciate the statuary and ornate ironwork and literally stumble upon many historic tombs.

Voodoo queen Marie Laveau purportedly rests here. Fittingly, mystery surrounds her crypt. A family tomb not far from the entrance has the names Glapion, Laveau and Paris (all branches of Marie Laveau's family) etched in its marble front, and a commemorative plaque identifies it as Laveau's 'reputed' resting site. Debates concerning *which* Marie Laveau – mother or daughter, if either – was actually buried here will never be resolved, but popular consensus has designated this as Laveau's memorial. People come to scratch an 'x' in the tomb's plaster, presumably to pay their 'respects' to the voodoo queen. However, living members of the Glapion family consider this practice vandalism – there is

MUSICIANS' VILLAGE

On an eight-acre tract along N Roman St in the Upper Ninth Ward, 81 houses have been built to house musicians who lost homes during Hurricane Katrina. The project is a collaboration between Branford Marsalis, Harry Connick Jr and Habitat for Humanity. The modest homes are the result of a community effort to ensure that New Orleans remains a city of musicians. Hundreds of construction workers volunteered their labor to help keep costs down. The centerpiece of this musical neighborhood is the Ellis Marsalis Center for Music, where cultural events and education seminars are held.

no spiritual significance to these chicken scratches, and visitors are strongly discouraged from desecrating this or any other tomb.

In the adjacent family tomb rests Ernest 'Dutch' Morial, New Orleans' first black mayor. Morial was mayor from 1978 to 1986, and he died in 1989.

Civil Rights–figure Homer Plessy also rests in the cemetery, as do real-estate speculator Bernard de Marigny, architect Henry Latrobe and countless others.

The Italian Mutual Benevolent Society Tomb is responsible for the tallest monument in the cemetery. Like a lot of immigrant groups in New Orleans, the Italians formed a benevolent association to pool funds and assist in covering burial costs. The tomb is large enough to hold the remains of thousands. In 1969, to the obvious shock of the families who own tombs here, a demented rape scene in the movie *Easy Rider* was filmed in St Louis Cemetery No 1. Take note of the headless statue called *Charity* on the Italian Society tomb – urban myth maintains that actor Dennis Hopper, who starred in the film, was responsible for tearing the head off.

The cemetery gates are open and you are free to wander around on your own. It can be hard to find all of the noteworthy sights, and a good organized walking tour (p134) will help you see all of them. Even if you are not interested in a tour, it's a good idea to coincide your visit with one in order to ensure that you are not alone within the cemetery walls. Vandalism and statuary theft are the most common crimes here, but solitary visitors within the secluded grounds might be risking their personal safety.

MORTUARY CHAPEL Map pp310-11
☎ 525-1551; 411 N Rampart St; donations accepted; 7am-6pm
An unfounded fear of yellow-fever contagion led the city to forbid funerals for fever victims at the St Louis Cathedral. Built in 1826 near St Louis Cemetery No 1, the Mortuary Chapel offered hasty services for victims, as its bell tolled constantly during epidemics. In 1931 it was renamed Our Lady of Guadeloupe Church. Inside the chapel you'll see a statue of St Jude, patron saint of impossible cases, and a curious statue of St Expedite, a saint who probably never existed (on the plaque there are quotation marks around his name).

FAUBOURG MARIGNY & BYWATER

Eating p185, Shopping p230, Sleeping p242

The old Creole faubourgs (suburbs) immediately downriver from the French Quarter are some of New Orleans' most colorful and lively neighborhoods. Faubourg Marigny and Bywater share a great deal of the lower Quarter's architectural and cultural heritage, with row upon row of Creole cottages and double-shotgun houses, and a population that is ethnically and demographically mixed. Frenchmen St in Faubourg Marigny, easily reached on foot from the French Quarter, is one of New Orleans' after-dark hubs.

Faubourg Marigny was the first Creole suburb of the old city when it was laid out in 1806 on the plantation of Bernard Xavier Philippe de Marigny de Mandeville. Monsieur Marigny, an unpredictable character, was the first to introduce the game of craps to New Orleans after acquiring a taste for the dice on a visit to London. Marigny unfortunately gambled away much of his fortune, but somehow survived some 27 duels. He chose whimsical names for the streets of his development, though many were changed decades ago. Originally, Burgundy St in the Faubourg Marigny was called Rue de Craps. Other street names in the district included Poets, Music, Love and Good Children.

Early inhabitants of the neighborhood included whites and free persons of color. By the 1840s, some 40% of the homes in the Marigny were owned by the black mistresses of white Creoles. Marriages between the races were not legal, but unions, called *plaçages,* were relatively common. Sometimes these mixed-race couples lived together, but more often the men bought property for the women and supported the children, who were considered legitimate offspring.

The Marigny today has a sizable gay population, and the neighborhood supports a vibrant bohemian scene as well. Faubourg Marigny's artistic leanings have naturally spilled down into the more working class Bywater, which has been 'up and coming' for years now. The neighborhoods are worthy of an afternoon stroll to observe the rustic elegance of the Creole architecture.

TRANSPORTATION

Bus The 5 bus runs down on Dauphine and back up Royal St through the Marigny and Bywater and extends through the Quarter on N Peters St. The 55 bus runs on Elysian Fields Ave and down Decatur St through the French Quarter. The 88 bus runs along the lakeside of the Bywater and Marigny, on St Claude Ave, and continues along Rampart St.
Streetcar The 2 Riverfront streetcar starts from Esplanade Ave (near the Faubourg Marigny) and edges the Quarter and the Warehouse District.
Parking Street parking, while not always easy to find, is all there is.

Orientation

From the French Quarter, cross Esplanade Ave and you're in the Faubourg Marigny. The Bywater is the next neighborhood down. Both are wedged between the river and St Claude Ave. The two neighborhoods are divided by the railroad tracks along Press St. The Bywater ends at Poland St, opposite the naval base, more than a mile below Esplanade Ave. Frenchmen St is the cultural hub of the Faubourg Marigny and within walking distance of the French Quarter. The Bywater is more spread out and less walkable.

TALES OF THE CRYPTS

New Orleans' necropolises exhibit all the diversity and style of the surrounding city. In death, as in life, the wealthy mingle with the poor with just enough elbow room for all to express some – or, in many cases, ample – personal style. Ornate marble tombs rise to the sky like Gothic churches amid rows of inner-city apartments for the dearly departed. Some neglected cemeteries exhibit all the hallmarks of postmortem ghettoes.

The vast majority of the graves in New Orleans are aboveground and while no small amount of grandiosity inspired the more extravagant high-rise tombs, this practice of building up rather than down originated out of necessity. As early New Orleanians discovered, the region's high-water table makes for wet digging; getting a buoyant wood coffin 6ft underground meant first scuttling it to ensure that it would sink. Even then a heavy rain could easily draw it back up to the surface again, and the dreadful sight of cadavers washing down flooded streets in the young city was not uncommon. So aboveground tombs constructed of brick and surfaced with plaster became the norm, ensuring that old Jean-Claude rested in peace.

There are several distinct styles of tombs. The wall vaults that surround many cemeteries are often called 'ovens.' Family tombs are the most common type of tomb. The cemetery equivalent of two-story, single-family homes, they are privately owned and typically house the remains of several generations. The grandest tombs are the society tombs, so called because they were funded by benevolent associations to ensure proper burial for members of specific communities. Many of these majestic monuments are dedicated to particular 19th-century immigrant groups, who pooled funds to take care of their dead. Professions, religious denominations and branches of the military are also commonly represented in the cemetery. The larger society tombs have more than 20 vaults and, as these are reused over time, the population within these monuments can reach staggering numbers.

What really makes New Orleans' cemeteries visually enthralling is the incredible array of expressive, creative and often strange statuary and ornamentation that adorn many of the crypts. Angels praying with slumped shoulders and wings, grieving mothers tenderly cradling lethargic (perhaps dead) babies, wrought-iron crosses and gates, and stained-glass mosaics all play on light and shadow to create glorious surroundings for the dead. Some cemeteries are rapidly decaying, with broken tablets and loose plaster falling about the tombs, making them decidedly eerie.

There are over 40 cemeteries in New Orleans. This book highlights just a few of them: St Louis Cemetery No 1 (p147), Lafayette Cemetery No 1 (p156), Metairie Cemetery (p163) and St Roch Cemetery (p150). Some of these can be dangerous to explore on your own – muggings have been common over the years. It's unclear if this is likely to change for the better in the smaller, post-Katrina New Orleans. Many companies offer informative cemetery walking tours (p134).

ST ROCH CEMETERY Map p316
☎ 945-5961; cnr St Roch Ave & N Roman St; 🕑 9am-4pm

Just a few blocks toward the lake from the Faubourg Marigny (driving is recommended), St Roch cemetery is one of New Orleans' most intriguing resting places. It is named after an obscure saint, a French native, whose prayers are said to have protected Rome from the Black Plague. During New Orleans' bouts with yellow fever, Catholics who prayed to St Roch (pronounced 'Rock') are believed to have been spared, and the small **chapel** within the cemetery grounds was raised in his honor.

Entering this walled necropolis, you pass through an elegant wrought-iron fence; the grounds' paved paths are lined with family and society tombs, some magnificent, some decrepit. The real fascination here is within the chapel itself.

The main reason to schlep out here is to cast your peepers on the curiosities displayed behind a small gated chamber, to your right as you enter the chapel. The strange collection of ceramic body parts (healed ankles, heads, breasts), prosthetics, leg braces, crutches and false teeth that hang from the walls and cover the floor are *ex-votos,* or testaments to the healing power of St Roch. Marble floor tiles are inscribed with the words 'thanks' and '*merci.*' Each of these items represents a prayer answered by the prolific, strangely named saint who, the decaying evidence suggests, is currently enjoying a semiretirement.

Tons of debris were hauled out of the cemetery after Hurricane Katrina, and the chapel was damaged. At the time of writing, the chapel was still closed and there was no indication it would reopen soon. Call if you're interested in visiting. The surrounding neighborhood was one of the most violent neighborhoods in the city, and some of the criminal element has crept back since Katrina – so be alert.

CBD & WAREHOUSE DISTRICT

Eating p187, Shopping p231, Sleeping p244

On the other side of Canal St from the French Quarter, the Central Business District (CBD) and the Warehouse District make up the American commercial sector that burgeoned following the Louisiana Purchase. But this district, originally called Faubourg St Mary, was established before the Americans arrived. Beltran Gravier subdivided the land here immediately after gaining it in 1788 through his marriage to a wealthy widow. Gravier is still remembered through the street that was named for him. Throughout the duration of the Spanish era, the Faubourg St Mary was a quiet suburb.

Soon after the Stars and Stripes were raised over the Cabildo, manufacturers, brokers and merchants from New England flooded into New Orleans and, with the advent of the steamboats, they industriously transformed the city into a bustling port. The Faubourg St Mary became the American sector, which became a nexus of offices, banks, warehouses and government buildings around Lafayette Sq.

Canal St was the dividing line between the French and American parts of New Orleans. The wide median down the middle of Canal St was considered part of neither the French nor American sector and for that reason came to be called the 'neutral ground' – in time, all medians in the city would be referred to by that idiosyncratic phrase.

Toward the lake, extending to Claiborne Ave, is the modern City Hall, the Louisiana Superdome and new office buildings and convention hotels. Most of this modern area was formerly part of the back o' town, primarily inhabited by African Americans. Jazz originated in the seamy nightclubs along Perdido St and Basin St, and in the adjacent Storyville red-light district. Louis Armstrong's birthplace, like every other house in the area, was bulldozed to make room for the characterless structures that now stand here.

During the 20th century, the Warehouse District faded in its importance as the port shrank in size, but over the past two decades former warehouses have been converted into galleries and nightclubs. The area closest to the river was redeveloped in the 1980s with a Convention Center and the Riverwalk shopping mall.

Orientation

The Central Business District is just above Canal St. It more or less extends out to S Claiborne Ave and to the elevated I-90

TRANSPORTATION

Bus The 11 bus runs from Canal St along the entire length of Magazine St, to Audubon Park. The 42 bus runs on Canal St through Mid-City all the way to City Park. The 10 bus runs on Tchoupitoulas St to Audubon Park.
Streetcar The 2 Riverfront streetcar runs along the river from the Convention Center and along the entire length of the French Quarter. When operating, the St Charles Ave streetcar runs from Canal St along St Charles Ave through the CBD, the Garden District and Uptown. The 45 streetcar runs on Canal St from the river through Mid-City (temporarily only as far as Crozat).
Parking There are public lots on nearly every block, with convenient parking at the Riverwalk Mall and near the CAC on Camp St. Metered parking is available on most streets.

freeway. Poydras St runs through the heart of the district, from the river on past the Superdome. Above Poydras St, the river side of the CBD is the warehouse district, which extends out to Magazine St or St Charles Ave, depending on who you ask. Julia St, running from the river and on past St Charles Ave, is known as 'Gallery Row' and is the heart of New Orleans' arts district. Lafayette Sq, the heart of the old American sector, is on St Charles Ave, a block above Poydras. The Riverwalk Mall is on the levee and the Convention Center is adjacent to it.

CBD

The Central Business District is New Orleans' modern skyscraper zone and has its share of bland government buildings. The area immediately surrounding Lafayette Sq is the heart of the former Faubourg St Mary, and has some places of historic interest.

GALLIER HALL Map pp308-9

545 St Charles Ave

Architect James Gallier Sr designed this monumental Greek-revival structure, which was dedicated in 1853. It served as New Orleans' city hall until the 1950s, and it far outclasses the city's current city hall (a few blocks away). Gallier Hall is a focal point for MG parades, most of which promenade past the grandstand that is put up along St Charles Ave.

NEW ORLEANS PUBLIC LIBRARY

Map pp308-9

☎ 529-7323; http://nutrias.org; 219 Loyola Ave; 11am-4pm Mon-Fri

The main library was badly damaged during Hurricane Katrina, when winds blew out windows and falling debris damaged the computer lab. The 1st floor suffered some flooding. However, it recovered and reopened within a few months. The library isn't one of the country's best, but its Louisiana Room, on the 3rd floor, is a respectable resource of regional history, with materials including books, maps and newspapers. The library's computer room is handy for anyone wanting to get online for free.

LOUISIANA SUPERDOME Map pp308-9

☎ 587-3663; www.superdome.com; Sugar Bowl Dr

Seemingly hovering like a giant, bronze-tinted hubcap amid the CBD skyscrapers and the elevated I-10 freeway, the Superdome is one of New Orleans' most easily recognized structures. The immense indoor stadium, with its sophisticated climate-control system, has hosted six Superbowls, presidential conventions and an address in 1987 by Pope John Paul II. The Rolling Stones performed before some 87,500 screaming fans in the dome in 1981. On New Year's Day the Sugar Bowl is played here, and the New Orleans Saints play home games in the Superdome each fall. The Superdome is built on top of an ancient burial ground, and some say unhappy spirits have cursed the Saints – how else can you explain the team's miserable performance for much of its 40-year history?

The Superdome gained regrettable notoriety in 2005 when it was designated a 'refuge of last resort' during Hurricane Katrina. Some 20,000 to 30,000 people huddled under the dome as Katrina's winds blew away part of the roof. Power went out and food and water supplies were quickly depleted as people lived in squalor (and at least one person died) and waited nearly a week for buses to arrive and take them out of the flooded city.

WAREHOUSE DISTRICT

The old warehouses that line most of the streets in this part of town have proved perfectly suitable for the arts district that now thrives here. The museums and galleries are joined by some of the city's finest restaurants (see p187).

AQUARIUM OF THE AMERICAS

Map pp308-9

☎ 581-4629; Canal St; adult/senior/child 2-12 yrs $16/13/9.50; 9:30am-5pm

Part of the Audubon Institute (also see Audubon Zoological Gardens, p158), the immense Aquarium of the Americas is one of the country's best places to come face to face with exotic sea creatures. The emphasis is loosely regional, with exhibits that delve beneath the surface of the Mississippi River, Gulf of Mexico, Caribbean Sea and far-off Amazon rain forest. Some 10,000 fish were lost when Hurricane Katrina wiped out the aquarium's filtration and temperature control systems, but the aquarium reopened the following year and continues to restock its depleted tanks.

Highlights in the aquarium include 'Spots,' a rare white alligator found in the swamps of Louisiana. There's usually a large crowd around the **Mississippi River Gallery** while this big guy suns himself. The **Caribbean Reef** has a 30ft-long glass tunnel that allows you to walk through a 130,000-gallon tank amid sea creatures without getting wet – or eaten. The sea-horse gallery and the warm-weather penguin colony afford visitors the opportunity to familiarize themselves with some of the world's most unusual creatures.

The air-conditioned aquarium is at the foot of Canal St, adjacent to Woldenberg Park and next to the Canal St Ferry. The Riverfront streetcar stops nearby. Be sure to pick up a program listing times for special presentations such as the penguin feed and diver shows. The gift shop is a good place to pick up books on Louisiana's natural history.

You can get a variety of combination tickets that include the zoo, the aquarium and the Zoo Cruise (p158). Other combination tickets good for the aquarium and adjacent **IMAX theater** (p215) offer a saving of about 15%.

CANAL ST FERRY Map pp308-9

A short ferry ride from the foot of Canal St to Algiers Point is the easiest way to get out on the Mississippi River and admire New Orleans from the traditional river approach. Ride on the lower deck next to the water, and you're likely to see the state bird, the brown pelican. The state-run ferry is free and runs between 6am and midnight, leaving Canal St on the hour and half-hour, and returning from Algiers on the quarter-hour.

CONFEDERATE MUSEUM Map pp308-9

☎ 523-4522; www.confederatemuseum.com; 929 Camp St; adult/senior & child $5/2; 10am-4pm Mon-Sat

Dedicated to presenting Louisiana life during the Civil War, this museum is housed in sturdy old Confederate Memorial Hall, designed by Thomas Sully. Opened to the public in 1891, it's the oldest operating museum in the state. Entering the hall, with

CBD LANDMARKS

Scattered about the CBD are historic buildings where some of the city's biggest (and, in some cases, most notorious) wheelers and dealers operated. Keep an eye out for them if you're wandering through the neighborhood.

New Orleans Cotton Exchange (Map pp308–9; 231 Carondelet St) Some would say New Orleans was built on cotton. In the mid-19th century, as one-third of all cotton produced in the US was routed through New Orleans, the receiving docks on the levee were perpetually covered by tall stacks of cotton bales ready to be shipped out. The Cotton Exchange was founded in 1871 to regulate trade and prices. The building here, dating to the 1920s, is the third Cotton Exchange to occupy this site.

United Fruit Company (Map pp308–9; 321 St Charles Ave) A cornucopia of tropical produce graces the entrance to this building, hinting at the business conducted within. The United Fruit Company, often reviled for its neocolonial practices in Central America, was based here from the 1930s until the 1970s. For many decades, the company held a virtual monopoly on the banana trade throughout much of the world. It's now part of Chiquita Brands International, based in Cincinnati, OH.

Factors Row (Map pp308–9; 806 Perdido St) Edgar Degas painted *The Cotton Market in New Orleans* while visiting his uncle's office in this building in 1873.

its exposed cypress ceiling beams and exhibition cases, is worth the price of admission alone, and the exhibit itself is likely to exceed expectations.

The museum makes little effort to reinterpret history, or lament past sins. The closest thing to a point of view are a few harsh words (mostly quoting federal officials in Washington, DC) about General Benjamin 'Beast' Butler, the locally reviled head of the Union forces that occupied New Orleans during the war. If there is an agenda, it would be to humanize those who fought on the losing side of a grisly war. The exhibits falter by neglecting unpleasant topics, including slavery. It's a huge omission that can only be explained by the paucity of material possessions slaves could have left behind.

For this museum is really a collection of *things*. The exhibit includes the expected rifles, swords, pistols and flags from the war, as well as other strangely beautiful artifacts of the industrial age. The museum really shines for its endless collection of personal effects that belonged to soldiers and officers, and their families back at home. Knapsacks, playing cards, tobacco pouches and undergarments are fastidiously arranged within the display cabinets. Display cases densely packed with curious items, such as Jefferson Davis' slippers and an impressive array of oddly styled hats, conjure up the past in a surprisingly touching way.

CONTEMPORARY ARTS CENTER

Map pp308-9

☎ 528-3805; www.cacno.org; 900 Camp St; adult/child $5/3, Thu free; 🕒 11am-5pm Tue-Sun

This huge exhibition and performance space occupies a renovated warehouse. The CAC lacks a permanent collection, but has established itself as an important showcase for contemporary local artists. The steel ceiling above the impressive central stairway honors prominent figures in local arts. Among the many acknowledged artists are painter and sculptor Fritz Bultman, visual artist and sculptor Enrique Alferez, architect Charles Rousseve and his wife, Noma, who was the first director of Xavier's Fine Arts Department, and Ellsworth Woodward, the first director of Newcomb's Fine Arts Department. Dozens of multimedia exhibits appear each year in the gallery spaces. Also featured on the two stages are performances of plays, performance art, dance programs, musical concerts and video screenings.

HARRAH'S CASINO Map pp308-9

☎ 533-600, 800-427-7247; 4 Canal St; 🕒 24hr

The national casino chain arrived in New Orleans in 1999, and while one would think all manner of vice would be welcome in the Big Easy, Harrah's, near the foot of Canal St, was not popularly received. In spite of its best efforts to fit in, with a stately new brick home and a perfunctory Mardi Gras parade every night, Harrah's still manages to make guests feel like they're in Sparks, Nevada – not exactly what tourists usually have in mind when they come to New Orleans. Nevertheless, people do trickle in for the casino gambling, buffet dining, free parking and hotel discounts.

LEE CIRCLE Map pp308-9

Called Place du Tivoli until it was renamed to honor Confederate General Robert E Lee after the Civil War, Lee Circle has lost some of its earlier cachet. Just a few dozen paces away, an elevated freeway structure disturbs some of the traffic circle's symmetry, and gas stations occupy two of its corners. Nevertheless, the **Robert E Lee monument** at its center, dedicated in 1884, still refuses to turn its back on the North – for that's the direction the statue faces.

Also on Lee Circle, **K&B Plaza** (1055 St Charles Ave; 🕒 8:30am-4:30pm Mon-Fri) is a modish office tower dating to 1963 with an indoor/outdoor sculpture gallery. The outdoor sculptures, featuring Isamu Noguchi's *The Mississippi,* can be viewed anytime.

LOUISIANA ARTWORKS Map pp308-9

☎ 523-1465; www.artscouncilofneworleans.org; 725 Howard Ave; admission $7; 🕒 10am-5pm Tue-Sat, noon-5pm Sun

A promising new addition to the arts district, this 90,000-sq-ft space was established by the Arts Council of New Orleans to bring working artists and lovers of art together. By providing artists with affordable studio spaces, the project hopes to foster a continuation of the city's growing arts scene, even as rents go up around town. The Arts Council hopes to promote the local arts by keeping the facility open to the public, thus giving visitors the opportunity to witness

WORTH A TRIP: BLAINE KERN'S MARDI GRAS WORLD

When there is no parade happening in New Orleans, you can get your fill of floats at **Mardi Gras World** (Map pp306–7; ☎ 361-7821, 800-362-8213; www.mardigrasworld.com; 233 Newton St, Algiers; adult/child $15/7.25; 🕑 8:30am-5pm), where most of the best parade floats are made and stored. It's across the river from the French Quarter, in historic Algiers Point. Getting there is a breeze: the Canal St Ferry gets you over the water and a free shuttle will take you the rest of the way.

The man behind the magic is Blaine Kern – 'Mr Mardi Gras' – who has been making parade floats since 1947. Kern learned the trade from his father and passed it down to his sons, who now help run the business. The company's 75,000-sq-ft warehouse is filled with dazzling floats and other props, all carefully crafted by some of the world's most talented float builders. Among the company's major accomplishments are the superfloats Leviathan and SS Captain Eddie, which are on display here when they're not running down the streets of New Orleans for the Endymion parade.

Tours include an introduction and a slice of king cake. Guests are invited to try on snazzy Mardi Gras costumes before being released for an unguided traipse through the world's largest fleet of parade floats. Larger-than-life artists and celebrities (Mick Jagger, Tina Turner and Salvador Dali, among others) rub their spray-painted elbows with a pantheon of gods and goddesses (Medusa, Apollo, Hercules et al). In some rooms you'll see carpenters, sculptors and painters creating new floats, all spangly and colorful and lit up like Christmas trees.

art being created. Tourists who appreciate art are the obvious target audience here. It's an interesting idea, and a positive step for the city as it attempts to rebuild its tourist-based economy without going the Mickey Mouse route.

LOUISIANA CHILDREN'S MUSEUM

Map pp308-9

☎ 523-1357; www.lcm.org; 420 Julia St; admission $7; 🕑 9:30am-4:30pm Tue-Sat, noon-4:30pm Sun

This educational museum is like a high-tech kindergarten. Generous corporate sponsors have helped create hands-on exhibits such as a supermarket, complete with stocked shelves and check-out registers, and a TV news studio, where young anchors can see themselves on monitors as they forecast a July snowstorm in New Orleans. In the rush to build newer, bigger and better exhibits, the museum has failed to maintain some of the existing displays – 'Mayday!' calls on the tugboat radio go unheard and most kids abandon ship. Overall, however, the nonprofit museum and volunteers have done a good job providing attractions for everyone from toddlers to 12-year-olds. Children under 16 must be accompanied by an adult.

The museum's roof was badly damaged by Hurricane Katrina, and the resulting water intrusion caused further harm to the building's interior. However, the real hardship facing the museum was the loss of 90% of its staff. At the time of research the Louisiana Children's Museum anticipated a slow recovery.

NATIONAL WORLD WAR II MUSEUM

Map pp308-9

☎ 527-6012; www.nationalww2museum.org; 945 Magazine St; adult/senior/child $14/8/6; 🕑 9am-5pm Tue-Sat

This monumental museum opened its doors in June 2000 to extraordinary fanfare. Stephen Ambrose, the museum's founder and best-selling WWII historian, was on hand as were filmmaker Stephen Spielberg, actor Tom Hanks and a gaggle of network news anchors. The museum, touted as the only one of its kind, is a 70,500-sq-ft structure presenting WWII with boats, planes, weapons and uniforms used in the Allied effort. A special feature with a local angle is a pair of Higgins boats, the landing craft that enabled the Allies to invade Normandy by sea. The boats were designed and produced by New Orleans–entrepreneur Andrew Higgins. According to Ambrose, General Dwight D Eisenhower once said that Higgins 'won the war for us.'

The upstairs exhibits are a narrative documentary. Authentic and replicated artifacts encased in glass serve to heighten the drama created in multimedia accounts of what happened on the ground at Normandy, Iwo Jima and elsewhere during WWII. Oral-history stations with recorded first-hand accounts, and the Academy Award–winning film *D-Day Remembered* (which screens daily) add context to the exhibits and help make this a worthwhile stop.

The museum is currently undergoing an ambitious expansion project, due to be completed sometime in 2009, that will quadruple it's size and also broaden its mission. The end result will be that the National WWII Museum will have exhibits on great campaigns of the war, a large theater and a USO-style canteen featuring latter-day Bob Hopes and Betty Grables as a tribute to the entertainers who helped keep troops' morale up during the Second World War.

OGDEN MUSEUM OF SOUTHERN ART

Map pp308-9

☎ 539-9600; www.ogdenmuseum.com; 925 Camp St; 🕙 10am-5pm Mon-Sat

Over the past four decades, New Orleans–entrepreneur Roger Houston Ogden has assembled one of the finest collections of Southern art – far too large to keep to himself. This large, modern facility houses Ogden's still-growing collection, and other private collections that the museum seems to gain with regularity. The Ogden Museum is also affiliated with the Smithsonian Institute in Washington, DC, giving it access to that bottomless collection. Overall it's a polished operation, with smartly presented exhibits. Before your visit have a look at the website, which offers a visual catalog of paintings.

PRESERVATION RESOURCE CENTER

Map pp308-9

☎ 581-7032; www.prcno.org; 923 Tchoupitoulas St; admission free; 🕙 9am-5pm Mon-Fri

For anyone with a special interest in the architecture of New Orleans, this center is a great place to stop and get a sense for the lay of the land. The PRC is a nonprofit organization whose chief mission is to restore and revitalize New Orleans' historic neighborhoods. Its headquarters, in the expansive Leeds-Davis building, has a street-level museum. The display is modest, but manages to impart key information in a very straightforward manner. Grab some free walking-tour maps and literature on virtually every part of town. The engaging staff can provide information on every-thing from cycling routes to how to secure low-interest loans to buy and restore your dream shotgun house. Upstairs, a library contains volumes on local history and architecture.

LOWER GARDEN DISTRICT

Eating p188, Shopping p231, Sleeping p246

The Garden District's unprecious neighbor is full of beautiful residential architecture, interesting history and some of Magazine St's liveliest blocks. On its many tree-lined thoroughfares stand a seemingly endless collection of Greek-revival houses that were once home to the city's elite. The neighborhood has come up a few notches in recent years after a long decline, but hasn't lost its healthy, creative edge.

The neighborhood was developed in the 1830s by surveyor Barthélémy Lafon, who envisioned a posh and sophisticated suburb that would be the envy of other classically obsessed planners of his day. Street names honored Greek gods, nymphs and muses, and attractive tree-lined canals along their median strips provided drainage to the river. The city's elite built their mansions here, also paying homage to the Greeks with columned galleries looking out over cultivated gardens burgeoning with pecan trees, banana trees and fish ponds. Gazebos and horse stables further announced that life was grand here. New Orleans' craze for cast-iron struck the mid-century denizens of the Lower Garden District, who adorned and fenced in their homes with ornate metallic designs, which today lend the area a rustic grace.

The neighborhood's glory was short-lived. The wealthy soon moved further uptown to the newer, more fashionable Garden District, and many of the larger residences of the Lower Garden District were divided into rental units to accommodate immigrants from Germany and Ireland, many of whom were employed on the docks. With the introduction of housing projects and the construction of an entrance to the

TRANSPORTATION

Bus The 11 bus runs along Magazine St from Canal St to Audubon Park. The 10 bus runs on Tchoupitoulas St, past Tipitina's nightclub, to Audubon Park.

Streetcar When operating, the St Charles Ave streetcar runs from Canal St along St Charles Ave through the CBD, the Garden District and Uptown.

Parking Metered parking is available on Magazine Street. Free parking can be found on side streets.

Mississippi River bridge, the neighborhood deteriorated. The bridge ramp has since been demolished.

Some of the old, crime-ridden housing projects have been replaced by the River Garden development for mixed-income residents. River Garden's faux traditional architecture has sparked its share of controversy, which for some signifies a step toward the 'Disneyfication' of New Orleans. Likewise, the inclusion of a huge Wal-Mart store as part of the development has not drawn universal praise.

Orientation

The Lower Garden District is upriver from the CBD. Its extents are the elevated I-90 freeway, St Charles Ave, Jackson Ave and the river. Magazine St is the main commercial thoroughfare.

GOODRICH-STANLEY HOUSE

Map pp312-13

1729 Coliseum St

This historic home was built in 1837 by jeweler William M Goodrich. Goodrich sold the house to the British-born cotton factor Henry Hope Stanley, whose adopted son, Henry Morton Stanley, went on to gain fame for finding the missing Scottish missionary, Dr David Livingston. It was Stanley who first uttered the legendary question, 'Dr Livingston, I presume?' He was subsequently knighted and founded the Congo Free States. The house originally stood a few blocks away, at 904 Orange St, and was moved to its current spot in 1981.

GRACE KING HOUSE Map pp312-13

1749 Coliseum St

Behind a handsome wrought-iron fence, this papaya-hued house was named for the Louisiana historian and author who lived here from 1905 to 1932. It was built in 1847 by banker Frederick Rodewald and features both Greek Ionic columns on the lower floor and Corinthian columns above.

ST VINCENT'S INFANT ASYLUM

Map pp312-13

1507 Magazine St

This large, red-brick orphanage was built in 1864 with assistance from federal troops occupying the city. It helped relieve the overcrowded orphanages filled with youngsters of all races who lost their parents to epidemics. The orphanage is now a hotel. A sign from the orphanage days still hangs from the finely styled cast-iron gallery in front.

GARDEN DISTRICT

Eating p188, Shopping p232, Sleeping p246

Wealthy English-speaking protestants, many of them transplants from New York and New England, built their mansions in the Garden District in the 1850s, and the neighborhood has lost none of its grace since then. It has a rare architectural cohesiveness, as most of the houses here reflect the tastes of that remarkably industrious decade. As advertised, many yards in the neighborhood are lushly landscaped and the streets are shaded by gorgeous old oak trees, whose powerful roots have lifted sections of the sidewalk.

Visitors come to the Garden District simply to walk its streets and admire the architecture. Commanders Palace (p190), one of the city's best loved restaurants, and elegant Lafayette Cemetery are the neighborhood's lead attractions. Everything else worth seeing is covered in the Walking Tours chapter (p168).

Orientation

The Garden District is a compact, rectangular grid. It's bound by St Charles Ave, Jackson Ave, Magazine St and Louisiana Ave. Magazine St and St Charles Ave are the primary commercial thoroughfares. Prytania St is the most scenic route through the neighborhood.

LAFAYETTE CEMETERY NO 1 Map pp312-13

Washington Ave at Prytania St; 9am-2:30pm

Established in 1833 by the former City of Lafayette, this cemetery is divided by two

TRANSPORTATION

Bus The 11 bus runs along Magazine St from Canal St to Audubon Park. The 12 bus runs the length of St Charles Ave.

Streetcar When operating, the St Charles Ave streetcar runs from Canal St along St Charles Ave through the CBD, the Garden District and Uptown.

Parking Metered parking is available on Magazine St and St Charles Ave. Free parking can be found on side streets.

intersecting footpaths that form a cross. Fraternal organizations and groups, such as the Jefferson Fire Company No 22, took care of their members and their families in large shared crypts. Some of the wealthier family tombs were built of marble, with elaborate detail rivaling the finest architecture in the district. But most tombs were constructed simply of inexpensive plastered brick. You'll notice many German and Irish names on the aboveground graves, testifying that immigrants were devastated by 19th-century yellow-fever epidemics. Not far from the entrance is a tomb containing the remains of an entire family that died of yellow fever.

The cemetery was filled within decades of it opening, and before the surrounding neighborhood reached its greatest affluence. By 1872, the prestigious Metairie Cemetery had already opened and its opulent grounds appealed to those with truly extravagant and flamboyant tastes.

An unusual event occurred at Lafayette Cemetery in July 1995, when author Anne Rice, who lived just a few blocks away, staged her own funeral here. She hired a horse-drawn hearse and a brass band to play dirges, and wore an antique wedding dress as she laid down in a coffin – because, she said, she wanted to experience her funeral *before* she was dead. (The newsworthy stunt coincided with the release of one of Rice's novels, so it wasn't pure frivolity.)

As with all the cemeteries in New Orleans, there is no security and lone visitors might be at risk within the secluded grounds. A good way to see the cemetery is to join a tour, or coincide your visit with a tour so that you're not alone on the grounds. The gates close early – don't get locked in!

IRISH CHANNEL

Across Magazine St from the Garden District, **Irish Channel** is another historic district of interest, though it's not nearly so posh as the Garden District. The Irish Channel was home to poor Irish immigrants who fled the potato famine in the 1840s. Irish laborers found ample work during New Orleans' mid-19th-century housing boom. Paradoxically, the wage-earning Irish were widely regarded as more economical than slaves, particularly for dangerous assignments, for it cost nothing to replace an Irish laborer who died on the job. The Irish Channel's humble shotgun houses and cottages are still home to a working-class community, and remnants of the city's Irish heritage can be felt on **St Patrick's Day** (p15), when a block party takes over Constance St, in front of **Parasol's Bar** (p189).

UPTOWN & RIVERBEND

Eating p190, Shopping p233, Sleeping p248

Uptown New Orleans is a splendid display of architectural extravagance. Block upon block of glorious mansions stand as symbols of the bustling trade and enterprise that made New Orleans one of the world's wealthiest cities in the mid-19th century.

Americans began to settle further beyond Canal St as development followed the streetcar tracks through the towns of Lafayette, Jefferson and Carrollton. Laid out on expansive plantations, these upriver towns were populated almost exclusively by English-speaking protestants who settled in New Orleans to capitalize on the burgeoning river trade. From the look of things, these folks were living the high life. Commodious street plans allowed for larger, more ostentatious houses and lush gardens. One by one, each of these towns became part of the city of New Orleans: Lafayette, annexed in 1852, was the first, followed by Jefferson in 1870 and, finally, Carrollton in 1874.

The presence of two private, side-by-side universities, Tulane and Loyola, ensures there is a constant influx of youth into the area, which otherwise might easily become stodgy.

TRANSPORTATION

Bus The 11 bus runs along Magazine St from Canal St to Audubon Park. The 12 bus runs the length of St Charles Ave. The 10 bus runs the length of Tchoupitoulas St, past Tipitina's.

Streetcar When operating, the St Charles Ave streetcar runs from Canal St along St Charles Ave from the Riverbend all the way to Canal St at the edge of the French Quarter.

Parking Metered parking is available on Magazine St and St Charles Ave. Free parking can be found on side streets.

Orientation

Uptown is the broad area above the Garden District. Maps of New Orleans rarely agree on the area's extents, but for the purposes of this book we'll say it includes everything above Louisiana Ave, between Magnolia to the river, including the Universities and Audubon Park. St Charles Ave, Magazine St and Tchoupitoulas St are the main routes that more or less follow the contours of the river. The Riverbend is the area above the campuses and Audubon Park. Where St Charles Ave meets S Carrollton Ave is the nexus of the area. Maple St and Oak St are narrow shopping strips that have some interesting restaurants and bars.

AUDUBON ZOOLOGICAL GARDENS

Map pp314-15

☎ 861-2537; www.auduboninstitute.org; adult/senior/child $12/9/7; 🕑 9am-5pm

The Audubon Zoo is among the country's best zoos. It is the heart of the Audubon Institute, which also maintains the Aquarium of the Americas (p152) and the Louisiana Nature Center.

The zoo is divided into distinct sections. **Louisiana Swamp** displays flora and fauna amid a Cajun cultural setting, which shows how the Cajuns harvested Spanish moss for use as furniture stuffing, among other details. The authentic fishing camp comes complete with shrimp trawls, crawfish traps and an oyster dredge. Alligators laze on the muddy bank of the bayou. Year-round in the exhibit, you'll see bobcats *(Lynx rufus floridamus),* red foxes *(Vulpes vulpes),* endangered Louisiana black bears *(Urses americanus luteolus)* and alligators snapping at a 200-pound giant turtle *(Macroclemys temminicki)* that wiggles its pink tongue as bait. Human intrusions into the swamp environment are poignantly represented with a *traånasee* cutter, used by fish and game trappers to create access across shallow swamps, and an 'Xmas Tree' oil-well cap, reminding us of the much larger corporate threat to the swamp environment.

The **Audubon Flight Exhibit** is best on quiet days, when you can enter the giant cage to sit and observe the bird species portrayed by ornithologist-artist John James Audubon in *Birds of America*. Of course, there are ducks galore, but you will be mesmerized by the brilliant plumage of species such as the scarlet ibis *(Eudocimus ruber)* and glossy ibis *(Plegadis falcmellus),* among others.

Most visitors are awed by the 'magnificent seven' in the **Reptile Encounter**, which displays representatives of the largest snakes in the world – from the king cobra that grows to over 18ft in length to the green anaconda that reaches 38ft. Many local species of nonpoisonous and poisonous snakes are also on display.

In the children's area, the centerpiece is the historic **Endangered Species Carousel** (adult/child $2/1), a spinning menagerie of elephants, rhinos, giraffes and other great and colorful creatures.

The zoo has added some high-tech attractions in recent years, including **Safari Simulator Ride** (adult/child $5/4), which works like a NASA simulator to make passengers experience the sensation of joining a jungle mission through a gorilla habitat. The same simulator is used to create virtual experiences like **H20 Odyssey**, in which passengers experience life as a raindrop. It's all good fun and educational too.

The **Swamp Train** (adult/child $4/3), which departs every 30 minutes from the Carousel train depot, offers a lazy tour of the zoo.

The Audubon Zoo, on the riverside of Magazine St and Audubon Park, is accessible from the French Quarter via the Zoo Cruise and the Magazine St bus 11, or you can take the St Charles Ave streetcar, if it's running, and walk 1½ miles through shady Audubon Park. Look for discount coupons in tourist magazines such as *Where*.

The **Audubon Zoo Cruise** (round-trip fare adult/child $17/8.50) offers a unique way to see the zoo and the Aquarium of the Americas in a day. Combined discount tickets for the riverboat cruise, zoo and aquarium are available. The boat departs the aquarium at 9am and 3pm. It leaves the zoo at 10am and 4pm (expect more departures as tourist numbers bounce back from Katrina).

TULANE UNIVERSITY Map pp314-15

☎ 865-4000; www.tulane.edu; 6823 St Charles Ave

The Tulane University was founded in 1834 as the Medical College of Louisiana in an attempt to control the repeated cholera and yellow-fever epidemics. In 1847, the University of Louisiana merged with the school. Paul Tulane's $1 million donation in 1883 initiated significant expansion –

plus it immortalized his name. The highly regarded medical school has since moved downtown to Tulane Ave. Tulane's law program is also well respected.

Tulane now boasts 22,000 students in 11 colleges and schools, including a law school and school of medicine. Among the university's most noted graduates are the president of France, Jacques Chirac, who wrote a thesis on the port of New Orleans, and former speaker of the US House of Representatives, Newt Gingrich, who opposed university censorship of the student newspaper in 1968.

The **University Center** features a bookstore, ATM and a **box office** (☎ 861-9283) that sells tickets for sporting and special events. Downstairs there's a bulletin board for information on apartment rentals, sublets and ride shares. *Hullabaloo,* the campus newspaper published during the school year, is a good source for campus happenings, such as free Friday open-air concerts and work opportunities.

The **Amistad Research Center** (☎ 865-5535; www.amistadresearchcenter.org; Tilton Memorial Hall; 9am-4:30pm Mon-Sat) is one of the nation's largest repositories specializing in African American history. Even if you haven't come to New Orleans to study, the rotating exhibits offer insight on ethnic heritage that you're not likely to get from any other source. The displayed works of art from the Aaron Douglas Collection are another reason to drop by – a few of the works are copied for sale.

Garden statue in Audubon Zoological Gardens

A specialized research library, the **Hogan Jazz Archive** (☎ 865-5688; 3rd floor, Joseph Merrick Jones Hall, 304 Freret St; 9am-5pm Mon-Fri) is worth visiting if you're writing a book about jazz, or are just seriously into jazz history. Most of its great wealth of material is not on exhibit; the librarian will retrieve items from the stacks for you. The collection includes stacks of 78rpm recordings, including early sides recorded by the Original Dixieland Jazz Band in 1917, and you can ask to listen to rare tracks if you like. There's also a wealth of oral histories, photos and early concert posters. Curator Bruce Raeburn is a great man to talk to if you've come with questions about jazz. For the more casual visitor, the Storyville Room, with its emphasis on Jelly Roll Morton (who played piano in the district's bordellos during the early 20th century) may be of interest.

The **Newcomb Art Gallery** (Woldenberg Art Center; admission free; 10am-5pm Mon-Fri, noon-5pm Sat & Sun) features a permanent exhibit of the college's collection, including Newcomb Pottery, rotating exhibits from the university's art collection, nationally recognized traveling exhibits and contemporary student and faculty exhibits. Flanking the gallery entrance are two important Tiffany stained-glass triptychs depicting figurative scenes, *The Resurrection* and *The Supper at Emmaus*.

LOYOLA UNIVERSITY Map pp314-15

☎ 865-2011; www.loyno.edu; 6363 St Charles Ave

Operated by Jesuits since 1904, and chartered in 1912, Loyola University is often overshadowed by its larger neighbor. Loyola educates just 5900 students, 3800 of them undergraduates. The cornerstone of Marquette Hall was laid in 1910. Loyola University is best known for its College of Music, School of Business and Department of Communications.

ESPLANADE RIDGE & BAYOU ST JOHN

Eating p194, Sleeping p249

Esplanade Ridge is a strip of subtly higher ground extending from Bayou St John along to the French Quarter. Early settlers in the area quickly recognized the many advantages of building their homes along here as a precaution against the seasonal floods that washed away the surrounding flatlands. The neighborhood abuts the Fair Grounds Race Track, and just below City Park is placid Bayou St John, where one of the original settlements of New Orleans stood.

Esplanade Ave, like St Charles Ave Uptown, is an exquisite residential concourse with neutral ground down the middle and a continuous oak canopy shading its lovely manses. The houses in this neighbourhood are less ostentatious than their Uptown counterparts, no doubt a reflection of the subtler tastes of the wealthy Creoles who built here.

There isn't much to entertain the sightseer, beyond an easy walk admiring the old homes. Upscale restaurants are clustered around the corner of Esplanade Ave and Ponce de Leon St. A visit to City Park, nearby, can easily segue into lunch or dinner around this culinary nexus.

Orientation

The area we're dealing with here is chiefly defined by Esplanade Ave and Bayou Rd, to the lakeside of Claiborne Ave. Where these two streets meet there is a cluster of restaurants and accommodations. There is another cluster of businesses on Esplanade Ave near the Fair Grounds. The historic Bayou St John neighborhood clings to the bayou in the area south of Esplanade Ave. (The actual bayou runs along the edge of City Park and crooks south of the park down to Mid-City.)

TRANSPORTATION

Bus The 91 bus runs up and down Esplanade Ave from City Park to Rampart St, where it skirts the lakeside of the French Quarter

Parking Street parking is generally easy to find on Esplanade Ave and on side streets.

FAIR GROUNDS RACE TRACK Map p317

☎ 944-5515; www.fairgroundsracecourse.com; 1751 Gentilly Blvd

The Union Race Course was laid out on this spot in 1852, and New Orleanians have been betting on the ponies pretty much nonstop ever since. The track was rechristened the Fair Grounds in 1863, during the Union occupation of New Orleans, and today the Churchill Downs Company (no relation to this author or to the legendary British prime minister) operates the track. Churchill Downs, of course, also hosts the USA's premier horse race, the Kentucky Derby, in Louisville, KY.

The Fair Grounds is the third-oldest track in the nation. During the Civil War, in addition to horse races, the Fair Grounds hosted bear fights and cavalry races. Today, the track is the site of the annual Louisiana Derby (in March), which many times has starred horses who have gone on to win bigger prizes at the Kentucky Derby and Preakness Stakes. Also held here, every April, is the **New Orleans Jazz & Heritage Festival** (p49), the second-largest event in the city after Mardi Gras.

The Fair Grounds' handsome gatehouse entryway was designed by James Gallier Jr in 1859 for an agricultural fair, and the stands were rebuilt following a disastrous fire in 1993. Buried in the infield here are derby winners from an era when New Orleans was one of the premier tracks in the country. The racing season runs from November to March on Wednesday through Sunday, with a 1:30pm post time.

ST LOUIS CEMETERY NO 3 Map p317

This relatively tidy looking cemetery was established in 1854 at the site of the old Bayou Cemetery and is worth strolling through for a few minutes (longer if you're a cemetery enthusiast). Of particular note here is the striking monument James Gallier Jr designed for his mother and father, who were lost at sea. James Gallier Sr was also a well-established architect who preceded his son in designing many of the city's landmark buildings. The cemetery's wrought-iron entrance gate is a beauty.

BAYOU ST JOHN

Graced with a variety of residential architectural styles, Bayou St John is a pleasant place to stroll through. French Canadians actually settled the area prior to the official founding of New Orleans. Long before that, Native Americans used the waterway to reach a ridge along what is now Esplanade Ave (or Esplanade Ridge), as this portage was the shortest route between the Mississippi River and Lake Pontchartrain. When explorers Iberville and Bienville learned of this path, they decided Bayou St John was the ideal place to settle. Later a canal built by Governor Carondelet extended the bayou to the edge of the French Quarter, nearly connecting the lake and the river. Navigation ended with the filling of the canal in 1927. A visit to this area is largely an opportunity to appreciate the beautiful houses that line the old waterway. Only one house, Pitot House, is actually open to the public.

At the Esplanade Bridge, you can see the entrance to City Park, on the left, and the **Beauregard Monument** (Map p317), dedicated to the French Creole Confederate general who ordered the first shots of the Civil War.

PITOT HOUSE Map p317

☎ 482-0312; 1440 Moss St; adult/senior/child $5/3/2; 🕑 10am-3pm Wed-Sat

This French-colonial plantation-style house was built in 1799. It is named for James Pitot, the first mayor of the incorporated city of New Orleans, who acquired it in 1810. Built entirely without corridors, the adjoining interior rooms allow air to circulate through the louvered shutters on the windows and upstairs back porch. The house also features a double-pitched roof and stucco-covered briquette *entre poteaux* construction.

OUR LADY OF THE ROSARY RECTORY Map p317

1342 Moss St

Built circa 1834 as the home of Evariste Blanc, Our Lady of the Rosary Rectory exhibits a combination of styles characteristic of the region. The high-hipped roof and wraparound gallery seem reminiscent of West Indies houses but were actually the preferred styles of the French Canadians who originally settled Bayou St John. However, it is the house's neoclassic details that make it obvious that this building is from a later period.

SANCTUARY Map p317

924 Moss St

This historic house was also built by Evariste Blanc, from 1816 to 1822, on land originally granted in 1720–1 to French Canadians. The once swampy property was later transferred to Don Andrés Almonaster y Roxas, the real-estate speculator who commissioned St Louis Cathedral on Jackson Sq in the French Quarter.

CITY PARK & AROUND

City Park (Map p317; ☎ 482-4888; www.neworleanscitypark.com), at 1300 acres, is the nation's fifth-largest urban park. Abutting the Bayou St John and the Bayou Metairie, the park is on the former Allard Plantation, which was acquired by the city of New Orleans in 1850. The park has dense groves of mature live oaks – thousands of them, some as old as 600 years – along with bald cypresses, Southern magnolias and many other magnificent species. Man-made amusements include a children's theme park, boating, fishing, horse stables, tennis courts, golf courses and a 400m track on which US Olympians have trained. Above all, the New Orleans Museum of Art is the most popular reason to visit the park.

City Park continues to recover from Hurricane Katrina, from which the park received a massive blow. Over 90% of the park was flooded by up to 8ft of salt water. Delicate plants in the Botanical Gardens were wiped out, ancient oaks split and uprooted, and nearly every blade of grass in the park turned a putrid yellow. While most of the park's attractions have reopened, many will be in various stages of recovery for years to come.

Orientation

City Park is a long (3 miles by 1 mile) strip of greenery that spans roughly a third of the distance between Lake Ponchartrain and the Mississippi River, with the lake forming the park's northern boundary. Esplanade Ave and Orleans Ave link it directly to the French Quarter. Most visitors just explore the lower third of the park, nearest Esplanade Ridge, where there are kiddy rides, caféterias and tennis courts, as well as the New Orleans Museum of Art.

TRANSPORTATION

Bus The 91 bus runs up and down Esplanade from the edge of the French Quarter to City Park. The 27 bus goes to City Park from the Garden District primarily via Louisiana and Washington Aves.

Parking Street parking is generally easy to find. There are lots near the museum and Storyland.

BOTANICAL GARDENS Map p317

☎ 482-4888; www.neworleanscitypark.com/nobg.php; adult/child $3/1; 🕑 10am-4:30pm Tue-Sun

This 12-acre garden has seen better days, but park workers are steadily restoring it after the near-total wipeout wrought by Katrina's flooding. Some parts of the garden were submerged for two weeks in 3ft of toxic saltwater. Not good for the vast majority of native and exotic species lovingly cultivated here. It was a cruel irony that many of the native species did not escape the fate of native wild plants dying out in Louisiana's disappearing wetlands. The garden's greenhouse species, such as orchids, bromeliads and gorgeous staghead ferns, perished when the electric-powered climate-control and watering systems failed.

As the gardens return to life, though, they'll be well worth visiting. Especially make a point to see the **Conservatory**, in which a simulated tropical rain forest includes hanging vines, a waterfall and a complement of snakes, geckos and tree frogs. A fossil exhibit includes dinosaur eggs and fossilized plants.

While you're here, also check out the **New Orleans Historic Train Garden**, a neat replica of old New Orleans through which G-gauge streetcars roll.

UPCOMING NOMA EXHIBITS

La Belle Femme Images of Women in French Society in the 19th Century from the National Museums of France (Mar 3-Jun 2, 2007)

Albert Durer Graphic Master Works (Jun 16-Aug 26, 2007)

Gaston Lachaise 1882–1935 (Sep 8-Oct 28, 2007)

Blue Winds Dancing The Whitecloud Collection of Native American Art (Nov 10, 2007-Feb 24, 2008)

Humans, Animals and the Spirit World Art from the Village and Tribal India, from the Figiel and Bhansali Collections (Mar 15-May 25, 2008)

The Baroque World of Fernando Botero (Jun 28-Sep 21, 2008)

Monet to Gauguin The Traveling Artist in the Age of Impressionism (Nov 8, 2008-Feb 1, 2009)

Zen Through Art The Paintings of Hakuin (Feb 21-May 2, 2009)

CAROUSEL GARDENS & STORYLAND Map p317

☎ 483-9382; admission $2, Christmas season $3; 🕑 usually 11am-2:30pm Wed-Sun

For children, the main attractions of City Park are these charmingly dated theme parks on Victory Ave.

The centerpiece of **Carousel Gardens** is a restored antique carousel, housed in a 1906 structure with a stained-glass cupola. In the 1980s, residents raised $1.2 million to restore the broken animals, fix the squeaky merry-go-round and replace the Wurlitzer organ. The results are naturally spectacular. Other rides on the grounds include a small roller coaster, a tilt-a-whirl and bumper cars. The City Park Railroad is also boarded here. Rides at Carousel Gardens cost an additional $1 each, however an $8 pass will allow you unlimited rides for the whole day.

Storyland has no rides, but the park's fairytale statuary is plenty of fuel for young imaginations. Children can play among – and climb upon – such larger-than-life figures as the Jabberwocky from *Alice in Wonderland*, or enter the mouth of the whale from *Pinocchio*. If these characters seem strangely similar to Mardi Gras floats, it's because they were created by master float-builder Blaine Kern. Storyland is open later on Saturday and Sunday. During the Christmas season, it's lit up like a Christmas tree.

DUELING OAKS Map p317

During the 19th century, hot-headed Creoles responded to challenges to their honor by arranging pistol duels behind St Louis Cathedral or here, in a shaded oak grove on the former Allard Plantation. There are some mighty old oaks here. Many of them were three centuries old when the French arrived.

A famous duel on this spot between a Baton Rouge newspaper editor and one Alcée La Branche refutes the notion that the pen is mightier than the sword. After three attempts in which the combatants missed each other from 40yd away, the fourth round felled the editor. Only one of the original Dueling Oaks still stands near the Museum of Art. You'll find more ancient oaks along the Bayou Metairie edge of the park.

Fortunately, Katrina's winds spared the lone surviving Dueling Oak, and the grove is still a good spot for a picnic without the interruption of formal firearm face-offs. Nowadays the city's vendettas are typically carried out elsewhere, and in the more casual drive-by style.

NEW ORLEANS MUSEUM OF ART Map p317

☎ 488-2631; www.noma.org; 1 Collins Diboll Circle; admission free; 🕑 10am-5pm Tue-Sun

The cultural focal point of City Park and one of the best art museums in all the South, NOMA was founded in 1910. It was a gift from philanthropist Isaac Delgado, and its permanent collection has grown to over 40,000 paintings, drawings, photographs, sculptures and decorative items. The collection is particularly strong in French and American art, including several works by Edgar Degas, who visited family in New Orleans and painted in the city. You'll also see paintings by Picasso, Braque, Dufy and Miro. NOMA also has an impressive and growing collection of African and Japanese art.

The 1st floor is where major traveling exhibits are shown (see Upcoming NOMA Exhibits opposite for more). These exhibits, which typically attract substantial crowds, usually feature associated lectures, films and workshops. If you're not here for a special exhibit, you might consider starting with the 3rd-floor permanent exhibits, where pre-Columbian art created by the Mayas and Incas sets the stage for European influences, which are shown on the 2nd floor.

The **Courtyard Café** offers lunch and snacks from 10:30am to 4:30pm.

SYDNEY AND WALDA BESTHOFF SCULPTURE GARDEN Map p317

☎ 488-2631; www.noma.org; 1 Collins Diboll Circle; 🕑 Fri-Sun

Just outside the New Orleans Museum of Art, the Besthoff Sculpture Garden opened in 2003 with some 45 pieces from the world-renowned Besthoff collection. The garden collection is growing – 55 works at the latest count – and includes mostly contemporary works by such artists as Antoine Bourdelle, Henry Moore and Louis Bourgeois.

METAIRIE CEMETERY Map pp306-7

☎ 486-6331; 5100 Pontchartrain Blvd; admission free

Having visited other New Orleans cemeteries doesn't quite prepare you for the stunning architectural splendor and over-the-top extravagance of Metairie Cemetery. Established in 1872 on a former race track (the grounds, you'll notice, still follow the oval layout), Metairie Cemetery is the most American of New Orleans' cities of the dead

Metairie Cemetery

and, like the houses of the Garden District, its tombs appear to be attempts at one-upmanship.

This is the final resting place for many of New Orleans' most prominent citizens, and some of the cemetery's inhabitants are fairly famous. William Charles Cole Claiborne, Louisiana's first American governor, is here, as is Confederate General PGT Beauregard. Jefferson Davis was laid to rest here, only to be moved to Richmond, Virginia, two years later. Trumpet player Louis Prima occupies a family tomb inscribed with the refrain from his signature song, *Just a Gigolo* – 'When the end comes they'll know/I was just a gigolo/Life goes on without me.'

But the real highlight here is the architecture. Many of the family tombs and monuments gracing Metairie Cemetery's concentric ovals are stunning, bringing together stone, bronze and stained glass. The statuary here is often elegant, touchingly sad and even sensual. Highlights include the **Brunswig mausoleum**, a pyramid guarded by a sphinx statue; the **Moriarty monument**, the reputed 'tallest privately owned monument' in the entire country; and the **Estelle Theleman Hyams monument**, with its stained glass casting a somber blue light over a slumped, despondent angel statue.

Visitors can drop by the funeral home on the grounds and select either the 'Soldier, Statesmen, Patriots, Rebels' or 'Great Families and Captains of Commerce' self-guided tours. You will be given a map and loaned a recorded cassette and tape player (no charge).

Seeing everything on the 150-acre grounds is most easily accomplished by car. Tape tours take about an hour, but stretching this out by getting out of your car for a closer look at the tombs is highly recommended.

Walking Tours

A Sober Stroll in the Quarter 166
Garden District & Irish Channel Walk 168
Spine-Tingling Tour 170
Nightlife Crawl 172

Walking Tours

New Orleans was made for walking. Tourists staying in or near the French Quarter will have little need for a car, bus or cab, except at night. So while, you're doing all that walking, you ought to be paying attention to what you're walking past. The city's blocks are short and densely packed with historic buildings that are interesting to look at. And behind the façades are intriguing stories, just as you would imagine.

Detail of cornstalk fence

In this chapter we'll outline four walking tours, beginning with a surface-scratching stroll through the French Quarter. By taking in some of the sights in the heart of the old Creole District, we hope you'll be inspired to explore the neighborhood more thoroughly on your own. We'll follow a similar tack in the historic Garden District, taking in the beautiful old houses that the neighborhood is famous for, and then wander Magazine St for some fun gallery hopping. This tour will also take in a bit of the Irish Channel.

We'll round things out with two thematic tours in the French Quarter that are best done in the evening – or even late at night. The Spine-Tingling Tour delves into the creepy lore of the old Quarter. The Nightlife Crawl is just a good boozer that easily avoids Bourbon St. Hey, you can find your own way to Bourbon St, pal.

A SOBER STROLL IN THE QUARTER

This walk explores the French Quarter's two main drags: Bourbon St and Royal St. Goofus and Gallant, if you will. Think of this as a quick introduction to the Quarter. Obviously, every block is worth a stroll if you're really into the architecture and atmosphere of this beautifully preserved historic district. We'll just sample a bit of the Quarter's architecture and some of its intriguing lore and then close out with a relaxing courtyard lunch.

WALK FACTS

Start Pirate's Alley
End Napoleon House
Distance 1 mile
Duration 45 minutes
Fuel Stop Stop for a drink at Lafitte's Blacksmith Shop (p201), finish with a courtyard snack at Napoleon House (p201)

Begin at **Pirate's Alley**, an inviting walkway that cuts through the shadow of St Louis Cathedral. The alley is supposedly where the pirate Jean Lafitte hawked goods plundered from Spanish ships. However, some city records indicate the alley did not open until 1831, long after Lafitte and his gang were gone. To the right is gated **St Anthony's Garden 1**, which lost some of its lushness in the hurricanes of 2005 but nevertheless remains a peaceful pocket in the bustling Quarter. Halfway up the alley, stop in at the small but charming **Faulkner House Bookstore 2** (p140). It opened in 1990 and very quickly became a focal point for New Orleans literary circles. It is so named because in 1925 author William Faulkner briefly lived in the house (the street was then called Orleans Alley).

Much of the alley is occupied by the **Labranche Buildings** (3; 622-624 Pirate's Alley), which wrap around Royal St to St Peter St. Slow down to admire the balconies, which display a variety of attractive cast-iron and wrought-iron styles. The houses were built by Jean Baptiste Labranche, a Creole sugar planter.

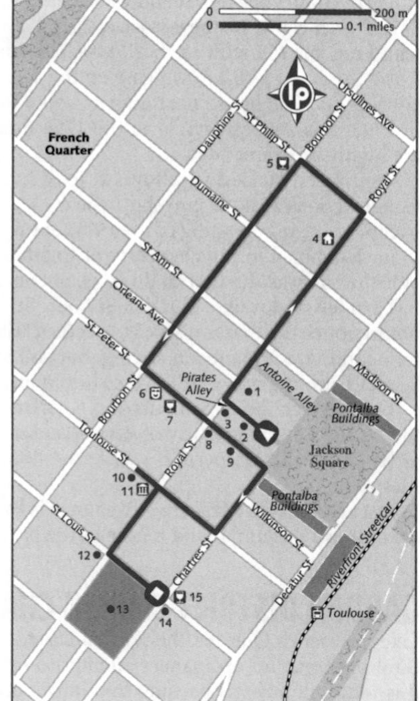

Turn right at Royal St. You'll soon notice that this street takes the cake when it comes to classic New Orleans postcard images. Many of the structures along the following blocks are graced by cast-iron galleries and potted plants hanging from the balconies. Take it slow and appreciate the details.

The **Cornstalk Hotel** 4 (p238) stands behind one of the most frequently photographed fences anywhere. The cast-iron fence with its cornstalk motif was manufactured in 1859 and has seen many coats of paint over the years but is looking pretty good.

Turn the corner at St Philip St and head towards Bourbon St. If you have ever had a bad experience with whiskey, saying the word 'bourbon' will probably make you belch. It's an appropriate response for the street as well. Most nights Bourbon St is crammed with accountants, librarians and book publishers unwinding after a long day at the convention center. And some of them are shamefully drunk! Those people mooning you from the balconies don't look much like librarians, so probably the population here might be a little more diverse than we're supposing.

The ramshackle one-story structure on the corner of St Philip St is a great little tavern called **Lafitte's Blacksmith Shop** 5 (p201). Legend has it pirate Jean Lafitte ran a blacksmith shop here with his brother, Pierre. If so, it would have been a front for their trade in stolen and smuggled goods. Although such stories are not necessarily true, the little relic looks like the real deal and indeed it is old enough. Architecturally, it stands out for its exposed brick-between-post construction. Most of the houses in the Quarter are built in this style, but the brick and framework is almost always concealed in stucco or wood. Have a drink to brace yourself for Bourbon St. We'll just stroll down it for a few blocks, speechless.

Turn left down St Peter St towards the river and we'll soon pass the rustic façade of **Preservation Hall** 6 (p207), where old-time jazz musicians perform nightly to a packed house. At nighttime, you'll hear the trumpets and trombones blaring through the open windows.

Practically next door is **Pat O'Brien's** 7 (p202), a bar famous for its syrupy signature beverage, the 'Hurricane.' You can walk through Pat's large scenic courtyard, take in the raucous scene or become part of it, before re-emerging on Bourbon St. If you do, be sure to loop back around to St Peter St, and head in the direction of Royal St.

At the corner of Royal, take a look at **LeMonnier Mansion** (8; 640 Royal St), which is commonly known to be New Orleans' first skyscraper. Begun in 1795, the structure grew to three stories tall by 1811 (a fourth floor was added in 1876). Until that time, building in New Orleans was generally limited to two floors, for fear that the swampy soil couldn't support taller structures. Notice that this building's one-time owner, Dr Yves LeMonnier, left his initials in the wrought-iron balcony that overlooks the street corner.

On the next block, the **Avart-Peretti House** (9; 632 St Peter St) is where Tennessee Williams lived in 1946–7 when he was writing his most famous play, *A Streetcar Named Desire*. Shout out 'Stella!' here. The neighbors love that sort of thing.

Turn left on Chartres St and walk a block, past a pretty row of antique shops, to Toulouse St and turn right. At the corner of Royal and Toulouse Sts stand a pair of houses built by Jean François Merieult in the 1790s. The corner house, called the **Court of Two Lions** (10; 541 Royal St), has a well-known gate on the Toulouse St side, flanked by marble lions atop the entry posts. The house next door is home to the **Historic New Orleans Collection** 11 (p139). Built in 1792, it is a rare survivor of the 1794 fire. Organized tours of the house and collection are highly recommended.

Continue a block down Royal St to St Louis St. On this corner, in what is now James H Cohen & Sons antique gun shop, the cocktail supposedly was invented. The premises were occupied at the beginning of the 19th century by **Peychaud's Apothecary** 12. Old Peychaud is said to have dabbled in the chemistry of imbibible spirits, and served his drinks to the public. Whether he was the first to do so is, of course, widely disputed.

Turn left and walk a block of St Louis St, back to Chartres. All the while, it's impossible not to notice the massive **State Supreme Court Building** 13. Opened in 1909, the white-marble and terracotta façade stands in jarring, but still attractive contrast with the rest of the Quarter. Scenes from the movie *JFK* were shot in and around the building.

The intersection of St Louis and Chartres is flanked by two noteworthy buildings. First there's the sobering history of **Maspero's Exchange** 14 (p141), a restaurant that once was known as La Bourse de Maspero. It was a slave-trading house and coffee shop operated by Pierre Maspero.

Just across from Maspero's Exchange is **Napoleon House** 15 (p201), where we'll end our tour over a bowl of gumbo and a beer in the beautiful courtyard.

GARDEN DISTRICT & IRISH CHANNEL WALK

Like the French Quarter, the Garden District is a National Historic District, where architectural preservation ordinances attempt to maintain the character of the area. So, naturally, this tour will have us pausing to admire some of New Orleans' most beautiful homes, all built during the city's wealthiest period, just prior to the Civil War. But relax, this tour isn't strictly about envying the neighborhood's impossibly rich residents. We'll also swing down to the workaday Irish Channel and take a jaunt down a few blocks of Magazine St to have a look at some art galleries and other interesting shops.

WALK FACTS

Start Corner Fourth St and St Charles Ave
End Corner Magazine and St Mary Sts
Distance 2 miles
Duration 90 minutes
Fuel Stop A fancy lunch at Commander's Palace (p190) or a po'boy at Parasol's (p189)

If you're taking the St Charles Ave streetcar out to this neighborhood, disembark at Third St and walk to the corner of Fourth and Prytania Sts.

Colonel Robert Short's House (1; 1448 Fourth St) was home to a Confederate officer. The house was seized by federal authorities during the Civil War, but was returned at the war's end to Short, who lived there until his death in 1890. Designed by architect Henry Howard, who is renowned in these parts, it is an exemplary double-gallery home with fine cast-iron details. It is further distinguished by a cornstalk cast-iron fence, identical to the more famous cornstalk fence in the French Quarter.

The lovely **Charles Briggs' House** (2; 2605 Prytania St) stands out for deviating dramatically from the local style. Designed by James Gallier Sr in 1849, the house's Gothic pointed-arch windows and Elizabethan chimneys are unique in the neighborhood.

The **Chapel of Our Lady of Perpetual Help** (3; 2521 Prytania St) is another Henry Howard design, built in 1856. It was commissioned by Henry Lonsdale, a merchant who made an incredible fortune trading gunnysacks and coffee.

The **Louise S McGehee School** (4; 2343 Prytania St) occupies one of the Garden District's most impressive mansions. Built in 1872 – later than other grand mansions in the district – the house combines decorative French second-empire and classic styles. The architect is unknown, but stylistic clues suggest it may have been James Freret. The building has been home to an all-girls academy since 1929.

Turn right at Jackson Ave for a good look at the largest house of the neighborhood. The **Buckner House** (5; 1410 Jackson St) was built in 1856 for cotton merchant Henry S Buckner. The architect was Lewis E Reynolds. Its wide galleries on all four sides are luxurious – the house seems to yawn contentedly in all directions.

Head back into the neighborhood, making your way down Chestnut St to the corner of First St. **Anne Rice's house** (6; 1239 First St), called 'Rosegate,' is no longer the home of the author of best-selling novels such as *Interview with the Vampire*. But she lived here for many years, and she regularly invited fans to tour the home. The place looks strangely free of spooks, but who knows what sort of goings-on disturbed the place at night while Rice slept here.

Also near this corner, the **Joseph Carroll House** (7; 1315 First St) is a glorious center-hall house with double galleries laced with cast-iron filaments. The house was designed by architect Samuel Jamison for Carroll, a cotton factor. Peer towards the back of the lot to see the similarly impressive carriage house.

Turn left on Coliseum and continue to Washington St for a rewarding lunch at **Commander's Palace** 8 (p190), long considered one of the best restaurants in America. Across the street, you can explore Lafayette Cemetery No 1 (p156).

We've had our fill of gorgeous buildings, so now follow Sixth St out to Magazine St. This is one of the city's most interesting and vital shopping districts, lined with creative shops and galleries.

Near the corner of Magazine and Sixth Sts, **Anton Haardt Gallery** 9 (p213) is a superb dealer of contemporary folk art from around the South. Drop in to see if Haardt is exhibiting works by celebrated outsider artists like Howard Finster or Clementine Hunter.

On the same block, **Christopher's Discoveries** 10 (p233) is an intriguing shop filled with unusual art and furnishings from Asia and the Middle East. The owner obviously has a finely honed sensibility, and the objects are well presented in the manner of an old curiosity shop.

While we're in the area, let's detour into the Irish Channel, another of the city's historic districts, by taking a right on Third St. The area was home to poor Irish immigrants who fled the potato famine in the 1840s, and many of these immigrants were laborers who built the Garden District nearby. It's still basically a working-class residential enclave, with streets lined with charming shotgun houses. The only place compelling a traveler to stop is **Parasol's** 11 (p189), on the corner of Constance and Third Sts. It's an exemplary neighborhood bar that also happens to be known for superior po'boy sandwiches.

Stroll a few blocks through the Irish Channel, then return to Magazine St via First St. **Simon of New Orleans** 12 (p213) is the shop of a groovy local painter known for his dazzling, sparkly signs. Be sure to make your way towards the rustic back courtyard, which is jam-packed with curiosities.

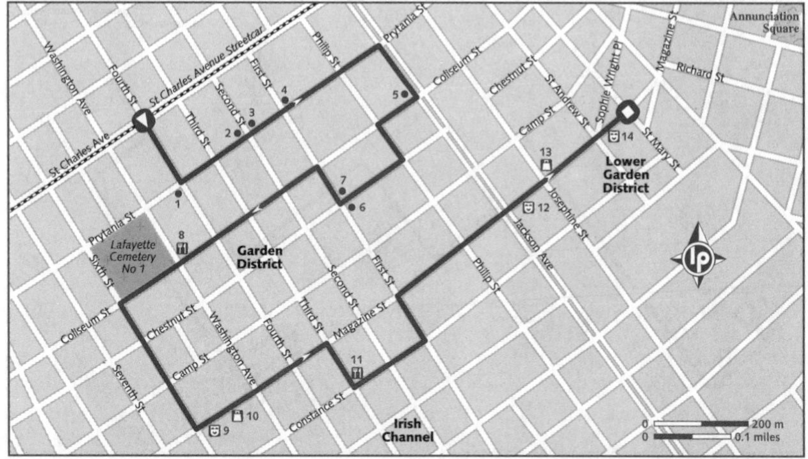

On the other side of the street, the **Southern Fossil & Mineral Exchange** 13 (p232) is always worth a stop to look at the collection of skulls, geodes and ancient miscellanea.

Stroll on by more galleries and antique shops until you reach the **Perrin Benham Gallery** 14 (p213), one of the city's best purveyors of vibrant contemporary art. You're in luck if they're showing works by the Brazilian painter Mauro Tambeiro, a major talent.

This'll give you a taste of what the neighborhood has to offer. You may want to linger longer, or even return to this part of town another day.

SPINE-TINGLING TOUR

There's a story for every ghost and a ghost for every house in New Orleans. Most of the stories were passed down orally until book collections and websites preserved them for posterity. While the most enduring stories all have a strong element of believability in them, few of them are verifiable.

If you have the opportunity, venture out into the French Quarter late on a rainy night, and you will become acquainted with the shuttered solitude of the old town. You'll encounter other live humans skulking the streets in a manner that suggests they too are communing with the French Quarter's darker, deeper side. Even if it's not raining, this tour is best done at night.

WALK FACTS

Start St Louis Cathedral, Jackson Sq
End St Louis Cemetery No 1
Distance 1.5 miles
Duration One hour, more with stops
Fuel Stop Stop for a courtyard lunch at Café Amelie (p181); when the tour is complete, have coffee at Café du Monde (p178)

You'll be pretty good and spooked by the time we finish this tour, so you might want to buddy up with someone now. If you want to chicken out now, go ahead. We'll forever consider you a coward, but we won't say no to drinks if you're paying.

St Louis Cathedral 1 (p137) is more than a starting place for us. It has its own scary stories, including one having to do with a singing ghost who is said to have been an 18th-century priest. On wet, blustery nights, the priest's song can be heard in the wind. He was Père Dagobert, and he no doubt made a compelling hero in French New Orleans more than two centuries ago. When Spain assumed control of Louisiana in 1762, a small group of French-speaking Creoles launched a rebellion that was easily crushed. All of the rebels were executed and denied a funeral by the Spanish, but Père Dagobert honored them with a proper funeral anyway. It is said he still keens in the rain and it is very sad, for few who hear him are moved by his story.

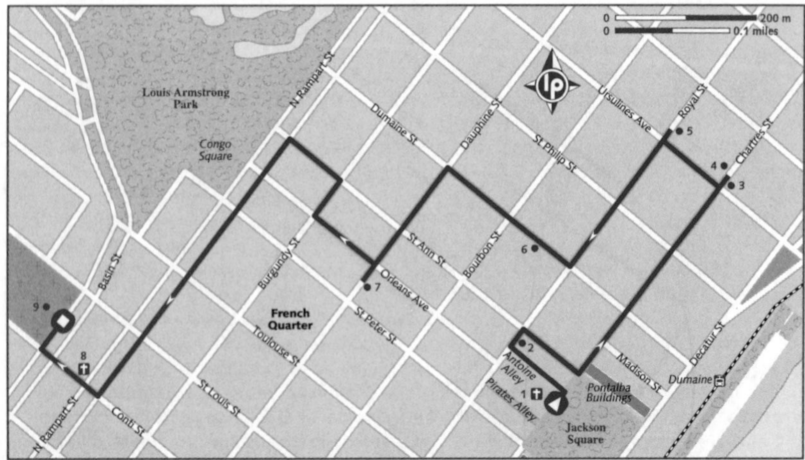

Now, let's grab hold of our wits and head up dark Antoine Alley. At the corner of Royal stands the **house of the octoroon mistress** (2; 734 Royal St). Her name was Julie and, like many octoroon (one-eighth black) women in old New Orleans, this apparition is said to have been the mistress of a white Creole man, and she had hopes that he would make an honest woman out of her. When he refused to marry her, Julie supposedly stripped naked and lay on the roof of this house on a cold December night. She caught her death of cold, and her spirit is said to linger around the place still. Over the years people have reported catching glimpses of her skirts as she playfully hides about the house. Look up at the gabled window coming out of the roof – maybe you'll spot her there.

Statue of Christ in front of St Louis Cathedral (p137)

After turning down St Ann then walking three blocks along beautiful Chartres St, we reach the **Ursuline Convent 3** (p142), haunted by vampires, some say. In the 18th century, when girls were sent from France to New Orleans to be educated by the Ursuline nuns, they brought their clothes in wooden crates – thus the girls became known as the 'casket girls.' Later, during yellow-fever epidemics, the notion took hold that the city was being ravaged by vampires who were spreading the disease. One thing lead to another, and it was concluded that the vampires had been brought over from Europe by these poor girls in their casket-like trunks.

Across the street, the **Beauregard-Keyes House 4** (p139) has one of the very best ghost stories in town. The house is reputedly haunted by its one-time resident, Civil War General PFT Beauregard, who along with some of his old cronies re-enacts the battle of Shiloh every now and then in the house's main hall. It happens rarely, and usually very late at night. Just keep an ear out for the sounds of canon fire, snorting mules, the clash of sabers and maybe even a marching band, and you'll know the general is having a grand old time in this historic house.

Walk up the block to **Madame Lalaurie's house** (5; 1140 Royal St), which is haunted by the victims of one of New Orleans' most grisly, gruesome crimes. In the 1830s Madame Lalaurie slaughtered her slaves in the house, set the place ablaze then disappeared into the night, never to be heard from again. By the 1920s, a low-income apartment house stood on the site, and a tenant reported seeing a man walking about the hallways carrying his head in his hand.

Head back along Royal and turn up Dumaine St. We'll pass the **Historic Voodoo Museum 6** (p140), which is certainly worth a stop during the day, though voodoo doesn't give non-practicioners the willies the way it once did.

Turn left on Dauphine. We're now looking for the **sultan's palace** (7; 716 Dauphine St), where another gruesome slaughter took place. The story involves a mysterious Turk who, during the 1860s, moved into the house with a group of beautiful women presumed to be his harem. The doors and windows of the place always remained shuttered, which drove the neighbors mad with curiosity, until one day it was discovered that everyone in the house, including the Turk, had been murdered. The ghosts in the house don't seem to be very upset about what happened to them. Every now and then people say they have heard the tinkling of bells and the plunking of stringed instruments coming from inside the house.

Make your way back to Rampart St to check out the voodoo temples there. Then cross over to the **Mortuary Chapel** 8 (p148). The church was specifically built in 1826 so that funerals for yellow-fever victims could be held here, across the street from the cemetery, rather than at St Louis Cathedral, in the center of town. Sources estimate anywhere between 7000 to 12,000 victims died of the disease in 1853 alone. Either way, it's a lot of funerals each day. While here, say a prayer before the statue of 'St Expedite,' the mysterious saint who was never canonized and probably never existed.

St Louis Cemetery No 1 9 (p147) is a pretty run-down, creepy sort of place. It's also stunningly beautiful. You'll notice the crypts are all above ground. The bodies in this cemetery rest within the crypt itself, rather than in the ground. Early French settlers here learned the hard way that it's difficult to keep the dead down when they're buried in such wet earth. After a little rain, bodies and boxes floated down the street. No wonder people in New Orleans are so easily spooked. While in the cemetery, be sure to pay your respects at the tomb of Marie Laveau. It's in the Glapion, Laveau and Paris family crypt. You'll observe the 'x' marks scratched on the tomb's plaster façade, along with offerings such as candles, little dolls and such. Marie Laveau's spirit is doubtless flattered by all this attention so long after her death in 1881. However, other members of the family take offense at all this nonsense.

Hope we didn't scare you too much. Pleasant dreams tonight.

NIGHTLIFE CRAWL

Hopefully this tour won't involve any actual crawling. Think of it as a fun outing through the French Quarter and Faubourg Marigny that's best done with a friend. You might keep each other from getting lost, and if your gait takes on a precarious tilt, you'll have someone to lean against. Needless to say, we're assuming you're not just taking this tour to *look* at the bars. Stop and linger awhile, enjoy a beer or a cocktail while appreciating New Orleans' wealth of fine drinking establishments.

Here's how we'll approach this thing. We'll start in the early evening, have a few drinks in the Quarter, fortify ourselves on tasty bar food, try and catch some live music on Frenchmen St, then maybe hop in a cab to a late show somewhere else in town.

WALK FACTS

Start Corner St Louis and Chartres Sts
End Corner Chartres and Frenchmen Sts
Distance 1 mile
Duration Several hours
Fuel Stop Casual Cajun food at Coop's Place (p179) or curry at Hookah Café (p186)

We'll start at **Napoleon House** 1 (p201) because it's historic and because it tends to close ridiculously early. This old bar's atmosphere conjures up all of the city's intriguing history. While relishing your first beer of the evening, ponder that the building's original owner, Mayor Nicholas Girod, supposedly plotted with the pirate Jean Lafitte to free Napoleon Bonaparte from his exile on the remote island of St Helena. These prominent New Orleanians intended to set up the deposed emperor in an apartment upstairs from this bar. The plot was foiled by the emperor's untimely death.

Enough history. Let's wander on through the Quarter, bracing ourselves for the hard work ahead. Stick to Chartres St for a few blocks, as Decatur St around Jackson Sq will only feel like a premature hangover. Lower Decatur St, however, has a row of excellent old dives that we'll want to duck into.

Lined up along a single block of Decatur are **Molly's at the Market** 2 (p201), **Coop's Place** 3 (p179) and the **Abbey** 4 (p200). All are great bars in their own manner, but we don't recommend drinking in all of these places. Pick one, maybe two. Coop's is a cut above the others on the strength of its stellar menu featuring filling and tasty Cajun dishes – like gas in the engine for the journey ahead.

Two blocks down, **Oswald's Speakeasy** 5 (p202) is a convivial spot on the very edge of the French Quarter. You enter through a narrow passageway, through a small courtyard, and into a dark bar room that looks like a stripped-down Victorian-era beer hall. A variety of entertainments is offered here. Someone may be tinkling the ivories, or owner Harry Anderson may be hosting one of his comical magic shows.

Cross Esplanade and you're in the Faubourg Marigny, which is always a lively part of town when the sun goes down. The trendy **Hookah Café** 6 (p186) might draw you in, particularly if you're in the mood for smoking some *shisha*. It's a perfectly legal indulgence imported from the Islamic world, but it'll make you woozy if you're not used to it. You can also drink booze or eat curries if the smoking option looks like too great a threat to your well-being.

Round the bend of Frenchmen St is one of the city's great nightlife zones, with a smattering of bars, clubs, cafés, restaurants and live-music venues. A good bet for music, even if it's still early in the evening, is the **Spotted Cat** 7 (p208). This small, friendly bar regularly crams blues or swing bands onto its tiny stage, beginning at 7pm.

Across the way is **d.b.a.** 8 (p203), a cosmopolitan sort of place with a stage. The selection of imported beers and microbrews from around the country is an unexpected taste

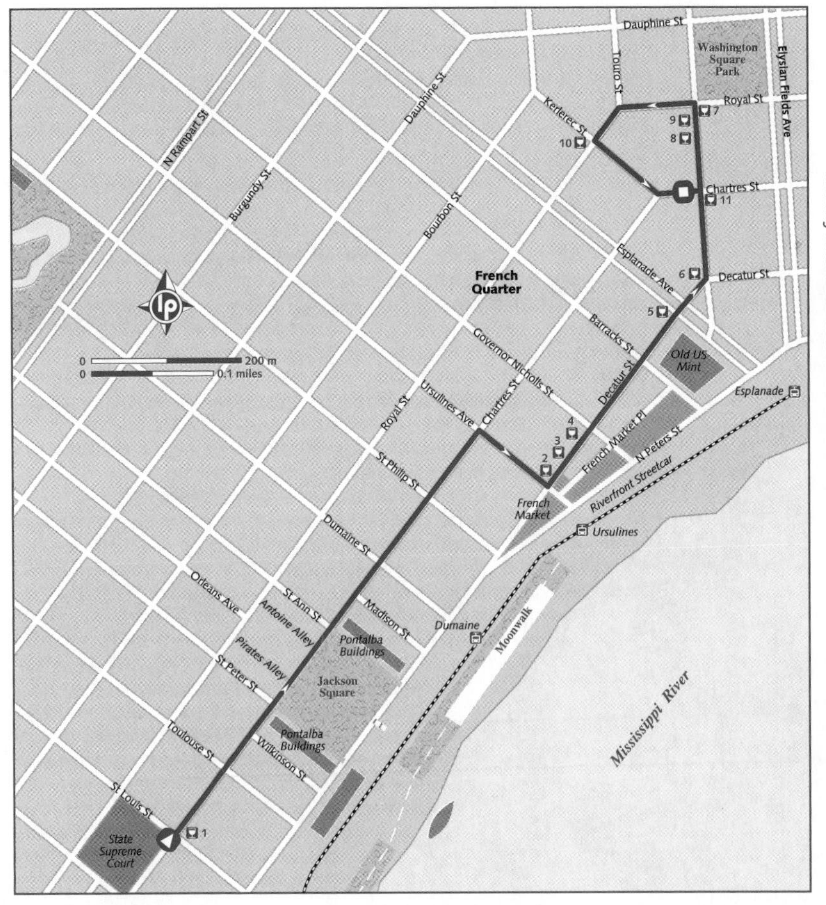

of globalism in this far-flung, waterlogged outpost. The music offerings here are always top-notch, so you might be induced to stay awhile.

For serious jazz, mosey on over to **Snug Harbor 9** (p208). It's the city's number-one jazz club, with little cocktail tables in front of a well-lit stage. Another great local tavern, the hip and funky **R Bar 10** (p203), is around the corner, down Royal St. If it's late and you're in more of a partying frame of mind, head on over to **Café Brasil 11** (p202). On the nights Fredy Omar's salsa big band is performing, you're set – no need for further plans.

If it's Thursday night, though, hop into a cab and head out to Vaughan's (p208) in the Bywater, where Kermit Ruffins kicks off around 11pm and keeps the bar hopping until very late.

Eating

French Quarter 178
Tremé District 185
Faubourg Marigny & Bywater 185
CBD & Warehouse District 187
Lower Garden & Garden Districts 188
Uptown & Riverbend 190
Esplanade Ridge 194

Eating

Food is one of New Orleans' biggest tourist attractions, and people big and small come to the Big Easy for a sublime feeding frenzy. Visitors can plan their entire itinerary around meals in this town, resigning themselves to the reality that they'll be a few pounds heavier when they get home.

New Orleans has rich and unique culinary traditions that run deeper than those of most North American cities. Beginning with the traditions of French cuisine, the chefs and household cooks of New Orleans created and gradually elevated their own style of cooking. Creole cuisine, one of the USA's most distinctive regional cuisines, originated here. Many venerated 19th-century eateries continue to satisfy the local palate – you can still dine at Antoine's, established in 1840, and experience pretty much the same meal that was served there more than a century ago.

Chef preparing the meals at Café Degas (p196)

But New Orleans' reputation as a gastronomic paradise doesn't rest solely on tradition. Many contemporary chefs are challenging the city's old culinary habits and winning over loyal new followings. Fresh and local, the bywords of contemporary American cuisine, are fully appreciated here. Some New Orleans chefs have pioneered creative culinary approaches to rival the cutting-edge trends of New York, San Francisco and Los Angeles. Asian, Mexican, Indian and European influences are creeping in, sometimes in surprising combinations. But new trends pass muster only if they appeal to the local population, which takes its food rather seriously and isn't easily impressed. The local audience won't go for food unless, above all else, it tastes great.

A good way to approach the local culinary landscape is to mix it up. Sample different types of eateries. Plan a traditional four-course meal at a classic Creole establishment, have po'boys at a casual neighborhood joint, try one of the city's excellent contemporary offerings, have an exquisite meal in a fine cottage bistro, pull all the stops for brunch or breakfast, see if you can finish a muffuletta sandwich. Surely you get the idea. Let's eat.

Opening Hours

Since Hurricane Katrina hit New Orleans opening hours for most businesses have been constantly changing. Many businesses are not fully staffed, while others simply aren't attracting enough business to stay open every day. So, while a restaurant may have served two or three meals six or seven days a week before Katrina, it may currently only be serving one or two meals four or five days a week. Some places known for staying open around the clock now are open for maybe eight hours instead. And the hours posted one week may change the next. Opening hours should stabilize in time (possibly before your visit), but the new hours are not likely to match pre-Katrina hours.

That said, most places that serve breakfast are open from 7am or 8am until around 10am or 11am. Some of these establishments also serve lunch, and make the breakfast and lunch menus available until 2pm or so. If fresh biscuits are on the menu, bear in mind they're likely to be fresh until about 9am or 10am in diners and mom-and-pop places. Brunch is available on Sundays from around 11am until 2pm or 3pm, though some places that stake their reputations on brunch keep it going all week long. Dinner hours generally start at 6pm and go until 9pm or 10pm. New Orleans has no shortage of eateries that keep their kitchens going past midnight, though. Some, but not all of the late-eats joints are bars.

How Much?

New Orleans is generally not so expensive as most other US cities. Many of the city's finest restaurants offer a range of main dishes for under $20. Some of New Orleans' signature dishes – like po'boys, red beans and rice, oysters on the half shell and gumbo – are widely available for under $10. The old-line Creole restaurants, however, are all rather expensive. Their à la carte menus tend to have mains starting around $25, and then you have to put down another $6 to $10 for side dishes. Start with a bowl of soup or a salad and you're looking at a meal of around $50. Add wine, dessert and coffee and of course it all mounts up.

PRICE GUIDE

$	under $15
$$	$15 to $30
$$$	more than $30

One way to save money is to do like the farmers do and make lunch your main meal of the day. Lunch menus in the city's best restaurants are usually abridged versions of the evening menu, with many of the same dishes considerably marked down in price. In the evening, you can still have a quality meal in a po'boy shop or even in a bar. Some of the city's bars serve excellent food.

Booking Tables

Some of New Orleans' restaurants are just too popular. Where reservations are really necessary, we'll say so in our listings in this chapter. It's generally best to call a day or two ahead. You can even try snagging a table with a call on the same afternoon. After all, business is slow in the new New Orleans, but expect that to change.

For some exceedingly popular places, it may be wise to call before you even arrive in New Orleans. If you're staying in a hotel with concierge service, ask if the hotel can book your tables for you.

Many restaurants have no-booking policies. Galatoire's (p182) and K-Paul's (p184) are two notable examples. This just means instead of calling ahead, you can expect to wait out on the sidewalk for a table to open up.

If no tables are available in your favorite restaurant, you might want to see for yourself if everyone's on the take in this town. An offer of $20 or so to the maître d' might make a table suddenly turn up. Our regrets if the Big Easy turns out to be not so easy. Take heart. This city has a *lot* of excellent restaurants!

Take-out & To Go

Take-out meals are widely available at all hours. Po'boy shops and delis do half their trade in 'to go' orders, as do many soul-food joints. Most coffee shops and diners will pack up a meal as well. Grocery stores often have a deli that will prepare sandwiches and the like.

The French Quarter has few parks, but you might want to have an impromptu picnic in Jackson Sq or on the levee of the Mississippi River. If your hotel room has a balcony that's not getting much use, you can set up some candles and unfold your take-out for a romantic meal. Elsewhere in town, parks are more common. Audubon Park, in the shade of oak trees, makes a particularly nice picnic ground. Same goes for City Park, once it has recovered from the devastation of Hurricane Katrina.

Tipping

You just have two thumbs, so we'll just provide two simple rules for you: tipping is not optional in sit-down restaurants; an adequate tip for your server is 15%. It needn't be any more complicated than that, but there are some finer points to bear in mind. Most over-the-counter establishments will have a tip jar with a note telling you it's bad karma not to tip. That may be so, but you're not obliged to. And if you feel like tipping a dude for pouring coffee into a paper cup for you, a little spare change will do. That little jangle in the jar will make him eternally grateful to you. Delis and po'boy shops operate on a similar basis.

By the way, 15% is merely a baseline. If you're really happy with the service, 20% or so is not out of line. Some places will charge an automatic 18% gratuity for large groups (usually of six or more people).

FRENCH QUARTER

The French Quarter offers the greatest number and variety of restaurants in town. Here you'll find all the old-line Creole restaurants you've already heard about, along with newer high-profile places run by Emeril Lagasse and Susan Spicer. Thrown into the mix are plenty of genuine neighborhood joints serving up high-quality fare for very little money. During peak seasons reservations at some of the more popular places can be difficult to get.

CAFÉ DU MONDE Map pp310-11 Café $

☎ 581-2914; www.cafédumonde.com; 800 Decatur St; beignets $2; 🕑 24hr

Coffee and beignets, folks, that's all they got. You can choose café au lait or take yours black.

Café du Monde is an admirable institution which, despite its fame and prime location opposite Jackson Sq, keeps its menu simple and its prices low. The atmosphere is equally straightforward and no less charming for it – a large, covered patio filled with little café tables all lightly dusted by powdered sugar. It's hours are easy to remember, too, because the place never closes – making this a good late-night stop if you're going around the clock yourself, or a final pit stop before you head to the airport for an early flight. Beignets, by the way, are light, square-shaped doughnuts dusted with powdered sugar.

CC'S COFFEE HOUSE

Map pp310-11 Café $

☎ 581-6996; 941 Royal St; pastries $2; 🕑 7am-late

Since 1919 Community Coffee has been a staple in most homes in Louisiana. This well-lit corner café is a French Quarter base for coffee addicts. A full complement of espresso and cappuccino drinks are available, as are free wi-fi service and occasional live music in the evenings.

VERTI MARTE Map pp310-11 Deli $

☎ 525-4767; 1201 Royal St; meals $2-6; 🕑 24hr

Handy for those who just want to eat a quick, sodium-rich meal on their hotel balcony after everything else is closed. The take-out menu seems endless, but stick with basics like po'boys, seafood sandwiches and the daily chef specials and you'll do all right. The main selling points here are the traditional seamy atmosphere and free delivery anywhere in the French Quarter and Faubourg Marigny.

CREOLE CLASSICS

Creole cuisine, combining French cooking techniques with local Louisiana staples and a significant African influence, is a deeply rooted tradition in New Orleans. The city's oldest restaurants are all Creole restaurants. Here's a rundown of the old-line establishments.

Galatoire's (p182) Join the locals in line for Friday lunch, and try the pompano.

Antoine's (p183) New Orleans' oldest restaurant (since 1840) is a historic experience. Order whatever is fresh from the sea.

Arnaud's (p183) Snazzy dining room and upbeat jazz bistro make the occasion special; the speckled trout meunière follows through.

Tujague's (p184) Since 1856, New Orleans' second-oldest restaurant is famous for its beef brisket.

Brennan's (p185) Breakfast at Brennan's is a local tradition that starts with an 'eye-opener' and can take a few hours.

CLOVER GRILL
Map pp310-11 American $
☎ 598-1010; www.clovergrill.com; 900 Bourbon St; dishes $3-8; ⏰ 24hr
Looks much like a '50s diner and serves that kind of food – tasty burgers, fries and other grill fare. The nostalgia stops there, however. A disco-caliber sound system booms out dance music, and the boys slinging the hash can be prima donnas at times. A mixed clientele files through all day long, but as the night goes on the Clover draws more gay clubhoppers.

CROISSANT D'OR PATISSERIE
Map pp310-11 Café $
☎ 524-4663; 617 Ursulines Ave; meals $3-5; ⏰ 7am-5pm
On the quieter side of the Quarter, this ancient and spotlessly clean pastry shop is where many locals start their day. Bring a paper, order coffee and a savory or sweet stuffed croissant and you'll feel like a local yourself. On your way in, check out the tiled sign on the threshold that says 'ladies entrance' – a holdover from pre-feminist days that is no longer enforced.

ROYAL BLEND Map pp310-11 Café $
☎ 523-2716; 621 Royal St; meals $4-6; ⏰ 7am-midnight
Has a pleasant courtyard in which to sip coffee and chew a toasted bagel and other baked goods. They also serve a passable gumbo and light lunch fare. The courtyard is a free–wi-fi zone.

JOHNNY'S PO-BOYS
Map pp310-11 Sandwiches $
☎ 524-8129; 511 St Louis St; dishes $4-8; ⏰ 9:30am-3pm
A local favorite since 1950, Johnny's is the only traditional po'boy joint in the French Quarter. It's a basic little joint with checkered tablecloths, and it always seems to be bustling with an equal proportion of eat-in and take-out patrons. Breakfast and an assortment of seafood platters are also served.

CAFÉ MASPERO Map pp310-11 American $
☎ 523-6250; 601 Decatur St; mains $5-10; ⏰ 11am-late
Maspero's is another New Orleans restaurant that oozes atmosphere without trying very hard. Its smoky, brick arches make its street-level eating rooms feel underground. Its large menu touches all the bases of cheap local cuisine: fried-catfish sandwiches, red beans and rice, cold Abita on tap delivered to your table by alert waitstaff. During peak tourist season out-of-towners are usually lined up on the sidewalk to get in, but during the slow season, many locals sneak back in to reclaim an old haunt. Cash only.

CAFÉ BEIGNET Map pp310-11 Café $
☎ 524-5530; 334B Royal St; meals $6-8; ⏰ 7am-5pm
In a shaded patio setting with a view of Royal St, this intimate café serves small meals over the counter. French-style omelettes stuffed with ham, Belgian waffles and beignets are all a good start to the day, while quiches and sandwiches make up the simple lunch fare.

ANGELI ON DECATUR
Map pp310-11 Pasta & Pizza $
☎ 566-0077; 1141 Decatur St; mains $6-12; ⏰ 11am-2am Sun-Thu, 11am-4am Fri & Sat
Angeli is a genuinely fun spot that stays open late. Pizzas, calzones, sandwiches, pita rolls and burgers sum up the straightforward menu. It's towards the lower end of Decatur, near several hip bars. The real draw is the early music sets by solid outfits like the New Orleans Jazz Vipers – a good way to launch your evening. Credit cards are not accepted.

LA MADELEINE FRENCH BAKERY & CAFÉ Map pp310-11 Bakery $
☎ 568-9950; 547 St Ann St; mains $6-12; ⏰ 7am-9pm
A convenient stop on Jackson Sq, with over-the-counter service and decent quiches, pastas and pizzas. An assortment of fresh-baked pastries and muffins makes this café equally popular for breakfast.

COOP'S PLACE Map pp310-11 Cajun $
☎ 525-9053; 1109 Decatur St; mains $6-15; ⏰ 11am-3am
Absolutely no thought went into the design of this neighborhood bar (est 1983), and the darkly lit cavern is put together like a maze to befuddle inebriated patrons. But over the years Coop's

has acquired a kind of well-worn appeal that no interior decorator could pull off. Most importantly for nonregular patrons (who are always in the minority at Coop's) is that the eating far exceeds the usual bar fare. The huge chalkboard menu includes chicken, battered and fried to perfection, jambalaya with rabbit meat (an authentic, rural touch), hot links over a mess of red beans and rice, and Louisiana nibbles like fried alligator bits. It is also a good place to grab a hefty burger and swill it down with beer off the tap. The kitchen is open until 2am.

ACME OYSTER AND SEAFOOD HOUSE

Map pp310-11 Seafood $

☎ 522-5973; www.acmeoyster.com; 724 Iberville St; mains $6-15; 🕑 11am-late

Locals and tourists line up to get into this casual holdover from the Old Quarter. It first opened in 1910, and it stands on its reputation for shucking out some of the city's best oysters ($4 for six on the half shell), along with po'boys, red beans and rice, and seafood gumbo. Overall, the joint is easy to like. But, being just around the corner from Bourbon St, Acme has willingly sacrificed some of its integrity in recent years (you can order gumbo in a hollowed out French bread bowl, à la Frisco's Fisherman's Wharf). When it's real busy, Acme keeps the line moving by serving up pre-shucked oysters – for novices this may be acceptable, but true zealots might want to take a pass.

CENTRAL GROCERY

Map pp310-11 Italian Deli $

☎ 523-1620; 923 Decatur St; sandwiches $7-10; 🕑 9am-5pm Tue-Sat

The mother church for the muffuletta is a requisite stop for visitors to New Orleans. The crazy sandwich, loaded with meats, cheeses and olive relish, was invented here in 1906. The grocery is an authentic relic from the Quarter's long-gone Sicilian community, with fat sausages overhanging the counter and bottles of olive oil shelved to the ceiling. The place smells heavenly, of course. A whole muffuletta and a Barq's root beer is a meal for two (solo diners can order half a muffuletta). Counters in back make it possible to eat and run, or pack your lunch out to the levee, a block away.

FIORELLA'S

Map pp310-11 Italian & Louisianan $

☎ 528-9566; 1136 Decatur St; mains $7-11; 🕑 11am-midnight Sun-Thu, 11am-2am Fri & Sat

A remnant of the old Sicilian community that used to populate the Quarter, Fiorella's has all the hallmarks of a neighborhood fixture: it's unpretentious with checkered tablecloths and candlelit tables, is seemingly oblivious to the tourism industry and, remarkably, continues to fit in on evolving, hipsterized lower Decatur St. The menu is a jumble of pretty much anything you'd want from such a place: spaghetti and meatballs, veal cutlets and po'boys. But top billing goes to the fried chicken, which some will have you believe is the best in town. That may be so in post-Katrina New Orleans.

GUMBO SHOP

Map pp310-11 Louisianan $

☎ 525-1486; 630 St Peter St; mains $7-19; 🕑 11am-11pm

Despite its tourist-trap status, the Gumbo Shop is a decent fallback where you can order passable regional classics – seafood gumbo, jambalaya and the like. It's a nice, open room with elegant frescoes of old New Orleans scenes. Out-of-towners eat here in astonishing numbers, and most of them seem to be satisfied.

PORT OF CALL

Map pp310-11 Grill $

☎ 523-0120; 838 Esplanade Ave; mains $7-21; 🕑 11am-late

Locals head here for hefty half-pound burgers, touted as the best in town, and piping-hot baked potatoes with slabs of melting butter. It's a basic bar and grill, but the kitchen serves up individual pizzas and steaks. Reservations are not accepted and waiting on the sidewalk is not uncommon.

LOUISIANA PIZZA KITCHEN

Map pp310-11 Pizza $

☎ 522-9500; www.louisianapizzakitchen.com; 95 French Market Place; mains $8-16; 🕑 noon-9pm Wed-Sun

Opposite the Old US Mint, this is a popular local chain offering wood-fired, individual pizza crusts ($8 to $11) that resemble toasted pita bread and are topped with a delicious array of ingredients. Try a Caesar salad and the pizza with garlic, sun-dried tomatoes and feta cheese. Pastas, wraps and salads round out the menu.

MONA LISA Map pp310-11 Pizza $

☎ 522-6746; 1212 Royal St; mains $9-14; 11am-11pm

An informal, quiet, local spot in the lower Quarter. Kooky renditions of da Vinci's familiar subject hang on the walls. In hair curlers, 50lbs heavier or in the form of a cow, she stares impassively at diners munching on pizzas, pastas and spinach salads. Bring your own wine for a budget candlelight dinner.

CRESCENT CITY BREWHOUSE

Map pp310-11 Louisianan $

☎ 522-0571; 527 Decatur St; mains $9-20; 4-9pm Mon-Thu, 4-10pm Fri, noon-10pm Sat, noon-9pm Sun

A microbrewery that produces passable pilsners and wheat beers. The menu features Louisiana standards with a seafood emphasis: redfish, soft-shell crabs, crabcakes, steaks and burgers. There's often live music. It's a lively, upbeat place that can take care of an entire family's needs.

CAFÉ AMELIE

Map pp310-11 French $$

☎ 412-8965; 912 Royal St; mains $10-21; 11am-9pm Wed-Fri, 9am-9pm Sat, 9am-4pm Sun

The French Quarter's best alfresco dining is to be found in this charmed spot. Amelie occupies an old carriage house, set deep within a beautiful courtyard surrounded by high brick walls and shaded by trees. Fresh seafood and local produce are the basis of a modest, ever-changing menu. When available, don't pass on the killer mussels served in a Pernod sauce. Pan-seared salmon and blackened rack of lamb make frequent appearances. Live music often livens up the courtyard in the evening. At lunchtime, Amelie is a quiet retreat for excellent sandwiches and highlights off the dinner menu.

PALACE CAFÉ Map pp310-11 Creole $$

☎ 523-1661; www.palacecafe.com; 605 Canal St; mains $12-31; 11:30am-2:30pm Tue-Fri, 5:30-10pm Tue-Sat, 10:30-2:30 Sun

Another dining establishment operated by the Brennan family, the Palace Café makes a strong first impression, with a striking interior that combines modern and classic designs. When it opened in 1990 in a former music store, the building's original tile floors and interior columns were retained and a corkscrew staircase was added. Businesspeople, conventioneers and office workers seem to have laid claim to the place. The food follows through with modern, nonexperimental approaches to classic Creole standards like Palace potato pie with a pork debris (a mess of shredded meat and gravy) and Gulf fish pecan. Occasional surprises, such as the herbed gnocchi with wild mushrooms starter served in a smoky chicken stock, add nice twists to the menu. Local products predominate.

OLIVIER'S Map pp310-11 Creole $$

☎ 525-7734; www.olivierscreole.com; 204 Decatur St; mains $16-20; 6-10pm Thu-Tue

Olivier's has loyal followers who appreciate authentic, inexpensive Creole food in the French Quarter. It's run by an African American–Creole family that's been in the restaurant business for five generations, and the recipes have been handed down and refined over decades. Share a gumbo sampler ($9), an education in local cuisine, before digging into specialties such as Creole rabbit, crabcakes and broiled catfish. Save room for bourbon-pecan pie.

IRENE'S CUISINE Map pp310-11 Italian $$

☎ 529-8811; 539 St Philip St; mains $16-20; 5:30-10pm Mon-Sat

Irene's is small and romantic and calls very little attention to itself. Its cozy, dimly lit dining rooms are conducive to intimate conversation, and the food is hearty. The menu straddles the Italian-French border and includes offerings such as a finely seasoned rosemary chicken, seared chops and pan-sautéed fish fillets. Sweet aromas waft from your plate before you take your first bite. Leave room for the decadent pecan-praline bread pudding. Reservations are not accepted and long waits are the norm.

CAFÉ SBISA

Map pp310-11 Contemporary Louisianan $$

☎ 522-5565; 1011 Decatur St; mains $17-25; 5:30-10:30pm daily, & 10:30am-3pm Sun

A Vieux Carré institution (since 1899), Café Sbisa remained closed for nine months after Hurricane Katrina damaged its façade. Nice to see this one come back. It has a reputation for innovative regional cuisine. Tasteful restoration of the ancient building, with exposed brick and strikingly decadent art above the long bar, helps make this one of New Orleans' most stylish dining rooms, while New American touches spruce up a solid menu, which includes speckled trout, bouillabaisse and huge steaks and chops. Café Sbisa also has a nice brunch on Sunday with a roving 'trad' jazz unit.

BACCO

Map pp310-11 Italian $$

☎ 522-2426; www.bacco.com; 310 Chartres St; mains $17-30; 🕑 11:30am-2:30pm & 6-10pm

Businesslike Bacco oozes conservative sophistication. There is no sentimentality about the contemporary décor, and the menu doesn't really push the envelope. But this is one of the city's best Italian restaurants, offering a medley of flavorful Italian and New Orleans dishes prepared with a light hand and served by congenial, professional staff. Fresh basil accents a fresh pesto served with shrimp and bowtie pasta, Louisiana asserts itself in hickory grilled redfish topped by a lump of crabmeat, and the Bacco shrimp is served in a Creole sauce spiked with Abita Amber beer. From the bar comes a nice selection of specialty cocktails (the Katrina Rita packs a wallop).

GALATOIRE'S Map pp310-11 Creole $$

☎ 525-2021; 209 Bourbon St; mains $17-32; 🕑 11:30am-10pm Tue-Sat, noon-10pm Sun

Galatoire's is a revered institution where the regulars are treated regally and tourists are sometimes dished out surprisingly average food. Local devotees so love this New Orleans establishment that to die here over a plate of, say, grilled pompano with almonds is considered a *belle mort*, or good death. (Fortunately, this doesn't happen very often.) The building has housed a restaurant since 1830 (it was called Victor's before Jean Galatoire bought it in 1905), and the history is palpable in the main dining room. Oysters Rockefeller, asparagus salad, 'chicken *clemenceau*' and the to-die-for pompano are good bets off the menu (or ask the waiter what's fresh). Expect a long wait outside before being seated, especially for lunch on Friday. Galatoire's stays open all afternoon, and a relaxed late lunch among natty waiters lounging at available tables can be a charming experience. Reservations accepted for tables in the unhistoric upstairs dining room.

MR B'S BISTRO

Map pp310-11 Contemporary Louisianan $$

☎ 523-2078; www.mrbsbistro.com; 201 Royal St; mains $18-28; 🕑 11:30am-3pm & 5:30-10pm Mon-Sat, 10:30am-3pm & 5:30-10pm Sun

Run by a branch of the Brennan family, Mr B's is a clubby, attractively designed restaurant that appeals to a variety of tastes. During the lull after Hurricane Katrina the restaurant remained closed for a year of remodeling. But expect sophisticated Creole dishes with rural Cajun overtones. The 'gumbo Ya-Ya' with chicken and andouille is excellent, and the barbecued shrimp, sautéed in a delicious buttery sauce, is a fun and messy dish served with a paper bib to protect your shirt. Chops, steaks, grilled fish and rabbit anchor the rugged menu.

COURT OF TWO SISTERS

Map pp310-11 Creole $$

☎ 522-7261; www.courtoftwosisters.com; 613 Royal St; mains $18-32; 🕑 9am-3pm Sat & Sun, 11:30am-2:30pm Mon, Tue, Thu & Fri, 5:30-9pm Mon & Thu-Sat

Brunch in the famous courtyard here is fine on a bright Sunday morning. It's a circus of Creole omelettes, Cajun pasta salads, grillades, grits, fresh fruits, carved meats and fruity cocktails. The alfresco ambience is wonderful, but when it rains, patrons are seated in one of several slightly faded (some actually drab) indoor dining rooms. The regrettably lackluster dinners cover all the traditional Creole standards. Ask for what's fresh and opt for the simplest preparation available.

MURIEL'S Map pp310-11 Contemporary Creole $$

☎ 568-1885; www.muriels.com; 801 Chartres St; mains $21-31; 🕑 5:30-10pm Mon-Sat, 11:30am-2:30pm & 5-10pm Sun

Good food, sultry atmosphere and location-location-location make Muriel's hard to pass up. You have your choice of settings: the main dining room evokes the lurid pomp of Storyville, with deep-red walls and chandeliers; in the eclectic bistro 19th-century art hangs from exposed brick walls; the courtyard bar exemplifies traditional tropical decadence with potted palms and marble-topped café tables; balcony seating affords an elevated view of Jackson Sq's motley krewe of musicians, magicians, painters and tarot readers. The kitchen

Street musicians entertain diners

tinkers with the Creole ethos enough to steer clear of stodginess without schooling nongourmand patrons. It's also a good spot for a steak.

PERISTYLE

Map pp310-11 French & New American $$

☎ 593-9535; 1041 Dumaine St; mains $22-25; 🕑 6-8:30pm Tue-Sat, 11:30am-1:30pm Fri

Peristyle is a warm and welcoming space, with a beautiful old bar and a lovely dining room with leather bench seating and romantic lighting. Though the restaurant opened its doors in only 1992, and its celebrated chef Anne Kearney has moved on, Friday lunch here is a well established tradition that hasn't let up, and reservations are a must anytime. New chef Tom Wolfe has retained much of the place's bistro quality, but his main courses include more chops and the like. Starters really shine, with escargot foie gras with duck sausage, and seared sea scallops.

ANTOINE'S Map pp310-11 Creole $$$

☎ 581-4422; www.antoines.com; 713 St Louis St; dinner mains $22-39; 🕑 11:30am-2pm & 5:30-9:30pm

New Orleans' oldest restaurant first opened for business in 1840. ('That is now over 165 years,' the menu kindly offers.) The dated atmosphere of its dining rooms (a brightly lit room for nonsmokers and a more ambient smoking room) might be just the ticket for a formal family gathering, particularly if older folks are involved. Dining here is certainly of historical interest, but in general the food fails to thrill the senses and contemporary palates might find the meat and fish dishes overburdened by staid sauces. Even the oysters Rockefeller, Antoine's own invention, lack spirit. As a general rule, ask your waiter what's fresh and follow suit. Jackets required; denim prohibited.

ARNAUD'S Map pp310-11 Creole $$

☎ 523-5433; www.arnauds.com; 813 Bienville St; mains $24-36; 🕑 6-10pm daily, 10am-2:30pm Sun

Here's one of the better places to go for traditional haute-Creole cuisine. Arnaud's was founded in 1918 by 'Count' Arnaud Cazenave, a French immigrant whose extravagant tastes are still evident here. The restaurant is an agglomeration of buildings that take up nearly an entire city block. It's a festive place where locals and tourists go for special occasions and to soak in New Orleans' past. The main dining room is much admired for its stately old-world elegance (which, in New Orleans, means hex-tile floors and cast-iron posts supporting the ceiling). The Jazz Bistro is more up tempo, with a classy acoustic jazz ensemble ($4 music charge). While it isn't the most scintillating dining, the kitchen surely handles its specialties well; they appear in red type on the menu – shrimp Arnaud, oysters Bienville (an original dish), speckled trout meunière (saved by a rich, gravy-like sauce) and a variety of steaks and fowl dishes. Show up early and have a mint julep at the bar. Men, jackets.

BAYONA Map pp310-11 Contemporary Louisianan $$

☎ 525-4455; 430 Dauphine St; mains $24-27; 🕑 11:30am-2pm Mon-Fri, 6-10pm Mon-Thu, 6-11pm Fri & Sat

One of the city's best all-around dining experiences. It is in a converted Creole cottage, with several former parlors serving as homey dining rooms. On pleasant-weather days, there's also alfresco dining on the back patio. Chef Susan Spicer's menu is always inventive, but rarely shocking. She pulls together local, European and Japanese concepts without muddying the waters. Representative entrées include a braised pork shank with sauerkraut and spaetzle, and red snapper with sweet potatoes and brown-butter satsuma sauce. The wine list is extensive and predominantly European.

K-PAUL'S LOUISIANA KITCHEN

Map pp310-11 Cajun $$

☎ 596-2530; www.kpauls.com; 416 Chartres St; mains $25-36; 🕑 11:30am-2pm Mon-Fri, 5:30-10pm Mon-Sat

Chef Paul Prudhomme is no longer active in the day-to-day operation of the kitchen, but the same food he created here in the 1980s is still available. The kitchen eschews shortcuts. Blackened twin beef tenders, a signature dish, come with an incredibly rich 'debris' gravy that's been slowly cooked over a two-day period. You can also get gumbo with hot andouille sausages made on the premises, and turtle soup, which has a nice flavorful snap to it. Jambalaya is simmered for hours with jalapeños and is hot indeed. Despite its popularity, K-Paul's retains a no-reservations policy downstairs, but takes reservations for its upstairs tables. For weekday lunches, you might be seated on arrival.

NOLA

Map pp310-11 Contemporary American $$

☎ 522-6652; 534 St Louis St; mains $26-35; 🕑 11:30am-2pm Sat, 6-10pm Wed-Sun

This is Chef Emeril Lagasse's French Quarter outpost. Lagasse's kitchen staff deftly cull local, Asian and Californian traditions for natural, subtle combinations. Fresh fish parts neatly under your fork, and roasted filet mignon, cooked rare, is so tender you can almost chew it with your eyebrows. NOLA also scores high for its wood-fired pizzas (a good starter for a group) and its 27-page wine list (with many affordable choices). Excessively noisy dining rooms and an energetic staff help make this an exciting place to eat.

TUJAGUE'S

Map pp310-11 Creole $$

☎ 525-8676; www.tujagues.com; 823 Decatur St; 6-course dinner $27; 🕑 11am-3pm & 5-11pm

Tujague's (*two* jacks) has been quietly holding down its corner forever (since 1856), making it the second-oldest eatery in New Orleans. It's classy and old-fashioned, but far more casual than institutions like Antoine's. Patrons enter the small dining room via a narrow barroom, where you can still envision a past century's mustachioed, jauntily hatted crowd. Dinner is a traditional six-course affair that highlights the joint's signature items: a piquant shrimp remoulade and a tender beef brisket with a simple Creole sauce for dipping. These items are required, while diners can select from four entrées based on the choice offerings from the butcher and the fish monger. Close out with pecan pie and coffee.

PAUL PRUDHOMME

Chef Prudhomme is to Cajun cuisine what Louis Armstrong was to jazz. He's an innovator and an ambassador of Louisiana culture. Certainly he is one of the most recognizable chefs in America.

Prudhomme was born in 1940 on a farm near Opelousas, LA (see p259), and learned to cook by helping his mother in the kitchen. By the early 1970s he was head chef at Commanders Palace (p190), which under his leadership became recognized as one of the finest restaurants in the country. In 1979, he and his late wife opened K-Paul's (above).

Before K-Paul's opened, Cajun cooking was a rural cuisine little known outside Louisiana. Prudhomme's celebrity, which came with daily TV shows and his own line of packaged seasonings, spread the gospel of Cajun cooking far and wide. Prudhomme's greatest contribution to American cuisine is the blackening technique, which he perfected with dishes like blackened redfish. Thanks to Prudhomme, blackened redfish became so popular the species was very nearly fished to extinction in the 1980s.

The blackening technique merely requires rubbing fish (or chicken) in spicy seasonings and then searing it in an intensely hot cast-iron skillet. Interestingly, blackening is not a standard practice in rural Cajun cooking, but you'd never know it now that blackened Cajun dishes pop up on menus all around the world.

Prudhomme is still a visible character in the French Quarter, where he is often seen riding around on his electric tricycle. He still owns K-Paul's, but is no longer overseeing the day-to-day activity in the kitchen. After Hurricane Katrina, K-Paul's quick reopening was seen as a significant morale boost for the city. The big man appeared on MSNBC, saying 'If you're hungry, we want to feed you…That's my job, to lift people up with great food.'

LATE NIGHT EATS

New Orleans' bars can stay open round the clock, which of course makes it possible to completely rearrange your schedule to whatever truly suits your night-owl soul. Only problem is, most restaurants close at 10pm. If you're likely to experience an undeniable hunger sometime past midnight, it's a good idea to commit the following late-night eateries to memory. Some of these joints aren't operating full hours currently, but look for 'em to bounce back as the Katrina shock fades.

Clover Grill (p179) Burgers and fries are flipped to order at any time.

Coop's Place (p179) Your best bet for Cajun, fried chicken or a plate of beans and rice 'til 2am.

Angeli on Decatur (p179) Pizzas, calzones, sandwiches 'til 2am weekdays, 'til 4am on the weekend.

Fiorella's (p180) Old lower-Quarter neighborhood joint dishes out fried chicken and pastas 'til 2am on the weekends.

La Peniché (right) In the wee hours this Marigny spot attracts a crazy crowd for seafood platters, chops and po'boys. It's closed Wednesday.

Red Eye Grill (p187) Convenient greasy spoon if your clubhopping in the Warehouse District.

Huey's 24/7 Diner (p187) Quality diner standards, round-the-clock hours and a full bar – what more could you ask for?

Trolly Stop (p189) A carbo-loading pit stop for Uptown clubhoppers that never closes.

Camellia Grill (p190) Look forward to seeing the return of the alert hash-slingers in this Riverbend classic.

Café du Monde (p178) You can get a coffee and sugar boost at any hour at this French Quarter institution.

BRENNAN'S RESTAURANT

Map pp310-11 Creole $$$

☎ 525-9711; www.brennansneworleans.com; 417 Royal St; 4-course dinner $45; ⏲ 8am-2:30pm & 6-10pm

Brennan's prides itself on having introduced the luxury breakfast to New Orleans. Indeed, breakfast in one of the restaurant's 12 elegant dining rooms or its lovely courtyard is no *petit déjeuner:* it's a virtual gastronomic extravaganza that could start with an 'eye-opener' (if you can imagine downing a Sazerac cocktail before breakfast), followed by a baked apple or turtle soup, any of about 20 egg dishes, and then dessert (bananas Foster is a Brennan's original). The dinner menu emphasizes Creole seafood dishes.

TREMÉ DISTRICT

There isn't a whole lot going on in this part of town, especially if you're hungry. Really, there's only one reason why your stomach would lead you into the Tremé, but it's a pretty damn good one.

POWELL'S

Map pp310-11 Soul Food $

☎ 598-9532; 1313 St Philip St; plate lunches $7; ⏲ 10am-5pm

You don't have to trek far from the French Quarter for honest-to-gosh soul food, but you do have to be somewhat adventurous. Powell's, just a few blocks from Rampart St and facing a side of Louis Armstrong Park, is down an unpromising stretch of vacant houses. Often, you'll know you're approaching it because it's the only place on the block you're likely to see people hanging out on the sidewalk. It's the real deal, where friendly folks are pleased to set you up with heaping plate lunches of red beans and rice, pork chops, smothered chicken and the like. It's all slid into a styrofoam container for your take-out pleasure.

FAUBOURG MARIGNY & BYWATER

An inviting selection of restaurants along colorful Frenchmen St entices many visitors away from the French Quarter for dinner. The range of cuisines here is varied enough to keep things interesting on repeated visits. The Bywater lacks a distinctive cultural strip like Frenchmen St, but a smattering of excellent eateries are to be found along some of its sleepy residential byways.

LA PENICHÉ Map p316 American $

☎ 943-1460; 1940 Dauphine St; mains $6-14; ⏲ 24hr Thu-Tue

In the lazy twilight hour, La Peniché qualifies as an unassuming corner restaurant, a few blocks from the Frenchmen St scene. But it's open 24 hours, and it tends to get interesting later on when night owls,

FIVE CHOICE NEIGHBORHOOD JOINTS

You weren't planning to eat all your meals in the French Quarter, were you? You want to get out around town, see what this city's all about, break bread with the locals. There's some good eating out there, some of it in very cool and casual little joints. (In addition to these, there are also fine dining experiences to be had in the cottage bistros Uptown, see Five Choice Cottage Bistros p191.)

Liuzza's By the Track (p191) Friendly po'boy joint near the Fair Grounds that feels like a corner bar. Worth the trek and the wait for a table.

Elizabeth's (below) Hugely popular lunch spot in the Bywater that is known for gargantuan portions and reasonable prices.

Camellia Grill (p190) The Taj Mahal of New Orleans diners is reachable by the St Charles streetcar line. Classic short-order fare, served with flair.

Domilise's (p191) When you stumble on this perfect little shack, on a quiet Uptown residential corner, you'll know you're in for a treat. Deep-fried shrimp and catfish po'boys and frosty schooners of cheap beer complement the ramshackle atmosphere.

Powell's (p185) It's just three blocks from the French Quarter, but this soul-food joint feels miles away. Heaping portions of gut-busting food are slid into take-out trays for your eating pleasure.

clubhoppers, drag queens and insomniacs file through its doors. Surly waiters serve seafood platters, fried chicken, steaks, chops and po'boys – none of it exceptional, all of it reasonably priced.

ELIZABETH'S Map p316 American $

☎ 944-9272; www.elizabeths-restaurant.com; 601 Gallier St; mains $6.50-18; 10:30am-2:30pm & 5-10pm Tue-Fri, 9am-2:30pm & 5-10pm Sat

The Bywater's hottest ticket is this welcoming spot facing the levee. It has been one of the city's favorite down-home lunch destinations since it opened in 1998, and regular customers still flock here for some of the biggest po'boys around and for heaping plate lunches of barbecue beef and pork, meat loaf and baked chicken. Dinner is a tad more refined but no less gratifying, with rib-eye steaks, chops, chicken livers and blackened catfish along with those big-ass burgers and po'boys. Weekend brunch is a fattening affair not to be missed.

HOOKAH CAFE

Map p316 Indian $

☎ 940-0722; www.hookah-cafe.com; 1407 Decatur St; mains $8-12; kitchen 5:30-11pm

Torn between eating and club-hopping? Hookah Cafe takes care of both needs with a full menu, a long, curved bar, seductive atmosphere and entertainment several nights a week (see p203). The food explores the culinary side of the land of hookahs: Indian and Middle Eastern with modest contemporary flair. Diners can nibble on sides (hummus platter, mango crabcakes), or have a quick bite such as a lamb burger with spicy Indian fries. Ideal post-beer plates like chicken tikka masala, lamb byranni and vindaloos will set you up for a late night.

ADOLFO'S Map p316 Italian $

☎ 948-3800; 611 Frenchmen St; mains $8-16; 6-11pm Mon-Sat

This might be just what you came looking for in New Orleans, a romantic little Creole-Italian restaurant upstairs from a bar. It's timeworn, dimly lit and the front tables look out over Frenchmen St. Folks from the neighborhood gather here for hearty, working-class Italian-Americano fare that has the requisite New Orleans zing. Pastas with Creole tomato sauces, chicken parmagiana and cheap reds by the caraf emerge from the kitchen and raise a diner's spirits.

PRALINE CONNECTION

Map p316 Soul Food $

☎ 943-3934; 542 Frenchmen St; mains $9-18; 11am-10:30pm Sun-Thu, 11am-midnight Fri & Sat

Here's where you can get soul food without venturing into the 'hood. In terms of atmosphere, Praline Connection is not exactly down home – it's well-lit, spotless and service is of the sit-down variety. But the kitchen gets it right where it counts. The fried chicken and fried catfish platters are aces, and greens come in all the right varieties – collards, mustards and cabbages. Also, diners can have their choice of red beans, white beans, lima beans or crowder peas, as well as stewed chicken, turkey necks and fried chicken livers. Not bad for a slick joint like this one. It's all served up by cool waiters decked out like Blues Brothers.

BANK CAFE Map p316 New Louisianan $$
☎ 371-5260; www.thebankcafe.com; 2001 Burgundy St; mains $16-24; 🕒 6-10pm Tue-Sat
Beautiful spaces such as this, with high ceilings, warm lighting and an impeccable art-deco bar, create a sense of anticipation. It's in a former bank, and has preserved the grandeur and dispensed with stodginess. The menu follows through wonderfully. It's Louisiana cooking with unintrusive updates. Fresh vegetables, while not qualifying as innovations, are welcomed for their snap and color. Dishes like Moroccan-braised lamb shanks, served with couscous and *gremoulata*, gently bend culinary categories. American classics like seared red snapper are accompanied by a bounty of veggies. The menu follows the seasons, and fresh and organic are the bywords here.

CBD & WAREHOUSE DISTRICT

New Orleans' business district is home to some highly acclaimed contemporary restaurants. In this part of town you'll also find many decent eat-and-run spots for smaller budgets.

LOUISIANA PRODUCTS Map pp308-9 Deli $
☎ 529-1666; 618 Julia St; meals $2-5; 🕒 8am-4pm Mon-Sat
On historic Julia Row, this place has the feel of an overcrowded country store, but it's really a deli with limited seating and inexpensive breakfasts and lunches. If you're headed to a nearby museum, join the construction workers and office workers for ham, eggs and cheese on a French roll for breakfast or a mini-muffuletta for lunch.

RED EYE GRILL Map pp308-9 Grill $
☎ 593-9393; 852 S Peters St; meals $5-8; 🕒 11am-late
A grungy bar in the Warehouse District (for those 21 years and up), the Red Eye is strictly for greasy burgers and fries. It's convenient if you're seeing a show at one of the nearby clubs.

MOTHER'S Map pp308-9 Southern Deli $
☎ 523-9656; 401 Poydras St; meals $6-13; 🕒 8am-8pm
Mother's is a no-frills institution that's justifiably famous for its hearty down-home breakfasts, which nobody ever finishes. But really you shouldn't leave New Orleans without having a heaping debris (roast-beef drippings) po'boy here. Service is over the counter, and everything is prepared to order. Loyal patrons happily endure long lines on the weekend, but that's easily avoided by dropping in weekdays just before peak lunch hour. Be sure to figure out what you're ordering before you get in line, as the counter people aren't crazy about indecisive patrons. Holds up the line, y'know?

HUEY'S 24/7 DINER
Map pp308-9 American $
☎ 598-4839; www.hueys247diner.com; 200 Magazine St; mains $7-16; 🕒 24hrs
For top-notch breakfast chow anytime of the day or night, Huey's is your place. It's a tad fancier than a traditional diner, with a huge menu to match. If you aren't up for gut-busting omelette platters, you can drop in for a thick burger or a sandwich. Huey's strays from the concept by including a full bar that never closes, so if you came here to sober up, you can always decide to get drunk again. Not a bad deal.

LIBORIO CUBAN RESTAURANT
Map pp308-9 Cuban $
☎ 581-9680; 322 Magazine St; mains $7-25; 🕒 11am-3pm Mon-Sat, 6-9pm Tue-Sat
Business lunchers crowd into this festive Warehouse District establishment for a taste of old Havana. Cuban pork sandwiches are ironed into a flat, melted, savory treat and served with plantains and black beans. You can also get *ropa vieja* ('old rope,' made with spicy, shredded roast beef), roast pork and seafood paella, all excellent.

LEMON GRASS CAFE
Map pp308-9 Contemporary Vietnamese $$
☎ 523-1200; www.lemongrassrest.com; 217 Camp St; mains $9.50-24; 🕒 11am-2pm Mon-Fri, 5-9pm Thu-Sat
In the International House Hotel, Lemon Grass is the chic culinary atelier of chef Minh Bui, whose highly original menu borrows freely from French cuisine as well as the cooking of his own native Vietnam. Main dishes change frequently, depending on what's locally fresh, but may include lacquered duck smoked with five spices and

served over black-bean sticky rice, or Viet bird nest, which is a bed of crispy yellow noodles piled high with sautéed seafood and vegetables. Many diners here graze on appetizers, such as summer rolls (a riff on traditional spring rolls, with avocado and a heavenly peanut sauce) and jumbo scallops seared and drizzled with a sweet chili sauce. For a light bite, the excellent *banh mi*, aptly described as a 'Vietnamese po'boy,' is a delicate French loaf stuffed with chopped barbecue pork tenderloin, cucumber and cilantro.

BON TON CAFÉ Map pp308-09 Cajun $$

☎ 524-3386; 401 Magazine St; mains $15-25; 11am-2pm & 5-9:30pm Mon-Fri

Bon Ton is a good-time, old-style Cajun restaurant that's been open for half a century. The dining room looks like a pizza parlor, but folks show up dressed to the nines. This is Cajun food from before Paul Prudhomme came along. Spices are used in tasteful moderation in gumbo, jambalaya and shrimp étouffée. Crawfish show up in so many dishes, it's a wonder they haven't joined Louisiana redfish on the endangered-species list. Don't pass on the rum-soaked bread pudding. And – what the hey? – Bon Ton is closed on weekends.

CUVÉE Map pp308-9 Contemporary Louisianan $$

☎ 587-9001; www.restaurantcuvee.com; 322 Magazine St; mains $18-35; 11:30am-2:30pm Mon-Fri, 6-10pm Mon-Sat

Cuvée is a high-class joint in a stylishly converted warehouse space. Its thoughtful, descriptive menu projects an understandable pride in fine ingredients and cooking methods. Influences range freely between Cajun, Creole and French cuisines for exotic originals that are to be admired and savored bite by bite. The dinner menu might include grilled redfish over andouille hash, mustard and herb-coated salmon, and seared sea scallops with toasted pearl pasta and truffle shellfish fumet.

RESTAURANT AUGUST

Map pp308-9 Contemporary Creole $$

☎ 299-9777; www.rest-august.com; 301 Tchoupitoulas St; mains $20-29; 11am-2pm Fri, 5:30-10pm Tue-Sat

In a 19th-century tobacco warehouse converted into a very swank, upscale dining room, August is a Warehouse District highlight. The emphasis here is Creole-French, and dishes aim to surprise and satisfy contemporary palates. Dinner standouts include tender slow-roasted pheasant with wild mushrooms and bread dumplings, Moroccan-spiced duck with polenta and foie gras, and prime filet of beef with short ribs and smoked marrow.

HERBSAINT

Map pp308-9 Contemporary Louisianan $$$

☎ 525-4114; www.herbsaint.com; 701 St Charles Ave; mains $22-26; 11:30am-2:30pm Mon-Fri, 5:30-9:30 Mon-Sat

Chef Donald Link's menu is a homage to traditional French-bistro fare, but with strong Louisianan inflections and subtle, contemporary innovations. Steak frites appear in the form of a grilled hanger steak with fries and a zesty pimento aioli, and frog legs in a light herbed batter are served on a starter plate. The dining room, warmly lit by windows, is especially pleasant for lunch. Reservations are a good idea.

EMERIL'S Map pp308-9 Contemporary Creole $$$

☎ 528-9393; www.emerils.com; 800 Tchoupitoulas St; mains $22-36; 11:30am-2pm Fri, 6-10pm Mon-Sat

In a converted warehouse in the Warehouse District, this is the flagship of chef Emeril Lagasse's restaurant empire. The noise level can be deafening, the service can be aloof and the chef is rarely in town, but nevertheless Emeril's remains one of New Orleans' finest dining establishments. The kitchen's strengths are best appreciated by ordering the daily specials, although you can't go wrong with mainstays like grilled *filet mignon au poivre*, which sounds like a contradiction but of course tastes wonderful. The full-on Emeril experience includes partaking of the cheese board with a selection from the restaurant's eclectic wine list.

LOWER GARDEN & GARDEN DISTRICTS

Food-lovers and hungry people have an interesting array of choices on and off St Charles Ave. Many places in the Lower Garden District are esteemed for their 24-hour breakfasts and late-night fixings, many bars serve decent food, and the Garden District is home to Commander's

BAM! IT'S EMERIL! (APPLAUSE)

Like Paul Prudhomme before him, Emeril Lagasse rose to fame as head chef at Commander's Palace. Then, in 1990, he *kicked it up a notch,* opening his own restaurant, **Emeril's** (opposite) and, *bam!,* skyrocketed to unprecedented celebrity heights for a chef. *Oh, yeah, babe.* (Well, shucks, we've exhausted Emeril's repertoir of signature catchphrases. Might as well add that if you want to be seen as a geeky tourist in New Orleans, fling these expressions at everyone you meet.)

A native of Fall River, MA, Lagasse (he pronounces his name 'la-*gah*-see') owns three restaurants in New Orleans (NOLA, Emeril's and Delmonico), along with two in Las Vegas, NV, two in Orlando, FL, and others in Miami, FL, and Atlanta, GA. But the true sources of his fame are the TV programs *Emeril Live* and *The Essence of Emeril,* which air on the Food Network and are seen in some 78 million homes daily. The shows are as much about the chef's spunk as they are about cooking. Emeril bams and kicks it up a notch for about half an hour, all the while snazzily conjuring up dishes that probably taste amazing. An Emeril-based sitcom, which debuted and flopped in 2001, did little to enhance his reputation, but his cookbooks, such as *From Emeril's Kitchens* (2003), fly off bookstore shelves.

'Homebase' is what Emeril calls his headquarters in New Orleans, but after Hurricane Katrina the gung-ho chef got himself in hot water by staying outta town a little too long. At a time when his presence would have added a welcome dash of pepper in the city's tepid bowl, Emeril was busy on a book-signing tour. Ah, well, he's back, his restaurants are open and New Orleans isn't a town that stews over spilled gravy.

Palace, one of the most highly acclaimed restaurants in the US.

RUE DE LA COURSE Map pp312-13 Café $

☎ 899-0242; 3121 Magazine St; pastries $2; ⏲ 7:30am-11pm

An ideal rest stop on a busy shopping block, Rue de la Course is your basic coffee shop where quality coffee and tea beverages are served in heavy mugs. The place has style, though, and attracts a diverse crowd. Many come with laptops, books or newspapers and spend hours at the sturdy wood tables. Cakes, brownies and biscotti are about all there is to eat, but they're good.

SLIM GOODIE'S DINER

Map pp312-13 American $

☎ 891-3447; http://slimgoodies.com; 3322 Magazine St; mains $2.50-10.50; ⏲ 9am-3pm

This hip retro diner was among the first restaurants to reopen after Hurricane Katrina. Burgers, shakes, all-American breakfasts and other short-order standards are on offer. A standout is the one-eyed bacon cheeseburger, a real eye-opener with a fried egg slipped into the bun. The extensive menu includes varied vegetarian delights, such as potato latkes and black-bean nachos.

JUAN'S FLYING BURRITO

Map pp312-13 Mexican $

☎ 569-0000; www.juansflyingburrito.com; 2018 Magazine St; mains $5-9; ⏲ 11:30am-3pm & 5-10pm Mon-Sat

Juan's is a hipster burrito hangout on a fun and busy block of Magazine St, in the Lower Garden District. Apart from a loud jukebox, which rocks the joint day and night, the atmosphere here is strictly post-industrial-utilitarian. But the hefty burritos are good, with some interesting experimental varieties, such as a selection of fajita burritos, a tasty jerk-chicken model and a fine little number called a 'veggie punk' burrito. You can also order platters of tacos, enchiladas and quesadillas, local and Mexican beers, and kick-ass margaritas.

TROLLEY STOP Map pp312-13 American $

☎ 523-0090; 1923 St Charles Ave; meals $5-10; ⏲ 24hr

This old standby has several virtues, none of which is the greasy food. First and foremost, the diner is set in a former gas station and locals now regard it as a filling station of another sort. New Orleanians of all stripes pull up to this convenient pit stop along the St Charles Ave corridor for ham and eggs and the usual assortment of sandwiches and burgers. There's always an interesting crowd on hand.

PARASOL'S Map pp312-13 Po'boys $

☎ 899-2054; 2533 Constance St; po'boys $6; ⏲ 11am-10pm

Locals have long insisted that this Irish Channel institution is one of the best places to get a po'boy sandwich. No argument here. The shredded roast beef po'boys are superb and eating one is a sloppy, joyful business. Fine catfish and other varieties are also available. Half of Parasol's is a casual eatery, usually jam packed with families

YELLOW SNOW (OTHER COLORS AVAILABLE)

Called snow cones elsewhere in the country, but more popular here than anywhere else, snowballs are a blast of winter on a steamy mid-summer afternoon in New Orleans. Shaved ice in a paper cup doused liberally with fruit-flavored syrup, they're a simple pleasure that appeals to children and adults alike. During the hot months, bare-bones shacks and portable trailers magically appear on the streets. You'll see 'em on Magazine St and Tchoupitoulas St Uptown, and elsewhere around the city. It's an impulse-buy you won't regret.

and old folks. The other half is a great little neighborhood bar where the patrons don't mind the flypaper hanging on the walls. The characters swivelling on the barstools are matched by the characters working the bar. You can eat on either side. The place is St Paddy's Day headquarters, when a huge block party happens on the street.

COMMANDER'S PALACE

Map pp312-13 Creole $$

☎ 899-8221; www.commanderspalace.com; 1403 Washington Ave; mains lunch $14-25, dinner $22-32, starters $8-10

In the heart of the Garden District, Commander's Palace has long been regarded as one of the USA's great restaurants. Owner Ella Brennan prides her ability to promote her chefs to stardom. (Paul Prudhomme and Emeril Lagasse are among her alumni.) It must be said that Commander's lives up to the hype and still makes its guests feel welcome. The service is impeccable and friendly, the décor tasteful and comfortable, and the food is splendorous. The main dining room is warmly lit through windows during lunch, but at night its artificial lighting is a little stale – try to reserve in the upstairs parlor or in the Garden Room, which looks out over Ella's lovely courtyard. The Creole menu includes regional soup specialties like turtle soup au sherry and starters such as shrimp remoulade and tasso shrimp. Main dishes are where Commander's really sells itself; the Colorado roast rack of lamb is prepared with a Creole mustard crust and an exquisite muscadine lamb sauce. Commander's lunch prices are mercifully reduced. Reservations are required and, for men, so are jackets.

UPTOWN & RIVERBEND

There are many reasons to head Uptown for a meal. Great little neighborhood eateries pop up along quiet blocks off the main St Charles Ave and Magazine St arteries. There are a few healthy options up this way, too. The Riverbend area should not be overlooked for its restaurants.

TEE-EVA'S CREOLE SOUL FOOD

Map pp314-15 Creole $

☎ 899-8350; 4430 Magazine St; snacks $1-3, mains $4-6; 🕑 11am-7pm

This colorful take-out stand serves snacks that can cool you off or satiate a sweet tooth. Snowballs and pralines are the specialties, but owner Tee-Eva often prepares hot lunches – baked chicken or plates of red beans and rice. She's a hot number herself, having sung backup vocals with the late, great Ernie K-Doe's Burn K-Doe Burn Band. When we dropped by Tee-Eva still wasn't up and running, but expect her to return.

SNOWIZARD SNO BALL STAND

Map pp314-15 Snowballs $

☎ 899-8758; 4001 Magazine St; snowballs $1.50-3.50; 🕑 noon-8pm Sun-Fri, noon-7pm Sat

A corner take-out stand worth finding when you're overheated. A shaved-ice snowball, with 80 different flavors to choose from, will cool you off right away. They can also provide you with milk shakes, cones and soft drinks. Cash only.

CAMELLIA GRILL Map pp314-15 Grill $

☎ 866-9573; 626 S Carrollton Ave; mains $2-8; 🕑 9am-1am Mon-Thu, 9am-3am Fri, 8am-3am Sat, 8am-1am Sun

Hurricane Katrina imposed an extended hiatus on this New Orleans classic, most likely due to the exodus of the staff. Here's hoping it's back up and running in the very near future. The Camellia's popularity hasn't wavered since it opened in 1946. Its secret? It simply refuses to change. Well-made American short-order fare (the burgers and omelettes stand out) is served by some of the city's snazziest (in black bow ties) and most entertaining waiters. That this is the South, there is no doubt. Regular folks feel right at home here. But the Camellia's fluffy omelettes and addictive pecan waffles have made regulars out of more than a few upper-crust Uptowners – not the sort of people you'd expect to encounter in a diner.

BLUEBIRD CAFÉ Map pp314-15 American $

☎ 895-7166; 3625 Prytania St; breakfast $4-7, lunch $3.50-5.50; 7am-3pm Mon-Fri, 8am-3pm Sat & Sun

Often packed with locals and staff from nearby hospitals, the Bluebird's calling card is breakfast. The menu goes beyond the traditional eggs-and-grits combos. The *huevos rancheros* are a spicy Mexican repast, and the 'powerhouse eggs' dish contains nutritional yeast, tamari and cheese. The Bluebird is also known for its malted pancakes and Belgian waffles. For lunch, sandwiches (burgers, vegie melts and BLTs) are available. Usually you'll wait for a table. Cash only.

FRANKIE & JOHNNY'S

Map pp314-15 Cajun $

☎ 899-9146; 321 Arabella St; mains $4-14; 11am-9pm

Down by the river you'll find this friendly neighborhood bar and restaurant. The joint really drives home the fact that you're in southern Louisiana. Come with a large group and expect to enjoy yourselves. In the spring, when crawfish are in season, order a platter of the boiled critters and a round of beers for your party. You can also choose starters like alligator pie and turtle soup, and mains like fried fish.

FIVE CHOICE COTTAGE BISTROS

It's gotten so you can't swing a cat Uptown without hitting an old shotgun house that's been converted into a restaurant. This is a good thing. Commonly called 'cottage bistros' or 'house bistros,' they offer some of the city's finest dining experiences, with excellent cooking and convivial environs.

Upperline Restaurant (p194) Diners will feel like invited guests in a refined home.

Dick & Jenny's (p192) A lively spot with a cool, upbeat atmosphere.

Martinique Bistro (p193) Seductive indoor/outdoor setting that evokes the Caribbean.

Brigtsen's (p193) An award-winning chef works wonders with Cajun cuisine.

Clancy's (p194) Creole food in an unpretentious setting, with great bar service.

COOTER BROWN'S TAVERN & OYSTER BAR Map pp314-15 Louisianan $

☎ 866-9104; www.cooterbrowns.com; 509 S Carrollton Ave; mains $5-13; 11am-midnight

A popular place to stop in for oysters on the half shell and sandwiches (like delicate fried catfish) that generally exceed bar-food standards. While you're here, check out the 'Hall of Foam.' After 8pm, the place turns into a rowdy college hangout. (See p205 for details on Cooter's virtues as a bar).

REGINELLI'S PIZZERIA Map pp314-15 Pizza $

☎ 899-1414; 741 State St; sandwiches $6-7, pizzas $10-15; 11am-11pm Sun-Thu, 11am-midnight Fri & Sat

A casual and upbeat place for lunch near Audubon Park. The crowd is a friendly mix of university students and gallery hoppers. Pizzas and focaccia sandwiches get the contemporary treatment, with ingredients such as sun-dried tomatoes, goat and feta cheeses, artichokes and roasted walnuts making frequent appearances.

TAQUERIA CORONA Map pp314-15 Mexican $

☎ 897-3974; 5932 Magazine St; mains $6-13; 11:30am-2pm & 5-9:30pm

A regular crowd of students jams into this casual spot for inexpensive Mexican fare. The menu features a variety of grilled meat and fish tacos prepared on soft, flour tortillas. They're small and packed with flavor, and many can put away two or three for a meal. The burritos are just the right size – not quite gut-busting – and are filled with rice and high-quality meats.

DOMILISE'S PO-BOYS

Map pp314-15 Sandwiches $

☎ 899-9126; 5240 Annunciation St; po'boys $7; 11am-7pm Mon-Sat

On a quiet corner near the river, where scattered white shells stand in for sidewalks, this bustling little shack churns out some of the city's best-loved sandwiches. The huge fryer announces a readiness to dunk a basket of shrimp or catfish to order. Watch 'em sizzle, or turn around and, lo and behold, there's a little bar in the next room where a friendly old gent draws frosty mugs of draught Dixie. It's drinkable when served this cold. All in all, a most gratifying experience. Cash only.

CASAMENTO'S

Map pp314-15 Seafood $

☎ 895-9761; http://casamentosrestaurant.com; 4330 Magazine St; mains $7-13; 11am-2pm & 5:30-9pm Tue-Sat fall-spring

Casamento's is where oyster fiends head for their fix of raw ones on the half shell. It's administered in a most impeccably clean setting and the environs are vintage 1949. Spotless, glowing white-tile floors and walls make it feel more like a laboratory than a family-owned eatery. Their oysters are always the freshest. The thick gumbo with Creole tomatoes and oyster loaf (a sandwich of breaded and fried oysters on white bread) also have faithful followers. Other traditions upheld here include closing up during the summer and trading only in cash.

PASCAL'S MANALE

Map pp314-15 Italian & Louisianan $

☎ 895-4877; 1838 Napoleon Ave; mains $10-20; 11:30am-10pm Mon-Fri, 4-10pm Sat, 4-9pm Sun fall-spring

When we last went by this place, a sign taped to the door said it was still 'Closed for Hurricane.' It didn't look like anyone had been back since Katrina blew through town, but we can't imagine the place keeping its doors closed forever. Pascal's Manale is an Uptown tradition, est 1913, with walls bedecked with black and white photos of staff, patrons and the odd celebrity. It claims to have invented the local take on barbecue shrimp that requires no grill. (It's sautéed in a garlicky sauce.) Specialties are mostly Italian standards – lotsa veal, seafood and steaks.

DICK & JENNY'S

Map pp314-15 Contemporary Creole $$

☎ 894-9880; 4501 Tchoupitoulas St; mains $13-22; 5:30-10pm Tue-Sat

In a converted cottage along the uptown frontage road, Dick and Jenny's is well worth the schlep and, on busy nights, the wait for a table. It's unfussy but cheery, the main dining room is lit by colorful lanterns that hang from the ceiling. Some of New Orleans' friendliest waiters bring out gratifyingly good Creole dishes that exhibit the flair and care of a gifted chef's home cooking. Highlights include pecan-crusted Gulf fish with smoked leeks and mushrooms, and succulent steaks drizzled with a simple wine-reduction sauce. Good food, good people, good fun – can't beat it.

HOW YA LIKE DEM ERSTERS?

Hard-core New Orleans oyster bars, such as Casamento's (above), can be a little intimidating for neophytes. There's a certain cultishness in the way experienced patrons stand before a cold marble bartop as half a dozen oysters (which some locals pronounce 'ersters') are shucked and laid out on the half shell. With restrained anticipation, often disguised by an air of ritualism, these oyster fiends dash lemon and a spot of hot sauce or a bit of horseradish onto the first of the oysters. They then slurp down the addictive bivalve, pausing to savor that first oyster's saltiness and to summon up a renewed sense of anticipation before turning their attention to the second one, and this behavioral pattern repeats itself until all six half shells lie empty on the counter. For many New Orleanians, this entire ritual is completed in about the length of time it takes to fill a tank of gas.

Naturally, people who hold oysters in such high esteem have come to attribute certain health-promoting qualities to them. According to one popular myth, eating oysters can increase a person's sex drive and enhance their sexual prowess.

Oysters also have a variety of ways of insinuating themselves into a leisurely classic New Orleans meal. In some people's minds, seafood gumbo must include oysters or be called something else. And the list of appetizers on many of the city's menus generally includes several baked-oyster dishes. The most famous local oyster dish, served with a devilish little fork, is oysters Rockefeller, an Antoine's (p183) restaurant creation that owes its success as much to an irresistible secret spinach sauce as it does to the well-hidden oysters.

Then, of course, oysters make the classic po'boy. The name, local parlance for 'poor boy', refers to the cheapness of oysters during the Great Depression. An oyster sandwich cost just 20¢ in those days. In some traditional quarters of the city you can still order an oyster loaf, which as some people may recall was once known as *'la mediatrice'* – the peacemaker – because bringing one home was considered an effective way for a guilty husband to appease an angry wife. The loaf is composed of oysters dipped in cornmeal, deep fried and served on white toast, and it appears to have gone out of fashion as divorces became more popular.

JACQUES-IMO'S CAFÉ

Map pp314-15 Louisianan $$

☎ 861-0886; www.jacquesimoscafe.com; 8324 Oak St; mains $14-21; 🕑 5:30-10pm Mon-Sat

Jack Leonardi's exceedingly popular restaurant (now with two New York City outlets) is just a few doors from the famous Maple Leaf Bar, and many people make an evening out of these two spots. Not that you need an excuse to dine at this lively Creole–soul food restaurant. Outward appearances give the impression that it's a dive, and it's that kind of local-bar atmosphere that has always made this such a fun place. The menu encompasses high and low as down-home dishes like smothered chicken clink against more exotic items like blackened tuna with oyster champagne brie sauce. The place is legendary for making creative food that literally makes diners laugh (for one dish, the claws of a crab stick out of a green tomato). Many complain about two-hour waits to get in (reservations are not accepted) and, after that, if the kitchen isn't completely on the beam it can be a little hard to take.

MARTINIQUE BISTRO

Map pp314-15 Bistro $$

☎ 891-8495; 5908 Magazine St; mains $17-23; 🕑 6-10pm Sun-Thu, 6-10:30pm Fri & Sat

French cuisine with a little snap from the island of Martinique. In pleasant twilight, when the doors to the lush courtyard are flung open, the atmosphere at this converted cottage is both exotic and convivial. The cooking has an accomplished simplicity. The chef here really knows how to conduct an orchestra and tease out genuine flavor from the ingredients. Hawaiian sunfish glazed with a Tabasco *buerre blanc*, sesame-crusted salmon filet drizzled with a cilantro-ginger-soy vinaigrette, curry Gulf shrimp – it all comes together perfectly in this place. Make reservations.

BRIGTSEN'S RESTAURANT

Map pp314-15 Contemporary Cajun $$

☎ 861-7610; www.brigtsens.com; 723 Dante St; mains $18-26; 🕑 5:30-10pm Tue-Sat

Despite all the critical acclaim that has been heaped upon chef Frank Brigtsen, this remains a decidedly unpretentious place. Set in a converted double-shotgun house, the restaurant feels homey and inviting. Service is attentive but never oppressive. Brigtsen terms his cooking 'modern Louisiana cuisine,' and those in search of haute-Cajun cuisine will not find a better restaurant in the city. Rabbit and duck are among his specialties. Look for the roast duck with cornbread dressing and honey-pecan gravy, or braised rabbit in phyllo pastry with creamed spinach, bacon, mushrooms, leeks, and white-truffle oil.

DANTE'S KITCHEN

Map pp314-15 Contemporary Louisianan $$

☎ 861-3121; www.danteskitchen.com; 736 Dante St; mains $18-26, brunch $8-12; 🕑 11:30am-2:30pm & 6-10pm Tue-Sat, 11:30am-2:30pm Sun

Only a few short paces from the Mississippi River levee, the patio tables here may serve as front-row seating for the next 100-year flood. The imaginative cuisine at Dante's is by turns basic and refined, and melds French, American and Louisiana trad itions. It can be difficult to choose from the menu's inviting selections: sautéed Gulf fish amandine, iron skillet-roasted chicken, roasted duck served with andouille cornbread dressing, pan-roasted thick-cut pork chops. The Sunday brunch here is lauded by fans as among the best in a city filled with famous brunch destinations. Debris and poached eggs on a caramelized onion biscuit and topped with a demi-glace hollandaise sauce is a pretty unbelievable way to start your day.

GABRIELLE Map pp314-15 Creole & Cajun $$

☎ 948-6233; www.gabriellerestaurant.com; 438 Henry Clay Ave; dinner mains $18-32; 🕑 11:30am-2pm Fri, 5:30-10pm Tue-Sat

At the time of writing, Gabrielle's original location on Esplanade Ave was closed after Hurricane Katrina, and owner-chef Greg Sonnier had announced plans to relocate to this historic social hall near Audubon Park. It's a relief to know one of the city's best restaurants hasn't become a Katrina casualty. Sonnier captures the attention of both locals and a national audience with his innovative Creole and Cajun dishes. Look for signature dishes like homemade sausages, slow-roasted duck and barbecue shrimp pie. And save room for dessert. Greg's wife, Mary, creates outstanding pastries. If the phone number we've listed here is no longer in service, check the website for current information.

PINCH DA TAIL, SUCK DA HEAD

Louisiana's official state crustacean is the crawfish, which back home you probably know as crayfish. Cajuns call them *écrevisses,* and many rural folks just call them mudbugs. Peeling and eating their delicate thumb-size tail meat is a Cajun ritual that goes well with drinking beer and telling tall tales to a crowd around a heaping platter of the miniature swamp lobsters. Some are harvested in the wild; others are farm-raised in rice ponds during the off-season. Local harvests first show up in the spring.

Two keys to tasty crawfish are boiling them live and using a good spicy boil made with red pepper and other seasonings. It takes a 7lb platter to yield about a single pound of tail meat. Real dives even provide tables with a disposal hole in the middle for the wasted head and shell. One such joint in New Orleans is Frankie and Johnny's (p191).

A few Cajuns seeking riches continue to search for ways to automate the peeling process; until that happens, the peeling is up to you. First, grab and uncurl the crawfish, snapping the head and body from the tail. Hold the tail with both hands, using your thumb and finger to crack the tail open and pinch out the meat. As an option, you can suck the head to taste the flavorful 'fat' from the orange-colored hepatopancreas organ.

LILETTE Map pp314-15 French $$

☎ 895-1636; www.liletterestaurant.com; 3637 Magazine St; mains $19-28; 🕒 11:30am-2pm Tue-Sat, 6-10pm Tue-Thu, 6-11pm Fri & Sat

Lillette is a lively little bistro with a very traditional European vibe. Tradition is not an obsession here, as Chef John Harris works wonders with familiar dishes, making them subtly new. Start your meal with the white-truffle parmagiana toast with wild mushrooms, then pick from a solid line up of entrées. Grilled hanger steak comes with fries and marrowed bordelaise sauce. Potato-crusted black drum is served with mushrooms, vegetables and *beurre rouge*.

CLANCY'S Map pp314-15 Creole $$

☎ 895-1111; 6100 Annunciation St; mains $19-29; 🕒 11:30am-2pm Tue-Fri, 5:30-10:30pm Mon-Thu, 5:30-11pm Fri & Sat

A most unassuming local favorite, Clancy's is fine dining in intimate surroundings – you'll feel like a welcomed stranger in a crowd of old friends here. Have a finely mixed cocktail while perusing the menu. You'll see nearby patrons sighing with pleasure over Clancy's beloved blue-crab specialty, smoked then sautéed, which should nudge you in that direction. Nightly specials are always solid and inventive takes on Creole classics. Icebox pie brings perfect closure.

UPPERLINE RESTAURANT

Map pp314-15 Contemporary Creole $$

☎ 891-9822; www.upperline.com; 1413 Upperline St; mains $20-27; 🕒 5:30-9:30pm Wed-Sun

This restaurant is an excellent choice for contemporary Creole food in romantic surroundings. Upperline's owner JoAnn Clevenger loves her city – its art, its architecture, its cuisine – and her restaurant reflects these passions. She plays the charming hostess, making sure every guest feels welcome in her beautiful old house, its walls covered with vibrant paintings. Diners are then treated to exquisite Creole dishes. Chef Ken Smith applies original touches without reinventing the wheel. But mostly, Upperline is about great food prepared with care. Dishes like grilled Gulf fish with warm salad Niçoise, and roast duck with garlic port are classics prepared with a contemporary sensibility. The people in the kitchen also do great things with beef and lamb. Finish your meal off with a slice of the delectable key lime pie.

ESPLANADE RIDGE

Restaurants in the vicinity of the Fair Grounds naturally attract huge crowds for dinner during Jazz Fest. But several places out this way are worth coming to no matter what time of year it is. You can easily combine a meal along Esplanade Ave with a trip to City Park or a stroll along Bayou St John.

WHOLE FOODS MARKET

Map p317 Grocery & Deli $

☎ 943-1626; 3135 Esplanade Ave; sandwiches $5-7; 🕒 8am-9:30pm

A popular source for a picnic lunch, this market has an excellent deli as well as a healthy selection of fresh fruits and dry bins filled with nuts and healthy snacks. Hefty sandwiches are made to order, with fresh breads stuffed with quality meats and a full range of condiments. You can also get small salads and beverages. It's just a few blocks from here to City Park or the Fair Grounds.

LIUZZA'S BY THE TRACK

Map p317 Po'boys $

☎ 943-8667; 1518 N Lopez St; mains $6-13; 🕒 11am-5pm Tue-Sat

This is a great little neighborhood joint with a friendly atmosphere – the sort of place people don't mind schlepping to from other parts of town. It has the atmosphere of a corner bar with tables.

The specialty is po'boys, and Liuzza's roasted meats, barbecue shrimp and deep-fried garlic oysters are legendary. Before ordering one of these huge sandwiches, though, first inspect the daily specials (red beans and rice, pork chops and the like), which are always up to scratch. Liuzza's is nearly impossible to squeeze into during Jazz Fest, natch.

LOLA'S Map p317 Spanish $$

☎ 488-6946; 3312 Esplanade Ave; mains $10-29; 🕒 6-10pm

Lola's is an energetic and fun little place serving good, inexpensive Spanish food. Cool, soothing gazpacho is a smart way to start. Elaborate paellas and *fideuas* (an angel-hair pasta variation on the rice-based paella) are the specialties here – they're feasts for the eyes as well as the stomach and great for sharing. Fish, meats and stews are also good and are reasonably priced. Lola's does not take reservations and lines are almost inevitable. It's BYO, so get a bottle of wine at Whole Foods across the street, have it uncorked and make the most of the wait.

RESTAURANT INDIGO

Map p317 Contemporary Louisianan $$

☎ 947-0123; www.restaurantindigo.com; 2285 Bayou Rd; mains $12-26; 🕒 5:30-10pm Tue-Sat

With its exquisite tropical suavity, Indigo creates a sultry mood. Restaurant Indigo is housed in a 19th-century corner grocery, a rustic touch that is played off and elevated by a veranda that opens to a garden filled with palmettos and other leafy plants that thrive in balmy climes. Colorful cocktails add a festive look on the tables. Polished service and Chef Michael Sichel's contemporary regional cuisine buoys the experience. Sichel's toned-down haute style is built on surf-and-turf mainstays that are prepared with sophistication. Keep an eye out for items like short ribs with marrow

The owner of Restaurant Indigo

mashed potatoes or whole fried redfish served with white beans and sautéed calamari.

CAFÉ DEGAS Map p317 French Bistro $$

☎ 945-5635; www.cafedegas.com; 3127 Esplanade Ave; mains $16-20; ⏲ 11am-2:30pm Wed-Sat, 10:30am-3pm Sun, 6-10pm Wed-Sun

A full-grown pecan tree thrusts through the floor and ceiling of the enclosed deck which serves as Café Degas' congenial dining room. This is a rustic and romantic little spot that warms the heart with first-rate French-bistro fare. The casual atmosphere is accentuated by the mildly eccentric, but exceedingly polite waitstaff. Meals that sound familiar on the menu – steak *frites au poivre*, parmesan-crusted veal medallions, seared duck breast with mushroom spaetzle – are arranged with extraordinary beauty on their plates. You might feel guilty for disturbing art like this, but it's a crime for which you will be amply rewarded.

Entertainment & Nightlife

Bars & Clubs 200
- French Quarter 200
- Faubourg Marigny & Bywater 202
- CBD & Warehouse District 204
- Lower Garden District 205
- Uptown & Riverbend 205

Live Music 206
- French Quarter 206
- Faubourg Marigny & Bywater 207
- CBD & Warehouse District 208
- Uptown & Riverbend 209

Art Galleries & Openings 210
- French Quarter 210
- CBD & Warehouse District 211
- Lower Garden District & Garden District 213
- Uptown & Riverbend 213

Classical Music, Opera & Dance 213

Theater 214

Cinemas 214

Sports & Activities 215
- Spectator Sports 215
- Activities 216
- Health & Fitness 218

Entertainment & Nightlife

Katrina be damned, New Orleans is still a funhouse. It's a town full of cornet players and painters, Dapper Dans and Champagne Charlenes. Sharp-dressed swingers, hipsters and gays are as ever drawn to the Crescent City's promise of stylized decadence. For many musicians, 'day job' means performing out on Jackson Sq in the afternoon. And day and night bars belch out drunken tourists wielding take-away drinks in plastic 'go cups.'

As elsewhere, however, New Orleans' finest entertainment is to be found behind closed doors. The better bars encourage patrons to stay awhile by providing a welcoming atmosphere and serving the drinks in glasses made of, well, glass. The selection of drinking establishments ranges from historic dives to swanky modern hotel bars. The most memorable shows are in neighborhood taverns like Vaughan's (p208) and legendary clubs like Tipitina's (p209).

The arts are flourishing like never before, and the city's galleries are hopping as people are drawn to the new burst of creative energy. Meanwhile, the future of the city's major sports teams remains in doubt after Katrina. They have returned to the city unsure if the smaller 'new' New Orleans will be able to fill such large venues as the Superdome and New Orleans Arena.

Your best sources for upcoming performances and reviews are the free monthly entertainment guide *Offbeat* and the weekly *Gambit*. The *Times-Picayune* entertainment section, 'Lagniappe,' is published on Friday. Tune into radio station WWOZ (90.7FM) for a round-the-clock education on southern Louisiana music, or call the station's events hotline, the **Second Line** (☎ 840-4040), for a daily listing of shows.

Tickets & Reservations

You generally won't need to purchase tickets in advance to see live music in a New Orleans club. Shows at **Tipitina's** (p209), for instance, will rarely require advance planning unless Dr John or someone else of that caliber is performing. If you are wanting to catch a high-profile touring band at **House of Blues** (p206) or even at a smaller joint such as **Snug Harbor**

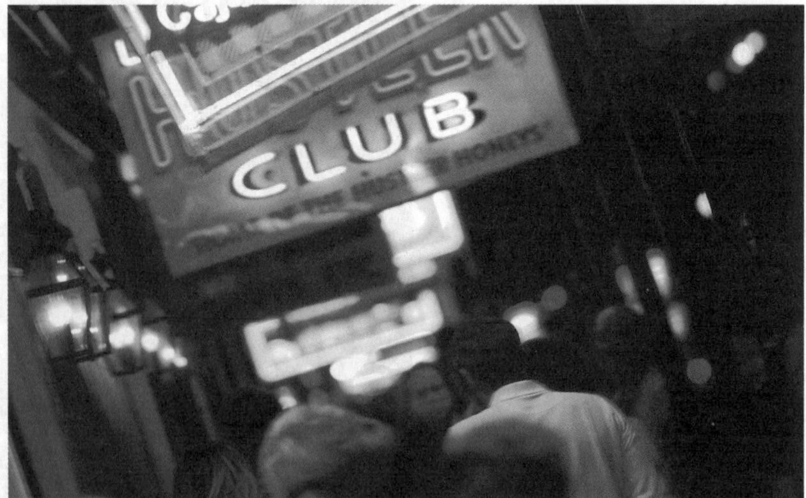

Strip of bars and clubs

(p208) or **One Eyed Jacks** (p207), just head over to the club's box office or bar a day or two ahead of time.

Additionally, **TicketMaster** (Map pp310–11; ☎ 522-5555; www.ticketmaster.com; 408 N Peters St) has information on, and sells tickets to, just about any major event in the city, including big music shows and sports events. This is a good option if you're purchasing tickets from home before you go to New Orleans. There is a TicketMaster outlet at Tower Records in the French Quarter.

GO CUPS

Guy walks into a bar and orders a drink. Bartender asks, 'Zat for here or to go?' True story. It is legal to walk the streets of New Orleans with a drink in your hand, as long as the drink is in a plastic 'go cup.' Wandering drinkers are prone to losing their grip on their drinks, leaving shattered glass on the sidewalk, so drinking from a real glass or bottle is strictly forbidden.

Festivals

New Orleans' ample holiday calendar includes many events that showcase the city's wonderful music, culture and nightlife. On these occasions, the city kicks it up a notch, just like Chef Emeril, and visitors' heads are guaranteed to spin for all the entertainment options.

Mardi Gras (Febuary or March) is very entertaining, of course, with parades and live music and fun costumed crowds filling the streets with their own spontaneous theater and burlesque. See the Mardi Gras & Jazz Fest chapter (p32) for more.

The **French Quarter Festival** (April) puts Jazz Fest on the streets of the French Quarter, while the real **Jazz Fest** (end of April, early May) amps it up at the Fair Grounds. During both festivals the clubs hop at night, with Jazz Fest's bigger crowds challenging fire codes and leaving little room for a slide trombone player.

The **Essence Festival** (July) is all about R&B and soul music, but it departed for Houston in 2006 and there's no indication whether it will ever be back in the Superdome. Never fear, the **Satchmo Summer Fest** (August) puts bands back on the streets of the French Quarter, which is more fun anyway.

Southern Decadence (August) is a gay festival that naturally ups the ante in the city's gay bars and generally turns the lower Quarter into a theatrical street party. The Halloween season is launched with the **Voodoo Music Experience** (October), which rocks the Crescent City with hard rock bands like Nine Inch Nails.

Club Strips & Neighborhoods

There are bars galore on Bourbon St, as you probably know. These places more or less blend into one another with little to recommend one over the other. Bourbon St is New Orleans' entertainment equivalent of the food buffet at Circus Circus. The amusements are slopped out with indifference while the patrons go hog wild like the donkey-boys on Pleasure Island. Those who keep their wits about them tend to look bemused or stunned. Most people just roam the street with their go cups, ducking into the nearest door (pretty much any will do) when they need another drink. Many bars feature live cover bands and some, at the lower end of the street, are gay discos.

Elsewhere in the Quarter it's possible to find lively local boozers and civilized jazz joints. For several blocks, Lower Decatur St is lined with varied bars, clubs and eateries where locals, musicians, tourists and the odd magician mix peacefully. Careful navigating over the legs of kids begging for change.

Over in the Faubourg Marigny, Frenchmen St puts on the best street party in town just about every night. It's a vibrant local scene that spans all age groups, races and genders. Things start up slowly during the cocktail hour with acoustic bands playing at the Spotted Cat (p208). By midnight Café Brasil (p202) is usually packed to the gills, and the crowd milling from bar to bar spills out onto the street.

Up in the Riverbend area, near Tulane and Loyola universities, a cluster of dives and music clubs draws a regular crowd of students. The Maple Leaf Bar (p209) on Oak St draws a more diverse crowd with its superior musical lineup.

BARS & CLUBS

As the great rock-and-roll songwriter Lee Hazelwood once noted, 'You won't find it on any map, but take a step in any direction and you're in trouble.' So it goes in New Orleans, a town with plenty of slippery slopes but no hills. On some blocks every other door's to be avoided for anyone hoping to lead a pious life. Hopefully that's not what you had in mind. Mud in your eye.

FRENCH QUARTER

There's a lot going on in the Old Quarter, from boozy Bourbon St to quiet Pirate's Alley. Head down to lower Decatur St for a collection of interesting dives.

ABBEY Map pp310-11

☎ 523-7150; 1123 Decatur St; 24hr

The riffraff congregating in this atmospheric Decatur St dive tend to dress in black. The place has a faded and jaded port of call feel to it, with blasé female bartenders, transient hipsters and shifty-eyed characters. You needn't be pierced or tattooed to fit in, but a little Joe Strummer/Suicide Girl swagger won't hurt. The jukebox reflects these sensibilities, but also includes rocking sides by the original Man in Black. And if you're seeking Lee Hazelwood's brand of trouble, the juke here has that covered too. At least stop by for a shot of Jack if you're prowling the Lower Quarter.

FIVE FAVORITE BARS

New Orleans' best watering holes are the ones you wish were just around the corner in your own town. While in New Orleans, you may end up a regular customer at any of the following.

R Bar (p203) Casual and funky Marigny hang-out with good beer, good juke and a pool table.

Napoleon House (opposite) Faded Vieux Carré sanctuary from Bonaparte's time.

Oswald's Speakeasy (p202) Magic shows, piano players and old flicks make this a fun spot in the Quarter.

St Joe's (p206) Fun little Uptown corner bar for a nip of sacramental booze.

Spotted Cat (p208) Intimate Marigny spot for a spot of beer and live blues and jazz.

BOMBAY CLUB Map pp310-11

☎ 586-0972; 830 Conti St; 5pm-late

If the name activates a craving for martinis, then you'll understand what this swank gin joint is all about. In complete defiance of the nearby Bourbon St jungle, Bombay is a study in British refinement, with overstuffed armchairs and candlelit tables. It's about sipping and savoring, rather than guzzling by the gallon. The list of over 100 martini cocktails, bound in leather, includes all those deadly vodka concoctions that veil the alcohol in frivolous fruity flavors. Of course, you can also order a stiff Churchill model (gin with just a whiff of vermouth). It's a friendly enough place, though cigar smoking is permitted and even encouraged. Live jazz combos perform most nights.

CAROUSEL BAR Map pp310-11

☎ 523-3341; 214 Royal St; 11am-late

At this smart-looking hotel bar, inside the historic Monteleone, everyone's a comic until they realize the barkeeps have heard 'em all before. No, you don't get to sit on a painted horse. Hey, how come the stools don't go up and down? What?! No blaring mechanical orchestra?! The circular bar does revolve and it is canopied by the top hat of the 1904 World's Fair carousel with running lights, hand-painted figures and gilded mirrors. Wednesday night is Louis Prima Night, with John Autin and Julie Jules standing in for Louis and Keely Smith. It takes 15 minutes for the bar to complete a revolution. If it's spinning too fast for you, then you really ought to ease up on the sauce, pal. Careful on your way out.

DUNGEON Map pp310-11

☎ 523-5530; 738 Toulouse St; cover $5; midnight-late

Got to admit, this place made us a little nervous at first. It doesn't open till the witching hour, and some of the bouncers have filed their teeth into pointy Dracula fangs. Then we observed the words 'Ye Olde' in small type on the sign out front. So this is really just 'Ye Olde Dungeon,' which doesn't sound so threatening after all. Having descended into the club's basement chambers, we found Goths outnumbered by yuppies and bikers. DJs keep things throbbing until dawn's early light (egads! sunlight!) and several barkeeps serve up ghoulish cocktails (with creepy names like the Witches Brew

ABSINTHE & HERBSAINT

When absinthe, the once insanely popular licorice-flavored liqueur, was outlawed in the early 20th century for its extreme addictive and psychoactive potential, addicts and purveyors of the drink tried to find a substitute for the bitter liquor. The French developed pastis and Pernod as safer alternatives to the wormwood-based absinthe. Not to be outdone, a New Orleans company developed its own wormwood-free absinthe with star anise replacing the forbidden herb.

The resulting yellowish-green Herbsaint replaced absinthe in cocktails and culinary preparations alike. A host of local specialties use Herbsaint as a primary ingredient or subtle flavoring, including local versions of oysters Rockefeller and the New Orleans signature cocktails such as Sazerac and Absinthe Suissesse.

and the Dragon's Blood), which the bar promises will help you 'leave your troubles behind.' Such caring, warmhearted sentiments! We had this place all wrong!

JEAN LAFITTE'S OLD ABSINTHE HOUSE Map pp310-11

☎ 523-3181; 240 Bourbon St; 10am-4am

A number of bars in New Orleans, including this one, served absinthe before it was outlawed in 1914. The mysterious beverage had a psychotropic allure – wormwood was the active ingredient – but it allegedly sent enthusiasts to the loony bin. Today, Herbsaint, a locally produced anisette, is a relatively safe stand-in for old absinthe-based drinks. You're probably also wondering about the bar. It is a historic spot, having opened in 1807, but the crowd is generally of the bottom-shelf Bourbon St variety.

KING BOLDEN'S Map pp310-11

☎ 525-2379; 820 N Rampart St; cover $5-10; 6pm-late

A smart looking club on Rampart St, King Bolden's mixes it up with DJs spinning soul, hip-hop and reggae early in the week, and live jazz and brass bands performing through the weekend.

LAFITTE'S BLACKSMITH SHOP Map pp310-11

☎ 523-0066; 941 Bourbon St; noon-late

Fashioned eons ago from a gutted brick cottage, this atmospheric haunt is purported to have been the workshop of the smuggler Jean Lafitte and his brother Pierre. Whether that tasty bit of lore is true or not, the ancient house did go up in the 18th century and it endured the fires that destroyed most of the French Quarter during the Spanish era. It feels like the real deal. In the afternoon, grab a small table near the open shutters, where you might catch a refreshing breeze. At night the joint is entirely lit by tabletop candles, and drunk tourists gather round the back-room piano and sing along to Fats Domino and Otis Redding tunes. Good for a few laughs.

MOLLY'S AT THE MARKET Map pp310-11

☎ 525-5169; 1107 Decatur St; 10am-6am

The unofficial Irish cultural center of the French Quarter draws a regular crowd of neighborhood characters and seldom-sober rovers. Former owner Jim Monaghan (whose ashes are kept in an urn behind the bar) inaugurated the wild St Patrick's Day parade that starts at Molly's. The bar doesn't bleed green, though, and in terms of décor makes no especial effort to re-create the atmosphere of the old sod. A worthwhile sanctuary.

NAPOLEON HOUSE Map pp310-11

☎ 524-9752; 500 Chartres St; 11am-5pm Mon, 11am-midnight Tue-Thu, 11am-1am Fri & Sat, 11am-7pm Sun

Just as the best emperors are the deposed ones, the best bars are those that have seen better days. Having opened its doors in 1797, Napoleon House is a particularly attractive example of what Walker Percy termed 'vital decay.' By all appearances, its stuccoed walls haven't received so much as a dab of paint in over two centuries, and the diffuse glow pouring through the open doors and windows in the afternoon draws out the room's gorgeous patina. The back courtyard is also pleasant, day or night. As an added bonus, the place has a colorful connection to Bonaparte himself. After the emperor was banished to St Helena, a band of loyal New Orleanians reputedly plotted to snatch him and set him up in this building's 3rd-floor digs. It didn't happen, but one can easily imagine Napoleon whiling away his last days in this pleasant spot, telling fishing stories about conquering Europe.

OSWALD'S SPEAKEASY Map pp310-11
☎ 218-5954; 1331 Decatur St; 🕑 6pm-midnight
Named for Kennedy's assassin, this 19th-century tavern is owned by Harry Anderson, the magician and actor best known as the star of the '80s sitcom *Night Court*. It's been turned into more of a variety theater than a clandestine drinking hall, and there's something interesting going on pretty much every night. The jocular Anderson, not so scrawny as he once was, presides over Tuesday night magic shows, and several nights a week lone piano players fill the old hall with familiar tunes we can't quite remember from days gone by. Our personal favorite event here is the weekly installment of the Zapruder Film Festival, when Anderson screens rare prints of film noir classics, some of which have yet to be released on DVD.

PAT O'BRIEN'S Map pp310-11
☎ 525-4823, 800-597-4823; 718 St Peter St; 🕑 10am-4am
New Orleans has dozens of tourist trap bars, but Pat O'Brien's is probably the only one you ever heard of and it's really the only one worth bothering with. The place has genuine atmosphere and history, though the gift shop does lend a whiff of commercialism and the Bourbon St boozeoisie has the run of the joint most nights. The back courtyard, lit by flaming fountains, has an obvious allure for anyone who remembers wanting to jump ship during the *Pirates of the Caribbean* ride at Disneyland. The bar's trademark drink, the Hurricane, is a lethal 29oz blend of rum, orange juice, pineapple juice and grenadine that will have you talking like a pirate without ever tasting the rum.

TONY SEVILLE'S PIRATE'S ALLEY CAFE Map pp310-11
☎ 524-9332; 622 Pirate's Alley; 🕑 noon-late
The narrow pedestrian alley hidden in the shadow of St Louis Cathedral is a natural spot for a tiny little bar, and Tony Seville's fits the bill perfectly. It's owned by friendly folk and has the atmosphere of a little Montparnasse hideaway with no claim to fame. You can snag a stool at the bar and meet the regular characters who seem to drop by every few minutes, or claim a table out on the alley and soak up the atmosphere of the Old Quarter.

FAUBOURG MARIGNY & BYWATER

Frenchmen St in Faubourg Marigny is perhaps the best entertainment strip in New Orleans, with a great mix of small locals, hipster havens and live music venues, as well as some decent restaurants. The strip's proximity to the Lower Quarter is another boon, making it possible to work your way from here back to lower Decatur in a fun-filled evening.

APPLE BARRELL Map p316
☎ 949-9399; 609 Frenchmen St; 🕑 5pm-late
This roughshod local seats about eight people, but good folks congregate here, so rubbing elbows isn't an unpleasant experience. Somehow the joint makes room for live musicians. Usually it's someone reliving Dylan's acoustic period. Upstairs is the casual Italian eatery Adolfo's (p186) and this is a good spot for a drink before dinner.

BACCHANAL Map p316
☎ 948-9111; 600 Poland Ave
Flouting the rules of wine snobbery, this laid-back little Bywater shop caters to cheapskates who have a taste for the grape. Owner Chris Rudge is a sommelier who seeks out great wines that he can put a fair price tag on – for under $10, say. His customers need not ask themselves 'Should I go with the $7 cabernet or should I take a chance on this $18 pinot noir?' They can ask Rudge. The real allure, however, is the wine bar, a friendly neighborhood spot where patrons can linger over a glass, and the krewe of regular customers here are good company.

CAFÉ BRASIL Map p316
☎ 947-9386; 2100 Chartres St; cover $5; 🕑 6pm-2am Sun-Thu, 6pm-4am Fri & Sat
When this large club gets cranking – around midnight most any night of the week – a lively crowd spills out onto the sidewalk and often clogs up Frenchmen St traffic. It's a hip, bohemian space with a colorful Caribbean vibe. The entertainment shuffles between live Latin jazz combos, funk, rock and reggae bands, suave crooners and DJs spinning heady grooves from around the world. Fredy Omar's salsa band gets the place jumping on Wednesday night, and you can drop by

early to cop free pointers on Latin dance steps. A lot of club-hoppers make a point of ending up here after surveying the scene elsewhere.

D.B.A. Map p316

☎ 942-3731; 618 Frenchmen St; 🕑 5pm-4am

A bona-fide cool spot, with an impressive selection of international beers and live music on most nights. D.B.A. has another outlet in New York's East Village, which may give you an idea of what it's aiming for. Hip, young professionals predominate around the bar, but a good live show will draw a mixed and friendly crowd. The musical lineup ranges wildly, but is generally good, with cool modern jazz combos, R&B singers, traveling country outfits and a local gypsy jazz combo. On Saturday night John Boutté's early show is the best way to get things rolling.

HOOKAH CAFE Map p316

☎ 943-1101; 500 Frenchmen St; 🕑 5:30pm-2am; cover free-$5

The hip Hookah is a swank-looking bar/supper club with a gimmick, which is that patrons can smoke hookahs at their table. For the uninitiated, a hookah is a groovy Middle Eastern water pipe that looks like an extraterrestrial musical instrument, or something pulled out of a goat. A full tobacco menu features *shisha* blends from far-off Saudi Arabia, Jordan and the UAE. Most people just drink here, or sup on Indian cuisine, but we encourage sharing a smoke ($11 to $20) with your friends. It's a rare pleasure. A good time to do it is Sunday night, when the Sisters of Salome Belly Dance troupe invades the aisles and raises the atmosphere bar a few hip-shifting notches. Between the 'backy' and the bellies your head will swirl.

IGOR'S CHECKPOINT CHARLIE Map p316

☎ 947-0979; 501 Esplanade Ave; 🕑 24hr

A grungy bar where you can order greasy grill food, do laundry, shoot a game of pool and play Elvis Pinball. The small stage is worked by unknowns passing through from far-off corners of the country, and often they're very good.

MIMI'S IN THE MARIGNY Map p316

☎ 947-8015; 2601 Royal St; 🕑 5pm-late

Mimi's is a comfortable local bar and a tapas restaurant. It has two floors, so you can decide if you're dining or just drinking. The bar has a pool table and the bartenders are known for spinning cool tunes. Mimi's is also known for fun theme nights when tango lessons are offered or old-school soul music is spun.

R BAR Map p316

☎ 948-7499; 1431 Royal St; 🕑 3pm-late

Sounds like a cattle brand, but merely by coincidence. The R Bar is just a damn good corner spot, several notches above a dive, that actually benefits from being a few blocks apart from the Frenchmen St scene. The regular crowd is generally single and seemingly savvy. The place has a friendly vibe and goofy ironic décor that's worth inspecting while your friends are using the john. For instance, a drum kit hangs upside-down from the ceiling, offering a unique perspective. The bar serves a wide selection of quality brews; campy films are shown on three monitors; and there's usually a casual game of pool in progress.

ERNIE K-DOE MOTHER-IN-LAW LOUNGE

Rhythm and blues singer Ernie K-Doe passed away in 2001, but his nightclub, **Ernie K-Doe Mother-in-Law Lounge** (☎ 947-1078; 1500 N Claiborne Ave; 🕑 5pm-2am), lives on. A visit here is an unforgettable experience for anyone who remembers the inimitable K-Doe, whose life was a remarkable up-and-down ride from the 1960s, when he recorded his number-one hit 'Mother in Law,' through to the 1990s, when he pronounced himself 'Emperor of the World.' His widow, Antoinette, keeps the K-Doe spirit alive in the bar, and she designs and sews flamboyant suits for the life-sized statue of her late husband that presides over the room. (And we always assumed they broke the mold when they made K-Doe.)

The joint was flooded by Hurricane Katrina, but Antoinette and the statue survived in the upstairs apartment. She set out to refurbish the place and at this writing she was optimistic she'd be reopening soon. Fans continue to flock to the place for live music, karaoke, film screenings and crazy parties. The Mother-in-Law Lounge is on Claiborne Ave, downriver from Esplanade by a couple of blocks. It's a sketchy neighborhood, so take a cab.

SATURN BAR Map p316

☎ **949-7532; 3067 St Claude Ave;** 🕑 **3pm-midnight**

The very definition of saturnine. The Saturn is admirable for going to so little effort to make its patrons feel at home. Light comes only from two cosmic neon lamps, boxes are stacked about the room and there is not a comfortable seat in the place. But locals have an enduring love for the Saturn, and often hold parties and events in the ramshackle back room. Late at night, hipsters are drawn here but haven't succeeded in colonizing it. All in all, a great bar.

CBD & WAREHOUSE DISTRICT

Amid this area's odd mix of convention hotels, office buildings and art galleries you might have a difficult time locating a bar stool with your name on it. Rest assured, though, good watering holes are to be found.

CIRCLE BAR Map pp308-9

☎ **588-2616; 1032 St Charles Ave;** 🕑 **4pm-late, shows 11pm**

In an old house between an empty lot and a vacant office building, the Circle Bar looks a little forlorn from the street. Inside, however, the dimly lit former bedrooms and parlors are jam packed with smartly dressed hipsters who come for live music and cocktails. The musical lineup is an eclectic mix of alt-rock, punk, jazz, funk and ironic blends of all the above. It's on Lee Circle, just around the corner from the Ogden Museum. You can look at some art and be here in time for happy hour.

LOA Map pp308-9

☎ **553-9550; 221 Camp St;** 🕑 **5pm-late**

Off the lobby of the fashionable International House Hotel, Loa is a great place to grab a daytime drink. Huge windows overlook the CBD's streetscape of dedicated worker bees, and watching them while getting drunk is a pleasure akin to munching on doughnuts among people sweating it out at the gym. In the evening, live music runs the gamut of world beats. And everyone looks good bathed in candlelight. If you practice voodoo, or just like the idea of a full-coverage plan, you can leave an offering at the voodoo altar on your way out.

GAY & LESBIAN CLUBS

New Orleans is gay friendly, with some longstanding bars and a very open scene. Big concentrations of gays live in the lower French Quarter and in the Marigny and Bywater. You'll notice the rainbow flags over businesses and hanging from balconies in these parts of town. There's always lots going on.

Bourbon Pub & Parade Disco (Map pp310–11; ☎ 529-2107; www.bourbonpub.com; 801 Bourbon St; cover $5; 🕑 24hr, disco 10pm-late) Smack dab on Bourbon St is this gay bar with a very popular happy hour. At night, it's a loud and bawdy scene that spills out onto the street. You can head to the upstairs dance club and watch the scene from the balconies.

Country Club (Map p316; ☎ 945-0742; 634 Louisa St; cover $5-10; 🕑 11am-1am) There's no golf course here. Down in the Bywater, this historic mansion has been converted into a gay frat house, replete with a large swimming pool in the back yard. It's a low-key hang out by day and more of a clubby scene by night. Clothing is not altogether forbidden on the patio, where guys and dolls tend to strip down and erase those tan lines. Indoors things are a bit more refined, with frequent shows.

Good Friends Bar (Map pp310–11; ☎ 566-7191; www.goodfriendsbar.com; 740 Dauphine St; 🕑 24hr) The crowd of regulars really are good friends, partly because the bar stools are so damn comfortable. Easy-on-the-eye bartenders make the bar's famous drink, the 'Separator' (Kahlúa ice cream, milk, brandy and coffee liqueur). The upstairs piano area, the 'Queen's Head Pub,' heats up with show tunes on Sunday night. The balcony is a good spot to chill.

Lafitte in Exile (Map pp310–11; ☎ 522-8397; www.lafittes.com; 901 Bourbon St; 🕑 24hr) A most venerable and popular gay bar in the quarter, Lafitte in Exile gets a vastly mixed and friendly crowd of all ages and sexes. The upstairs balcony is one of the best and as you'd expect the drink specials just keep coming.

Oz (Map pp310–11; ☎ 593-9491; 800 Bourbon St; cover free-$5; 🕑 24hr) Even Uptown debs have been seen shaking their tail feathers at this mixed dance club. The bump-and-grind area is surrounded by a cast-iron balcony and the bar is manned by buff, shirtless bartenders. In the wee hours, clothing becomes more of a concept than a reality.

LOWER GARDEN DISTRICT

The Lower Garden District seems to be getting better all the time. A few bars in the neighborhood are worth stopping into after an afternoon spent shopping and gallery hopping on Magazine St.

HALF MOON Map pp312-13

☎ 522-7313; 1125 St Mary St; 11am-4am

On an interesting corner, just half a block from Magazine St, the Half Moon beckons with a cool neighborhood vibe. The place is good for a beer, short order meal or an evening shooting stick.

IGOR'S LOUNGE Map pp312-13

☎ 522-2145; 2133 St Charles Ave; 24hr

A good old joint with a greasy grill, pool tables and washing machines. Igor's constant rotation of characters makes it a good place to drop in if you're making your way up or down St Charles Ave. Or make this your terminus if you're staying nearby.

UPTOWN & RIVERBEND

Tulane and Loyola universities obviously pump some young energy into the nightlife in this part of town, but there's more going on here. Some of the area's best bars are covered under Live Music, p206.

COLUMNS HOTEL Map pp314-15

☎ 899-9308; 3811 St Charles Ave; 3pm-midnight Mon-Thu, 3pm-2am Fri, 11am-2am Sat, 11am-midnight Sun

Uptown society converges on the dignified drinking environs of the Columns' Victorian Lounge and on its broad front porch. It's a see-and-be-seen locus for local professionals, and suits and gowns abound. Ordinary out-of-town folk won't feel unwelcome, although men might want to comb their hair and don a jacket to fit in. Over the clinking glasses the murmur of the crowd grows louder as the night goes on.

COOTER BROWN'S TAVERN & OYSTER BAR Map pp314-15

☎ 866-9104; www.cooterbrowns.com; 509 S Carrollton Ave; 11am-late

Cooter's is a Riverbend local that takes its beer seriously, serving over 40 draft brews and hundreds of international bottled brews. College kids, local characters and Uptown swells drop in for a few brews and freshly shucked oysters, or to shoot pool or watch sports on TV. While you're joining them in any of the above activities, pause to appreciate the tavern's 'Beersoleum & Hall of Foam' – a gallery of 100 plaster bas-relief statuettes of everybody from Liberace to Chairman Mao, each holding a bottle of beer (Albert Einstein, Mother Theresa and Andy Warhol also appear). This curious, still-growing exhibit is the work of the uniquely talented Scott Conary.

F&M PATIO BAR Map pp314-15

☎ 895-6784; 4841 Tchoupitoulas St; 24hr

It's remote and not particularly impressive looking, but lots of locals take the trouble to work F&M into their Saturday night plans. It's an all-around fun spot with a very laid-back atmosphere. College kids and restaurant workers come for the lively back patio scene and good jukebox, and to shoot casual games of pool.

RIVERSHACK TAVERN Map pp306-7

☎ 834-4938; 3449 River Rd; 11am-midnight Mon-Thu, 11am-3am Fri & Sat

In Jefferson, upstream from Riverbend beside the levee, is an advertisement-adorned roadhouse that probably hit its prime in the 1940s. It's packed with students, older bikers and hospital staff (hopefully not heading back to the surgery room). It has a good selection of beers on tap. If you're hungry, the lunch specials are pretty good.

SIP Map pp314-15

☎ 894-7071; www.sipwinenola.com; 3119 Magazine St; 10am-8pm Mon-Sat, noon-6pm Sun

Sip is a wine shop that was scheduled to open in September 2005. Although Hurricane Katrina delayed that plan, the owners opened shop as soon as possible, an act of faith that locals were quick to praise. The place hopped from the git-go, and hasn't stopped since. The wine selection includes many fine and economical choices, and you can just stop in for a glass. But the real draw is the pleasant, no-fuss atmosphere. Neighbors seem to be in the habit of dropping by to say hello to the friendly proprietors. Friday nights are really all right when Sip has free wine tastings (starting at 6pm). The place is also packed for Tuesday night's 'Sip 'n Spin,' a classy wine party with DJs spinning cool tunes.

ST JOE'S BAR Map pp314-15

☎ 899-3744; 5535 Magazine St; 🕑 5pm-late

You gotta love a saint named Joe, even if he preferred to be called Joseph. This neighborhood boozer is pretty down to earth but manages to feel classy and even a little churchlike. The narrow front room broods with hand-carved wooden crosses and church pews, but the piety stops there. The stereo plays jazz and swing, and seems strangely lacking in Gregorian chants. The ordinary Joes who pack into the place – many of 'em working stiffs in their early 30s – have a good time and don't appear to be feeling at all guilty about it. Past the pool table you'll find a door to the intimate patio, lit by votive candles and colorful lanterns – a sweet spot where you can loosen your collar and not have to worry about spilling your drink on someone.

LIVE MUSIC

New Orleans can shake, rattle and roll with the best of cities. At times, it seems musicians have everyone else outnumbered. But the Big Easy does things its own way. Where else can you get down to the funky grooves laid down by a tuba player? Live performances in jazz, R&B, rock, country, Cajun, zydeco, funk, Mardi Gras Indians, soul and genre-defying experimentation are on every night of the week.

FRENCH QUARTER

You've got your choice of white-haired trad jazz at Preservation Hall, funky brass at Donna's and big name touring acts at House of Blues. Many bars and restaurants also feature live music.

DONNA'S BAR & GRILL Map pp310-11

☎ 596-6914; www.donnasbarandgrill.com; 800 N Rampart St; cover $5-10; 🕑 shows 10pm-late Thu-Mon

Walk down St Ann St toward the lighted arches of Louis Armstrong Park and you'll end up at this humble little sweatbox. Everyone knows about Donna's. It is the premier brass-band club in the city, with a nonstop lineup of top jazz and funky second-line outfits playing weekly gigs. The cats who aren't on the bill – someone who copped a gig with a touring band, say – frequently drop in to jam, which always ups the ante. Friday night's Tremé Brass Band gig is an opportunity to hear bass drummer Uncle Lionel Batiste, a local living legend. The fine drummer from Shannon Powell's quartet holds things down on Sunday Night, and the joint also cooks on Monday when Bob French takes the stage and free barbecue is served between sets. (You can pay for the good stuff any other night.)

WEEKLY GIGS

Some musicians in New Orleans are regular as clockwork, showing up at the same clubs at the same time every week. Many of the weekly gigs have a very social atmosphere. They can be like parties with a regular crowd of friendly people – and musicians do not take entertaining their friends lightly.

Sunday Shannon Powell Quartet at Donna's (left).

Monday Bob French and Friends at Donna's (left); New Orleans Jazz Vipers at the Spotted Cat (p208); Charmaine Neville at Snug Harbor (p208).

Tuesday Rebirth Brass Band at Maple Leaf (p209); New Orleans Jazz Vipers at Angeli on Decatur (p179).

Thursday Kermit Ruffins and the Barbecue Swingers at Vaughan's (p208).

Wednesday Fredy Omar con Su Banda at Café Brasil (p202).

Friday Joe Krown at Le Bon Temps Roule (p209); Tremé Brass Band at Donna's (left); Ellis Marsalis at Snug Harbor (p208); Fredy Omar con Su Banda at Café Brasil (p202).

Saturday John Boutté at d.b.a. (p203); Washboard Chaz at the Spotted Cat (p208).

HOUSE OF BLUES Map pp310-11

☎ 529-2583; 255 Decatur St; tickets $7-25; 🕑 8pm-2am nightly, gospel brunch 9:30am-4pm Sun

There's no denying that HOB is one of the best live-music venues in the city for rock, alt-rock and alt-country. A full calendar of headliner acts, from the hottest local talent to major touring bands, makes this congenial space a winner just about every night of the week. On Sunday morning HOB's Gospel Brunch will fortify your soul. A few doors down, a small auxiliary club, the **Parish** (Map pp310–11; ☎ 529-2583; 229 Decatur St), features mostly local acts.

PALM COURT JAZZ CAFÉ Map pp310-11

☎ 525-0200; 1204 Decatur St; cover $5; 🕐 7-11pm Wed-Sun

A mature crowd of trad jazz fans enjoys this supper club alternative to Preservation Hall. No sitting on the floor for the shows in this roomy club. Palm Court has an excellent music calendar with a regular lineup of local legends. Shows start at 8pm.

PRESERVATION HALL Map pp310-11

☎ 522-2841; 726 St Peter St; cover $5; 🕐 8pm-midnight

The large crowds that file into this historic kitty club are always fully satisfied with the traditional New Orleans jazz performances. White-haired grandpas on tubas, trombones and cornets raise the roof here every night – they are clearly jazzed by what they're doing. It's worth the discomfort of sitting on the floor for an entire set. 'When the Saints Go Marching In' is always a memorable moment. Barbara Reid and Grayson 'Ken' Mills formed the Society for the Preservation of New Orleans Jazz in 1961, at a time when Louis Armstrong's generation was already getting on in years. Get in line early to snag a good seat. When it's warm enough to leave the window shutters open, those not fortunate enough to get in can join the crowd on the sidewalk to listen to the sets. No booze or snacks are served in the club.

ONE EYED JACKS Map pp310-11

☎ 569-8361; www.oneeyedjacks.net; 615 Toulouse St; cover $5-15; 🕐 2pm-6am

This club hips up the heart of the Quarter. The swanky front barroom is no slouch, with the plush wallpaper and lurid paintings of a Storyville parlor. Acoustic bands – gypsy jazz and the like – play early shows. The main theater is a stunner, recapturing early-20th-century style with chandeliers, an oval-shaped bar and little tables with little tabletop lamps. The setting is particularly suitable for the retro burlesque shows that take place here. The booking isn't strictly retro, however, as punk legends and post-punk up-and-comers pass through.

FAUBOURG MARIGNY & BYWATER

The city's finest jazz club and a number of little taverns with great local acts are found on Frenchmen St in the Faubourg Marigny. In the Bywater, Kermit Ruffins' Thursday night gig at Vaughan's is legendary.

RAY'S ROOM NEW ORLEANS Map p316

508 Frenchmen St

Trumpeter Kermit Ruffins and a partner opened this nightclub/restaurant/art gallery in the Faubourg Marigny during Jazz Fest 2006. Knowing Kerm, this ought to be a fun addition to the Frenchmen St scene.

Jazz at Preservation Hall

NEW CLUB TO LOOK FOR

Big Chief Bo Dollis of the Wild Magnolias opened his own bar, **Handa Wanda's** (Map pp312–13; 2425 Dryades St), in 2006, just a few blocks from the Garden District. Very likely the club will serve as a neighborhood hang-out for the African American community. But during Jazz Fest and around Carnival time you can expect some events here to have a broader appeal. From November to February Mardi Gras Indian gangs will practice here during the buildup to Carnival season. During Jazz Fest 2006 the club featured live music and Indian performances most nights.

SNUG HARBOR Map p316

☎ 949-0696; 626 Frenchmen St; cover $5-25; 🕓 5pm-3am

New Orleans' premier contemporary jazz venue regularly books headliner talent. There really isn't a bad seat in the place, upstairs or down, and the room's acoustics are unparalleled in town. Local performers who regularly appear here include pianist Ellis Marsalis (Winton and Branford's dad) and R&B singer Charmaine Neville (of *that* Neville family), and touring jazz acts usually play here when in New Orleans. The main floor serves as a restaurant with a menu featuring burgers and steaks.

SPOTTED CAT Map p316

☎ 943-3887; 623 Frenchmen St; 🕓 4pm-late

It's always worth checking in at this friendly space while on Frenchmen St. The Spotted Cat is about as intimate as it gets, with a 1ft-high stage crammed into a room full of tables and an upbeat crowd congregating in the bar and out on the sidewalk. Shows often start early here (6pm or 8pm), making this a good place to start the evening and a convenient link between dinner and visiting the clubs on Frenchmen St. The New Orleans Jazz Vipers hold down the fort on Friday night (7pm) and The Washboard Chaz Blues Band grind it out on Saturday (7pm).

VAUGHAN'S Map p316

☎ 947-5562; 800 Lesseps St; cover $7-10; 🕓 11am-3am daily, shows 11pm Thu

On Thursday night Vaughan's is as good as New Orleans gets. That's the night trumpeter Kermit Ruffins raises the roof here. The weekly gig regularly features Ruffins' band, the Barbecue Swingers, and drummer Shannon Powell, who is an amazing performer. Anyone might show up to sit in – Wynton Marsalis has dropped by, and when pianist Henry Butler shows up the bar's poor little upright piano darn near explodes. The crowds spill out onto the street and between sets Kerm often dishes out barbecue from the smoker on the back of his pickup truck. The rest of the week Vaughan's quietly serves the neighborhood well.

CBD & WAREHOUSE DISTRICT

A couple of New Orleans' edgiest rock clubs, completely free of any historic or overt touristy appeal, are to be found in the Warehouse District.

HOWLIN' WOLF Map pp308-9

☎ 522-9653; www.howlin-wolf.com; 907 S Peters St; cover $5-15; 🕓 3am-late Mon-Fri

One of New Orleans' best venues for live blues, alt-rock, jazz and roots music, the Howlin' Wolf always draws a lively crowd. It started out booking local progressive bands, but has become a regular stop for name touring acts like the Smithereens and Hank Williams III. Cracker played here a few years back. Look for more of the same as the club regains its footing after a post-Katrina lull.

LE CHAT NOIR Map pp308-9

☎ 581-5812; 715 St Charles Ave; cover free-$20; 🕓 4pm-2am Tue-Sat, shows 8pm

At this smartly accoutered bar and cabaret the beverage of choice is the martini and the entertainment ranges from Edith Piaf reincarnations to comic stage productions. CBD office workers prevail during 'happy hour' (4pm to 8pm), and a well-heeled mature audience turns out for the evening shows.

REPUBLIC NEW ORLEANS Map pp308-9

☎ 528-8282; 828 S Peters St; cover $5-15; 🕓 3am-late Mon-Fri

In a space formerly occupied by Howlin' Wolf, Republic New Orleans offers much of the same fare but with a greater emphasis on regular gigs by New Orleans artists. Funk and blues bands, including Walter 'Wolfman' Washington, frequently take the stage.

UPTOWN & RIVERBEND

New Orleans' best-loved music club, Tipitina's, is in this part of town, and there is a well-known concentration of live music venues in the Riverbend, anchored by the Maple Leaf Bar. Other worthy bars and clubs are to be found along the Uptown corridors. Cabs and cars are really the only way to get around at night.

CARROLLTON STATION Map pp314-15

☎ 865-9190; www.carrolltonstation.com; 8140 Willow St; cover $5-10; ⏰ noon-late

An old stalwart on the Riverbend club scene, Carrollton Station has the tumble-down exterior you'd expect from a Mississippi Delta juke joint. The club's musical offerings don't really deliver on that promise. You'll generally encounter a very young, white crowd shakin' it to bluesy bar bands. Just a good co-ed party atmosphere.

DOS JEFES UPTOWN CIGAR BAR Map pp314-15

☎ 891-8500; 5535 Tchoupitoulas St; cover free-$10; ⏰ 6pm-late

Long touted as one of New Orleans' better venues for modern jazz, Dos Jefes is also a great spot for a smoke. Patrons can select from a list of 40 fine cigars, light up, and puff plumes of sweet-smelling smoke into the room. The club has broadened its appeal of late with the addition of blues and roots performers. Coco Robicheaux makes frequent appearances.

LE BON TEMPS ROULÉ Map pp314-15

☎ 895-8117; 4801 Magazine St; ⏰ 11am-3am

A neighborhood bar – a very good one at that – with a mostly college and post-college crowd drawn in by two pool tables and a commendable beer selection. Late at night, high-caliber blues, zydeco or jazz rocks the joint's little back room. The Hammond organist Joe Krown rattles the rafters with his Leslie speakers on Friday night.

MAPLE LEAF BAR Map pp314-15

☎ 866-9359; 8316 Oak St; cover $5-10, Mon free; ⏰ 3pm-4am

The premier nighttime destination in the Riverbend area. The legendary Maple Leaf has a solid musical calendar and its dimly lit, pressed-tin caverns are the kind of environs you'd expect from a New Orleans juke joint. Scenes from the film *Angel Heart*, in which the late, great blues man Brownie McGhee starred, were shot here. You can regularly catch performances by local stars such as bluesman Walter 'Wolfman' Washington, zydeco squeezebox impresario Rockin' Dopsie Jr, and the funky Rebirth Brass Band. Slide guitarist John Mooney also plays here often, and on Monday night (when there's no cover charge) a traditional piano player sets the tone. You can choose to work up a sweat on the small dance floor directly in front of the stage or relax at the bar in the next room. There's also a nice back patio in which to cool your heels. The crowd is a healthy mix of college students, tourists and music lovers of all stripes.

TIPITINA'S Map pp314-15

☎ 895-8477, concert line 897-3943; www.tipitinas.com; 501 Napoleon Ave; cover $8-20; ⏰ 5pm-late

'Tips,' as locals refer to it, is a musical mecca. The legendary nightclub, which takes its name from Professor Longhair's 1953 hit single, is the site of some of the city's most memorable shows, particularly

ROCK & BOWL

There aren't many reasons to head out to Mid-City. But amid the post-Katrina wreckage is one of New Orleans' most popular live music venues, **Mid-City Lanes Rock & Bowl** (Map p317; ☎ 482-3133; 4133 S Carrollton Ave; admission $5-10; ⏰ noon-2am, shows usually 10pm)

What we have here is the unlikely marriage of live music and a bustling bowling alley. The clincher is that owner John Blancher consistently books quality artists from around southern Louisiana. Two-stepping to the sounds of a hot zydeco ensemble accompanied by the crash of bowling pins is an unreal experience. (Other musical styles include rockabilly, R&B and blues.) Add to this perky teenage bar staff and unusual side acts·(lip-synching black Elvis impersonators, anyone?), and you begin to get the idea that Blancher (who *looks* fairly normal) is a genius of the absurd. He claims he was on the road to visit a religious shrine when he had an epiphany to buy the bowling alley. Hurricane Katrina flooded the building but the club, luckily, is upstairs. With the surrounding neighborhood a ghost town, Rock & Bowl feels even more surreal than ever.

LIVE MUSIC FOR THE WHOLE FAMILY

If you're traveling with kids, you don't need to delete live music from your itinerary. Nor do you need to settle for second-rate offerings at tourists trap restaurants. New Orleans has many live music options outside the usual bar and nightclub realm, and many of these gigs take place at a reasonable hour.

Mid-City Lanes Rock & Bowl (p209) is a bowling alley with a great live music calendar. It's the ideal place to introduce the kids to zydeco or R&B music. If they don't dig it, just send 'em down to the lanes while mom and pop boogie the night away.

The Louisiana Music Factory (p226) is a record and CD shop that has live music on its stage every Saturday afternoon. The artists tend to specialize in the regional gumbo of jazz, R&B and blues, and are always good. The crowd, assembling among the CD bins, is high spirited – free music and free beer tend to have that effect on people.

The **Big Top Gallery and Three Ring Circus** (p141) is an art gallery that makes a special effort to appeal to kids. Not only does the gallery offer arts and crafts workshops for kids, it also frequently has live music shows early Saturday night (starting around 7pm) and on Sunday afternoon (starting at 2pm).

The **New Orleans Jazz National Park** (p142) puts on free afternoon shows nearly every day. These tend to have an educational nature, but often feature local musical stars.

A number of restaurants in town feature live music during the dinner hour. A good one for families to check out is **Angeli on Decatur** (p179), a pizza and pasta restaurant that has entertaining jazz ensembles many nights.

Local singer-songwriter **Johnette Downing** (www.johnettedowning.com) performs music for children. Her songs draw on local traditions in Cajun music, blues, boogie-woogie and Caribbean sounds, and children in her audience often sing along. Check the calendar on her website to see if she's doing any shows while you're in town.

when big names like Dr John come home to roost. Outstanding music from the local talent pool still packs 'em in yearround, and, after Hurricane Katrina, Mardi Gras Indians practiced here on Sunday nights. (Not sure if that will become a tradition; if so, look for it in December and January – it will surely blow your socks off.) The joint really jumps in the weeks prior to Mardi Gras and during Jazz Fest, when Dr John and a bevy of Fess-inspired piano players take over.

ART GALLERIES & OPENINGS

Hurricane Katrina did little to impede the growth of New Orleans' art scene, which has been on the upswing for several years now. The galleries are worth visiting for the varied art they present, which ranges from outsider folk art to the works of well-known 19th-century masters. Galleries of local celebrity painters are concentrated in the French Quarter. The historic Warehouse District, now commonly called the arts district, has some of the city's most highly respected galleries on Julia St. There's a funky mix of exciting works in galleries all along Magazine St from the Lower Garden District up to Audubon Park.

FRENCH QUARTER

Galleries are all over the Quarter, particularly on Royal and Chartres Sts.

A GALLERY FOR FINE PHOTOGRAPHY Map pp310-11

☎ 568-1313; www.agallery.com; 241 Chartres St; 🕐 10am-6pm Thu-Sat, noon-4pm Sun & Mon

This impressive gallery usually has prints such as William Henry Jackson's early-20th-century views of New Orleans and EJ Bellocq's rare images of Storyville prostitutes, made from the photographers' original glass plates. The gallery also regularly features Herman Leonard's shots of Duke Ellington and other jazz legends, as well as the occasional Cartier-Bresson enlargement (available at second mortgage prices).

ANIMAZING GALLERY Map pp310-11

☎ 525-0744; www.animazing.com; 906 Royal St; 🕐 noon-5pm Thu-Sun

You won't find local art here. This national dealer specializes in very cool works by legendary illustrators and animators. Chuck Jones' cells from classic Looney Toon cartoons, rare and personal art pieces by Dr Seuss and the finished doodlings of *Simpsons* creator Matt Groening are but a few examples of what you're likely to encounter here.

HAROUNI GALLERY Map pp310-11

☎ 299-8900; www.harouni.com; 829 Royal St; ⏲ noon-5pm Thu-Sat

Artist David Harouni is a native of Iran who has lived and worked in New Orleans for several decades. He creates works of absorbing depth by painting and scraping multiple layers.

KURT E SCHON LTD GALLERY

Map pp310-11

☎ 524-5462; www.kurteschonltd.com; 510 St Louis St; ⏲ 9am-5pm Mon-Fri, 9am-3pm Sat

For moneyed art collectors, and the rest of us who just like to look at great artwork, Kurt E Schon is an immense gallery and storehouse that purveys fine paintings from the 19th century. The gallery is like a small museum showcasing the works of the lesser-known contemporaries of the master impressionists, and most of the works on display here are pieces of remarkable beauty.

MICHALOPOULOS GALLERY

Map pp310-11

☎ 558-0505; www.michalopoulos.com; 617 Bienville St

Michalopoulos has become one of New Orleans' most popular painters in recent years, in part on the strength of his best-selling Jazz Fest posters. His shop showcases his colorful and expressive architectural studies. The gallery holds frequent openings on Friday night. Check out the website for specific events.

RODRIGUE STUDIO Map pp310-11

☎ 581-4244; www.georgerodrigue.com; 721 Royal St; ⏲ noon-5pm Wed-Sun

Cajun artist George Rodrigue's gallery is the place to go to see examples of his unbelievably popular 'Blue Dog' paintings. He just keeps painting and painting that darn dog. Look for topical works, in which the dog quietly comments on the post-Katrina issues.

CBD & WAREHOUSE DISTRICT

With the most impressive concentration of serious galleries in New Orleans, Julia St is the core of New Orleans' Arts District. Nearby, the excellent Ogden Museum of Southern Art (p155) and the Contemporary Arts Center (p153) are easily worked into an afternoon of gallery hopping.

JEAN BRAGG GALLERY OF SOUTHERN ART Map pp308-9

☎ 895-7375; www.jeanbraggantiques.com; 600 Julia St; ⏲ 10am-5pm Mon-Sat

This is a good source for the Arts and Crafts–style Newcomb Pottery, which originated at New Orleans' own Newcomb College. Bragg also deals in classic landscapes by Louisiana painters and every month she features the work of a contemporary artist.

ARTHUR ROGER GALLERY Map pp308-9

☎ 522-1999; www.arthurrogergallery.com; 432 Julia St; ⏲ 10am-5pm Mon-Sat

One of the district's most prominent galleries, Arthur Roger represents several dozen artists from around the South, including Simon Gunning, whose landscapes are haunting records of Louisiana's disappearing wetlands.

BERGERON STUDIO & GALLERY

Map pp308-9

☎ 522-7503; www.bergeronstudio.com; 406 Magazine St; ⏲ 10am-5pm Mon-Sat

This gallery has a superb collection of historic photographs by key artists who worked in New Orleans over the past century, from Pops Whitesell to Michael P Smith.

GEORGE SCHMIDT GALLERY Map pp308-9

☎ 592-0206; www.georgeschmidt.com; 626 Julia St; ⏲ 10am-5pm Mon-Sat

New Orleans artist George Schmidt describes himself as a 'historical' painter.

MUSEUM GIGS

The Ogden Museum of Southern Art (p155) hosts **Ogden After Hours**, a Thursday night happy hour with live music amid some fine Southern art. The entertainment is always top notch and starts at 6pm. Check out the O's calendar online if you want to know what's planned while you're in town. The Contemporary Arts Center (CAC; p153) hosts the more formal **Made In New Orleans**, a music series on Saturday night. Again, some stellar acts, often from out of town, perform in the CAC's theater.

Indeed, his canvasses evoke the city's past, awash in a warm romantic light. His Mardi Gras paintings are worth a look.

HERIARD-CIMINO GALLERY Map pp308-9
☎ 525-7300; www.heriardcimino.com; 440 Julia St; 10:30am-5:30pm Tue-Fri, 10am-5pm Sat
Established contemporary artists from across the US are represented in this elegant space. The emphasis is on abstract and figurative paintings, but you might also encounter photography and sculpture here.

LEMIEUX GALLERIES Map pp308-9
☎ 522-5988; www.lemieuxgalleries.com; 332 Julia St; 10am-6pm Mon-Sat
Gulf Coast art is the emphasis in this nationally recognized gallery, and it's a good place to get a handle on the breadth of the regional arts scene. Paintings here include Kate Samworth's sardonic grotesqueries and Jesse Poimbeuf's depictions of birds.

NEW ORLEANS GLASSWORK & PRINTMAKING STUDIOS Map pp308-9
☎ 529-7277; www.neworleansglassworks.com; 727 Magazine St; 11am-5pm Mon-Sat
In an immense 25,000ft brick building, New Orleans Glasswork & Printmaking Studios is a combination studio and gallery space primarily for glassblowers and stained-glass artisans. Not only can you admire and purchase works here; you might also watch artists blow glass, which is an impressive sight to behold. Saturday afternoon is a good time to come and catch artists in action.

SOREN CHRISTENSEN GALLERY
Map pp308-9
☎ 569-9501; www.sorengallery.com; 400 Julia St; 10am-5:30pm Tue-Fri, 11am-5pm Sat
This impressive space showcases the work of nationally renowned painters and sculptors. The gallery is known for its nontraditional sensibility.

LEARN SOMETHING NEW

Hey, a visit to New Orleans can't be all booze all the time, can it? Or, maybe it can, but that's really not good for you. A fun way to add lasting value to time spent in the Crescent City is to take a class. You've come to enjoy the food and the arts in this creative city, so why not participate in these pursuits? You'll head home with new skills along with tales to tell of your exploits in the Big Easy.

Cookin' Cajun (Map pp308–9; ☎ 586-8832; www.cookincajun.com; Riverwalk Mall; classes adult/child $20/10) Offers entertaining cooking courses for the entire family. Hands-on courses are also available. Call for the daily schedule.

Dark Room (Map pp312–13; ☎ 522-3211; www.neworleansdarkroom.com; 1927 Sophie Wright Pl; courses around $500) This is one of the city's premier printing labs, and it offers workshops (usually three full days in length) in shooting and printing, some taught by well-known photographers. One of the more interesting courses offered here explores the Storyville milieu and antiquated techniques of EJ Bellocq. See the website for a schedule of events.

New Orleans Glasswork & Printmaking Studios (Map pp308–9; ☎ 529-7277; www.neworleansglassworks.com; 727 Magazine St; 10am-4pm Sat & Sun Oct-May) Shaping and coloring hot glass is a rare skill. This studio offers unique two-day courses in glassblowing for absolute beginners.

New Orleans Jazz National Historic Park (Map pp310–11; ☎ 877-520-0677; 916 N Peters St; admission free; 9am-5pm) Free music courses are offered nearly every day in the afternoon, usually delving into New Orleans' rich music history and traditions. Local musicians are on hand to illustrate the point.

New Orleans School of Cooking (Map pp310–11; ☎ 525-2665, 800-237-4841; www.neworleansschoolofcooking.com; classes $27; 10am-12:30pm Wed-Sun) Offers a fun 2½-hour lunch class delving into regional classics like gumbo, jambalaya and bread pudding. Students are treated to a full meal and an Abita beer. Hands-on courses are also available.

Savvy Gourmet (Map pp314–15; ☎ 895-2665; www.savvygourmet.com; 4519 Magazine St; classes from $50) This modern facility offers nightly courses in a variety of cuisines, but with a contemporary sensibility. The courses are slanted toward the interests of aspiring gourmets, but often cover the basics of southern Louisiana cuisine. On some nights the emphasis is on wine, or food and wine pairings. Some courses are demonstrations, others are more hands on. See the website for a schedule.

LOWER GARDEN DISTRICT & GARDEN DISTRICT

Magazine St gets into high gear in this part of town with some excellent art galleries. While you're here, you also ought to have a look in some of the shops, many of which specialize in creative clothing and jewelry (see p231 for more).

ANTON HAARDT GALLERY Map pp312-13
☎ 891-9080; www.antonart.com; 2858 Magazine St; noon-5pm Fri & Sat
Among the finest galleries anywhere to specialize in contemporary folk art from the Deep South. The gallery has featured the works of well-known artists such as Howard Finster and Clementine Hunter, but you are more likely to come across Lamar Sorrento's cool portraits of blues musicians or Jimmy Lee Sudduth's striking earth-tone figures. Alabama artist Haardt quietly mixes her own accomplished work into the gallery.

BARRISTER'S GALLERY Map pp312-13
☎ 525-2767; www.barristersgallery.com; 1724 Oretha Castle Haley Blvd; 10am-5pm Tue-Sat
A little ways beyond the Lower Garden District, this gallery has some edge to it. It has represented the works of Julie Crozat, who gained some notice for her lurid and visually stunning 'Deadly Sins' series. The gallery also specializes in works by African American and Haitian artists.

PERRIN BENHAM GALLERY Map pp312-13
☎ 565-7699; 1914 Magazine St; 11am-5pm Mon-Sat
Typifying the neighborhood's exciting sensibilities, this small gallery features some locally renowned painters, but really makes its mark with stellar works by lesser-known artists. A case in point is the Brazilian painter Mauro Tambeiro, who the gallery has introduced to North America. Tambeiro's lush technique and warm, jazzy images are a soothing tonic against the desolation so much in vogue in contemporary New Orleans art.

SIMON OF NEW ORLEANS Map pp312-13
☎ 561-0088; 2126 Magazine St; 10am-5pm Mon-Sat
Local artist Simon (no last name) has made a name (though only a first name) for himself by painting groovy signs that are hung like artwork in restaurants all over New Orleans. You'll probably recognize the distinctive stars, dots and sparkles that fill the spaces between letters on colorfully painted signs such as 'Who Died & Made You Elvis?' The gallery is a ramshackle indoor/outdoor affair. Out back, a tabletop box contains hand-painted Zulu coconuts – collectors' items in these parts.

UPTOWN & RIVERBEND

Magazine St goes in spurts for miles. The blocks between Louisiana and Napoleon Aves are particularly strong on galleries.

BERTA'S & MINA'S ANTIQUITIES
Map pp312-13
☎ 895-6201; 4138 Magazine St
This cluttered gallery, with paintings seemingly tumbling out onto the sidewalk, specializes in regional folk art, especially the works of the late Nilo Lanzas. His daughter operates the shop. Lanzas began painting at age 63, and produced an impressive body of work up until his death just a few years ago. Museums and serious collectors have snatched up many of Lanzas' paintings already, but there are dozens of nice pieces, all very eye-catching and worthy of homes. Lanzas' work is, in fact, very easy to like. His daughter, Mina, also paints and her works show alongside her father's and a few other artists from the city and its surrounds.

COLE PRATT GALLERY Map pp312-13
☎ 891-6789; www.colepratgallery.com; 3800 Magazine St; 11am-4pm Wed-Sat, 1-5pm Sun
Contemporary Southern artists are showcased in this fine art gallery. Paintings here might include Lea Barton's earthy abstractions or Gustave Blanche's warmly rendered still lifes.

CLASSICAL MUSIC, OPERA & DANCE

New Orleans makes a deeper musical impression in its nightclubs than in its concert halls. But the city does have a philharmonic orchestra, an opera and a ballet. You might want to have a look at upcoming events to see if anything strikes your fancy.

The **New Orleans Opera** (☎ 529-2278; www.neworleansopera.org; tickets $30-120) rarely causes much of a stir, but remains an important part of the local culture. Productions are held at the Mahalia Jackson Theater (Map pp310–11) in Louis Armstrong Park.

The **Louisiana Philharmonic Orchestra** (☎ 523-6530; www.lpomusic.com; box office 6th fl, 305 Baronne St; tickets $11-36) temporarily lost its home, the **Orpheum Theatre** (129 University Pl), which was badly damaged by Hurricane Katrina. But during the spring 2006 season the Philharmonic made appearances at other venues around town, such as Loyola University's Roussell Hall, Tulane University's Dixon Hall and at City Park.

The **New Orleans Ballet Association** (NOBA; ☎ 522-0996; wwwnobadance.com; tickets $30-75) usually runs a few productions annually. The season is very short, and is fleshed out with presentations by visiting dance companies from around the world. Performances are at the Mahalia Jackson Theater in Louis Armstrong Park.

THEATER

New Orleans has a strong theatrical bent, but the local scene took a momentary dive after Hurricane Katrina. Things appear to be rebounding and should be back to normal by the time you read this. The city has numerous local theater companies and a few large theatrical venues for touring productions. Student plays are frequently performed at the **UNO Downtown Theatre** (Map pp308–9; ☎ 539-9580; 619 Carondelet St) and Tulane University's **Lupin Theatre** (Map pp314–15; ☎ 865-5105).

CONTEMPORARY ARTS CENTER

Map pp308-9

☎ 523-1216; www.cacno.org; 900 Camp St

In the Warehouse District, stages some of New Orleans' most cutting-edge and interesting performances.

LE CHAT NOIR Map pp308-9

☎ 581-5812; www.cabaretlechatnoir.com; 715 St Charles Ave; admission $12-20

At this classy cabaret-theater the entertainment ranges from full-blown musicals to Edith Piaf reincarnations. It's a small joint so it's very intimate, and the crowd here is pretty enthusiastic.

LE PETIT THÉÂTRE DU VIEUX CARRÉ

Map pp310-11

☎ 522-2081; www.lepetittheatre.com; 616 St Peter St; admission $21-26

Going strong since 1916, Le Petit Théâtre is one of the oldest theater groups in the US. In its Jackson Sq home the troupe offers an interesting repertory, with a proclivity for Southern dramas as well as special children's programming. Shows are sometimes followed by an informal cabaret performance, with the cast and audience mingling over drinks.

SAENGER THEATRE Map pp310-11

☎ 524-2490; 143 N Rampart St

New Orleans' premier site for major touring troupes. It's worth the price of a ticket just to see the ornate interior of this fine 1927 theater.

SOUTHERN REPERTORY THEATER

Map pp310-11

☎ 861-8163; www.southernrep.com; 3rd fl, 161 Canal Place; admission $15-30

Though its home in a shopping mall isn't particularly reassuring, this company has established itself as one of the city's best. Founded in 1986, the company performs original works by Southern playwrights. There's not a bad seat in the 150-seat theater.

OKRA TRUE BREW PLAYHOUSE

Map pp308-9

☎ 800-595-4849; 200 Julia St

In the Warehouse District, this is an added feature of the popular coffee shop. The group performs seasonal classics such as Dickens' *Christmas Carol* along with original works, which typically explore local themes with a sharp satirical sensibility.

CINEMAS

New Orleans has a few quality cinemas scattered about, but the city could really use a decent art house or two. Making up for this deficiency are sporadic screenings in some bars and clubs, which can be a fun way to take in a flick. But on the whole, New Orleans doesn't get independent movies until months after they've screened in major coastal cities, and many films never make it here at all.

CANAL PLACE CINEMAS Map pp310-11
☎ **581-5400; 3rd fl, 333 Canal St; adult/child $7/5**
New Orleans' best all-around multiplex in a convenient downtown location. The cinema features first-run art and mainstream movies.

ENTERGY IMAX THEATER Map pp308-9
☎ **581-4629; Canal St; adult/child $8/6**
Part of the Audubon Institute complex at the foot of Canal St. IMAX stands for 'image maximum,' and its films are shown on a 74ft by 54ft screen. It's all about the size of the image, and indeed cinematography at this scale can be very impressive. Films such as *The Living Sea* and *Antarctica* are guaranteed to capture your attention. Shows begin on the hour between 10am and 8pm.

PRYTANIA THEATRE Map pp314-15
☎ **891-2787; 5339 Prytania St; adult/student $7/6**
This old movie house has been around since the 1920s and screens independent and art films. The owner has talked about opening another venue closer to downtown that would screen alternative films.

SPORTS & ACTIVITIES

SPECTATOR SPORTS

New Orleans is a major league sports city, but just barely. The city has its beloved and beleaguered NFL team – the Saints – and an NBA basketball team, but with the population in flux after Hurricane Katrina, the future of these teams is uncertain. The city's numerous colleges also have sports teams, and the racetrack is a vaunted tradition in New Orleans.

Tickets for most professional sports events are handled by Ticketmaster.

Football

The National Football League's **New Orleans Saints** (www.neworleanssaints.com; tickets $42-80) play eight home games (plus a preseason exhibition game) from August through December at the gigantic Louisiana Superdome (p151).

The **Louisiana State University Tigers** (www.lsusports.net) play home games at their 92,000-seat Tiger Stadium in Baton Rouge. The Tulane Green Wave plays NCAA Division I football at the Superdome. The best and most exciting Tulane game is a battle with long-standing rival Louisiana State University (LSU) from Baton Rouge.

The hottest college football ticket is the **Sugar Bowl** (p14), which is played on January 1 in the Superdome. New Orleans has also hosted nine Super Bowls, more than any other city, but doesn't figure in the NFL championship game's plans for the foreseeable future. Meanwhile Miami, with eight Super Bowls under its belt, is scheduled to host in 2007 and 2010, which will put it ahead of the Crescent City.

Basketball

The National Basketball Association's **New Orleans Hornets** (www.nba.com/hornets; tickets $25-100) is a fairly recent transplant, having moved to the Big Easy from Charlotte, NC, in 2002. The team hadn't really made itself at home in New Orleans when Hurricane Katrina forced it to play all but

WHEN THE SAINTS GO MARCHING

Football isn't exactly a turn-the-other-cheek game, which may explain why the Saints haven't been particularly successful since the team joined the NFL in 1967. In the team's first two decades it never enjoyed a winning season, and fans made a regular habit of watching the games with paper bags over their heads – such was their shame at being loyal to these lovable losers. The Saints had a good run in the late 1980s, making the play-offs four times. Of late, however, it has been business as usual. Several years ago, a voodoo priestess attempted to lift the hex that seems to be dragging the team down, but her antidote lasted for just one game.

As if things haven't been bad enough, Hurricane Katrina blew part of the roof off the Superdome, forcing the Saints to hit the road for the entire 2005 season. With talk of the city's population plummeting to half its pre-Katrina numbers, it was questionable whether New Orleans could support a professional football team. (The NBA Hornets faced similar questions.) The team vowed to return for the 2006 season, but beyond that it remained to be seen whether ticket sales and TV revenue would justify the team's staying. But surely deserting the battered city would amount to apostasy. Saints don't do that sort of thing, do they?

a few of its 2005-06 home games in Oklahoma City. The team's coach expressed a desire to stay in OKC, and the team's play showed much improvement there. However, the Hornets pledged to return to New Orleans the following season, although how long it will remain in New Orleans Arena remains to be seen. What is certain is that the NBA All-Star game will be held in New Orleans in 2008. Check the NBA website (www.nba.com) for details.

The **LSU Tigers** (www.lsusports.net) are the biggest college team around these parts. NBA star Shaquille O'Neal is an alumnus. They play at Maravich Assembly Center in Baton Rouge. LSU also has a women's team. Both Tulane and UNO have men's and women's teams as well.

Baseball

With 72 home games from April to September, you can catch the minor league **New Orleans Zephyrs** (☎ 734-5155; www.zephyrsbaseball.com; 6000 Airline Hwy; tickets $5-9.50) playing at intimate Zephyr Field at the junction with Hickory Ave. Games between the Zephyrs (a Milwaukee Brewers affiliate) and other Triple-A clubs in the Southern League begin at 7:05pm, except on Sunday, when games begin at 6:05pm.

Tulane and UNO baseball games are worth spending a lazy afternoon watching. Tulane plays on campus, while UNO games take place in the larger **Privateer Park** (Map pp306–7). In late February, baseball teams from Louisiana face off against Mississippi teams in the Winn-Dixie Showdown, a three-day series of triple-headers in the Superdome.

Horse Racing

Fair Grounds Race Track (Map pp306–7; ☎ 944-5515; 1751 Gentilly Blvd), which opened in 1872, is the third-oldest track in the nation. The racing season runs from November to March on Wednesday through Sunday, with a 1:30pm post time.

ACTIVITIES

New Orleans doesn't necessarily conjure up images of getting fit, but for those who like to counter their nightly sins with a little bit of physical contrition the city does offer a few options. Louisiana is, after all, the 'sportsman's paradise.' Some of the following activities can even be done while drinking beer.

Bicycling

New Orleans is a great city to bicycle in – it's flat and compact. Just watch out for those mammoth potholes that can swallow skinny tires. And be careful riding into devastated areas, which includes some of the routes from the French Quarter to City Park. For casual bicycling, pedal through City Park (during daylight hours only as the park is closed at night), around the lakefront, in a loop around Audubon Park and in the riverside Levee Park. See p272 for bicycle-rental information and for details about touring either on your own or with a group.

Residents typically follow either Burgundy or Dauphine Sts to traverse the French Quarter between the CBD and Faubourg Marigny, where the bicycle is the travel mode of choice. Esplanade Ave is somewhat busy, but the cars can go around you as you pedal from the French Quarter to the Fair Grounds or City Park. At City Park you should avoid Weisner Blvd where it crosses I-610 and instead travel through the western side of the park to Lakeshore Dr. Roads and paths along the lake are typically bicycle friendly. Racers favor workouts in City Park on the Roosevelt Mall oval and along Lakeshore Dr.

Many visitors travel from the French Quarter through the Warehouse District on Magazine St. Prytania St is a good choice for crossing through the Lower Garden District. The rest of Uptown is readily traversed, from Jackson Ave to Audubon Park, on quiet residential streets such as Camp and Chestnut Sts. A complete circuit of town can be completed from Uptown by following either Napoleon Ave to Octavia St, or State St to the neutral ground bike path on Jefferson Davis Parkway leading to Bayou St John. Return to the French Quarter on Esplanade Ave. It's a good idea to have a bike light if you plan to return in the evening (especially during the shorter winter daylight hours).

From S Carrollton Ave the river levee offers a continuous off-road bicycle route upriver to near the airport.

You can also take the Canal St Ferry to Algiers, follow the levee downriver on Patterson Rd and detour around the US Navy Hospital before returning to Patterson Rd via Odean St. Continue to the Chalmette Ferry, but beware that returning on the St Bernard Hwy is not for beginners – you may want to return in the same direction.

Golf

New Orleans has many courses that can be played on without early reservations.

AUDUBON PARK GOLF COURSE

Map pp314-15

☎ 865-8260; dawn-dusk

Only a streetcar ride from downtown, this 18-hole golf course is open to the public. It's one of the city's more popular courses and tee times need to be reserved up to a week ahead.

BAYOU OAKS GOLF COURSE

Map p317

☎ 483-9396; Zachary Taylor Dr; dawn-dusk

City Park is home to this golf course, with tee fees ranging from $10 to $18. Across from the clubhouse you'll find the **driving range** (☎ 483-9394; 9am-10pm Mon-Fri, 8am-10pm Sat & Sun) where a large bucket of balls costs $6.

Horseback Riding

CASCADE STABLES Map pp314-15

☎ 891-2246; 535 Calhoun St

This stable offers a 45-minute horse ride ($20) and lessons ($25 per hour) in Audubon Park.

EQUEST FARM Map pp306-7

☎ 483-9398; 1001 Filmore Ave; ½hr lesson $35-45; 8am-6pm Tue-Fri, 8am-4pm Sat & Sun

In City Park, this little ranch offers lessons for individuals and small groups. Riders must be over six years old and be wearing hard-soled boots.

Tennis

AUDUBON PARK TENNIS COURTS

☎ 895-1042; 6320 Tchoupitoulas St; court hire per hr $6; 8am-7pm Mon-Fri, 8am-6pm Sat

Well-maintained courts are open to the public.

CITY PARK TENNIS CENTER

Map p317

☎ 483-9382; court hire per hr $6-8; 7am-10pm Mon-Thu, 7am-7pm Fri-Sun

In all there are 36 lighted courts available to the public here, including hard and soft courts, and locker rooms, racquet rental, a pro shop and lessons from USPTA pros.

Jogging

The best uninterrupted jogging paths are along either the levee above Audubon Park or the West Bank levee. Joggers have also worn pathways between the St Charles Ave streetcar tracks. When they are back up and operating, be sure to run facing the approaching streetcar so you will be aware of its approach and be able to step aside while it passes. Many joggers also circle the Superdome on the plaza level – each lap is slightly more than a quarter mile.

Beware that pedestrians do not have the right-of-way and will find their lives in danger should they attempt to challenge motorists. Local motorists consider it a courtesy to honk at pedestrians in the street before speeding by – only out-of-state drivers are inclined to slow down or stop.

See p281 for more information on pedestrian safety.

Equest Farm in City Park s

HEALTH & FITNESS

Traveling can be hard work, and although it's fun to eat and drink and stay out late in the French Quarter, such activities can leave you feeling ragged the next day. Sometimes you just have to sweat it out with exercise machines or have professionals with strong hands knead it out of your body.

BELLADONNA DAY SPA Map pp312-13

☎ 891-4393; www.belladonnadayspa.com; 2900 Magazine St; massage from $50, spa packages $175-210; ⏲ 9am-6pm Tue, Fri & Sat, 9am-8pm Wed & Thu

If you have no qualms about treating yourself well, spend a few hours here. You can be restored with a full-body massage and have the glow put back in your skin with a body buff. The spa offers a full range of mud baths, aromatherapy treatments and seaweed detox rituals. Wow. Cool.

AVENUE PLAZA RESORT & SPA

Map pp312-13

☎ 566-1212; 2111 St Charles Ave; day use $10, massage from $40; ⏲ 6am-9pm Mon-Fri, 8am-5pm Sat & Sun

If you want to rub elbows with real professionals, head for this place in the Avenue Plaza Resort. It has a full complement of training equipment, a sauna and a staff of massage and body therapists. Aromatherapy, body scrub, mud facial mask – name your poison and they'll give it to you.

DOWNTOWN FITNESS CENTERS

Map pp310-11

☎ 525-2956; Suite 380, Canal Place, 1 Canal St; day use $12; ⏲ 6am-9pm Mon-Fri, 9am-6pm Sat, 9am-3pm Sun

This place has weight machines, treadmills and aerobics classes, including Pilates. There's also a sauna and the center offers massage therapy.

Shopping

French Quarter 223
Faubourg Marigny & Bywater 230
CBD & Warehouse District 231
Lower Garden District 231
Garden District 232
Uptown 233

Shopping

Shop vendor in the Farmer's Market, French Quarter

New Orleans has some of the goofiest tourist curios to be found anywhere. Wares in some of the tacky shops on Bourbon St and Decatur St include tropical snow domes (which we personally recommend), shiny, polyurethane alligator heads (neat looking, but would you still want it a week after you got home?) and T-shirts that let the world know your judgment has been severely impaired ('Katrina Gave Me A Blow Job I'll Never Forget').

But if you're not enticed by the city's mighty impressive array of cheeseball offerings, well, you can still shop up a tropical storm in New Orleans. Naturally, this is a great city in which to hunt down music recordings (whether you like CDs, LPs, 45s or 78s), as well as rare posters and photographs of musicians past and present.

Lovers of art, antiques, antiquarian books and unique designer clothing will delight in bountiful shopping strips like Royal, Chartres, lower Decatur and Magazine Sts. If you're a voodoo practitioner, or just intrigued by the colorful paraphernalia, New Orleans is probably the best city to stock up on supplies. The availability of Mardi Gras costumes and masks often inspires out-of-town visitors to start planning their next Halloween party.

Shopping Areas

FRENCH QUARTER

The Quarter is lined with great strips that are well suited to window shopping and sticking your nose into people's businesses.

Many regard Royal St as the 'Main St' of the French Quarter. Portions of Royal St are closed to automobiles during daytime shopping hours. Between Iberville and St Ann Sts visitors will find a number of distinguished galleries and shops selling antiques and collectibles. These shops inhabit buildings that have been prominent commercial addresses since before the 1803 Louisiana Purchase.

In shopping terms, Chartres St is Royal St's equal. It's lined with interesting small shops dealing in antiques, art and expensive curiosities. More recently, clothing boutiques and other small shops have extended the Royal St shopping area into the lower Quarter to St Philip St. Lower Decatur, below Governor Nicholls St, is lined with interesting antique and junk shops, boutiques and some good bars where you can get loaded after shopping.

Upper Decatur St is where all the T-shirt shops and cheap tourist bric-a-brac is sold. About the only worthwhile things sold in these stores are plastic snow domes that bring together charming incongruities such as alligators and snow.

CANAL PLACE

A standard-issue shopping mall right at the edge of the French Quarter? That's right, but as it's just below the towering Wyndham New Orleans Hotel you'd hardly notice it if you weren't looking for it. Obviously this is where you'll want to go if your shoe suddenly implodes or if your only suit has to be shipped off to the cleaners after a gin-fizz mishap. The upscale mall (Map pp310–11) is anchored by a Saks Fifth Avenue store; supporting roles are played by Kenneth Cole, Ann Taylor, Laura Ashley, Brooks Brothers and Banana Republic. A multiplex cinema and a performing-arts theater are on the 3rd floor. The mall parking lot is convenient and has reasonable rates.

JACKSON BREWERY

It once really was a brewery, but despite having Bourbon St a few blocks away the company failed. Must have been some mighty fine brew. The old brick structure, on Decatur St just a block or so from Jackson Sq, was converted into a shopping mall long ago. It has dozens of shops and eateries, most of them singing siren songs to unwary tourists. Proceed with caution or your next credit card statement will include charges for such items as Cajun golf clothing (?!), novelty ties, old-timey photographic portraits of you and your cousin Archie, and other various merchandise that says 'cash dump' all over it. However, if you're looking for a crawfish T-shirt for your cool niece Henrietta or a new pair of sunglasses, or are just in need of a toilet, come on by. There's an ATM on the sidewalk.

WAREHOUSE DISTRICT

Art is the name of the game in this part of town. The main drag for galleries is Julia St, between Commerce and Baronne Sts. Drop by the Contemporary Art Center (p153) or any gallery to pick up a comprehensive guide to the area's art dealers.

RIVERWALK

An unappealing by-product of the 1984 New Orleans World's Fair, Riverwalk provides a sanitized, air-conditioned alternative to the Quarter's shops and restaurants. In fact, many Quarter shops have outlets in the mall or its food court. The mall lacks an anchor store but does have branches of Banana Republic, Sharper Image and other mall standards. Many stores have shorter operating hours than the mall. If you don't want to walk there, take the Riverfront streetcar.

NEW ORLEANS CENTRE

Adjoining the Superdome at La Salle St and Poydras St, this is another downtown air-conditioned shopping emporium (Map pp308–9). Macy's is the big department store and fashion chains such as Gap also here. New Orleans Centre also affords foreign tourists the opportunity to experience a typical American shopping mall food court.

FRENCH MARKET

Truth be told, from a shopping standpoint, the French Market is a bit of a disappointment. It no longer plays a vital role in French Quarter life, and locals do not rely on it as they once did for their foodstuffs. For the most part the French Market caters to tourism. Still, it's an atmospheric old market with a range of shops and vendors, and is a hive of activity most days, but especially on weekends.

The market is split into two sections – the Farmer's Market and Flea Market – and neither is particularly special. In a pinch, the French Market will supply the visitor with cheap gimcracks to give away back home, but for quality shopping you'll have to look elsewhere.

Shoppers can pick up some unique southern Louisiana products at the Flea Market any day of the week. There is a motley assortment of T-shirt and sunglasses vendors, as well as African art (obviously mass-produced), inexpensive silver jewelry, chintzy Mardi Gras masks and dolls, musical tapes and CDs of dubious origin, and enough preserved alligator heads to populate a polyurethane swamp. Most prices at the Flea Market are negotiable. Officially the Flea Market is open 24 hours, however, most vendors keep their own hours and are open from 9am to 5pm.

Only a vestige of former market activity remains at the Farmer's Market, where large freezer trucks have replaced the small trucks of farmers. Still, you might occasionally see a beat-up pickup truck on sagging springs heading from the market to sell a load of fresh produce on an Uptown street.

Merchants in the Farmer's Market offer fresh fruit and vegetables, including green beans, mangos, papayas, bananas, plantains, peaches, strawberries, watermelons, apples and pecans, as well as cold drinks. In addition, there are lots of kitchen supplies, spices (including a large selection of hot sauces), garlic and chili strings, and cookbooks for the tourist trade. The Farmer's Market opens up early every morning and gradually peters out in the afternoon.

GARDEN DISTRICT & UPTOWN

Rink (Map pp312–13), opposite Lafayette Cemetery No 1 at Prytania St and Washington Ave in the heart of the Garden District, houses a small group of upscale shops including a bookstore and coffee shop.

Riverside Market Shopping Center (Map pp314–15; cnr Jefferson Ave & Tchoupitoulas St) is a modern surprise that primarily serves the locals' grocery, video rental, liquor and drugstore needs. The 10 Tchoupitoulas bus goes there from downtown.

MAGAZINE STREET

For the true-blue shopper, New Orleans doesn't get any better than Magazine St. For some 6 miles the street courses through the Warehouse District and along the riverside edge of the Garden District and Uptown, lined nearly the entire way with small shops that sell antiques, art, contemporary fashions, vintage clothing and other odds and ends. The street hits its peak in the Lower Garden District (near Jackson Ave), the Garden District (between 1st and 7th Sts) and Uptown (from Antonine St to Napoleon Ave).

RIVERBEND

An interesting area is the fashionable shops and restaurants fronting a small square on Dublin St near S Carrollton Ave where it meets St Charles Ave. To get here, take the St Charles Ave streetcar (or bus 12) to the Riverbend near Camellia Grill.

Student-oriented shopping is centered on Maple St, which is also accessible by the St Charles Ave streetcar line. Here, bookstores, coffee shops and restaurants make for a happening district.

On the riverside of S Carrollton, Oak St is an older neighborhood commercial zone intersecting with the streetcar line. It's reasonably compact for strolling and offers a few interesting businesses, along with a few restaurants and the stellar Maple Leaf Bar (p209).

CLOTHING SIZES

Measurements approximate only; try before you buy

Women's Clothing						
Aus/UK	8	10	12	14	16	18
Europe	36	38	40	42	44	46
Japan	5	7	9	11	13	15
USA	6	8	10	12	14	16
Women's Shoes						
Aus/USA	5	6	7	8	9	10
Europe	35	36	37	38	39	40
France only	35	36	38	39	40	42
Japan	22	23	24	25	26	27
UK	3½	4½	5½	6½	7½	8½
Men's Clothing						
Aus	92	96	100	104	108	112
Europe	46	48	50	52	54	56
Japan	S		M	M		L
UK/USA	35	36	37	38	39	40
Men's Shirts (Collar Sizes)						
Aus/Japan	38	39	40	41	42	43
Europe	38	39	40	41	42	43
UK/USA	15	15½	16	16½	17	17½
Men's Shoes						
Aus/UK	7	8	9	10	11	12
Europe	41	42	43	44½	46	47
Japan	26	27	27½	28	29	30
USA	7½	8½	9½	10½	11½	12½

Opening Hours

Common shop hours are Tuesday through Saturday from 10am or 11am until 5pm or 6pm. Independently owned shops can keep odd hours. For instance, a shopkeeper might not feel any compunction about arriving an hour late to open. Some might even stay closed on the odd day or two each week. Many bookstores are open daily, and some keep later hours in the evening.

Taxes & Refunds

There is a 9% sales tax on goods sold in the city. International visitors can get refunds on sales taxes from Louisiana Tax Free Shopping (LTFS) stores; look for the sign in the window. Foreign visitors must show participating merchants a valid passport (Canadians may show a birth certificate or driver's license) to get a tax-refund voucher. To get your refund at the refund center in the New Orleans International Airport present the voucher(s), sales receipt(s), your passport and round-trip international ticket indicating less than 90 days' stay. Refunds under $500 are made in cash; otherwise, a check will be mailed to your home.

Check out www.louisianataxfree.com for a directory of businesses participating in the LTFS program.

FRENCH QUARTER

Regardless what you are after in New Orleans, you'll want to check out the shopping in the Quarter. You'll find fine art and antiques on Royal St, unheralded outsider art and rummage shops on lower Decatur, and record shops, galleries, bookstores, frilly dress shops and voodoo shops scattered about the neighborhood. Fascinating stuff is being sold just around every corner.

FIVE UNFORGETTABLE SOUVENIRS

- Local music from **Louisiana Music Factory** (p226)
- Outsider art from Magazine St and Decatur St galleries
- Carnival mask from **Maskarade** (p227)
- Plaster of Paris bust of Louis Armstrong from **Zombie's House of Voodoo** (p229)
- Beer belly, spare tire etc, from your favorite bars and restaurants

A&P MARKET Map pp310-11 Groceries

☎ 523-1353; 701 Royal St

Smack in the heart of the French Quarter, this is an economic alternative to the 'minibars' that commit hotel-room robbery in so many accommodations around town. A&P is convenient for cold beer, bottled water and snacks along with various sundry items. Best of all, it's open 23 hours a day (closing at 3am for just an hour of cleaning and restocking). A&P is also a fine place to go to stock up on Cajun spices and pepper sauces at lower prices than those of the Farmer's Market.

ARCADIAN BOOKS & ART PRINTS

Map pp310-11 Antiquarian & Used Books

☎ 523-4138; 714 Orleans Ave

In the French Quarter is a small, crowded little shop that's filled with Southern literature and history, as well as many volumes in French. Owner Russell Desmond speaks French fluently and is a wonderful, yet cynical, ambassador to New Orleans.

ARTISTS' MARKET Map pp310-11 Art

☎ 561-0046; 85 French Market Pl

With a back entry on antique-mad lower Decatur St, this sizable emporium is a conglomerate of consignment dealers and artists who sell their own work. A walk-through is like snorkeling through a dense reef of art. You'll find yourself surrounded by paintings, prints, handmade glass beads, original lamps, candle holders, cast-iron designs and one-of-a-kind Mardi Gras masks. A few of the artists work on site. In all, the works of some 70 artists are sold here.

BECKHAM'S BOOKSTORE

Map pp310-11 Antiquarian & Used Books

☎ 522-9875; 228 Decatur St

In the French Quarter, across the street from House of Blues, this large, neatly organized store has two floors of used books. The store also sells used classical LPs. It's definitely worth a browse.

BOURBON STRIP TEASE

Map pp310-11 Risqué Clothing

☎ 581-6633; 205 Bourbon St

If you've just asked to be excused while you 'slip into something more comfortable,' but haven't actually packed anything more comfortable, sneak on down to this shop. It has all manner of dainty things to put on before you take 'em off, starting with lacy lingerie and progressing to edible undies and sleazy toys.

CENTRAL GROCERY

Map pp310-11 Groceries

☎ 523-1620; 923 Decatur St

A hyper-busy store offering many of the cooking ingredients typically found in Louisiana kitchens: Zatarain's Creole Seasoning and Crab Boil (even Chef Emeril uses it), McIlhenny Tabasco or Crystal hot sauce, chicory coffee and filé for making gumbo. While you're here, grab a jar of Central Gro Co's famous olive relish, the not-so-secret weapon of the muffuletta sandwich.

CENTURIES

Map pp310-11 Antique Prints & Maps

☎ 568-9491; 408 Chartres St

OK, it's a little on the stodgy side, with its selection of 19th-century lithographs and old maps. But wait. Flip through the inventory (all of it well organized by theme, date or locale) and you just might find yourself slowing down to look things over. It's like perusing a historical coffee-table book, with no cheesy reproductions. Particularly interesting are the 'Civil War' and 'Black

History' sections. And if you're the type who likes to ride shotgun so you can while away a drive studying a detailed highway map, then you're sure to be absorbed by the ancient maps here, beautifully drawn with outdated demarcations and occasional glaring cartographic errors.

CIVIL WAR STORE Map pp310-11 Coins

☎ 522-3328; 212 Chartres St

If you're looking for old 'Dix' bills printed by the short-lived Confederacy, then duck into this tiny shop. It's about as big as a walk-in closet, and it will take but a few minutes to assess the wares. The shop also carries a minimal selection of ancient firearms, in case you've been challenged to a duel and don't object to the possibility of a weapons malfunction.

COLLECTIBLE ANTIQUES

Map pp310-11 Antiques

☎ 566-0399; 1232 Decatur St

Some people love this sort of place simply because the possibilities seem limitless. You never know what you'll find between the piles of old furniture stacked along the walls of this large, garagelike emporium of tantalizing junk. Perhaps you collect old photographic portraits from long defunct studios, the subjects looking dapper, frilly or severe in their Victorian finery. You might find everything you need for that tiki bar you're slapping together in the basement. Or maybe you're just after an art-deco martini shaker, an old dented trumpet, a Pewee Herman doll from the 1980s, a heavy Army surplus coat, some silverware that needs polishing or a lady's hat from the 1920s. Remarkably, the entire assemblage is not just a heaping mess. Every piece is lovingly contextualized to add interest, and browsing through the wares here is somewhat like a visit to a grab-bag museum.

COLLECTION Map pp310-11 Books & Art

☎ 598-7147; 533 Royal St

The little gift shop at the Historic New Orleans Collection (p139) has a quality selection of new and used books on the region's history, politics, art and architecture. There's also a small selection of art and art reproductions from the Historic Collection's impressive archive. This is also a good spot to pick up some classy postcards.

CRESCENT CITY BOOKS

Map pp310-11 Antiquarian & Used Books

☎ 524-4997; 204 Chartres St

You'll want to include this two-story concern in your tour of the city's book shops. Crescent City stocks a healthy blend of hard-to-find, out-of-print titles and newly published volumes. Prices are generally reasonable.

DAVID'S Map pp310-11 Antiques & Interesting Junk

☎ 568-1197; 1319 Decatur St

Squeezed in among the numerous antique stores and clothing boutiques along lower Decatur is this small rummage shop filled with found objects, collectibles, funky lamps, swanky duds, bar accoutrements, jewelry and other odds and ends. Worth checking out.

FAULKNER HOUSE BOOKSTORE

Map pp310-11 Specialty Books

☎ 524-2940; 624 Pirate's Alley

Both a business and a bona-fide literary attraction, Faulkner House is an essential stop for any lover of books. It's a pleasant space, with beautifully crafted shelves packed from floor to ceiling lending it the dignified atmosphere of a private library. It's not a large store – if there are more than five or six customers at a time, the place starts to feel crowded – but it offers a commendable mix of new titles and first editions. The selection of books by local and Southern authors is particularly strong, and naturally William Faulkner is a staple. The shop is something of a literary hub, and local authors (Richard Ford, Andrei Codrescu etc) regularly stop by to chat with owner Joe DiSalvo and maybe sign a few copies of their latest works. (Also see p140.)

FLEUR DE PARIS

Map pp310-11 Haute Couture

☎ 525-1899; www.fleurdeparis.net; 712 Royal St

Some of the stores in New Orleans exist simply to indulge the most eccentric and particular interests a person can possibly have. This boutique in the Labranche Building is a case in point. The woman who wants to appear ready for the 1904 St Louis World's Fair need look no further. The custom hats are bouquets of plumage, fur felt, lace and, here and there, a snatch of black netting. Once selected and paid for, the hats are packed into extravagant hat boxes with loving care. The evening gowns are devastating showstoppers guaranteed to make a dapper Dan in spats swoon. The store's website suggests wearing one to the Academy Awards, if you happen to have been nominated for something. Failing that, you'll want to promenade around a city park or at least have your picture taken in such finery.

FLORA SAVAGE Map pp310-11 Florist

☎ **581-4728; 1301 Royal St**

In town for an anniversary? Met someone you want to impress in a hurry? Take care of your floral needs here. You'll soon be festooning your hotel room with romantic aromas and colors, and your sweetheart will be swooning with romantic feelings for you.

GARGOYLE'S Map pp310-11 Goth Duds

☎ **529-4384; 1201 Decatur St**

At times in New Orleans it seems there must be a Gothic convention in town, so great is the concentration of guys and dolls in black from head to toenail. If you're looking a little too cheery for such company, you can always swing by this shop for some sinister boots and black garb. You'll be welcomed into the coven with open arms.

HOVÉ PARFUMEUR Map pp310-11 Perfume

☎ **525-7827; 824 Royal St**

Grassy vetiver, bittersweet orange blossoms, spicy ginger – New Orleans' exotic flora has graciously lent its scents to Hové's house-made perfumes for over 70 years. A brief sniffing visit will leave your head swirling with images of the Vieux Carré's magnificent past. Thus intoxicated, you can ask staff to custom mix a fragrance for you.

JAMES H COHEN & SONS

Map pp310-11 Antiques & Interesting Junk

☎ **522-3305; 437 Royal St**

From the sidewalk windows, you might be inclined to pass this one by if you're not interested in guns. To be sure, Cohen & Sons does sell antique guns for people who like to play cowboys and Indians with authentic hardware. The choice of firearms here includes some remarkable specimens of flintlocks, colts, Winchester '73s and even a French musket or two. Suitable for that manly room in the house where Grandpa likes to drink his sherry. But weapons are not all there is here. The place is a repository of relics and historical curiosities, with many fascinating artifacts on view in glass display cases. Duck in for a look at the ancient coins from Celtic and Hellenic cultures worn smooth by human hands millennia ago. Or disturbing slave documents and notarized bills of sale for the transfer of human chattel. The store's unique selection of campaign buttons for US presidential elections spans back to the 1900 contest in which incumbent William McKinley outlegged William Jennings Bryan. (Incidentally, McKinley was shot dead a year later by Leo Czolgosz with a .32 caliber Johnson revolver.)

THE GIFT OF FOOD

Customs won't always allow you to take sacks of groceries back home with you. But New Orleans does offer the gourmand many tempting and unique edibles that make nice gifts for the loved ones back home.

By the way, local parlance for grocery shopping is 'making groceries.' As you stroll the aisles of a store, be sure to tell everyone you meet that this is what you're doing. They might smile at you nervously and quickly turn down another aisle, but they'll know what you mean.

Pralines are a local confection that never really caught on anywhere else in the country. They make a nice treat for friends and co-workers. Freshness really counts, though, so buy a box on your last day in New Orleans and don't wait a week to unpack. Good places to buy pralines are **Leah's Pralines** (p226) and **Southern Candy Makers** (p228).

Crawfish are another delicacy under-appreciated everywhere outside of Louisiana. Though the tasty little crustaceans thrive throughout the US, they're hard to find. You can buy them at **Big Fisherman Seafood** (p232) and have them shipped back home. (Weird as it may sound, out-of-state crawfish fiends do this all the time.) If the **St Roch Seafood Market** (Map pp310–11) ever recovers from damage wrought by Hurricane Katrina you'll be able to buy crawfish there too. It's one of New Orleans' classic markets, a real treasure.

Louisiana hot sauces – Tabasco, Crystal etc – are available in grocery stores throughout America, but judging by the great number of souvenir shops selling these products there must be places in the world where you can't get this stuff. If you live in such a place, grab a few bottles at the **French Market** (p221) or **A&P Market** (p223) and your condiments shelf will have a new zing to it.

JOHNNY DONNELS

Map pp310-11 Art & Photography

☎ 525-6438; 634 St Peter St

This is the gallery of a fine local photographer, whose work turns up in galleries, museums and publications across the country. The collection is anchored by some touchingly beautiful shots of the French Quarter, as well as revealing portraits of musicians and people in New Orleans. Donnels has a fine eye and he's been shooting New Orleans for years.

KABOOM BOOKS

Map pp310-11 Antiquarian & Used Books

☎ 529-5780; 915 Barracks St

In the far reaches of the lower Quarter, Kaboom is a great bookstore to visit for its large and varied collection. Prices are often well below what you would expect, and the paperback shelves are packed with thousands of classics, mysteries and recent best-sellers. You'll find something to read here, for sure.

LEAH'S PRALINES

Map pp310-11 Pralines

☎ 523-5662; 714 St Louis St

In the heart of the Quarter, this old candy shop specializes in that special Creole confection, the praline. Here you'll get some of the very best in town. If you've already tried pralines elsewhere and decided you didn't care for 'em, we suggest you try some at Leah's before making up your mind. The creamy pralines are deadly. Try one with rum in it if you don't mind a nice extra zing. Grab a whole box and have it expressed to your friends back home. And throw in some of the pecan brittle or rum pecans while you're at it.

LE GARAGE

Map pp310-11 Antiques & Interesting Junk

☎ 522-6639; 1234 Decatur St

Got to admit, we liked the name better when it was simply 'The Garage.' But why quibble over a little ironic Frenchness? The place is still a garage loaded with interesting stuff to paw through. Things for sale here include odd items of clothing, hats, army surplus, curtains, yellowed pool balls, tattered Mardi Gras costumes from yesteryear, knitted Coors-can caps, furniture, and oodles of objets d'art to ogle or even buy. Treasures galore, we tell you. Dive in.

LIBRAIRIE BOOKS

Map pp310-11 Antiquarian & Used Books

☎ 525-4837; 823 Chartres St

A jam-packed little shop of delights for the avid bookworm and collectors. The emphasis here is squarely on very old (and sometimes dusty) volumes. You might dig up an ancient copy of Herbert Asbury's *The French Quarter*, or other tales of old New Orleans. And there are scholarly texts and ample material of more general interest as well.

LOUISIANA MUSIC FACTORY

Map pp310-11 Records & CDs

☎ 586-1094; 210 Decatur St

Here's your first stop if you're looking for music. The selection of new and used CDs delves deep into New Orleans and Louisiana musical culture, with recordings from the 19-noughts all the way up to this week. You're sure to walk out of this store with sacks of CDs from the region's bottomless talent pool. Get your jazz here, from King Oliver and Jellyroll to the Marsalises to Los Hombres Calientes. Get your R&B from Fess to K-Doe to the Meters to John Boutté. Get your Cajun and zydeco here, from the Hackberry Ramblers to Boozoo to Clifton Chenier to Buckwheat. Brass bands? Get 'em here. The listening stations are a great way to familiarize yourself with local artists. There's also a nice selection of cool T-shirts that you won't find elsewhere, along with books, DVDs and posters. Live performances on Saturday afternoons really rock the joint.

LUCULLUS Map pp310-11 Antiques

☎ 528-9620; 610 Chartres St

Take a peek in the window of this shop and you'll see a battery of ancient copper pots that appear to have generations of dents tinkered out of their bottoms. Owner Patrick Dunne is an advocate of using, not merely collecting, culinary antiques and that's what his shop specializes in. Follow his advice and add more ritual and elegance to your life with an antique café au lait bowl or an absinthe spoon for creating your evening cocktails. Don't just pop open your champagne and pour it; chill it in a silver bucket. You get the idea. A visit to this shop can turn an ordinary dinner party into the classiest, most exotic to-do.

MARY JANE'S EMPORIUM

Map pp310-11 Tobacco & Pipes

☎ 525-8004; 1229 Decatur St

Alack and alas, no Mary Jane is sold here. (New Orleans may be permissive, but it's still in the USA, where pot-smokin' is done on the QT.) Nevertheless, this is an essential stop for smokers of legal tobacco products, including finer brands of cigarettes not sold at your basic corner store. Also, a variety of apparatus for the smoking of unsanctioned herbal products and such is sold here. All right, it's basically a head shop.

MASKARADE Map pp310-11 Masks

☎ 568-1018; 630 St Ann St

Definitely the place to go if you've cottoned on to the local penchant for masking. This shop deals in high-quality masks by local and international artisans, and the selection includes everything from classic commedia dell'arte masks from Venice to more way-out designs for your wigged-out end-of–Mardi Gras state of mind. If your nose is too small, many of the selections here can correct the problem. Maskarade also sells beguiling hand-crafted gifts as well. How about a little demon paperweight for your office mate?

COSTUMES & MASKS

Mardi Gras and Halloween give New Orleanians two excuses to disguise themselves, but the preponderance of shops specializing in duds for such occasions suggests that the locals are playing dress up more often than that. Out-of-towners can get with the program right quickly in a fun-filled shopping excursion that ought to include some or all of the following shops.

Uptown Costume & Dancewear (p234) In a pinch, this place can address all your needs.

Gargoyle's Black duds for sinister occasions (p225).

Le Garage (opposite) Frumpy old MG costumes, hats, army surplus.

Maskarade (above) Great selection of high-quality Mardi Gras masks.

Mardi Gras Mask Market (p49) On Mardi Gras weekend vendors and artisans from around the country converge on the French Market for what basically amounts to the Olympics of handmade masquerade wear.

MOSS ANTIQUES Map pp310-11 Antiques

☎ 352-1744; 411 Royal St

Watch your head when you enter this gallery of low-hanging chandeliers. Oof! Too late! Moss is a Royal St institution in the local antiques trade. Only the finest quality antiques and objets d'art are sold here. You'll find the perfect thing for your Garden District mansion. Or perhaps you can take home the busted chandelier they made you pay for.

MS RAU ANTIQUES Map pp310-11 Antiques

☎ 523-5660; 630 Royal St

With a massive 30,000ft showroom (you'd never know it by passing by on Royal St), and after nearly a century of doing business, MS Rau ranks among New Orleans' most venerated dealers of antiques. It's a little over-serious – these are the sorts of frosty antiques that require their own insurance policies – but it's a family business and the professional salespeople are quite approachable. And for that very special trinket for that once-in-a-lifetime occasion this is a pretty good bet. You'll find fine art, jewelry, music boxes, clocks, Judaica, 19th-century globes – all in impeccable condition and unbelievably expensive. Nothing's keeping you from just having a look, though.

PHOTO WORKS

Map pp310-11 Art & Photography

☎ 593-9090; 839 Chartres St

This is a polished showroom for the accomplished photographer Louis Sahuc (*Sigh*-ook), who has been shooting New Orleans for years and years. Sahuc's beautiful prints capture timeless images of the city. They are vantages upon which even Hurricane Katrina failed to impose change.

QUARTER PAST TIME

Map pp310-11 Antiques & Interesting Junk

☎ 410-0010; 606 Chartres St

This quiet little shop carries a selection of beautiful timekeepers. We didn't see any grandfather clocks, but they seemed to have everything else covered – wristwatches, pocket watches, wall-mounted clocks etc. Also, some nifty old radios of Jack Benny and the Brooklyn Dodgers vintage. You can buy, sell or trade, and if your watch ain't winding properly they'll fix it for you.

ROCK & ROLL COLLECTIBLES

Map pp310-11 Records & CDs

☎ **561-5683; 1214 Decatur St**

In this cluttered and very exciting shop you'll find the French Quarter's largest selection of vinyl (that's old-timey 33rpm long-playing records, pal). Come to think of it, this is the only shop selling records in the Quarter anymore. After two-plus decades of CDs and the emergence of eBay as the primary marketplace for used LPs, this place keeps things humming. (Though the store does have a presence on eBay.) Rock, blues and R&B are the primary areas of interest here, spanning everything from highly collectible 1940s jump blues to those latter-day Stones albums nobody seems to want. The store also carries a limited supply of rare 78rpm discs, and the walls are covered with vintage concert posters that are for sale.

SANTA'S QUARTERS

Map pp310-11 Christmas Ornaments

☎ **581-5820; 1025 Decatur St**

Finding ourselves puzzling over this store pretty much every time we walk by, we decided to go in and check it out for you. Sure enough, the place keeps the Christmas spirit alive yearround, with ornaments, lights and every festive trinket imaginable. Now, you have to wonder about people who love Christmas so badly they might be tempted to purchase Christmas ornaments on one of August's most sultry days. And you have to wonder about the zero receipt days this shop surely endures for much of the year. So is this shop a front for something more sinister? Or is it simply a vanity concern for St Nick? And, if so, why's it New Orleans? Or is the fat man indulging a local filly he's keeping on the side? Anyway, on with your shopping...

SIDESHOW: THE OLD CURIOSITY SHOP

Map pp310-11 Interesting Junk

☎ **581-2012; 828 Chartres St**

In the tradition of rummage stores of earlier times, this shop aims not just to sell you stuff, but to dazzle you as well. It does so simply by stocking oddities you'd expect to encounter in a sideshow tent (two-headed ducks, skulls of mythological creatures and other mind-bending items). You can also buy magician's supplies, snazzy decks of risqué playing cards and a bevy of other guilty pleasures from another age. It's owned and operated by Elizabeth Anderson, wife of actor Harry Anderson (himself a magician).

SOUTHERN CANDY MAKERS

Map pp310-11 Pralines

☎ **523-5544; 334 Decatur St**

Sweet-smelling confections with a Southern accent are created in this neat little shop. A visit is guaranteed to put a big ol' Dolly Parton smile on your face. The toffee is divine and the pralines are to die for. The shop does special candies for every holiday (fat Santas for Christmas, fat bunnies for Easter, chocolate hearts for Valentines) and you can have something sent off to loved ones around the country.

STARLING BOOKS & CRAFTS

Map pp310-11 Voodoo & Occult

☎ **595-6777; 1022 Royal St**

This place is about the serious side of the occult, lest we've got the idea the whole thing's been cooked up for our own amusement. This scholarly shop sells books concerning voodoo and the occult, and also has a few shelves of potions and voodoo dolls. The staff are knowledgeable, so fire away with questions if you're genuinely interested. Otherwise, walk on by.

STONE AND PRESS

Map pp310-11 Art & Photography

☎ **561-8555; 238 Chartres St**

Here's a cool shop for enthusiasts of fine-art mezzotints, lithographs, wood engravings and etchings by modern American artists. Mezzotints are the emphasis here, and flipping through the huge collection (filed away in bins like records in a record store) is a good way to gain an appreciation for a largely under-appreciated art form. Naturally, most of the work here has a soft, antiquated look, and much of the imagery is plucked from the past – old photos, newspaper clippings and the like. But most of the artists featured here are contemporary, and some are clearly pushing the envelope, exploring new possibilities and techniques. A startling range in texture, tone and definition is achieved in black and white and sepia hues. All works are original and printed in limited editions. Spend a little time in this shop. You'll be glad you did.

TOWER RECORDS

Map pp310-11 Music & Books

☎ **529-4411; 408 N Peters St**

This huge music chain has an immense store near Jackson Sq. Commendably, Tower reopened soon after Hurricane Katrina, showing more moxie than the innumerable chains that shied away for months afterwards. Here you'll find the usual complement of CDs in almost every genre (with a special room dedicated to regional artists), along with underground comics, magazines and obscure publications.

TRASHY DIVA Map pp310-11 Risqué Clothing

☎ **581-4555; 829 Chartres St**

Not really as scandalous as the name suggests, except maybe by Victorian standards. The specialty at this place is sassy Belle Epoque undergarments – lots of corsets and lacy, frilly stuff for ladies and gentlemen who enjoy those drawn-out undressing rituals. The shop also features Kabuki-inspired dresses with embroidered dragons and racks of retro tops, skirts and shawls reflecting styles plucked from just about every era. There's another store in the Lower Garden District (p232).

VIEUX CARRÉ WINE & SPIRITS

Map pp310-11 Groceries

☎ **568-9463; 422 Chartres St**

This is a densely stocked shop run by two Italian-born brothers who can often be found socializing at a table near the front door. It has an impressive selection of wines from California, Australia, France and Italy, and a commendable choice of international beers. If you're really serious about wine and willing to pay good money for it, ask to see the back room, where the rare vintages are kept.

INTERESTING JUNK

New Orleans rewards the shopper who appreciates that a surprising number of things just get better with age, including old lamps, ashtrays, toys and the kind of bric-a-brac that once was considered worthless. The best parts of town to go looking for these sorts of treasures are on lower Decatur St in the French Quarter and along Magazine St in the Garden District and Uptown. You could easily spend an entire afternoon browsing the Decatur St shops, or an entire day on Magazine St.

Trashy Diva

ZOMBIE'S HOUSE OF VOODOO

Map pp310-11 Voodoo & Occult

☎ **486-6366; 723 St Peter St**

Just around the corner from Bourbon St (and with another outlet, actually on Bourbon), this voodoo shop gamely makes its pitch amid the drunken hordes. You might see it as a mission in the devil's hand basket, but step inside and it's plain to see this is one religion that's not bent on snuffing out the party. There's an altar at the entry with a serious note not to disrespectfully take photos, and then there is the truly splendiferous display of plaster of Paris statuettes imported from the Santeria realms of Brazil. All of them are fun and charming, and many are simply beautiful. Works of folk art are mass produced. They laugh at death, celebrate sex and honor great figures in history. Some make great gifts to take back home – such as the smiling bust of Louis Armstrong. You can also choose your pick of potions and browse the selection of books on the occult. If you don't find what you're looking for here, try **Marie Laveau's House of Voodoo** (Map pp310–11; ☎ 581-3751; 739 Bourbon St), which carries similar stock. Shipping is available from either store.

FAUBOURG MARIGNY & BYWATER

For so fun and creative a neighborhood as the Marigny there is surprisingly little in the way of shopping. Most of what you'll find here is along Frenchmen St, among the clubs and restaurants. There are galleries and art-related shops scattered throughout the Bywater.

BACCHANAL Map p316 — Wine

☎ 948-9111; 600 Poland Ave

Flouting the rules of wine snobbery, this laid-back little Bywater shop specializes in a good deal. The owner, Chris Rudge, is a sommelier who seeks out great wines that he can put a fair price tag on – for under $10, say. He does the research and the buying so his customers don't need to ask themselves, 'should I go with the $10 cabernet or should I take a chance on this $18 pinot noir?' The real allure, however, is that Bacchanal is just your friendly neighborhood spot where patrons can linger over a glass of wine. Chris Rudge and his krewe of regular customers provide good company.

DR BOB'S STUDIO

Map p316 — Art & Interesting Junk

☎ 945-2225; 3027 Chartres St

Self-taught outside artist Dr Bob is a fixture in the Bywater, and you're sure to recognize his signature work – the 'Be Nice or Leave' signs that appear in restaurants and bars around town. Dr Bob's work also turns up in the House of Blues (p206) and museums throughout the South. In addition to the signs, he's known for his alligator carvings and sculptures of assembled found objects. Garbage-can lids, bottle caps, pieces of junked musical instruments and essentially anything that strikes Dr Bob's weird sensibility is turned into art. His gallery is really a fascinating junkyard of art, with a sculpture garden comprising spray-painted lawn ornaments. The man himself is a bit ornery, and he's not always in – call ahead.

ELECTRIC LADYLAND Map p316 — Tattoos

☎ 947-8286; 610 Frenchmen St

New Orleans is an old port filled with bars, right? Then a tattoo is just about the coolest souvenir you can get here. Day or night you'll spot people whose florid and lurid body art indicates business is not at all bad here at Electric Ladyland. It's a clean, brightly lit spot where young tattoo artists can set you up with a classic set of dice ('born to lose'), a growling wolf or a naked woman sashaying beneath a coconut palm. Customized designs can also be arranged.

FAUBOURG MARIGNY BOOK STORE

Map p316 — Specialty Books

☎ 943-9875; 600 Frenchmen St

The South's oldest gay bookstore is a ramshackle, intellectual spot and a good place to pick up local 'zines and catch up on the local scene.

NEW ORLEANS ART SUPPLY

Map p316 — Art Supplies

☎ 949-1525; 3620 Royal St

If you're one who likes to sketch while traveling, as a growing number of people do, here's a good place to go for a fresh supply of pencils and pads. Surprisingly, it's the most central art store in New Orleans, and it's not a bad one. The selection isn't huge, but it's of high quality. The shop is an annex of the New Orleans Conservation Guild.

A CONFLUENCE OF ARTISTS

A fun monthly event, the **Bywater Art Market** (☎ 944-7900; www.bywaterartmarket.com; Mickey Markey Park, Piety St; 9am-4pm 3rd Sat monthly), between Royal and Dauphine Sts, is a good place to seek out original works of art at reasonable prices. The number of local artists on hand ranges from 50 to 120, with some of the city's finest artists setting up shop next to unheralded folk artists. Rest assured, the artists are juried in, so none of the works offered here are by your Uncle Rufus' dog Elroy. No prints are sold.

By bringing artists and collectors together on a regular basis the market has contributed to the growing buzz around New Orleans' arts scene. As a result, some previously unsung artists have gained well-deserved recognition and an obvious boost in sales. For customers (free admission) the market is a great opportunity to score quality décor for your apartment, add value to your collection or just tap into the creative veins of the city and meet interesting people. Musicians and food vendors add a festive air.

PORCHÉ WEST GALLERY

Map p316 Art & Photography

☎ 947-3880; cnr Burgundy & Louise Sts

In the Bywater, this is the rustic shop and studio of photographer Christopher Porché West. Pathos defines Porché West's black-and-white images of the people of New Orleans, and his photos of the Mardi Gras Indians are among the best. Call for an appointment.

CBD & WAREHOUSE DISTRICT

This part of town is chiefly concerned with business and art. It's not good for window shopping, but if you know what you're looking for you may find yourself zeroing in on a little shop that specializes in something of interest to you.

MEYER THE HATTER Map pp308-9 Hats

☎ 525-1048; 120 St Charles Ave

This place is a cluttered asylum for people who are mad about hats. If that doesn't include you, then we'll have you know that New Orleans is a hat town, and hats are good. A brim shades the forehead, covers up the sweaty mess New Orleans turns your hair into and makes you look fuckin' cool. This shop, just a half block from Canal St, has a truly astounding inventory of world-class headwear. Biltmore, Dobbs, Stetson and Borsalino are just a few of the classy hatmakers represented. Those hip-hoppy Kangol Player hats are also sold here. Fur felts dominate in the fall and winter, and flimsy straw hats take over in the spring and summer. The clerks shoo away interlopers who come looking for the wrong type of hat at the wrong time of year.

INTERNATIONAL VINTAGE GUITARS

Map pp308-9 Musical Instruments

☎ 524-4557; 646 Tchoupitoulas St

In the Warehouse District, this is a small shop specializing in used guitars and amps. The collection usually features a few showpieces, but its stock generally consists of new Fenders, Epiphones and a few Gibsons. It's a convenient place to grab new strings if you busted yours while busking in the Quarter.

EAT YOUR GREENS (AND OTHER GOOD STUFF)

The **Crescent City Farmers Market** (www.crescentcityfarmersmarket.org) runs a series of popular green markets around town several days a week. Most accessible and fun is the Saturday morning **market** (700 Magazine St; 🕑 8am-noon Sat) in the Warehouse District. Farmers and bakers from all over southern Louisiana sell fruit, produce, tasty snacks, flowers, potted plants and coffee. Arrive before the 10am chefs' cooking demonstration. The Tuesday **market** (200 Broadway) is near Audubon Park Uptown Sq parking lot. Before Katrina, markets took place four days a week. Check the website to see if the number of markets is back up from the current two.

NEW ORLEANS SCHOOL OF GLASSWORKS Map pp308-9 Art

☎ 529-7277; 727 Magazine St

This school and gallery impressively fills 25,000 sq ft of an old brick warehouse. Glassworks is the sister school of the Louvre Museum of Decorative Arts and excellent pieces are sold here. On Saturday afternoon you'll usually see artists at work, and the blowing of glass is always worth seeing. Artists also specialize in stained glass, fine silver alchemy, copper enameling, printmaking, paper sculpture and bookbinding.

LOWER GARDEN DISTRICT

Magazine gets cooking in the Lower Garden District. There is a heady concentration of galleries, boutiques, restaurants and other shops between St Mary St and Jackson Ave.

AIDAN GILL FOR MEN

Map pp312-13 Men's Coiffure

☎ 587-9090; 2026 Magazine St

Metrosexual headquarters for Orleans Parish, smartly dressed mobsters of the Prohibition era would have felt at home in these clubby environs. It's all about looking not just neat, but stylish – in a well-heeled, masculine sort of way. High-end shaving gear, smart cufflinks and colorful silk ties are sold in front, and there's a popular barber shop ($35 for a trim; reserve a week ahead) in back.

BIG LIFE TOYS/WINKY'S

Map pp312-13 Retro Fashion & Toys

☎ 568-1020; 2038 Magazine St

Toys and retro clothing for childish adults – we mean that in the best possible way, of course. Fun stuff sold here includes tiki paraphernalia, tools of the cocktail hour and actual toys. The swinging casual duds for men and women and even children are worth trying on.

DARK ROOM

Map pp312-13 Photo Processing

☎ 522-3211; 1927 Sophie Wright Pl

New Orleans is photogenic and the city is home to hundreds of photographers, so it stands to reason there would be a place to get some very high-quality print work done. Dark Room is it. It's a center for the photographic arts, and you can take classes in photography and printing too, if you're interested.

HOUSE OF LOUNGE

Map pp312-13 Fashion

☎ 671-8300; 2044 Magazine St

Its name doesn't exactly have a svelte ring to it, but House of Lounge has its big vampish heart in the right place. The shop sells just about everything you would need to turn your foreplay into a classy burlesque review. The lingerie is sexy and shameless, the 'baby doll' assemblages are cute as all get-out (and gettin' out's the idea) and the feather fans will keep everything coyly covered after you've lost at strip poker. For the femme fatale who really knows how, the shop also sells cigarette holders and flasks. House of Lounge also carries smoking jackets for Hugh Hefner wannabes.

JIM RUSSELL'S RECORDS

Map pp312-13 Records & CDs

☎ 522-2602; 1837 Magazine St

A dense emporium of used 45s, with some highly rare, collectable and expensive disks featuring all the blues, R&B and soul stars of the past. (Collecting Johnny Adams' singles? This is the place.) The used LPs have mostly given way to CDs, with an uneven selection available. Turntables make it possible to assess the quality of your purchases before you lay down the crisp greenbacks.

SOUTHERN FOSSIL & MINERAL EXCHANGE

Map pp312-13 Interesting Junk

☎ 523-5525; 2049 Magazine St

The SFME is a store that can induce nightmares of the bone-rattling variety. It's a curiosity museum where most everything's got a price tag on it. So if you're impressed by the selection of skulls from all creatures great and small, you can take some home with you. Something to raise the eyebrows of the guards at the airport when your luggage goes through the X-ray machine. More subdued are the rocks on which ancient life forms have imprinted images of themselves. Pretty cool, actually, even if it just ends up as a paperweight on your desk. A selection of animal puppets is just the thing to appease your terrified children.

THOMAS MANN GALLERY I/O

Map pp312-13 Jewelry

☎ 581-2113; www.thomasmann.com; 1812 Magazine St

The 'IO' in this gallery's name stands for 'insightful objects.' Local craftsman Thomas Mann specializes in jewelry and sculpture, and his gallery is a smorgasbord of glass and metal. Mann's necklaces and bracelets make nice gifts.

TRASHY DIVA

Map pp312-13 Risqué Clothing

☎ 581-4555; 2048 Magazine St

It isn't really as scandalous as the name suggests, except by Victorian standards. Its specialty is sassy Belle Epoque undergarments – lots of corsets and lacy, frilly stuff for the Suicide Girl of yesteryear. The shop also features Kabuki-inspired dresses with embroidered dragons, and retro tops, skirts and shawls reflecting styles plucked from just about every era. There's another store in the French Quarter (p229).

GARDEN DISTRICT

On Magazine St, where it forms the riverside extent of the Garden District, you'll find another intriguing pack of shops.

BIG FISHERMAN SEAFOOD

Map pp312-13 Crawfish

☎ 897-9907; 3301 Magazine St

If you're in New Orleans in the spring, when it's crawfish season, you may have developed a taste for the little mudbugs. But you haven't really had the full-on crawfish experience unless you've been invited to a crawfish boil in someone's backyard. If that hasn't happened for you, send some crawfish back home and invite your friends over. This busy little shop will pack and ship crawfish to anywhere in the USA. The price fluctuates widely from season to season, so call ahead for prices.

CHRISTOPHER'S DISCOVERIES

Map pp312-13 Antiques & Interesting Junk

☎ 899-6226; 2842 Magazine St

Time spent in here might inspire you to rethink the layout of your pad back home. The shop has a loosely connected inventory that can only be attributed to the owner's cool sensibilities. Two large rooms in an old converted house are filled with choice artifacts, paintings, groovy lamps and exotic art (mostly of olive-skinned women) from Asia and the Middle East.

FUNKY MONKEY

Map pp312-13 Vintage Clothing

☎ 899-5587; 3127 Magazine St

Vintage attire for club-hoppers is what's sold in this funhouse of frippery. Worth a stop if you're making the rounds. The shop also sells wigs, shades and cheap jewelry.

GARDEN DISTRICT BOOKSHOP

Map pp312-13 General Books

☎ 895-2266; 2727 Prytania St

In the Rink, this place offers a select collection of first-edition works. It also stocks mostly new books about the region.

MAGAZINE ANTIQUE MALL

Map pp312-13 Antiques & Interesting Junk

☎ 895-5451; 3017 Magazine St

Hard-core rummagers are likely to score items of interest in the dozen or so stalls here, where independent dealers peddle an intriguing and varied range of antique bric-a-brac. Bargain hunters aren't likely to have much luck, though.

NEW ORLEANS MUSIC EXCHANGE

Map pp312-13 Musical Instruments

☎ 891-7670; 3342 Magazine St

It's high time you learned how to play trumpet. This large shop, specializing mostly in second-hand instruments, is the place to go for a nice used horn. There's an entire room of brass and woodwinds, all priced fairly. But to find it, you must weave through a maze of guitar and bass amps. It also sells guitars, guitar strings and all that other stuff. But you really ought to go for the trumpet.

Funky Monkey in the Garden District

UPTOWN

Keep following the Magazine St trail all the way up to Audubon Park. There are lots of interesting shops, cafés and galleries to poke your nose in here, with a particularly dense and varied concentration between Louisiana Ave and Upperline St. That's a lengthy haul, so be prepared for some walking.

IL NEGOZIO

Map pp314-15 Antiques & Interesting Junk

☎ 269-0130; 3607 Magazine St

You may be fed up with closet-sized boutiques offering a selection of three dresses all in size zero, but you needn't avoid this stylish store. It's in a large old house with a lush garden out front. The merchandise includes an assortment of dresses, skirts, pants and blouses by European and American designers.

FASHION MONGERS UNITE!

In the wake of Hurricane Katrina, many local and independent clothing designers banded together and formed the **New Orleans Fashion Collaborative** (www.nolafashion.com; 8316 Oak St; 3-8pm Sat) and began staging a weekly fashion bazaar at the Maple Leaf Bar (p209) in the Riverbend. Many of the vendors here sell their goods in shops around town, particularly on Magazine St, but this big stylish event brings it all together, with a wide selection of women's and men's apparel. The sensibilities run the gamut from hip to casual, way-in to way-out, with lots of groovy retro styles woven into the fabric. Costumes, hats, shoes and jewelry are also sold. The low overhead means better deals for shoppers, and it's an excellent opportunity to assemble your party duds for later in the evening.

Clothes hounds might also want to check out the **Kingpin Flea Market** (☎ 891-2373; 1307 Lyons St; noon-5pm Sun), a weekly flea market where vendors sell vintage and designer clothing and a whole host of interesting stuff. It's on the neutral ground between Lyons and Upperline Sts.

MAPLE STREET BOOKSTORE

Map pp314-15 General Books

☎ 866-4916; 7529 Maple St

Shopkeeper Rhonda Kellog Faust advocates for antiracism group Erace and she is a storehouse of local knowledge. The business, which includes a children's bookstore, was founded by her mother and aunt more than 30 years ago.

MIGON FAGET'S BOUTIQUE

Map pp314-15 Antiques & Interesting Junk

☎ 865-7361; 710 Dublin St

The shop of celebrated jewelry designer Faget, a native of New Orleans and a Newcomb College alumnus whose original designs are often inspired by patterns she observes in the natural world. Animals, flowers, seashells and coral are common motifs in her work.

MISS CLAUDIA'S

Map pp314-15 Vintage Fashion

☎ 897-6310; 4204 Magazine St

This shop will serve as your wardrobe department if the look you're after is straight out of Matt Helm movies or *77 Sunset Strip*. Try on some old suits, ties, striped shirts, knee-high boots, fake-fur coats and short skirts, whip out the credit card and shimmy on down Magazine St.

MUSICA LATINA DISCOTECA

Map pp314-15 CDs

☎ 895-4227; 4714 Magazine St

With a growing Spanish-speaking population and well-established cultural ties to the Caribbean, it makes sense that New Orleanians would have an appreciation for the exciting music of Latin America. That's all this jam-packed, one-room shop sells. It has everything covered, from the musical traditions of Cuba to Argentina. The mambo greats are thoroughly stocked and there's a smattering of mariachi and salsa artists from the ages.

RETROACTIVE

Map pp314-15 Vintage Jewelry

☎ 895-5054; 5414 Magazine St

This little glad-rag grotto is spilling over with eye-catching treasures. Once you've ducked in through the vintage handbags and crazy hats that literally hang from the ceiling, slow down a bit to inspect the jaw-dropping selection of costume jewelry. Beautiful glass and Bakelite pieces plucked from the middle of the 20th century cost anywhere from $20 to $500. You're sure to find a snazzy little something to pin to your sweater.

UPTOWN COSTUME & DANCEWEAR

Map pp314-15 Costumes & Masks

☎ 895-7969; 4326 Magazine St

A one-stop emergency room for anyone caught completely unprepared for Mardi Gras, Halloween or any other occasion that calls for an utterly frivolous disguise. It's an emporium of goofy get-ups, packed to the rafters with boas, tiaras, masks, Elvis capes, ballerina tutus and a truly astounding selection of cheap-ass wigs. Guaranteed to keep you from blending into the woodwork. Fun stuff for the entire family.

Sleeping

French Quarter 238

Faubourg Marigny & Bywater 242

CBD & Warehouse District 244

Lower Garden & Garden Districts 246

Uptown 248

Esplanade Ridge 249

Sleeping

Many visitors to New Orleans stay in the French Quarter, which for most is really the best way to go. You're likely to spend much of your time in this part of town anyway, and it can be a real pleasure walking back to your room at night after a leisurely meal or spending time in bars. If you're looking for hotels in the more residential lower Quarter, you should also consider staying in the Faubourg Marigny, an arty neighborhood just below the Quarter with good nightlife.

The CBD and the Warehouse District are where you'll find most of the chain hotels that accommodate business travelers. These range from boutique to corporate, and, with a few notable exceptions, generally lack New Orleans character. Budget seekers may want to look into hotels in this part of town, as when things are slow the big behemoths are forced to drop their prices to unexpected lows.

Hotel in Toulouse St, French Quarter

Elsewhere around town myriad options are worth exploring. In particular, the Garden District and Uptown offer grand old guesthouses within a block or two of the historic St Charles streetcar line, which links visitors to the French Quarter and most Uptown sights. Esplanade Ridge is home to historic mansions that have been converted into magnificent B&Bs that are particularly convenient for Jazz Festers.

Room rates vary depending on the time of year, with peaks during Mardi Gras and Jazz Fest and to a lesser degree around New Year's Eve. Advance reservations are recommended well ahead of time during these periods. New Orleans' very busy convention calendar also influences room rates. Off-season discounts kick in when occupancy rates drop. When it's really slow, top-end hotels sometimes let out their rooms for as low as $100 per night.

B&Bs

New Orleans has hundreds of B&Bs, many of them in Creole cottages and town houses with not so much as a sign out front to indicate that their rooms are available to travelers. Their obvious selling points are intimate surroundings, historic architecture, generally convivial hosts, early morning victuals and, in many cases, a traditional Creole courtyard in which to escape the maddening crowds. Some of these hidden B&Bs are right in the French Quarter. Other neighborhoods in which to consider seeking out your home away from home are the Faubourg Marigny, Esplanade Ridge and the Garden District.

You can get help finding a B&B from **Bed & Breakfast, Inc** (☎ 488-4640, 800-729-4640; www.historiclodging.com) and **Louisiana B&B Association** (☎ 225-346-1857, 800-395-4970; www.louisianabandb.com). Check out the websites for pictures and descriptions of amenities.

PRICE GUIDE

$	under $100
$$	$100 to $200
$$$	more than $200

Apartments & Long-term Stays

If you're settling in for awhile, or even for just a week, you'll do well to find an apartment. Many are set up with travelers in mind. You'll experience homeyness and space not to be found in hotels, and the price is often reasonable. Fairly luxurious spreads are often available in fashionable neighborhoods such as the French Quarter, the Faubourg Marigny and the Garden District.

Two companies serve the needs of travelers looking for apartments with flexible commitment plans: **Vacation Rentals by Owner** (www.vrbo.com) and **Vacation Rentals Online** (www.vacationrentalsonline.com).

Check-in & Check-out Times

Check-out times vary from 10am to noon. Often these can be flexible if you discuss them beforehand. Check-in times are relative, allowing time for cleanup, and range from 2pm to 4pm. It's best to alert the hotel if you're arriving late in the evening, so that your room is held for you. Smaller hotels and B&Bs often need to know when you are arriving in order to ensure staff are on hand to check you in.

Reservations

It's good policy to have room reservations before you arrive in New Orleans. For festivals such as Mardi Gras or Jazz Fest, or even for fun holidays such as New Years or Halloween, you'll want to reserve three to six months in advance to have a decent choice of good rooms in convenient locations.

During slower periods throughout the year (but especially in summer) you can get good deals by arriving in New Orleans with no hotel reservation. Many hotels have midweek specials, some as low as $59 for a double. The big convention hotels regularly drop their rates when they're not busy.

If you're driving into New Orleans from out of state, be sure to stop by the State Welcome Centers, off most highways near the state line, to check out the accommodations boards. Cheap deals are often available, and phone calls to the hotels are free. If you're already in town, some hotels turn over a portion of their last-day bookings, at reduced rates, to the **New Orleans Welcome Center** (Map pp310–11; ☎ 566-5031; 529 St Ann St; 9am-5pm).

BOOK ACCOMMODATION ONLINE

For more accommodation reviews and recommendations by Lonely Planet authors, check out the online booking service at www.lonelyplanet.com. You'll find the true, insider lowdown on the best places to stay. Reviews are thorough and independent. Best of all, you can book online.

HISTORIC HOTELS

There's nothing like an old building to make you feel a connection to the past. And since New Orleans' past is especially intriguing, you're right to seek out historic digs in which to rest your head at night. George Washington didn't hang his wig in any of these places, but the walls surely have stories to tell.

House on Bayou Road (p250) – It dates all the way back to 1798, and it's on the oldest road in New Orleans.

Hotel Monteleone (p241) – Capote was practically born here. Authors from William Faulkner to Richard Ford slept here. Liberace tinkled the ivories and twinkled his eyes in the bar here.

Degas House (p250) – The famed French painter Edgar Degas resided in this house while on an extended visit with his cousins. The ground-floor gallery showcases reproductions of the artist's work.

Columns Hotel (p205) – Still grand after all these years, the Columns stood in for a Storyville brothel in the film *Pretty Baby*. But it was never really a working woman's workplace.

Fairmont Hotel (p246) – Huey P Long hung out here in the 1930s, calling the shots while downing Sazerac cocktails at the bar. Someone shot at the governor in the bar, but missed. Ask the barkeep to point out where the bullet hit the wall.

FRENCH QUARTER

If you are looking for the historic flavor of the Old Quarter, a general rule of thumb is the further away you stay from Canal St the better. You might also want to avoid Bourbon St. The Lower Quarter is more residential, with guesthouses and smaller hotels, and staying down here is not inconvenient. The upper French Quarter has a concentration of large hotels with all the conveniences you would expect from high-end tourist accommodations, but some of these buildings feel out of scale for the charming old district, and the streets in this area have more T-shirt shops and take-out daiquiri bars.

GENTRY QUARTERS Map pp310-11 $

☎ 525-4433; www.gentryhouse.com; 1031 St Ann St; r $71-125

A charming old Creole house with six homey rooms, some with kitchens. This one has its loyal fans, with some guests staying a spell every year. It has changed ownership, but the couple who run it now liked it the way it was and are making just a few tasteful changes to update things. Most rooms open up onto a lush garden patio inhabited by a cat, a friendly dog and several dozen geckoes. Furnishings are modest but comfortable, giving the rooms a lived-in feel, while linens and towels are fresh and clean. Some rooms are large enough for families.

TOP FIVE TOWN HOUSES

These are some of the top converted town houses to be found around town. They tend to have a homey stylishness with unique décor, personable management, private courtyards and a tangible connection to the alluring history of New Orleans.

Soniat House (p241) – Creole elegance at its unassuming best.

Terrell House (p248) – Impeccable lodgings in a converted Georgian revival town house.

Josephine Guest House (p247) – Beautiful, if slightly eccentric, guesthouse.

Creole House Hotel (right) – Welcoming accommodations with home-style furnishings.

Villa Convento (opposite) – A classic French Quarter town house.

CORNSTALK HOTEL Map pp310-11 $

☎ 523-1515; www.travelguides.com/bb/cornstalk; 915 Royal St; r $75-185; Ⓟ

The Cornstalk Hotel is famous for its cast-iron fence, which is quite possibly the most photographed fence in the United States. The rooms inside the landmark Victorian house are attractive, with high ceilings, antique furnishings and private bathrooms. The colorful cornstalks were cast in 1859 and they continue to attract a steady stream of admirers. This is a regular stop along the horse-and-buggy tours that roam the French Quarter, so if there's a drawback to staying here, it might be the occasional, though reasonably inoffensive aroma of mules. Hey, that's what the 19th century was like.

CREOLE HOUSE HOTEL Map pp310-11 $

☎ 524-8076, 800-535-7858; www.acreolehouse.com; 1013 St Ann St; d from $80

Three historic houses make up this hotel on the lakeside of the Quarter, a little beyond where most of the tourists hang out. The hotel's old façade and courtyards have that painterly French Quarter elegance. Rooms are welcoming, with home-style furnishings and beds warmed by patchwork quilts. Here and there graceful touches, such as chandeliers, are hints of an ancient Creole elegance. A block away, Donna's Bar & Grill (p206) is a good place to go for live music, and more jazz clubs may soon be opening along Rampart St. After Hurricane Katrina, Creole House endeared itself to scores of locals by accommodating for several months those made homeless by the flooding.

URSULINE GUEST HOUSE Map pp310-11 $

☎ 525-8509, 800-654-2351; 708 Ursulines Ave; d from $85

The appeal here is unadorned accommodations in the laid-back lower Quarter. The buildings here date back to the Spanish era. Don't expect fussy preservationist charm, or luxury, although the bathrooms are fairly modern. The shuttered front rooms are just a short step up from the sidewalk, perhaps too close to the neighborhood's stream of yammering late-night pedestrians. Rooms in back are much quieter. This place is for adults only. Same-sex couples will feel welcome.

LE RICHELIEU Map pp310-11 $$

☎ 529-2492, 800-535-9653; www.lerichelieuhotel.com; 1234 Chartres St; r $85-180, ste from $200; P

A very convivial spot, on the quiet side of the Quarter. Le Richelieu's red-brick walls once housed a macaroni factory, but extensive reconstruction in the early 1960s converted it into a conservative-looking hotel. Its rooms are handsomely decorated in quasi-baroque stylings (Liberace on a subdued day) and the price includes parking. At night, guests can admire the phosphorescent swimming pool while having a drink on the patio.

ANDREW JACKSON HOTEL

Map pp310-11 $$

☎ 561-5881, 800-654-0224; www.frenchquarterinns.com; 919 Royal St; d from $100;

From the attractive mustard and federal blue façade to the high-ceilinged rooms within, this is a good traditional choice in the Quarter. The 22 rooms range in size from small to not-so-small. Best are the ones right up front with access to the 2nd-floor balcony. It's next to the Cornstalk Hotel, so the horses trot by day and night (a nice sound for the Old Quarter). Its rooms are spacious and comfortable and overlook a scenic courtyard and a swimming pool.

NINE-O-FIVE ROYAL HOTEL

Map pp310-11 $$

☎ 523-0219; www.905royalhotel.com; 905 Royal St; d from $110

Even the most diminished of characters should be able to find their way home if they can just remember its name. Not that that's the sort of person who stays in this low-key charmer in the heart of the Quarter. Next door to the Cornstalk Hotel, on a particularly scenic block, the 905 eschews much of the usual NOLA schtick and opts instead for the timeless comfort you'd expect to find if the house belonged to a dignified old aunt. Front rooms with balconies are the choice for those who want to survey the always entertaining Royal St scene, but for real seclusion, get a room off the cute little courtyard out back. All rooms include cable TV and small kitchen areas.

HOTEL ST MARIE Map pp310-11 $$

☎ 529-7142, 800-366-2743; www.hotelstmarie.com; 830 Conti St; d from $120;

Built from scratch as a modern hotel, the St Marie looks historic from the outside but is contemporary on the inside. Its best feature is the large and inviting courtyard, where you'll find a swimming pool and umbrella-covered tables amid lush plantings. The guest rooms with reproductions of antiques are somewhat lacking in authentic character, but are quite spacious and more than serviceable. Fabrics and carpets are something of a riot of patterns that may be unsettling in the morning if you're hung over. Just around the corner, Bourbon St is at its sleaziest, but of course there are diamonds in the rough, such as Galatoir's restaurant (p182).

HOTEL VILLA CONVENTO

Map pp310-11 $$

☎ 522-1793, 800-887-2817; www.villaconvento.com; 616 Ursulines Ave; d from $120

Classic New Orleans in every sense, the Villa Convento is a French Quarter town house built in 1833. It has a three-story red-brick façade with wrought-iron balconies. Out back in the annex, probably the former servants' quarters, there are more rooms. It's all very low-key, perfect for this residential part of the lower Quarter. According to a growing number of unreliable storytellers, this was the legendary 'House of the Rising Sun' made famous in the old ballad. Chances are, if you stay here, it won't lead to your ruin. Furnishings are basic but comfortable. The 25 rooms vary from small to not-so-small, and those in front open to balconies.

HOTEL PROVINCIAL Map pp310-11 $$

☎ 581-4995, 800-535-7922; www.hotelprovincial.com; 1024 Chartres St; d from $120; P

Behind its stately beige stucco façade, this hotel fills much of the block with a series of buildings and courtyards, and a large parking area. It has 93 rooms in a cluster of finely restored buildings. The best rooms have high ceilings and open onto interior courtyards (one with a pool), while some others can be cramped and dark. Décor ranges from commercial standard to ornately historic. Check out a few rooms for choosing. The excellent on-site restaurant, Stella!, is much more mellow than Brando's hollering in *A Streetcar Named Desire*.

HISTORIC FRENCH MARKET INN Map pp310-11 $$
☎ 561-5621, 888-211-3447; www.neworleansfinehotels.com; 501 Decatur St; d from $120;
On a particularly busy block of Decatur St, not far from excellent restaurants and the Café du Monde's aromatic chicory coffee (p178), is this fairly basic hotel with 95 rooms. Room sizes range from minute to relatively spacious, many get little daylight – a boon if you're only getting home at daybreak – and furnishings are purely functional. Check out a few before deciding. A courtyard and simple pool are found deep in the complex.

HOTEL ROYAL Map pp310-11 $$
☎ 524-3900, 800-776-3901; www.melrosegroup.com; 1006 Royal St; d from $120
It's in a historic town house on the quiet end of Royal St, and the Hotel Royal is suitably dignified. Furnishings are decidedly modern and attractive, each one designed uniquely. Some have exposed brick and some have balcony access. Fragrant chicory coffee is available and muffins and pastries are served in the morning.

CHATEAU HOTEL Map pp310-11 $$
☎ 524-9636; www.chateauhotel.com; 1001 Chartres St; d from $130; P
Several 1800s buildings have been combined to form this large hotel in the heart of the Quarter. Nothing is cookie cutter here; rooms range in size from roomy to scrawny. They have varying décor, but many feature wrought-iron beds that echo the street-side balconies. Though they're on the small side, we'd opt for the courtyard rooms, which are cool and peaceful and open up to a pool. You can slip in for a dip in the morning and fall in again on your way back to the room at night. It's on the residential end of the Quarter, but a block away Decatur St is at its neighborly best.

OMNI ROYAL ORLEANS Map pp310-11 $$
☎ 529-5333, 800-578-0500; www.omniroyalorleans.com; 621 St Louis St; d from $140; P
In the very heart of the French Quarter, the Omni Royal offers some of the best furnishings and in-room amenities of any large hotel in the Quarter. The cheapest rooms can be small and dark, while rooms with balcony access regularly go for more than $200 a night. On a clear day you can almost see Mississippi – the state, not the river – from the unique rooftop deck. Services include a beauty salon, barber shop and baby-sitting. This part of Royal St is lined with interesting boutiques, galleries and funky little shops, and K-Paul's (p184) is just around the corner.

OLIVIER HOUSE Map pp310-11 $$
☎ 525-8456; www.olivierhouse.com; 828 Toulouse St; d from $140;
Its main house was built in 1838 by Marie Anne Bienvenu Olivier, a wealthy planter's widow, and is an uncommon beauty with Greek-revival touches. Two elegant town houses expand the hotel's capacity. Each of the 42 rooms has its own style, but most have furnishings that evoke the early 19th century. Rooms range from the small and relatively economical to the elaborate with balconies and kitchens. Guests can enjoy the stately sitting room, with an impressive marble fireplace mantle. Out back the main courtyard is lush with mature trees, thick vines and numerous flowers. A second courtyard has a small pool. Thoughtful touches abound, including free local phone calls. Best of all, the house is within a few minute's walk of darn near everything.

W FRENCH QUARTER Map pp310-11 $$
☎ 581-1200, 888-625-5144; www.whotels.com; 316 Chartres St; d from $150; P
Like all W Hotels, this one wears its style on its trendy, businesslike sleeve. Whether it jibes with the French Quarter is questionable, but this is the flashier, less residential side of the district so maybe it does. (Mercifully, the Bourbon St racket is two blocks away.) Rooms come in varying sizes and color schemes, but all have that sleek contemporary slickness. The best are airy spaces that open onto an inner patio. Here you can ponder the pool's azure waters, or just enjoy a breeze while checking your email or watching a large screen TV. Bacco (p182), the Brennan family's trendiest restaurant, serves up classy Italian fare in a modern on-site dining room.

PLACE D'ARMES HOTEL Map pp310-11 $$
☎ 524-4531, 800-366-2743; www.placedarmes.com; 625 St Ann St; d from $150; P
Nine buildings from the 1830s combine to form a fine midrange hotel in the very

heart of the Quarter. Everything famous about the French Quarter is within a five-minute walk. Rooms are not exceptional (it pays to look at a few before choosing) but they are comfortable and you simply cannot beat the location. The courtyard and pool are pluses as well.

BOURBON ORLEANS HOTEL Map pp310-11 $$

☎ 523-2222, 800-521-5338; www.wyndhambourbonorleans.com; 717 Orleans Ave; d from $160; Ⓟ

Don't be put off by the name, which makes the place sound like frat-boy holidayland. The Bourbon Orleans, a large hotel operated by the Wyndham chain, has genuine elegance. The hotel combines several buildings that mostly date from the early 1830s, and its exterior hasn't made any unsightly bows to modernity. Rooms feature especially comfortable beds, good work-desks and marble bathrooms. Note, however, that room size varies greatly: standard rooms set a new standard for smallness. In contrast, deluxe rooms are quite large. Most rooms along the exterior have access to the classic wrought-iron balconies. On the Bourbon St side, needless to say, it can get noisy.

LAFITTE GUEST HOUSE Map pp310-11 $$

☎ 581-2678, 800-331-7971; www.lafitteguesthouse.com; 1003 Bourbon St; d from $180

This elegant three-story Creole town house, built in 1849, is down at the quieter end of riotous Bourbon St. Its 14 guest rooms are lavishly furnished in period style. Lafitte's Blacksmith Shop (p201), one of the street's more welcoming drinking taverns, is on the opposite corner.

WYNDHAM NEW ORLEANS AT CANAL PLACE Map pp310-11 $$

☎ 566-7006; www.wyndham.com; 100 Iberville St; d from $190; Ⓟ

Reaching as high as 29 stories, the Wyndham (once the Westin) has aged well in its two decades as one of the Crescent City's top hotels. The lobby is a stunner, a soaring two-story affair that begins on the 11th floor and showcases a worthwhile collection of antiques and art (ask for a brochure). The lobby and some of the rooms also have some of the best views of the Mississippi River. (In the wee hours, watching the passing parade of huge freighters, tankers and barges beats TV.) Rooms are large and have good desks for working, as well as small sitting areas. There's a rooftop pool that, needless to say, has more good views. Service is accommodating and gracious.

HOTEL MONTELEONE Map pp310-11 $$$

☎ 523-3341, 800-535-9595; www.hotelmonteleone.com; 214 Royal St; d from $200

This has been the hotel of choice for writers for many decades running, as you'll see from the glassed-in literary display in the Monteleone's grand lobby. It's one of the city's venerable old hotels, and it's also the French Quarter's largest. (Not long after the Monteleone was built, preservationists put a stop to building on this scale below Iberville St.) The narrow streets hardly allow one to stand back to admire its handsome, white, terracotta exterior. The rooms were brought up to date a decade ago, and rates drop significantly during the summer. The classic Carousel Bar (p200) is a clever revolving contraption from the early 20th century, churning somewhat more slowly than a merry-go-round but a jolly spot nevertheless.

ROYAL SONESTA Map pp310-11 $$$

☎ 586-0300, 800-766-3782; www.royalsonestano.com; 300 Bourbon St; d from $200; Ⓟ

Ground Zero for the tourist excesses of Mardi Gras – when they grease the pillars to keep revelers from climbing up to the balconies this hotel has a gracious charm at other times of year. It's a vast place that fills the block behind its traditional façade. Its nearly 500 rooms are well appointed, even classy, retreats from the strip clubs and lousy cover bands outside. The hotel offers many different types of rooms – right off the pool, balcony, courtyard etc – so you might want to check out a few. The Mystic Den is a dignified old bar that's the perfect venue for a civilized gin and tonic.

SONIAT HOUSE Map pp310-11 $$$

☎ 522-0570, 800-544-8808; www.soniathouse.com; 1133 Chartres St; d from $240, ste from $425

The three town houses that make up this hospitable hotel in the lower Quarter epitomize Creole elegance at its unassuming best. The place projects that elusive blend of warmth and creative style. It's run with congenial efficiency, with secret weapons like fresh biscuits in the morning to make guests feel right at home.

Soniat House (p231)

You enter via a cool loggia, which leads directly to a calming courtyard with ferns, palmettos and a trickling fountain. Some rooms open up onto the courtyard, while winding stairways lead to elegant upstairs quarters. Rooms vary in size and décor, (you can view photos on the website). Furnishings are antiques, well chosen and not off-putting, and the walls are graced by paintings on loan from the New Orleans Museum of Art. Bathrooms are of a quality that never goes out of date, with well-lit marble counters softened over time. This is a genuinely romantic spot (children under 12 are not permitted to stay here). Before heading off to dinner you can switch on a balcony ceiling fan and relax with a glass of wine or a splash of whiskey while mules clip-clop lazily by. Decatur St shops and galleries only reinforce the arty mood, and some of the Quarter's better watering holes are within a block.

FAUBOURG MARIGNY & BYWATER

Immediately below Esplanade Ave, the Faubourg Marigny is an attractive alternative to the Quarter. Its grid-defying street pattern is speckled with colorful old cottages, many of which have been converted into homey B&Bs. Savvy night owls feel the pull of the lively Frenchmen St scene (and the bars along lower Decatur St, in the lower Quarter). Same-sex couples are also drawn to the neighborhood by accommodations that make a special effort to cater to them.

Immediately below the Marigny, Bywater is another creative neighborhood that stays on the low-rent side of the spectrum – although, with blocks of historic shotgun houses and Creole cottages, that's subject to change. From either neighborhood, it is possible to walk to the Quarter, but it's more than a mile from the Bywater to the lower Quarter. Cabs are recommended after dark.

FRENCHMEN Map p316 $

☎ 948-2166, 800-831-1781; www.french-quarter.org; 417 Frenchmen St; d $49-250; P

The three thoroughly refurbished 1850s houses that comprise this smart hotel are clustered around a courtyard with a swimming pool and Jacuzzi. The real selling point is its proximity to some great bars and nightclubs. Some of the rooms have balconies, and some have rustic exposed brick, but most are fairly unremarkable, with serviceable furnishings and stiff polyester bedspreads we all recognize from spiffy 1970s motels. High ceilings are a luxurious remnant from the buildings' more elegant past. Concierge service is an upscale touch for this bargain hotel.

LIONS INN B&B Map p316 $

☎ 945-2339; www.lionsinn.com; 2517 Chartres St; d $50-110, q $110-120;

On a quiet block in the Marigny, the Lions Inn is bright and friendly and suitable for gays and straights. Nine guest rooms are furnished simply with splashes of vibrant color and no fussy antiques. Some rooms have a private bathroom, so be sure to clarify that before reserving. The choice space is the Sun Room, which can accommodate four and has a bank of windows overlooking the back courtyard. A crazy-shaped swimming pool and Jacuzzi will lure you in for a soak. Continental breakfast is served in the rooms. It's a couple blocks from Frenchmen St, and about five blocks from the Quarter. The owners, Floyd and

Stuart, also operate the exceedingly popular Elizabeth's Restaurant (p186) in the Bywater, just in case you're after a more substantial breakfast.

LAMOTHE HOUSE Map p316 $

☎ 947-1161, 800-367-5858; www.new-orleans.org; 621 Esplanade Ave; d from $59; P

This is one of the very best deals in town. On lovely, oak-shaded Esplanade Ave, it's a prime jumping-off point for prowling the nightlife of Frenchmen St and the lower Quarter. Its charms are slightly faded, but Lamothe House doesn't lack for character or elegance. The guest rooms are tastefully furnished with antiques of a quality that you won't feel guilty about bumping into, and thick curtains keep the sun out when you're sleeping off a big night. If you're determined to revive in the AM, a dip in the pool and the continental breakfast will get you going. The cheapest rooms are slender, though not all that cramped, and open onto a long courtyard. More elaborately accoutered suites somehow suggest Bellocq's beautiful Storyville photographs without being lurid or seedy. If the main house's 11 rooms are booked, you might be offered a room just around the block, at Lamothe's smaller, Marigny Guest House (Map p316; same room rates).

TOP FIVE HOTEL BARS

When you're just about drunk enough to not know your way back to the hotel, you'll wish you were staying and drinking in one of these fine establishments, where groovy cocktail lounges are just an elevator ride away from dreamland. (* = substitute stairs for elevator.)

Carousel Bar (p200) – Hotel Monteleone is the home of this revolving bar beneath a carousel top complete with lights.

Loa (p204) – Huge windows overlook the CBD's streetscape of dedicated worker bees in this International House bar.

Sazerac Bar (p246) – This swanky bar in the Fairmont was frequented by governor Huey Long in the 1930s.

Columns Hotel* (p205) – A swell place to tie one on with Uptown swells.

Mystic Den (p241) – The perfect venue for a civilized gin and tonic in the Royal Sonesta.

BYWATER BED & BREAKFAST Map p316 $

☎ 944-8438; www.bywaterbnb.com; 1026 Clouet St; d from $65

This artsy B&B, particularly popular with lesbians, is about as homey and laid-back as it gets. It's a restored double-shotgun, very colorful, with a kitchen and parlors in which guests can cook or loiter. The walls double as gallery space, showcasing a collection of vibrant outsider art. The owners enjoy steering guests in the right direction, whether you're looking for a great po'boy, live music or gay bars. The four guest rooms are simple and comfortable with more cheery paint and art on the walls. All have shared bathroom.

HOTEL DE LA MONNAIE Map p316 $$

☎ 947-0009; 405 Esplanade Ave; ste from $140; P

Built in the 1980s to look much older on the outside than it really is, this is the largest hotel in this part of town. But it doesn't really smell like money. It has five floors of suites, each with minikitchens and surprisingly dated and mundane furnishings. (Think family-friendly and easy to clean.) Rooms are large, and can sleep four to six people. The interior courtyards are lush with spindly Hollywood palms and deck chairs, and rooms on the top floor enjoy wonderful views of the Mighty Mississippi flowing by. If you're traveling with a group or family, this place makes real sense.

MELROSE MANSION Map p316 $$$

☎ 944-2255, 800-650-3323; www.melrosemansion.com; 937 Esplanade Ave; ste $225-450; P

One of New Orleans' premier crash pads. This is an exquisite 1884 Victorian mansion that really stands out even among its stately neighbors along beautiful Esplanade Ave. This is a retreat for well-heeled honeymooners and slick Hollywood swells, not for families. Rooms are luxurious, airy spaces, with high ceilings and large French windows. Fastidiously polished antique furnishings reflect impeccable taste, with four-poster beds, cast-iron lamps and comfortable reading chairs in every room. Bathrooms have deep tubs and are fully equipped. Fresh-baked pastries are served in the guest rooms, and nightly cocktails are mixed up in the parlor. Full concierge service is available round the clock. Obviously, guests are pampered to death here, but it's an exquisite way to go.

CBD & WAREHOUSE DISTRICT

This is not the part of town to stay in if you're looking for that distinctive New Orleans atmosphere. The hotels here tend to be modern, utilitarian chains or posh high-rises catering to business people on expense accounts. Even the Warehouse District, despite its promising artistic leanings, caters mostly to the conventioneer set. Reasons to stay in these parts of town include: proximity to the French Quarter; you've found a sweet deal; Mardi Gras parades pass through this part of town; you want a view of the Superdome; your employers are paying the bill and this is where they chose to put you.

That said, there are a handful of truly outstanding exceptions. During slower periods, prices for nicer midrange places come down to 'budget' levels, so try these before resorting to the rinky-dink chains.

DOUBLETREE HOTEL NEW ORLEANS

Map pp308-9 $$

☎ 581-1300; www.neworleans.doubletree.com; 300 Canal St; d from $110; P

One of the better choices among the chain hotels on Canal St, the Doubletree manages to feel almost a bit intimate given it has 363 rooms as opposed to some places nearby with room totals in the four digits. Like most properties in this group, rooms are sizable if generic. Rooms on the higher of the 17 floors have good views, especially those facing the river, which is not far away. Patrons range from package groups from middle America to professionals from middle management.

LAFAYETTE HOTEL Map pp308-9 $$

☎ 524-4441, 888-211-3447; www.neworleansfinehotels.com; 600 St Charles Ave; d from $140

A small and luxuriant hotel right on Lafayette Sq, this is the most charming place to stay in this part of town. It was built in 1916, and the surrounding blocks have a classic feel that's generally lacking in most of the modern CBD. (Lafayette Sq was the center of the American Faubourg St Mary, developed after the Louisiana Purchase.) Its 44 rooms are poshly furnished with dark woods, antiques and king-size beds. The walls are painted in rich, classic colors, and the bathrooms are roomy and finished in marble. Service is tops and the hotel has a loyal following. The Julia Row arts district is a short walk from here, as are numerous cutting-edge restaurants. The French Quarter is a few blocks away and, when operating, the St Charles Ave Streetcar rattles down the street often, leading to Uptown excursions.

COUNTRY INN & SUITES BY CARLSON

Map pp308-9 $$

☎ 324-5400, 800-456-4000; www.countryinns.com/neworleansla; 315 Magazine St; d from $140; P

Seven historic buildings, most of them former warehouses built in the 19th century, have been converted into this huge hotel. It is spotlessly clean, with a small pool, exercise room and a friendly cocktail lounge. The guest rooms are smallish and utilitarian, but come with desks and free high-speed Internet connections. Canal St and the French Quarter are just a block and a half away.

QUEEN & CRESCENT HOTEL

Map pp308-9 $$

☎ 587-9700, 800-975-6652; www.queenandcrescent.com; 344 Camp St; d from $140

Two early 1900s commercial buildings make up this hotel, in a part of the CBD now dominated by midrange chains. The Q&C is not small (it has 196 rooms), and its grey-painted brick façade doesn't scream out luxury, but the place manages to stand apart. The windows facing the street are wide, allowing maximum light inside. In the main building, rooms above the 8th floor often have interesting city views. All rooms have a certain European charm, but vary greatly. You might want to leave the bags in the lobby while you peruse.

LE PAVILLON Map pp308-9 $$

☎ 581-3111, 800-535-9095; www.lepavillon.com; 833 Poydras St; d from $145; P

Looking a little like an overblown wedding cake with its gleaming white façade and fluted columned carport, Le Pavillon may be a little too rich for some people's tastes. The hotel's motto – 'Imagination governs the world,' attributed to Napoleon – is all ambition and romance. But we haven't revealed half of it yet. Furnishings in many of the suites rightly belong in museums (watch what you're doin' with that gin fizz, Bub), and the lobby and rooms are redolent with historic portraits, magnificent chandeliers, marble floors, blah blah, etc etc. You'll be amazed. The doorman wears white gloves and a top hat, and doesn't look ridiculous. Get the picture? This place really sells it. The rooms are extravaganzas of color, heavy drapery, four-poster beds, striped wallpaper and the like. Just when you're getting the idea that this is some sort of asylum for deposed world conquerors, out comes the plate of peanut butter and jelly sandwiches, the perfect midnight snack, served every night in the lobby at 10pm. Rates are unexpectedly low for a hotel of this quality. During slow periods Le Pavillon offers some astounding deals, and at all times the website offers to beat any comparable room rates by 10%.

SHERATON NEW ORLEANS

Map pp308-9 $$

☎ 525-2500; www.sheratonneworleans.com; 500 Canal St; d from $150; (P) (wheelchair)

To be sure, there's nothing intimate about this 1100-room conventioneer hotel. It's a behemoth, with a lobby that seems bigger than the terminals at Louis Armstrong Airport. In the rooms you'll find nicely designed furniture and subtle color schemes that are easy on the eyes. And needless to say high floors mean fabbo views. But we're digressing from our main point, which is that prices plummet when there's no convention in town, meaning fantastic deals for guests who appreciate Sheraton's quality service.

HAMPTON INN NEW ORLEANS DOWNTOWN Map pp308-9 $$

☎ 529-5077, 800-292-0653; www.neworleanshamptoninns.com; 226 Carondelet St; d from $150; (P)

It's in the Carondelet Building, considered the Big Easy's first skyscraper, but the Hampton Inn stays close to its modest chain roots by offering good-value accommodation and a convenient central location. It's two blocks from the Quarter, and the streetcar begins its Uptown run just around the corner. Inside, the 187 rooms will be instantly familiar to anyone who has stayed at the one of its oodles of properties located at interstate interchanges from coast to coast. In addition, per Hampton protocol, there's a complimentary breakfast buffet in the morning where you'll end up waffling over your choice of waffles, pancakes and more. On weeknights there's a free happy hour, which is much loved by business travelers.

EMBASSY SUITES HOTEL Map pp308-9 $$

☎ 525-1993, 800-362-2779; www.embassyneworleans.com; 315 Julia St; d from $150; (P)

This architectural flight of fancy astonishes with its vast size and cacophony of angles, but the eccentric design grows on the people who stay here. It is a large, modern hotel, built in 1984, and the soaring atrium is indeed impressive. Every room is a large suite and no two are exactly the same. Most have balconies, and rooms on the higher floors have views of the city and the river. Some rooms, in an adjoining historic loft building that was once a cotton warehouse, have very high ceilings and exposed brick walls – good for families. Art galleries and fine restaurants such as Emeril's (p188) and Herbsaint (p188) are nearby.

LOEWS NEW ORLEANS HOTEL

Map pp308-9 $$$

☎ 595-3300; www.loewshotels.com; 300 Poydras St; d from $200; (P) (wheelchair)

In a converted office building formerly occupied by a steamship company, Loews is a luxury hotel offering a boatload of amenities with a relaxed and unfussy style. The 285 rooms are larger than average and many have superb views. Rooms are decorated and furnished with understated yet elegant modernism. It's one of the very few major hotels in New Orleans that welcomes pets. There's an indoor lap pool and health centre plus a noted spa. In a bar off the lobby, dubiously called Swizzle Sticks, live jazz is performed many nights.

INTERNATIONAL HOUSE

Map pp308-9 $$$

☎ 553-9550; www.ihhotel.com; 221 Camp St; d from $210; (no smoking)

This boutique hotel offers easily the most stylish and hip accommodations in the CBD. Rooms (119 of them) are lavish, with an array of amenities including floral arrangements of local wildflowers, CD players with jazz CDs, ceiling fans (in addition to the aircon), and two-headed showers. The lobby is hang-out worthy, with its over-the-top arrangement of flowers amid soaring columns and plush furniture. The lobby bar, Loa, is one of New Orleans' most fashionable. There's even an iMac for those who want to check their email. Should budget allow, go for the penthouse rooms with sweeping terraces.

W NEW ORLEANS Map pp308-9 $$$

☎ 525-9444; www.whotels.com; 333 Poydras St; d from $210; P

You have to hand it to W when it does things right, as it tends to do, but you also have to snicker at the wunderkinds behind this suave hotel chain for trying so damn hard to impress their guests. This one is housed in a tower that was once a bland office building. After a wave of the magic W wand it became the modern hotel equivalent of Buddy Love: too cool for school, pops. The W offers a high level of service and likes to boast about getting you 'whatever, whenever' including 'the city's best beignet brought directly to your bath.' Now, who would want that? The rooftop pool is nice, but management insists on calling it 'The Big Blue.' Perhaps we're splitting hairs. Overall, the W offers quality accommodations, and not just for people who once were nerds, made some money and, presto, became hip.

FUN HOTELS

The whole damn town's fun, but some people don't want the fun to stop even when they're sleeping. A few accommodations go all out trying to keep the good times rolling, whether with goofy architecture, crazy décor or some other intangible quality that appeals to happy-go-lucky guests.

International House (p245) – Over the top décor and a hip bar make Loa an unforgettable choice.

Lamothe House (p243) – It's old-fashioned, but not stodgy, and is around the block from some of the city's best nightlife.

India House Hostel (p249) – This flophouse for the young takes its fun seriously.

Columns Hotel (p205) – Swank and lively digs upstairs, and a boisterous bar downstairs make an unbeatable combo.

Embassy Suites (p245) – An architectural flight of fancy amid galleries and fine restaurants.

FAIRMONT HOTEL Map pp308-9

☎ 529-7111, 800-441-1414; www.fairmont.com; 123 Baronne St; rates not available at press time; P

With its majestic, block-long lobby, this was the city's elite establishment in days gone by. It opened in 1893 and by the 1930s, when it was called the Roosevelt Hotel, its swanky bar was frequented by governor Huey Long. The Fairmont still has an imposing presence. The curvaceous bar is as stylish as ever, the guest rooms have been tastefully remodeled, and the rooftop swimming pool affords an impressive downtown view. After Hurricane Katrina the Fairmont closed for a year while renovation and restoration work was done. We didn't have an opportunity to check it out, but as it is a local landmark and part of a highly respected international hotel chain, we figured it likely to return in fine shape.

WINDSOR COURT HOTEL Map pp308-9 $$$

☎ 523-6000, 888-596-0955; www.windsorcourthotel.com; 300 Gravier St; d from $280; P

It's architecturally an ugly duckling from the 1980s, but the toney and sumptuous Windsor Court more than makes up for it inside. The public areas feature a long list of artworks and antiques. Lavish floral displays add immeasurable charm while a harpist sets the tone. Service is superb, rooms large and comfy, and the bars and restaurants are local destinations. If it sounds a little British, well, it is meant to. You're sure to wonder what famous people have stayed here, and your bellman is likely to mention such dignitaries as Rod Stewart. But surely Mr 'Hot Legs' stands about midway up the hotel's social ladder? A large pool, Jacuzzi, health club, in-room massage services – these are the sorts of things you (and Rod) can expect from one of New Orleans' finer accommodations.

LOWER GARDEN & GARDEN DISTRICTS

For much of its length, St Charles Ave is one of the USA's most attractive thoroughfares, with oak trees arcing across its neutral ground, down which historic streetcars jangle their way Uptown. Most of these neighborhoods' accommodations are to be found along this main stem. Prytania St is in some ways the prettier street, with less traffic and just as many trees. Many old homes along or just off Prytania have been converted into guest houses.

This part of town also boasts a youth hostel, Marquette House, which is still good value for budget travelers.

HI MARQUETTE HOUSE HOSTEL

Map pp312-13 $

☎ **523-3014; hineworle@aol.com; 2253 Carondelet St; dm from $17, d from $39**

The cheapest place around and not a bad place to lay your head. The hostel is around the block from St Charles Ave and the Garden District, heading toward a rough area. But this block of Carondelet St is fairly quiet. The large facility consists of four buildings with 21 rooms that are kept impressively clean. Dorm rooms and private rooms sleep up to four people. Some have private bathrooms, others share. Picnic tables in the backyard are an ideal place to meet fellow travelers. Internet access is available in the lobby, and there are two laundries nearby (one is in a bar). Once the St Charles streetcar line is running, the hostel's location means that you can easily reach downtown or uptown. Street parking is easy.

AVENUE GARDEN HOTEL Map pp312-13 $

☎ **521-8000, 800-379-5322; www.avenuegarden hotel.com; 1509 St Charles Ave; d from $80;** Ⓟ

This hotel is on an uncharacteristically drab and treeless block of St Charles Ave, but that's not all you can say for it. Its 30 rooms are scattered across a cluster of buildings of various vintages, mostly from the 19th century. Rooms are not fancy but as you'd expect from such an idiosyncratic place, some are a lot better than others. Bargain-hunters will prefer rooms 15, 23 and 24, while those looking for air will like the balcony on 47. If you and your partner like to admire yourselves (and tend to rotate while, er, sleeping), try 31 with its round bed and mirrored ceiling. There is a small courtyard in back.

GARDEN DISTRICT HOTEL

Map pp312-13 $$

☎ **566-1200, 800-265-1856; www.gardendistrict hotel.com; 2203 St Charles Ave; d from $100;** Ⓟ

You'll find none of the eccentric charm of the namesake Garden District within the walls of this nine-story, modern hotel block. You will find corporate-standard rooms that could really be almost anywhere. However, some have good city views and, best of all, the hotel is barely a hop and definitely less than a skip from the actual Garden District. Frequent special rates are a real draw.

JOSEPHINE GUEST HOUSE

Map pp312-13 $$

☎ **524-6361, 800-779-6361; 1450 Josephine St; d from $100**

On the corner of Prytania St, the Josephine has many loyal repeat visitors who enjoy the beautiful old house and its hospitable environment. You'll feel like guests of fun relatives who are somewhat wealthy but have slightly eccentric taste. The house has six lovely rooms, each with its own charms, antique furnishings and Oriental rugs. Every room has a balcony or opens onto a gallery, and all have plush private bathrooms. Reserve well ahead for this one, and while you're at it, ask about restaurants that may require early reservations (the owners are a fount of such information).

PRYTANIA PARK HOTEL Map pp312-13 $$

☎ **524-0427, 888-674-6764; www.prytaniapark hotel.com; 1525 Prytania St; d from $100;** Ⓟ

A modern motel adjoined to a restored 1850s guesthouse, the Prytania Park has 49 nicely appointed rooms, each with refrigerators and microwaves. Some of the larger rooms, in the historic part of the hotel, have spiral staircases winding up to extra sleeping quarters and are well suited to families. The newer rooms are fairly standard. It's on a beautiful, oak-shaded street, one block from the streetcar line, and the hotel offers a free shuttle to the French Quarter. This place is always worth checking for last-minute reservations, as the room rates tend to bottom out when things are slow.

SULLY MANSION B&B Map pp312-13 $$

☎ **891-0457, 800-364-2414; www.sullymansion.com; 2631 Prytania St; d from $110**

This historic house is surrounded by lush gardens and a cast-iron fence, and pretty much lives up to everything the Garden District is cracked up to be. The seven guest rooms are elegantly put together, each with a fireplace and antique four-poster beds. Curtains and art on the walls are oddly underwhelming. You'll want to spend more of your downtime in a wicker chair out on the mansion's curved porch, which harks back to the Old South. Oddly enough, this is the only B&B in the Garden District, and it's at the heart of things, among the historic homes and gardens for which the neighborhood is internationally famous.

MAISON ST CHARLES Map pp312-13 $$

☎ 522-0187, 800-831-1783; www.maisonstcharles.com; 1319 St Charles Ave; d from $120; P

A hodgepodge of historic and newer buildings set around gorgeous courtyards makes up this hotel that's clearly geared toward the practical-minded traveler. Rooms are very midrange, furnishings lean toward heavy burgundies with the odd antique touch here and there. But there's wi-fi throughout and the larger rooms come with kitchenettes. Given the variety here, you may want to look at more than one of the 130 rooms before making your selection. The pool is decent-sized and there's a hot tub that can fit up to 12 people depending on how well you know or wish to know your companions. This is on the slightly scruffy end of St Charles Ave, not far from the Hwy 90 overpass and Lee Circle.

TERRELL HOUSE Map pp312-13 $$

☎ 247-0560, 866-261-9687; www.terrellhouse.com; 1441 Magazine St; d from $135;

An 1858 Georgian-revival house is in the Lower Garden District, just a few blocks away from some of the neighborhood's jammin' art galleries and restaurants. It's impeccable. It's a two-level house with cast-iron galleries, a spacious brick courtyard and exquisite galleries filled with art, antiques and potted plants. Rooms in the main house are designed with period furnishings, silk draperies and Oriental rugs but still manage to feel cozy. Some even have fireplaces with marble mantle pieces. Upstairs rooms have fairly low ceilings – something to ask about while reserving. The carriage house out back was fully restored just a few years ago, and its rooms are among the hotel's finest offerings. All rooms have private bathroom and include a full breakfast and cocktails. Other amenities include cable TV, wi-fi, coffeemakers and bottled water.

PONTCHARTRAIN HOTEL Map pp312-13 $$

☎ 524-0581, 800-777-6193; www.pontchartrainhotel.com; 2031 St Charles Ave; d from $140; P

Like an aged entertainer who's unimpressed by flashy newer talents, the Pontchartrain has a certain timeless air. And in keeping with this character, the hotel honors long-ago visits by the likes of Carol Channing and Richard Burton by naming suites after them. Built in 1927, the 12-story Pontchartrain was originally an apartment hotel, where guests stayed by the month or year but enjoyed the services of a hotel. Many of the rooms are still apartment sized. Regular guests prefer the rooms on the front above the 8th floor for their light and views. The trees out front are suitably twisted and gnarled, and you can sip a coffee on the heavy iron tables and chairs near the entrance outside. The hotel's ageless Bayou Bar is dramatically beamed with huge old cypress wood.

AVENUE PLAZA RESORT & SPA

Map pp312-13

☎ 566-1212, 800-535-9575; www.avenueplazahotel.com; 2111 St Charles Ave; rates not available at press time; P

Just outside the Garden District proper, but along a very attractive block of St Charles Ave, this large hotel is one of the grander choices in the neighborhood. It's as much noted for its spa, with a full complement of massage and salon treatments available. Guest rooms are all suites, smartly furnished with king-size beds and kitchenettes. There's also a courtyard swimming pool at the back. During Hurricane Katrina this hotel suffered some flooding in its basement, which caused electrical problems and pointed out the need for some construction work to buffer against future flooding. We were unable to view it, but it will reopen soon.

UPTOWN

Uptown is where St Charles Ave really flourishes. It's lined with historic mansions surrounded by carefully manicured gardens. There are some lovely places to stay in this part of town, though the pickings are slim.

LAGNIAPPE B&B Map pp314-15 $

☎ 899-2120, 800-317-2120; www.lanyappe.com; 1925 Peniston St; d from $99; P

This restored Creole house has very stylish rooms, all with high ceilings and private bathrooms. Furnishings are a mix of antiques and well-made reproductions. Owners Helene and Ken Barnett claim their goal is to spoil guests rotten, but really these are just nice people who know how to make their guests comfortable. Fresh fruit, fresh flowers, cold beer in the fridge, wine on the porch and a wonderful breakfast in the morning are just some of the ways in which guests are pampered. Concierge services are also available. The Lagniappe is in a transitional neighborhood, but only three blocks off St Charles Ave.

PARK VIEW GUEST HOUSE

Map pp314-15 $$

☎ 861-7564, 888-533-0746; www.parkviewguesthouse.com; 7004 St Charles Ave; d from $120

Next to Audubon Park, this ornate wooden masterpiece was built in 1884 to impress people attending the World Cotton Exchange Exposition the following year. Antique furnishings abound in the lounge and guest rooms. The 22 rooms have private bathroom and cable TV. Furnishings are of the stodgy, heavy wood variety. From the wraparound veranda you can enjoy up-close views of stately oaks grizzled with Spanish beards on St Charles Ave and Audubon Park. Tulane and Loyola Universities are just blocks away, and many of the hotel's guests appear to be visiting parents.

COLUMNS HOTEL Map pp314-15 $$

☎ 899-9308, 800-445-9308; www.thecolumns.com; 3811 St Charles Ave; d from $160

Built in 1883, this is one of New Orleans' great establishments, with a magnificent mahogany stairwell leading to tidy, unpretentious rooms. Adding to the fun, the downstairs bar and patio is a swell place to tie one on with Uptown swells. On the 2nd and 3rd floors are 20 rooms of various sizes from smallish doubles to the two-room 'Pretty Baby Suite' (named for the Louis Malle film shot here in the 1970s). Elaborate marble fireplaces, richly carved armoires and clawfoot tubs are among the highlights. To absorb the late-night revelry take a front room on the 2nd floor; room 16 has a balcony overlooking the front entry and St Charles Ave. The public spaces are equally grand, with high ceilings and numerous details and artworks to catch and hold the eye. A lavish breakfast is included.

ESPLANADE RIDGE

Esplanade Ridge, near City Park and the Fair Grounds, is rife with old and beautiful homes that now accommodate guests looking for some of that Southern grandeur we've all heard about. This part of town is along a natural levee that survived the storms of 2005. However, within blocks of Esplanade Ave, in either direction, the floods were disastrous. It's a strange contrast, but by the time you visit, the area may be busy with contractors making new homes for the new New Orleans.

Of course, this part of town is the ideal area to stay in if you've come for Jazz Fest – the Fair Grounds are only a short walk away. The neighborhood is also home to some of the city's finest restaurants. It's a couple of miles from this area to the French Quarter, but buses run regularly down Esplanade Ave.

There's not much going on in Mid-City besides the post-Katrina recovery. But the hostel out this way was fairly quick to get back on its feet, and seems to be poised for the neighborhood's renewal. Streetcars run down Canal St from the French Quarter.

INDIA HOUSE HOSTEL Map p317 $

☎ 821-1904; www.indiahousehostel.com; 124 S Lopez St; dm $17, d $45;

Half a block off Canal St in Mid-City, this place has a free-spirited party atmosphere. A large aboveground swimming pool and cabana-like patio décor add ambience to the three well-used old houses that serve as dorms. Bunk beds include linen and tax. For a unique experience, ask about the private Cajun shacks out back, which come with pet alligators. Guests can use the washer and dryer, and log onto the Internet. Children are not permitted to stay at this hostel.

BENACHI HOUSE Map p317 $$

☎ 525-7040, 800-308-7040; www.nolabb.com; 2257 Bayou Rd; d $105-135; P

Half a block off Esplanade Ave, this truly spectacular Greek revival mansion was built in 1858 for Nicolas Benachi, a wealthy cotton broker. The house retains many of its original details with high ceilings, banded cornices, black marble mantles, rococo-revival chandeliers and heart pine floors. Furnishings are true to the building's vintage, with much mahogany and rosewood. There are just four bedrooms, none of which equals the splendor of the house's public rooms, and only one has a private bathroom. The house occupies a spacious lot with landscaped gardens, an ornate cast-iron fence and the original carriage house and cistern.

DEGAS HOUSE Map p317 $$

☎ 821-5009, 800-755-6730; www.degashouse.com; 2306 Esplanade Ave; d from $125

Edgar Degas, the famed French impressionist, lived in this 1852 Italianate house when visiting his mother's family in the early 1870s. During his stay here he produced the city's most famous painting, *The Cotton Exchange in New Orleans*. Rooms recall the painter's stay with reproductions of his work and period furnishings. The suites have balconies and fireplaces, while the less expensive garret rooms are the cramped top-floor quarters that once housed the Degas family's servants. All rooms have private bathroom, wi-fi, bottled water and cable TV. Continental breakfast is included.

HOUSE ON BAYOU ROAD Map p317 $$

☎ 945-0992, 800-882-2968; www.houseonbayouroad.com; 2275 Bayou Rd; d from $135; P

The true gem of the neighborhood is this 1798 Creole plantation house. It was built for diplomat Domingo Fleitas, an émigré from the Canary Islands who wanted his new home fashioned in a familiar West Indies Creole style. No doubt he was satisfied. The house is airy and warmly lit, with wide galleries and French doors that open onto thick tropical gardens. In the evening, the place oozes sultry atmosphere. Three rooms in the main house are elegant and cozy, with four-poster beds and other antiques splashed with natural light from the windows. You'll feel like you're waking up in the country. Four more rooms in the Kumquat House, also on the grounds, are in no way a compromise, maintaining the same quality atmosphere, style and comfort. For a really private and charming experience, a small Creole cottage with its own gallery and porch (and your own rocking chair) is also hidden away on the grounds. This one has a fireplace. All rooms have private bathroom, many with Jacuzzi tubs. Some have private screened porches, making it possible to enjoy the chirp of crickets at night without being slaughtered by mosquitoes. A large swimming pool will keep you cool and Restaurant Indigo (p195), next door, impresses diners in much the same way. You'll hear the clinking of silverware and want to wander on over.

AIRPORT HOTELS

Lots of flights out of New Orleans depart at the crack of dawn. Not an easy schedule if you've been tempted to make a full night of it in the French Quarter during your last hours in the Big Easy. Nervous, conscientious types might opt for staying as near the tarmac as possible. Many airport chains have free shuttles that take just a few minutes to reach the terminals.

Best Western (☎ 800-528-1238; www.bestwestern.com)

Doubletree (☎ 800-222-8733; www.doubletree.com)

Hilton (☎ 800-872-5914; www.hilton.com)

Sheraton (☎ 800-325-3535; www.sheraton.com)

ESPLANADE VILLA Map p317 $$

☎ 525-7040, 800-308-7040; www.nolabb.com; 2216 Esplanade Ave; ste $135; P

Owned by the same people who run Benachi House (p249), this is an attractive alternative just a few skips away. The house and grounds are not as impressive as those at Benachi, but the rooms are far superior – spacious, colorful, well lit and elegantly furnished with sturdy antiques. All have sitting rooms and private bathroom with pedestal sinks and cast-iron tubs. Bubbles are provided for bath-time frivolity. This is a good place for families to stay. The larger suites can accommodate three or four people comfortably.

Eat the South 253
Cajun Country Ramble 254
Rhythm of the River 254

Plantation Country 254
Along the East Bank 255
Along the West Bank 256

Cajun Country 257
Cajun Wetlands 258
Cajun Prairie 259

Southward to the Swamp 263

Baton Rouge 264

Mississippi Delta 265

Memphis 268

Excursions

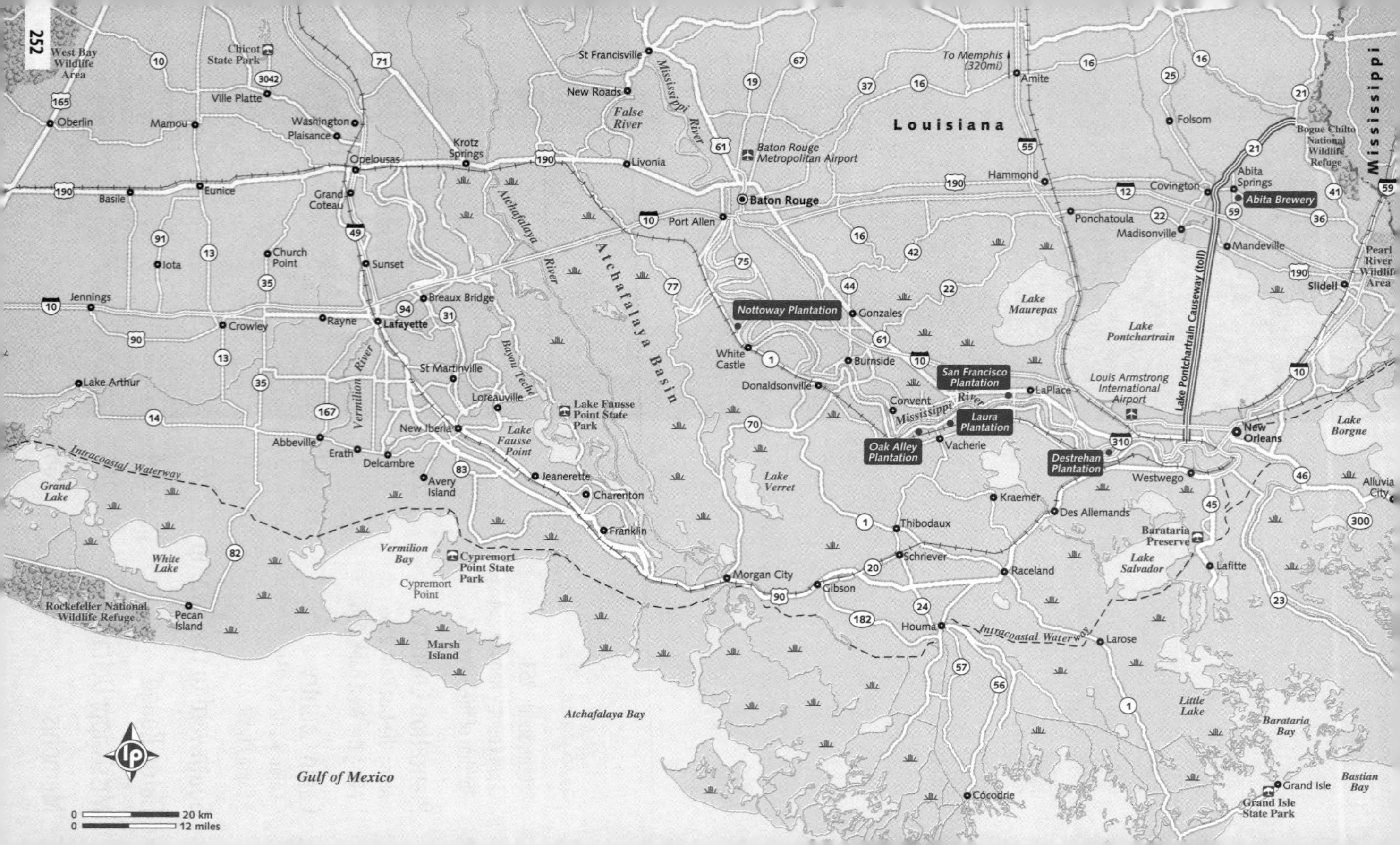

Louisiana
Mississippi
Gulf of Mexico
Atchafalaya Basin
Atchafalaya Bay
Atchafalaya River
Mississippi River
Vermilion River
Bayou Teche
False River
Intracoastal Waterway
Lake Pontchartrain
Lake Pontchartrain Causeway (toll)
Lake Maurepas
Lake Borgne
Lake Verret
Lake Salvador
Little Lake
Barataria Bay
Bastian Bay
Vermilion Bay
Grand Lake
White Lake
Marsh Island
Cypremort Point
Lake Fausse Point
Nottoway Plantation
San Francisco Plantation
Laura Plantation
Oak Alley Plantation
Destrehan Plantation
Abita Brewery
Baton Rouge
Baton Rouge Metropolitan Airport
Louis Armstrong International Airport
New Orleans
Lafayette
To Memphis (320mi)
St Francisville
New Roads
Livonia
Port Allen
Krotz Springs
Opelousas
Washington
Plaisance
Ville Platte
Chicot State Park
Mamou
Oberlin
West Bay Wildlife Area
Basile
Eunice
Grand Coteau
Sunset
Church Point
Iota
Jennings
Crowley
Rayne
Breaux Bridge
St Martinville
Loreauville
New Iberia
Lake Fausse Point State Park
Lake Arthur
Abbeville
Erath
Delcambre
Avery Island
Jeanerette
Charenton
Franklin
Cypremort Point State Park
Morgan City
Gibson
Houma
Schriever
Thibodaux
Raceland
Kraemer
Des Allemands
Larose
Cocodrie
Grand Isle
Grand Isle State Park
Lafitte
Barataria Preserve
Westwego
Alluvia City
Vacherie
Convent
LaPlace
Donaldsonville
Burnside
White Castle
Gonzales
Hammond
Amite
Ponchatoula
Madisonville
Mandeville
Covington
Abita Springs
Folsom
Bogue Chitto National Wildlife Refuge
Slidell
Pearl River Wildlife Area
Rockefeller National Wildlife Refuge
Pecan Island
0 20 km
0 12 miles

Excursions

New Orleans is a unique city within a fascinating region. Many travelers who come to New Orleans set aside a few days to get out to the hinterlands of southern Louisiana, and some even take the opportunity to scoot up through the Mississippi Delta and Memphis. While there are a few worthy destinations within day trip distance (two hours' drive from the city), most really require at least an overnight stay.

Crawfish pond in Cajun Country (p257)

Day trip options include driving south to paddle a canoe through the swamp at the Jean Lafitte National Historic Park; heading southwest to the Cajun Wetlands and coming face to face with a gator on a swamp tour; driving across Lake Pontchartrain and having a beer at the Abita Brewery; or wending your way up the River Rd for a glimpse of antebellum opulence.

The Cajun Prairie, where there is so much music and dancing on the weekend, is a bit further away. Lafayette, where everything from zydeco music to jambalaya is feted with weekend street parties, is also an overnight excursion. Why rush through such exotic country, where alligators bask in the sun, ice-cold beer awaits in a cinderblock roadhouse just around the bend, accordion music beckons in a pumped-up waltz and spicy boiled crawfish promises to induce a healthy sweat?

Heading further afield, as many travelers do while following the great Blues Hwy, from New Orleans to Memphis, will require at least two nights – or even longer if you're really into American roots music, Elvis, barbecue pork shoulder, big-ass American cars, juke joints and tooling down the lost highways of the rural South.

EAT THE SOUTH

Once you've had your fill of trout meunière, oysters Rockefeller and muffuletta sandwiches, you might be ready to move on out of New Orleans and see what the rest of Louisiana tastes like. Up the River Rd, 'filling station' gets a new meaning at **Hymel's Seafood** (p256), where a turtle sauce piquant and soft-shell crabs will put a little gas in your tank. You can eat Cajun in New Orleans, of course, but the real deal is just two hours' drive away. In New Iberia, you can shovel some jambalaya through your pie hole in unfussy **Victor's Cafeteria** (p262), with fictional detective Dave Robicheaux seated somewhere in the room. Or you can dig into an honest pile of chicken fricassee at **Brenda's Diner** (p261). Over at **Prejean's Restaurant** (p262), outside Lafayette, tuck into a plate of fried catfish as couples two-step to a live Cajun ensemble. Up in Mississippi you'll say, 'Now, this is really the South' when a plate lunch is slid before you at **Walnut Hills** (p267) in Vicksburg, or mouthwatering pulled pork is served on a cheap-ass hamburger bun at **Abe's** (p267) in Clarksdale. Detour slightly over to Greenwood for a meal at **Lusco's** (p267) or **Crystal Grill** (p267) and you'll feel like you've walked onto the set of *O Brother, Where Art Thou?* Have the fish and don't talk to one-eyed strangers. Up in Memphis, you're in barbecue heaven. Try some chopped pork shoulder sammies at **Cozy Corner** (p270) or **Tops Bar-B-Q** (p270), or the dry-rubbed ribs at **Charlie Vergo's** (p270). Then have an Elvis gastronomic experience at **Arcade** (p270). While you're busting your gut, you might also want to do the Cajun Country Ramble or the Rhythm of the River tours.

CAJUN COUNTRY RAMBLE

Alligators don't creep in the gutters of the French Quarter and New Orleanians don't speak French, so if that's what you're after you'll have to have your own personal *grand dérangement*. Do like the Cajun people did in the 1700s: head out into the swamps, the bayou, the Cajun Prairie, and experience a unique culture that exists right here in the US of A. Start out by dipping a paddle into the water at the **Barataria Preserve** (p263), where the pirate Jean Lafitte hid out two centuries ago. In Houma, **Alligator Annie's Son** (p259) will dazzle you by feeding chicken to alligators, those beady-eyed kings of the swamp. Have a sobering look at some toppling slave quarters and trapper shacks at the **Laurel Valley Village** (p259). Lafayette's a gas during the **Festival International de Louisiane** (p257). While in town, eat jambalaya at **T-Coon's** (p262), then wheel on over to St Martinville for a gander at **Evangeline Oak** (p260). Nearby New Iberia is the setting for James Lee Burke's novels and **Shadows on the Teche** (p261), a magnificent old mansion overlooking the bayou. In Opelousas, you can shake your crazy ass to zydeco music at **Slim's Y-Ki-Ki** (p262). At Mamou's **Fred's Lounge** (p262) you can get drunk with some old Cajun characters at 8am on Saturday morning while a live band plays traditional dances. Son of a gun, if it ain't good fun.

RHYTHM OF THE RIVER

Must be something about the drinking water they've been siphoning out of the Big Muddy. Along the Mississippi, America's best music sprouted up out of the ground and spread like vines. Blues, jazz, soul, gospel, Cajun, zydeco, rhythm and blues, rock and roll. It all happened on the Old Man's floodplain.

Of course, New Orleans is part of this tour. Once you've done jazz at **Donna's** (p206), Thursday night at **Vaughan's** (p208), trad jazz at **Preservation Hall** (p207), modern jazz at **Snug Harbor** (p208) and R&B at the **Mid-City Lanes Rock & Bowl** (p209), head upstream.

You'll want to make it up to the Cajun Prairie on the weekend. Friday and Saturday nights are good bets for live zydeco at either **Slim's Y-Ki-Ki** (p262) or **Richard's Club** (p262) in Opelousas. Saturday morning presents a tough choice, both options involving live Cajun music: if you feel like getting drunk before lunch, head to **Fred's Lounge** (p262) in Mamou. If you have a strict rule about not drinking before the morning fog lifts, head to **Savoy Music Center** (p261), where living legend Marc Savoy plays some lovely old tunes on his accordion.

The Mississippi Delta is just a few hours north by car. You'll soak up the languid, bluesy vibe of the place just by driving through the Delta's sleepy old towns. Once you reach Clarksdale, head to **Ground Zero** (p267) for live music or to **Red's** (p267) for a real juke joint experience. Up in Memphis, you'll catch more blues at **BB King's** (p270) and bow to the rock and roll gods at **Graceland** (p269) and **Sun Studio** (p269). The **Stax Museum** (p269) honors the city's soul music legacy.

PLANTATION COUNTRY

Elaborate plantation homes line the banks of the Mississippi River between New Orleans and Baton Rouge along the River Rd. Here, relatively simple French-Creole plantation homes, like those found at Vacherie, stand in stark contrast with the Greek-revival mansions built by American settlers after the Louisiana Purchase in 1803.

No matter what the architectural style on the River Rd, the stories of plantation slave society get short shrift. Instead, the emphasis is on the glory of days past, when black men and women of bondage labored at the behest of white masters. Save for the River Rd African American Museum and the Laura Plantation tours, you will get a feel for what life was like for the master and missus, but rarely will you catch a glimpse of life out the back of the big house, where slaves made the bricks, raised the roofs, tended the fires and worked the fields. Expect costumed guides leading interior tours of 45 to 60 minutes, which focus on the lovely architecture, ornate gardens and genteel lifestyle of antebellum Louisiana. Admission usually includes a guided tour of the main house and self-guided tours of the grounds with their enormous moss-draped live oaks.

To understand the area, you must know a bit about agriculture. Throughout the French colonial stewardship, rice and indigo were the principal plantation crops. But, in 1795, with the introduction of the open-kettle process, which enabled sugar to be reduced to more easily transportable crystals, the agricultural economy was transformed. Sugarcane planting expanded exponentially during the antebellum period – as did slave ownership. Financial success led to the proliferation of grand plantation homes for which River Rd is now known. On the eve of the Civil War in 1861, Louisiana had 1200 plantations producing 95% of the sugar in the US.

Following the war, less than 200 plantations remained. Blacks and whites alike left the plantations in droves, heading north and west in search of jobs. Today many of the grand homes are open to the public, although the setting is far different than it once was. Where once stretched mile after mile of sugarcane fields, now sit myriad chemical plants and refineries, belching sulfurous clouds of smoke morning, noon and night – suffocating the surrounding countryside in a wet blanket of industrial fog. It's a truly surreal juxtaposition of old and new.

Looking at a map, the East Bank is the area above the Mississippi River, which curves in an easterly direction here. The West Bank is the area below the river. 'Downriver' means heading southeastward, as the river flows toward New Orleans. 'Upriver' means northwestward, against the river's flow, toward Baton Rouge.

River Rd is a name given, not to one particular road, but to the various routes that follow the sinuous levees. As an example, traveling upriver on the east bank, River Rd will show up on a map as Hwy 48, then Hwy 44 and then Hwy 942, yet few of the towns you pass through will display any signage to indicate the change in highway numbers. Sound confusing? It isn't. Just keep the river in sight, and remember that ferry crossings are offered frequently. Should you stop to ask directions, memorize the difference between upriver and downriver, East Bank and West Bank before you ask.

TRANSPORTATION

Car Between New Orleans and Baton Rouge, I-10 provides motorists with the quickest access to the winding, river-levee roads. Alternately, parallel to I-10, Hwy 61, once the primary artery north, offers a glimpse of the US roadside past. Ferries still outnumber bridges across the Mississippi River. Don't despair if you're still on the road at 6pm and have 8pm dinner reservations in New Orleans. Even the distant upriver plantations are not much more than a one-hour drive from the city via I-10.

Ferry A few motorists and all bicyclists use the state-operated ferries ($1 toll traveling westward, free eastward) to cross the river.

ALONG THE EAST BANK

Only 12 miles from New Orleans International Airport, **Destrehan Plantation**, downriver from I-310, is the oldest plantation home remaining in the lower Mississippi Valley. Indigo was the principal crop in 1787 when Antoine Robert Robin DeLongy hired a mulatto builder to construct the original French colonial–style mansion, using *bousillage* (mud- and straw-filled) walls supported by cypress timbers. The house features a distinctive African-style hipped roof – no doubt a tip of the hat to the builder's ancestry. When DeLongy's daughter, Celeste, married Jean Noel Destrehan, they added the present Greek-revival façade. Tours by costumed guides cost $10 for adults, $5 for teens and $3 for children.

The stunning 'steamboat Gothic' **San Francisco Plantation**, 20 miles upriver from I-310, is on a 1700-acre site purchased in 1830 by Edmond B Marmillion from Elisee Rillieux, a free person of color. With $100,000 and 100 slaves, Marmillion's son, Valsin, built a grand sugar plantation. Today, only the architectural confection of the house and metal-domed cisterns remain. The surrounding fields where sugarcane once grew now sprout smokestacks. Tours of the ornately furnished interior are $10 for adults, $5 for teens and $3 for children.

Three impressive homes upriver can be admired from the road. **Houmas House**, 4 miles upriver from the Sunshine Bridge, was named for the Native American tribe that once inhabited the area. It offers a postcard image of the great Greek-revival plantation home that has long been associated with Louisiana. The original structure, built in the 1790s, now forms the back end of the main house, which was built in 1840. Another 2 miles and 3 miles along are two private antebellum homes worth a drive-by: **Bocage Plantation House**, built in 1801 and remodeled in 1840, and the **Hermitage Plantation House**, built in 1812 by Marius Bringier, a Haitian builder responsible for many of the region's homes, including Whitehall, Tezcuco and Bocage. Its impressive Tuscan brick columns were added in 1838.

Information

Ascension Parish Tourist Center (☎ 225-675-6550; cnr Hwys 22 & 70) In the purposefully quaint Cajun Village, near I-10 exit 182, this info stop offers state and local maps and information.

Sights

Destrehan Plantation (☎ 985-764-9315; www.destrehanplantation.org; 13034 Hwy 48; adult/child $10/5; 9:30am-4pm)

San Francisco Plantation (☎ 985-535-2341; www.sanfranciscoplantation.org; Hwy 44; adult/child $10/5; 10am-4pm)

Eating

Airline Motors Restaurant (☎ 985-652-9181; 221 E Airline/Hwy 61, La Place; 4am-10pm Mon-Thu, 24hr Fri-Sun) This is a rough-edged art-deco palace embellished with enough glass blocks, chrome and neon to send you reeling. Grab a seat at the counter and take it all in while enjoying a cup of surprisingly good chicken-andouille gumbo ($3) or a BLT.

Cabin Restaurant (☎ 225-473-3007; cnr Hwys 44 & 22, Burnside; dishes $5-11; 11am-3pm Mon, 11am-9pm Tue-Sat, 11am-6pm Sun) Two miles from the River Rd, this rustic old joint is in a collection of slave dwellings and other dependencies rescued from the demolished Monroe, Welham and Helvetia plantations. The interior walls are papered with old newspapers in the same manner that slaves once insulated the rough-sawn walls of their cabins. Besides po'boys you can get dishes such as red beans and rice with sausage, an omelette filled with crawfish étouffée, or a broiled or fried seafood plate. Even though the restaurant is geared toward serving the tourist crowds, the food is actually pretty good.

Hymel's Seafood (☎ 225-562-7031; 8740 Hwy 44, Convent; dishes $5-10; 11am-2:30pm Tue-Thu, 11am-10pm Fri & Sat, 11am-8pm Sun) A local favorite for over 40 years, this former filling station serves a fine platter of soft-shell crab, as well as turtle sauce piquant and weekday lunch specials. It is 4 miles downriver from the Sunshine Bridge.

ALONG THE WEST BANK

Laura Plantation, at Vacherie, is a comparatively unassuming West Indies-style plantation home, built in 1805 by Guillaume Duparc and named for his granddaughter, Laura Locoul. Rather than a pristine showplace, Laura Plantation is a work in progress, an ongoing historical experiment, wherein visitors are invited to imagine life as it existed for both slave and master. Here, thanks to the ongoing restoration efforts that give you a carpenter's-eye view of repairs, you will come to understand how these monstrous homes were constructed, and what back-breaking labor was required for their upkeep. A 2004 fire damaged more than half the house, and rebuilding efforts have been underway since, but the tours are still worthwhile, primarily for the history they convey.

Just upriver of Laura Plantation, **Oak Alley Plantation** features the most dramatic approach of all the plantations: a quarter-mile canopy of majestic live oaks running from the River Rd to the house. The 28 trees, 14 on each side of the driveway, predate the house by 100 years. More symmetry awaits at the plantation house, which is built in Greek-revival style: 28 columns, each 8ft in diameter, frame the scene. Tours are offered daily.

Donaldsonville is a pleasant little town with a surprising collection of good restaurants, making it by far the best place to stop for a meal. It's also home to the **Historic Donaldsonville Museum**, a charming paean to small-town life set in a majestic, white masonry building that was once home to the Lemann Department Store.

The **River Road African American Museum** was started by Kathe Hambrick, a local African American woman who, after visiting a plantation several years ago, decided that someone needed to tell the story of the slaves. This growing museum details the history of the rural blacks of Louisiana. The emphasis is not only on the indignity of slavery, but also on the achievements of black doctors, artists and others throughout history.

But the premier attraction in town, indeed one of the premier attractions on the River Rd, is **Rossie's Custom Framing**, where the works of folk artist Alvin Batiste are on display. His depictions of life in his hometown will take your breath away. And the prices are more than reasonable, with most pieces falling between the $100 to $500 range. Most days, he sets up his easel in the shop's window, so he can watch the street life passing by. Hours vary, but afternoons are the best time to catch him in.

For sheer size, **Nottoway Plantation**, 2 miles north of White Castle and built between 1849 and 1859 by Virginian sugar planter John Hampton Randolph, is the finest on the river.

The largest plantation house in the South, it has 64 rooms covering 53,000 sq ft. Guides don't wear costumes and don't deliver any drama, yet the tours are rich in personal history. The house has original furnishings and period pieces. Wide galleries with rocking chairs are accessible to visitors who wish to sit and gaze out upon the river.

Sights

Historic Donaldsonville Museum (☎ 225-746-0004; cnr Railroad & Mississippi Sts; 🕑 10am-4pm Tue, Thu & Sat)

Laura Plantation (☎ 225-265-7690; www.lauraplantation.com; 2247 Hwy 18, Vacherie; adult/child $10/5; 🕑 Mon-Sun)

Nottoway Plantation (☎ 225-545-2730; www.nottoway.com; Hwy 1; adult/child $10/4; 🕑 9am-5pm)

Oak Alley Plantation (☎ 225-265-2151; www.oakalleyplantation.com; 3645 Hwy 18, Vacherie; adult/child $10/5; 🕑 9am-5pm)

River Road African American Museum (☎ 225-474-5553; www.africanamericanmuseum.org; 406 Charles St, Donaldsonville; admission $4; 🕑 10am-5pm Wed-Sat, 1-5pm Sun)

Rossie's Custom Framing (☎ 225-473-8536; www.alvinbatiste.com; 510 Railroad Ave, Donaldsonville; 🕑 9am-5pm Mon-Sat, 10am-3pm Sun)

Eating

B&C Seafood Market & Cajun Deli (☎ 225-265-8356; 2155 Hwy 18, Vacherie; meals $5-9; 🕑 9am-6pm Mon-Sat) If you stick to fried seafood po'boys, you'll eat well here. It's convenient to Laura Plantation and Oak Alley Plantation.

First & Last Chance Café (☎ 225-473-8236; 812 Railroad Ave, Donaldsonville; meals $3-20; 🕑 9am-midnight Mon-Sat) A relic of the time when this trackside joint was the only place to grab a drink on the rail trip from New Orleans to Baton Rouge. Great burgers and toothsome steaks smothered in garlic sauce are the best bets.

Railroad Café (☎ 225-473-8513; 212 Railroad Ave, Donaldsonville; meals $5-9; 🕑 10am-2pm Mon-Wed, 10am-7:30pm Thu-Sat) In an old grocery store, this casual spot is perfect for a plate lunch or a fried oyster po'boy.

CAJUN COUNTRY

Although much of Cajun Country is beyond the traditional driving distance (two hours) for a day trip, the sights, sounds and smells of the region often draw travelers away from New Orleans for two or three days. It's a land of rural French-speaking farmers and fishers, of Cajun and zydeco dancehalls and a unique cuisine that influences chefs worldwide.

In 1755, *le grand dérangement,* the British expulsion of the rural French settlers from L'Acadie (now Nova Scotia), created a homeless population of Acadians who searched for decades for a place to settle. In 1785 seven boatloads of exiles arrived in New Orleans. By the early 19th century some 3000 to 4000 Acadians, or Cajuns as they became known, lived in southern Louisiana. Early German peasant farmers also produced crops for the New

CAJUN COUNTRY CALENDAR

Louisiana's smaller towns seem to be in a constant state of celebration. A local festival – be it a church fair, a Christmas festival or a competitive gumbo cook-off – can provide great opportunities to rub shoulders with the locals and explore the state's regional specialties. For a full calendar with dates and details, check the website of the **Louisiana Association of Fairs & Festivals** (www.laffnet.org).

February – La Grande Boucherie, St Martinville; Courir de Mardi Gras, Mamou

April – Ponchatoula Strawberry Festival, Ponchatoula; Festival International de Louisiane, Lafayette

May – Breaux Bridge Crawfish Festival, Breaux Bridge

July – Greater Mandeville Seafood Festival, Mandeville; Catfish Festival, Des Allemands

August – Delcambre Shrimp Festival, Delcambre

September – Southwest Louisiana Zydeco Festival, Plaisance; Frog Festival, Rayne; Festival Acadiens, Lafayette; Louisiana Sugarcane Festival, New Iberia

October – Andouille Festival, LaPlace; Yambilee, Opelousas; St Martinville Pepper Festival, St Martinville

Orleans market in the vicinity of Thibodaux. In about 1780, Isleños (Canary Islanders) arrived on the upper Bayou Lafourche, and by 1800, Acadians and Americans extended down the bayou to Thibodaux. Today the entire polyglot mix has a tendency to proudly call themselves Cajuns.

Some occupied the swamplands southwest of New Orleans, where they eked out a living based upon fishing and trapping, while others settled further inland in the prairie region, where animal husbandry and farming were the primary vocations. Thus, two distinct subregions developed with substantially different cultures. Lafayette, the self-proclaimed capital of French Louisiana, straddles both.

Cajun Country encompasses a 22-parish region of southern Louisiana: a triangle bound by the Mississippi River Delta and the wetlands south of New Orleans, the uplands near Ville Platte and the Texan borderlands west of Lake Charles. The region is home to the largest French-speaking minority in the US.

CAJUN WETLANDS

The maze of bayous and swamps arching southwest of New Orleans and up to Lafayette is where the first Cajuns settled. Their traditional lifestyle is still in evidence, though now it's mostly older folks who speak French and fish the waterways. As their culture fades away, the land itself is disappearing. Louisiana's coastal waterways are eroding at an alarming rate, due in part to natural subsidence, which happens when silty alluvial land compresses under its own weight. As the land sinks, the Gulf of Mexico moves in, denuding freshwater ecosystems with the saltwater intrusion. Annually, an area the size of Manhattan is lost forever along Louisiana's coast and, as the Gulf of Mexico inches its way north, some of the smaller fishing villages along Bayou Lafourche are literally disintegrating.

But enough of the doom and gloom. Let's appreciate the Cajun Wetlands while we can and hope that slack politicians wake up and approve funding to correct the region's environmental imbalance.

Positioned at the confluence of Bayou Lafourche and Bayou Terrebonne, **Thibodaux** (*ti-buh-dough*; population 14,400) was, at a time when water travel was preeminent, the most important town between New Orleans and Bayou Teche. It has been the Lafourche Parish seat since 1820. The copper-domed **courthouse** (cnr 2nd & Green Sts), was built in 1855 and remains a testament to Thibodaux's glory days.

Laurel Valley Village, about 2 miles east of town on Hwy 308 down Bayou Lafourche, is a sugar plantation that was established in 1785. Among the cane fields is one of the best-preserved assemblages of plantation slave structures in the state. Overall, some 60 structures survive, including the old general store and a school house. On your way out, stop by the store, which you'll find halfway between Laurel Valley and town, to get information and see some local crafts.

The **Wetlands Cajun Cultural Center** is a spacious museum and gallery operated by the National Park Service (NPS). Exhibits cover virtually every aspect of Cajun life in the wetlands, from music to the environmental impacts of trapping and oil exploration. Visitors learn about 'the time of shame,' from 1916 to 1968, when the Louisiana Board of Education discouraged speakers of Cajun-French. Cajun musicians jam at the center from 5pm to 7pm on Monday evenings.

The economic hub of the Cajun Wetlands region is **Houma**, a town of 30,000. It was named for the Houma tribe of Native Americans who were displaced in the mid-19th century by the Acadians. Driving into town, up and over the many bridges that crisscross the numerous bodies of water wending their way through the city center (Bayou Black, Little Bayou Black, the Intracoastal Waterway and Bayou Terrebonne), you come to appreciate Houma's self-styled moniker, Venice of America. That said, the city itself offers little of interest to visitors, save functioning as a way station for travelers heading to the docks just west of town, from where two of the area's best swamp tours depart.

Annie Miller's Son's Swamp and Marsh Tours is run by the son of Alligator Annie, a local legend in the swamp-tour business. He, and his mom before him, have been feeding chicken drumsticks to the alligator babies for so long that they're now conditioned to respond to the sound of his approaching motor and rise from the muck to take a bite. No matter whether you take advantage of the moment as a photo opportunity or plunge headlong for the opposite side of the boat, it's great fun. It's 8 miles west of town. Call ahead for reservations.

Cajun Man's Swamp Cruise is run by Black Guidry, who serenades his passengers with a bit of accordion music, while piloting them through a scenic slice of Bayou Black with his trusty dog Gator Bait at his side. It's 10 miles west of Houma.

Information

Thibodaux Chamber of Commerce (☎ 985-446-1187; 1048 E Canal St, Thibodaux) Stop by here for maps and information on local events.

Visitor center (☎ 985-868-2732; cnr Hwy 90 & St Charles St, Houma) West of the town limits, this info center is operated by the local tourist commission.

Sights

Annie Miller's Son's Swamp and Marsh Tours (☎ 985-868-4758, 800-341-5441; www.annie-miller.com; 3718 Southdown Mandalay Rd, Houma; adult/child $15/10)

Cajun Man's Swamp Cruise (☎ 985-868-4625; Hwy 90; adult/child $15/10)

General Store (Hwy 308; 10am-3pm Tue-Fri, noon-3pm Sat & Sun)

Laurel Valley Village (☎ 985-446-7456; Hwy 308, Thibodaux; 10am-4pm Tue-Fri, 11am-5pm Sat & Sun)

Wetlands Cajun Cultural Center (☎ 985-448-1375; 314 St Mary St, Thibodaux; 9am-7pm Mon, 9am-6pm Tue-Sun)

TRANSPORTATION

Car Thibodaux is 60 miles west of New Orleans, best reached by taking I-10 to the I-310 crossing of the Mississippi River, and then following Hwy 90 to Hwy 1, which parallels Bayou Lafourche for 17 miles to Thibodaux. Houma is 60 miles west of New Orleans. Take I-10 west to I-310, cross the Mississippi River and follow Hwy 90 south into town. Thibodaux is just 20 miles northwest of Houma by way of Hwy 24.

Eating

A-Bear's Café (☎ 985-872-6306; 809 Bayou Black Dr, Houma; meals $6-12; 7am-5pm Mon-Thu, 7am-10pm Fri, 7am-2pm Sat) It looks and feels like an old country store. Although it caters to the tourist trade, you'll find a good measure of locals inside, tucking into plates of red beans and rice, po'boys and plate lunch specials, topped off with a slice of icebox pie. On most Friday nights there's a live Cajun band.

Bayou Delight Restaurant (☎ 985-876-4879; Hwy 90, Houma; meals $9-14; 11am-10pm) About 7 miles west of Houma, this place may display shellacked alligator snouts in the showcase by the register, but don't let that dissuade you; it's not really a tourist trap. Start with homemade onion rings, followed by a plate of white beans and rice with fried catfish. Most Friday and Saturday nights, it offers live Cajun or country music.

Gros Place (☎ 985-446-6623; 710 St Patrick St, Thibodaux; 9am-midnight) A popular spot set in an old service station where locals gather to shoot pool and quaff beer after beer. Stop by on a Friday evening and you're likely to get a chance to sample some deep-fried turkey, which the proprietor cooks for the crowd.

Rob's Donuts (☎ 985-447-4080; cnr St Mary & Tiger Sts, Thibodaux; 24hr) For breakfast, this is the place to try for praline-stuffed pastries oozing with pecans and syrup.

CAJUN PRAIRIE

Northwest of Lafayette is the Cajun Prairie, an area of cattle ranches and rice and crawfish farms settled by Acadians and Creoles. Most importantly, this part of Louisiana is where you're most likely to find Cajun and zydeco music.

Known as the 'Hub City,' **Lafayette** (population 115,000) is best treated as a base from which you can explore the rural Cajun communities. There are nearly 4000 hotel and 60 B&B rooms in the city, with the usual chains at or near exits 101 and 103, off I-10. Lafayette becomes a destination in itself when one of the city's great music festivals are on (see Cajun Country Calendar, p257).

This is not an easy town to navigate, so here's a primer: I-10 traverses the north side of town; Evangeline Thruway bisects I-10 along parallel one-way streets.

The NPS-run **Acadian Cultural Center** has interactive displays that give life to local-folk ways. The highlight is the Cajun joke-telling booth.

Vermilionville is a living history and folk-life museum. It is a bit corny, with docents in period costumes guiding you through a 19th-century Cajun village. Bands perform in the barn, and there are cooking demonstrations and tastings. Less glitzy is **Acadian Village**, where you follow a brick path around a rippling bayou to restored houses, craft shops and a church. Be sure to check out the display dedicated to Dudley LeBlanc, the man behind Hadacol, an infamous patent medicine peddled as a quack's cure to gullible folks.

St Martinville is a picture-postcard beautiful town, worthy of an hour or two of ambling about. Massive **Evangeline Oak**, poised along Bayou Teche just off Main St, has become a lodestar for those seeking a connection to the Acadians deposed during *le grand dérangement*. Thanks go, in large part, to Henry Wadsworth Longfellow's 1847 epic poem *Evangeline*, which recounts the story of star-crossed French lovers Evangeline and Gabriel. To gain a deeper understanding of the events that compelled Longfellow to write his ode and to grasp how African Americans have made this region their own, visit the **Museum of the Acadian Memorial and African American Museum**, which is alongside Evangeline Oak. At **Longfellow-Evangeline State Historical Site**, a former sugar plantation, the lush grounds boast huge moss-draped trees, a narrow bayou and a restored, raised Creole cottage (1815) that is open for tours. It's a mile north of town on Hwy 31.

Shadows on the Teche plantation

New Iberia was settled by the Spanish in 1779 and the town prospered on the sugarcane of surrounding plantations. Today the town's best-known native son is mystery writer James Lee Burke, whose page-turning Detective Dave Robicheaux novels take place in and around New Iberia. A stroll down Main St, past the courthouse and **Victor's Cafeteria**, puts you squarely inside Robicheaux's world. You might even run into Burke, who still winters in the town. Any walk around should start at **Shadows on the Teche**, a grand, Greek-revival plantation house set on the banks of Bayou Teche. End your tour in City Park along the bayou.

Drive southwest of New Iberia along Hwy 329 through cane fields to **Avery Island**, home of the **McIlhenny Tabasco factory** and a wildlife sanctuary. The island is actually a salt dome that extends 8 miles below the surface. The salt mined here goes into the sauce, as do the locally grown peppers. The peppers and salt mixture ferments in oak barrels before it's mixed with vinegar, strained and bottled. At the factory gift shop, order a bag of the 'Tabasco dregs,' which are the lees strained when making the sauce, and you'll gain a fine seasoning mix and get a free tour to boot. Nearby, at **Jungle Gardens** you can drive or walk through 250 acres of subtropical jungle flora and view an amazing array of water birds (especially snowy egrets, which nest here), turtles and alligators. Watch for turtles and peacocks crossing the road.

Opelousas is the epicenter of Louisiana zydeco club culture. You have not really experienced this music until you've made the trek to **Slim's Y-Ki-Ki** or **Richard's Club**, two of the most venerable venues in the state. Although it might be best to call ahead, you can almost be assured that, on the weekends, these wobbly wood-frame buildings will be featuring local acts of international renown. These are the kinds of clubs where if you aren't dancing, someone will pull you out of your chair and onto the dancefloor.

COURIR DE MARDI GRAS

In 1950, Mamou citizens revived the Cajun Mardi Gras traditional, where, instead of tossing beads from floats, celebrants mount horses and tear off through the countryside, often collecting the ingredients for a gumbo from nearby farmers. The garb worn (colorful suits, spooky wire-mesh masks) adds to the mystique. Mamou hosts a street party on the Monday night of Mardi Gras and sends its riders out at 7am on Tuesday morning, welcoming drunken celebrants back to 6th St at around 3pm that afternoon.

Outlanders are welcomed with open arms. If you're keen on learning a bit more about zydeco, stop by the **Opelousas Museum and Interpretive Center**, where they house a collection of recordings.

Eunice is the unofficial capital of prairie Cajun heritage. The best day to visit is Saturday, when the **Liberty Theater** is open. Built in 1924, the theater is best known for its Rendez-vous des Cajuns, which is a Saturday-night performance broadcast on local radio stations. The Rendez-vous des Cajuns features traditional Cajun music in a variety-show format. **Savoy Music Center**, 3 miles east of town, houses the accordion factory of musician Marc Savoy. On most Saturday mornings, Savoy hosts a Cajun-music jam session here from around 9am to noon; his wife, Ann, a guitarist, often joins him. Look for the huge Savoy Music Company sign west of the Cajun Campground. The **Cajun Music Hall of Fame**, showcasing Cajun instruments and other musical memorabilia, is also worth a peek.

Mamou is a rough-and-tumble prairie town that has seen better days. The main drag, 6th St, is a ragtag collection of sleepy businesses and boarded storefronts. And yet, this little backwater calls itself the 'Cajun music capital' and backs its claim with a crazy 8am Saturday morning booze fest at **Fred's Lounge**. A live, traditional Cajun band plays charming country waltzes for a jovial crowd getting awfully merry in the wee hours. Mamou is on Hwy 13, about 12 miles north of Hwy 190. Eunice is 15 minutes away, and Opelousas 25 minutes.

Information

Acadian Cultural Center (☎ 337-232-0789; 501 Fisher Rd, Lafayette; admission free)

Eunice Chamber of Commerce (☎ 337-457-2565, 800-222-2342; Hwy 13, Eunice) Operates a visitors center downtown.

Lafayette Visitor Center (☎ 318-232-3737; Evangeline Thruway, Lafayette)

Prairie Acadian Cultural Center (☎ 337-457-8490; cnr Third St & Park Ave, Eunice)

Sights

Acadian Village (☎ 337-981-2364; www.acadianvillage.org; 200 Greenleaf Dr, Lafayette; adult/child $7/3; 🕑 10am-4pm)

African American Museum (☎ 337-394-2258; St Martinville; adult/child $2/1; 🕑 10am-4pm)

Cajun Music Hall of Fame (☎ 337-457-6534; 240 S CC Duson Dr, Eunice; admission free; 🕑 9am-4pm Tue-Sat)

Jungle Gardens (☎ 337-365-8173; Avery Island; adult/child $6/4; 🕑 9am-5pm)

Liberty Theater (☎ 337-457-7389; cnr S Second St & Park Ave, Eunice; adult/child/teen under 12 $5/free/3; 🕑 ticket office 4-6pm Sat, shows 6-7:30pm Sat)

Longfellow-Evangeline State Historical Site (☎ 337-394-3754; 1200 N Main St, St Martinville; admission $2; 🕑 9am-5pm)

McIlhenny Tabasco (☎ 337-365-8173; Avery Island; admission free; 🕑 tours 9am-4pm)

Museum of the Acadian Memorial and Opelousas Museum and Interpretive Center (☎ 337-948-2589; 315 N Main St, Opelousas; admission free; 🕑 9am-5pm Mon-Sat)

Savoy Music Center (☎ 337-457-9563; www.savoymusiccenter.com; Hwy 190, Eunice; 🕑 9am-4pm)

Shadows on the Teche (☎ 337-365-5213; www.shadowsontheteche.org; 317 E Main St, New Iberia; adult/child $6/3)

Vermilionville (☎ 337-233-4077; www.vermilionville.org; 300 Fisher Rd, Lafayette; adult/student $8/5; 🕑 10am-4pm Tue-Sun)

Eating

Borden's (☎ 337-235-9291; 1103 Jefferson Blvd, Lafayette) At this classic ice creamery, order a sundae or milkshake, slide into a red-vinyl booth beneath the Elsie the Cow portrait and enjoy.

Brenda's Diner (☎ 337-367-0868; 409 W Pershing St, New Iberia; dishes $6-12) For soul food and plate lunches duck into this beautiful little shack. Whether you're hankering for fried chicken, fried pork chops, sausages, candied yams, chicken fricassee or smothered okra – your gut will bust and you'll be happy. Call ahead, as hours are irregular.

TRANSPORTATION

Bus Greyhound runs from New Orleans to Lafayette (☎ 337-235-1541; cnr Clinton & Lee Sts) and Opelousas (☎ 337-942-2702; 1210 W Landry St).

Car Lafayette is an hour west of Baton Rouge and two hours west of New Orleans by way of I-10. St Martinville is about 15 miles southeast of Lafayette. New Iberia is 30 minutes southeast of Lafayette by way of Hwy 90. To get to Opelousas from Baton Rouge, take Hwy 190 west for 45 miles. Eunice is 20 miles west of Opelousas on Hwy 190 and about 20 miles north of I-10 exit 80 at Crowley.

THE CAJUN BOUCHERIE *Pableaux Johnson*

If you're squeamish about slaughter and prefer not to see your food in extremely raw form, you'd better skip the early stages of the traditional Acadian *boucherie* (communal pig butchering). Once a critical part of any Cajun community's culinary life, the *boucherie* is now less of a family affair than a large-scale festival celebrating the noble pig and its contribution to Louisiana cuisine. The most well-known celebration, La Grande Boucherie, is held every February in the small Acadian town of St Martinville.

In the early morning hours a pig is killed; its throat slit and the blood caught in a basin, to be used in the production of boudin rouge (pork-blood sausage). Since boudin rouge cannot be sold commercially due to health regulations, a *boucherie* may be the only place where you can enjoy this Cajun specialty.

Next, the pig is split, scraped and skinned, and the fatty hide is rendered in black-iron cauldrons over open fires to make cracklings (known as gratons in local French-Cajun dialect). Much early-morning beer drinking accompanies this bloody work – both for the workers and onlookers.

The carcass is then hoisted up onto a table and butchered into its various components. The head, shoulders and feet are placed in a pot to cook all day for hog's head cheese (a chunky, gelatinous sausage made from the meat of the pig's head). The backbone is made into a stew called *reintier de cochon*, the ribs are used for the barbecue and all the remaining meat is ground up to make the various specialty sausages, including boudin blanc, boudin rouge and andouille.

Before the advent of refrigeration, *boucheries* were regular events during the cooler months in southern Louisiana. As the fresh meat could not be kept for too long, families would gather together to slaughter a hog, prepare the meat and divide it up among themselves. The following week another family's pig would be slaughtered and the whole bloody process would begin again.

It takes all day to slaughter and prepare the animal but a *boucherie* is traditionally a family event and everybody pitches in – preparing seasonings, piping filling into the clean sausage casings, playing music and cooking the cracklings. The day traditionally ends with a plate of backbone stew, some fresh boudin, music and an informal *fais do-do*. The modern variation of the *boucherie* resembles the other cultural festivals of the area, where most of the spectators show up to eat, dance and toast a few beers to their friend the pig.

Old Tyme Grocery (☎ 337-235-8165; 218 W St Mary St, Lafayette; meals $5-7; 🕑 8am-10pm Mon-Fri, 9am-7pm Sat) For shrimp or roast beef po'boys at lunch or dinner, this no-frills joint is the best in town. In summer, swing round the back for a refreshing snowball treat.

Palace Café (☎ 337-942-2142; Hwy 190, Opelousas; meals $8-12; 🕑 11am-9pm) A downtown Opelousas institution, the Palace has been in business since 1954 and is famous for onion rings and fried chicken.

Prejean's Restaurant (☎ 337-896-3247; 3480 I-29 N, Lafayette; dishes $9-22; 🕑 8am-10pm) It's a fancified food barn with checkered tablecloths, but Prejean's does fine Cajun standards (good gumbo) and fried fish plates, and here and there offers up innovations. Local families cram the joint, especially on Saturday night when a live Cajun band cranks it up.

Ruby's Café (221 W Walnut Ave, Eunice; dishes $3-10; 🕑 8am-2pm) In business since 1958, Ruby's is a traditional lunch counter where stewed shrimp on rice is tops.

T-Coons (☎ 337-232-3803; 740 Jefferson Blvd, Lafayette; meals $5-12; 🕑 11am-2pm Mon-Fri) Lafayette's lunchtime favorite for hefty smothered pork chops or jambalaya.

Victor's Cafeteria (☎ 337-369-9924; 109 E Main St, New Iberia; dishes $5-14; 🕑 6am-2pm Mon-Fri, 6am-10am Sat, 6:30am-2pm Sun) James Lee Burke's detective Dave Robicheaux likes to drop by this place, and so do his fans. Locals and tourists alike line up at the counter to order favorites such as gumbo and fried shrimp, and home-style Cajun standards in this laid-back little landmark.

Entertainment

Fred's Lounge (☎ 337-468-5411; 420 6th St, Mamou)

Richard's Club (☎ 337- 543-6596; Hwy 190 W, Opelousas)

Slim's Y-Ki-Ki (☎ 337-942-9980; Hwy 167 N, Opelousas)

Sleeping

Estorage-Norton House (☎ 337-365-7603; 446 E Main St, New Iberia; r $60-90) In a historic district, this is a comfortable 100-plus-year-old home with four comfortable bedrooms. Prices include a full breakfast.

Howard's Inn (☎ 337-457-2066; 3789 Hwy 190, Eunice; r $45-55) Outside Eunice, this bargain has clean rooms.

Teche Hotel (☎ 337-369-3756; 1830 E Main St, New Iberia; r $50) East of downtown New Iberia, this classic cottage-style place is on the cheaper side without having any dubious no-tell vibe.

T'Frere's B&B (☎ 337-984-9347, 800-984-9347; www.tfreres.com; 1905 E Verot School Rd, Lafayette; r $95-110) This tidy old brick house has a covered porch and a country feel. It offers six rooms, all with private bathroom. Breakfast is served on the porch.

SOUTHWARD TO THE SWAMP

Below New Orleans, the Mississippi River flows 90 miles to the bird's foot-shaped delta, where river pilots board ships entering from the Gulf. Rather than drive for hours to Venice, the furthest downstream point accessible by automobile, you can satisfy the same desire to travel to the end of the road at **Barataria Preserve** or Lafitte, less than an hour's drive from New Orleans. For those in search of a wetlands adventure, the Barataria Preserve beckons. In the little fishing village of Lafitte, about 10 miles or so south of Barataria down Hwy 45, you will find a wonderful country inn and two great seafood shacks in a setting more reminiscent of the Mosquito Coast than suburban New Orleans.

The Barataria Preserve, a unit of southern Louisiana's Jean Lafitte National Historic Park, is set in an area originally settled by Isleños in 1779. It offers hiking and canoe trips into the swamp and a good introduction to the wetlands environment. It is not a pristine wilderness, as canals and other structures offer evidence of human activity, yet wild animals and plants are abundant. Even a brief walk on the boardwalks that wend their way through the swamp will yield sightings of gators and egrets. Trails in the preserve are open daily from 7am to 5pm, with extended hours during daylight-savings time. Ranger-led walks around Bayou Coquille are offered daily at 2pm. Other activities, which require reservations, include a guided canoe trek on Saturday at 8:30am. On evenings around a full moon, moonlight canoe treks are offered.

After you cross the high-rise bridge and double back onto Hwy 45 heading south, you will first come to the little town of **Jean Lafitte**. Quaint and remote though it may be, it has nothing on the little fishing village of **Lafitte**, some 8 miles further down the road. Soon the road narrows and you can almost feel the swamplands closing in around you. Due to frequent flooding, even the mobile homes down this way are set on stilts, and the Spanish moss hangs heavy – like green streamers tossed pell-mell onto the boughs of the live oak trees. This was once the province of the pirate Jean Lafitte and is now home to a hardy camp of commercial fishers. Around these parts, 90% of the locals still make their living from the waters, and life owes its design to the patterns of the seasons and the sea. Although there are no typical tourist attractions to visit, the abundant waterside funk is worthy of an hour or so of wandering.

Sights & Information

Barataria Preserve/National Park Service Visitors Center (☎ 589-2330; 6588 Barataria Blvd, Marrero; 🕒 9am-5pm) The best place to start a visit to the park is this office, 1 mile west of Hwy 45, where you can pick up a map of the 8 miles of hiking trails and 9 miles of dedicated canoe routes.

Bayou Barn (☎ 689-2663; 2hr canoe rental $15; 🕒 9am-5pm Thu-Sun) This shack, on the Bayou de Familles just outside the Barataria Preserve, has a large supply of canoes for hire. It was once also a restaurant with a fun Sunday afternoon Cajun dance. Call to see if they've reopened that end of the business.

TRANSPORTATION

Bus Infrequent bus services to and from New Orleans are available.

Car To reach the Barataria Preserve take Business Hwy 90 across the Greater New Orleans Bridge to the Westbank Expressway and turn south on Barataria Blvd (Hwy 45) to Hwy 3134, which leads to the national park entrance. The trip takes about 30 minutes. To reach Lafitte, continue south on Hwy 45 past the turnoff for the park. Take a switchback turn on a high-rise bridge and then pass through the town of Jean Lafitte before reaching land's end at Lafitte. Total travel time is 45 minutes or so.

Eating

Restaurant de Familles (☎ 689-7834; meals $8-17; 🕒 noon-8pm Wed-Sun) Behind Bayou Barn, near the Barataria Preserve, de Familles offers upscale dining in a rustic setting. It's a reward for a day of hiking or paddling. The dining room overlooks the bayou, and the menu really shines when soft-shell crabs are in season.

Sleeping

Jean Lafitte Inn (☎ 689-3271; cnr Hwys 45 & 3134; cabins $75-90) Modern cabins are just outside the entrance to the Barataria Preserve, with rustic Earl's Bar next door being one of the real selling points (walk in to Earl's for cabin info and check-in). The inn also rents canoes for use in the preserve; $25 gets you a canoe seating up to three people plus a drop-off and pick-up service in the preserve.

ABITA BREWERY

On the north shore of Lake Pontchartrain you'll find well-to-do bedroom communities like Mandeville, Covington and the former spa town of Abita Springs. It's nice driving the area's rural two-lane blacktops, and it's not far from New Orleans if you're wanting a quick jaunt into the country. The natural springs that attracted health-conscious vacationers to the area are still burbling, but now provide water for the more vital commodity of Abita Beer.

What we're trying tell you is, if you need an incentive for heading up this way, look no further than the **Abita Brewery** (☎ 985-893-3143; www.abita.com; 21084 Hwy 36; admission free; tours 1pm & 2:30pm Sat, 1pm Sun), just a mile or so west of Abita Springs.

This microbrewery produced its first batch in 1986 and has been pumping out fresh, flavorful beers ever since. From its standard amber ale to more ambitious Mardi Gras bock and seasonal Jockimo stout, Abita beers provide a welcome local alternative to the usual corporate lagers.

The crew at Abita are also canny enough to play the intriguing name game with their products; try the dark and malty TurboDog, or the raspberry-enhanced wheat beer Purple Haze. Abita's brewers also vary their offerings according to season by offering a nice bock beer during Mardi Gras, an autumnal Oktoberfest brew, and a thick stout to chase off the winter chill. The brewery also bottles a microbrewed root beer sweetened with cane sugar rather than the more prevalent corn sweeteners.

The once-tiny concern also boasts an adjoining **brewpub** (☎ 985-892-5837; meals $7-19; 11am-10pm Mon-Sun).

The Inn was put out of commission by Hurricane Rita, but try calling as it may have reopened in time for your visit.

Victorian Inn (☎ 689-4757; www.victoriainn.com; Lafitte; r $100-115) On the southern side of the bridge, this place has 14 rooms in two West Indies–style plantation homes surrounded by gardens. Just over the levee looms a lake, known as 'The Pen,' complete with a private dock (which was damaged by Hurricane Rita – hopefully repaired by now!). Some of the rooms are cramped, but the innkeepers are welcoming and extremely knowledgeable about the area, and the surroundings are sure to please guests in search of a respite from cookie-cutter motels.

BATON ROUGE

Baton Rouge suddenly became the largest city in the state when Hurricane Katrina blew thousands of New Orleanians north. The city's population, numbering about 227,000 before the storm, is now estimated at well over 300,000. Thus many New Orleanians who once scoffed at their state's capital now live in it – the rest continue to scoff, however. You have to work hard to find something interesting to do hereabouts, but it can be done. And, in case you were wondering, the city's name, which translates from French as 'red stick,' is said to derive from a Native American practice of painting cypress poles with blood to mark off the boundaries of hunting territories.

The new and old state capitols, casinos and a riverfront entertainment complex are downtown, off I-110. Louisiana State University (LSU) is in the southwest quadrant of the city, off I-10. The neighboring streets are home to parks, inexpensive restaurants, nightclubs, movie theaters and shops. Highland Rd is the main college thoroughfare.

The **Louisiana Capitol**, an art-deco skyscraper built during the height of the Great Depression at a cost of more than $5 million, is populist Governor Huey Long's most visible legacy. Today, the 34-story capitol, a towering palace of marble, is a beauty to behold. On the 27th floor there is an **observation tower** offering sweeping views of the city and the barges chugging by on the river.

Facing the capitol is a massive **monument** to Long. The left hand of Long's bronze likeness rests on a marble replica of the capitol as if it were a scepter. His body is buried beneath. The inscription on the sculpture boasts that he was 'an unconquered friend of the poor who dreamed of the day when the wealth of the land would be spread among the people.'

A few blocks away you'll find the **Old State Capitol**. The imposing Gothic structure now serves as the Center for Political & Governmental History. Worth a look is a 20-minute film bolstered by interactive exhibits, the best of which allows you to stand at a lectern, call up a speech by Huey Long, and then watch and listen as the performance is projected on a screen in front of you while the text scrolls by on a teleprompter.

The state's largest university, **Louisiana State University**, sits on a 650-acre plateau southwest of town and is reached by way of Highland Rd. For visitor information, call ☎ 225-388-5030; for a fall football schedule and tickets, call ☎ 225-388-2184. The **LSU Rural Life Museum** depicts everyday life in the 19th century. You can view a collection of rural buildings typically found on sugar plantations including slave cottages, a commissary, shotgun-style and dogtrot houses, an overseer's home and a sugar house with a 'Jamaica train' of open kettles. The oddest 'attraction' is the controversial sculpture known as 'Uncle Jack,' a tribute to the 'good darkies of Louisiana,' which was originally cast in 1927 and is now on display at the museum's entrance. You may view the sculpture without paying an entrance fee.

Sights

Louisiana Capitol (☎ 225-342-7317; admission free; 🕒 9am-4pm)

LSU Rural Life Museum (☎ 225-765-2437; http://rurallife.lsu.edu; 4600 Essen Lane; adult/child/senior $5/3/4; 🕒 8:30am-5pm)

Old State Capitol (☎ 225-342-0500; 100 North Blvd; adult/child $4/2; 🕒 10am-4pm Tue-Sat, noon-4pm Sun)

TRANSPORTATION

Bus Greyhound buses serve Baton Rouge from New Orleans.

Car Traveling from New Orleans, I-12 merges into I-10 on the eastern periphery of Baton Rouge, at which point I-10 continues westward toward Lafayette. Travel time is around 1¼ hours.

Eating

Fleur-De-Lis Cocktail Lounge (☎ 225-924-2904; 5655 Government St; individual pizzas $5-11; 🕒 10am-10pm Tue-Sat) A funky Baton Rouge favorite that's been in business since the 1940s. The Pepto Bismol–pink exterior and art deco–tinged interior are a kick, and the 'Roman' pizzas are tasty. It doesn't accept credit cards.

Poor Boy Loyd's (☎ 225-387-2271; 205 Florida St; meals $5-11; 🕒 7am-2pm Mon-Fri, 6-10pm Fri) This nondescript downtown eatery is chockablock with political memorabilia. Locals flock in for po'boy, and fried fish and shrimp plates.

Silver Moon (☎ 225-387-3345; 206 W Chimes St; meals $5-10; 🕒 6:30am-6pm Mon-Fri, 11am-5pm Sat) Just across the tracks from Louisiana State University, Silver Moon is the place to go to get the best soul food in Baton Rouge. Seabell Thomas piles white beans and rice, smothered pork chops and other classic soul food favorites on your plate and ladles out turnip greens by the generous bowlful.

MISSISSIPPI DELTA

The Mississippi Delta is haunted by the ghosts of those who created the distinctive Delta blues. Charlie Patton, Robert Johnson, Muddy Waters, BB King and dozens of others lived, worked and performed in the Delta. Their blues, usually a simple combination of vocals and complex guitar finger-picking, were by turns tragic, disquieting, weary, spiritual, belligerent and uplifting. Most visitors come looking for remnants of this past.

Mostly what you'll encounter here is a third-world montage of cotton fields and small, impoverished towns. Economic stagnation is evident in the rows of abandoned shops and run-down houses and groups of people hanging around street corners and on front porches. Long abandoned commissaries and rusted farm equipment pop up along the road, while painted signs fade away on the sides of buildings.

The Delta stretches for 250 miles from Vicksburg to Memphis. Technically it's an alluvial plain rather than a river delta. Regular blues festivals occur in towns throughout the Delta, and local performers play small 'juke joints' most weekends.

Vicksburg (population 27,500) is generally considered the southern tip of the Delta. The town is mostly remembered as a strategic focal point in the Civil War, when Union General Ulysses S Grant besieged the city for 47 days. Upon the city's surrender on July 4, 1863, the North gained the dominant hand on the Mississippi River. The major sights are readily accessible from I-20 exit 4B (Clay St). North of I-20 on Clay St, the **National Military Park & Cemetery** is the city's main attraction. The park preserves 1858 acres where the Union army laid siege to Vicksburg. An 18-mile driving tour passes historic markers explaining key events that occurred here. The cemetery, in which nearly 17,000 Union soldiers are buried, is in the northern end of the park. A museum relates some fascinating, oft-overlooked history.

Vicksburg's most important landmark structure is the **Old Court House Museum**, designed and built in 1858 by skilled slaves. Exhibits relate Vicksburg history in colorful, sometimes overly rosy terms, particularly where the subject of slavery is concerned. Amid shocking Klan hoods and old yellow newspapers are some genuinely lighthearted curiosities, such as an exhibit on the 'Minnié Ball Pregnancy,' which maintains that in a battle at Raymond, MI, a shot pierced through a soldier's reproductive organs and continued on into the reproductive organs of a female observer. Naturally, the ball successfully impregnated the woman.

As you drive Hwy 61 north of Vicksburg, you can't help but notice the huge red, yellow, white and pink towers that engulf **Margaret's Grocery**. Pull off and inspect this more closely. The Rev HD Dennis has obsessively created a religious folk art monument here, fashioning a chapel from an old school bus and scrawling Bible verses throughout the compound.

Driving up Hwy 61 will get you to **Clarksdale** in about three hours, passing through small towns like Rolling Fork, Leland and Cleveland along the way. There are few reasons to stop, unless you're a true blues aficionado (in which case you'll need more than a few days' excursion to explore the Delta's smaller two-lane blacktops).

A regular photo-op stop on Delta blues pilgrimages is **Dockery Farm**, a few miles east of Cleveland along Hwy 8. A big wooden cotton gin, visible from the highway, has a large sign on one side that lets you know you're there. This is where Charlie Patton lived on and off for about 30 years. A young Howlin' Wolf also lived on the Dockery Plantation and learned from Patton. Roebuck 'Pops' Staples, of the gospel-singing family, also grew up here.

At the northern end of the Delta, Clarksdale celebrates its blues heritage more than any other Delta town, making it a good base for blues travelers. Clarksdale was a jumping-off point for blacks catching trains to Memphis or Chicago. Muddy Waters lived near here, and Bessie Smith died in Clarksdale. Downtown is the few blocks where the railroad tracks meet the Sunflower River. At the town's south side, Hwys 61 and 49 meet at what locals refer to as the **crossroads**. You can't miss the tin guitars that mark the spot. Does this busy intersection look like a good place to sell your soul to the devil? Some locals will have you believe Robert Johnson did just that, right here.

In the old train station, the **Delta Blues Museum** is a must-see for blues pilgrims. You can get maps and charts that plot musical milestones, see a wax likeness of Muddy Waters in the sharecroppers cabin he lived in and peruse a collection of guitars and other artifacts. In 1937 singer Bessie Smith died in the **Riverside Hotel**, then a black medical clinic. She was brought to the clinic after being injured in a car wreck on the highway. Visit the hotel and if the proprietor is in a talkative mood he'll share stories from the old days, when musicians lived in the hotel, and show you the room in which Bessie is believed to have died.

Musical events are sporadic and often publicized by word of mouth. A reliable starting point is **Ground Zero**, near the Blues Museum. It's a huge and friendly hall owned by actor Morgan Freeman, who lives near Clarksdale. For an authentic juke joint experience head to **Red's**. A faded sign out front indicates that this was once the Laverne Music Center, and only a hand-scrawled sign on the wall above the huge barbecue pit tells us it's now Red's. (If the pit's smoking, order whatever's cooking.) The joint jumps when live music is on – sometimes Friday night and during festivals.

Swing by **Cat Head Delta Blues & Folk Art.** This gallery shows the paintings of outsider artists like Lamar Sorrento, whose portraits of blues legends are understandably popular. It's also the de-facto cultural info desk for the entire Delta – check out the website for upcoming juke joint gigs and events.

BLUES FESTIVALS

The only time towns in the Delta really come alive is during music festivals. Not only is there music in the streets, but all the jukes get cranking at night. Here's a calendar. See the Cat Head website (www.cathead.biz) for more information.

Juke Joint Festival – Clarksdale, mid-April.

Mississippi Delta Blues & Heritage Festival – Greenville, mid-May.

Crossroads Blues Festival – Rosedale, May.

BB King Hometown Homecoming – Indianola, early June.

Hwy 61 Blues Festival – Leland, mid-June.

Sunflower River Blues & Gospel Festival – Clarksdale, early August.

King Biscuit Blues Festival – Helena, AR, early October.

Information

Vicksburg Visitors Center (☎ 601-636-9421, 800-221-3536; cnr Clay & Washington Sts, Vicksburg)

Sights

Cat Head Delta Blues & Folk Art (☎ 662-624-5992; www.cathead.biz; 252 Delta Ave, Clarksdale)

Delta Blues Museum (☎ 601-627-6820; www.deltabluesmuseum.org; 1 Blues Alley, Clarksdale; admission $6; ⌚ 10am-5pm Mon-Sat)

Margaret's Grocery (☎ 601-638-1163; 4535 N Washington St, Vicksburg; ⌚ vary)

National Military Park & Cemetery (☎ 601-636-0583; www.nps.gov/vick; Vicksburg; per car $5; ⌚ 8am-5pm)

Old Court House Museum (☎ 601-636-0741; www.oldcourthouse.org; 1008 Cherry St, Vicksburg; adult/child $5/3; ⌚ 8:30am-4:30pm Mon-Sat, 1:30-4:30pm Sun)

Eating

Abe's (☎ 662-624-9947; 616 State St, Clarksdale; dishes $3-6) At the crossroads look for the sign with the black pig in a bowtie. Abe's has been providing Clarksdale with mouthwatering pork sandwiches since 1924.

Crystal Grill (☎ 662-453-6530; 423 Carrollton Ave, Greenwood; dishes $5-17; ⌚ 11am-8pm) In Greenwood, near the junction of Hwys 49 and 82, family-owned Crystal Grill is a landmark from the 1930s. Steaks, seafood and fresh vegetables anchor a diverse menu. Some locals have been eating here all their lives, and some of the waitresses have been working here for decades. Worth a detour.

Delta Amusement Blues Café (☎ 662-627-1467; 348 Delta Ave, Clarksdale; dishes $3-8; ⌚ 8am-2pm Mon-Sat) This local favorite slings some sturdy hash for breakfast and lunch. We're talking tasty soul food. During festivals, the place moonlights as a juke joint, and sometimes late on Saturday afternoons a jam session gets going.

Lusco's (☎ 662-453-5365; 722 Carrollton Ave, Greenwood; dishes $7-20; ⌚ 6-9pm Tue-Sat) Another fine Greenwood landmark from the '30s, Lusco's is often rated among Mississippi's best restaurants. It qualifies as a set designer's idea of how a Delta eatery should look: gracefully aged, with tables hidden in curtained booths. The steaks are broiled to perfection and the pompano is to die for. Reservations are a good idea.

Madidi ☎ 662-627-7770; 164 Delta Ave, Clarksdale; mains $18-34; ⌚ 6pm Tue-Sat) Actor Morgan Freeman hails from the Clarksdale area and still lives nearby. Having decided the area needed an upscale restaurant to satisfy his refined tastes, he opened Madidi with a local businessman. The food is French with a Mediterranean flair, and the atmosphere is reserved but pleasant. Reservations recommended.

TRANSPORTATION

Bus Greyhound buses stop in Vicksburg and Clarksdale.

Car Hwy 61 is the 'Blues Hwy' through the Delta. I-55 offers a high-speed alternative from New Orleans: for Vicksburg, switch to westbound I-20; for Clarksdale, switch to westbound Hwy 278 at Batesville. More scenic are Hwy 1, which meanders along the river north of Rolling Fork, and Old Hwy 61 (where you can still find traces of it).

Walnut Hills (☎ 601-638-4910; 1214 Adams St, Vicksburg; dishes $7-12; ⌚ 11am-9pm Mon-Fri, 11am-2pm Sun) Your best bet in Vicksburg is this charming old house near downtown, where daily menus include old faves like fried chicken, country-fried steak, Southern-cooked vegetables, biscuits and cornbread.

Entertainment

Red's (☎ 662-627-3166; 395 Sunflower Ave, Clarksdale; ⌚ usually Fri & Sat night)

Ground Zero (☎ 662-621-0990; www.groundzeroblues club.com; 387 Delta St, Clarksdale)

Sleeping

Battlefield Inn (☎ 601-638-5811, 800-359-9363; www.battlefieldinn.org; 4137 I-20 Frontage Rd, Vicksburg; r $45-80; P) It looks like your average roadside motel, but Battlefield Inn pampers its visitors with free cocktails and snacks in the early evening and a free buffet breakfast in the morning. The rooms here are tidy and comfortable and it's very close to the National Military Park.

Delta Cotton Club Apartment (☎ 662-645-9366; www.groundzerobluesclub.com; 387 Delta St, Clarksdale; r $75) Upstairs from the Ground Zero nightclub are basic rooms in about the most convenient location you could imagine.

Riverside Hotel (☎ 662-624-9163; 615 Sunflower Ave, Clarksdale; r $30-40;) Very basic accommodations are available in this historic site.

Shack Up Inn (☎ 662-624-8329; www.shackupinn.com; Hwy 49, Clarksdale; shacks $50-75, r $65; P) A night or two in one of the Shack Up's refurbished sharecropper cabins offers a totally unique experience that'll immerse you in Delta life. The cabins are filled with old furniture and musical instruments and the more expensive ones sleep up to four people. The old commissary is an atmospheric site for frequent live music performances, and the owners are great sources of information. Opt for a shack over the modern Cotton Gin rooms.

OVER TO OXFORD

Oxford, home of the University of Mississippi (Ole Miss), is about an hour's drive east of Clarksdale, via Hwy 6. It's a prosperous college town that once was home to William Faulkner, and it feels much less intense than the impoverished Delta.

Literary pilgrims head directly to **Rowan Oak** (☎ 662-234-3284; admission free; 🕑 10am-4pm Tue-Sat, 2-4pm Sun), the graceful 1840s home of William Faulkner, who authored so many brilliant and dense novels set in northeastern Mississippi. Faulkner lived here from 1930 until he died in 1962. A trail leads through the grounds to the cemetery where **Faulkner's grave** stands. Rowan Oak is near the University, off Old Taylor Rd.

While in town, have dinner at **Taylor Grocery** (☎ 601-236-1716; Old Taylor Rd; dishes $10-14; 🕑 6-10pm Thu-Sat), in a beautifully rusticated grocery store. It serves up some of the state's best fried catfish and hush-puppies. To get there, drive about 10 minutes from downtown Oxford, south on Old Taylor Rd, to the tiny town of Taylor.

MEMPHIS

This is where rock and roll got rolling. It's where soul music dug its grooves into the American consciousness. Elvis Presley made this city the seat of his power. Memphis is a carnivore's paradise, with some of the USA's best barbecue joints slinging savory pulled pork sandwiches and heavenly dry-rubbed ribs. And, on a more sobering note, the great Martin Luther King, Jr was murdered here at the height of the Civil Rights movement. Little wonder so many travelers are intrigued by Memphis.

For an utterly fascinating insight into a great American success story, do not miss the chance to see **Graceland**. Elvis bought the house and 500-acre farm surrounding it in 1957, after recording a string of number-one hits for RCA Records. Tours of the house inevitably draw a mix of die-hard worshippers, casual fans, earnest sociology professors and the perversely curious. There's a jungle room with green shag carpeting on the ceiling, a swank TV room with three monitors (which Elvis is rumored to have enjoyed shooting at) and an immense, unsightly racquetball gym in the backyard, where hundreds of gold and platinum discs now hang above mannequins sporting the King's sequinned threads from his flamboyant cape-donning days. Elvis is buried on the grounds, in a prayer garden next to the swimming pool.

For some fans, Memphis' number one musical shrine is **Sun Studio**. It offers a simple 30-minute tour that packs a punch because so many events took place here during the 1950s. Some say rock and roll took its first flight here when Elvis Presley recorded his legendary 'Sun Sessions' in 1954. Others argue rock began in 1951, when Jackie Brenston's 'Rocket 88' was recorded here. Blues artists Howlin' Wolf, BB King and Ike Turner, and rockabilly innovators Jerry Lee Lewis, Carl Perkins, Johnny Cash and Roy Orbison, all recorded here.

If the **Stax Museum** fails to give visitors goose pimples it's because the original building was demolished long ago. The museum stands at the original address, however, and looks the same, with a theater marquee emblazoned with the words 'Soulsville USA.' Indeed, this was soul music's epicenter in the 1960s, when Otis Redding, Carla Thomas, Booker T & the MGs and Wilson Pickett recorded here. It's worth visiting for the photos, displays of '60s and '70s peacock clothing and, above all, Isaac Hayes' 1972 Superfly Cadillac outfitted with shag fur carpeting and 24k-gold exterior trim.

From the street, the **Lorraine Motel**, where Martin Luther King Jr was fatally shot on April 4, 1968, appears eerily frozen in time. 1960's Cadillacs are parked in front and a memorial wreath hangs on the balcony in front of Room 6, where Dr King spent his last night. Inside, the hotel has been disemboweled and is part of the monumental **National Civil Rights Museum**. Five blocks south of Beale St, it brings to light one of the most significant moments in modern American history. Documentary photos and audio displays chronicle key events in civil rights history.

The **Beale St** strip from 2nd to 4th Sts is filled with clubs, restaurants, souvenir shops and neon signs – a veritable theme park of the blues. It's easy and safe to walk around. **BB King's** anchors the Beale St scene. It always has great live music and there's usually no cover, but the beer's expensive. **Mr Handy's Blues Hall**, the most atmospheric club on Beale St, has live blues every night. The original **A Schwab's** dry-goods store has three floors of voodoo powders, 99¢ neckties, clerical collars and a big selection of hats. **WC Handy's House** has memorabilia recalling the songwriter and composer's career.

The Smithsonian's **Rock 'n' Soul Museum** examines the social and cultural history that nurtured the music of Memphis and the Delta. Next door, **Gibson Beale Street Showcase** gives 30-minute tours of its factory, where blocks of wood are transformed into prized Gibson guitars.

Sights

A Schwab's (☎ 907-523-9782; 163 Beale St; admission free; 🕑 9am-5pm Mon-Sat)

Gibson Beale Street Showcase (☎ 800- 444-4766; 145 Lt George W Lee Ave; admission $10; tours 1pm Sun-Wed, 11am, noon, 1pm & 2pm Thu-Sat)

Graceland (☎ 901-332-3322, 800-238-2000; www.elvis.com; 3734 Elvis Presley Blvd; admission mansion adult/child $22/9, all attractions $30/15; 🕑 9am-5pm Mon-Sat & 10am-4pm Sun Mar-Oct, 10am-4pm daily Nov, 10am-4pm Mon & Wed-Sun Dec-Feb)

National Civil Rights Museum (☎ 901-521-9699; www.civilrightsmuseum.org; 450 Mulberry St, Memphis; admission adult/child $12/8.50; 🕑 9am-5pm Mon-Sat, 1-5pm Sun)

Sun Studio (☎ 901-521-0664, 800-441-6249; www.sunstudio.com; 706 Union Ave; admission $9.50; 🕑 10am-6pm)

Stax Museum (☎ 901-942-7685; www.staxmuseum.com; 926 E McLemore Ave; adult/child $9/4; 🕑 10am-4pm Mon-Sat, 1-4pm Sun)

Rock 'n' Soul Museum (☎ 901-543-0800; www.memphisrocknsoul.org; 145 Lt George W Lee Ave; admission $8.50; 🕑 10am-6pm)

WC Handy's House (☎ 901-527-3427; 352 Beale St; admission $3; 🕑 Tue-Sat)

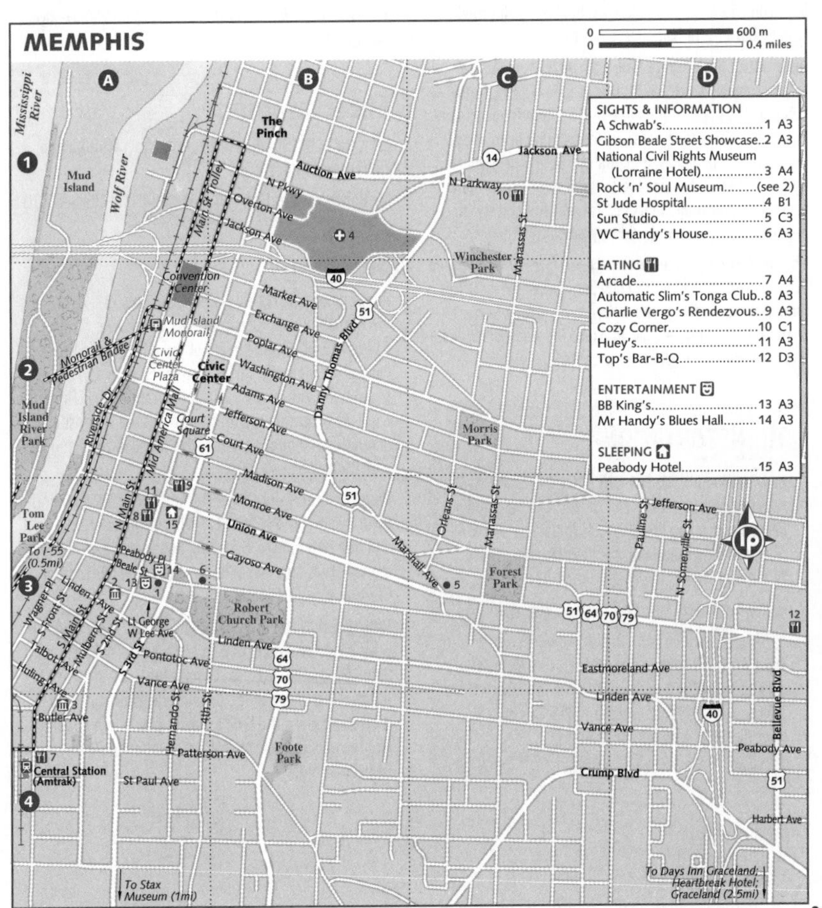

ELVIS WEEK

Each year in mid-August Memphis is flooded – not by the Mississippi River, but by Elvis impersonators of all ages. They are joined by devoted pilgrims, retro '50s swingers, average Joes and paparazzi. They come to mark the latest anniversary of the King's death on August 16, 1977. They congregate around Graceland, where they add to the graffiti on the brick wall out front. They strut, they weep, they laugh, they make spectacles of themselves. In other words, the fans steal the show. To become a part of this extraordinary event, plan ahead – reserve accommodations, get those sideburns started, have a sequined cape tailored. Check the Elvis website (www.elvis.com) for dates.

Eating

Arcade (☎ 901-526-5757; 540 S Main St; dishes $5-8; 🕑 7am-3pm Sun-Thu, 7am-9pm Fri & Sat) Fans of movie director Jim Jarmusch will want to duck into this classic restaurant where scenes from *Mystery Train* were filmed. The menu features standard short-order hash, along with some standout meatloaf and Southern-cooked vegetables, but the main draw is the atmosphere. Elvis is reputed to have come to Arcade to satiate his hankerings for fried peanut-butter-and-banana sandwiches.

Automatic Slim's Tonga Club (☎ 901-525-7948; 83 S 2nd St; mains lunch $8-14, dinner $17-27; 🕑 11am-2:30pm Mon-Fri, 5-10pm Mon-Thu, 5-11pm Fri-Sat) Memphians flock here for creative upscale dining in an artsy atmosphere. The food is a highfalutin Southern-Caribbean hybrid: jerked meats, voodoo seafood stew, green-market vegetables and Tonga martinis. This is a fun and stylish departure from the smoky, bluesy side of town.

Charlie Vergo's Rendezvous (☎ 901-523-2746; 53 S 2nd St; dishes $8-20; 🕑 lunch Fri & Sat, dinner Tue-Sat) This jumping establishment specializes in dry ribs, which are charcoal broiled rather than smoked. The service is friendly and the family atmosphere very upbeat.

TRANSPORTATION

Bus Greyhound (☎ 901-523-1184; 203 Union Ave) runs frequent buses to New Orleans. The Sun Studio Shuttle runs a free hourly circuit to the city's music sites including Graceland, the Stax Museum, Beale St and Sun Studios.

Car I-55 connects Memphis to New Orleans. It's five or six hours' drive.

Train Amtrak (☎ 901-526-0052; 545 S Main St) goes to Memphis from New Orleans. The Main St Trolley (fare 60¢) runs vintage trolley cars on a loop from the Amtrak station up Main St.

Cozy Corner (☎ 901-527-9158; 745 N Parkway; dishes $5-10) A nondescript and very friendly neighborhood barbecue joint, Cozy Corner is well worth the five-minute drive from downtown.

Huey's (☎ 901-527-2700; 77 S 2nd St; dishes $5-9; 🕑 until 3am) Long favored for creating the best burgers in town, Huey's is a good bet for casual pub food right on the edge of the Beale St action.

Tops Bar-B-Q (☎ 901-725-7527; 1286 Union Ave; dishes $6-10) A Memphis favorite for cheap barbecue since 1952.

Entertainment

BB King's (☎ 901-524-5464; http://memphis.bbkingclubs.com; 143 Beale St)

Mr Handy's Blues Hall (☎ 901-528-0150; 182 Beale St)

Sleeping

Peabody Hotel (☎ 901-529-4000, 800-732-2639; www.peabodymemphis.com; 149 Union Ave; r from $169; P ✖) In the heart of the city, the landmark Peabody is Memphis' prize accommodation and a social hub, with a classy bar in its grand lobby. This is early-20th-century grandeur, with all the steamship amenities you might expect. Plus it has ducks living in a penthouse pen.

Days Inn Graceland (☎ 901-346-5500; 3839 Elvis Presley Blvd; d $50-70; P ✖ 🏊) With its guitar-shaped pool and free Elvis movies, this chain bends over backwards to make Elvis fans feel at home. Just a few blocks from Graceland.

Heartbreak Hotel (☎ 901-332-1000, 877-777-0606; www.heartbreakhotel.net; 3677 Elvis Presley Blvd; r from $99; P ✖ 🏊) OK, so it's not at the end of Lonely St but the Heartbreak Hotel, behind Graceland's parking lot, is all about Elvis. The King's movies play in every room and the pool is shaped like a heart. Free shuttle to Beale St at night.

Directory

Transportation 272

Air 272
Bicycle 272
Boat 272
Bus 273
Car & Motorcycle 274
Streetcar 275
Taxi 275
Train 275

Practicalities 276

Accommodations 276
Business Hours 276
Children 276
Climate 277
Customs 277
Disabled Travelers 277
Electricity 277
Embassies 277
Emergency 277
Gay & Lesbian Travelers 277
Health 278
Holidays 278
Internet Access 278
Internet Resources 278
Legal Matters 278
Maps 279
Medical Services 279
Metric System 279
Money 279
Pharmacies 280
Photography 280
Post 280
Safety 281
Tax & Refunds 281
Telephone 282
Television 282
Time 282
Tipping 282
Toilets 283
Tourist Information 283
Visas 283
Women Travelers 284
Work 284

Directory

TRANSPORTATION

The compact and level nature of the French Quarter and downtown riverfront areas make walking and bicycling the preferred ways to get around for most visitors. As in other cities throughout the USA, public transit in New Orleans has deteriorated as transportation funds have been diverted to subsidize motorists. Hurricane Katrina was of course a blow to the city's transit systems. Nevertheless, visitors will find that the buses, streetcars and ferries generally serve the most popular attractions. In fact, the streetcars and ferries themselves are attractions.

AIR

New Orleans is not a major airline hub and it is not a big center for national commerce, so direct flights are not always available, even from major travel centers like the Bay Area. International travelers will almost certainly need to change flights somewhere else within the US before connecting to flights to New Orleans (and the connection may require an additional stopover en route).

The cheapest flights can often be found on the web. Sites worth checking include **Expedia** (www.expedia.com), **Cheap Tickets** (www.cheaptickets.com), **Smarter Travel** (www.smartertravel.com) and **Travelzoo** (www.travelzoo.com). Ever reliable **STA Travel** (Map pp314–15; ☎ 866-1767; www.statravel.com; 6363 St Charles Ave), at the Loyola University Student Center, also offers a full range of travel services.

Airlines

The following airlines offer regular service to New Orleans.

AirTran (☎ 800-825-8538; www.airtran.com)

American Airlines (Map pp308–9; ☎ 800-433-7300; www.aa.com)

Continental Airlines (☎ 523-9739, 800-732-6887; www.continental.com)

Delta Air Lines (☎ 800-221-1212; www.delta.com)

Jet Blue (☎ 800-538-3583; www.jetblue.com) Connects MSY with JFK in NYC.

Northwest Airlines (☎ 800-225-2525; www.nwa.com)

Southwest Airlines (☎ 464-9240, 800-435-9792; www.southwest.com)

United Airlines (☎ 800-241-6522; www.united.com)

Airport

Louis Armstrong New Orleans International Airport (MSY; ☎ 464-0831; www.flymsy.com) is in the suburb of Kenner, 20 minutes west of the city along the I-10 freeway. In the aftermath of Hurricane Katrina, the airport remained dry and its concourses served as an impromptu triage center. In June 2006 the airport was serving 60% of its pre-Katrina traffic volume. Few services and concessions were up and running. Some airlines, including Continental and some smaller commuter lines, were already at pre-Katrina levels. Jet Blue was only operating a flight to/from JFK in New York.

BICYCLE

On the positive side of the ledger for riders, New Orleans is flat and relatively compact. On the negative side are heavy traffic and potholes, which make fat tires a near necessity. Oppressive summer heat and humidity also discourage some bicyclists.

All state-operated ferries offer free transportation for bikes. Bicyclists board ahead of cars by walking down the left lane of the ramp to the swinging gate. You must wait for the cars to exit before leaving.

The Regional Transit Authority (RTA) doesn't allow bikes on buses or streetcars.

Bikes can be rented for around $25 a day at **Bicycle Michael's** (Map p316; ☎ 945-9505; http://bicyclemichaels.com; 622 Frenchmen St, Marigny).

BOAT

Ferry

The cheapest way to cruise the Mississippi River is aboard one of the state-run ferries. The most popular line, the Canal St Ferry, operates between Canal St and the West Bank community of Algiers from 6am to

GETTING INTO TOWN

Louis Armstrong New Orleans International Airport is 11 miles west of the city center. Shuttles and cabs depart regularly from the curb outside the baggage claim area.

Bus

If your baggage is not too unwieldy and you're in no hurry, **Jefferson Transit** (☎ 818-1077; www.jeffersontransit.org) offers the cheapest ride downtown aboard its Airport Downtown Express, for $1.10. At the airport the bus stops along the median on the second level, near the Delta counter. The ride to New Orleans follows city streets, pausing for stoplights every few minutes, and will only get you as far as the corner of Tulane ST and Carrollton Ave. From there, you can transfer to an **RTA** (☎ 827-7433; www.norta.com) bus. Bus 27 will get you to St Charles Ave in the Garden District; bus 39 follows Tulane Ave to Canal St, just outside the French Quarter.

Car

The quickest way to drive between the airport and downtown is to take I-10. If you're coming from downtown on I-10, take exit 223 for the airport; going to downtown, take exit 234, as the Superdome looms before you.

Shuttle

Most visitors take the **Airport Shuttle** (☎ 522-3500; www.airportshuttleneworleans.com) to and from the airport. It's a frequent service between the airport and downtown hotels for $13 per passenger each way. It's a cheap and courteous introduction to the city, although it can be time-consuming, especially if your hotel is the last stop. At the airport, buy tickets from agencies in the baggage claim area. For your return to the airport, call a day ahead to arrange for a pickup, which you should schedule at least two hours prior to your flight's departure.

Taxi

A taxi ride from the airport costs a flat rate of $28 for one to two passengers. Each additional passenger costs another $12. No more than four passengers are allowed in a single cab.

midnight daily. Another ferry stops at Jackson Ave, near the Irish Channel, and leads to the suburb of Grena. The ferries are free for pedestrians and cyclists, and just $1 for vehicles.

Riverboat

Visitors to New Orleans during Mark Twain's time arrived by boat via the Mississippi River. This once-common mode of travel continues to be offered by a few paddle-wheel riverboats and ocean-going cruise ships. The costs are high compared with other travel modes. River travel is now typically offered as a package tour or excursion that includes top-end food and lodging.

With headquarters in New Orleans, the **Delta Queen Steamboat Company** (Map pp308–9; ☎ 586-0631, 800-543-1949; www.deltaqueen.com; 30 Robin St Wharf) offers paddle-wheel riverboat travel to and from ports on the Mississippi River, including St Paul, MN (14 nights); St Louis, MO (seven nights); and Memphis, TN (five nights). It also connects New Orleans with river ports such as Pittsburgh, PA (12 nights); Nashville, TN (nine nights); and Chattanooga, TN (10 nights). All times are for downriver travel – add at least one day for each five days to head upriver.

Riverboat fares generally start at $800 per person for a three-night journey in a simple double-occupancy berth and include all meals and entertainment. For the more posh state rooms you can pay as much as $2350 for a three-night trip. Additional fees include port and departure taxes ($90 to $100). Obviously, if you are considering a riverboat trip you will want to check out the website, request brochures and plan several months ahead.

BUS

Local

The **Regional Transit Authority** (RTA; ☎ 827-7433; www.norta.com) offers decent bus and streetcar (see p275) services. Since Katrina disrupted so much of the city's infrastructure, service is constantly changing and, along some lines, infrequent. The RTA website has complete bus route and schedule information. On the upside, riding the buses is free since Hurricane Katrina. Fares of $1.25 to $1.50 are likely to be reintroduced at some point.

No buses run through the heart of the French Quarter, so most visitors only use them when venturing Uptown or out to City Park. In the Sights chapter (p132), convenient bus routes are indicated for all parts of town in the 'Transportation' boxes.

Long-Distance

Greyhound (☎ 800-231-2222; www.greyhound.com) buses arrive and depart at **New Orleans Union Passenger Terminal** (Map pp308–9; 1001 Loyola Ave), which is also known as Union Station. It's seven blocks upriver from Canal St. Greyhound regularly connects to Lafayette, Opelousas and Baton Rouge, LA; Clarksdale, MS; and Memphis, TN, en route to essentially every city in the USA.

CAR & MOTORCYCLE

Driving

A car is not a bad thing to have in New Orleans. Having one makes it easy to fully experience the entire city, from the Faubourg Marigny on up to the Riverbend, and out along Esplanade Ave. If you are planning to spend most of your time in the French Quarter, though, don't bother with a car. You'll just end up wasting money on parking.

Drivers in New Orleans are not overly aggressive, although you can always expect the car behind you to get within a few feet of your rear bumper. It's just a herd impulse, though. Pause a few beats at a green light, and that same tailgater is likely to wait patiently for you to catch on that the light has changed. On the other hand, as in many parts of the United States, drivers in New Orleans cannot resist speeding up for a yellow light to make it through an intersection before the light turns red. More often than not, the light is red by the time they are zipping through, so if you are in cross-bound traffic, do not rush into an intersection immediately after your light turns green.

Visitors from some countries may find it wise to back up their national driver's license with an International Driving Permit, available from their local automobile club.

Hire

Most of the big car-rental companies are found in New Orleans, particularly at the airport. Typically you must be at least 25 years of age and have a major credit card, as well as a valid driver's license, in order to rent a car.

Rates go up and availability lessens during special events or large conventions. A compact car typically costs $30 to $40 a day or $150 to $200 a week. On top of that, there is a 13.75% tax and an optional $9 to $15 a day loss/damage-waiver or LDW (insurance). If you already have auto insurance you're probably covered, but check with your insurance company first.

Agencies in or near the downtown area include:

Avis (☎ 523-4317, 800-3311-1212; 2024 Canal St)

Budget Rent-a-Car (Map pp310–11; ☎ 565-5600, 800-527-0700; 1317 Canal St)

Hertz (Map pp308–9; ☎ 568-1645, 800-654-3131; 901 Convention Center Blvd)

Parking

Downtown on-street parking is typically for short-term use. In some parts of town, look for the solar-powered parking meters. One meter often serves an entire block, so if there's no meter on the curb immediately beside your car, don't assume it means parking is free. And of course there are all kinds of restrictions for street cleaning that limit when you can park on certain streets. Be sure to read all parking signs on the block before leaving your car. Enforcement is particularly efficient in the French Quarter and the CBD and Warehouse districts.

Vehicles parked illegally are frequently towed in the Quarter. If you park your car in a driveway, within 20ft of a corner or crosswalk, within 15ft of a fire hydrant or on a street-sweeping day, you will need to pay about $75 (cash or credit card) plus cab fare to retrieve your car from the **Auto Pound** (☎ 565-7450; 400 N Claiborne Ave).

Free street parking is available on many blocks in the lower Quarter (or try along Esplanade Ave). For more-central parking, you might have to pay. Try the **U-Park Garage** (Map pp310–11; ☎ 524-5994; 721 Iberville St), near the upper end of Bourbon St. Most hotels in the Quarter and the CBD have parking garages where you can park with in–out privileges for around $20 to $30 a day.

STREETCAR

Streetcars have made a comeback in New Orleans with three lines serving key routes in the city. As on the city buses, riding the streetcars is currently free. A fare of $1.25 to $1.50 is likely to be reinstated at some point.

Canal Streetcar Lines

Bright red streetcars began running up and down Canal St in 2004. They look old, but aren't. All are fully modern, air-conditioned light-rail cars custom designed and built locally. The entire original fleet incurred extensive water damage during the hurricanes of 2005 and the cars essentially had to be rebuilt. The line continued to run with the antique St Charles Ave streetcars (see below), which were unharmed during the hurricanes.

Two slightly different lines follow Canal St to Mid-City. Both run from the French Market and up the levee before heading up Canal St. The 47 line goes all the way to City Park Ave. More useful for tourists is the 8 line, which heads up a spur on N Carrollton Ave, ending up at the Esplanade Ave entrance to City Park. The cars run from 6am to 11pm.

Riverfront Streetcar Line

In 1988 the wheelchair-accessible Riverfront streetcar line began operating vintage red cars on the old dockside rail corridor wedged between the levee and flood wall. The 2-mile route runs between the French Market, in the lower end of the French Quarter near Esplanade Ave, and the upriver Convention Center, crossing Canal St on the way. It operates from 6am to midnight.

St Charles Ave Streetcar Line

When the St Charles Ave streetcar route opened as the New Orleans & Carrollton Railroad in 1835, it was the nation's second horse-drawn streetcar line. The line was also among the first systems to be electrified when New Orleans adopted electric traction in 1893. Now it is one of the few streetcars in the US to have survived the automobile era.

The line's fleet of antique cars survived the hurricanes of 2005, but the tracks and power lines did not. Currently, the cars are running on the Canal St tracks. RTA has not announced plans to repair the St Charles Ave tracks.

The important thing is that you can still enjoy a ride on one of these extraordinary streetcars, which employ technology that's intriguingly out of date. There is no need to worry about breakdowns when you hear the intermittent thunka-thunka sound – it's just the air compressor. The streetcars' brakes, doors and even the fare box operate on compressed air. Unfortunately, these old streetcars are not wheelchair accessible.

TAXI

If you are traveling alone or at night, taxis are highly recommended. **United Cab** (☎ 522-9771) is the biggest and most reliable company in New Orleans. You might have to call for a pickup, unless you are in a central part of the French Quarter, where it is relatively easy to flag down a passing cab, or to find a taxi stand. Taxis can almost always be found in front of the Omni Orleans Hotel (Map pp310–11), on St Louis St. Uptown and in neighborhoods like the Bywater you will have to call. For an early morning ride to the airport, call and book one the night before.

Fares within the city start with a $2.50 flag fall charge for one passenger (plus $1 for each additional passenger). From there it's $1.20 per mile. Practically speaking, this amounts to fares of around $8 from the French Quarter to the Bywater and $10 or more to the Garden District. Don't forget to tip your driver 10% to 15%.

High demand for taxis during Jazz Fest and Mardi Gras means availability is severely limited.

TRAIN

Three **Amtrak** (☎ 800-872-7245) trains serve New Orleans at the **Union Passenger Terminal** (Map pp308–9; ☎ 528-1610; 1001 Loyola Ave). The *City of New Orleans* train runs to Memphis, TN; Jackson, MS; and Chicago, IL. Alternatively, the *Crescent Route* serves Birmingham, AL; Atlanta, GA; Washington, DC; and New York City. The *Sunset Limited* route between Los Angeles, CA, and Miami, FL, also passes through New Orleans.

PRACTICALITIES

ACCOMMODATIONS

New Orleans accommodations come in several varieties, with the most common choices being between large purpose-built hotels and more-intimate lodging in converted town houses and cottages. The names of hotels rarely indicate what you can expect in this regard – an old Creole town house might be called an 'inn' or a 'hotel.' Some smaller establishments offer breakfast, but don't necessarily have 'B&B' in their name. Among the purpose built, many are fairly bland convention hotels that fail to reflect New Orleans' beautiful architectural heritage. As in many cities, quite a few newer purpose-built properties are boutique hotels with designer rooms and hip bars. Websites with photos are commonplace for accommodations in New Orleans, so it's wise to have a look before you book.

Rates fluctuate with the seasons, but New Orleans is peculiar for being slow during the summer (due to the oppressive heat) and busy during the shoulder seasons (spring and fall). Busiest, of course, are Mardi Gras (February or March), Jazz Fest (late April to early May) and other holidays and festivals (p14). Expect hotels to charge the highest rates during these periods.

Room availability has been reduced by the Hurricane Katrina recovery effort, as many rooms continue to be occupied by contractors and displaced workers. Many hotels are charging more than they did before Katrina. That said, while researching this edition, we found many fine accommodations starting under $100 per night.

Booking Services

The number of online booking services is staggering. Here are a few worth checking.

Hotel Discounts (www.hoteldiscounts.com)

Last Minute Travel (www.lastminutetravel.com)

Lonely Planet (lonelyplanet.com)

Places to Stay (www.placestostay.com)

BUSINESS HOURS

New Orleans has always been a 24-hour center of activity, but as business slowly creeps back after Katrina many shops continue to keep reduced hours of operation. It's really on a per-shop basis right now, and for many individual shops the hours fluctuate week by week. Perhaps the biggest contributing factor to the unstable business hours situation is the drastic drop in the city's population. Along with the slow recovery of the tourism industry, this means fewer customers for everyone. But, just as significant, it also means a shrunken workforce. Some places – restaurants in particular – can't resume their pre-Katrina hours simply because they don't have enough staff to operate every day.

So, for the foreseeable future, expect museums to open Thursday to Sunday or even just on weekends. Expect restaurants to have cut back on breakfast and lunch, and possibly to remain shut two or three nights a week. Some nightclubs, at the time of writing, weren't open every night either.

Very likely it will take several years before the city's opening hours are stabilized.

CHILDREN

Before Hurricane Katrina came along, national travel magazines such as *Condé Nast Traveler* were touting New Orleans as the USA's best family destination. The hurricane didn't really affect any of the city's family-oriented sights and activities, so there's no need to re-evaluate that assessment. It's a city of zoos, museums, riverboat cruises and fun entertainment. We've included information in the Sights (p141) and Entertainment (p210) chapters detailing interesting places for parents and children to visit.

Babysitting

Most major hotels offer on-site babysitting arrangements. Smaller hotels are also familiar with parents' needs and can often provide the name of recommended child-minding services. You might want to inquire about this while making your hotel reservations.

Accent on Children's Arrangements (Map pp308–9; ☎ 524-1227; www.accentoca.com; Ste 303, 615 Baronne St) is a service that takes the kids off your hands and engages them in organized activities. This might include a child-oriented tour of the city or educational entertainment. They are able to custom services for varying age groups and to meet your personal needs.

CLIMATE

New Orleans' climate is fairly simple: it's hot and humid in the summer, and not so hot and humid the rest of the year. The humidity is enough to drive some locals out of town for lengthy summer vacations in more pleasant climes, and to keep tourists away. In December temperatures can fluctuate from 40°F to 70°F. Snowfall is extremely rare. The wettest months are July and August and the driest month is October.

Perhaps all you really want to know is when hurricane season starts and ends. Hurricanes can come off the Gulf of Mexico anytime from June to December, though the peak season is in August and September.

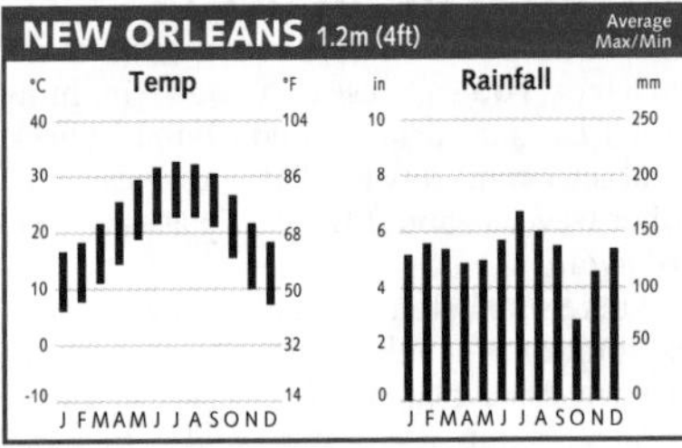

CUSTOMS

US Customs (www.customs.gov) allows each person over the age of 21 to bring 1L of liquor and 200 cigarettes duty-free into the USA. Non-US citizens are allowed to enter the US with $100 worth of gifts from abroad. There are restrictions on bringing fresh fruit and flowers into the country and there is a strict quarantine on animals. If you are carrying more than $10,000 in US and foreign cash, traveler's checks, money orders or the like, you need to declare the excess amount. There is no legal restriction on the amount that may be imported, but undeclared sums in excess of $10,000 may be subject to confiscation.

DISABLED TRAVELERS

Unfortunately, New Orleans is a little lax in this department. Sidewalk curbs rarely have ramps, and many historic public buildings and hotels are not equipped to meet the needs of the wheelchair bound. The disabled will find their way around, though, if they can tolerate such inconveniences. Modern hotels adhere to standards established by the federal Americans with Disabilities Act, with ramps, elevators and accessible bathrooms. A few of the RTA buses offer a lift service; for information about paratransit service (alternate transportation for those who can't ride regular buses), call the **RTA** (☎ 827-7433). The Riverfront streetcar line features Braille kiosks, platform ramps and wide doors that allow anyone to board easily. However, the St Charles Ave streetcar line has not been modified for wheelchair passengers. While these old cars are used on the Canal St line, wheelchair accessibility will not be available there either.

ELECTRICITY

Electric current in the USA is 110–115V, 60Hz AC. Outlets may be suited for flat two-prong or three-prong grounded plugs. If your appliance is made for another electrical system, you will need a transformer or adapter; if you didn't bring one along, buy one at Radio Shack (which has several locations around town) or another consumer electronics store.

EMBASSIES

There aren't any embassies in New Orleans, but several countries have consulates and honorary consuls in town. Canada's nearest consulate is in Miami, FL.

France (Map pp308–9; ☎ 523-5772; www.ambafrance-us.org; 1340 Poydras St)

Japan (Map pp308–9; ☎ 529-2101; www.neworleans.us.emb-japan.go.jp; Ste 2050, 639 Loyola Ave)

UK Honorary Consul (Map pp308–9; ☎ 524-4180; 10th fl, 321 St Charles Ave)

EMERGENCY

Ambulance ☎ 911

Fire ☎ 911

Police (emergency) ☎ 911

Police (nonemergency) ☎ 821-2222

Rape Crisis Line ☎ 483-8888

GAY & LESBIAN TRAVELERS

The gay community in New Orleans is most visible in the French Quarter, to the lakeside of Bourbon St. Gays are present but keep a lower profile in the Faubourg Marigny and Bywater and elsewhere in town. For gay visitors, finding a place to stay, eat or party in New Orleans will not be a problem. See Gay & Lesbian Clubs (p204) for listings.

Southern Decadence (p17) is a gay festival that draws a huge crowd to the Quarter in late August or early September. Halloween and Mardi Gras also have a strong gay component in New Orleans.

The **Faubourg Marigny Book Store** (Map p316; ☎ 943-9875; 600 Frenchmen St) is the South's oldest gay bookstore and is a good place to learn about the local scene. Several websites provide information geared toward the gay community in New Orleans, as well as gay travelers.

Ambush Mag (www.ambushmag.com)

Gay New Orleans (www.gayneworleans.com)

Gay New Orleans Guide (www.gayneworleansguide.com)

HEALTH

Health is a concern in New Orleans only if you drink too much, get too much sun out at the Fair Grounds during Jazz Fest or plan to venture into the Dead Zone. The Dead Zone, the vast area flooded after Hurricane Katrina, may have toxic residues, airborne mold spores and the risk of tetanus from the rusted hulls of cars and from nails protruding from demolition debris. Proceed through these areas very cautiously.

HOLIDAYS

Note that when national holidays fall on a weekend, they are often celebrated on the nearest Friday or Monday so that everyone enjoys a three-day weekend. For further information on New Orleans' holidays and festivals see p14. The following are all national holidays.

New Year's Day January 1

Presidents' Day Third Monday in February

Memorial Day Last Monday in May

Independence Day July 4

Labor Day First Monday in September

Columbus Day Second Monday in October

Veterans Day November 11

Thanksgiving Fourth Thursday in November

INTERNET ACCESS

Many hotels offer Internet access, but it's not yet something you can assume – be sure to confirm while making reservations. Wi-fi hot spots (free access for those carrying laptops with wireless capability) are becoming increasingly common in cafés.

Wi-fi hot spots include **Coop's Place** (p179), **Cooter Brown's Tavern & Oyster Bar** (p191), **dba** (p203) and **Huey's 24/7 Diner** (p187).

If you're not traveling with your own laptop, try **Bastille Computer Café** (Map pp310–11; ☎ 581-1150; e@netzero.net; 605 Toulouse St; 10am-11pm), located in the heart of the Quarter. **New Orleans Public Library** (Map pp308–9; ☎ 529-7323; http://nutrias.org; 219 Loyola Ave), near City Hall, has terminals for free Web access.

INTERNET RESOURCES

The World Wide Web is a rich resource for travelers. You can research your trip, hunt down bargain airfares, book hotels, check weather conditions or chat with locals and other travelers about the best places to visit (or avoid!).

There's no better place to start your Web explorations than the Lonely Planet website at www.lonelyplanet.com. Here you'll find succinct summaries on traveling to most places on earth, postcards from other travelers, and the Thorn Tree bulletin board, where you can ask questions before you go or dispense advice when you get back. You can also find travel news and updates to many of our most popular guidebooks, and the Subwwway section links you to the most useful travel resources elsewhere on the Web.

Other useful websites, many of which serve as gateways to an infinite number of interesting links:

Food Fest (http://foodfest.neworleans.com)

Gambit Weekly (www.bestofneworleans.com)

Jazz Festival (www.nojazzfest.com)

Louisiana Music Factory (www.louisianamusicfactory.com)

Offbeat Magazine (www.offbeat.com)

New Orleans Menu (www.nomenu.com)

WWOZ Radio (www.wwoz.org)

Times-Picayune (www.nola.com)

LEGAL MATTERS

Although it may seem that anything goes, even New Orleans has its limits. Common tourist-related offenses include underage drinking, drinking outdoors from a bottle rather than a plastic go cup, teen curfew violations and, probably the most common, flaunting of private parts of the anatomy.

Drink-driving is obviously something people with cars are more likely to do in New Orleans. About two drinks will put enough alcohol into your bloodstream to make you legally drunk – so don't drive if you're drinking.

The legal drinking age is 21. Anyone under the age of 18 on the streets after 11pm is violating the city's curfew. Most bars will offer your drink in a plastic cup, so accept it if you're going to wander off with your drink. Bourbon St flashers rarely get in serious trouble for exposing their private parts, but repeatedly doing so in front of the cops is asking for trouble. If you aren't flashing, be careful not to grope those who are. That's a no-no.

The legal age for gambling is also 21, and businesses with gaming devices (usually video poker machines) out in the open are closed to minors. Even cafés with gaming devices are off-limits to minors, unless the games are contained within private rooms or booths.

MAPS

Good-quality maps of New Orleans are available from most bookstores, but free maps from a variety of sources are generally OK for most visitors. Car-rental agencies have heaps of maps, and so does the New Orleans Welcome Center (see p283) on Jackson Sq.

Lonely Planet's handy laminated *New Orleans City Map* has all the key neighborhoods, a street index and sights placed on the map. The map was designed to nicely complement this book.

Member of the American Automobile Association (AAA) using their *New Orleans & Vicinity Map* will appreciate the detailed 'metropolitan' coverage of the CBD and French Quarter, but the greatly simplified map of the city is disappointing.

MEDICAL SERVICES

If you need immediate medical attention and you are in your hotel, your first call should be to the front desk. Some of the larger hotels have agreements with on-call doctors who can make house calls if necessary. In really urgent situations, you can call an **ambulance** (☎ 911), which will deliver you to a hospital emergency room.

If you can get to an emergency room with the help of a friend, your best bet is the **Tulane University Medical Center** (Map pp308–9; ☎ 988-5800; 1415 Tulane Ave), located in the CBD.

METRIC SYSTEM

New Orleans residents resist the metric system. Draft beer is commonly offered by the pint. Dry weights are in ounces (oz), pounds (lb) and tons, but liquid measures differ from dry measures. One pint equals 16 fluid oz; 2 pints equal 1 quart, a common measure for liquids such as milk, which is also sold in half-gallons (2 quarts) and gallons (4 quarts). Gasoline is measured in the US gallon, which is about 20% smaller than the imperial gallon and equivalent to 3.79L. Distances are in feet (ft), yards (yd) and miles. Three feet equals 1yd (0.914m); 1760yd (5280ft) equals 1 mile. Temperatures are in degrees Fahrenheit, whereby 32°F is freezing. There is a conversion chart on the inside front cover of this book.

MONEY

There are three straightforward ways to handle money in the US: cash, US-dollar traveler's checks and credit or bank cards, which can be used to withdraw cash from the many automatic teller machines (ATMs) across the country. US dollars are the only accepted currency in New Orleans.

ATMs

With a Visa card, MasterCard or a bank card affiliated with the Plus or Cirrus networks you can easily obtain cash from ATMs all over New Orleans. The advantage of using ATMs is that you do not need to buy traveler's checks in advance, you do not have to pay the usual 1% commission on the checks and, if you're from a foreign country, you may actually receive a better exchange rate. However, most ATMs charge a $2 or $3 service charge for each withdrawal. It doesn't make sense to grab $40 several times a day.

There are four ATMs at the airport: in the east lobby near Concourse B, next to the Whitney National Bank; and two in the baggage claim areas on the lower level.

The **Whitney National Bank** (☎ 838-6492; 🕒 8:30am-3pm Mon-Thu, 8:30am-5:30pm Fri) is located in the ticket lobby next to the U.S. Post Office. Services offered include cash advances on credit cards, traveler's checks, money orders, foreign currency exchange, and ATMs.

TravelEx America Business Center (☎ 465-9647; 🕒 6am-5pm) is located in the ticket lobby near the U.S. Post Office. It offers travel insurance, foreign money exchange, photocopies, fax services, emergency cash and wire money transfers. The Money Gram section of the office closes at 4:30pm.

Changing Money

Most major currencies and leading brands of traveler's checks are easily exchanged in New Orleans. You will also find various independent exchange bureaus. When you first arrive at the airport terminal you can change money at TravelEx America Business Center, which you'll find in the ticket lobby. TravelEx charges a sliding service fee ($2 for amounts up to $20, $4 for greater amounts). Nearby, Whitney National Bank also changes money, charging a flat $5 service fee. Since the exchange counters are only feet apart, get quotes from both.

Better exchange rates are generally available at banks in the CBD. Typical opening hours are 10am to 5pm Monday to Thursday, 10am to 6pm Friday and 10am to 1pm Saturday. The **Hibernia National Bank** (Map pp308–9; ☎ 533-5712; 313 Carondelet St) and the main office of the **Whitney National Bank** (Map pp308–9; ☎ 586-7272; 228 St Charles Ave) both buy and sell foreign currency.

For exchange rates see the Quick Reference page.

Credit & Debit Cards

Major credit cards are widely accepted by car-rental agencies and most hotels, restaurants, gas stations, shops and larger grocery stores. Many recreational and tourist activities can also be paid for by credit card. The most commonly accepted cards are Visa, MasterCard and AmEx. However, Discover and Diners Club cards are also accepted by a large number of businesses.

If your debit card is affiliated with a major credit-card company, businesses will accept it as they do a credit card. Unlike a credit card, a debit card deducts payment directly from your account, so be aware of your balance when using it. At some establishments (such as supermarkets, drugstores and gas stations) you can withdraw additional cash when you use your debit card.

Traveler's Checks

ATMs and debit cards have nearly rendered traveler's checks obsolete, but if your bank isn't affiliated with one of the common bank networks such as Cirrus or Plus, the old-fashioned way can be pretty handy. Some younger waitstaff and shop clerks might be unsure how to react to them, though.

But they are still virtually as good as cash in the US. And they can still be replaced if lost or stolen. Both AmEx and Thomas Cook, two well-known issuers of traveler's checks, have efficient replacement policies.

You'll save yourself trouble and expense if you buy traveler's checks in US dollars.

PHARMACIES

Nonprescription medications and contraceptives can be purchased in the pharmacy section of drugstores like **Walgreens** (Map pp310–11; ☎ 525-7263; 619 Decatur St) in the French Quarter.

PHOTOGRAPHY

For film, batteries and poor quality prints (either digital or traditional film) go to a drugstore such as Walgreens in the French Quarter. For camera equipment, printing and slide processing, head to **Moldaner's Camera & Imaging** (Map pp314–15; ☎ 486-5811; 622 S Carrollton Ave) in the Riverbend. For a selection of professional film and quality B&W processing go to **Dark Room** (Map pp312–13; ☎ 522-3211; www.neworleansdarkroom.com; 1927 Sophie Wright Pl) in the Lower Garden District.

POST

New Orleans' **main post office** (Map pp308–9; ☎ 589-1135; 701 Loyola Ave) is near City Hall. There are smaller branches throughout the city, including the **Airport Mail Center** (☎ 589-1296) in the passenger terminal; the **World Trade Center** (Map pp308–9; ☎ 524-0033; 2 Canal St); and in the CBD at Lafayette Sq (Map pp308–9; ☎ 524-0491; 610

S Maestri Place). Post offices are generally open 8:30am to 4:30pm Monday to Friday and 8:30am to noon Saturday.

The French Quarter branch is currently closed, but there are independent postal shops, including the **Royal Mail Service** (Map pp310–11; ☎ 522-8523; 828 Royal St) and the **French Quarter Postal Emporium** (Map pp310–11; ☎ 525-6651; 1000 Bourbon St). These shops will send letters and packages at the same rates as the post office.

Postal Rates

Postal rates frequently increase, but at the time of writing the rates were 39¢ for 1st-class mail within the USA for letters up to 1oz (24¢ for each additional ounce) and 24¢ for postcards.

It costs 63¢ to send a 1oz letter and 55¢ to send a postcard to Canada and Mexico. International airmail rates to any other foreign country are 84¢ for a 1oz letter and 75¢ for a postcard.

The **US Postal Service** (☎ 800-222-1811; www.usps.gov) also offers a Priority Mail service, which delivers your letter or package anywhere in the USA in two days or less. The cost is $4.05 for 1lb. For heavier items, rates differ according to the distance mailed. Overnight Express Mail starts at $14.50.

Receiving Mail

If you don't want to receive mail at your hotel, you can have mail sent to you at the main post office, marked c/o General Delivery, New Orleans, LA 70112. General Delivery is US terminology for what is known as poste restante internationally. General Delivery mail is only held for 30 days. It's not advisable to try to have mail sent to other post offices in New Orleans.

Sending Mail

If you have the correct postage, you can drop your mail into any blue mailbox. However, to send a package that weighs 1lb or more, you must take it to a post office or postal shop.

SAFETY

After Hurricane Katrina cleared out New Orleans, the city went from one of the most dangerous cities in America to the safest. The murder rate went down to zero. The peace has not lasted completely, as law-abiding citizens and criminals have gradually returned to the city, but clearly New Orleans is far safer today than it was in the summer of 2005. Just the same, visitors are still occasionally targeted by stick-'em-up thugs, some of whom can be unnecessarily trigger-happy. Exercise the caution you would in any US city.

The possibility of getting mugged is something to consider even in areas you'd think are safe (eg the Garden District). Naturally, solo pedestrians are targeted more often than people walking in groups, and daytime is a better time to be out on foot than nighttime. Avoid entering secluded areas such as cemeteries alone, especially those in the Tremé.

Large crowds typically make the French Quarter a secure around-the-clock realm for the visitor. However, if your hotel or vehicle is on the margins of the Quarter, you might want to take a taxi back at night. The CBD and Warehouse District have plenty of activity during weekdays, but they're relatively deserted at night and on weekends. The B&Bs along Esplanade Ridge are near enough troubled neighborhoods to call for caution in the area at night. In the Quarter, street hustlers frequently approach tourists. You can simply walk away.

Pedestrians crossing the street do not have the right of way and motorists (unless they are from out of state) will not yield. Whether on foot or in a car, be wary before entering an intersection, as New Orleans drivers are notorious for running yellow and even red lights.

TAX & REFUNDS

New Orleans' 9% sales tax is tacked onto virtually everything including meals, groceries and car rentals. For accommodations, room and occupancy taxes add an additional 12% to your bill plus $1 to $3 per person, depending on the size of the hotel.

Some merchants in Louisiana participate in a program called **Louisiana Tax Free Shopping** (☎ 568-5323; www.louisianataxfree.com). Look for the snazzy red-and-blue 'Tax Free' logo in the window or on the sign of the store. Usually these stores specialize in the kinds of impulse purchases people are likely to make while on vacation. In these stores, present a passport to verify you are not a US citizen and request a voucher as you make your purchase. Reimbursement centers are located in the **Downtown Refund Center** (☎ 568-3605; Riverwalk Marketplace; ⏲ 10am-6pm Mon-Sat, 11am-6pm Sun) and the main lobby of the **Louis Armstrong Airport** (☎ 467-0723; ⏲ 7am-6pm Mon-Fri, 7am-3pm Sat & Sun).

TELEPHONE

New Orleans' telephones are run by BellSouth. The *Yellow Pages* has comprehensive business listings, organized alphabetically by subject. The New Orleans area code is ☎ 504, which includes Thibodaux and the surrounding area. Baton Rouge and its surrounding area use the area code ☎ 225. Area code ☎ 318 applies to the northern part of the state.

When dialing another area code, you must dial ☎ 1 before the area code. For example, to call a Baton Rouge number from New Orleans, begin by dialing ☎ 1-225. At pay phones, local calls start at 50¢, but long-distance charges apply to 'nonlocal' calls even within the same area code – to Thibodaux, for example – and costs rapidly increase once you dial another area code. Hotel telephones often have heavy surcharges.

Toll-free numbers start with ☎ 1-800 or ☎ 1-888 and allow you to call free within the USA. These numbers are commonly offered by car-rental operators, large hotels and the like. Dial ☎ 411 for local directory assistance, or ☎ 1 + area code + 555-1212 for long-distance directory information; dial ☎ 1-800-555-1212 for toll-free number information. Dial ☎ 0 for the operator.

If you're calling from abroad, the international country code for the USA (and Canada) is ☎ 1.

To make an international call direct from New Orleans, dial ☎ 011 + country code + area code (dropping the leading 0) + number. For calls to Canada, there's no need to dial the international access code ☎ 011. For international operator assistance, dial ☎ 00.

Cell Phones

The USA uses a variety of cell (mobile) phone systems, only one of which is compatible with systems used outside North America. This is the Global System for Mobile telephones (GSM), which is becoming more commonly available worldwide. Many popular phone services, including T-Mobile, Vodafone and Orange, offer GSM service. Check with your local provider to determine whether your phone will work in New Orleans.

Fax

Besides hotel fax machines, services in the French Quarter include **French Quarter Postal Emporium** (Map pp310–11; ☎ 525-6651; fax 525-6652; 1000 Bourbon St), at St Philip St. In the CBD there is a **Kinko's FedEx Office Center** (Map pp308–9; ☎ 581-2541; fax 525-6272; 762 St Charles Ave; ⏲ 24hr).

Phonecards

Phonecards are readily sold at newsstands and pharmacies. They save you the trouble of feeding coins into pay phones, and are often more economical as well.

TELEVISION

Broadcast and cable channels are available in most hotels and in many bars. The local channels have nothing to offer that would keep you from having fun on the town, but if you're tethered to a particular US network program, chances are you can find a way to avoid missing it while in New Orleans.

TIME

New Orleans Standard Time is six hours behind GMT/UTC. In US terms, that puts it one hour behind the East Coast and two hours ahead of the West Coast. In early April the clocks move ahead one hour for Daylight Saving Time; clocks move back one hour in October.

TIPPING

Tipping is not really optional. In bars and restaurants the waitstaff are paid minimal wages and rely on tips for their livelihoods. The service has to be absolutely appalling before you consider not tipping. Tip at least 15% of the bill or 20% if the service is great. You needn't tip at fast-food restaurants or self-serve caféterias.

Taxi drivers expect a 15% tip. If you stay at a top-end hotel, tipping is so common you might get tennis elbow from reaching for your wallet constantly. Hotel porters who carry bags a long way expect $3 to $5, or $1 per bag; smaller services (holding the taxi door open for you) might justify only $1. Valet parking is worth about $2, and is given when your car is returned to you.

TOILETS

A recording by Benny Grunch, 'Ain't No Place to Pee on Mardi Gras Day,' summarizes the situation in the French Quarter. While tour guides delight in describing the unsanitary waste-disposal practices of the old Creole days, the stench arising from back alleys is actually far more recent in origin.

Public rest rooms can be found in the Jackson Brewery mall (Map pp310–11) and in the French Market (Map pp310–11). Larger hotels often have accessible rest rooms off the lobby, usually near the elevators and pay phones.

TOURIST INFORMATION

Right next to popular Jackson Sq in the heart of the Quarter, the **New Orleans Welcome Center** (Map pp310–11; ☎ 566-5031; 529 St Ann St; 🕑 9am-5pm), in the lower Pontalba Building, offers maps, up-to-date pocket guidebooks, listings of upcoming events and a variety of brochures for sights, restaurants and hotels. The helpful staff can help you find accommodations in a pinch, answer questions, and offer advice about New Orleans.

Information kiosks scattered through main tourist areas offer most of the same brochures as the Welcome Center, but their staff tend not to be as knowledgeable.

Information on Louisiana tourism can be obtained through the mail from **Louisiana Office of Tourism** (☎ 342-8119, 800-414-8626; PO Box 94291, Baton Rouge, LA, 70804).

VISAS

With the exception of Canadians, who only need proof of Canadian citizenship, all foreign visitors to the USA must have a valid passport and most visitors must also have a US visa. It's a good idea to keep photocopies of these documents; in the case of theft, they'll be a lot easier to replace.

Your passport should be valid for at least six months longer than your intended stay in the USA. Documents of financial stability and/or guarantees from a US resident are sometimes required, particularly for visitors from third world countries.

A reciprocal visa-waiver program applies to citizens of certain countries who may enter the USA for stays of 90 days or less without obtaining a visa. Currently these countries include Andorra, Australia, Austria, Belgium, Brunei, Denmark, Finland, France, Germany, Iceland, Ireland, Italy, Japan, Liechtenstein, Luxembourg, Monaco, the Netherlands, New Zealand, Norway, Portugal, San Marino, Singapore, Slovenia, Spain, Sweden, Switzerland and the UK. Under this program you must have a round-trip ticket on an airline that participates in the visa-waiver program, proof of financial solvency, a signed form waiving the right to a hearing of deportation and you will not be allowed to extend your stay beyond 90 days. Consult with your travel agency or contact the airlines directly for more information.

Other travelers will need to obtain a visa from a US consulate or embassy. In most countries the process can be done by mail.

Visa applicants may need to 'demonstrate binding obligations' that will ensure their return home. Because of this requirement, those who are planning to travel through other countries before arriving in the US are generally better off applying for their US visa while they are still in their home country, rather than doing so while on the road.

The most common type of visa is a Nonimmigrant Visitors Visa (B1 for business purposes, B2 for tourism or visiting friends and relatives). A visitors visa is good for one or five years with multiple entries, and it specifically prohibits the visitor from taking up paid employment in the USA. The validity period for US visitor visas depends on what country you're from. The length of time you'll be allowed to stay in the USA is ultimately determined by US immigration authorities at the port of entry.

Tourist visitors are usually granted a six-month stay on first arrival. If you try to extend that time, the first assumption will be that you are working illegally, so come prepared with concrete evidence that you've been traveling extensively and will continue to be a model tourist. A wad of traveler's checks looks much better than a solid and unmoving bank account. Extensions are handled by the US Justice

Department's **Immigration & Naturalization Service** (INS; Map pp308–9; ☎ 800-375-5283; Rm T8011, 701 Loyola Ave; ⏲ 7:30am-2:15pm Mon-Fri) in the main post office.

WOMEN TRAVELERS

Intoxicated bands of young men in the Quarter and along parade routes are a particular nuisance for women. Otherwise respectable students and businessmen are transformed by New Orleans – they expect to drink and carouse in a manner that is not acceptable in their home towns. Women in almost any attire are liable to receive lewd comments. More-provocative outfits will lead to a continuous barrage of requests to 'show your tits.' This occurs on any Friday or Saturday night, not just during Mardi Gras. Many men assume that any woman wearing impressive strands of beads has acquired them by displaying herself on the street.

Conducting yourself in a common-sense manner will help you avoid most problems. For example, you're more vulnerable if you've been drinking or using drugs than if you're sober; you're more vulnerable alone than if you're with company; and you're more vulnerable in a high-crime urban area than in a 'better' district. Of course, any serious problems you encounter (including assault or rape) should be reported to the **police** (☎ 911). The YWCA offers a **Rape Crisis Hotline** (☎ 483-8888), as well as a **Battered Women's Hotline** (☎ 486-0377).

The New Orleans branch of **Planned Parenthood** (Map pp314–15; ☎ 897-9200; 4018 Magazine St) provides health-care services for women, including pregnancy testing and birth-control counseling.

WORK

It perhaps goes without saying that New Orleans is not a magnet for migrating professionals. Tourism puts butter on most people's bread in this town, and passers-through might score a low-paying job in a bar, restaurant or youth hostel. Of course, overseas visitors must have the proper work visas in order to work in the US.

Skills in construction, electricity or plumbing are particularly in demand for the foreseeable future. Show up in town with a truck full of tools and very likely you'll find work as an independent contractor.

You probably don't need a work visa to volunteer in the rebuilding effort in town. Some organizations, such as **Habitat For Humanity** (www.habitat.org), claim to have more workers than they need, but it can't hurt to check in with them.

See p320 for a list of possible charitable organizations.

Glossary

Glossary

andouille – (ahn-*doo*-we) a French sausage made with tripe; Creole versions are made from ground pork in casings of smoked pig intestines; also known as chitterlings

bayou – a canal of sluggish and marshy water removed from the main river channel

beignet – (ben-*yea*) a deep-fried pastry, which is New Orleans' version of the doughnut; typically covered with powdered sugar and is sweet, although savory variations also exist

Big Easy – nickname for New Orleans that suggests the city is on the take: to make things happen your way, just pay off the right people

boudin – *Cajun* sausage usually filled with pork, pork liver and rice

café au lait – mixture of coffee and steamed milk

Cajun – a corruption of the word Acadian; the term refers to a Louisianan descended from French-speaking Acadia, but may also apply to other rural settlers that live amid Cajuns; also relating to food and music

carpetbagger – a derogatory name given to itinerant financial or political opportunists, particularly Northerners in the reconstructed South, who moved in with their possessions in heavy cloth satchels; their Southern accomplices were branded 'scalawags'

Code Noir – the 'Black Code' adopted by the French administration in 1724 that governed the conduct of free people of color and prescribed how masters should treat slaves and under what conditions freedom should be granted; free people of color were accorded the rights of full citizenship except that they could neither vote, hold public office nor marry a white person

Confederacy – the nation formed by the Southern states that seceded from the USA prior to the Civil War. With the South's defeat in 1865 came the end of the Confederacy

Creole – a free person of French, Spanish or African descent born in Spanish America; during the 19th century whites of French or Spanish descent used Creole to exclusively refer to whites; however, following the Civil War the term also came to encompass the free Creoles of color; its definition has shifted with time – now people descended from any of the above cultures are regarded as Creole (from the Spanish *criollo*, meaning native to the locality); also relating to food and music

dirty rice – small quantities of giblets or ground pork, along with green onions, peppers and celery, fried with rice

Dixie – nickname for the South derived from the French term *dix* (10)

dressed – a 'dressed' *po'boy* comes with mayonnaise, mustard, lettuce and tomato

fais do-do – *Cajun* house dance

faubourg – French for suburb; it's what Creoles called the neighborhoods they developed beyond the boundaries of the French Quarter

FEMA – Federal Emergency Management Agency

gallery – a balcony or roofed promenade

gens de couleur libre – French phrase for the 'free people of color' during the antebellum period; after the Civil War they were known as *Creole*s of color

go cup – plastic container provided for patrons so they can transfer an alcoholic beverage from a bottle or glass as they leave a bar; it is legal to drink alcoholic beverages in the street but illegal to carry an open glass container

grand dérangement – literally 'forced migration;' used to describe the great dispersal of Acadians; following the 18th-century colonial wars between England and France, 10,000 Acadians were deported from Nova Scotia by the English in 1755

gris-gris – magical objects used in voodoo, which have curative, protective or evil powers

grits – coarsely ground hominy prepared as a mush; served throughout the South, it picks up the flavor of whatever is ladled over it, often butter or gravy

icebox pie – a cold, often creamy, pie

jambalaya – a one-dish meal of rice cooked with onions, peppers and celery along with ham; Louisiana chefs waste nothing – any leftovers go into this dish

krewes – clubs that sponsor Mardi Gras parades and events; ersatz Old English spelling for 'crews'

lagniappe – literally 'a little something extra;' small gift from a merchant or resident

levee – a French word meaning 'raised' or 'elevated' that applies to the natural or artificial riverbanks that guard the floodplain

Louisiana Purchase – the deal through which the US acquired the entire Louisiana territory, including New Orleans, from Napoleon Bonaparte in 1803

muffuletta – Italian dock workers were once sustained with this enormous sandwich of ham, hard salami, provolone and olive salad piled onto a round loaf of Italian bread and liberally sprinkled with olive oil and vinegar

NCAA – National Collegiate Athletic Association

neutral ground – a median; the Canal St median served as a neutral meeting space dividing the *Creole* and American communities

NOLA – the abbreviation for New Orleans is NO, for Louisiana it's LA; put 'em together and you get NOLA

NPS – National Park Service

picayune – used to refer to something of little value; also a coin formerly used by the Spanish in the South

pirogue – a dugout canoe that was traditionally carved by burning the center of a log and scraping out the embers; modern pirogues are shallow-draft vessels that can be made from plywood

po'boy – a submarine-style sandwich served on fresh French bread; fried oysters, soft-shell crab, catfish or deli meats are used as fillings

praline – confection made from pecans, sugar and butter

quadroon – a person who is one-quarter black; the term was used to refer to light-skinned free women of color in the 18th and 19th centuries

R&B – abbreviation of rhythm & blues; a musical style developed by African Americans that combines blues and jazz

red beans and rice – spicy bean stew made with peppers, many seasonings and a hunk of salt pork, or tasso, often served over white rice with *andouille* sausage

réveillon – a traditional *Creole* Christmas Eve dinner

roux – a mixture of flour and oil or butter that is heated slowly until it browns; used as a thickener in *Cajun* soups and sauces

second line – the partying group that follows parading musicians; the resulting parade is often called a 'second line,' while joining in is called 'second-lining'

trad jazz – traditional jazz, as it was played before the Swing era

Union – generally the Union means the entire US, including the North and the South. However, it often specifically means those parts of the country fighting to preserve the Union during the Civil War; the Southern states, which had seceded, were not considered part of the Union during that period, while the north was

Vieux Carré – French for 'old square;' it refers to the French Quarter; original walled city of New Orleans bounded by Canal St, N Rampart St, Esplanade Ave and the Mississippi River

zydeco – fast, syncopated *Creole* dance music, influenced by *Cajun*, African American and Afro Caribbean cultures; zydeco is often a combination of *R&B* and *Cajun* with French lyrics; bands typically feature guitar, accordion and frottoir

Behind the Scenes

THE LONELY PLANET STORY

The story begins with a classic travel adventure: Tony and Maureen Wheeler's 1972 journey across Europe and Asia to Australia. There was no useful information about the overland trail then, so Tony and Maureen published the first Lonely Planet guidebook to meet a growing need.

From a kitchen table, Lonely Planet has grown to become the largest independent travel publisher in the world, with offices in Melbourne (Australia), Oakland (USA) and London (UK). Today Lonely Planet guidebooks cover the globe. There is an ever-growing list of books and information in a variety of media. Some things haven't changed. The main aim is still to make it possible for adventurous travelers to get out there – to explore and better understand the world.

At Lonely Planet we believe travelers can make a positive contribution to the countries they visit – if they respect their host communities and spend their money wisely. Every year 5% of company profit is donated to charities around the world.

THIS BOOK

This guidebook was commissioned in Lonely Planet's Oakland office, and produced by the following:

Commissioning Editor Jay Cooke

Coordinating Editor Lauren Rollheiser

Coordinating Cartographer Joshua Geoghegan

Coordinating Layout Designer Indra Kilfoyle

Managing Editor Melanie Dankel

Managing Cartographer Alison Lyall

Assisting Editors Lutie Clark, Helen Koehne, Joanne Newell

Assisting Cartographer Emma McNicol

Cover Designer Gerilyn Attebery

Project Manager Rachel Imeson

Thanks to Sally Darmody, Pableaux Johnson, Wayne Murphy, Charmaine O'Brien, Raphael Richards, Celia Wood

Cover photographs Jazz trumpet player New Orleans, Louisiana, Miles Ertman/Masterfile (top); A lime green Antique store on Magazine St in the Garden District Richard, Cummins/Lonely Planet Images (bottom).

Internal photographs p6 (#2, 3), p7 (#2), p86, p93 Jerry Alexander/Lonely Planet Images; p7 (#1) Michael Aw/Lonely Planet Images; p121 APL/Corbis; p2, p3, p5 (#3), p6 (#1), p8, p12, p43 (#1, 2, 3), p56, p68, p76, p111, p159, p236 Richard Cummins/Lonely Planet Images; p4 (#3), p42 (#1), p46 (#1, 3), p72, p147, p163 Thomas Downs/Lonely Planet Images; p207, p253, p260 John Elk III/Lonely Planet Images; p124 EPA/AAP; p5 (#1), p106, p132, p140, p183 Lee Foster/Lonely Planet Images; p41 Rick Gerharter/Lonely Planet Images; p7 (#3) Peter Hendrie/Lonely Planet Images; p46 (#2), p47 (#2), p48 Pableux Johnson; p4 (#1, 2), p5 (#2), p21, p28, p39, p42 (#2), p45 (#1, 2, 3), p47 (#1), p51, p63, p83, p96, p176, p195, p198, p217, p220, p229, p233, p242 Ray Laskowitz/Lonely Planet Images; p32 John Neubauer/Lonely Planet Images; p166 Margie Politzer/Lonely Planet Images; p171 Stephen Saks/Lonely Planet Images; p18 Neil Setchfield/Lonely Planet Images; p44 Witold Skrypczak/Lonely Planet Images; Many of the images in this guide are available for licensing from Lonely Planet Images: www.lonelyplanetimages.com.

THANKS

TOM DOWNS

So many people helped me in New Orleans, despite all they and their city have been going through. I hope in some small way this book contributes to the return of New Orleans. Thanks to old friends Ryan Ver Berkmoes and Erin Corrigan for eating and drinking with me in New Orleans, and especially for providing indispensable material for the Sleeping and Shopping chapters. Rob Florence, as always, was a sagacious local friend who kept me abreast of Katrina issues with innumerable emails and phone conversations. I'll never forget our harrowing trek through the Lower Ninth Ward. Christine DeCuir of the NOMCVB was, as always, a solid professional contact. She helped me line up media contacts and hotel rooms at a time when it seemed most hotels were booked by FEMA operatives. Terri Kaupp and Larry Lovell, PR people working long hours to bring back New Orleans tourism, offered tons of information that would not have been easy for me to gather in the post-Katrina upheaval. John Callaway and Trish Cruse brought me up to date on Jazz Fest. Alan Gutierrez helped me to new hangouts in the Marigny and Bywater. Bonnie Warren shared invaluable anecdotes, insight and contacts. At Lonely Planet, commissioning editor Jay Cooke dove into this project with both feet, even traveling to New Orleans in December 2005 to scope things out. His brief was detailed and intelligent. I had a purely positive experience with editor Lauren Rollheiser, who handled the project with sensitivity and in an impressive, orderly fashion. Thanks also to Lutie Clark, who edited many chapters. Cartographers Alison Lyall and Josh Geoghegan obviously did a superb job on the maps and were a pleasure to work with. I'd like to tip my hat to the wife and kids for their undying love and support. Fawn, Mai, Lana and Liam - I love you.

OUR READERS

Many thanks to the travelers who used the last edition and wrote to us with helpful hints, useful advice and interesting anecdotes:
Allen Armer, Lella Baker, Geoff Beardshall, Anne Berns, Anna Bolteus, John Carey, Nicole Geiger, Tony Goodbody, Joseph Grynbaum, Silvia Guiu, Stuart Hale, Tom Hall, Kevin Hawkins, Stefanie Henkel-Hagmann, Elizabeth Hogg, Nicole Ives, Massoud Javadi, Shawn Kairschner, Jeroen Kruis, Thomas Lowenburg, Stefan Lucke, Cynthia McKnight, Carrie Mogged, Heather Monell, Jacques Noel, Sonia Ortiz, Daniel Pearce, Genevieve Peterson, Dierdre Price, Tanya Ragan, Judy Robinson, Linda Scira, Karl Siemsen, Kate Simister, Nicolle Singer, Jane Skalisky, Peter & Gillian Sleight, Christopher Smejkal, Paul Stangroom, William Swinerton, Thor & Mary Swope, Henry Tobias, N Tomich, Matthew Ulyatt, Frank van der Heijden, Jaime Wayne-Smith, Stacey Wisdom

ACKNOWLEDGEMENTS

Many thanks to the following for the use of their content:
Orleans Parish Route Map © NORTA 2006

SEND US YOUR FEEDBACK

We love to hear from travelers – your comments keep us on our toes and help make our books better. Our well-traveled team reads every word on what you loved or loathed about this book. Although we cannot reply individually to postal submissions, we always guarantee that your feedback goes straight to the appropriate authors, in time for the next edition. Each person who sends us information is thanked in the next edition – and the most useful submissions are rewarded with a free book.

To send us your updates – and find out about Lonely Planet events, newsletters and travel news – visit our award-winning website: www.lonelyplanet.com/feedback.

Note: We may edit, reproduce and incorporate your comments in Lonely Planet products such as guidebooks, websites and digital products, so let us know if you don't want your comments reproduced or your name acknowledged. For a copy of our privacy policy visit www.lonelyplanet.com/privacy.

Notes

Notes

Notes

Notes

Notes

Notes

Index

See also separate indexes for Eating (p301), Entertainment (p301), Shopping (p302) and Sleeping (p302).

1850 House Museum 137

A

Abita Brewery 264
Acadian Village 259, 262
accommodations 236-50, 276, *see also* Sleeping subindex 302
  apartments 237
  B&Bs 236
  check-in 237
  costs 236, 276
  reservations 237
activities 216-18
air travel 272
airport 272
  to/from airport 273
Algren, Nelson 62
alligators 152, 263, **5**
ambulance services 277
Amistad Research Center 159
Anderson, Harry 173
Anderson, Sherwood 61
Aquarium of the Americas 152
architecture 68-74
  American style 71-2
  artisans 73
  beaux arts 72-3
  federal style 71
  French colonial 69
  Gothic revival 72
  Greek revival 71
  influences 70-1, 111
  ironwork 73, **2**
  Italianate 72
  Katrina aftermath 68, 73-4
  second empire 73
  shotgun style 71
  Spanish colonial 69-70
  useful terms 70
Ardoin, Amadé 83
area codes, *see inside front cover*
Armstrong, Louis 77-78
  Satchmo SummerFest 17
arts 56-66, *see also* galleries, literature, painting
  ballet 64
  courses 212
  dance 213-14
  Katrina aftermath 63, 64
  markets 56, 230
  museums 59
  opera 64
  photography 59-60
  pottery 61
  theater 63, 214
ATMs 279-80
Audubon Institute
  Aquarium of the Americas 152
  Entergy IMAX theatre 215
  Audubon Zoological Gardens 158
Audubon, John James 57

B

babysitting organizations 276
Backstreet Cultural Museum 80, 146
Barataria Preserve 263, 264
bars 200-6, 243, *see also* Entertainment subindex 301
Bartholomew, Dave 80
baseball 23, 215-16
basketball 23, 216
bathrooms 283
Batiste, Uncle Lionel 206
Baton Rouge 264-5
Battle of New Orleans 110, 112
Bayou St John 160-1, **317**
Beauregard, General Pierre Gustave Toutant 139, 171
  gravesite 164
  monument 161
Beauregard-Keyes House 139, 171
beer 98, 264
Bellocq, Ernest J 59, 60
Better than Ezra 83
bicycling 216-17, 272
Blanco, Kathleen 122, 128
boat travel 272-3
Bocage Plantation House 255
Bolden, Charles 'Buddy' 77
Bonaparte, Napoleon 111, 172, 201
books 14, 61-2
  environment 29
  history 107
  music 80
  photography 60
  Robicheaux novels 62
  vampire chronicles 63
Botanical Gardens 162
Bourbon St 167, **7**
Brennan, Ella 190
Brigtsen, Frank 193
Bring New Orleans Back Commission 13-14, 30, 129, 130
Brown, Michael 125, 126, 128
Burke, James Lee 62
bus travel 273-4
Bush, George W 125, 127-8
business hours 276, *see also inside front cover*
  restaurants 176-7
  shops 222
Butler, Henry 79, 208
Butler, Major General Benjamin 115
Bywater **316**
  accommodations 242-3
  attractions 148-50
  bars & clubs 202-4
  bus travel 149
  eating 185-7
  live music 207-8
  shopping 230-1
  streetcars 149

C

Cabildo 138
Cable, George Washington 61
Cajun country 257-62
  prairies 259-62
  wetlands 258-9
Cajun Music Hall of Fame 261, 262
Cajuns 113-14
  food 86-7, 118
  le grand dérangement 114, 257, 260
  music 82-3
Canal Place 220
Canal St Ferry 152
Canal streetcar 275
Capote, Truman 62
car travel 274
Carnival, *see* Mardi Gras
Carousel Gardens & Storyland 162
carpetbaggers 115
Cat Head Delta Blues & Folk Art 266, 267
cathedrals 137, 170
Catholicism 21
CBD **308-9**
  accommodations 244-6
  attractions 150-5
  bars & clubs 204
  bus travel 151
  eating 187-8
  galleries 211-12
  live music 208
  shopping 231
  streetcars 151
cell phones 282
cemeteries 149
  Lafayette Cemetery No 1 156-7
  Metairie Cemetery 163-4
  National Military Park & Cemetery 265
  St Louis Cemetery No 1 147, 172
  St Louis Cemetery No 3 160
  St Roch Cemetery 150
charitable organizations 320
Charles Briggs' House 168
chemists 280
Chenier, Clifton 83
Chertoff, Michael 125, 128
Chez Vodun 144

000 map pages
000 photographs

children, travel with 276
attractions 141
babysitters 276
food 103-4
Jazz Fest 53
live music 210
Chopin, Kate 61
Christmas 19, 100
churches 147
cinemas 214-15
City Park 161-4, **4**
Civil Rights 116
Civil War 114-15
Claiborne, Governor WCC 110
Clarksdale 266, 267
climate 27, 277
clubs 200-6, *see also* Entertainment subindex
cocktails 97-8
Code Noir 112-13
Codrescu, Andrei 62
coffee 98-9
Company of the West 109
Confederate Museum 152
Congo Sq 112
Connick, Harry, Jr 36, 39, 78, 148
consulates 277
Contemporary Arts Center 153
Convention Center 126
convicts 109
costs 12, 25-6, *see also inside front cover*
accommodations 236, 276
food 177
taxes 222
tipping 178
courses 212
Crawford, Davell 82
credit cards 280
Creoles 113-14
culture 113
food 86-7, 178
history 111
Mardi Gras 34
music 116
Crewes, Harry 62
culture 19-25
customs regulations 277
cycling 216-17, 272

D

de La Salle, Nicolas 109
de Marigny de Mandeville, Bernard Xavier Philippe 148
de Pauger, Adrien 109, 136
de Pineda, Alonso Alvarez 109
de Soto, Hernando 109
de Ulloa, Antonio 110
Degas, Edgar 57, 250
Delta Blues Museum 266
demographics 13, 19, 20, 130
historic 113-14
post-WWII 117
desegregation 117, *see also* segregation
Destrehan Plantation 255
disabled travelers 277
Dockery Farm 266, 267
Dr John 82
Domino, Fats 80, 125
Donaldsonville 256, 257
Dopsie, Rockin', Jr 209
drinks 97-9
absinthe 201
beer 98, 264
cocktails 97-8
coffee 98-9
Herbsaint 201
root beer 99
drugstores 280
Dueling Oaks 162-3

E

economy 25-6, 107
early 20th century 117
early trade 111
tourism 118
egrets 263
electricity 277
embassies 277
emergencies 277, *see also inside front cover*
environmental issues 27-9
Esplanade Ridge **317**
accommodations 249-50
attractions 160-1
bus travel 160
eating 194-6
Essence Music Festival 17
Eunice 261
Evangeline Oak 260
Evans, Walker 60
events 14-19
Battle of New Orleans Celebration 15
Feux de Joie 19
Halloween 18
Independence Day 17
Martin Luther King, Jr Day 15
New Year's Eve 19
Sugar Bowl 14-15
Tales of the Cocktail 17
Voodoo Music Experience 18
Wine & Food Experience 16-17
exchange rates, *see inside front cover*

F

Factors Row 152
Fair Grounds Race Track 52-3, 160, 216
Falcon, Joe 82
fashion 22-3, *see also* Shopping subindex 302
Faubourg Marigny **173**, **316**
accommodations 242-3
attractions 148-50
bars & clubs 202-4
bus travel 149
eating 185-7
live music 207-8
shopping 230-1
streetcars 149
walking tour 172-4
Faulkner House 140, 166, 224
Faulkner, William 61
gravesite 268
Federal Emergency Management Agency (FEMA) 122, 125
trailers 146
Ferdinand, Roy 58
ferries 152, 272-3
festivals 14-19, 199, *see also* Jazz Fest, Mardi Gras
All Saints Day 18
Celebration in the Oaks 18-19
Elvis week 270
Essence Music Festival 17
French Market Creole Tomato Festival 17
French Quarter Festival 16
Indian Sunday 16
Louisiana Crawfish Festival 16
St Patrick's Day 15-16, 101
Satchmo SummerFest 17
Southern Decadence 17
Tennessee Williams Literary Festival 16
films 64-6, 107
fire services 277
fishing 23
fitness centers 218
Fitzgerald, F Scott 61
Fontenot, Adam 83
food 86-104, 225, **6**, *see also* Eating subindex 301
Cajun 86-7, 118
celebrations 99-101
children 103-4
costs 177
courses 212
Creole 86-7, 178
culture 88-9
fruits & vegetables 95
gumbo 92, 104
history 87-8
influences 86-9
itineraries 253
jambalaya 93
meats 91-2
muffulettas 93
po'boys 92-3
recipes 104
restaurants 101-3, 176-96
seafood 89-91, 192, 194
snowballs 190
soul food 86-7
specialties 89-97
sweets 96-7
traditions 88-9
vegetarians & vegans 103
football 23, 215
Forbes, Justin 59
Frank, Robert 60
French Market 138, 221
French Quarter **167**, **170**, **173**, **310-11**, **4**
accommodations 238-42
attractions 135-45
bars & clubs 200-2
bus travel 136
eating 178-85
ferries 136
French Quarter Festival 16
galleries 210-11
ghost tour 170-2
live music 206-7
shopping 220, 223-9
streetcars 136
walking tours 166-8, 172-4
Friedlander, Lee 60

G

galleries 56, 210-13
  Cat Head Delta Blues & Folk Art 266, 267
  Contemporary Arts Center 153
  Louisiana ArtWorks 153-4
  New Orleans Museum of Art 162, 163
  Newcomb Art Gallery 159
  Ogden Museum of Southern Art 155
Gallier Hall 151
Gallier House Museum 139, **2**
Gallier Sr, James 168
Garden District **169**, **312-13**
  accommodations 246-8
  attractions 156-7
  bus travel 156
  eating 188-90
  galleries 213
  shopping 222, 232-3
  streetcars 156
  walking tour 168-70
gardens, *see* parks & gardens
gay travelers 277-8
  bars & clubs 204
  Southern Decadence 17-18
geography 27-8
Gibson Beale Street Showcase 269
golf 217
Goodrich-Stanley House 156
government & politics 26, 106-7
Grace King House 156
Graceland 268, 269
Grau, Shirley Ann 62
Guillemard, Gilberto 137

H

Haardt, Anton 58, 169, 213
Harrah's Casino 153
health 218, 278
Heldner, Knute 58
Hermann-Grima House 140
Hermitage Plantation House 255
Historic New Orleans Collection 139
Historic Voodoo Museum 140, **5**
history 106-18, *see also* Hurricane Katrina
  antebellum period 111-12, 114
  Battle of New Orleans 110, 112
  Civil Rights movement 116
  Civil War 114-15
  Code Noir 112-13
  early colonization 109-11
  European exploration 109
  free people of color 112-13
  French rule 109-10
  immigration 109, 113-14
  Jazz Age 116
  Jim Crow law 116
  le grand dérangement 114, 257, 260
  Louisiana Purchase 111
  Native Americans 108
  plaçage 113
  post-WWII 117-18
  Reconstruction 115-16
  slavery 110, 112-14, 141
  Spanish rule 110-11
  World War II 117
holidays 278
  Christmas 19, 100
  Thanksgiving 100
Hornets 23, 215-16
horseback riding 217
Houma 258, 259
Houma people 108
Houmas House 255
Hula Mae's Laundry 141
Hunter, Clementine 58
hurricanes
  flood protection 29
  future infrastructure 130
  geographic vulnerability 28
  hurricane parties 123
  major hurricanes 120-2
  Saffir-Simpson Scale 120
  storm surges 28-9, 122
Hurricane Katrina 3, 108, 120-30
  aftermath 126-30
  artworks 56
  Bring New Orleans Back Commission 13-14, 30, 129, 130
  conspiracy theories 127
  Convention Center 126
  crime 126
  demographic shift 19
  devastated areas 135
  economic effects 25
  emergency response 125-6
  environmental impacts 26-9, 129
  environmental issues 129
  evacuation 126
  floods 123, 124-5
  initial response 122
  levees 27, 124-5
  military response 128-9
  political response 125-6, 127-8, 130
  population 129
  racial divides 13, 127-8
  redevelopment 12-14, 29-30, 73-4, 130, 148
  refugees 130
  storm surges 122
  Superdome 126, 151
  tropical storm 122
Hurricane Rita 128-9

I

immigration 109, 113-14
Indian Sunday 16
insurance 274, 280
Internet access 278
Internet resources 24, 278
  accommodations 237, 276
  cultural 24
  news 24
Irish Channel 157
  walking tour 168-70
itineraries 133-4, 253-4

J

Jackson, Andrew 112
Jackson Brewery 221
Jackson Square 136, **5**, **310-11**
Jackson, William Henry 59
jazz 77-9
  brass 79
  gigs 81
  New Orleans Jazz National Historic Park 142
  pioneers 77-8
  resurgence 78-9
Jazz Fest 16, 32, 49-54, **46-8**
  children 53
  Fair Grounds Race Track 52-3, 160, 216
  food & drink 53-4, 100
  history 50
  musicians 53
  off-site venues 54
  planning 50-2
  shopping 54
  tents & stages 52-3
  tickets 50
Jean Lafitte town 263-4
Jefferson, Thomas 111
Jewish people 114
Jim Crow law 116
jogging 217
Jollain, François Gérard 57
Jungle Gardens 260, 262

K

Keyes, Francis Parkinson 62, 140
King, Martin Luther, Jr 268-9
krewes 34-5, 38
  Bacchus 36, 39
  Endymion 36, 38
  Iris 35, 38
  Krewe du Vieux 37
  Mistick Krewe of Comus 34
  Momus 34
  Orpheus 36, 39
  Petronius 35
  Proteus 34, 39
  Rex 39
  Tucks 38
  Zulu 39
Krown, Joe 209
Ku Klux Klan 115

L

Lacen, Anthony 'Tuba Fats' 80
Lafayette 259-62
Lafayette Cemetery No 1 156-7
Lafitte, Jean 110, 112, 166, 167, 172
Lafitte town 263-4
Lagasse, Emeril 184, 188-9, 190
Lalaurie, Madame 171

000 map pages
000 photographs

Landrieu, Mitch 13
language 24-5
Lanzas, Nilo 58, 213
Laura Plantation 256, 257
Laurel Valley Village 258
Laveau, Marie 137, 143, 147-8
Law, John 109
le grand dérangement 114, 257, 260
Le Moyne, Jean-Baptiste 109
Le Moyne, Pierre 109
Lee Circle 153
legal matters 278-9
  Jim Crow law 116
  Mardi Gras 40
  Napoleonic Code 111, 114
Leonard, Elmore 62
lesbian travelers 277-8
  bars & clubs 204
  Southern Decadence 17-18
levees 27, 124-5
Liberty Theater 261
libraries 151
literature 14, 61-2, *see also* books
Long, Earl 26
Long, Huey P 26
Longfellow, Henry Wadsworth 260
Longfellow-Evangeline State Historical Site 260, 262
Longhair, Professor 80
Louis Armstrong Park 146
Louisiana ArtWorks 153-4
Louisiana Capitol 264, 265
Louisiana Children's Museum 154
Louisiana Purchase 111
Louisiana State University 265
Lower Garden District **312-13**
  accommodations 246-8
  attractions 155-6
  bars & clubs 205
  bus travel 155
  eating 188-90
  galleries 213
  shopping 231-2
  streetcars 155
Loyola University 159

M

Madison, James 112
Magazine St 222
magazines 24
Mamou 261
maps 279
Mardi Gras 21, 32-9, 48-9, **42-5**
  balls 49
  Creole influences 34
  exhibits 137
  fashion 23, 49, 227
  food 99, 100
  future dates 49
  history 33-7, 112
  Indians 33, 35, 36-7
  krewes 34-5, 38
  legal matters 40
  Mamou 260
  masks 49, 227
  parades 15, 37-40
  planning 37, 40, 49
  post-Katrina 36-7
  superkrewes 35-6, 38-9
  throws 37
  walking parades 40, 48-9
Mardi Gras World 154
markets
  arts 56, 230
  farmers 231
  fashion 234
Marsalis, Branford 78
Marsalis, Ellis 78, 208
Marsalis, Wynton 78
Maspero's Exchange 141
McCrady, John 58
McIlhenny tabasco 260
measures 279, *see also inside front cover*
media 23-4
medical services 279
Memphis, TN 268-70, **269**
Metairie Cemetery 163-4
metric conversions 279, *see also inside front cover*
Michalopoulos, James 59, 211
Millet, Clarence 57
Mississippi Delta 265-7
Mississippi flood 117
Mississippi River 144-5, 254-7, **4**
Mississippi River Gulf Outlet 124
mobile phones 282
money 279-80, *see also inside front cover*
Montana, Allison 'Tootie' 106
Mooney, John 209
Morial, Ernest 'Dutch' 26, 117, 148
Morial, Marc 26, 117
Morton, Jelly Roll 78
Mortuary Chapel 148
motorcycle travel 274
museums
  1850 House Museum 137
  Backstreet Cultural Museum 146
  Cabildo 138
  Confederate Museum 152-3
  Delta Blues Museum 266, 267
  Gallier House Museum 139
  Historic Donaldsonville Museum 256, 257
  Historic New Orleans Collection 139
  Historic Voodoo Museum 140, **5**
  Louisiana Children's Museum 154
  LSU Rural Life Museum 265
  Musée Conti Historical Wax Museum 141
  Museum of the Acadian Memorial & African American Museum 260, 261
  National Civil Rights Museum 268, 269
  National World War II Museum 154-5
  New Orleans Museum of Art 162, 163
  New Orleans Pharmacy Museum 140
  Ogden Museum of Southern Art 155, 211
  Old Court House Museum 266, 267
  Old US Mint 142
  Opelousas Museum and Interpretive Center 261, 262
  River Road African American Museum 256, 257
  Rock 'n' Soul Museum 269
  Stax Museum 268, 269
  Wetlands Cajun Cultural Center 258, 259
music 76-84, *see also* jazz
  blues 80
  children 210
  classical music 64, 213-14
  courses 212
  fesitvals 266
  funk 80-2
  gigs 81, 206-10, 211, 254
  hip-hop 84
  indie 83-4
  influences 76, 82-3, 116
  opera 213-14
  playlist 77
  post-Katrina 76
  R&B 80-2
  reservations 198-9
  rock 83-4
  roots 83-4
  tickets 198-9
  zydeco 82-3
Musicians' Village 148

N

Nagin, Ray 13, 106-7, 108, 122-3, 125, 128, 129
Napoleon House 172
Napoleonic Code 111, 114
National Civil Rights Museum 268, 269
National Military Park & Cemetery 265, 267
National World War II Museum 154-5
NBA 215-16
Neville, Aaron 81
Neville, Art 82
Neville, Charmaine 208
New Iberia 260, 262
New Orleans & Carrollton Railroad 112
New Orleans Centre 221
New Orleans Cotton Exchange 152
New Orleans Jazz National Historic Park 142
New Orleans Museum of Art 162, 163
New Orleans Pharmacy Museum 140
New Orleans Public Library 151
Newcomb Art Gallery 159
Newcomb pottery 211

newspapers 23-4
NFL 14-15, 23, 215
Nottoway Plantation 256

O

Oak Alley Plantation 256
Ogden Museum of Southern Art 59, 155, 211
Old State Capitol 264, 265
Old US Mint 142
Opelousas 260, 262
O'Reilly, General Alejandro 110-11
Our Lady of the Rosary Rectory 161
Oxford, MI 268

P

painting 56-9, *see also* galleries
  contemporary 58-9
  historic 57
  museums 59
  outsider art 58
parks & gardens
  Botanical Gardens 162
  Carousel Gardens & Storyland 162
  City Park 161-4, **4**
  Louis Armstrong Park 146
  Sydney & Walda Besthoff Sculpture Garden 163
Payton, Nicholas 79
Penn, Sean 64
Percy, Walker 62
Peters, Samuel Jarvis 111
pharmacies 280
philosophy 20-1
photography 280
  courses 212
Pitot House 161
plaçage 113, 148-9
plantation country 254-7
plantations
  Bocage Plantation House 255
  Destrehan Plantation 255, 256
  Houmas House 255
  Laura Plantation 256
  Laurel Valley Village 258, 259
  Nottoway Plantation 256, 257
  Oak Alley Plantation 256, 257
  San Francisco Plantation 255, 256
  Shadows on the Teche 260, 261
Plessy, Homer 116, 148
police services 277
politics 26, 106-7
Pontalba, Madame Micaëla 137-8
population 12-13, 130
  post-Katrina 129
postal services 280-1
Powell, Shannon 208
Presbytère 137
Preservation Resource Center 155
Presley, Elvis 268, 270
Prima, Louis 78
  gravesite 164
Prudhomme, Paul 118, 129, 184, 190

Q

Quinapisa people 108

R

radio 24, 82, 102
Reconstruction 115-16
religion 21-2
restaurants 101-3, 176-96, *see also* Eating subindex 301
  costs 177
  opening hours 176-7
  reservations 177
  tipping 178
Reznor, Trent 84
Rice, Anne 63, 157, 169
River Rd 254-7
Riverbend **314-15**
  attractions 157-9
  bars & clubs 205-6
  bus travel 157
  eating 190-4
  galleries 213
  live music 209-10
  streetcars 157
riverboats 145, 273, **8**
Riverfront streetcar 275
Riverwalk 221
Robichaux, Coco 209
Rodrigue, George 59
Rowan Oak 268
Royal St 138
Ruffins, Kermit 21, 79, 207, 208

S

safety 281
Saffir-Simpson scale 120
St Augustine's Church 147
St Charles Ave streetcar 275
St Louis Cathedral 137, 170
St Louis Cemetery No 1 147, 172
St Louis Cemetery No 3 160-1
St Martinville 260, 262
St Roch Cemetery 150
St Vincent's Infant Asylum 156
Saints 23, 215
San Francisco Plantation 255, 256
Sanctuary 161
Saturday Night Live 65
Savoy Music Center 261
Schmidt, George 211-12
segregation 116-15, *see also* desegregation
Shadows on the Teche 260, 261
shopping 220-34
  business hours 222
Short, Colonel Robert 168
Simon 213
slavery 110, 112-14
  auctions 113, 141
  Civil War 114-15
  culture 112
  Reconstruction 115-16
Smith, Michael P 60
souvenirs 223
spas 218
sports
  baseball 23, 215-16
  basketball 23, 215-16
  fishing 23
  football 14-15, 23, 215
  horse racing 160, 216
  tennis 217
Stanley, Henry Morton 156
storm surges 28-9, 122
Storyville 60, 116
streetcars 275
Sugar Bowl 14-15, 215
Sun Studio 268, 269
Superdome 126, 151
Sydney & Walda Besthoff Sculpture Garden 163

T

taxes 222, 281-2
taxis 275
Tchefuncte people 108
telephone services 282
television 65, 282
tennis 217
Thanksgiving 100
theater 63, 214
theft 281
Thibodaux 258, 259
Thomas, Irma 81
time 12, 282
Times-Picayune 23, 125
tipping 178, 282-3
toliets 283
Toole, John Kennedy 62
tourism 25, 118
tourist information 283
tours
  bus 135
  carriage 135
  swamp 258-9
  walking 134-5, 166-74
Toussaint, Allen 81
traditions 21, 88-9
train travel 275
transportations 272-5
traveler's checks 280
Tremé District **310-11**
  attractions 145-8
  bus travel 146
  eating 185
Tulane University 158-9

U

United Fruit Company 152
universities 158-9
Uptown **314-15**
  accommodations 248-9
  attractions 157-9
  bars & clubs 205-6
  bus travel 157
  eating 190-4
  galleries 213
  live music 209-10
  shopping 233-4
  streetcars 157
Ursuline Convent 142, 171
Ursuline nuns 109-10, 171
US Civil War 114-15
US Custom House 143

V

vacations 278
vegetarians & vegans 103
Vermilionville 259, 262

000 map pages
000 photographs

Vicksburg 265, 267
visas 283
volunteering 320
  organizations 284
voodoo 22, 114
  Chez Vodun 144
  Historic Voodoo Museum 140
  Laveau, Marie 137, 143, 147-8
  Voodoo Spiritual Temple 143
  Zombie's House of Voodoo 229

W

Warehouse District **308-9**
  accommodations 244-6
  attractions 150-5
  bars & clubs 204
  bus travel 151
  eating 187-8
  galleries 211-12
  live music 208
  shopping 221, 231
  streetcars 151
Warren, Robert Penn 62
Washington, Walter 'Wolfman' 209
WC Handy's House 268
weather 277
websites, *see* Internet resources
weights 279, *see also inside front cover*
Wetlands Cajun Cultural Center 258, 259
Williams, Tennessee 16, 63, 64, 65, 167
Williams, Walter 65
Winans, Fonville 60
Winn-Dixie Showdown 23
women travelers 284
Woodward, Ellsworth 58
Woodward, William 58
work 284
Works Progress Administration (WPA) 138
WWII 117
  National World War II Museum 154-5
WWOZ (FM90.7) 24, 82

Y

yellow fever 114, 172

Z

Zephyrs 23, 216
zoos 158

EATING

A-Bear's Café 259
Abe's 267
Acme Oyster and Seafood House 180
Adolfo's 186
Airline Motors Restaurant 256
Angeli on Decatur 179
Antoine's 183
Arcade 270
Arnaud's 183
Automatic Slim's Tonga Club 270
B&C Seafood Market & Cajun Deli 257
Bacco 182
Bank Cafe 187
Bayona 183
Bayou Delight Restaurant 259
Bluebird Café 191
Bon Ton Café 188
Borden's 261
Brenda's Diner 261
Brennan's Restaurant 185, 193
Cabin Restaurant 256
Café Amelie 181
Café Beignet 179
Café Degas 196
Café du Monde 178
Café Maspero 179
Café Sbisa 181
Camellia Grill 190
Casamento's 192
CC's Coffee House 178
Central Grocery 180
Charlie Vergo's Rendezvous 270
Clancy's 194
Clover Grill 179
Commander's Palace 190
Coop's Place 179-80
Cooter Brown's Tavern & Oyster Bar 191
Court of Two Sisters 182
Cozy Corner 270
Crescent City Brewhouse 181
Croissant d'Or Patisserie 179
Crystal Grill 267
Cuvée 188
Dante's Kitchen 193
Delta Amusement Blues Café 267
Dick & Jenny's 192
Domilise's Po-Boys 191
Elizabeth's 186
Emeril's 188
Fiorella's 180
First & Last Chance Café 257
Fleur-De-Lis Cocktail Lounge 265
Frankie & Johnny's 191
Gabrielle 193
Galatoire's 182
Gros Place 259
Gumbo Shop 180
Herbsaint 188
Hookah Cafe 186
Huey's 24/7 Diner 187, 270
Hymel's Seafood 256
Irene's Cuisine 181
Jacques-Imo's Café 193
Jean Lafitte Inn 263, 264
Johnny's Po-Boys 179
Juan's Flying Burrito 189
K-Paul's Louisiana Kitchen 184
La Madeleine French Bakery & Café 179
La Peniché 185
Lemon Grass Cafe 187
Liborio Cuban Restaurant 187
Lilette 194
Liuzza's By the Track 195
Lola's 195
Louisiana Pizza Kitchen 180
Louisiana Products 187
Lusco's 267
Madidi 267
Martinique Bistro 193
Mona Lisa 181
Mother's 187
Mr B's Bistro 182
Muriel's 182
NOLA 184
Old Tyme Grocery 262
Olivier's 181
Palace Café 181, 262
Parasol's 189
Pascal's Manale 192
Peristyle 183
Poor Boy Loyd's 265
Port of Call 180
Powell's 185
Praline Connection 186
Prejean's Restaurant 262
Railroad Café 257
Red Eye Grill 187
Reginelli's Pizzeria 191
Restaurant August 188
Restaurant de Familles 263
Restaurant Indigo 195
Rob's Donuts 259
Royal Blend 179
Ruby's Café 262
Rue de la Course 189
Silver Moon 265
Slim Goodie's Diner 189
SnoWizard Sno Ball Stand 190
Taqueria Corona 191
T-Coons 262
Tee-Eva's Creole Soul Food 190
T'Frere's B&B 262
Tops Bar-B-Q 270
Trolley Stop 189
Tujague's 184
Upperline Restaurant 194
Verti Marte 178
Victor's Cafeteria 262
Victorian Inn 264
Walnut Hills 267
Whole Foods Market 194

ENTERTAINMENT

Abbey 200
Animazing Gallery 210
Anton Haardt Gallery 213
Apple Barrell 202
Arthur Roger Gallery 211
Audubon Park Golf Course 217
Audubon Park Tennis Courts 217
Avenue Plaza Resort & Spa 218
Bacchanal 202
Barrister's Gallery 213
Bayou Oaks Golf Course 217
BB King's 268, 270
Belladonna Day Spa 218
Bergeron Studio & Gallery 211
Berta's & Mina's Antiquities 213
Bombay Club 200
Bourbon Pub & Parade Disco 204
Café Brasil 202
Canal Place Cinemas 215
Carousel Bar 200

Carrollton Station 209
Cascade Stables 217
Circle Bar 204
City Park Tennis Center 217
Cole Pratt Gallery 213
Columns Hotel 205
Contemporary Arts Center 211, 214
Cooter Brown's Tavern & Oyster Bar 205
Country Club 204
d.b.a. 203
Donna's Bar & Grill 206
Dos Jefes Uptown Cigar Bar 209
Downtown Fitness Centers 218
Dungeon 200
Entergy IMAX theater 215
Equest Farm 217
F&M Patio Bar 205
Fred's Lounge 261
Gallery for Fine Photography 210
George Schmidt Gallery 211
Good Friends Bar 204
Ground Zero 266
Half Moon 205
Handa Wanda's 208
Harouni Gallery 211
Heriard-Cimino Gallery 212
Hookah Cafe 203
House of Blues 206
Howlin' Wolf 208
Igor's Checkpoint Charlie 203
Igor's Lounge 205
Jean Bragg Gallery of Southern Art 211
Jean Lafitte's Old Absinthe House 201
King Bolden's 201
Kurt E Schon Ltd Gallery 211
Lafitte in Exile 204
Le Bon Temps Roulé 209
Le Chat Noir 208, 214
Le Petit Théâtre du Vieux Carré 214
Lemieux Galleries 212
Loa 204
Louisiana Philharmonic Orchestra 214
Lupin Theatre 214
Maple Leaf Bar 209
Michalopoulos Gallery 211
Mid-City Lanes Rock & Bowl 209
Mimi's In the Marigny 203
Molly's at the Market 15, 201
Mr Handy's Blues Hall 268, 270
Napoleon House 201
New Orleans Ballet Association 214
New Orleans Glasswork & Printmaking Studios 212
New Orleans Opera 214
Okra True Brew Playhouse 214
One Eyed Jacks 207
Orpheum Theatre 214
Oswald's Speakeasy 173, 202
Oz 204
Palm Court Jazz Café 207
Pat O'Brien's 202
Perrin Benham Gallery 213
Preservation Hall 207
Prytania Theatre 215
R Bar 203
Ray's Room New Orleans 207
Red's 266
Republic New Orleans 208
Richard's Club 260
Rivershack Tavern 205
Rodrigue Studio 211
Saenger Theatre 214
St Joe's Bar 206
Saturn Bar 204
Simon of New Orleans 213
Sip 205
Slim's Y-Ki-Ki 260
Snug Harbor 208
Soren Christensen Gallery 212
Southern Repertory Theater 214
Spotted Cat 208
Tipitina's 209-10
Tony Seville's Pirate's Alley Cafe 202
UNO Downtown Theatre 214
Vaughan's 208

000map pages
000 photographs

SHOPPING

A&P Market 223
Aidan Gill for Men 231
Arcadian Books & Art Prints 223
Artists' Market 223
Bacchanal 230
Beckham's Bookstore 223
Big Fisherman Seafood 232
Big Life Toys/Winky's 232
Bourbon Strip Tease 223
Bywater Art Market 230
Central Grocery 223
Centuries 223
Christopher's Discoveries 233
Civil War Store 224
Collectible Antiques 224
Collection 224
Crescent City Books 224
Crescent City Farmers Market 231
Dark Room 232
Dr Bob's Studio 230
Electric Ladyland 230
Faubourg Marigny Book Store 230
Faulkner House Bookstore 224
Fleur de Paris 224
Flora Savage 225
Funky Monkey 233
Garden District Bookshop 233
Gargoyle's 225
House of Lounge 232
Hové Parfumeur 225
Il Negozio 233
International Vintage Guitars 231
James H Cohen & Sons 225
Jim Russell's Records 232
Johnny Donnels 226
Kaboom Books 226
Leah's Pralines 226
Le Garage 226
Librairie Books 226
Louisiana Music Factory 226
Lucullus 226
Magazine Antique Mall 233
Mary Jane's Emporium 227
Maskarade 227
Meyer the Hatter 231
Migon Faget's boutique 234
Miss Claudia's 234
Moss Antiques 227
Ms Rau Antiques 227
Musica Latina Discoteca 234
New Orleans Art Supply 230
New Orleans Music Exchange 233
New Orleans School of Glassworks 231
Photo Works 227
Porché West Gallery 231
Quarter Past Time 227
Retroactive 234
Rock & Roll Collectibles 228
Rossie's Custom Framing 256
Santa's Quarters 228
Sideshow: The Old Curiosity Shop 228
Southern Candy Makers 228
Starling Books & Crafts 228
Stone and Press 228
Tower Records 229
Trashy Diva 229, 232
Uptown Costume & Dancewear 234
Vieux Carré Wine & Spirits 229
Zombie's House of Voodoo 229

SLEEPING

Andrew Jackson Hotel 239
Avenue Garden Hotel 247
Avenue Plaza Resort & Spa 248
Battlefield Inn 267
Benachi House 249
Best Western 250
Bourbon Orleans Hotel 241
Bywater Bed & Breakfast 243
Chateau Hotel 240
Columns Hotel 249
Cornstalk Hotel 238
Country Inn & Suites By Carlson 244
Creole House Hotel 238
Days Inn Graceland 270
Degas House 250
Delta Cotton Club Apartment 267
Doubletree 244, 250
Embassy Suites Hotel 245
Esplanade Villa 250
Estorage-Norton House 262
Fairmont Hotel 246

Frenchmen 242
Garden District Hotel 247
Gentry Quarters 238
Hampton Inn New Orleans Downtown 245
Heartbreak Hotel 270
HI Marquette House Hostel 247
Hilton 250
Historic French Market Inn 240
Hotel de la Monnaie 243
Hotel Monteleone 241
Hotel Provincial 239
Hotel Royal 240
Hotel St Marie 239
Hotel Villa Convento 239
House on Bayou Road 250
Howard's Inn 262
India House Hostel 249
International House 245
Josephine Guest House 247
Lafayette Hotel 244
Lafitte Guest House 241
Lagniappe B&B 248
Lamothe House 243
Le Pavillon 244
Le Richelieu 239
Lions Inn B&B 242
Loews New Orleans Hotel 245
Maison St Charles 248
Melrose Mansion 243
Nine-O-Five Royal Hotel 239
Olivier House 240
Omni Royal Orleans 240
Park View Guest House 249
Peabody Hotel 270
Place d'Armes Hotel 240
Pontchartrain Hotel 248
Prytania Park Hotel 247
Queen & Crescent Hotel 244
Riverside Hotel 266
Royal Sonesta 241
Shack Up Inn 267
Sheraton New Orleans 245
Soniat House 241
Sully Mansion B&B 247
Teche Hotel 262
Terrell House 248
Ursuline Guest House 238
W French Quarter 240
W New Orleans 246
Windsor Court Hotel 246
Wyndham New Orleans at Canal Place 241

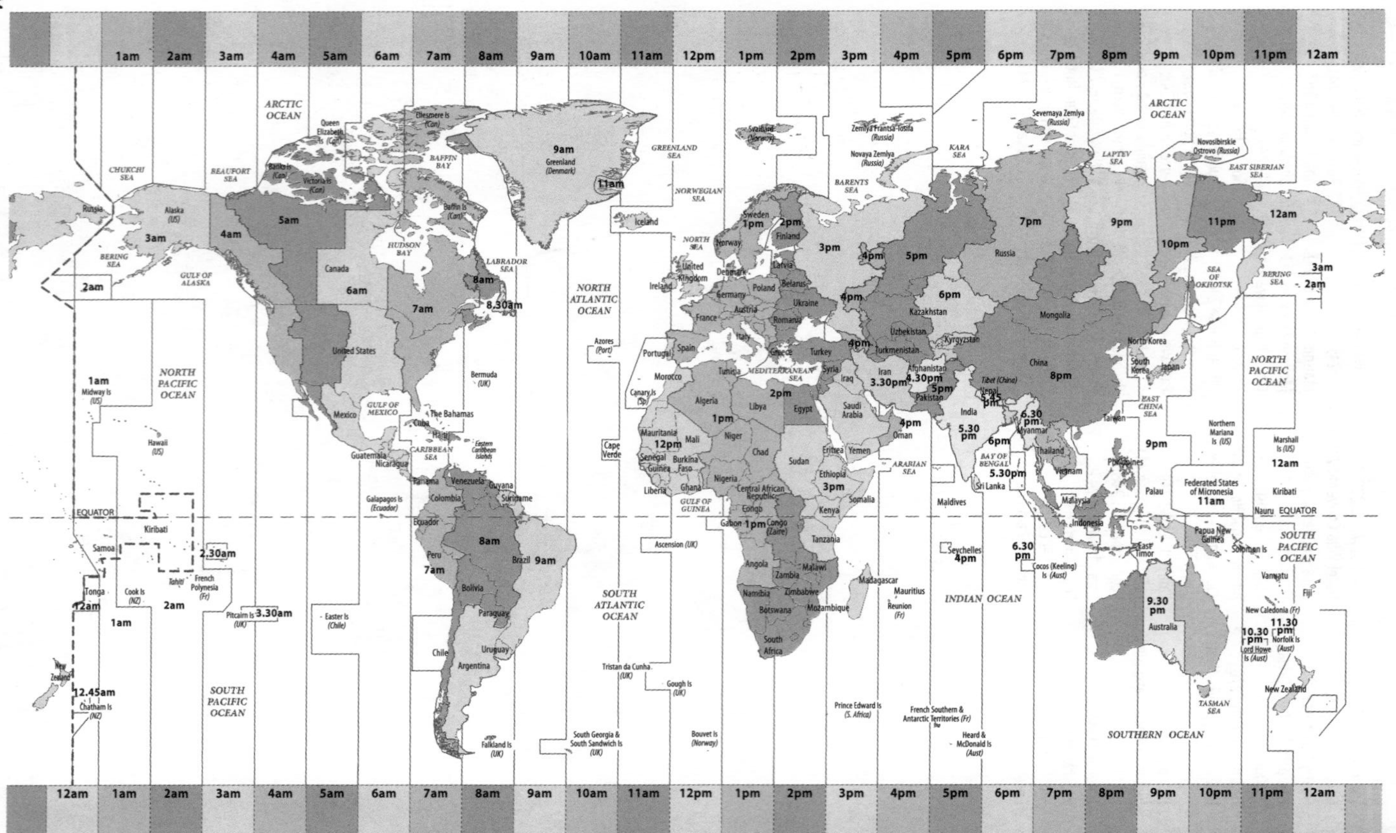

1am
2am
3am
4am
5am
6am
7am
8am
9am
10am
11am
12pm
1pm
2pm
3pm
4pm
5pm
6pm
7pm
8pm
9pm
10pm
11pm
12am
ARCTIC OCEAN
CHUKCHI SEA
BEAUFORT SEA
Russia
Alaska (US)
3am
BERING SEA
GULF OF ALASKA
2am
4am
5am
Queen Elizabeth Is (Can)
Banks Is (Can)
Victoria Is (Can)
Ellesmere Is (Can)
BAFFIN BAY
Baffin Is (Can)
HUDSON BAY
Canada
6am
7am
LABRADOR SEA
8am
8.30am
Greenland (Denmark)
9am
11am
GREENLAND SEA
NORWEGIAN SEA
Iceland
United States
Bermuda (UK)
GULF OF MEXICO
Mexico
The Bahamas
Cuba
Haiti
CARIBBEAN SEA
Eastern Caribbean Islands
Guatemala
Nicaragua
Panama
Venezuela
Guyana
Suriname
Colombia
Ecuador
Peru
7am
8am
Brazil
9am
Bolivia
Paraguay
Chile
Uruguay
Argentina
Falkland Is (UK)
Galapagos Is (Ecuador)
Easter Is (Chile)
NORTH PACIFIC OCEAN
1am
Midway Is (US)
Hawaii (US)
EQUATOR
Kiribati
Samoa
2.30am
Tahiti
French Polynesia (Fr)
Tonga
12am
Cook Is (NZ)
2am
1am
Pitcairn Is 3.30am (UK)
New Zealand
12.45am
Chatham Is (NZ)
SOUTH PACIFIC OCEAN
NORTH ATLANTIC OCEAN
Azores (Port)
Canary Is (Sp)
Cape Verde
SOUTH ATLANTIC OCEAN
Ascension (UK)
Tristan da Cunha (UK)
Gough Is (UK)
South Georgia & South Sandwich Is (UK)
Bouvet Is (Norway)
NORTH SEA
United Kingdom
Ireland
Portugal
Spain
France
Morocco
Algeria
Tunisia
Mauritania
12pm
Mali
Senegal
Guinea
Burkina Faso
Liberia
Ghana
GULF OF GUINEA
Sweden
1pm
Norway
Denmark
Germany
Poland
Austria
Italy
Niger
1pm
Nigeria
Chad
Central African Republic
Congo
Gabon 1pm
Angola
Namibia
Botswana
South Africa
Finland
2pm
Latvia
Belarus
Ukraine
Romania
Greece
MEDITERRANEAN SEA
Libya
2pm
Egypt
Sudan
Congo (Zaire)
Zambia
Malawi
Zimbabwe
Mozambique
Tanzania
Svalbard (Norway)
Zemlya Frantsa-Iosifa (Russia)
Novaya Zemlya (Russia)
BARENTS SEA
3pm
4pm
Turkey
Syria
Iraq
Saudi Arabia
Eritrea
Yemen
Ethiopia
3pm
Somalia
Kenya
Madagascar
Mauritius
Reunion (Fr)
Prince Edward Is (S. Africa)
KARA SEA
5pm
4pm
4pm
Kazakhstan
6pm
Uzbekistan
Turkmenistan
Kyrgyzstan
Iran
3.30pm
Afghanistan
4.30pm
5pm
Pakistan
4pm
Oman
ARABIAN SEA
India
5.30 pm
Nepal
5.45 pm
Tibet (China)
BAY OF BENGAL
6pm
5.30pm
Sri Lanka
Maldives
Seychelles
4pm
6.30 pm
Cocos (Keeling) Is (Aust)
INDIAN OCEAN
French Southern & Antarctic Territories (Fr)
Heard & McDonald Is (Aust)
Severnaya Zemlya (Russia)
Russia
7pm
Mongolia
China
8pm
6.30 pm
Myanmar
Thailand
Vietnam
Malaysia
Indonesia
Philippines
Taiwan
LAPTEV SEA
ARCTIC OCEAN
Novosibirskie Ostrova (Russia)
EAST SIBERIAN SEA
9pm
10pm
11pm
12am
SEA OF OKHOTSK
BERING SEA
3am
2am
North Korea
South Korea
Japan
EAST CHINA SEA
9pm
Palau
East Timor
Papua New Guinea
Australia
9.30 pm
NORTH PACIFIC OCEAN
Northern Mariana Is (US)
Marshall Is (US)
12am
Federated States of Micronesia
11am
Kiribati
Nauru EQUATOR
Solomon Is
SOUTH PACIFIC OCEAN
Vanuatu
Fiji
New Caledonia (Fr)
11.30 pm
Norfolk Is (Aust)
10.30 pm
Lord Howe Is (Aust)
New Zealand
TASMAN SEA
SOUTHERN OCEAN
12am
1am
2am
3am
4am
5am
6am
7am
8am
9am
10am
11am
12pm
1pm
2pm
3pm
4pm
5pm
6pm
7pm
8pm
9pm
10pm
11pm
12am

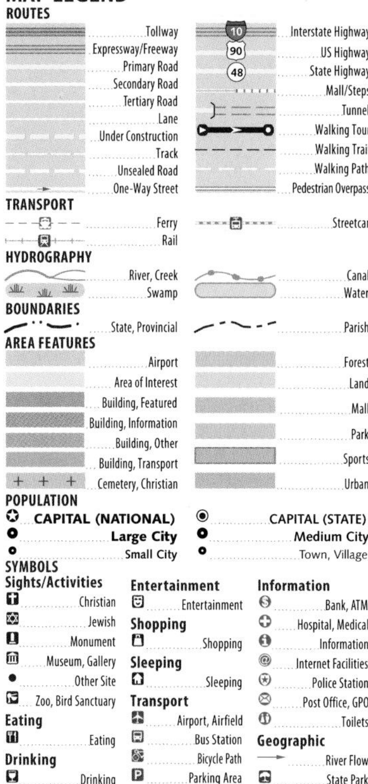

Maps

New Orleans 306

CBD & Warehouse District 308

French Quarter, Jackson Square & Tremé 310

Lower Garden & Garden Districts 312

Uptown & Riverbend 314

Faubourg Marigny & Bywater 316

Mid-City, Esplanade Ridge & Bayou St John 317

New Orleans Transit Map 318

NEW ORLEANS

Lake Pontchartrain
New Orleans Lakefront Airport
Hayne Blvd
To Slidell (25mi)
Morison Rd
Dwyer Rd
Downman Rd
To New Orleans East (6mi)
Chef Menteur Hwy
Almonaster Ave
Intracoastal Waterway
Lower Ninth Ward
To St Bernard Parish (12mi)
Judge Perez Dr
Inner Harbor Canal
Lakeshore Dr
Pontchartrain Park
Southern University of New Orleans
Peoples Ave
Franklin Ave
N Claiborne Ave
Almonaster Ave
N Claiborne Ave
St Claude Ave
See Faubourg Marigny & Bywater Map (p316)
See French Quarter, Jackson Square & Tremé Map (pp310–11)
University of New Orleans
Greek Orthodox Cathedral of the Holy Trinity
Elysian Fields Ave
Gentilly Blvd
Elysian Fields Ave
Dillard University
Gentilly
Prentiss St
Fillmore St
Mirabeau Ave
St Bernard Ave
Paris Ave
St Bernard Ave
N Broad Ave
DeSaix Blvd
Fair Grounds Race Track
Esplanade Ave
Wisner Blvd
City Park
Equest Farm
Lakeshore Park
Orleans Ave
Bienville St
Canal St
N Carrollton Ave
Banks St
Tulane Ave
See Mid-City, Esplanade Ridge & Bayou St John Map (p317)
Argonne Blvd
Robert E Lee Blvd
Canal Blvd
Harrison Ave
City Park Ave
Pontchartrain Blvd
Metairie Cemetery
Bellaire Rd
Fleur De Lis Dr
West End Park
West End
17th Street Canal
Garden Ln
Bamboo Rd
Metairie Rd
Metairie
Airline Hwy
Earhart Expwy
Bonnabel Place
To Mandeville (17mi); Covington (20mi)
Lake Pontchartrain Causeway (toll)
W Esplanade Ave
Veterans Memorial Blvd
To Baton Rouge (75mi); Lafayette (80mi)
Causeway Blvd
Jefferson
To Zephyr Field (2mi); Louis Armstrong International Airport (8mi)

Tavern
Jefferson Parish
Orleans Parish
Claiborne Ave
3139
Police Department
Pontchartrain Expwy
N Galvez St
Poydras Ave
N Rampart St
Canal St
Mississippi River
To Chalmette (3mi)
Riverbend
Algiers
New Orleans Naval Support Activity
Bridge City
Levee Park
Broadway
Tulane University
Martin Luther King Jr Blvd
Blaine Kern's Mardi Gras World
Whitney Ave
General Meyer Ave
Loyola University
Jefferson Ave
See CBD & Warehouse District Map (pp308–9)
Greater New Orleans Bridge
Behrman Memorial Park
To Houma (48mi)
River Rd
Loyola St
Louisiana Ave
Jackson Ave
Magazine St
Franklin St
Holiday Dr
Bridge City Ave
St Charles Ave
Napoleon Ave
General De Gaulle Dr
MacArthur Blvd
Audubon Park
See Lower Garden & Garden Districts Map (pp312–13)
Gretna
Westwego
Magazine St
Tchoupitoulas St
See Uptown & Riverbend Map (pp314–15)
Fourth St
Lafayette St
West Bank Expwy
Orleans Parish
Jefferson Parish
Mississippi River
Harvey
Bayou Segnette State Park
Louisiana St
Drake Ave
4th St
Harvey Tunnel
Belle Chasse Hwy
West Bank Expwy
Marrero
Manhattan Blvd
Terry Pkwy
Behrman Hwy
Lapalco Blvd
Ames Blvd
Barataria Blvd
Peters Rd
Harvey Canal
To Jean Lafitte National Historic Park (5mi); Barataria Unit (5mi); Visitor Center (5mi)
Lapalco Blvd
Wall Blvd
0 3 km
0 2 miles

CBD & WAREHOUSE DISTRICT

SIGHTS & ACTIVITIES (pp132–64)
- Aquarium of the Americas............1 G3
- Big Top Gallery and Three Ring Circus..............2 D5
- Confederate Museum....................3 E5
- Contemporary Arts Center............4 E5
- Cookin' Cajun..............................5 G4
- Creole Queen................................6 G3
- Factors Row..................................7 E3
- Gallier Hall....................................8 E3
- Harrah's Casino.............................9 F3
- K&B Plaza....................................10 E5
- Louisiana Artworks.......................11 E4
- Louisiana Children's Museum.......12 F4
- Louisiana Superdome...................13 C3
- National D-Day Museum..............14 E5
- New Orleans Cotton Exchange.....15 E2
- New Orleans Public Library..........16 D2
- Ogden Museum of Southern Art..17 E5
- Preservation Resource Center......18 F5
- Robert E Lee Monument..............19 E5
- United Fruit Company.................20 E3

EATING (pp176–96)
- Bon Ton Café..............................21 F3
- Cuvée..22 F3
- Emeril's.......................................23 F4
- Herbsaint....................................24 E4
- Huey's 24/7 Diner.......................25 F3
- Lemon Grass Cafe........................26 F3
- Liborio Cuban Restaurant............27 F3
- Louisiana Products.......................28 E4
- Mother's......................................29 F3
- Red Eye Grill...............................30 F5
- Restaurant August.......................31 F3

DRINKING (pp198–218)
- Circle Bar....................................32 E5
- Loa...(see 55)
- Republic New Orleans.................33 F5

ENTERTAINMENT (pp198–218)
- Arthur Roger Gallery....................34 F4
- Bergeron Studio & Gallery............35 F3
- Entergy IMAX Theater.................(see 1)
- George Schmidt Gallery................36 E4
- Heriard-Cimino Gallery................37 F4
- Howlin' Wolf................................38 F5
- Jean Bragg Gallery of Southern Art...39 E4
- Le Chat Noir................................40 E4
- Lemieux Galleries.........................41 F4
- New Orleans Glasswork & Printmaking Studios.................42 F4
- Okra True Brew Playhouse...........43 F4
- Orpheum Theatre.........................44 E2
- Soren Christensen Gallery............45 F4
- UNO Downtown Theatre..............46 E3

SHOPPING (pp220–34)
- International Vintage Guitars.......47 F4
- Meyer the Hatter..........................48 E2
- New Orleans Centre.....................49 D3
- New Orleans School of Glassworks...........................(see 42)

SLEEPING (pp236–50)
- Country Inn & Suites by Carlson..50 F3
- Doubletree Hotel New Orleans....51 F3
- Embassy Suites Hotel...................52 F4
- Fairmont Hotel.............................53 E2
- Hampton Inn New Orleans Downtown....................................54 E3
- International House......................55 F3
- Lafayette Hotel.............................56 E4
- Le Pavillon...................................57 E3
- Loews New Orleans Hotel...........58 F3
- Queen & Crescent Hotel..............59 F3
- Sheraton New Orleans.................60 F2
- W New Orleans...........................61 F3
- Windsor Court Hotel....................62 F3

TRANSPORT (pp272–5)
- American Airlines Office............(see 53)
- Delta Queen Dock.......................63 G6
- Hertz...64 F5
- Mississippi Queen Dock.............(see 63)
- New Orleans Union Passenger Terminal.....................................65 C4

INFORMATION
- Accent on Children's Arrangements..........................66 D3
- French Consulate.........................67 D3
- Hibernia National Bank................68 E3
- Immigration & Naturalization Service.......................................69 C4
- Japan Consulate...........................70 D3
- Kinko's FedEx Office Center........71 E4
- Main Post Office..........................72 D4
- Post Office...................................73 G3
- Post Office...................................74 E4
- Tulane University Medical Center..75 D1
- UK Honorary Consul....................76 E3
- Whitney National Bank................77 E3

See Lower Garden & Garden Districts Map (pp312–13)

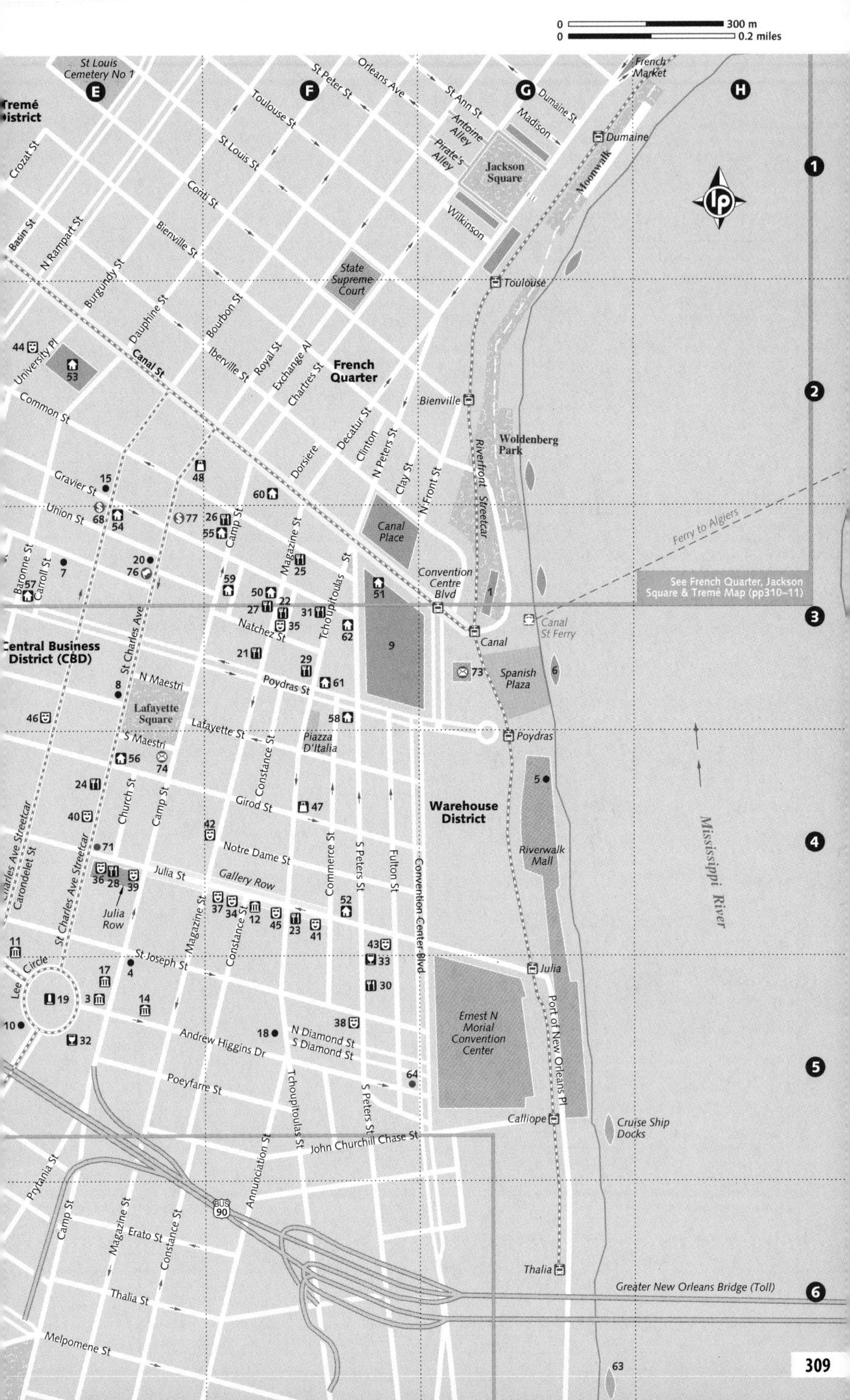
0 300 m
0 0.2 miles
St Louis Cemetery No 1
Tremé District
French Market
Dumaine
Jackson Square
Moonwalk
State Supreme Court
Toulouse
French Quarter
Bienville
Woldenberg Park
Riverfront Streetcar
Canal Place
Ferry to Algiers
Convention Centre Blvd
See French Quarter, Jackson Square & Tremé Map (pp310–11)
Canal
Canal St Ferry
Central Business District (CBD)
Spanish Plaza
Lafayette Square
Poydras
Piazza D'Italia
Warehouse District
Riverwalk Mall
Mississippi River
Julia Row
Gallery Row
Julia
Ernest N Morial Convention Center
Calliope
Cruise Ship Docks
Thalia
Greater New Orleans Bridge (Toll)
Lee Circle
Canal St
Common St
Gravier St
Union St
Poydras St
Lafayette St
Girod St
Julia St
Notre Dame St
St Joseph St
Andrew Higgins Dr
Poeyfarre St
John Churchill Chase St
Erato St
Thalia St
Melpomene St
St Charles Ave
Camp St
Magazine St
Tchoupitoulas St
Convention Center Blvd
Port of New Orleans Pl

FRENCH QUARTER, JACKSON SQUARE & TREMÉ

SIGHTS & ACTIVITIES (pp132–64)
1850 House Museum.....1 G3
Backstreet Cultural Museum.....2 E1
Beauregard-Keyes House.....3 G2
Cabildo.....4 F4
Cajun Queen.....5 G6
Chez Vodun.....6 E2
Congo Square.....7 D2
French Market.....8 G3
Gallier House Museum.....9 G2
Hermann-Grima House.....10 E4
Historic New Orleans Collection..11 E4
Historic Voodoo Museum.....12 F3
Houma Indian Arts Museum....(see 27)
Hula Mae's Laundry.....13 E2
Jackson Monument.....14 F3
Jean Lafitte National Historic Park Office.....15 F5
John James Audubon Riverboat..16 G6
Louis Armstrong Park.....17 D2
Louis Armstrong Statue.....18 E2
Lower Pontalba Buildings.....19 G3
Madame John's Legacy.....20 F3
Maspero's Exchange.....21 F4
Merieult House.....(see 11)
Mortuary Chapel.....22 D3
Municipal Auditorium.....23 D2
Musée Conti Historical Wax Museum.....24 D4
New Orleans Jazz Exhibit.....(see 27)
New Orleans Jazz National Historic Park.....25 H2
New Orleans Pharmacy Museum.26 F4
Old US Mint.....27 H2
Perserverance Hall.....28 E1
Presbytère.....29 F3
St Augustine's Church.....30 E1
St Louis Cathedral.....31 F3
St Louis Cemetery No 1.....32 C3
Steamboat Natchez.....33 G4
Upper Pontalba Buildings.....34 F4
Ursuline Convent.....35 G2
US Custom House.....36 E6
Voodoo Spiritual Temple.....37 E2
Williams Research Center.....38 E4

EATING (pp176–96)
Acme Oyster and Seafood House.....39 D5
Angeli on Decatur.....40 G2
Antoine's.....41 E4
Arnaud's.....42 D4
Bacco.....(see 170)
Bayona.....43 E4
Brennan's Restaurant.....(see 135)
Café Amelie.....44 F3
Café Beignet.....45 E4
Café du Monde.....46 G4
Café Maspero.....47 F4
Café Sbisa.....48 G3
CC's Coffee House.....49 F2
Central Grocery.....50 G3
Clover Grill.....51 F2
Coop's Place.....52 G2
Court of Two Sisters.....53 F4
Crescent City Brewhouse.....54 F4
Croissant d'Or Patisserie.....55 G2
Fiorella's.....56 H2
Galatoire's.....57 D5
Gumbo Shop.....58 F4
Irene's Cuisine.....59 G3
Johnny's Po-Boys.....60 F4
K-Paul's Louisiana Kitchen.....(see 112)
La Madeleine French Bakery & Café.....61 F3
Louisiana Pizza Kitchen.....62 H2
Mona Lisa.....63 G2
Mr B's Bistro.....64 E5
Muriel's.....65 F3
NOLA.....66 F4
Olivier's.....67 E5
Palace Café.....68 D5
Peristyle.....69 E2
Port of Call.....70 G1
Powell's.....71 D1
Royal Blend.....72 F4
Tujague's.....73 G3
Verti Marte.....74 G2

DRINKING (pp198–218)
Abbey.....75 G2
Bombay Club.....(see 159)
Bourbon Pub & Parade Disco.....76 F3
Carousel Bar.....77 E5
Dungeon.....78 E4
Good Friends Bar.....79 E3
Jean Lafitte's Old Absinthe House.....80 D4
King Bolden's.....(see 6)
Lafitte in Exile.....81 F2
Lafitte's Blacksmith Shop.....82 F2
Molly's at the Market.....83 G3
Napoleon House.....84 F4
Oswald's Speakeasy.....85 H2
Oz.....86 F3
Pat O'Brien's.....87 F3
Tony Seville's Pirate's Alley Cafe.88 F3

ENTERTAINMENT (pp198–218)
A Gallery for Fine Photography..89 E5
Animazing Gallery.....90 F3
Canal Place Cinemas.....(see 111)
Donna's Bar & Grill.....91 E2
Downtown Fitness Centers....(see 111)
Harouni Gallery.....92 F3
House of Blues.....93 E5
Kurt E Schon Ltd Gallery.....94 E4
Le Petit Théâtre du Vieux Carré.95 F4
Mahalia Jackson Theatre.....96 D1
Michalopoulos Gallery.....97 E5
New Orleans School of Cooking.98 F4
One Eyed Jacks.....99 F4
Palm Court Jazz Café.....100 H2
Parish.....101 E5
Preservation Hall.....102 E3
Rodrigue Studio.....103 F3
Saenger Theatre.....104 C4
Southern Repertory Theater...(see 111)
TicketMaster.....(see 145)

SHOPPING (pp220–34)
A&P Market.....105 F3
Alternatives Shop.....106 F2
Arcadian Books & Art Prints.....107 F3
Artists' Market.....108 H2
Beckham's Bookstore.....109 E5
Bourbon Strip Tease.....110 D5
Canal Place.....111 E6
Centuries.....112 E5
Civil War Store.....113 E5
Collectible Antiques.....(see 108)
Collection.....(see 11)
Crescent City Books.....114 E5
David's.....115 H2
Farmer's Market.....116 H2
Faulkner House Bookstore.....117 F3
Flea Market.....118 H2
Fleur de Paris.....119 F3
Flora Savage.....120 G1
Gargoyle's.....121 H2
Hové Parfumeur.....122 F3
Jackson Brewery.....123 F4
James H Cohen & Sons.....124 E4
Johnny Donnels.....125 F3
Kaboom Books.....126 G1
Le Garage.....127 H2
Leah's Pralines.....128 E4
Librairie Books.....129 F3
Louisiana Music Factory.....130 E5
Lucullus.....131 F4
Marie Laveau's House of Voodoo.....132 F3
Mary Jane's Emporium.....133 H2
Maskarade.....134 F3
Moss Antiques.....135 E4
MS Rau Antiques.....136 F4
Photo Works.....137 F3
Quarter Past Time.....138 F4
Rock & Roll Collectibles.....139 H2
Santa's Quarters.....140 G3
Sideshow: The Old Curiosity Shop.....141 F3
Southern Candy Makers.....142 F5
Starling Books & Crafts.....143 G2
Stone and Press.....144 E5
Tower Records.....145 F5
Trashy Diva.....146 F3
Vieux Carré Wine & Spirits.....147 E4
Zombie's House of Voodoo.....148 F3

0 300 m
0 0.2 miles
Tremé District
Faubourg Marigny
Washington Square Park
French Quarter
Jackson Square
State Supreme Court
Moonwalk
Woldenberg Park
Mississippi River
Riverfront Streetcar
Ursulines
Dumaine
Toulouse
Bienville
Ferry to Algiers
See Faubourg Marigny & Bywater Map (p316)
See CBD & Warehouse District Map (pp308–9)
Tremé St
St Claude Ave
N Rampart St
Governor Nicholls St
Ursulines Ave
St Philip St
Dumaine St
St Ann St
Orleans Ave
St Peter St
Toulouse St
Dauphine St
Bourbon St
Royal St
Chartres St
Decatur St
Esplanade Ave
Barracks St
French Market Pl
N Peters St
Decatur St
Antoine Alley
Pirates Alley
Madison St
Wilkinson St
Exchange Pl
Dorsiere
Clinton
Clay St
N Front St
Iberville St
Canal St
Magazine St
Tchoupitoulas St
SLEEPING (pp236–50)
Andrew Jackson Hotel 149 F3
Bourbon Orleans Hotel 150 F3
Chateau Hotel 151 G3
Cornstalk Hotel 152 F3
Creole House Hotel 153 E2
Gentry Quarters 154 E2
Historic French Market Inn 155 F4
Hotel Monteleone 156 E5
Hotel Provincial 157 G3
Hotel Royal 158 G2
Hotel St Marie 159 E4
Hotel Villa Convento 160 G2
Lafitte Guest House 161 F2
Le Richelieu 162 G2
Nine-O-Five Royal Hotel 163 F3
Olivier House 164 E3
Omni Royal Orleans 165 E4
Place d'Armes Hotel 166 F3
Royal Sonesta 167 E4
Soniat House 168 G2
Ursuline Guest House 169 G2
W French Quarter 170 E5
Wyndham New Orleans at Canal Place 171 E6
TRANSPORT (pp272–5)
U-Park Garage 172 D5
INFORMATION
ATM 173 E4
ATM 174 F5
Bastille Computer Café 175 F4
French Quarter Postal Emporium 176 F2
Louisiana State Bank 177 E4
New Orleans Welcome Center 178 F3
Royal Mail Service 179 F3
Walgreens 180 F4

LOWER GARDEN & GARDEN DISTRICTS

SIGHTS & ACTIVITIES (pp132–64)
Charles Briggs House...............1 C4
Goodrich-Stanley House..........2 E2
Grace King House....................3 E2
House of Broel.........................4 D3
Lafayette Cemetery No 1.........5 B4
St Vincent's Infant Asylum.......6 F3

EATING (pp176–96)
Commander's Palace..............7 C4
Juan's Flying Burrito................8 E4
Parasol's.................................9 D5
Rue de la Course....................10 B6
Slim Goodie's Diner................11 B6
Trolley Stop...........................12 D2

DRINKING (pp198–218)
Half Moon...............................13 E3
Handa Wanda's........................14 C2
Igor's Lounge..........................15 D3

ENTERTAINMENT (pp198–218)
Anton Haardt Gallery.............16 C5
Avenue Plaza Resort & Spa ..(see 36)
Barrister's Gallery..................17 D1
Belladonna Day Spa...............18 C5
Perrin Benham Gallery............19 E4
Simon of New Orleans...........20 E4

SHOPPING (pp220–34)
Aidan Gill For Men.................21 E4
Big Fisherman Seafood...........22 B6
Big Life Toys/Winky's............23 E4
Christopher's Discoveries.......24 C5
Dark Room..............................25 E3
Funky Monkey.........................26 B6
Garden District Bookshop....(see 31)
House of Lounge....................27 E4
Jim Russell's Records.............28 F3
Magazine Antique Mall..........29 B6
New Orleans Music Exchange.30 B6
Rink..31 B4
Southern Fossil & Mineral Exchange..........................32 E4
Thomas Mann Gallery I/O.....33 F3
Trashy Diva............................34 E4

SLEEPING (pp236–50)
Avenue Garden Hotel.............35 E1
Avenue Plaza Resort & Spa....36 D2
Garden District Hotel.............37 D3
HI Marquette House Hostel...38 C3
Josephine Guest House..........39 D3
Maison St Charles..................40 E1
Pontchartrain Hotel...............41 D2
Prytania Park Hotel................42 E1
Sully Mansion B&B................43 C4
Terrell House.........................44 F2

INFORMATION
ATM.......................................45 E2
New Orleans General Hospital.46 F5

0
400 m
0
0.2 miles
E
F
G
H
Calliope St
Warehouse District
Convention Center Blvd
Carondelet St
Thalia St
Erato St
Martin Luther King Jr Blvd
Terpsichore St
St Charles Ave
St Charles Avenue Streetcar
Prytania St
Camp St
Magazine St
Constance St
Annunciation St
Tchoupitoulas St
S Peters St
Pontchartrain Expwy
Erato St
Thalia St
Melpomene St
Terpsichore St
Euterpe St
Henderson Pl
Coliseum Square
Coliseum St
Urania St
Felicity St
St Mary St
Race St
Orange St
Annunciation Square
Richard St
Chestnut St
Sophie Wright Pl
Camp St
Lower Garden District
Chippewa St
Market St
St James St
St Thomas St
Josephine St
Felicity St
Religious St
Jackson Ave
Annunciation St
Chippewa St
Philip St
St Thomas St
Rousseau St
Tchoupitoulas St
Mississippi River
Jackson Ave Ferry
To Gretna (400m)
1
2
3
4
5
6

Carrollton

Riverbend

Levee Park

Mississippi River

Newcomb College

Carrollton Cemetery

Audubon Park

Ursuline College & Convent

To Rivershack Tavern (2mi)

0 500 m
0 0.3 miles
E
F
G
H
1
2
3
4
5
6
SIGHTS & ACTIVITIES (pp132–64)
Amistad Research Center.............1 C3
Audubon Zoological Gardens......2 B5
Hogan Jazz Archive.....................3 C3
Loyola University........................4 C3
Loyola University Student Center.5 C3
Newcomb Art Gallery..................6 C2
Tulane University.........................7 C3
EATING (pp176–96)
Bluebird Café..............................8 G5
Brigtsen's Restaurant..................9 A2
Camellia Grill.............................10 B2
Casamento's...............................11 F6
Clancy's.....................................12 C6
Cooter Brown's Tavern & Oyster Bar..........................13 A2
Dante's Kitchen..........................14 A2
Dick & Jenny's.............................15 F6
Domilise's Po-Boys.....................16 D6
Frankie & Johnny's.....................17 D6
Gabrielle.....................................18 B6
Jacques-Imo's Café......................19 B1
Lilette..20 G5
Martinique Bistro........................21 C5
Pascal's Manale...........................22 F4
Reginelli's Pizzeria......................23 C5
SnoWizard Sno Ball Stand..........24 F6
Taqueria Corona.........................25 C5
Tee-Eva's Creole Soul Food........26 F6
Upperline Restaurant..................27 E5
Whole Foods...............................28 D6
DRINKING (pp198–218)
Cooter Brown's Tavern & Oyster Bar.............................(see 13)
F&M Patio Bar...........................29 E6
St Joe's Bar.................................30 D5
Sip...31 H5
ENTERTAINMENT (pp198–218)
Audubon Park Golf Course........32 C4
Berta's & Mina's Antiquities.......33 F6
Carrollton Station.......................34 B1
Cascade Stables..........................35 B6
Cole Pratt Gallery.......................36 G6
Dos Jefes Uptown Cigar Bar......37 D6
Le Bon Temps Roulé...................38 E6
Lupin Theatre.............................39 C3
Maple Leaf Bar...........................40 B1
Prytania Theatre.........................41 D5
Savvy Gourmet...........................42 F6
Tipitina's.....................................43 F6
SHOPPING (pp220–34)
Il Negozio...................................44 G5
Maple Street Bookstore.............45 B2
Mignon Faget's Boutique..........46 A2
Miss Claudia's............................47 F6
Moldaner's Camera....................48 A2
Musica Latina Discoteca............49 E6
Retroactive.................................50 D6
Riverside Market Shopping Center..................................51 D6
Uptown Costume & Dancewear............................52 F6
SLEEPING (pp236–50)
Columns Hotel...........................53 G5
Lagniappe B&B..........................54 G4
Park View Guest House.............55 C3
INFORMATION
ATM...56 B1
Children's Hospital.....................57 B6
De Paul Hospital........................58 C5
Planned Parenthood..................59 F6
STA Travel...............................(see 5)
US Marine Hospital...................60 B6
Fontainbleau Dr
S Rendon St
S Lopez St
S Salcedo St
S Gayoso St
S Dopre St
S White St
Eden St
Elba St
S Broad St
Jena St
Gen Pershing St
Louisiana Ave
Vincennes St
Nashville Ave
Rocheblave St
Tonti St
Miro St
Galvez St
Johnson St
Prieur St
Roman St
Derbigny St
Gen Taylor St
Delachaise St
Joseph St
Jefferson Ave
Lyons St
Cadiz St
Octavia St
S Claiborne Ave
Willow St
Clara St
Robert St
Upperline St
Valence St
S Robertson St
Freret St
La Salle St
Liberty St
Loyola St
Saratoga St
Danneel St
Dryades St
Baronne St
Carondelet St
Milan St
Marengo St
Dufossat St
Soniat St
Bordeaux St
Constantinople St
Peniston St
Amelia St
Foucher St
Brainard St
Toledano St
St Charles Avenue Streetcar
St Charles Ave
Third St
Second St
Fourth St
Washington Ave
Sixth St
Seventh St
Eighth St
Lafayette Cemetery No 1
Louisiana
Uptown
Napoleon
Prytania St
Coliseum St
Garden District
Harmony St
Pleasant St
Pitt St
Perrier St
Chestnut St
Camp St
Napoleon Ave
Antonine St
Aline St
Ninth St
See Lower Garden & Garden Districts Map (pp312–13)
Magazine St
Constance St
Laurel St
Annunciation St
Tchoupitoulas St
Austerlitz St
BUS 90

FAUBOURG MARIGNY & BYWATER

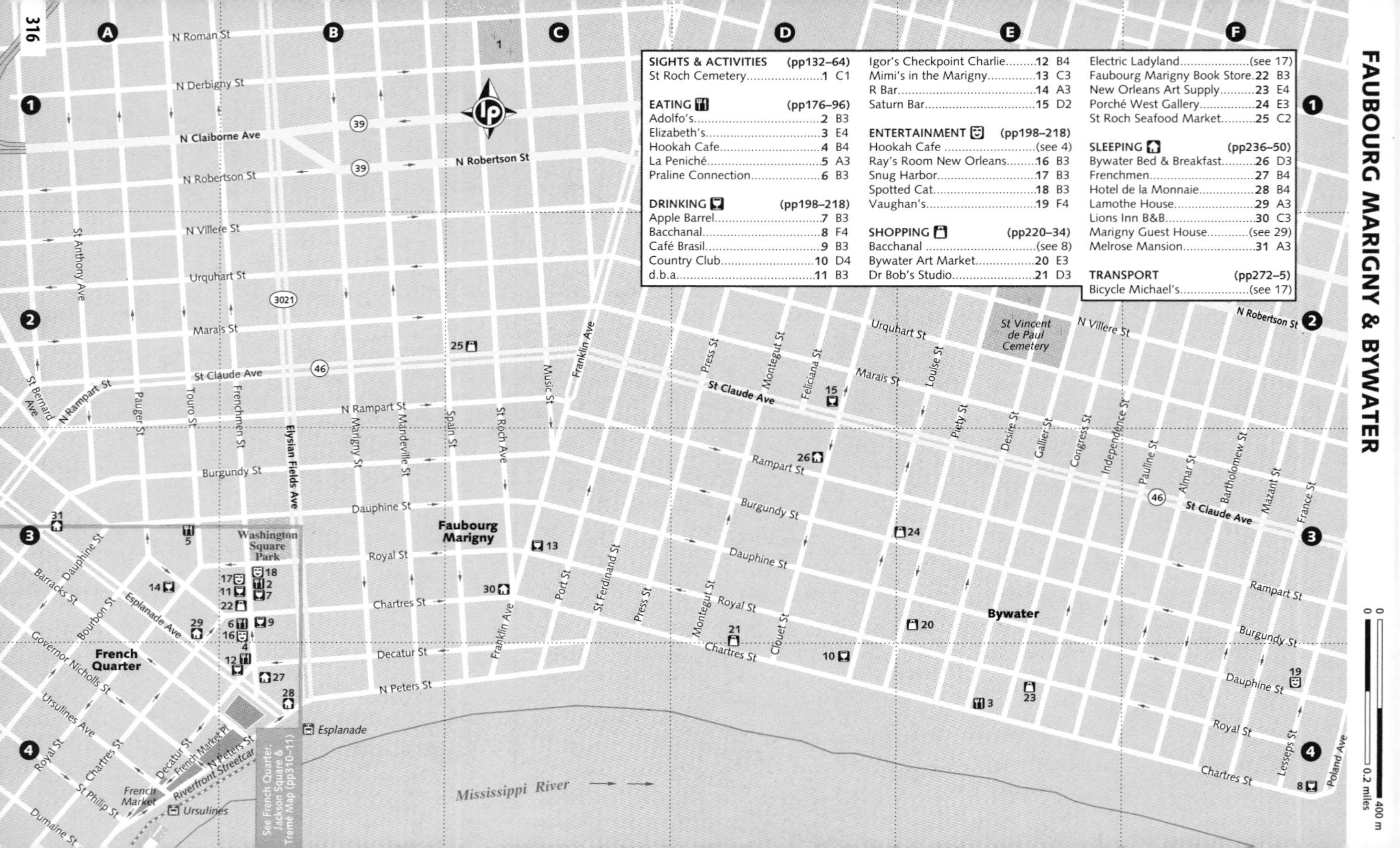
0 400 m
0 0.2 miles
SIGHTS & ACTIVITIES (pp132–64)
St Roch Cemetery 1 C1
EATING (pp176–96)
Adolfo's 2 B3
Elizabeth's 3 E4
Hookah Cafe 4 B4
La Peniché 5 A3
Praline Connection 6 B3
DRINKING (pp198–218)
Apple Barrel 7 B3
Bacchanal 8 F4
Café Brasil 9 B3
Country Club 10 D4
d.b.a. 11 B3
Igor's Checkpoint Charlie 12 B4
Mimi's in the Marigny 13 C3
R Bar 14 A3
Saturn Bar 15 D2
ENTERTAINMENT (pp198–218)
Hookah Cafe (see 4)
Ray's Room New Orleans 16 B3
Snug Harbor 17 B3
Spotted Cat 18 B3
Vaughan's 19 F4
SHOPPING (pp220–34)
Bacchanal (see 8)
Bywater Art Market 20 E3
Dr Bob's Studio 21 D3
Electric Ladyland (see 17)
Faubourg Marigny Book Store 22 B3
New Orleans Art Supply 23 E4
Porché West Gallery 24 E3
St Roch Seafood Market 25 C2
SLEEPING (pp236–50)
Bywater Bed & Breakfast 26 D3
Frenchmen 27 B4
Hotel de la Monnaie 28 B4
Lamothe House 29 A3
Lions Inn B&B 30 C3
Marigny Guest House (see 29)
Melrose Mansion 31 A3
TRANSPORT (pp272–5)
Bicycle Michael's (see 17)
Bywater
Faubourg Marigny
French Quarter
Washington Square Park
St Vincent de Paul Cemetery
Mississippi River
See French Quarter, Jackson Square & Treme Map (pp310–11)
Elysian Fields Ave
St Claude Ave
N Claiborne Ave
Esplanade Ave
Franklin Ave

MID-CITY, ESPLANADE RIDGE & BAYOU ST JOHN

SIGHTS & ACTIVITIES (pp132–64)

Beauregard Monument..............1 D2
Botanical Gardens.......................2 C1
Carousel Gardens & Storyland....3 B1
Dueling Oaks..............................4 C1
Fair Grounds Race Track.............5 E2
New Orleans Museum of Art......6 C1
Our Lady of the Rosary Rectory..7 D2
Pitot House.................................8 D2
St Louis Cemetery No 3.............9 D1
Sanctuary...................................10 D3
Sydney and Walda Besthoff Sculpture Garden.................11 C1

EATING (pp176–96)

Café Degas..................................12 E2
Courtyard Café........................(see 6)
Liuzza's by the Track................13 E2
Lola's..14 D2
Restaurant Indigo......................15 F3
Whole Foods Market..................16 D2

ENTERTAINMENT (pp198–218)

Bayou Oaks Golf Course...........17 D1
City Park Tennis Center............18 B1
Mid-City Rock & Bowl..............19 A4

SLEEPING (pp236–50)

Benachi House...........................20 F3
Degas House..............................21 F3
Esplanade Villa..........................22 F3
House on Bayou Road...............23 F3
India House Hostel....................24 C4

New Orleans Regional Transit Authority
Orleans Parish route map effective April 2, 2006

This map shows only a general overview of route patterns, and does not include every street traveled. For detailed route maps and Downtown New Orleans, see individual flyers at *http://www.norta.com*.

For the latest NORTA route and schedule information, please check *http://www.norta.com*, or call: (504) 248-3900 Mon–Fri, 8am–4pm.

All information is subject to change without notice.

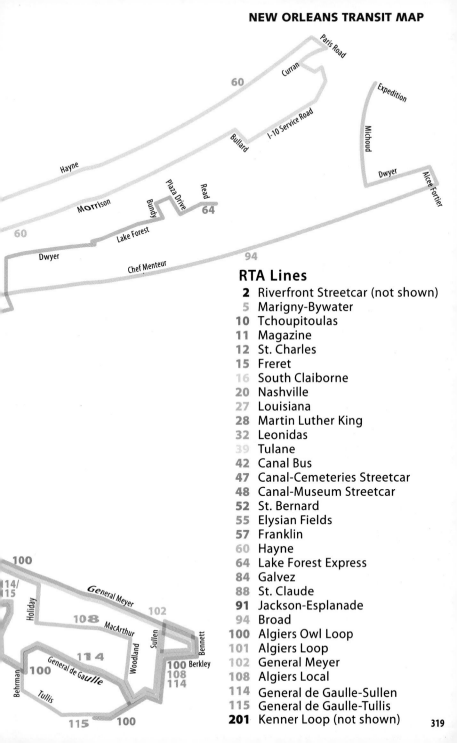

RTA Lines

2 Riverfront Streetcar (not shown)
5 Marigny-Bywater
10 Tchoupitoulas
11 Magazine
12 St. Charles
15 Freret
16 South Claiborne
20 Nashville
27 Louisiana
28 Martin Luther King
32 Leonidas
39 Tulane
42 Canal Bus
47 Canal-Cemeteries Streetcar
48 Canal-Museum Streetcar
52 St. Bernard
55 Elysian Fields
57 Franklin
60 Hayne
64 Lake Forest Express
84 Galvez
88 St. Claude
91 Jackson-Esplanade
94 Broad
100 Algiers Owl Loop
101 Algiers Loop
102 General Meyer
108 Algiers Local
114 General de Gaulle-Sullen
115 General de Gaulle-Tullis
201 Kenner Loop (not shown)

Rebuilding New Orleans

Want to help rebuild New Orleans? Many worthwhile organizations are on the job – here's a far-from-inclusive list.

Arts Council of New Orleans (www.artscouncilofneworleans.org) Assists visual artists, writers and performers with grants, housing relief and studio space.

Audubon Nature Institute (www.audubon institute.org) Restoring and supporting Audubon Zoo and Aquarium.

Bush-Clinton Katrina Fund (www.bushclinton katrinafund.org) Two former presidents offering grants for restoration and rebuilding projects in Louisiana, Mississippi and Alabama.

Children's Hospital (www.chnola.org) Not-for-profit pediatric acute care facility shuttered since Katrina.

Coalition to Restore Coastal Louisiana (www.crcl.org) Restoring and preserving coastal wetlands to prevent future Katrinas.

Common Ground (www.commongroundrelief.org) Grassroots Katrina relief group actively rebuilding the city.

Greater New Orleans Foundation (Rebuild New Orleans Fund; www.gnof.org) Longtime local foundation focused on education, job training and racial equality.

Habitat for Humanity (www.habitat-nola.org) Leading the way in New Orleans housing reconstruction with a musician's village and anti-poverty agenda.

Jazz Foundation (www.jazzfoundation.org) Musicians aid group focused on helping elderly jazz and blues players.

Katrina Krewe (Krewe Aiding Trash Removal in the New Orleans Area; www.cleanno.org) New Orleans based volunteer group clearing up trash and debris, block by block.

KIDsmART (www.kidsmart.org) In-school art therapy and arts training for low-income youth including those affected by Katrina.

Louisiana Disaster Recovery Foundation (www.louisianahelp.org) Supporting statewide economic redevelopment, housing, health care and legal services.

New Orleans City Park (www.neworleanscitypark.com/katrina.php) Focal point for a number of projects including the restoration of high school football's Tad Gormley Stadium (with the help of Saints phenom Reggie Bush), replenishing the urban forest and restoring City Park.

New Orleans Community Bike Project (www.bike project.org/planb) Bike advocacy group offering free and low-cost bikes and repairs.

Preservation Resource Center of New Orleans (www.prcno.org) Promoting the preservation of New Orleans architecture and neighborhoods.

Rebuild New Orleans Public Library (www.nutrias.org) Rebuilding public libraries devastated by Katrina.

Restaurant Employee Relief Fund (www.lra.org) Helping food service employees return home.

Save Our Cemeteries (www.saveourcemeteries.org) Restoring a unique aspect of New Orleans heritage and culture.

Tipitina's Foundation (www.tipitinasfoundation.org) Provides instruments for New Orleans students, and housing and business support for the city's musicians.